eBook and Digital Course Materials for

A History of Africa

COMBINED VOLUME

Toyin Falola

Timothy Stapleton

This code can be used only once and cannot be shared!

Carefully scratch off the silver coating to see your personal redemption code.

If the code has been scratched off when you receive it, the code may not be valid. Once the code has been scratched off, this access card cannot be returned to the publisher. You may buy access at **www.oup.com/he/falola-stapleton1e**.

The code on this card is valid for 2 years from the date of first purchase. Complete terms and conditions are available at **learninglink.oup.com.**

Access length: 6 months from redemption of the code.

UNIVERSITY PRESS

Directions for accessing your e-Book and Digital Course Materials

 link

www.oup.com/he/falola-stapleton1e

Select the edition you are using and the student resources for that edition.

Click the link to upgrade your access to the student resources.

Follow the on-screen instructions.

Enter your personal redemption code when prompted.

VIA YOUR SCHOOL'S LEARNING MANAGEMENT SYSTEM

Log in to your instructor's course.

When you click a link to a protected resource, you will be prompted to register for access.

Follow the on-screen instructions.

Enter your personal redemption code when prompted.

For assistance with code redemption or registration, please contact customer support at **learninglink.support@oup.com.**

About the Cover

Held in Ghana, the Yam Festival commemorates the first yam harvest, thanks the gods and ancestors for their bounty, and traditionally presents yams for sale and consumption. Known as the Fofie Yam Festival in the Techiman region, the Asante Yam Festival by the Asante and the Asogli Te Za in the Ho Municipality area, the festival is held annually between September and December. Music and dance are important aspects of this festival, as shown in this color lithograph from the 1820s. Locals dress in their best clothes, especially those made of the traditional Kente material.

A History of Africa

A History of Africa

COMBINED VOLUME

Toyin Falola
UNIVERSITY OF TEXAS AT AUSTIN

Timothy Stapleton
UNIVERSITY OF CALGARY

New York   Oxford
OXFORD UNIVERSITY PRESS

Oxford University Press is a department of the University of Oxford.
It furthers the University's objective of excellence in research, scholarship,
and education by publishing worldwide. Oxford is a registered trade mark of
Oxford University Press in the UK and certain other countries.

Published in the United States of America by Oxford University Press
198 Madison Avenue, New York, NY 10016, United States of America.

Library of Congress Cataloging-in-Publication Data

Names: Falola, Toyin, author. | Stapleton, Timothy J. (Timothy Joseph),
  1967- author.
Title: A history of Africa / Toyin Falola, University of Texas at Austin,
  and Timothy Stapleton, University of Calgary.
Description: [Combined edition] | New York : Oxford University Press,
  [2022] | Includes bibliographical references and index. | Summary: "A
  higher education text on the history of Africa"—Provided by publisher.
Identifiers: LCCN 2021029437 (print) | LCCN 2021029438 (ebook) | ISBN
  9780190690991 (paperback) | ISBN 9780197543009 | ISBN 9780197543016
  (epub) | ISBN 9780190691011 (pdf) | ISBN 9780197571477 (v. 1 ; epub) |
  ISBN 9780197571460 (v. 1 ; pdf) | ISBN 9780197571491 (v. 2 ; epub) |
  ISBN 9780197571484 (v. 2 ; pdf)
Subjects: LCSH: Africa—History—Textbooks.
Classification: LCC DT20 .F348 2022 (print) | LCC DT20 (ebook) | DDC
  960--dc23
LC record available at https://lccn.loc.gov/2021029437
LC ebook record available at https://lccn.loc.gov/2021029438

Printing number: 9 8 7 6 5 4 3 2 1
Paperback printed by Marquis, Canada

For Olatunde Falola and Oceane Kayitesi-Stapleton

Brief Contents

PART TWO: AFRICA SINCE 1870

Detailed Contents

List of Maps

Acknowledgements

We would like to thank Professors Mohammed Bashir Salau and Aribidesi Usman, as well as Luis Cataldo, Damilola Osunlakin and Devon Hsiao for their assistance. At Oxford University Press we extend our gratitude to Charles Cavaliere and Danica Donovan for their work in polishing the manuscript and assembling its many various elements. We also wish to acknowledge the reviewers commissioned by the Press. Their sagacious critiques greatly improved the final draft:

Esperanza Brizuela-Garcia, *Montclair State University*

Tyler Fleming, *University of Louisville*

Henry B. Lovejoy, *University of Colorado, Boulder*

Raphael C. Njoku, *Idaho State University*

Kwaku Nti, *Armstrong State University*

Priscilla M. Shilaro, *Virginia Commonwealth University*

Bridget A. Teboh, *University of Massachusetts Dartmouth*

Christopher Tounsel, *Pennsylvania State University*

Dawne Y. Curry, *University of Nebraska—Lincoln*

Anne Ruszkiewicz, *Sullivan County Community College*

Kevin Butler, *University of Arkansas at Pine Bluff*

Willis Okech Oyugi, *Sam Houston State University*

Support Material

Adopters of *A History of Africa* have access to Power Point slides of all the images in the text, a test-item file, and an Oxford Learning Link Direct course cartridge at https://learninglink.oup.com.

Formats

The text is available in multiple formats to accommodate various classroom settings and to provide students with choices:

- The Combined Volume includes Parts One and Two, and is available in paperback, loose-leaf, and eBook formats
- Volume One includes Part One and is available as an eBook
- Volume Two includes Part Two and is available as an eBook

The ebook for *A History of Africa* includes enhancements designed to increase student engagement, including end-of-chapter quizzes, notetaking guides, and timeline activities. Please visit www.redshelf.com or www.vitalsource.com to learn more about eBook purchasing options.

About the Authors

Toyin Falola is Professor of History, University Distinguished Teaching Professor, and the Jacob and Frances Sanger Mossiker Chair in the Humanities, the University of Texas at Austin. He is an Honorary Professor, University of Cape Town, and Extraordinary Professor of Human Rights, University of the Free State in South Africa. He has served as the General Secretary of the Historical Society of Nigeria, the President of the African Studies Association, Vice-President of the UNESCO Slave Route Project, and the Kluge Chair of the Countries of the South, Library of Congress. He has received over 30 lifetime career awards, 14 honorary doctorates, and a series of major teaching awards.

Timothy Stapleton is Professor in the Department of History and fellow of the Center for Military, Strategic and Security Studies at the University of Calgary, and series editor of "Africa: Missing Voices" at the University of Calgary Press. He has held various academic appointments at universities in South Africa, Zimbabwe, Zambia, and Botswana, and is currently Visiting Professorial Fellow at the Nigerian Defence Academy. He is the author of a dozen sole-authored books on African history.

A History of Africa

Introduction

This book introduces undergraduate university or college students to the history of Africa. While it is not possible to discuss every event that ever happened in African history, the book comprises a historical narrative emphasizing key trends and processes illustrated by some detailed examples. It represents a chronological and empirical history based on scholarly research and reconstructions of Africa's past. As a continental history, it seeks to cover all regions of Africa, including North Africa, often seen as culturally and historically different from the rest. Further, the narrative summarizes changing views and academic debates concerning aspects of African history, and at the same time, it seeks to avoid getting bogged down in technical matters. Focusing on the continental history of Africa, the work outlines factors that led to the movement of African peoples to other parts of the world, particularly during several intercontinental slave trades, but it does not have sufficient space to explore of the history of the **African Diaspora**. Structurally, the book consists of two parts of 14 chapters each. Aside from this introductory chapter discussing images, geography, and changing historical perceptions of Africa, the first part explores Africa's precolonial period, from earliest times to the late nineteenth century. Important precolonial topics include the spread of agriculture and ironworking, the rise of centralized states, and African involvement in intercontinental trade such as the trans-Saharan, transatlantic, and Indian Ocean networks. The book's second part covers the period from the European colonial conquest of Africa at the end of the nineteenth century to the independent era of the late twentieth and early twenty-first centuries. In this part, significant themes include African reactions to colonial conquest, social and economic change during colonial rule, Africa's experience of the world wars, African nationalism and decolonization, the rise of popular culture, globalization, and the

Zanzibar. Located off the coast of Tanzania, Zanzibar became an important point of exchange in the Indian Ocean trade system.

3

impact of the Cold War and its end. While the chapters on precolonial history focus mainly on specific regions of the continent, enabling readers to concentrate on topics such as West Africa's engagement with transatlantic trade and East Africa's with Indian Ocean trade, most of the chapters on colonial and postcolonial Africa adopt a more continental approach. Each chapter ends with a timeline of important events and key terms, and a chapter-by-chapter list of some relevant scholarly publications for students seeking more in-depth information is provided at the end of the book.

Images and Stereotypes

When venturing into the study of African history, it is impossible to avoid confronting a series of stereotypes and tropes about the continent. Novelists, journalists, filmmakers, and others often portray Africa as a mysterious, unknown, and unknowable place, or the **Dark Continent**. Some wildlife documentaries on television make it seem like all of Africa is a vast wilderness inhabited by exotic and awe-inspiring animals and almost no people. Presenting Africans as primitive savages and sometimes cannibals, old and even new Hollywood movies create a fictional Africa where a Victorian British castaway becomes a superhero called Tarzan and European explorers search for mythical lost cities of supposedly extra-African origin. On television and the Internet, international news reports and charity fundraising efforts focus on Africa's humanitarian disasters, dwelling on the now common image of malnourished African children with swollen stomachs or child soldiers who appear tiny compared to the assault weapons they carry. There is a common perception of Africa as a violent place where people fight wars because of innate and inexplicable ethnic hatreds.

The historical reality is very different. While contemporary Africa is home to many large and unpopulated national parks, these wilderness areas were created by European colonial regimes that evicted indigenous communities who now live on the fringes of these zones, contending with many dangerous animals and dense bush that breeds tropical disease-bearing insects. European explorers mapped Africa in the nineteenth century, but they were dependent upon the goodwill of their African hosts and the expertise of local guides who already knew the geography of their regions. Lost cities were found, but historic African people had built them all. While Africa has experienced more than its share of human suffering and conflict, and it would be misleading to minimize this aspect of African history, these events have logical explanations, and they have not happened everywhere on the continent at all times.

Geography

To understand Africa's history, it is important to know about its geography and climate. The continent consists of specific regions with characteristic environmental features, including deserts, plains, rivers, wetlands, forests, and mountain ranges. Some describe North Africa as an island separated from southern Europe by the Mediterranean Sea and from the rest of Africa by the **Sahara Desert**. This basic geographic reality means that the history of North Africa, while influenced by other parts of the continent, has been distinct. A central feature of the geography of the eastern part of North Africa is the Nile River, originating in the **Great Lakes** region of East Africa and the highlands of Ethiopia and flowing south through modern Sudan and Egypt. Northwestern Africa, called the **Maghreb**, comprises portions of the Mediterranean and Atlantic coasts, and a hinterland dominated by the Sahara. West Africa consists of a series of environmental zones running along a west–east axis. The first of these zones is a tropical forest that grows along most of the region's Atlantic coast, separated by a forest gap around present-day Benin. Further north, the forest thins out, giving way to a **savanna** zone with mixed grassland and trees, then the grassland of the **Sahel**, and lastly the Sahara Desert. West Africa contains several major rivers, such as the Senegal and Gambia Rivers that flow west toward the Atlantic coast, and the great Niger River winding through the Sahel and savanna, splitting into a large delta in modern Nigeria as it enters the Atlantic. At the heart of Central Africa is one of the world's largest tropical rainforests, bordered by savanna to the north and south, and mountains and great lakes to the east. The Congo River circles through Central Africa, emerging on the Atlantic coast in the west. East Africa comprises an Indian Ocean coastline; the open grasslands of the **Great Rift Valley**; the Great Lakes of Africa, such as Victoria (Nyanza), Tanganyika, and Malawi; and mountain ranges that include active volcanos along the modern border of Rwanda and the Democratic Republic of Congo (DRC). Southern Africa extends south from the Zambezi River, which flows from the western part of present-day Zambia eastward to the Indian Ocean. Just below the Zambezi, the **Kalahari Desert** and the **Zimbabwe Plateau** dominate the middle of this region. In the southeast, below the Limpopo River, the Drakensberg Mountains separate an interior high-altitude grassland called the **Highveld** from the eastern coast on the Indian Ocean. The region's arid Atlantic coast on the west side and the comparatively verdant Indian Ocean coast on the east meet at the Cape, which represents the continent's most southerly point, divided from the rest of Southern Africa by the **Great Karoo Desert**. It is worth noting that Africa's regional designations can overlap with, for example, the modern country of Zambia located just above the

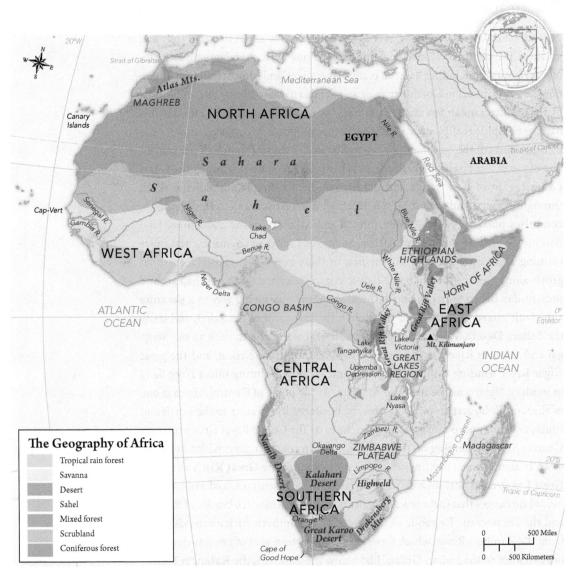

The Geography of Africa

- Tropical rain forest
- Savanna
- Desert
- Sahel
- Mixed forest
- Scrubland
- Coniferous forest

≡ MAP 1

Zambezi River, commonly referred to as both a Central and Southern African state. While the far north and south areas of Africa have temperate climates, West, Central, East, and the upper parts of Southern Africa comprise tropical environments in which tropical diseases such as malaria are endemic. As discussed in subsequent chapters, these environmental differences have had a huge impact on the course of African history.

Periodization and Evidence

The history of Africa is commonly divided into three periods: precolonial, colonial, and postcolonial. The **precolonial era** is extremely long, including many thousands of years from the earliest known human societies in any given area to the start of European colonial conquest of most of Africa in the late nineteenth century. The ending of the precolonial period can differ from place to place, as, for example, Dutch colonialism at the southern tip of Africa started in 1652 while the British conquered the Darfur sultanate of western Sudan only in 1916. What historians know about the precolonial history of different parts of Africa is very uneven due to varying types and amounts of historical evidence. For example, the survival of hieroglyphics from ancient Egypt means that historians know a great deal about that society that existed from around 5,000 years ago, but the lack of similar textual sources related to Rwanda means we know little about the inhabitants of that area before around 200–300 years ago. The reconstruction of Africa's precolonial history has been challenging for historians. Written historical records survive for only a few areas, such as ancient Greek and Roman texts for North Africa; medieval Arabic texts for North Africa, parts of the Sahara and Sahel, and the East African coast; and ancient Ge'ez script for the Horn of Africa, particularly modern Ethiopia and Eritrea. As such, historians have been able to delve back many centuries into the history of these areas. However, the languages spoken by **indigenous** societies in Southern and Central Africa as well as the coastal region of West Africa and the interior of East Africa did not have written scripts before European and African Christian missionaries created them in the early colonial era. To reconstruct the precolonial history of these areas, modern historians have relied on **oral traditions** whereby African communities have remembered historical information and passed it down from one generation to the next. Over the past few decades, and as discussed in some of the following chapters, historians have argued over the veracity of African oral traditions, with some seeing them as authentic historical records and others as manipulated legends and myths. Historians of precolonial Africa have also employed archaeological evidence, linguistic analysis, and rare historical documents authored by literate visitors, and they are beginning to look at DNA studies. Since they contend with such a long period, scholars of precolonial African history divide it into relatively shorter periods such as the Stone Age, Early Iron Age, and Later Iron Age, relating to archaeological discoveries of metallurgy.

The **colonial period** refers to the era when almost all of Africa fell under the rule of European imperial powers or settler states. It began with a continent-wide European colonial conquest in the late nineteenth and early twentieth century that came to be known as the **Scramble for Africa**. In most parts of the continent, the colonial period lasted around 70 or 80 years, beginning in the late nineteenth

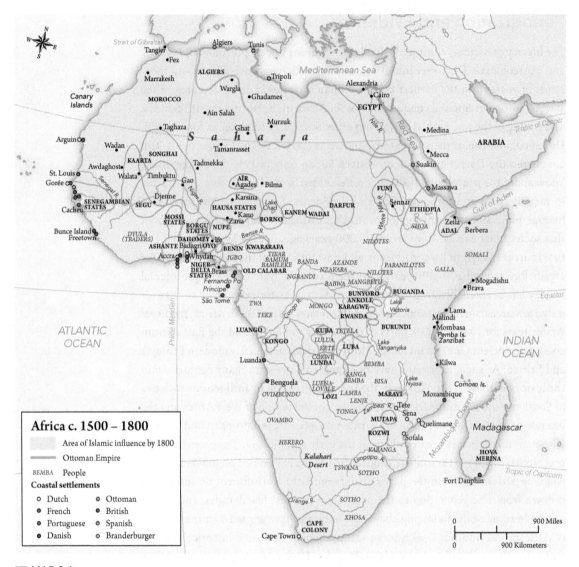

Africa c. 1500 – 1800

	Area of Islamic influence by 1800
	Ottoman Empire
BEMBA	People

Coastal settlements

○	Dutch	○	Ottoman
●	French	●	British
●	Portuguese	○	Spanish
●	Danish	○	Branderburger

≡ MAP 2 A

century and ending around 1960. To illustrate the brevity of this period, some people who were born just before the advent of colonial rule lived to see it end. This was an era of rapid change when external conquerors imposed what would become the modern political borders of Africa. Although many aspects of precolonial African society and culture survived, Western-style administrative systems developed, colonial capitalist economies emerged, and there was rampant social and cultural change. Historians working on Africa's colonial past have

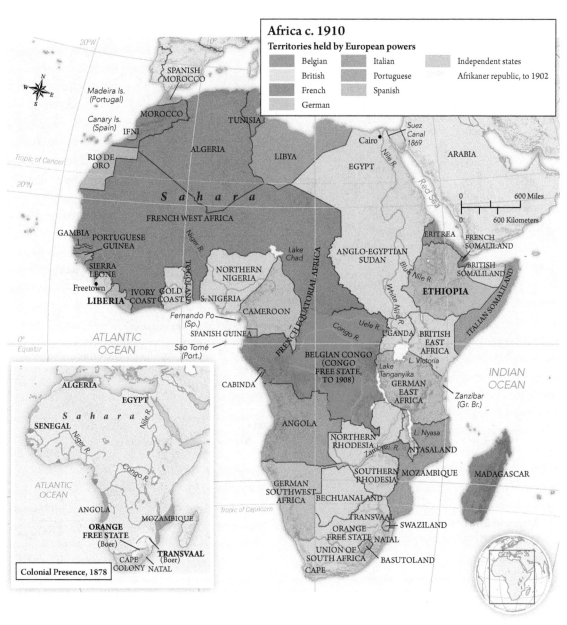

≡ **MAP 2 B**

mostly relied on written documents authored by European officials, soldiers, and missionaries—and sometimes by literate Africans—and on African oral histories, including eyewitness accounts. Given that most colonial documentary evidence was created by racist Europeans who usually could not speak or understand

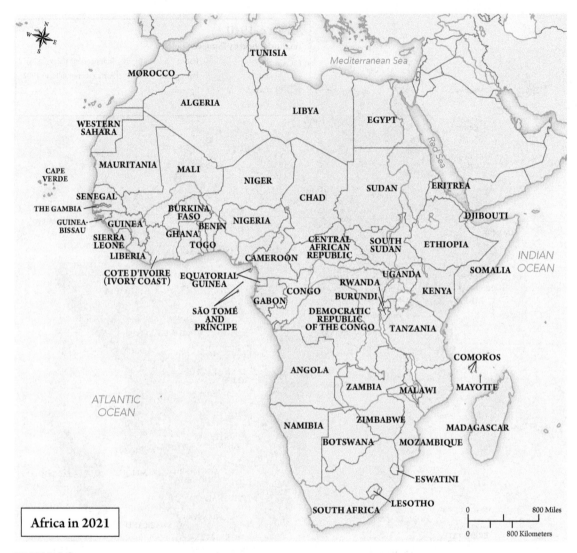

Africa in 2021

≡ MAP 2 C

local African languages, it has been difficult, but not impossible, for historians to reconstruct the experience of ordinary African people under colonial rule.

The **postcolonial** or independence period refers to Africa's history since the European-ruled colonies of the continent became independent states, mostly in the late 1950s and 1960s. Most African countries have now been independent for at least 60 years. However, in some places colonialism and white minority regimes lasted longer, with the Portuguese colonies gaining independence in 1974–75, South African–occupied Namibia becoming independent in 1990, and white minority regimes in Zimbabwe (Rhodesia) and South Africa ending in 1980 and 1994, respectively. For students beginning to look at African history, it is important to realize that the withdrawal of European rule did not mean that African countries went back to the governments, economies, and societies that existed before colonial conquest. The foreign-ruled colonies transformed into sovereign states with the same borders, administrative systems, security forces, economies, social structures, and often the same laws. The main difference was that African politicians operating within Western-style political and legal systems copied from the former European rulers now governed African people. Although this is the most recent period of African history and well within living memory, historians have sometimes struggled to study this era as many independent African states have not maintained good archives given lack of resources and secretiveness. As such, oral history continues to represent an important source for historians of contemporary Africa.

Historiography

E.H. Carr famously wrote that it is important to "study the historian before you begin to study the facts." While Carr was a British historian of international relations and the Soviet Union, his statement is instructive for students of all fields of history, including African history. History is not a set of objective facts about the past but a body of knowledge constructed by numerous historians who have made different contributions over time. As with all human beings, historians possess conscious or unconscious biases, opinions, agendas, life experiences, and approaches that influence what they write about the past. Just as history itself is always changing, the influences at work on historians are also constantly shifting, which means that historians working and living in different times, places, and socioeconomic contexts produce very different histories. Different generations of historians usually offer quite dissimilar versions and interpretations of the same historical event, topic, or process. This is why the study of history is always evolving and history is always contested. For instance, a white American historian living in the southern United States in the 1920s, a Nigerian historian living in West Africa in the 1960s, and an African-American historian living in Asia in the early 2000s were very likely to produce entirely different histories of the transatlantic slave trade (c. 1500–1860). As such, someone seeking to learn about a historical topic for the first time, as Carr advised, should become aware of the possible influences at work on the historians who wrote the relevant books, chapters, and journal articles. This awareness of different historians and their contexts comprises historiography. **Historiography** is the study of how history has developed as an academic discipline, or, simply put, it is the history of historians.

Before studying the history of Africa, therefore, it is vital to know something about the historians who have produced that history. The first historians of Africa were Africans who related, discussed, analyzed, and debated information about their communities' past. Before the era of European colonial rule that started in most parts of Africa in the late nineteenth century, most African societies did not have written scripts for their languages. In this context, people remembered, communicated verbally, and passed information about the past from one generation to the next as oral tradition. Such oral histories usually took the form of narratives or stories about the past, genealogies, songs, and praise poems of notable people. In many African societies, there were (and still are) specialists in oral tradition, such as the **griot** of West Africa and the **imbongi** (praise singer) of Southern Africa's Xhosa and Zulu peoples. For instance, in the kingdom of Rwanda during the eighteenth and nineteenth centuries, male warriors at the king's court were expected to learn, compose, and recite heroic stories and songs about the past. Although oral histories were performed for entertainment, they usually served the function of legitimizing the sociopolitical status quo—by, for example, explaining why a royal dynasty came to power. Of course, sometimes praise poems could tell awkward truths, and to some extent alternative oral traditions related subversive views.

Writing about the African past dates back to the origins of written history. Some 2,000 years ago, writers such as the Greek historian Herodotus, who is often called "the father of history" (and who visited Africa), the Greco-Roman geographer Strabo, and the Roman historian Tacitus wrote about events that had taken place in North and Northeast Africa, and about the people and geography of these regions. The spread of Islam across North and parts of West and East Africa, which began in the seventh and eight centuries CE, led to some historical writing about Africa in Arabic or in local languages using Arabic script by both foreign and indigenous authors. Prominent examples of this genre include the travel writings of the Moroccan Ibn Battuta during the 1300s and the Iberian–North African Leo Africanus during the 1500s. In the late 1300s the famous Arab-Tunisian scholar Ibn Khaldun wrote about North African history, but his cultural chauvinism prompted him to compare Black

≡ **A Senegalese griot c. 1910.** He is holding a *kora*, a stringed musical instrument widely played throughout West Africa.

Africans from south of the Sahara to animals. In Ethiopia, from around the 1200s, historians used the Ge'ez script to write royal biographies and dynastic chronicles that linked the kingdom's history to the biblical King Solomon and the early history of Christianity. From about the 1500s to the late 1800s, European explorers, officials, merchants, and missionaries wrote accounts of their activities in parts of Africa that sometimes mentioned historical aspects. While later historians of Africa used these early written records as source material, the Greco-Roman, Arabic, and early European explorer/missionary accounts did not consciously seek to write histories of Africa or parts of Africa, and the history of the continent was usually tangential to their work.

The emergence of distinct genres or schools of written African history, comprising historians working in similar contexts and producing histories with common characteristics, began with the

☰ **Historical document**. A fifteenth-century Ethiopian prayer book written in the Ge'ez script.

colonial conquest of Africa in the late nineteenth century. European colonial historians, who lacked formal academic training in the field, were often retired colonial officials or military officers writing about the parts of Africa they had worked in. An example of a historian from this colonial genre is Hugh Marshall Hole, who participated in the British colonial conquest of Southern Rhodesia (Zimbabwe) in the 1890s and later wrote celebratory books like *The Making of Rhodesia* (1926) and *The Passing of the Black Kings* (1932). Similarly, French colonial historians portrayed North Africa as a place of barbarism civilized by the rule of France, which was seen as heir to the ancient Roman Empire.

Although they were among the first to approach the history of Africa as a continental entity with common features, colonial historians expressed the white **racism** of their era. As such, they were most interested in the history of Europeans in Africa and focused on colonial wars of conquest and subsequent colonial development, such as the building of railways, roads, and administrative structures. For the most part, European colonial historians viewed Africa as having no significant history before the arrival of outsiders. Like most European historians of the late nineteenth and early twentieth centuries, they thought that history could only be reconstructed through information gleaned from written documents, which meant that they viewed African oral culture as **ahistorical** and primitive. The myth that

Africa had no history lasted for a long time: in 1790, German philosopher Frederick Hegel claimed that "it was no historical part of the world" and in 1965, at a time when many African colonies had recently gained independence, British historian Hugh Trevor Roper wrote, "there is only the history of Europeans in Africa."

During the period of colonial rule in Africa, when the dominant historians expressed the belief that Africa had no history before European conquest, some African and African-American historians began to author alternative genres of historical writing about the continent. Products of early Christian missionary education in colonial Africa, a few members of the emerging Westernized African elite, including clergy and teachers, researched and wrote detailed histories of their ethnic groups that focused on the precolonial era. While these rich local and regional histories clearly show the historical nature of African society, the mission background of the authors meant that they generally saw the coming of Christianity and Western "civilization" as positive developments. Furthermore, and similar to most colonial historians, the African-mission writers were amateur historians who lacked professional training and, therefore, did not document their sources of information. Nonetheless, they wrote and published extensive works in European and African languages. One of the most prominent examples of this type of historian is Samuel Johnson, a man of Nigerian Yoruba ancestry who was born in Sierra Leone, and who researched and wrote about Yoruba history and culture while working in western Nigerian as a missionary during the 1890s. After Samuel Johnson died in 1901, his brother Dr. Obadiah Johnson used his notes to compile an epic study entitled *A History of the Yorubas from Earliest Times to the Beginning of the British Protectorate*, published in 1921. There are many other examples of such historians for every region of Africa. Apollo Kaggwa, who had led the Protestant faction during the Buganda Civil War of the 1890s, and allied with the British colonizers of Uganda, in the 1920s wrote books in the Luganda language about the culture and history of the kingdom; some of these works were later translated into English. In the early twentieth century, the history of the Xhosa people of South Africa became the subject of Walter Rubusana, who compiled and edited an anthology of historical traditions called *Zemk'inkomo Magwalandini* ("The Cattle are Running Away, You Cowards"), published in 1906. Also in South Africa, J.H. Soga, son of the first Xhosa ordained minister and himself a clergyman, wrote and published *The Southeastern Bantu* in 1930, and *AmaXhosa: Life and Customs* in 1932. Around the same time, and on the other side of the Atlantic, African-American scholars began to write about the history of their ancestral homeland within the context of continued racial oppression in the Americas and particularly in the United States. With a much broader continental approach than the African mission elite historians, early African-American writings on African history reflected the emergence of **Pan-Africanism**, the idea that all Africans and people of African descent should unite to undo the separation brought about by the African Diaspora. In his 1946 book *The World and Africa*, pioneering Pan-Africanist and African-American academic W.E.B. du Bois showed how Africa's important contributions to world history had been obscured by the terrible ordeal of the transatlantic slave trade and anti-Black racism.

The professionalization of academic African History in the 1950s and 1960s is directly connected with the independence of African countries and the emergence of the civil rights movement in the United States. The new African universities established in the late colonial era or by the recently independent African governments, along with many universities in the United States, began to offer formal courses on African history. Universities in Europe, including some with older academic centers founded to study colonies in Africa, followed this trend. These developments stimulated the training of graduate students in African history,

Walter Rubusana

W.E.B. du Bois

≡ **Pioneering Historians** *Left*. Walter Rubusana, a South African educator, journalist, and politician, compiled an anthology of historical traditions called *Zemk'inkomo Magwalandini* ("The Cattle Are Running Away, You Cowards") that was published in 1906. *Right*. In 1946, African-American academic and activist W.E.B. du Bois published a book entitled *The World and Africa*.

who then became lecturers and professors at these institutions, conducted further specialized research on various aspects of the discipline, and disseminated their research findings as academic publications. As a result, scholarly African history journals appeared such as the *Journal of the Historical Society of Nigeria* in 1956, the UK-based *Journal of African History* in 1960, and the US-based *International Journal of African Historical Studies* in 1969.

It has become common to describe the first generation of professional historians of Africa that emerged in the 1960s as the "nationalist school of African history." Historians based at the University of Ibadan in Nigeria, such as Kenneth Dike, who was the first Black African to complete a PhD in history, and others at the University of Dar-es-Salaam in Tanzania, such as British academic Terence Ranger who initially trained in Irish history, played a key role in this new historical approach. Influenced by the broad optimism about the future of newly independent African countries, these historians attempted to overturn the prevalent colonial view that Africa had no history worth studying other than the history of European colonialism. They wished to use history to promote a **national identity** within Africa. The Dar-es-Salaam–based historians focused largely on revising views about the history of African resistance to colonial conquest in the late nineteenth and early twentieth centuries. While colonial historians had considered African resistance as negative reactions against modernization brought by Europeans, the nationalist historians glorified historic African resistance fighters and exaggerated the degree of unity against colonial conquest. The nationalist historians viewed African resistance during the Scramble as forming a continuum of different types of African resistance that would culminate in the modern, mass nationalist movements of the 1950s and 1960s. As such, this approach to African history sought to provide historical legitimacy to the African nationalist politicians who had sought independence and then formed African governments. The nationalist scholars of the 1960s also wanted to inspire African nationalist fighters struggling against stubborn settler minority regimes in Southern Africa. Thematically,

≡ **Kenneth Dike.** A key figure in the professionalization of African History, Kenneth Dike (1917–1983) earned a PhD from King's College London. During the 1950s and 1960s he developed what became known as the "Ibadan School of History" at the University of Ibadan, Nigeria.

the nationalist historians mostly focused on politics and warfare. Examples of books written by nationalist historians of this era include Kenneth Dike, *Trade and Politics in the Niger Delta, 1830–1885: An Introduction to the Economic and Political History of Nigeria* (1956) and Terence Ranger's *Revolt in Southern Rhodesia, 1896–97: A Study in African Resistance* (1967).

Another important development in the field of African history during the 1960s was the use of oral tradition as evidence to reconstruct Africa's precolonial past. The foremost advocate of this approach was Belgian historian-anthropologist Jan Vansina, who originally studied European medieval history but then focused on Central Africa. Vansina's early and influential works included *Oral Tradition: A Study in Historical Methodology* (1956) and *Kingdoms of the Savanna* (1966). Over many years, he trained a series of historians of Africa at the University of Wisconsin-Madison in the United States.

By the start of the 1970s, as military coups, wars, and worsening poverty gripped the continent, the optimism about Africa characteristic of the 1950s and early 1960s gave way to disappointment and pessimism. This changing attitude had an impact on the study of African history. Informed by similar concepts in Latin American studies, historians and other scholars began to see that Africa had been shaped into an underdeveloped continent to support the industrial development of Western Europe and North America. According to these **underdevelopmentalist** scholars, this situation did not change after independence because Africa had been granted a fake type of independence designed to guarantee the continuation of Western economic exploitation under what was now called **neocolonialism**. Such scholars saw African governments not as heirs of a long tradition of heroic resistance, as the nationalist historians had presented them, but as puppets of manipulative and exploitative external powers. In his polemic *How Europe Underdeveloped Africa*, published in 1972, the Guyanese historian Walter Rodney explained how Europe had drained Africa of its wealth over a number of centuries from the days of the transatlantic slave trade to the present. Furthermore, Rodney argued that the only way for Africa to prosper was to completely break its economic ties with the Western world and find its own way of developing. Although it is hard to deny that the Western world gained much from its exploitation of Africa, and some former colonial powers attempted to control their former colonies, some aspects of neocolonial theory seem like an unprovable conspiracy theory.

The discipline of African history expanded enormously in the 1970s and 1980s, influenced by broader intellectual trends in Western Europe and North America. At this time, many historians of Africa looked to materialist interpretations of history, partly in an effort to move away from the obvious subjectivity of the colonial and nationalist schools. Informed by the late-nineteenth-century writing of German

≡ **Walter Rodney.** Historian and activist Walter Rodney (1942–1980) wrote the controversial book *How Europe Underdeveloped Africa* (1972). He was assassinated in his home country of Guyana in 1980.

philosopher Karl Marx, **materialist** history looks at the material conditions of society rather than ideas as the main driving force of human development. For historians of Africa, this new focus combined with a larger trend that moved away from studying the great leaders and big events of the past to examine the daily experience of ordinary people. The result was a flourishing of scholarly works on African social, economic, and labor history. A good example of this materialist approach is Bill Freund's *The Making of Contemporary Africa*, which was published in 1984 and became an influential textbook for African history university courses. Eventually, materialist historians would be criticized for underemphasizing ideology and religion as historical factors. Simultaneously, the rise of **feminism**, the women's rights movement, and women's history in the West also inspired historians of Africa, who began to research and write about the experience of African women. One of the central points of African women's history, as a field, is that colonialism had weakened the position that African women held in precolonial societies.

Beginning in the 1990s, simultaneous with the end of the Cold War and the fall of Marxist regimes in Eastern Europe, a series of new intellectual concepts became popular among some historians of Africa. **Postmodernism** expressed skepticism about established historical facts and narratives, seeing them as constructions of specific social and cultural contexts, and claimed that it is impossible to reconstruct history. Similarly, **postcolonialism** sought to address the cultural legacy of colonialism and imperialism. Within African history, and other disciplines, tensions developed between scholars who wanted to pursue this "cultural turn" by placing culture at the center of historical study and others who continued with empirical and materialist interpretations. By this time, and in reaction to Eurocentric views of history, some scholars developed the concept of **Afrocentrism**, which sought to place Africa and African people at the center of world history. Informed by a belief that racist white historians had purposefully downgraded Africa's important historical contributions, Afrocentric scholars claimed, for example, that Africans had arrived in the Americas before Christopher Columbus and influenced the development of indigenous American societies. During the 1990s, a major academic debate erupted over Afrocentric claims about the possible African origins of ancient Greek civilization. Overall, Afrocentrism faced criticism for inventing evidence and making unsubstantiated claims, and for seeking to replace unipolar Eurocentrism with a similarly inaccurate and narrow theory. Research on precolonial African history began to wane from the 1990s onward as the limitations of oral tradition became apparent, historians became interested in social and cultural topics for which it is difficult to find evidence relating to the precolonial era, and it was simply much easier to do research in colonial or postcolonial documentary archives. With some important exceptions such as the transatlantic slave trade, African history became dominated by studies of the twentieth century.

South African Historiography

Given its long history of European settlement, South Africa presents a slightly different historiography than tropical Africa. South African oral traditions and the country's African-mission historians of the early twentieth century were essentially the same as in the rest of the continent. Formal historical writing began in South Africa with the settler historians of the late nineteenth and early twentieth century, who shared the racist attitudes of their colonial counterparts further north but differed in that they were interested in the history of African communities before European settlement. The main settler historians of South Africa were Canadian-born George McCall Theal, who became the first official archivist of the Cape Colony and wrote dozens of volumes on South African history, and British-born George Cory, who was a chemistry professor and archivist and wrote the three-volume *Rise of South Africa*. While the settler historians prolifically chronicled the dates and events of South African history, the early liberal historians of the 1920s and 1930s were the country's first professional historians and sought to study history to seek a better understanding of contemporary issues. William M. MacMillan, a history professor at the University of the Witwatersrand in Johannesburg and author of *Bantu, Boer and Briton* (1929), was among the first to study South Africa as a single society, which prompted hostility from academic and government authorities and resulted in his leaving the country in the early 1930s. At the same time, the rise of nationalism among **Afrikaners**, the descendants of the early Dutch settlers previously called **Boers**, inspired an Afrikaner nationalist history promoted in new Afrikaner universities and celebrated by an Afrikaner government during the era of strict racial segregation called **apartheid** from 1948 to the early 1990s. This apartheid historical view saw Afrikaners as the founders of South Africa, who had brought Christianity and civilization but who constantly strove for their freedom against supposedly barbaric Africans and oppressive British colonialism.

From the 1960s to 1980s, historians of South Africa engaged in a debate concerning the origin of the apartheid system. Liberal historians such as Leonard Thompson and Monica Wilson saw apartheid as the product of the outmoded ideology of Afrikaners whose descendants had arrived in South Africa before the European Enlightenment with its ideas about human equality and freedom. For the liberals, what they saw as the natural integrative tendencies of a free market economy as outlined by eighteenth-century economist Adam Smith would eventually lead to the dismantling of apartheid. Conversely, Marxist or radical historians understood apartheid as rooted in South Africa's distinctive form of racial capitalism, which relied on the white-owned mining industry exploiting cheap Black labor. From this perspective, apartheid would only end with an anticapitalist revolution and the creation of an egalitarian socialist society. The collapse of Marxist regimes in Eastern Europe and the Soviet Union, the end of the Cold War, the rise of a neoliberal world order, and the negotiated end of apartheid in the early 1990s seemed to undermine the radical view of South African history. From the 1990s, with the end of this debate, South African historians seemed to lack purpose and history teaching became a low priority in the post-apartheid era. In recent years, given the lack of economic transformation in the country more than 25 years after the advent of majority rule, many South Africans have begun to ask questions about the transition from apartheid to democracy, wondering if apartheid really ended or if it simply took another form.

Terminology

African history can present students with a minefield of problematic terms. Scholars and others question some terms or words frequently appearing in older academic works or contemporary journalism on Africa. The most common of

≡ **Monica Wilson.** Monica Wilson (1908–1982) was a pioneering South African anthropologist and historian. In this photo from 1945, she is flanked by colleagues from University College of Fort Hare, where she taught from 1944 to 1946.

these questionable terms is the word **tribe**, which is often used to describe African precolonial societies and current ethnic groups. However, "tribe" is a pejorative term in that it connotes images of primitiveness and savagery, and the word is not applied equally to all parts and peoples of the world. For example, it is typical to hear or read about Nigeria's "Yoruba tribe" or South Africa's "Zulu tribe," but it would be very strange to hear or read about the French tribe or the Russian tribe. Yet, these are exactly the same concepts denoting broad ethnic identities with common languages and cultures. In a clearly racist double standard, African ethnic identities are labeled as tribes while European ones are seen as nations. In addition, the word "tribe" is rather vague. With regard to African history, it has been used to refer to all sorts of entities, from centralized states to broad ethnic-cultural identities. When someone uses the term "Zulu tribe," it is not clear if they are referring to the nineteenth century Zulu kingdom or the wider Zulu identity of the twentieth and twenty-first centuries. It is much better to use accurate terms such as "state," "community," "society," "ethnicity," or "identity." That said, it is not unusual to hear the word "tribe" spoken on the African street, where people don't have time to consider its negative connotations. Similarly, "native" is often seen as a derogatory colonial term. In the 1950s, colonial administrations, responding to criticism from emerging African political leaders, began to replace it with the term "African." Of course, these terms are also employed in other parts of the world, such as in the United States, where "tribe" denotes an indigenous community. While "native" remains an acceptable term with reference to indigenous people in the United States, the word's colonial associations led to it falling out of favor in Canada.

The settler colonial society in Southern Africa generated its own racial terminology used in older written works but now highly offensive to people in that region. Many North Americans may have never encountered these words. In addition, their meanings changed over time. While the word "kaffir" originated from Arabic for "unbeliever" and was used by the nineteenth century British in South Africa to refer specifically to the Xhosa people, the meaning of the term changed and broadened during the twentieth century, when it became a racist epithet to refer to a Black person. Other potentially offensive Southern African terms include "Hottentot," which was a colonial epithet for the Khoisan people, and **Coloured**, which means a person of mixed European and African heritage and remains widely used in the region but which can be confused with an obsolete and racist American word for any Black person.

Students venturing into African history for the first time should be mindful of the changing names of African states. The precolonial kingdom of Benin existed in what is now southern Nigeria, while the French colony of Dahomey, the location of another precolonial African state called Dahomey, is now the independent

Republic of Benin. The name Benin, therefore, can refer to two different locations and periods. Similarly, the name Ghana refers to a precolonial state located in what is now Mali, while the British colony of the Gold Coast renamed itself Ghana on independence in 1957. Precolonial Ghana and postcolonial Ghana are two different entities that existed in different periods and were/are located in different parts of West Africa. There are many other examples. Over the course of the twentieth century, the Congo Free State became the Belgian Congo, and then the Democratic Republic of the Congo (DRC), and then Zaire, and then back to DRC. In Southern Africa, colonial Southern Rhodesia became Rhodesia, which became Zimbabwe-Rhodesia, which became the current Republic of Zimbabwe. The name Zimbabwe derives from a famous archaeological site bearing the same name and located in the same country.

Lastly, several prominent names associated with Africa, including the name Africa itself, originate with outsiders. The ancient Greeks and Romans, followed by the Arabs, employed terms like Africa and Libya to refer to parts or all of North Africa. Furthermore, the ancient Greeks called the land south of the Sahara Aethiopia (Ethiopia), meaning land of the dark-skinned or people with burnt faces. For Europeans of the early modern era, roughly 1500–1800 CE, the term Guiné or Guinea referred to a land of Black people comprising all of West Africa below the Sahara and the source of most enslaved Africans for the transatlantic slave trade. Around the same time, with the advent of cartography and the definition of continents, Europeans and others began to use "Africa" as a term that described the entire continent. Other names, like Libya, Ethiopia, and Guinea, came to refer to specific regions of the African continent.

KEY TERMS

African Diaspora 3	feminism 18	Kalahari Desert 5
Afrikaners 19	Great Karoo Desert 5	Maghreb 5
Afrocentrism 18	Great Lakes 5	materialist 18
ahistorical 13	Great Rift Valley 5	national identity 16
apartheid 19	griot 12	neocolonialism 17
Boers 19	Highveld 5	oral traditions 7
colonial period 7	historiography 11	Pan-Africanism 15
Coloured 21	imbongi 12	postcolonial 10
Dark Continent 4	indigenous 7	postcolonialism 18

postmodernism 18

precolonial era 7

racism 13

Sahara Desert 5

Sahel 5

savanna 5

Scramble for Africa 7

tribe 21

underdevelopmentalist 17

Zimbabwe Plateau 5

STUDY QUESTIONS

1. Why have novelists, journalists, filmmakers, and others often portrayed Africa as the "Dark Continent"?

2. Why is it important to understand Africa's geography and climate to study its history?

3. What three periods do scholars use to divide African history? To reconstruct the precolonial past, which type of evidence do researchers commonly use?

4. What is historiography? Why do different generations of historians usually offer dissimilar versions and interpretations of the same historical event, topic, or process? What are the main developments in African historiography since the colonial era? Why does South Africa have its own distinctive historiographical tradition?

5. Why is "tribe" a pejorative term? Why should students of African history be mindful of the names of countries?

Please see page FR-1 for the Further Readings for this chapter.
For additional digital learning resources please go to
https://www.oup.com/he/falola-stapleton1e

Part One

Africa to 1880

Equestrian Oba and Attendants, c. 1600. Over the course of the sixteenth and seventeenth centuries, a remarkable series of some 900 rectangular brass plaques were cast in relief at the Court of Benin for display across the facade of the royal palace. In this example, the mounted king is flanked by attendants who are rendered on a hierarchical scale that designates their relative rank.

1

Earliest Times

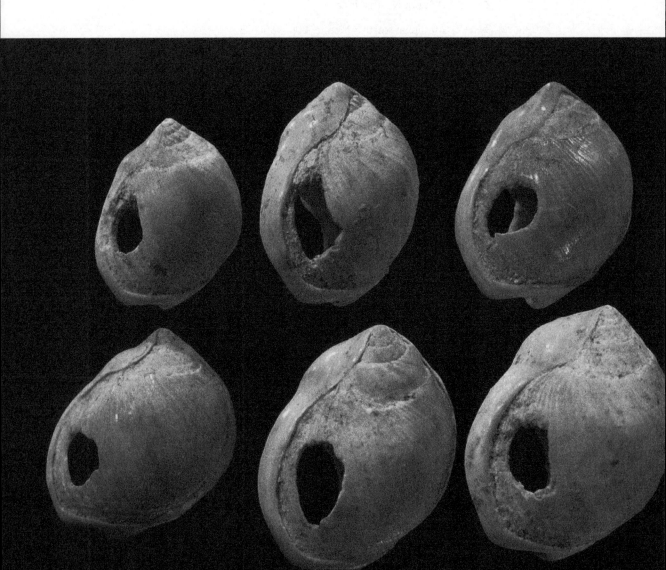

Human Origins in Africa

Humans evolved in Africa and, from there, moved out to the rest of the world. Beginning around four or five million years ago, various types of archaic humans emerged in East Africa's Rift Valley and spread to Southern Africa. As such, Africa represents the location for the oldest archaic human fossils, among the most important of which is a skull called the "Taung Child," discovered in South Africa in the 1920s and dating to around 2.3 million years ago, and a partial skeleton called "Lucy," found in Ethiopia during the 1970s and dating to 3.2 million years ago. The Sterkfontein Caves in South Africa, close to Johannesburg, have yielded archaic human fossils that are between 2 and 2.6 million years old including "Mrs. Ples," which represents the most complete skull of *Australopithecus Africanus.* In Olduvai Gorge in Tanzania, fossils indicate the presence of a series of archaic humans, including *Homo habillis* around two million years ago, Australopithecines around 1.8 million years ago, and *Homo erectus* around 1.2 million years ago. Evidence from the gorge also shows the development of stone tool making by these archaic humans. Around 2 million years ago, archaic humans, starting with *Homo erectus*, began to move out of Africa to parts of Europe and Asia and evolved into other archaic human species such as Neanderthals.

Anatomically modern humans—*Homo sapiens*—who looked the same as humans today, originated in Africa more than 300,000 years ago. Some of the oldest fossils of anatomically modern humans in Africa include the "Omo Remains" discovered in Ethiopia in the 1960s and 1970s, which are around 200,000 years old, and the "Florisbad Skull" found in South Africa in the 1930s, which is around 260,000 years old. These finds led scholars to believe that *Homo sapiens*, like their forbears, evolved in East and Southern Africa. More recently, however, the discovery of the oldest fossils of *Homo sapiens* in a cave in Morocco suggests that they were spread across other parts of Africa by 300,000 years ago and did not necessarily evolve in East Africa. A recent DNA study contends that anatomically modern humans first emerged around an ancient lake in northern Botswana and Namibia and that climate change caused the opening of a vegetated corridor enabling them to leave Southern Africa and move to other parts of the

Perforated shell beads from Blombos Cave, South Africa, created about 75,000 years ago. They are among the oldest known artifacts made by humans.

EARLY HUMANS IN AFRICA

Top left: Discovered in South Africa's Sterkfontein Caves, near Johannesburg, the fossil known as "Mrs. Ples" represents the most complete skull of *Australopithecus Africanus* and is between 2 and 2.6 million years old. *Top right:* Located in northern Tanzania, Olduvai Gorge has yielded some of the oldest known fossils of archaic humans, dating back around 2 million years. *Bottom:* Jebel Irhoud in Morocco—the site of the discovery of the oldest remains of anatomically modern humans. *Center left:* A cast of a skull of an anatomically modern human male found at Jebel Irhoud in Morocco and dating to around 300,000 years ago. *Center right:* Stone tools found at Jebel Irhoud in Morocco.

continent and beyond. However, critics pointed out that the researchers looked at just one part of the human genome and therefore produced an overly simplistic view of human origins ignoring other possible homelands in Africa. Around 200,000 years ago anatomically modern humans began to move to Europe and Asia, where they mixed with existing populations of archaic humans, and they eventually proceeded to the Americas and Australia.

The Advent of Herding and Farming

Some of the earliest developments in African history involved the emergence of herding and farming. Scholars

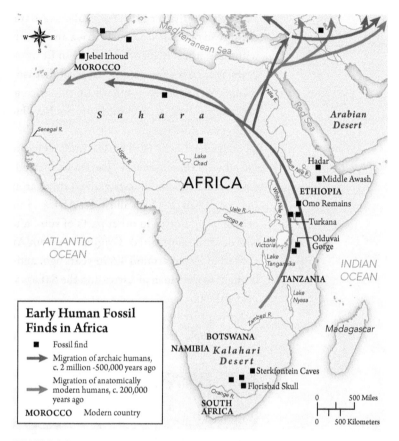

Early Human Fossil Finds in Africa

- ■ Fossil find
- → Migration of archaic humans, c. 2 million -500,000 years ago
- → Migration of anatomically modern humans, c. 200,000 years ago
- MOROCCO   Modern country

≡ **MAP 1.1**

disagree about the origins of livestock raising in Africa. Some maintain that this began when people in North Africa began domesticating wild animals, including wild cattle called **aurochs**. Dating to around 9,300 years ago, cattle bones discovered in western Egypt may represent evidence for some of the earliest known domesticated cattle in world history. Evidence from dung and cave paintings suggest that hunter-gatherers living in western Libya around the same time kept wild Barbary sheep in pens, using them for meat and ritual purposes. Other academics believe that domesticated livestock like cattle, goats, and sheep (different from Barbary sheep) originated in western Asia and arrived in North Africa and the Sahara grasslands around 7,500 years ago.

The spread of livestock raising to the rest of Africa resulted from environmental change. Around 4,500 years ago, pastoralists left the Sahara region as it was turning into a desert and moved south into the Sahel grassland and savanna, where the drier conditions meant the retreat of **tsetse flies** that carry Trypanosomiasis, a disease deadly to cattle. Tropical disease transmitted by wild animals delayed the spread of cattle into East Africa and Southern Africa by around 1,000 years, with the earliest evidence for cattle in Ethiopia dating to around 2,000 or 3,000 years ago. Less impacted by tropical disease, small stock preceded cattle with sheep arriving at the southern tip of Africa almost 2,000 years ago. While the earliest breeds of African cattle did not have humps and acquired some immunity to Trypanosomiasis given long exposure, other types of South Asian humped cattle arrived in East Africa via the Indian Ocean trade around 1,000 years ago and mixed with the older varieties. Domesticated donkeys existed in Egypt around 4,400 years ago and horses arrived there around 3,500 years ago and spread to the rest of North Africa and West Africa. However, there is limited evidence for people using horses in other parts of sub-Saharan Africa, and the African zebra was never domesticated. Originating from Arabia, a limited number of camels arrived in Egypt around 4,500 years ago, and around 2,000 years ago they were brought to the Horn of Africa and the Sahara where they became the main transport animal.

Agriculture in Africa began around 7,000 to 4,000 BCE in the Sahara region, where people transitioned from gathering edible wild plants to cultivating

≡ **Nabta Playa.** Cattle bones unearthed at Nabta Playa, in the Egyptian Sahara, date to approximately 7,000 BCE. Archaeologists have also unearthed a calendar circle that dates to about 5,000 BCE (see above), and which was aligned with the summer solstice.

☰ **Ancient Rock Art in the Sahara** This ancient rock art from Tadrart, Algeria, shows that the Sahara Desert was once a savanna where humans hunted wildlife such as giraffes.

domesticated plants, including wild sorghum and melons. At that time, the Sahara experienced much higher rainfall than today and consisted of savanna and grassland environments. It is likely that agriculture spread from the Sahara to other parts of the continent. Since archaeological research shows that domesticated versions of indigenous African plants like sorghum, cowpeas, and pearl millet grew in India around 2000 BCE, it is likely that these crops were produced in Africa before that time despite a lack of evidence. The earliest archaeological evidence for the cultivation of domesticated sorghum in East Africa, where it became a very important food source, dates to around 500 BCE in Nubia, in what is now Sudan. Crops from outside Africa also spread into the continent such as western Asian wheat, barley, peas, and lentils that grew in Egypt from around 4500 BCE and formed the basis of agriculture in the Nile valley and other parts of North Africa. In West Africa, the earliest evidence for the cultivation of pearl millet dates to between 2000 and 1500 BCE in Mauritania, Mali, and northern Ghana, and around 1200 BCE people in Nigeria utilized wild rice. Furthermore, northern Ghana is also home to the earliest evidence for the cultivation of cowpeas and the harvesting of palm oil in the region. The origin of tuber crops such as yam that became essential in the West African forest zone is more difficult to determine. Originating in Southeast Asia, bananas arrived in Africa more than 2000 years ago and became important in the advent of farming in forest areas of Equatorial Africa. In general, the gradual spread of farming over a few thousand years caused African people to change from living in small bands of hunters and gatherers and/or pastoralists to organizing larger semi-permanent settlements.

The Beginnings of Metallurgy

The spread of ironworking represents another foundational development in early precolonial African history. Archaeologists and other scholars intensely debate the origins of iron usage in ancient Africa. At the center of the debate is the archaeological technique of **radiocarbon dating**, invented in the 1950s, which can determine the approximate age of organic materials. Since historic African ironworkers used charcoal as fuel for smelting and forging, modern archaeologists date iron-smelting sites by subjecting remnants of charcoal to radiocarbon testing. The older academic view of the origin of iron technology in Africa is that it arrived in Egypt from the Middle East about 3,000 years ago, then spread west to Carthage on the Mediterranean coast (present-day Tunisia), and then south to the rest of the continent. Continuing its north–south **diffusion**, evidence for ironworking at Nok in Central Nigeria and at Meroë in Sudan has been dated to around 500 BCE, and in Southern Africa to around 400 CE. Unlike the Mediterranean region and the Middle East, however, most of sub-Saharan Africa lacked a transitional "Bronze Age" during which people experimented with working a softer metal (bronze is a combination of copper and tin) before developing iron technology, and this seemed proof that African knowledge of iron came from outside the continent. After all, it seems unrealistic that Africans jumped from making stone to making iron tools. Conversely, since the 1960s, other scholars have argued for an independent invention of iron in ancient Africa. Over the years, the discovery of ancient iron-smelting sites in the Sahara or further south that predate similar sites in North Africa seem to refute the north to south diffusion theory. In particular, evidence for ironworking in Rwanda dates to the 800s BCE, in Niger to around 1500 BCE, in eastern Nigeria to 750 BCE and 2000 BCE, and in the Central African Republic to about 2000 BCE. The 2000 BCE dates, if correct, represent the oldest evidence of ironworking in the world. However, critics point out, for instance, that at times the tested charcoal was much older than the associated iron objects, that researchers misidentified charred tree stumps as iron smelting sites, and that there are inherent technical problems in radiocarbon dating anything in the range of 800 to 400 BCE given irregularities in the atmosphere at that time. The diffusion versus independent invention debate remains unresolved.

Although many scholars commonly use the terms "Stone Age" and "Iron Age" to describe phases of early history involving the transition to metallurgy, these can present an overly simplistic picture, as the change was gradual and did not happen everywhere at the same time, and the use of old and new technologies overlapped. Although the situation was complex and diverse, the introduction of ironworking may have contributed to gender divisions of labor in parts of Africa. While producing iron became a highly ritualized activity compared to a woman giving birth, ironmaking and knowledge around it became dominated by older men who also

≡ **Terracotta Heads.** *Left:* Dating to around 500 BCE, this terracotta head discovered at Nok in Central Nigeria was created by people who knew how to make iron tools. *Right:* A terracotta sculpture from Ife in western Nigeria that dates to somewhere between the twelfth and fourteenth centuries.

became kings and rainmakers. At the same time, women commonly focused on making pottery, which enjoyed less ritual importance.

In West Africa, the transition to metals did not interrupt a long-established cultural continuity. For example, terracotta figures associated with the 2,500-year-old **Nok** culture of Central Nigeria seem culturally related to 700- or 800-year-old terracotta and bronze pieces discovered at Ife in western Nigeria. Several examples from different parts of West Africa show a lack of disruption caused by the gradual changes brought about by ironworking. A community in southwestern Cameroon, near present-day Bamenda, made chipped-stone hoes and pottery around 7,000 years ago; ground stones to make hoes and axes, and preserved nuts around 3,000 years ago; and began producing iron tools around 2,500 years ago. In northeastern Nigeria, on the plains around Lake Chad, people lived in settlements of wooden buildings with clay floors, raised cattle and goats, and engaged in fishing and hunting between 3,000 and 4,000 years ago. The absence of rock in the area prompted the inhabitants to make tools out of bone, and ironworking started just under 2,000 years ago, which is later than other parts of West Africa like Central Nigeria or southwestern Cameroon.

In parts of East, Central, and Southern Africa, the advent of ironworking represented a more dramatic transition. In East Africa, herders speaking early **Cushitic** languages (part of the larger Afroasiatic language family) and using stone tools entered the Rift Valley from the north around 4,000 or 5,000 years ago, settling among existing hunter-gather populations. The region's first iron-using communities, who were primarily cultivators but also raised some livestock, emerged in the Great Lakes area west of Lake Victoria in what is now northwestern Tanzania, Rwanda, and Burundi around the 700s or 600s BCE. Identified by their characteristic **Urewe** pottery that have been found at several archaeological sites, around 1,000 years later these communities expanded to the eastern side of Lake Victoria, settling next to rivers or lakes or in woodlands. Indeed, the people of the Urewe tradition used their iron tools to cut firewood and clear land for cultivation and therefore changed the environment in much of East Africa, pushing back the forest. On the eastern side of the Rift Valley, older hunter-forager and pastoral communities remained strong and interacted with more recently established iron-using farmers. Population growth drove the expansion of settled farming communities identified by remains of their distinctive pottery styles, and archaeologists generally associate pottery with cultivation. By the second or third century CE, ironworking farmers settled East Africa's coastal hinterland and set the foundations for the emergence of the Swahili civilization. During the 200s and 300s CE, in what may have been a relatively rapid process, ironworking farmers spread south to what is now Zambia and Malawi. In the Central African rainforest, the introduction of ironworking sometime between around 100 BCE and 400 CE

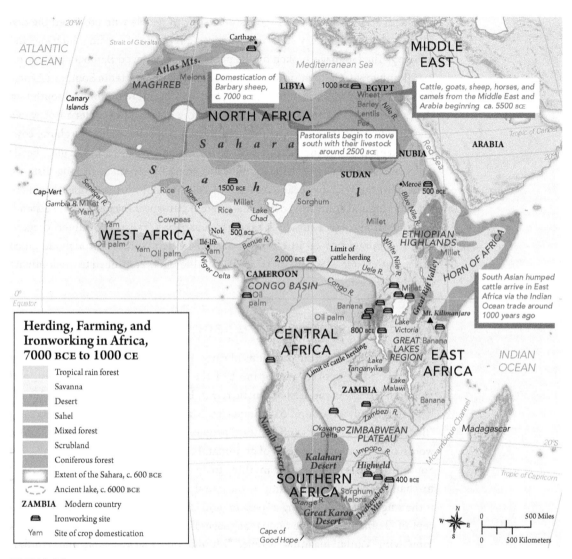

Herding, Farming, and Ironworking in Africa, 7000 BCE to 1000 CE

- Tropical rain forest
- Savanna
- Desert
- Sahel
- Mixed forest
- Scrubland
- Coniferous forest
- Extent of the Sahara, c. 600 BCE
- Ancient lake, c. 6000 BCE
- **ZAMBIA** Modern country
- Ironworking site
- Yam Site of crop domestication

≡ **MAP 1.2**

augmented the adoption of banana growing by enabling the expansion of farming communities, though hunting and gathering remained essential.

In Southern Africa, livestock raising and cultivation began in the northern part of the region around the Okavango Delta and Zambezi River, spreading from Central Africa, and on the coast of Mozambique, where crops from Asia and Southeast Asia arrived via Indian Ocean trade. While hunter-gatherer communities existed in Southern Africa since earliest times, cattle and sheep arrived from the north around 2,000 years ago, associated with people who produced the distinctive **Bambata** pottery style and practiced a mixture of herding, hunting, and foraging. The language spoken by the people who produced Bambata pottery remains unknown. Cultivation and metallurgy began much later in Southern Africa. Between around 600 and 1000 CE, people from Central Africa moved south into the Zambezi and Limpopo river valleys and the grassland of eastern Botswana. They produced iron and copper tools, cultivated crops like millet, sorghum, cowpeas and melons, and introduced goats to the region. The discovery of glass beads and seashells in their settlements indicates some involvement in long-distance trade with the Indian Ocean coast. As discussed below, it is possible that these ironworking and cultivating newcomers were Bantu-speaking people who expanded by absorbing older Khoisan-speaking groups of pastoralists and hunter-foragers. While communities of ironworking farmer-herders spread throughout much of the eastern side of Southern Africa, pastoral-foragers continued to predominate in the drier western half of the region.

The Expansion of Bantu Languages

One of the most enduring questions of early African history is how Bantu languages came to be spoken among most of the inhabitants of Central, East, and Southern Africa. In modern linguistic terms, Bantu languages comprise a broadly related family of around 650 languages. Many Bantu languages use the term "Bantu" or a very similar word to mean "people," and they share many other similar words and the same basic rules of grammar. For instance, in the Zulu language of South Africa, the root word for anything to do with humans is "ntu." Adding a prefix changes the word so "Abantu" is the plural form meaning "people," "Umuntu" is the singular form meaning a "person" and "Ubuntu" refers to the abstract concept of "humanity." In the Shona language of Zimbabwe, the root for human is "nhu" with "Vanhu" meaning "people," "Munhu" meaning a "person" and "Hunhu" meaning "humanity." The Zulu word "Abantu" and the Shona word "Vanhu" both mean "people" and are linguistically very similar. Many Bantu languages share such common vocabulary commonly involving, but not limited to, names of animals, body parts, and elements like fire and water. At the same time, they also contain diverse elements and only a few of them are mutually intelligible.

Linguists believe that the current 650 Bantu languages developed from a common ancestor language now called "proto-Bantu." During the 1960s, historical **linguists** used different linguistic theories based on the modern status of languages to debate where in Africa the original Bantu language emerged. They thought that if they could determine the historical home of Bantu languages then they could trace the spread and evolution of the broader Bantu language family across sub-Equatorial Africa. While some scholars identified the proto-Bantu home as the Benue River Valley of eastern Nigeria and Cameroon given the area's modern linguistic diversity, others claimed that the relative linguistic homogeneity of Katanga in southern DRC pointed to this area as the Bantu language homeland. Over the years, a consensus emerged that modern eastern Nigeria and Cameroon represented the historical location of proto-Bantu language and therefore the center of a historical linguistic expansion that occurred over more than several thousand years.

If Bantu languages originated in eastern Nigeria/Cameroon, how did they expand across Central, East, and Southern Africa? In the late twentieth century, academics believed that the historic people who spoke Bantu languages represented a biologically and culturally distinct population. Scholars portrayed the **Bantu expansion** as a vast movement of Bantu people who settled across much of the continent. According to this view, the Bantu were seen as possessing advanced ways of living, such as agriculture, and superior technology, such as ironworking. Therefore, as they expanded, they absorbed smaller preexisting groups of comparatively primitive hunter-gatherers such as the Twa of the Central African forest and the Khoisan of Southern Africa. Combining linguistics and archaeology, scholars traced and dated the Bantu expansion by examining the remains of particular types of pottery associated with the Bantu and remnants of ironworking. Many African History textbooks contained maps illustrating this Bantu expansion with an "X" marking the Bantu homeland in Cameroon and then bold arrows pointing to the various regions of Africa that they moved to and settled. Given more recent research and critical inquiry, many contemporary scholars now question the validity of this basic narrative of Bantu expansion.

Linguists, archaeologists, and geneticists find it increasingly difficult to reconcile the divergent evidence. Linguists push back the origin of Bantu languages to well over 3,000 years ago, which is long before the advent of iron usage in most of the regions currently dominated by Bantu-speaking populations. Furthermore, scholars have questioned whether or not it is accurate to associate a particular pottery style with people who speak a certain language. Most significantly, there is no evidence of any kind to indicate a substantial population movement into much of Central, East, and Southern Africa. While the imagined large-scale expansion of Bantu settlers across the continent probably did not happen, there may have been relatively small-scale Bantu expansions into places like the Central African rainforest and in the far south of Africa. Overall, movements of individuals or small groups as well as trade likely meant that Bantu languages expanded into existing communities and replaced and/or fused with older linguistic forms. A prominent

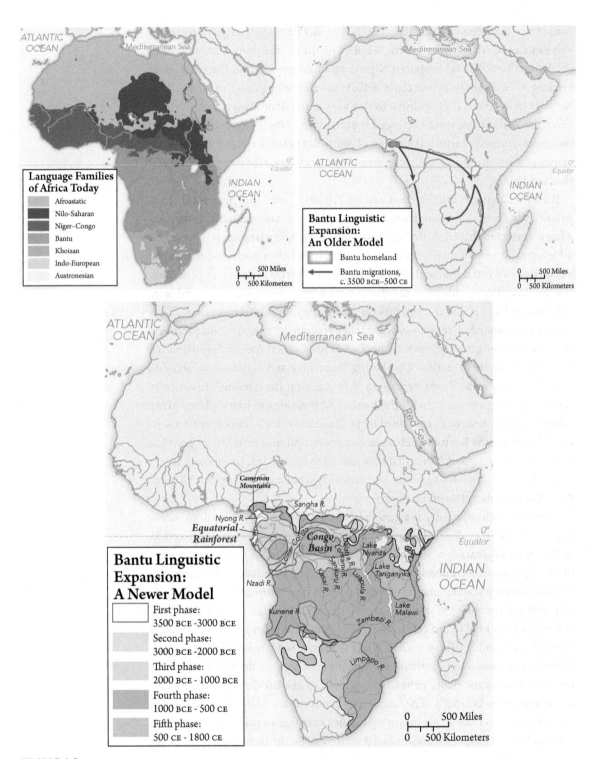

≡ **MAP 1.3**

Timeline

4–5 million years ago—Emergence of archaic humans in East Africa

2 million years ago—Archaic humans begin to migrate out of Africa

300,000 years ago—Rise of anatomically modern humans in Africa

200,000 years ago—Anatomically modern humans begin to migrate out of Africa

9,000 years ago—Beginning of herding in North Africa

9,000 to 6,000 years ago—Origins of agriculture in the fertile Sahara

7,500 years ago—Earliest evidence of herding in the fertile Sahara

6,500 years ago—Western Asian crops introduced to Egypt

4,000 to 5,000 years ago—Cushitic-speaking pastoralist enter East Africa's Rift Valley

4,500 years ago—Pastoralists migrate from the Sahara regions, moving to other parts of Africa

4,000 to 3,500 years ago—Earliest evidence of cultivation in West Africa

3,500 years ago—Contested evidence for earliest ironworking in Niger—Origin of Bantu languages in Cameroon

3,000 years ago—Introduction of iron to Egypt

2,600 to 2,700 years ago—Rise of Urewe ironworking agricultural communities in East Africa

2,500 years ago—Evidence of ironworking at Nok in Nigeria and Meroë in Sudan

2,000 or 3,000 years ago—Cattle arrive in Ethiopia

2,100 to 1,600 years ago—Spread of ironworking in Central African forest

2,000 years ago—Introduction of banana cultivation to Central Africa; cattle and sheep brought to Southern Africa; camels introduced to the dry Sahara

1,800 to 1,700 years ago—Spread of ironworking farmers into Zambia and Malawi

1,400 to 1,000 years ago—Beginning of ironworking and cultivation in northern part of Southern Africa

example of this is contained in Southern Africa's Nguni languages, including Zulu and Xhosa, which belong to the Bantu linguistic family but also contain distinct click sounds inherited from the Khoisan language family associated with historic hunter-gatherers and pastoralists. This indicates that the ancestors of today's Zulu and Xhosa people must have experienced long and intimate interaction with the Khoisan, whose languages declined in the region.

Though it could be seen as simplistic, historical linguists use the differences between the two broad branches of Bantu languages, western and eastern, to chart their expansion. The heterogeneity characteristic of western Bantu languages probably took a very long time to develop. Beginning more than 3,000 years ago, the original speakers of western Bantu languages spread slowly across the diverse riverine and forest environment of the Atlantic side of Central Africa. Given the region's many rivers and wetlands, it may have taken some time for people to learn how to live along the banks of one river before some of them moved on to another and then another. Conversely, the relative homogeneity of eastern Bantu languages, including those spoken in Southern Africa, seems to indicate a more rapid expansion from what is now Cameroon across the top of the rainforest into East Africa and then down into Central and Southern Africa. This process may have started around 2,000 or more years ago and was likely facilitated by easier movement of people and livestock across the open savannas and grasslands of these regions. Recent DNA studies indicate a great deal of genetic diversity among today's Bantu speakers and suggest that the dispersal of Bantu languages was more complex than previously thought, with numerous western and eastern expansions, and a later eastern expansion within the past 2,000 years.

Conclusion

Emerging in Africa, humans developed over several millions of years, and a number of archaic species, such as *Australopithecus Africanus*, *Homo habilis*, and *Homo erectus*, preceded anatomically modern humans. Gradually, our ancestors acquired the skills to manipulate the natural surroundings for their own purposes. After millions of years gathering foodstuffs available in the wild, between 9,000 and 6,000 years ago African peoples began to control the growth of plants and animals through farming and herding. Crops, such as wheat and barley, and domesticated animals, such as sheep and goats, were introduced to Egypt from the Middle East around 6500 BCE. A few thousand years later, pastoralists from the Sahara migrated to other parts of Africa, bringing both their animals and cultural practices with them. The development of metallurgy in Africa is contested, and the debate over whether it spread through diffusion or was independently invented in several locations at different times remains unsettled. Similarly, one of the most enduring questions of early African history is how Bantu languages came to be spoken among most of the inhabitants of Central, East, and Southern Africa. In contrast to an older view that a vast movement of Bantu people settled across much of the continent, many scholars now believe that Bantu languages expanded into existing communities and replaced and/or fused with older linguistic forms.

KEY TERMS

aurochs 29

Australopithecus Africanus 40

Bambata 36

Bantu expansion 37

Cushitic 34

diffusion 32

Homo habilis 40

linguists 36

Nok 34

radiocarbon dating 32

Urewe 34

STUDY QUESTIONS

1. What physical and behavioral adaptations and innovations characterized human evolution? Where did the first humans originate? Where and how did they spread?

2. How did environmental change affect the spread of animal herding and livestock raising in early Africa? Where are the earliest sites of agriculture in Africa? What crops were domesticated?

3. How is the spread of ironworking a foundational development in early precolonial African history?

What evidence refutes the north–south diffusion theory? What techniques do researchers use to date ancient metallurgy?

4. How do the remains from pottery provide crucial evidence of our understanding of ancient African societies?

5. How do scholars use historical linguistics and archaeology to reconstruct the Bantu expansion? How does today's view of Bantu expansion differ from older theories?

Please see page FR-1 for the Further Readings for this chapter.
For additional digital learning resources please go to
https://www.oup.com/he/falola-stapleton1e

2

Ancient North Africa

Comprising present-day Morocco, Algeria, Tunisia, Libya, and Egypt, North Africa has a history that is somewhat distinct from the rest of the continent. The existence of written records, such as Egyptian **hieroglyphs** and Latin and Greek texts, as well as extensive archaeological excavation, provide a great deal of information about North Africa's very distant past. In general, it is the only large region of Africa where historians can engage in detailed discussions about the societies, states, and economies as well as specific events and people of two, three, or even four thousand years ago. Furthermore, North Africa's geographic location on the southern shore of the Mediterranean Sea and its past physical connection to the Middle East via the Sinai Desert means that its history has always been closely connected with that of southern Europe and Western Asia. Ancient North Africa was home to indigenous African civilizations such as Egypt, Nubia, and the Berbers, but the region also attracted many external forces such as Phoenicians from present-day Lebanon, Assyrians from present-day Iraq, Persians from present-day Iran, and Greeks, Romans, and Arabs, who brought their cultures, languages, technologies, governments, armies, and religions. Of course, ancient North Africa was connected to the rest of Africa, but influences from the south, while significant, became comparatively limited by the expansion of the Sahara Desert. While all this meant that historic North African societies became incredibly diverse and the region became a cultural melting pot, it was not just a recipient of outside imports. North Africans also affected the histories of other parts of the ancient world.

Roman city. The ruins of the ancient Roman city of Timgad, founded around 100 CE in present-day Algeria.

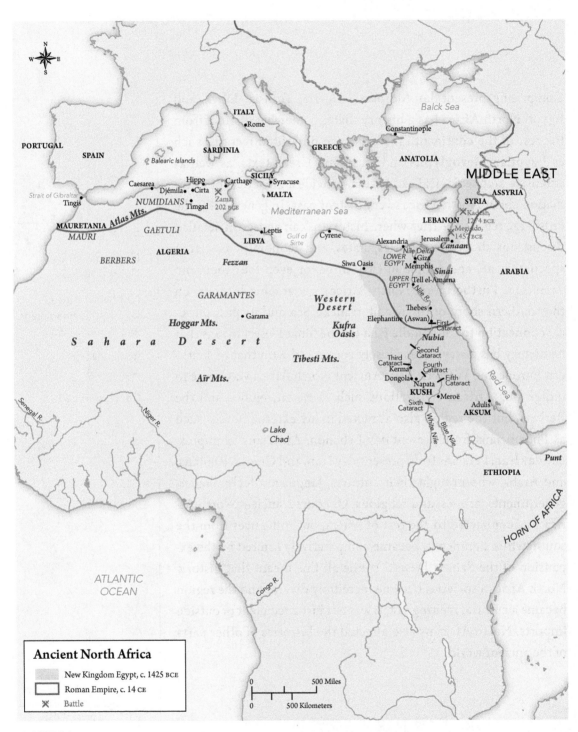

Ancient North Africa

New Kingdom Egypt, c. 1425 BCE

Roman Empire, c. 14 CE

✕ Battle

0 ———— 500 Miles

0 ———— 500 Kilometers

≡ MAP 2.1

Northeast Africa: Egypt

Egypt was the location of an ancient African civilization. Like comparable societies around the same time in India, China, and Mesopotamia, Egyptian civilization grew along the banks of a great river. The emergence of ancient Egypt was facilitated by the Nile River with its predictable patterns of flooding that eventually became important for farming. As far back as 120,000 years ago, bands of hunter-gatherers lived along the Nile, which was a much wetter area than today, consisting of a savanna with abundant wildlife. As North Africa's environment became hotter and drier, more people came to live along the great river, which became an important water source. These Nile communities were protected from attack by deserts to the east, west, and south, and the Mediterranean Sea to the north. By around 5000 BCE, Nile communities had developed agriculture such as growing barley and wheat, and livestock raising involving cattle and sheep, and they manufactured stone tools, pottery, and jewelry made from copper, ivory, and quartz. From around 4400 to 3000 BCE, the **Naqada** culture established a centralized state and engaged in trade with Ethiopia and Nubia to the south, desert dwellers to the west, and the eastern Mediterranean coast of the Middle East. In the last part of this era, the Naqada or "pre-dynastic" culture began developing elements that would become central to later ancient Egyptian civilization, such as hieroglyphic writing, royal symbols, and royal cemeteries. Around 3000 BCE a semi-mythical king called Narmer or Menes united the northern Nile's Delta region (Lower Egypt) with the southern Nile (Upper Egypt). From the new capital of Memphis located at the strategic point just before the Nile separates into a delta, the kings of Egypt's "Early Dynastic Period" (c. 3000–2686 BCE) controlled labor, resources, and land. Subsequently, Egyptian civilization was governed by 30 royal dynasties and experienced three long eras of stability called the Old Kingdom (2686–2181 BCE), Middle Kingdom (2055–1650 BCE), and New Kingdom (1550–1069 BCE).

≡ **The Pyramids.** *Left:* The Step Pyramid of Djoser is the oldest colossal stone building in Egypt, built during the Third Dynasty (c. 2686 BCE–c. 2613 BCE). *Center:* From left to right, the Pyramid of Menkaure, the Pyramid of Kafre, and the Great Pyramid of Khufu. *Right:* The Great Sphinx, constructed around 2500 BCE.

These Bronze Age kingdoms were separated by shorter intervals of instability called "intermediate periods."

Egypt's **Old Kingdom**, comprising the Third through the Sixth Dynasties, is famous for the massive pyramid tombs that its kings constructed. This building tradition began with Djoser (Zoser), first ruler of the Old Kingdom and a member of the Third Dynasty, who directed an official or priest called Imhotep to design and construct what would become the 200-foot-tall Step Pyramid. The largest pyramids were constructed at Giza during the Fourth Dynasty (2613–2494 BCE) which is considered the golden era of the Old Kingdom. Built for King Khufu, the largest pyramid stands 430 feet tall and is known as the Great Pyramid of Giza. King Khafre, Khufu's son, was responsible for the erection of the second tallest pyramid and probably the nearby Great Sphinx statue. During this era, the people of Egypt came to worship the kings as living gods responsible for the annual flooding of the Nile that was central to agricultural production. Old Kingdom rulers stood at the top of a centralized administrative hierarchy of officials and priests who collected taxes, maintained a justice system, coordinated irrigation to boost crop production, and mobilized peasant labor for ambitious construction projects. However, by the time of the Sixth Dynasty (2345–2181 BCE) the increasingly large central administration, in which officials and temples were given land grants by the king, was no longer sustainable and it gradually lost power to a network of regional rulers. The Old Kingdom collapsed amidst civil war and drought that prevented the flooding of the Nile and led to famine. During the First Intermediate Period (2181–2055 BCE), Egypt was divided between two separate kingdoms based in the north and south.

The **Middle Kingdom** (2055–1650 BCE) began when Mentuhotep II, a member of the Eleventh Dynasty that ruled southern or Upper Egypt and was based at Thebes, conquered northern or Lower Egypt reuniting the country and initiating a new era of stability in which kings regained divine status. The new rulers moved their capital from Thebes north toward the start of the Nile Delta. While the Middle Kingdom built a mostly defensive military focusing on frontier fortifications, it launched armed expeditions south into Nubia and northeast into Sinai to restore Egyptian dominance in these areas that had been lost after the fall of the Old Kingdom. Furthermore, Middle Kingdom rulers sent several naval expeditions down the Red Sea to Punt, an area believed to be in present-day Somalia. The construction of a navigable canal through the Nile's first **cataract** facilitated Egypt's southward expansion into Nubia, discussed below, and it appears that there was an attempt to dig a canal that would join the Nile Delta with the Red Sea. Scholarly views on the fall of the Middle Kingdom have evolved. Originally, academics believed that a foreign group called the **Hyksos**, probably from Western Asia, invaded from the east and used new weapons such as the horse-drawn chariot and composite bow to conquer Egypt. However, more recent research has concluded that this was not a sudden military invasion but a long process of migration by Canaanite settlers from around what is now Lebanon and Israel into Egypt perhaps to work in Egyptian mines or construction projects. As floods and overly ambitious building projects weakened the authority of the Middle Kingdom, these Canaanite immigrants also called Hyksos gradually asserted more control over the Nile Delta. It appears there is no evidence of battles during this period. Losing the north to the Hyksos and the far south to Nubia's Kingdom of Kush, the weakened Egyptian government withdrew to Thebes, thus ushering in the Second Intermediate Period (1650–1550 BCE).

The **New Kingdom** (1550–1069 BCE) began with the Egyptian re-conquest of the northern and southern territories by the rulers Kamose and Ahmose, who launched the Eighteenth Dynasty. Gaining military momentum, subsequent kings who were now called **pharaohs** embarked on expansionist campaigns that made Egypt the center of a vast empire stretching from the Nile's fourth cataract in Nubia to northern Syria. The New Kingdom developed a formidable military consisting of infantry archers and fast light chariots supported by a logistical service, led by professional officers and transported by a navy on the Mediterranean and Red Seas. In history's first recorded battle, Pharaoh Thutmose III led an Egyptian army across the Sinai Desert to defeat a Canaanite force at **Megiddo** or Armageddon in what is now Israel-Palestine around 1457 BCE. Hatshepsut, Egypt's second female pharaoh, ruled jointly with her stepson Thutmose III for 20 years, from 1478 to her death in 1458 BCE. During this time, she re-established Egyptian trade including with Punt in East Africa and embarked on one of the most audacious building programs in ancient Egyptian history, erecting many monuments and temples. Later male pharaohs, though probably not Thutmose III, tried to erase the history of this important queen by destroying her image including as statues and inscriptions on stonewalls, and removing her name from records. Despite this, Hatshepsut was one of the first prominent and powerful female rulers in world history. From the 1350s to 1330s BCE, at the height of New Kingdom wealth and power, Pharaoh Akhenaten attempted to replace the traditional polytheistic religion of Egypt with belief in the supremacy of the Sun god Aten and he created a new capital called Akhetaten (Amarna). After Akhenaten's death, successive pharaohs restored the old religion, moved the capital back to Thebes and tried to erase evidence of this short experimental period. Around this time, the newer but also Bronze Age Hittite Empire in Asia Minor, modern Turkey, clashed with New Kingdom Egypt over control of what is now Syria, Lebanon, and Israel-Palestine. In 1274 BCE, Pharaoh Ramesses II led an Egyptian army against the Hittites at the Battle of Kadesh where both sides employed a total of around 5,000

≡ **Hatshepsut.** Egypt's second female pharaoh, Hatshepsut ruled jointly with her stepson Thutmose III for 20 years, from 1478 BCE to her death in 1458 BCE.

to 6,000 horse-drawn chariots. Although Ramesses returned home claiming a great battlefield victory, the engagement resulted in a military stalemate and prompted the Egyptians and Hittites to sign the world's first known peace treaty.

From around 1000 BCE, New Kingdom Egypt gradually lost its empire as Libyans advanced into the western part of the Nile Delta, mysterious "Sea Peoples" raided the north, and Egyptian priests of the god Amun undermined the pharaohs and gained control of the south. In a process known as the **Late Bronze Age Collapse**, New Kingdom Egypt declined at around the same time as other eastern Mediterranean Bronze Age civilizations, like the Hittites and Mycenaean Greece, that gave way to new powers with ironmaking technology.

During the subsequent Third Intermediate Period (1069–653 BCE) Egypt experienced several waves of foreign invasion and conquest. In 727 BCE, the kingdom of Kush, based in what is now Sudan, captured Thebes and then the Nile Delta, and established Egypt's Twenty-Fifth Dynasty, or the Nubian dynasty, which synthesized Nubian and Egyptian cultures. From 671 to 667 BCE, the Assyrian Empire, a power centered in modern Iraq and Syria that used iron weapons and horse cavalry as well as chariots, invaded Egypt and pushed its Nubian rulers back to the south. The Assyrians established a regime of vassal Egyptian Saite kings who, in 653 BCE, asserted their independence with the help of Greek mercenaries, beginning a long history of Greek influence in Egypt.

Given its geographic position linking Africa and Western Asia, and the Mediterranean and Red Seas, Egypt would experience repeated external invasions and conquests over the next 1,000 years. Although the Saite kings led a brief economic and cultural resurgence in Egypt, the country was occupied by the Persian Empire in 525 BCE, with Persian emperor Cambyses II making himself pharaoh but ruling from Persia. In 402 BCE, Egypt regained independence but the Persians invaded again in 343 BCE and overthrew Nectanebo II who was the last Egyptian pharaoh and Egypt's last indigenous ruler until 1952 CE. In 332 BCE, Alexander the Great, leader of the expanding Macedonian–Greek Empire, took over Egypt without encountering much resistance. Alexander proclaimed himself son of the Egyptian god Amun, and established the port city of Alexandria as a new capital and an important trade and cultural center. With the death of Alexander in 323 BCE, his long-time friend and general Ptolemy I Soter, also a Macedonian, made himself pharaoh of Egypt, founding the **Ptolemaic Kingdom**. In Ptolemaic Egypt, Greeks formed an elite class, and aspects of Greek and Egyptian culture and religion were combined. This incited a series of Egyptian rebellions which were suppressed. Ptolemaic Egypt clashed with the neighboring Seleucid Empire, a similar successor state of Alexander that dominated much of the Middle East including Persia, and the city state of Rome in Italy became dependent on Egyptian grain imports, which drew this rising Mediterranean power into Egyptian politics.

In 30 BCE, the new Roman Empire incorporated Egypt following the defeat of allied Roman and Egyptian forces led by Marc Antony and Cleopatra VII, respectively, at the hands of the Roman forces of Octavian, who became Emperor Augustus. With the death of Cleopatra, Egypt's Ptolemaic dynasty ended and the country became a Roman province administered by Roman officials. The Romans clashed with the kingdom of Kush to the south, and oppressive Roman taxation in Egypt prompted a series of uprisings. During the period of Roman rule, Christianity spread into Egypt and eventually replaced Egyptian and Greco-Roman religions and led to the abandonment of Egyptian hieroglyphic writing in favor of Greek and Latin script. The meaning of Egyptian hieroglyphs was lost until

≡ **Cleopatra VII** (69–30 BCE) was the last ruler of Egypt's Ptolemaic dynasty.

1799 CE, when the discovery in Memphis of the **Rosetta Stone**, which dates to the Ptolemaic period and is inscribed with Egyptian and Greek text, enabled scholars to decipher Egyptian symbols and therefore study ancient Egyptian history. After the 300s CE, with the division of the Roman Empire into eastern and western sections, Egypt became part of the Eastern Roman or Byzantine Empire based at Constantinople (today's Istanbul); Greek became the administrative language and Christianity the official imperial religion. However, the Sassanid Empire, based in what is now Iran, occupied Egypt from 618 to 628 CE, when the country was briefly recovered by the Byzantine Empire. The Roman-Byzantine period concluded in 639–641 CE, when invading Arab armies, converts to the new religion of Islam, conquered Egypt, using it as a staging area for later westward expansion across the rest of North Africa and south into Nubia.

Northeast Africa: Nubia

Geographically, ancient Nubia straddled what is now southern Egypt and northern Sudan. It was centered on the Upper Nile, stretching from the first cataract (or rapids) at Aswan in modern Egypt to the sixth cataract, just north of present-day Khartoum, the modern capital of Sudan. A society that was very similar to pre-dynastic Egypt and that traded with the Egyptians existed between the Nile's first and second cataracts from around 3800 to 3100 BCE. As with neighboring peoples in East Africa, cattle-raising became very important for the ancient Nubians. From around 3000 to 2500 BCE, as in Egypt, the region dried out, prompting nomads from the Sahara to move to the fertile banks of the Nile and adopt a settled way of life though this seemed to cause a period of conflict and dislocation in Nubia. While Nubia had long served as a channel for trade between Egypt and sub-Saharan Africa, this economy expanded after around 2500 BCE, with gold, ivory, ebony, and exotic animals transported north along the Nile. Ancient Nubians developed a reputation as skilled archers, with the ancient Egyptians referring to the area as "the Land of the Bow"; and, beginning in the era of the Old Kingdom, Nubian mercenaries regularly served in Egyptian armies.

By 1700 BCE, the city of Kerma, located just south of the Nile's third cataract in what is now northern Sudan, contained an urban population of around 10,000 people and was the capital of a highly centralized state that controlled Nubia between the first and fourth cataracts. The wealthy elites of Kerma supervised a kingdom engaged in agriculture, extensive livestock-raising, gold mining, and regional trade along the Nile, and kings mobilized labor to build large royal tombs. It is thought that the Kerma people spoke Cushitic languages common to the Horn of Africa. The Kerma kingdom reached the height of its influence and wealth around the same time that Middle Kingdom Egypt, its northern trading partner and rival, went into decline. Taking advantage of Egyptian problems with the Hyksos in the north, Kerma invaded Egypt from 1575 to 1550 BCE, inflicting such a humiliating defeat on the Egyptians that subsequent pharaohs tried to eliminate any mention of it in historical records. However, around 1500 BCE, a resurgent New Kingdom Egypt invaded and conquered Kerma and ruled Nubia to just beyond the fourth cataract of the Nile. The Egyptians appointed a governor of Nubia and built a new capital of Napata near the Nile's fourth cataract. Nubia became the location of Egyptian temples and settlements, enslaved labor was used to mine gold that was sent north to support the Egyptian Empire, and Nubian society and religion became partly Egyptianized.

Around 1000 BCE, the collapse of New Kingdom Egypt and the withdrawal of Egyptian authority from Nubia led to the rise of the kingdom of Kush based at Napata. During the 720s and 710s BCE, King Piye of Kush, a devotee of the Egyptian god Amun, led an invasion of Egypt taking advantage of its political fragmentation to establish a Nubian dynasty there. The Nubian pharaohs embarked on fresh building programs and constructed the first new pyramid royal tombs since the Middle Kingdom with many

≡ **Taharqa.** A member of Egypt's Twenty-Fifth Dynasty, Taharqa ruled both Egypt and Nubia from 690 to 664 BCE.

≡ **Meroë.** From around 500 BCE to 350 CE, Meroë served as capital of the Nubian Kingdom of Kush in what is now Sudan, where the Nubians produced iron and built pyramid tombs for their kings.

of these located in what is now northern Sudan. In the 670s and 660s BCE, the Nubian-Egyptian pharaoh Taharqa became involved in wars with the Assyrians in present-day Israel-Palestine and this eventually led to the Assyrian invasion of Egypt which overthrew Nubian rule. During the 500s BCE, Egyptian and Persian raids into Nubia prompted the kingdom of Kush to shift its capital from Napata further south to Meroë, south of the Nile's fifth cataract, which became a major center for the new technology of iron production and the location of a large pyramid tomb complex. The royal court of Kush initially employed Egyptian hieroglyphs but from around 180 BCE it developed a distinct **Meroitic script** that combined hieroglyphs and an alphabet and which is yet to be decoded by modern scholars. The kingdom of Kush was a matrilineal society in which the king's sister became a powerful queen mother as her son would become the royal heir. Around 27 BCE, Queen Mother Amanirenas led an armed incursion into the southern part of Roman-ruled Egypt and returned to Meroë with a bronze bust of the Roman Emperor Augustus later found by archaeologists. In revenge, a Roman army advanced into Nubia, destroyed the old Kushitic capital of Napata and established a frontier outpost at Primus (Qasr Ibrim) between the first and second cataracts. Meroë and Rome negotiated a treaty in 21 or 20 BCE, which initiated several centuries of peaceful relations and expanded trade between the two states. Following many years of decline, the kingdom of Kush collapsed around 350 CE, and some scholars believe that an invading army from the kingdom of Aksum in what is now Ethiopia and Eritrea destroyed Meroë.

During the late 300s CE, after the fall of Kush, Nubia was divided between three small kingdoms located along the Upper Nile: Nobatia in the north, Makuria in the center, and Alodia in the south. Christianity had already entered Nubia from Egypt, and in the sixth century CE the Byzantine Empire, eager to secure allies

≡ **Faras Cathedral.** This wall frieze from Faras Cathedral in Nubia, which dates to around 800–1000 CE, depicts Nubian Bishop Petros standing in front of Saint Peter.

against Sassanid Persia, dispatched Christian missionaries who converted the kings of Nubia. The Nubian Christian church used both Greek and Egyptian Coptic languages in its liturgy, and constructed churches and monasteries. With its capital at Dongola, the Makuria kingdom grew in power, cultivating strong religious and trade contacts with the Byzantine Empire. Sometime during the 600s, it absorbed its northern neighbor of Nobatia, which was weakened, perhaps, by the Persian occupation of adjacent Egypt. Christian Nubia became one of the few places in the region to thwart the expansion of Arab Muslim power between c. 640 and 710 CE. With their successful takeover of Egypt, Arab Muslim armies invaded Christian Makuria in 641–42 and 651–52 CE but could not overcome stubborn Nubian resistance. After the Arabs failed to capture Dongola, the Arabs and Makuria negotiated a treaty called the **Baqt** which established peaceful relations but required Nubia to send 380 enslaved workers per year to Egypt. The agreement lasted for around 700 years, making it perhaps the world's most enduring peace treaty. In 707 CE, the Nubian Bishop Paulos and the Makurian King Merkuiros sponsored construction of the great Faras Cathedral in northern Nubia, which was excavated in the early 1960s just before the area was flooded to create modern Egypt's Aswan Dam.

Northwest Africa: Berbers, Carthaginians, and Romans

Originating in present-day Lebanon, the Phoenicians were sailors and merchants who established a chain of outposts along the Mediterranean coast of southern Europe and North Africa sometime between 1500 and 300 BCE. Sometime between around 830 and 800 BCE, Phoenician seafarers founded the city of Carthage on the coast of present-day Tunisia, and some accounts attribute this to the exiled Phoenician Queen Elissa (also called Dido). By around 500 BCE, Carthage had become an independent city-state with a powerful navy and controlled parts of the Western Mediterranean coasts of North Africa and Iberia, and the islands of Sicily, Sardinia, and Malta, as well as the Balearic Islands. In North Africa, the Carthaginians collected tribute from indigenous Berber communities in the hinterland. Levies of Berber cavalry became an important component of Carthage's army. Carthage became a trade intermediary between the Berbers—who acquired goods and enslaved workers further south via the trans-Saharan trade network—and the rest of the Mediterranean. Seafarers from Carthage ventured out into the Atlantic, exploring the coast of Morocco and perhaps further south to Senegal, and north to Portugal, and perhaps, even to northwestern Europe. During the 400s and 300s BCE, Sicily was the scene of numerous conflicts between Carthage and the Greek colony of Syracuse backed by city states in Greece. Between 310 and 307 BCE, the Greek ruler of Syracuse, Agathocles, led an unsuccessful military expedition

≡ **Carthage.** A modern representation of the ancient city shows a thriving port and ordered streets.

to North Africa to attack Carthage. Pyrrhus, ruler of the Greek state of Epirus in the western Balkans, fought against the Carthaginians in Sicily from 289 to 275 BCE but conflict with local Greek settlers compelled him to return home before launching a planned expedition against Carthage itself.

Carthage clashed with the rising Roman Republic over control of the Western Mediterranean. Three **Punic Wars**, named after the Roman word "Punicus" which means "Phoenician," were fought between these two powers. During the First Punic War (264–241 BCE), Rome built a navy that challenged Carthaginian control of the Mediterranean. Roman victory resulted in Carthage withdrawing from Sicily and paying the Romans a large indemnity. Fought from 218 to 201 BCE, the Second Punic War involved a Carthaginian army led by **Hannibal**, who marched through Spain and crossed the Alps to invade Italy. The long war ended with a Roman expedition under Scipio Africanus that landed near Carthage where it achieved victory at the climactic **Battle of Zama**. During the conflict, Hannibal employed trained North African war elephants as a shock force, but eventually the Roman infantry devised tactics to counter them. Decisively defeated, Carthage signed a treaty that deprived it of its empire in Spain, limited the size of its navy, forbade it to raise an army, and compelled it to make a huge payment to Rome. A resurgence of Carthaginian power led to the Third Punic War (149–146 BCE) in which Rome dispatched an expeditionary force that destroyed the city and created the Roman province of Africa that included present-day eastern Algeria, Tunisia, and the western Libyan coast. This total Roman victory meant that there are no Carthaginian sources related to the Punic Wars, the history of which is dominated by Roman accounts.

Cave paintings reveal that **Berbers**, the ancestors of most people who now live in northwestern Africa, inhabited present-day Morocco, Algeria, Tunisia, and Libya from around 10,000 BCE, when the region was a savanna. By the time of Carthage, the Berbers were herders and farmers who had developed several distinct groups, such as the **Numidians** who lived south and west of Carthage in present-day Tunisia and Algeria, and the Mauri who lived further to the west in what is now western Algeria and Morocco. There were also the Garamantes Berbers who inhabited the Libyan hinterland in what is now the Fezzan region and developed a sophisticated irrigation system in the dry northern Sahara. During the Second Punic War (218–201 BCE), the Numidians comprised two rival kingdoms; the Masaesyli to the west who were led by Syphax, and the Massylii in the east who were led by Masinissa. Syphax initially allied with the Romans and Masinissa with the Carthaginians, but they eventually switched sides, with Masinissa and his Numidian cavalry playing a major role in the ultimate Roman victory at Zama. With Roman support, Masinissa took territory from a weakened Carthage and united the Numidians into a single kingdom with the city of Cirta (present-day Constantine in Algeria), as its capital. Renewed conflict between Masinissa's Numidian kingdom and Carthage prompted Roman military intervention that destroyed the latter during the Third Punic War. Based in their new North African province that was once Carthage, the Romans began backing competing leaders in an unfolding civil war in neighboring Numidia. This led to the Jugurthine War (112–106 BCE) in which the Romans fought a long and troubled campaign against the Numidian leader Jugurtha who had previously served as a Roman ally in Spain. While the Romans occupied Numidian towns, they found it difficult to counter the mobile guerrilla tactics and speed of the Numidian light horsemen. The conflict ended when the Romans convinced the Mauri Berbers of King Bocchus, who had been helping the Numidians, to betray Jurgurtha, who was captured and brought to Rome, where he was paraded through the streets and then starved to death in prison. As a result, the Mauri gained control of part of western Numidia and eastern Numidia was divided among several Numidian rulers.

During the Roman Civil War of 49–45 BCE, the eastern Numidian King Tuba I sided with Roman general Pompey, who was eventually defeated by the forces of Julius Caesar. Consequently, in 46 BCE, Caesar annexed eastern Numidia as the Roman province of Africa Nova. In 25 BCE, the Mauri kingdom, also known as Mauritania, became a vassal state of Rome under the Roman-appointed Numidian King Juba II who married Cleopatra Selene II, the daughter of Cleopatra and Marc Antony, and ruled from the city

≡ **Juba II,** the Roman-appointed Numidian King who married Cleopatra Selene II.

of Caesarea which is now the Algerian coastal town of Cherchell. Under Juba and Cleopatra, Mauritania became a center for Greco-Roman scholarship and the arts, and a wealthy exporter of dyes, wood, and animal products to the Roman Empire. However, the Mauritanian kingdom's stability was rocked by a series of Berber rebellions from 17 to 24 CE at the end of Juba's reign. In 40 CE, another rebellion broke out in Mauritania after the assassination of its king Ptolemy, son of Juba and Cleopatra, during a visit to Rome and on the orders of Roman Emperor Caligula. The Romans suppressed the insurrection and then, around 44 CE, annexed the kingdom as two Roman provinces: Mauretania Caesariensis, based at Caesarea in what is now Algeria, and Mauretania Tingitana, based at the city of Tingis, which is today's Tangiers in Morocco and sits on the Atlantic side of the **Strait of Gibraltar**. By this time, the original Roman North Africa provinces of Africa Vetus, formerly Carthage, and Africa Nova, formerly eastern Numidia, had been combined into the large province of Africa Proconsularis. All of North Africa, including Egypt, was now under Roman rule.

Roman North Africa

Although the Romans mainly ruled coastal North Africa, they occasionally ventured south into the Sahara either retaliating against inland raiders or in search of gold and other valuable commodities. The first southward Roman expedition occurred in 19 BCE, when a Roman army under Cornelius Balbus, starting at the city of Sabratha in present-day western Libya, marched some 400 miles inland to occupy the Garamantes Berber capital of Garama (today's Germa in Libya) and then dispatched a smaller expeditionary force further south. It possibly reached the Niger River in what is now Mali. In 41 CE, Suetonius Paulinus led a Roman army across Morocco's Atlas Mountains, with some of his troops making it as far south as the Senegal River. Setting out from the Libyan coast in 50 CE, a Roman expedition under Septimius Flaccus passed through Garamantes Berber territory and arrived at Lake Chad, which was much larger than today. In 70 CE, Valerius Festus took a Roman force south to explore the Hoggar Mountains in southern Algeria and the Aïr Mountains in northern Niger, and some historians believe they might have reached the Niger River. In 90 CE, another Roman expedition led by Julius Maternus started out at the Gulf of Sirte on the Libyan coast, travelled inland to the Kufra oasis in southern Libya, and then explored the Tibesti Mountains in what is now northern Chad.

North Africa became a chief supplier of food for the rest of the Roman Empire. Beginning in the first century CE, North Africa exported half a million tons of grain per year as well as significant amounts of olive oil, wine, and livestock. The region was also a source of wool produced by the Berbers; glass made in Egypt; commodities acquired south of the Sahara, such as leather, enslaved people, and exotic wildlife for Roman public events such as gladiatorial games; and Asian goods such as silks arriving via ships in the Red Sea. Under Roman rule, North African urban life expanded as older cities like Alexandria thrived and new ones were constructed. In 29 CE, the Romans rebuilt Carthage, which became a celebrated intellectual center and one of the Mediterranean's most populous cities, and later they founded Timgad and Djémila in present-day eastern Algeria. During the Roman era, Northwestern Africa was the location of between 500 and 600 cities. Linked by a road network, Roman cities in North Africa featured sporting facilities, amphitheaters, baths, elite homes, and complex systems to supply water. While the urban population became Romanized adopting the Latin language, Berber culture and language survived in some rural areas and on the imperial periphery. To discourage frontier raiding and maintain internal security, Roman legions garrisoned North Africa, bringing soldiers and camp followers from across the Mediterranean and other parts of Europe and adding to the region's diversity. In addition, North Africans travelled to other parts of the Roman Empire such as the Numidian cavalrymen who helped the Romans conquer Britain.

As in Egypt, Christianity spread into Northwest Africa during Roman times. The pagan Roman state initiated violent persecutions of African Christians around 200 CE, but the young religion continued to flourish. Around 235, the first known Christian bishop of Carthage hosted a council of 18 fellow bishops from Numidia. Beginning in the 200s, some devout Christians in Egypt moved into the desert to remove themselves from worldly life and focus on prayer, which formed an important part of

≡ **Syncletica of Alexandria** was a Christian saint and Desert Mother who lived in Roman Egypt in the fourth century CE.

the development of Christian monasticism. Known as **Desert Mothers**, Egyptian women such as Syncletica of Alexandria, Sarah of the Desert, and Mary of Egypt, who became the patron saint of penitents, played a central role in this early Christian **asceticism** during the 300s and 400s.

However, early Christianity in North Africa experienced serious divisions. Originating with the Roman persecutions of the early 300s, Christianity in North Africa split between the **Donatists**, who believed that priests who had renounced their faith to avoid violence could no longer administer the sacraments, and the mainstream or **Catholic Church**, which maintained that this did not matter as sacraments came from God. **Augustine** (354–430 CE), who was born in eastern Algeria and served as bishop of the city of Hippo Regis, became one of the most influential thinkers in the history of Christianity. His strong opposition to the Donatists was central to the faction's decline. In 451 CE, theological disagreement over the nature of Christ, and popular Egyptian discontent over centuries of Greek dominance, prompted the Egyptian **Coptic Church** to split from the Byzantine Christian Church. This led to the Egyptian Coptic language replacing Greek as the main language of Christianity in Egypt.

As the Western Roman Empire collapsed, a Germanic group called the **Vandals**, led by King Gaiseric, moved through Spain and crossed into the western part of North Africa in 429 CE. Over the next few years the Vandals built a kingdom in western North Africa by capturing Roman cities and building a navy which enabled them to occupy the Mediterranean islands of Corsica, Sardinia, Malta, and Sicily, and the Balearic Islands. They even sacked Rome in 455. While the Romans portrayed the Vandals as destructive barbarians—reflected in the word "vandalism"—life in North Africa's cities under Vandal rule continued much the same as before, and the Vandals cultivated amicable relations with Berber communities who became important military allies. However, religious conflict continued in North Africa, as the ruling Vandals were **Arian Christians** who believed that God the Father and God the Son were separate deities, and they sometimes persecuted local Trinitarians (including Catholics and Donatists) who maintained that God comprised the Father, Son, and Holy Spirit.

In 533 CE, Emperor Justinian I, ruler of the surviving Eastern Roman Empire that was now the Byzantine Empire, launched a military campaign to recover western North Africa from the Vandals. Making an amphibious landing near Carthage, a Byzantine army under the able general Belisarius defeated the Vandals in several battles and obliged the surrender of the Vandal King Gelimer. As western North Africa returned to Roman rule from Constantinople, the Vandals either joined the Byzantine army, fled to Europe, or integrated into the broader North African population. Chafing under the restored Roman/Byzantine regime, the Berbers staged rebellions that were violently suppressed throughout the latter half of the sixth century CE. As it was before under Rome, North Africa became an important source of food for the Byzantine Empire, with Carthage and Alexandria as major centers of trade and naval power. At the start of the 600s, Carthage became a staging area for an insurgent military campaign that overthrew the existing dynasty in Constantinople and installed Heraclius, son of the governor of western North Africa, as the new Byzantine emperor. Under Heraclius, the Byzantines fought a series of wars against the Sassanid Persians, who besieged Constantinople and occupied Egypt for a decade.

In 647, shortly after they had seized Egypt from the Byzantines, the Muslim Arabs began what would turn into a long sequence of military campaigns to conquer northwest Africa. While some Berbers converted to Islam and joined the Arab army, many tenaciously resisted Arab conquest, including the Berber warrior queen and priestess Dihya (Kahina in Arabic) of Tunisia/eastern Algeria, who was killed in battle around 700. In 698, the Arabs destroyed Carthage, which had changed hands several times during that decade, as they thought it was vulnerable to attack by the Byzantine navy. They established the new regional capital of Tunis, which was more easily defended. By 710, with the help of a newly formed Arab navy, the Arabs were in control of all northwest Africa, from Libya to the Atlantic coast of Morocco, and they subsequently continued their conquests north into Spain. Christianized just a few centuries earlier, North Africa was now, in the span of a few decades, under the rule of Muslims.

Conclusion

Forming the southern rim of the ancient Mediterranean world, North Africa was the location of many classical civilizations of antiquity, including the Egyptians, Nubians, Carthaginians, Greeks, and Romans. Egypt and Nubia, both emerging along the Nile, are not only the oldest known African civilizations, they are also among the most ancient in the world, predating Greece and Rome by around 2,000 years. Around the time the Roman Empire was established in 30 BCE, Old Kingdom Egypt was as far back in history as ancient Rome is to us today. While it is common to see ancient Greece and Rome as having laid the foundations of modern Western civilization, the more ancient peoples of North Africa represent even deeper roots. In addition, the ancient Greco-Roman world, with all its cultural achievements, also included North Africa. Toward the end of the ancient period, North Africa served as the venue for the early expansion and development of two new religions, Christianity and Islam, which would eventually spread around the world.

Timeline

c. 5000 BCE—Nile communities developed agriculture

c. 4400–3000 BCE—Naqada culture in Egypt

c. 3000 BCE—Unification of Upper and Lower Egypt

2686–2181 BCE—Old Kingdom Egypt

2055–1650 BCE—Middle Kingdom Egypt

c. 1700–1500 BCE—Kerma kingdom in Nubia

1550–1069 BCE—New Kingdom Egypt

1478–1458 BCE—Reign of Hatshepsut

1457 BCE—Battle of Megiddo

1274 BCE—Battle of Kadesh

c. 1000 BCE—Rise of the kingdom of Kush in Nubia

830–800 BCE—Foundation of Carthage by Phoenicians

727 BCE—Kingdom of Kush conquers Egypt

671–667 BCE—Assyrian invasion of Egypt

525 BCE—Persian invasion of Egypt

c. 500s–300s BCE—Capital of Kush moved from Napata to Meroë

343 BCE—The last indigenous Egyptian pharaoh Nectanebo II overthrown by Persians

332 BCE—Alexander the Great conquers Egypt and builds Alexandria

323 BCE—Beginning of Ptolemaic dynasty in Egypt

310–307 BCE—Greek leader Agathocles attacks Carthage

264–241 BCE—First Punic War (Carthage vs. Rome)

218–201 BCE—Second Punic War

c. 180 BCE—Earliest known Meroitic script

149–146 BCE—Third Punic War

112–106 BCE—Jurgurthine War (Numidia vs Rome)

30 BCE—End of Ptolemaic dynasty and incorporation of Egypt into the new Roman Empire

27–20 BCE—War between Rome and Kush-Meroë

25 BCE—Mauritanian kingdom becomes vassal state of Rome

19 BCE—First Roman expedition into Sahara Desert

29 CE—Romans rebuild city of Carthage

44 CE—Roman Empire annexes ancient Mauritania

50 CE—Roman expedition reaches Lake Chad

200s+ CE—Spread of Christianity into western North Africa

285 CE—Division of Eastern and Western Roman Empire

350 CE—Fall of kingdom of Kush

354–430 CE—Life of Augustine, Bishop of Hippo Regis

300s–400s CE—Collapse of Western Roman Empire; Eastern Roman Empire becomes Byzantine Empire

429 CE—Vandals arrive in western North Africa and establish a kingdom

455 CE—Vandals sack Rome

533—Byzantine Empire recovers western North Africa from the Vandals

500s CE—Conversion of Nubian kings to Christianity

618–628 CE—Sasanid Persians occupy Egypt

639–641 CE—Arab Muslim conquest of Egypt

641–42 and 651–52—Arab Muslim invasions of Christian Nubia

647 CE—Start of Arab Muslim invasion of western North Africa

652C CE—Baqt treaty between Arab Egypt and Nubia

698 CE—Arabs destroy Carthage and build Tunis

707 CE—Construction of Faras Cathedral begins in Nubia

710 CE—Arab conquest of North Africa complete

KEY TERMS

Arian Christians 58

asceticism 58

Augustine 58

Baqt 53

Battle of Zama 54

Berbers 54

cataract 46

Catholic Church 58

Coptic Church 58

Desert Mothers 58

Donatists 58

Hannibal 54

hieroglyphs 43

Hyksos 46

Late Bronze Age
   Collapse 48

Megiddo 47

Meroitic script 52

Middle Kingdom 46

Naqada 45

New Kingdom 47

Numidians 54

Old Kingdom 46

pharaohs 47

Ptolemaic kingdom 49

Punic Wars 54

Rosetta Stone 50

Strait of Gibraltar 56

Vandals 58

STUDY QUESTIONS

1. How did geography influence Egyptian civilization? What was the relationship between gods and humans in ancient Egypt? What problems did Egypt face in the Late Bronze Age? Which peoples and empires invaded Egypt after the decline of the New Kingdom?

2. What factors led to the rise of the kingdom of Kush? What obstacles did it face? How did Christianity and Islam influence Nubian culture?

3. Why did Carthage become a leading Mediterranean power by 500 BCE? Why did Carthage clash with Rome? What was the outcome of the Punic Wars? How did the Roman and Byzantine Empires interact with North Africa?

Please see page FR-2 for the Further Readings for this chapter. For additional digital learning resources please go to https://www.oup.com/he/falola-stapleton1e

3

Medieval North Africa, c. 800–1500 CE

The term "medieval" is often used by historians of Europe, the Middle East, and North Africa to refer to a middle historical period of about 1,000 years that divides the ancient and modern eras. There are no specific events or dates that mark the start and end of the **medieval era** or Middle Ages. It is, however, common to date its beginning from roughly the fall of the Western Roman Empire in the 400s and its end to events that took place in the 1400s, such as the destruction of the Byzantine Empire by the Ottomans in 1453 or the Christian seizure of the last Muslim stronghold in Spain in 1492. For North Africa, specifically, the Muslim Arab conquest of the region from c. 630 to 710 and the Ottoman occupation of Egypt in 1517 serve as useful benchmarks for understanding the chronology of the medieval era. During this period, North African societies experienced profound change involving Islamization and Arabization. At the start of the medieval era, most North Africans were Christians, or to a lesser extent Jews, who spoke a variety of languages, including Berber dialects in the northwest, Coptic in Egypt, and Nubian along the Upper Nile, as well as Greek and Latin among urban elites. By the end of the Middle Ages, Islam had become the dominant religion in North Africa. Christians and Jews formed marginalized minorities, and Arabic language and script spread widely, replacing older languages and their written forms. While North Africa and southern Europe were part of an integrated Mediterranean cultural and religious world at the start of the medieval period, these regions were significantly divided by the events of the subsequent centuries. The rising Muslim and Arab powers of North Africa and the Middle East, though certainly experiencing conflicts among themselves, became increasingly at odds with the Christian powers of medieval Europe. At the same time, relations between North Africans and peoples to the

Al-Qarawiyyin Mosque and university in Fez, Morocco. Founded in 859 CE, for centuries it was one of the leading spiritual and educational centers of the Islamic world.

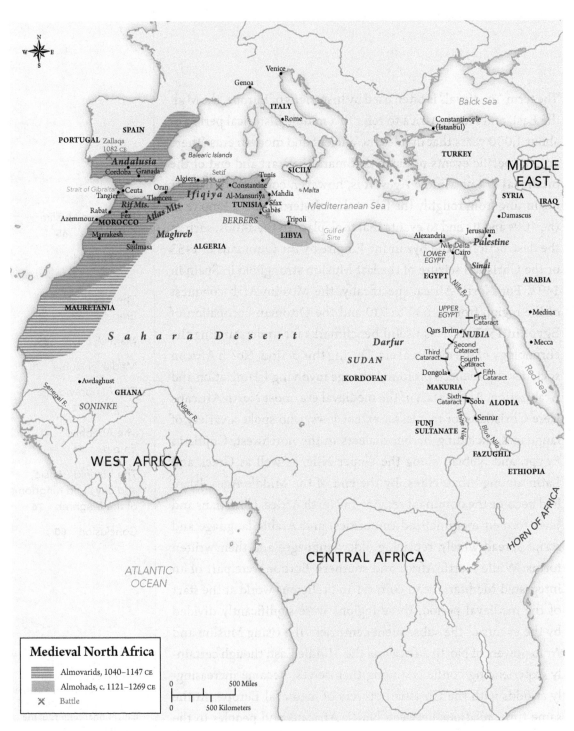

MAP 3.1

south, beyond the Sahara into West Africa, expanded during this era and forms the subject of another chapter. In surveying the medieval history of North Africa, this chapter essentially begins with Egypt and Nubia (modern Sudan) and progresses west to look at the western part of the region, also known as the Maghreb, which includes what is now Libya, Tunisia, Algeria, and Morocco.

Early Arab Muslim Caliphates

The Muslim Arab conquest of North Africa was mainly conducted by the **Umayyad Caliphate**, which, based in the Middle Eastern city of Damascus, established one of the world's largest empires of the time, stretching from Persia to Morocco and Spain between 661 and 750 CE. In this period, Islam divided into two main branches: the **Shi'a**, who maintained that the Prophet Mohammed had designated his cousin and son-in-law Ali to succeed him as head of the faithful, thus believing that only God could appoint the religious-political leader of Islam or caliph; and the **Sunni**, who rejected this claim. The Umayyad Empire was ruled by a relatively small group of Sunni Muslim Arabs, while most of the population consisted of Christians and Jews who paid a special tax to the state. However, non-Arab converts to Islam, such as the Berbers of western North Africa, became discontented as they were not granted equality with Muslim Arabs. While Arabs controlled the administration and military, and lived in special fortresses, non-Arab Muslims were excluded from state positions and required to pay the same tax as non-Muslims. In 750, as a result, the Umayyad rulers were overthrown by a widespread rebellion that united Shi'a Muslims and non-Arab Sunni Muslims. Some remnants of the Umayyad dynasty fled to Spain, where they founded a new state. With this revolution, the Middle East and North Africa came under the new **Abbasid Caliphate**, ruled by a Sunni Arab royal family that claimed descent from the Prophet Mohammed's uncle, and created a new capital of Baghdad. Given difficulties in governing such a huge empire, smaller independent states broke away, such as the Idrisid kingdom in Morocco in the 790s and the Aghlabid kingdom in Algeria and Tunisia in the 830s. In Morocco, the Idrisid dynasty founded the city of Fez around 790 that became a haven for Arabs expelled from Tunisia and Andalusia in Spain, and in 859 it became the location of the **University of Al-Qarawiyyin**, which is currently the world's oldest continually operating university. In 868, the Abbasid ruler in Baghdad appointed a Turkish military commander named Ahmad Ibn Tulun as governor of Egypt, but within a few years, he also created an independent state that eventually conquered Syria. This Tulunid dynasty ruled Egypt until 905, when the country was re-conquered by the Abbasids. Both the Umayyad and Abbasid caliphates were embroiled in regular warfare with the declining Christian Byzantine Empire—centered on Constantinople in what is now Turkey—which had once ruled most of North Africa and the Middle East.

The Fatimid Empire

Originating in Iraq and Syria, the Fatimid movement claimed descent from Fatima, who was the Prophet Mohammed's daughter and wife of his alleged successor Ali, and as such, they practiced the Shi'a interpretation of Islam. During the 800s, the movement relocated to western North Africa to escape persecution by the Abbasid dynasty, which subscribed to Sunni Islam. Rallying the oppressed Berbers of the Maghreb, the Arab Fatimid leaders launched a military offensive against the Arab dominated states of the region, eventually taking over what is now Morocco, Algeria, Tunisia, and Libya. The **Fatimids** planned to use the Maghreb as a staging area for the seizure of Egypt and then overthrow the Abbasid dynasty in Baghdad. After their initial invasion of Egypt failed in the 910s, the Fatimids strengthened and expanded their empire in western North Africa and occupied the island of Sicily. However, the Fatimid Empire was challenged during the 930s and 940s by a rebellion of the Khariji movement, which advocated that any Muslim, regardless of descent, could become leader of the faith. In 947, the Fatimids led by Ismail al-Mansur crushed the Khariji rebels and built a new capital called Al-Mansuriya, located in Tunisia and modeled on Baghdad. In 969, the Fatimids used their Berber army to conquer Egypt, where they founded the new capital of Al-Qahira, or Cairo, meaning "victorious." Egypt became the center of the Fatimid Empire, which expanded into Palestine, Syria, and the western side of the Arabian Peninsula, including the Muslim holy sites of Mecca and Medina. In Egypt, the Fatimids established an effective administrative system, promoted education, and exported flax, glassware, and ceramics in long-distance trade networks that stretched from Spain to China. While the Fatimids built the famous **Al-Azhar** mosque-university in Cairo to spread Shi'a Islam, they did not force this belief on the mostly Sunni Muslim Egyptians, and Jews and Christians were employed as state officials.

As the Fatimid Empire shifted eastward to Egypt, Berber subordinate rulers were appointed to govern parts of western North Africa or the Maghreb. Subsequently, western North Africa became fragmented between the Berber Zirid dynasty ruling Tunisia and the Hammadid dynasty ruling Algeria, and in the early 1000s these kingdoms adopted Sunni Islam to secure greater autonomy from the Shi'a Fatimids in Egypt. In response, the Fatimids in Egypt encouraged Arab nomads there, such as the Banu Hilal, Banu Sulauym, and Banu Ma'qil, to move west into the Maghreb, where they clashed with the Berber states. This second Arab invasion of western North Africa had a huge impact, as the replacement of Berber agriculture with Arab pastoralism meant that the Maghreb's interior cities were abandoned because of lack of food and the Arabic language expanded across the region.

During the 1060s, Fatimid Egypt experienced severe problems. First, the regular Nile River floods were unusually low, which caused drought and famine. Second, a civil war broke out among the ethnic factions of the Fatimid army with the Turkish and Sudanese soldiers fighting each other and the Berbers switching allegiance between these two sides. Although the Fatimid leaders restored order in 1072, Fatimid Egypt never fully recovered from these disasters. In the late 1090s, the Christian European military occupation of the "Holy Land" in present-day Palestine-Israel, known as the First Crusade, fatally weakened the Muslim Fatimid Empire in the Middle East, pushing it back to Egypt. At the same time, the vassals of the Fatimids in Tunisia and Algeria broke away

≡ **Al-Azhar mosque** The construction of Cairo's Al-Azhar mosque-university was commissioned in 970 CE by the Fatimid Dynasty. It is now the second oldest continually operating university in the world.

from the empire, and Christian Normans from southern Europe captured enclaves along the Western North African coast and seized Sicily.

The Ayyubid Empire

During the 1160s, **Salah al-Din ibn Ayyub** (known as Saladin in the West), a Kurd from present-day Iraq, worked as a military leader for the Fatimids directing battles against the Christian crusaders and putting down a rebellion of Sudanese Nubian troops within the Fatimid army. In 1171, Salah al-Din used his military to overthrow the Fatimids and seize power, establishing his own **Ayyubid** dynasty in Egypt. Under Salah al-Din, in the 1170s Egypt sent armies west into Libya, where they evicted the Normans from Tripoli and fought with the growing Almohad Empire (see below), and southeast to western Arabia and Yemen to secure Red Sea trade. Egyptian forces also moved south into Nubia, where they captured the town of Aswan at the Nile's first cataract and briefly occupied the Nubian center of Qasr Ibrim between the first and second cataracts. Throughout the 1170s and 1180s, Salah al-Din's armies expanded northeast into Palestine and Syria, where they fought both Christians and Muslims. After Salah al-Din took Jerusalem from the Christian crusaders in 1187, England's King Richard the Lionheart led a new crusader campaign that ultimately stalemated and produced a peace treaty whereby Muslims would rule the holy city but grant access to Christian pilgrims. Within Egypt, the fall of the Fatimids meant the end of Shi'a Islam among the elites and the revival of the Sunni interpretation. As such, Cairo's Al-Azhar University changed from a Shi'a to a Sunni scholarly center, and Egypt's expanding education system emphasized Sunni views. While Salah al-Din opposed the Christian European crusaders, his regime tolerated Egyptian Coptic Christians and Jews, and traded with Italian cities such as Venice and Genoa. Salah al-Din's personal physician was Moses ben Maimon, also known as Maimonides, who had fled Almohad persecution in Spain and became the leading Jewish scholar of the medieval world. After Salah

≡ **Salah al-Din.** A modern statue of Salah al-Din (1137–1193 CE), founder of Egypt's Ayyubid dynasty, located in Damascus, Syria.

al-Din's death in 1193, his sons fought over power, leading to the fragmentation of the Ayyubid Empire as crusader incursions continued and territories in Arabia became independent. In 1229 the Ayyubid ruler of Egypt, Al-Kamil, returned control of Jerusalem to Christian crusaders to thwart the ambitions of his Baghdad-based Abbasid rivals in nearby Syria. Attempting to re-establish Egyptian control over Palestine and Syria during the 1240s, the Ayyubid ruler As-Salih expanded the employment of Turkish and Central Asian enslaved soldiers called **Mamluks**, who had been dislocated from their homes by the expansion of Mongol horsemen from the east. The Mamluks were horse-mounted archers who could win their freedom by bravery in battle and advance to high military rank. In Egypt, the Mamluks became increasingly powerful, and by 1260 they had overthrown the Ayyubid dynasty and established their own military regime. Furthermore, by this time major cultural changes had taken place in Egypt. While the Umayyad dynasty of the 700s had imposed Arabic as the administrative language of Egypt, Coptic survived as the language of Egyptian communities living outside the capital. By the 1200s, however, Coptic had been almost completely replaced by Arabic in Egypt.

Mamluk Egypt

The Mamluk rulers of Egypt mostly did not create a royal dynasty; instead, each leader arose from among the commanders of the enslaved soldier army. The period of Mamluk rule in Egypt can be divided into two phases. First, the Bahri Mamluks, named after their barracks on an island in the Nile, were Kipchak Turks from the part of Eurasia where the Volga River flows into the Caspian Sea, and they ruled Egypt from 1260 to 1383. Second, the Burgi Mamluks were Circassian Turks from the Caucasus Mountains and ruled from 1383 to 1517. The Mamluk ruler Baybars I played a central role in the defeat of another Christian European crusade in 1250 and the halt of the Mongol invasion of Syria in 1260. Governing Egypt from 1260 to 1277, Baybars I sent armies to gain control of Syria and Palestine by destroying crusader fortresses there, to defeat the Christian Nubian kingdom of Makuria, which became a vassal, and to harass the Mongols in Anatolia in modern Turkey. Since the invading Mongols had devastated Baghdad and Persia, Mamluk Cairo became the center of the Muslim world, with a population of around 500,000. The Mamluks built aqueducts and canals, educational centers, mosques, and Mansuri Hospital, which became one of the greatest medical facilities of the medieval period. In 1347–48, Mamluk Egypt was greatly weakened by the arrival of the bubonic plague pandemic, called the Black Death, which killed around a quarter of the population and undermined agricultural production. Subsequently, in 1517, the expanding Ottoman Empire conquered Mamluk Egypt.

Medieval Nubia

Although the Muslim Arab conquerors of Egypt and the Nubian Christian kingdom of **Makuria** to the south had agreed a treaty in the 650s, the two neighboring powers engaged in periodic conflict during the medieval era. In 747, Makuria mounted a military incursion into Egypt to secure the release of the imprisoned Egyptian Coptic Christian Patriarch. During the 800s, Makuria suspended its regular export of enslaved people to Egypt, a requirement of the peace treaty between the two states, but it was reinstated through negotiation. Around the same time, east of Makuria, Arabs from Egypt expanded into the lands of the Beja people near the Red Sea in what is now Sudan and expanded Islam in that region.

Despite these challenges, Christian Makuria flourished. At Dongola, its capital, a large palace or "Throne Hall" and a 28-meter-tall "Cruciform Church" were constructed. While Makuria launched military campaigns into southern Egypt during the early 900s, the Fatimid conquest of Egypt led to peace as the new Shi'a Muslim rulers in Cairo wanted Christian Nubian support against their Sunni Muslim enemies in the Middle East. With stability on its northern frontier, Makuria was able to expand its influence west into Kordofan and south into the other Christian Nubian kingdom of Alodia. Furthermore, during the 1000s, Makuria's

≡ **Throne Hall, Nubia.** Located in Dongola, the "Throne Hall" was built during the 800s and served as the royal palace for the Christian Kingdom of Makuria. After the collapse of Makuria in the 1300s, the "Throne Hall" was converted into a Mosque.

rulers promoted a sense of Nubian nationalism by expanding the use of the written Nubian language to counter the growth of written Arabic, venerating dead Nubian kings and bishops, creating Nubian saints, and building new churches. Since Nubian society was matrilineal, women played a central part in medieval Makuria, with the queen mother and the sister of the king, who would be the mother of the next king, holding authority, and wealthy Nubian women owned land, which they passed on to their daughters, while also sponsoring the creation of religious art in churches. Most Nubians in Makuria were farmers along the Nile, growing crops like millet and barley, and raising cattle, and some were artisans making leather or metal goods. The kingdom's main export was enslaved people captured further south and sent north to Egypt in exchange of luxury items.

In the early 1170s, the context of warfare between Muslims and Christian crusaders in the Middle East and northeast Africa, and the rise of Salah al-Din, led to renewed conflict between Muslim-ruled Egypt and Christian Makuria. While Makuria took advantage of the fall of the Fatimids by raiding into southern Egypt, Salah al-Din responded by dispatching an army into Makuria that destroyed churches and then withdrew as the Nubians organized a response. Since Ayyubid Egypt remained at peace with Nubia for the next century, Arab nomads and merchants moved south into Makuria, leading to gradual Arabization and Islamization in the Christian kingdom. With the declining Makuria unable to fulfill its treaty obligations to prevent people like the Beja from raiding Egypt, the Mamluk rulers in Cairo became more involved in Nubian politics. In 1276, a Mamluk army conquered Makuria and put a puppet Christian king on the throne. However, in 1312, after their Christian vassal was overthrown, the Mamluks invaded again and installed a Muslim member of Makuria's royal family as the new ruler. In 1317, given the official Islamization of the kingdom, which included transforming the Dongola Throne Hall into a mosque, civil war erupted in Makuria, with power changing hands several times between Muslim and Christian leaders over the next few decades. Although the details remain vague, it is very likely that the bubonic plague that hit Egypt in the 1340s spread south into Nubia, devastating the Nubian population and contributing to the decline of Christianity in the area. By the mid-1500s, the kingdom of Makuria had disappeared and its churches had fallen into ruin.

From the 800s to 1100s, to the south of Makuria, the Christian Nubian kingdom of **Alodia** was a wealthy, large, and powerful state, with its capital of Soba located close to present-day Khartoum at the confluence of the Blue and White Nile. At this time, there were 400 churches throughout the kingdom, with a particularly large one at Soba. Alodia's decline began in the 1200s, when it experienced several invasions by Nilotic-speaking people from the south who may have destroyed the town of Soba. Other factors that undermined Alodia included drought, over-grazing and over-cultivation, and the development of new trade routes to the East African coast that redirected commerce away from the kingdom and the north-ward trade route along the Nile. By the end of the 1200s, it appears that Alodia was starting to fragment with sections of the state declaring independence. After the collapse of its northern neighbor Makuria in the late 1300s, nomadic Arabs from Egypt expanded south along the Nile into Alodia and then moved west into Kordofan and Darfur. It is possible that the bubonic plague devastated the settled Nubian communities of Alodia, therefore facilitating an Arab nomadic takeover in many places. While the immigrant Arab Muslims initially paid tribute to the Christian rulers of Alodia, the former gradually asserted more authority as the latter split into small, weak states. During the 1400s, there was conflict between the Arabs and the kingdom of Alodia, and at the end of that century, an Arab alliance led by Abdallah Jammah destroyed the remnants of this last Nubian Christian state. At the start of the 1500s, the Arabs were defeated by the newly arrived Funj people, pastoral horsemen from what is now South Sudan and Ethiopia, who converted to Islam and established the Funj sultanate with its capital at Sennar. The Funj rulers used their cavalry army to collect tribute from Nubian farmers along the Nile who were left under their own leaders. The collapse of Alodia led to the Arabization of Nubia as the Nubian language was replaced by Arabic and Christianity was replaced by Islam. Some refugees from Alodia fled south along the Blue Nile and founded the kingdom of Fazughli, which continued to be ruled by Christians in what is now the Sudan–Ethiopia frontier. Involved in the local gold trade, the Fazughli state was conquered by Ethiopia and then Funj during the 1600s.

The Almoravid Empire

Beginning in the 1040s, a Muslim revitalization movement known as the **Almoravids** united the Berbers of Western North Africa. Since the movement originated at a frontier fortress-monastery, or ribat, its members became known as al-Murabitun or "those of the ribat." They are commonly remembered by the Spanish version of this term: Almoravid. Led by the fervent Abdallah ibn Yasin, the Almoravids believed in a literal interpretation of the Qu'ran, the Muslim holy text, and maintained that it was not sufficient for Muslims to live by the teachings of Islam but that they had a religious duty to eliminate any sort of deviation. Consisting of a mass of infantry spearmen supported by horse and camel cavalry, the large Almoravid army made up for its lack of discipline with speed and religious fervor. In the mid-1050s, the Al-moravids captured the Moroccan town of Sijilmasa, which was the most important northern terminus of the burgeoning trans-Saharan trade, and Awdaghust in the south, in what is now southern Mauritania, which gave them control of gold coming from the West African kingdom of Ghana. In 1059, Almoravid leader Abdallah ibn Yasin was killed in a battle during the conquest of the Berghouata Berbers of southern Morocco. Although Abdallah was succeeded by his brother Abu-Bakr ibn Umar, the Almoravid Empire had become too vast to be governed by one person. Consequently, Abu-Bakr traveled south to lead the continuing military struggle against the Soninke people of the Ghana kingdom and his cousin Yusif ibn Tashfin crossed north of the Atlas Mountains to direct the conquest of northern Morocco and southern Spain. While medieval Arab writers claimed that the Almoravids conquered Ghana around 1076 and forcibly converted its people to Islam, modern historians disagree over whether or not this actually happened. In 1087, Abu-Bakr died, possibly in battle, on the southern frontiers of the Almoravid Empire. In northwest Africa, the Almoravids established the city of Marrakesh in 1062 and made it their capital, and they captured Fez in 1069 and a built a fortress there. From these centers in Morocco, they expanded east into today's Algeria in the 1070s, and by 1082 they had gained control over the region up to Algiers. In 1086, the Almoravids sent an army to Spain at the invitation of Muslim rulers there who needed assistance against local Christian kingdoms. That year, the now 80-year-old Tashfin led an Almoravid army that defeated Christian Spanish forces at the Battle of Zallaqa. Subsequently, during the 1090s the Almoravids conquered the Iberian Muslim states that had called for their assistance. Furthermore, Tashfin embarked on military reforms that transformed the Almoravid army from an ad hoc collection of desert nomads into a heterogeneous imperial military. The Almoravids also built a navy and captured the Balearic Islands. Under Tashfin, who died in 1106, the Almoravid Empire reached the height of its power ruling a large part of northwest Africa and the southern half of Iberia. Playing a central role in early Almoravid history, a wealthy Moroccan Berber woman called **Zaynab an-Nafzāwiyyah** initially married Abu-Bakr but then divorced him to marry Tashfin, convincing the two leaders to divide their territory during the 1070s. Unusual for medieval Muslim states, she became Tashfin's queen and main diplomatic advisor, setting a precedent that allowed elite women to participate in politics and education under the Almoravids. During the early 1100s, Iberian Christians began to gain momentum in their struggle with the Almoravids. The Almoravid Empire became overextended fighting wars in both Iberia and northwest Africa, and their employment of Spanish Christian mercenaries and the rulers' adoption of the Andalusian culture of southern Spain weakened their claims to Islamic purity and therefore undermined their popularity.

≡ **Jemaa-el-Fna market and square, Marrakesh.** One of the great public spaces of the Muslim world, the square dates to the eleventh century CE.

The Almohad Empire

Beginning in the early 1120s, a new Berber Muslim revitalization movement called the **Almohads** emerged in the Atlas Mountains of Northwest Africa and challenged the Almoravid Empire. Criticizing the Almoravids for attributing human qualities to God, the Muslim scholar Muhammad Abdullah ibn Tumart preached the spiritual oneness of God and his followers became known as Muwahhidun, or Unitarians, whom the Spanish called Almohads. The charismatic Tumart eventually claimed to be the Mahdi, a prophesied redeemer of Islam. Attempting to contain the Almohad rebellion, the Almoravids built forts on the northwestern slopes of the Atlas Mountains and imported more Christian mercenary cavalry, further undermining their Islamic legitimacy. In 1129, the Almoravids fortified the city of Marrakesh after an Almohad attack. After Tumart's death around 1130, the new Almohad leader Abdul Mu'min bin Ali launched a series of wars that created a new empire and founded an imperial dynasty. Enlarging the army by recruiting and making alliances with Berber groups, Abdul Mu'min extended Almohad influence in the Atlas and Rif mountains of northern Morocco, and eventually challenged the Almoravids on the open plains. In turn, many Berbers deserted the Almoravids. In 1144, near the city of Tlemcen in Algeria, the Almohad army routed an Almoravid force and an allied Christian contingent. The Almohads subsequently captured the main towns of northwest Africa, including Oran in 1145, Fez in 1146, and Marrakesh in 1147, and destroyed Almoravid mosques and palaces. In 1146, Abdul Mu'min founded the city of Rabat, short for Ribat al-fat or "stronghold of victory," on the Atlantic coast of Morocco that served as a staging area for military operations in Iberia and later became the Almohad capital. Shortly after their seizure of Marrakesh, the Almohads sent an army to occupy southwestern Spain. However, the 1148 capture of the North African ports of Mahdia, Gabès, and Sfax in what is now Tunisia by Christian Norman knights based in Sicily, who had previously taken Tripoli and Jirba Island, provoked the Almohads to redirect their military energy from Iberia to the eastern Maghreb. In 1151, Abdul Mu'min led a major Almohad army, originally meant for Spain, eastward where it took Algiers and defeated the forces of local Muslim rulers in a battle on the plain of Sitif in 1153. Once he suppressed rebellion in Morocco in the late 1150s, Abdul Mu'min again advanced east with a massive army marching overland and a navy sailing parallel along the coast. By 1160, the Almohads had conquered Tunisia and evicted the Normans from North Africa. Although the Almohads maintained a governing council with representatives from the original Berber groups who had founded the movement, Abdul Mu'min was protected by a bodyguard from his own Kumya Berber community and his sons gained senior military positions. He also established a class of professional administrators who, as young men, underwent instruction in law, scholarship, archery, horsemanship, swimming, and athletics.

Unlike the Almoravids who tolerated Christians and Jews if they paid a special tax, the Almohads persecuted non-Muslims living under their rule. By the late 1100s, the Almohads ruled an empire stretching from the Atlantic coast of Morocco to Libya, and up into southern Spain. The Almohads constructed large and impressive fortresses and mosques, including the unfinished Hassan Tower in Rabat that was intended to become the largest minaret in the world, and the Almohad rulers sponsored Muslim scholars. However, in the 1200s internal divisions, rebellion in the eastern Maghreb, and the expansion of Christian Iberian kingdoms caused the Almohad Empire to split into three rival states—Marinid, Hafsid, and Zayyanid. The power of the Berber Almoravid and Almohad empires meant that the ancient Berber language of northwest Africa survived the Islamization of the medieval period but its ancient written form was replaced by Arabic script.

≡ **Hassan Tower, Rabat.** Intended to be the world's tallest minaret, the Hassan Tower in Rabat, Morocco, was commissioned by Almohad ruler Abu Yusuf Yaqub al-Mansur in 1195, but construction was halted after his death and it remains unfinished.

The Marinid, Hafsid, and Zayyanid Kingdoms of the Maghreb

With its capital in Tunis, the **Hafsid dynasty** ruled the region that the Arabs called Ifriqiya, consisting of present-day Tunisia, eastern Algeria, and western Libya. Since they had started out as provincial governors appointed by the Almohad caliph at the start of the 1200s, the Hafsid rulers saw themselves as the true successors of the Almohads. The Hafsid kingdom emerged in 1228 when Abu Zakariya, the Hafsid governor at Tunis, declared himself an independent ruler and launched expansionist military wars to the west and east. By the 1250s, the Hafsid kingdom was widely regarded as the primary western Muslim power. Hafsid authority was undermined by the brief occupation of Tunis in 1270 by Christian French crusaders, the arrival of Muslims who had fled Spain given the Christian expansion there, and Marinid invasions from Morocco in 1347 and 1357. Although the Hafsids engaged in maritime trade with the Christian powers of southern Europe, they were also involved in naval warfare on the Mediterranean, including a large Hafsid raid on Malta in 1429 and retaliatory raids on Hafsid ports in North Africa by Christian Spanish and Venetians. The Hafsids were also invested in overland trade with Egypt to the east and the trans-Saharan trade to the south. Under the Hafsids, Tunis was fortified and became a major economic and educational center, and with a population of around 100,000 it was one of the largest cities in the world. In this period, Tunis was the birthplace of **Ibn Khaldun** (1332–1406), a famous scholar who served the rulers of the Hafsid, Zayyanid, and Marinid kingdoms and Mamluk Egypt. By 1500, rebellion by interior Berbers and some cities meant that the Hafsid kingdom consisted only of Tunis and Constantine.

In 1236, with the breakdown of the Almohad Empire, the Berber governor of the western Algerian city of Tlemcen, Yaghmurasen ibn Zyan, declared independence and founded what became the **Zayyanid dynasty**. Constantly embroiled in conflict with the neighboring Marinid kingdom to the west in Morocco and the Hafsid kingdom to the east in Tunisia, the Zayyanid rulers of the 1300s made alliances with both Muslim and Christian powers in Spain. Tlemcen, the Zayyanid capital, was a center for both the trans-Saharan trade through Sijilmasa to the southwest and the Mediterranean trade through the port of Oran in the northeast. While the Zayyanids and Marinids fought over the trans-Saharan terminus of Sijilmasa, caravans from there continued to take merchandise to Tlemcen as it was too difficult for them to cross the Atlas Mountains to Fez in Morocco. As an important point from where southern European merchants acquired gold produced south of the Sahara, Tlemcen became a wealthy town with palaces, business offices, mosques, schools, and markets. Tlemcen was occupied by the Hafsid kingdom during the late 1330s and 1340s, and by the Marinid kingdom in 1360 and 1370, but these invaders withdrew because of local rebellions that restored Zayyanid rule. However, by the start of the 1500s the Zayyanid dynasty was confined to Tlemcen and the Spanish Christian kingdom of Aragon captured Oran in what is now Algeria in 1509.

During the 1210s, there was conflict between the Almohad Empire and the Marinid Berbers who were trying to establish control over eastern Morocco. As a

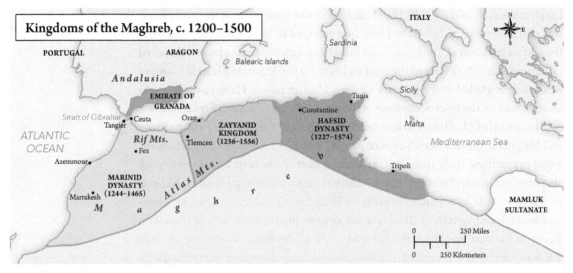

Kingdoms of the Maghreb, c. 1200–1500

≡ **MAP 3.2**

result, the **Marinids** were driven into the Rif Mountains. Taking advantage of the collapse of the Almohad Empire, the Marinids emerged from the mountains and launched an offensive in 1244 capturing important Moroccan towns such as Fez in 1248 and Marrakesh in 1269. Subsequently, Fez expanded as the capital of the new Marinid kingdom. With help from the Marinids, the Muslim kingdom of Granada was able to survive the Christian offensive in southeastern Spain that prompted the Christian Spaniards, in 1260 and 1267, to attempt invasions of Morocco. Furthermore, during the late 1200s the Marinids fought against Spanish Christians for control of the important trading area around Gibraltar. From 1337 to 1348, the Marinid ruler Abu al-Hasan Ali led an expansionist military campaign that defeated both the Zayyanid and Hafsid kingdoms and almost conquered all of the Maghreb but this was undermined by rebellions and continued conflict with Iberian Christians. In the early 1400s, political power in Morocco shifted from the Marinid kings to their prime ministers who were appointed from Berbers of the Wattasid family. This inspired tensions that prompted a Marinid attempt to massacre the Wattasids in 1459. The Marinid decline happened within the context of the increasing Christian Iberian incursions on the northern Moroccan coast including the Portuguese capture of Ceuta in 1415 and Tangiers in 1471 and the Christian Spanish conquest of Granada that was the last Muslim enclave in Iberia in 1492, and the growing independence of Moroccan towns such as Marrakesh and Azemmour. In 1471, the last Marinid ruler was overthrown by Abu Abd Allah al-Sheihk Muhammad ibn Yahya, a survivor of the 1459 Wattasid massacre, who established a new Wattasid royal dynasty in northern Morocco.

Timeline

661–750—Umayyad Empire rules North Africa and Middle East

750—Rise of Abbasid Caliphate in Baghdad

790—Establishment of the city of Fez

790s—Rise of Idrisid kingdom in Morocco

800s—Fatamid movement relocated from Middle East to Northwest Africa

830s—Rise of Aghlabid kingdom in Algeria and Tunisia

859—Founding of the University of Al-Qarawiyyin in Fez, Morocco

868–905—Tulunid dynasty in Egypt

969—Fatimids in northwest Africa conquer Egypt and found Cairo

1000s (early)—Spread of Arab nomads into western North Africa

1040s—Rise of Almoravid movement in Northwest Africa

1062—Almoravids establish city of Marrakesh in Morocco

1096–99—First Crusade

1121—Rise of the Almohad movement in Northwest Africa

1148—Capture of North African ports by Christian Normans

1150s—Establishment of Almohad Empire; fall of Almoravid Empire

1171—Takeover of Egypt by Salah al-Din; start of Ayyubid dynasty

1187—Capture of Jerusalem from crusaders by Salah al-Din

1189–92—Third crusade attempts to recapture Jerusalem

1200s—Decline of Almohad Empire in Northwest Africa

1200s—Decline of Nubian Christian kingdoms of Makuria and Alodia; Arabization and Islamization

1228—Establishment of Hafsid kingdom in Tunisia

1236—Independence of Zayyanid kingdom in western Algeria

1244—Expansion of Maranid kingdom in Morocco

1260—Start of Mamluk rule in Egypt

1300s—Zayyanid, Hafsid, and Maranid kingdoms struggle for control of trade center of Tlemcen

1347–48—Egypt hit by bubonic plague (Black Death)

1415—Portuguese capture of Ceuta

1429—Hafsid slave raid on island of Malta

1471—Marinid dynasty overthrown in Morocco—rise of Wattasid dynasty

1471—Portuguese capture Tangiers

1492—Christian Spanish conquer last Iberian Muslim center of Granada

1509—Christian Spanish seize Oran

1517—Conquest of Mamluk Egypt by Ottoman Empire

Conclusion

Medieval North Africa experienced serious and continuous religiously inspired conflict. Adherents to the Shi'a and Sunni interpretations of Islam struggled for control of the region, with the latter eventually winning out; a series of Muslim purification movements such as the Almoravids and Almohads swept across the Maghreb and beyond; and Christian Europeans such as crusaders and Normans launched military offensives against Muslim powers along the North African coast. The Muslim–Christian divide was not absolute as Shi'a Muslims worked with Christians against Sunni Muslims, the Almoravids employed Christian mercenaries, and Egyptian Muslims allied with Christian crusaders against their Muslim rivals in the Middle East. Simultaneously, medieval North Africa surged ahead of Europe in many respects. The great cities of Cairo, Fez, and Marrakesh were established, universities and medical centers were founded, architectural and technical marvels were built, and business thrived with the region serving as a meeting point for Mediterranean, Red Sea, and trans-Saharan trade involving products from China, South Asia, sub-Saharan Africa, the Middle East, and Europe.

KEY TERMS

Abbasid Caliphate 65

Al-Azhar 66

Almohads 74

Almoravids 72

Alodia 71

Ayyubid 67

Fatimids 66

Hafsid dynasty 76

Ibn Khaldun 77

Makuria 70

Mamluks 69

Marinids 77

medieval era 63

Salah al-Din ibn
   Ayyub 67

Shi'a 65

Sunni 65

Umayyad Caliphate 65

University of
   Al-Qarawiyyin 65

Zaynab
   an-Nafzāwiyyah 73

Zayyanid dynasty 77

STUDY QUESTIONS

1. What distinguishes the Sunni and Shi'a sects of Islam? How did Islam expand across North Africa under the Umayyad and Abbasid Caliphates?

2. Why did Egypt and Makuria come into conflict? What are some of the unique features of Nubian society? What explains the rise and fall of Alodia?

3. Who were the Fatimids? What impact did the Crusades have on Fatimid rule? What successes did Salah al-Din enjoy as a military leader? What role did the Mamluks play in the dissolution of the Ayyubid dynasty?

4. How did the Mamluk style of leadership contrast with previous models? What were some of the cultural contributions of the Mamluks?

5. What impact did the Almoravids and Almohads have on North Africa? Why are they known as revitalization movements?

Please see page FR-2 for the Further Readings for this chapter.
For additional digital learning resources please go to
https://www.oup.com/he/falola-stapleton1e

West Africa and the Trans-Saharan Trade, c. 400–1700 CE

The **trans-Saharan trade** refers to the historic north–south commerce between Mediterranean North Africa and Atlantic West Africa. Although the Sahara Desert long represented an obstacle between these two regions, overland traders transported goods across it before the advent of the Roman Empire. In ancient times, however, the trans-Saharan trade was limited as merchants were dependent on pack animals like oxen, donkeys, and horses that were not well suited for long, grueling journeys in dry desert conditions. This situation changed around 300 or 400 CE, or perhaps earlier, with the introduction of camels to the Sahara by the Romans or Berbers who brought them from Arabia. With its ability to survive long desert excursions by storing fat in its hump and its wide padded feet that move well in the sand, camels provided a much better method of transportation for trade goods across the Sahara and their advent in the region greatly boosted trans-Saharan interaction. The Tuaregs, popularly called the "blue people" because of their indigo dyed robes, became specialists in desert transportation and organized caravans consisting of sometimes several thousand or more camels that took about 60 to 90 days to traverse the Sahara. North Africa's Berbers were also involved in trans-Saharan transport. On either side of the desert, a series of trading towns developed where people brought various goods to exchange, caravans arrived to deliver their cargos and new caravans were assembled for the outward north or south journey.

Mansa Musa. This detail from the *Catalan Atlas* (1375) shows the king of Mali seated on his throne, holding a large gold coin or nugget as a rider on a camel approaches.

The Muslim Arab conquest of North Africa, which took place from around 630 to 710, happened just as the trans-Saharan trade was expanding and added a new element to the impact of this commercial system on West Africa. In the context of their growing businesses, West African merchants and rulers found it very useful to record inventories of trade goods and enter into written contracts which meant that written Arabic and the use of Arabic text to write some West African languages spread south along the Sahara trade routes. In addition, Muslim merchants, scribes, and teachers from North Africa traveled south across the desert establishing Muslim quarters in the trading towns of the West African interior and gradually spreading Islam in that region. As such, the growth of the trans-Saharan trade facilitated the expansion of Islam into West Africa in a generally top-down process whereby elite rulers, merchants, and artisans in towns were the first to convert while nearby rural farmers adopted a syncretic combination of Islam and traditional beliefs. Nevertheless, the expansion of Islam in West Africa was mostly limited to the areas intimately involved in the trans-Saharan trade and people living in remote parts of the hinterland and in the coastal forest retained their original religion and culture.

The inhabitants of each of West Africa's geographic belts contributed specific products to the burgeoning trans-Saharan trade. At the southern edge of the trade system, communities living in West Africa's coastal forest exported kola nuts which are a stimulant, animal products, and enslaved people, with some places like Bambuk, Bure, and Akan producing gold, which became the most sought-after commodity. Indeed, West Africa became one of the most important sources of gold for medieval North Africa, the Middle East, and Europe. While exports of enslaved people from West Africa were limited to a few thousand captives every year and the slave trade did not dominate this economy, scholars estimate that almost five million captives were sent north over the Sahara between around 650 and 1600. As Muslim law technically forbade the enslavement of fellow Muslims,

≡ **Camel caravan.** Camels loaded with salt are led by a camel driver in the Sahara, present-day Mali.

the Muslim slave traders of the Sahara targeted traditionalist southerners from the coastal zone but also ignored the rules and enslaved their co-religionists. Enslaved labor was also used within West Africa, where it supported activities like gold mining and farming.

The hinterland savanna and grassland of the Sahel became the location of the main trans-Saharan trading towns such as Gao, Timbuktu, and Djenne, which were also positioned along the Niger River, enabling goods to be delivered and picked up by canoe. Since the Sahel contained the region's major commercial centers and was inhabited by significant populations of farmers and herders who produced food, this region became the scene of a succession of large West African empires that flourished by taxing trans-Saharan merchants. An important aspect in the power of these empires was the expansion of the military use of horses in the Sahel. While the speed and endurance of horses was well suited to the open grasslands and enabled rulers to supervise and protect long trade routes, the presence of tropical diseases like **trypanosomiasis** (sleeping sickness) made it difficult to breed large horses in West Africa. Young horses were vulnerable to such diseases, and as a biological adaptation to this environment, horses would become physically smaller over generations and therefore less useful for warfare. This meant that the Sahelian empires became dependent on constantly acquiring large adult horses from North Africa. At the same time, the savanna and Sahel farmers exported grains like millet and rice to the Sahelian towns and north to the drier desert areas.

The desert itself represented another important geographic belt in the trans-Saharan trade system. Salt was produced by some desert communities and became heavily in demand to both the north and south, and it has been theorized that the trans-Saharan trade may have begun in ancient times with people venturing into the desert in search of this resource. Within the Sahara, centers of salt extraction and scattered oases became desert stopovers and watering points for Tuareg camel caravans. For example, the desert oasis of Awdaghust and the salt-production center of Taghaza became important trading towns along the Saharan trade routes.

In North Africa, caravan reception centers such as Sijilmasa in Morocco and Tlemcen in Algeria emerged along the edge of the Sahara and became hugely significant for powers based on the coast. From North Africa, goods such as textiles, swords, glass, leather, and horses, and, with the spread of Islam, writing materials and written texts were sent south. The impact of the trans-Saharan trade was wide as, for example, gold from the West African forest arrived in northwestern Europe and goods from the Middle East, Europe and Asia were delivered to West Africa.

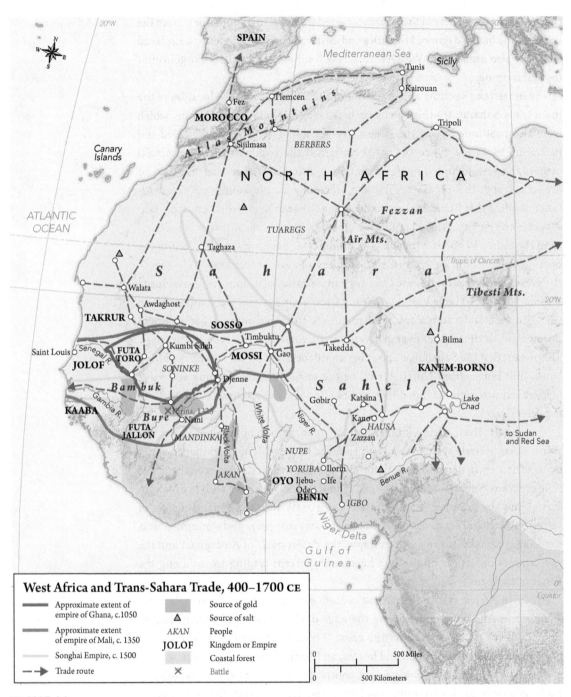

West Africa and Trans-Sahara Trade, 400–1700 CE

- Approximate extent of empire of Ghana, c.1050
- Approximate extent of empire of Mali, c. 1350
- Songhai Empire, c. 1500
- Trade route
- Source of gold
- △ Source of salt
- *AKAN* People
- **JOLOF** Kingdom or Empire
- Coastal forest
- ✕ Battle

0   500 Miles
0   500 Kilometers

≡ **MAP 4.1**

Empires of the Sahel: Ghana, Mali, and Songhai

By at least 700 CE, a centralized state had emerged on the grasslands between the Senegal and Upper Niger rivers in what is now southern Mauritania and western Mali. Known as Wagadou, or more commonly **Ghana** after the title of its ruler, the kingdom was inhabited by the area's Soninke-speaking farmers. During the 700s and 800s, Muslim geographers in Spain, North Africa, and the Middle East were aware of Ghana and mentioned it in their writings. While the exact origins of Ghana remain unknown, it was likely related to the ability of the Soninke to make iron tools and weapons which started around 400 CE and to their banding together to defend themselves from nomadic Berber pastoralists who were moving south as the Sahara dried out and expanded. Ghana became a center for trans-Saharan trade as it was strategically located between salt-producing Taghaza to its north and gold-producing Bambuk to its southwest. Establishing a capital at Kumbi Saleh, the Soninke kings of Ghana became wealthy collecting a tax in gold on imports and exports of salt and gold and gathering tribute in food and hunting products from neighboring subordinate Soninke communities. Most residents of the capital lived in wooden and mud houses with thatched roofs but the king stayed in a stone palace with glass windows that was surrounded by a fence. As the increasing commercial ties with North Africa led to the arrival of Muslim merchants, scribes, and scholars in Ghana, a Muslim neighborhood complete with stone houses, Qur'anic schools, and mosques developed in Kumbi Saleh. Trade expanded, with glass, mirrors, horses, blades, and salt arriving from the north and kola nuts, ostrich feathers, enslaved people, and gold coming in from the forests to the south. Calling on levies from vassal groups, Ghana could assemble an army of around 200,000 men, many of whom were archers. While horses were present in Ghana, it seems that they were not used extensively by the kingdom's military other than by a few of its leaders who rode horses decorated with gold. By around 1050, and likely well before, the successful trading empire of Ghana took over the Berber town of Awdaghust in the Sahara. The Soninke people of Ghana initially practiced an African traditional religion, but sometime around 1100 they converted to Islam. While some historians maintain that the expanding Morocco-based Almoravid Empire conquered Ghana in 1076 and forcibly converted the kingdom to Islam, other scholars question the evidence for this claim and believe that the residents of Ghana became Muslims through peaceful interaction with visitors from North Africa. Despite limited evidence, it appears that two factors contributed to the decline of Ghana during the 1200s. First, the continuing expansion of the Sahara and overgrazing by Berber pastoralists degraded the soil and made it difficult for the Soninke farmers to grow food. Second, new trans-Saharan trade routes were developed to the east, which deprived Ghana of tax revenue, and the discovery of new sources of gold at Bure to the south empowered the southern Soninke of the Sosso kingdom of Sumangura Kante, who led an invasion of Ghana that destroyed Kumbi Saleh around 1224–25.

The next major power to dominate the trans-Saharan trade was the empire of **Mali**. Around 1235, the expansion of the Sosso kingdom was checked by Sundiata Keita, who rallied a number of small states composed of Mandinka people. After defeating the Sosso army under Sumangura at the Battle of Kirina fought near the present-day city of Bamako, Sundiata's force destroyed the fortified Sosso capital. From his own capital of Niani, located on a tributary of the Upper Niger River and within the Bure gold-producing area, Sundiata directed the expansion of what came to be called the Mali Empire, becoming its first emperor or "mansa." To the west, Mali conquered the Jolof kingdom in present-day Senegal, turning it into a vassal state, and the growing empire established the subordinate Kaaba kingdom located in what is now Guinea-Bissau. Mali also extended southward, exercising influence over the Upper Senegal River and the forest fringe. After Sundiata's death around 1255, his son Ouali Keita became mansa and initiated eastward expansion, taking the important trading town of Gao on the Niger River Bend. Following a civil war in the 1270s, Mansa Sakura, a former enslaved person turned military leader, seized control of the empire, reasserted its authority over insubordinate vassals such as Gao, and expanded west by conquering the Takrur kingdom located in contemporary Senegal and Mauritania, and north by subjugating the copper producing center of Takedda in what is now Niger. When Sakura died around 1300, Mali was an immense empire stretching from the Niger Bend in the east to the Atlantic coast in the west. Controlling most of the trans-Saharan trade routes of the late 1200s and 1300s, the rulers of Mali became extremely wealthy through taxing gold, copper, and salt. While it seems that Sundiata practiced traditional religion, all the subsequent rulers were Muslims, and many of them, including Sakura, embarked on pilgrimages to the holy sites in Arabia. The most famous of these journeys was carried out by Mansa Musa Keita who, in 1324–25, organized a huge camel caravan including 100 camels laden with gold, and when this entourage arrived in Cairo its lavish spending caused inflation. Mansa Musa returned from his pilgrimage with North African scholars and architects who founded mosques and centers of learning in the Niger towns of Gao, Djenne, and Timbuktu. Among these buildings projects was Timbuktu's famous Djinguereber Mosque, which was constructed entirely out of earth and local organic materials and became one of three mosques to comprise the Muslim scholarly center collectively known as the University of Timbuktu. Mansa Musa may have also brought back large Middle Eastern horses along with saddles and bridles that boosted the use of cavalry in warfare in the Sahel zone. Unusual for precolonial African states, Mali maintained a permanent army consisting of a core of elite cavalrymen armed with lances and swords, and regional units of infantry equipped with spears and bows and arrows. This army kept Mali's many subordinate states in line and protected the empire's trade routes. Nevertheless, during the late 1300s and early 1400s a series of internal succession conflicts undermined the Mali Empire, enabling provincial rebellions and external threats. The Jolof kingdom regained independence in the 1360s, Takedda and Gao rebelled in the 1370s, and Djenne gained autonomy in the 1430s. From the late 1300s, Mossi horsemen from south of the Niger Bend raided Mali's towns and in the 1430s Tuaregs seized the important trans-Saharan trade hubs of Timbuktu and Walata. These troubles deprived Mali of the wealth it had previously earned from the trans-Saharan trade. Shortly thereafter, new forces appeared along the coast. During the 1440s and 1450s, Mali's vassal states in what is now Senegal and the Gambia fought Portuguese coastal raiders leading to a 1456 peace agreement between Portugal and Mali in which the former promised to limit itself to coastal trade. During the 1500s, the newer Songhai Empire took territory from declining Mali, which split into three separate and feuding Mandinka kingdoms.

The last and greatest trans-Saharan trade empire was **Songhai**. By the 800s, Songhai-speaking fishermen along the middle Niger River established a small state that engaged in river trade and adapted canoes for military campaigns. Increasingly involved in trans-Saharan commerce, the Songhai people made the trading town of Gao their capital and converted to Islam around 1000. While Gao and many Songhai communities came under the authority of the Mali Empire during the 1300s, the decline of that power allowed the Songhai to assert their autonomy during the next century. Organizing a large military with cavalry and war canoes, the Songhai king Sonni Ali directed westward expansion, capturing Timbuktu from the Tuaregs in 1468, seizing Djenne in 1480 after a long siege, and driving Mossi raiders south of the Niger. With Sonni Ali's death in 1492, a Songhai commoner and military leader called Muhammad Turi took over the expanding empire. Eventually called Askia the

≡ **Djinguereber Mosque in Timbuktu.** As shown in this early-twentieth-century postcard, Djinguereber Mosque is built entirely out of earth. It was constructed in 1327 after the return of Mansa Musa, ruler of the Mali Empire, from pilgrimage to Mecca.

Great, he organized the administrative structure of the newly conquered territories, revived the trans-Saharan trade, and strengthened Islam in the empire by building mosques and schools and hosting Muslim scholars from North Africa and the Middle East. It was in the Songhai era that Timbuktu became a thriving academic center famous for its collections of manuscripts. Songhai military expansion continued with a **jihad** against the Mossi to the south, which also resulted in the capture and enslavement of many people who were exported, and wars against the desert Tuaregs led to the seizure of Aïr in the east and salt-producing Taghaza in the north. Furthermore, Songhai subjugated the **Hausa** states of Kano, Katsina, and Gobir to its southeast in what is now northern Nigeria, and sent an army far west to Takrur close to the Atlantic coast of Senegal. Surpassing its regional predecessors Ghana and Mali, Songhai became the largest empire in the history of Africa and one of the largest land-based empires in world history. Although it fought many wars, Songhai did not maintain a permanent military, instead relying on provincial governors to raise armies when needed. Since West African gold exports across the Sahara declined in the 1500s due to the transatlantic shipment of American gold to Europe, Songhai became more involved in the slave trade both in terms of providing labor for its own growing agricultural projects along the Niger and for export to North Africa and beyond.

From the 1540s and 1550s, Songhai and Morocco clashed over control of the Sahara trade center of Taghaza. In the 1580s Morocco, under Ahmad al-Mansur, saw an opportunity to intervene in Songhai as the empire was distracted by a civil war and Spain, Morocco's main rival, had been defeated at sea by England. In 1590–91, a 4,000-strong Moroccan expeditionary force, consisting of many European and Turkish mercenaries armed with guns and cannon and supported by 8,000 supply camels, marched across the vast Sahara to invade Songhai. In March 1591, the Moroccan force led by the formerly enslaved Spanish-born Judar Pasha gunned down a large Songhai army comprising 18,000 cavalry and 30,000 infantry, none of whom had firearms. The technological disparity between the two forces was reminiscent of the Spanish conquest of the Aztec and Inca empires in the Americas earlier in the century. While the Moroccan troops subsequently occupied the Niger commercial towns of Gao and Timbuktu, they did not find as much gold as anticipated, and Moroccan military resources continued to be drained by Songhai guerrilla resistance and tropical disease. In the 1610s, Morocco, unable to sustain its occupation of a distant land, cut off direct administration of Songhai, and the Moroccan governors of the Niger towns became autonomous and conflicting rulers. The Moroccan invasion caused Songhai to break into a network of small states, and though these wars boosted exports of enslaved people from the area, they generally disrupted the trans-Saharan trade, which moved further east to new routes.

The Trans-Saharan Trade Moves East

Throughout its history, the trans-Saharan trade gradually moved east to avoid taxation from empires and exploit new sources of gold from Bambuk to Bure and then Akan. The last eastward shift of the trans-Saharan trade during the 1500s and 1600s boosted the power of the Hausa kingdoms of what is now northern Nigeria. Located on the north side of the Niger River, Hausa-speaking people had founded centralized states with capital towns by around 1000. Beginning in the mid-1300s, and in the context of their growing involvement in trans-Saharan trade in which they were exporting leather, dyed fabrics, and enslaved people, the rulers of the Hausa city-states such as Kano and Katsina converted to Islam, inspiring them to build mosques and host visiting Muslim scholars. This led to the emergence of an urban Muslim Hausa culture distinct from surrounding rural communities. As emerging military powers, the Hausa states employed cavalry armies and built defensive walls around their towns. While Kano tended to dominate these polities, Queen Amina of Zazzua (today's Zaria) led expansionist campaigns against the other Hausa states and south toward the Niger and Benue rivers during the late 1500s and very early 1600s.

East of the Hausa, around Lake Chad, the Kanem state emerged around 1000 and originated among pastoral nomads who gradually converted to Islam. Kanem engaged in the eastern section of the trans-Saharan system and by the 1200s, it controlled these routes up to Fezzan in what is now Libya. Building a formidable cavalry army, Kanem launched jihads against traditionalist communities to its south to capture and enslave people who were then exported north in exchange for horses. Around 1400, Kanem moved its capital southwest of Lake Chad to the subordinate Borno state, from where it traded with the Hausa emirates to the west, supplying them with horses and salt in return for gold from Akan. At the end of the 1500s, as Morocco was invading Songhai and the trans-Saharan trade was moving east toward Lake Chad, the **Kanem-Borno** ruler Idris Aloma modernized his army by importing Turkish mercenaries and firearms from Ottoman Tripoli, but also expanding the use

≡ **Queen Amina of Zaria.** Queen Amina was ruler of the city state of Zazzau (present-day Zaria) in northern Nigeria during the late 1500s and early 1600s.

AFRIQUE OCCIDENTALE — Guerriers en tenue de combat

≡ **Borno cavalrymen** photographed at the end of the nineteenth century.

of horse and camel mounted troops and canoes for carrying supplies and crossing rivers. As such, during the late 1500s and early 1600s, Kanem-Borno expanded to the east side of Lake Chad and conquered the trans-Saharan trading center of Aïr to the northwest and some of the Hausa states to the southwest. This series of wars provided Kanem-Borno with more enslaved people and, in turn, more horses. The increasing importance of slave trading is illustrated by one of Aloma's campaigns around Lake Chad in which 1000 women and 2000 men were captured and 400 free Muslim prisoners were executed as Islam forbade their enslavement. In addition, Aloma transformed his kingdom's administrative and legal systems and strengthened Islam there by encouraging pilgrimages, constructing mosques, and bringing in Muslim intellectuals. Though Aloma was assassinated while on a military campaign in the early 1600s, the intensive slave and horse trade between Lake Chad and Libya continued for a century.

The Coastal Forest

Although the people living in West Africa's coastal forest zone provided key trade items such as gold and kola nuts to the trans-Saharan network, much less is known about their history in this period than about the empires of the Sahel. While the history of Mali and Songhai has been derived from Arabic documents written by Muslim scholars, reconstructing the precolonial history of the coastal zone relies largely on oral tradition and archaeology. In general, the early history of the coast's comparatively small centralized states is somewhat clearer than that of the area's many decentralized communities.

During the 1300s and 1400s, Akan farmers on the savanna-forest fringe in present-day northern Ghana withdrew deeper into the forest to escape encroachment by the Mali Empire from the north. After relocation, the Akan used slave labor to clear forest areas for agriculture and gold mining, and they founded a series of small states, each centered on a town. The Akan became major gold exporters, competing with the established gold producers at Bambuk and Bure and contributing to the eastward movement of the trans-Saharan trade to Niger River towns like Gao and Timbuktu. In the late 1400s, with their gold exports flowing north and new European seagoing customers arriving along the southern coast, the Akan experienced further political centralization with the creation of larger kingdoms like Denkyira and Akwamu that competed for gold deposits and trade routes.

Around 1000, Yoruba-speaking farmers who inhabited the savanna and forest south of the lower Niger River in what is now western Nigeria began a process of state formation. Believed to be the original Yoruba town, Ife was located in a rich farming area that produced enough food to allow some of its residents to become expert artists, carving wood and ivory and making metal castings. Ife became the cultural and spiritual capital of a complex of autonomous Yoruba states. Among these kingdoms was Oyo-Ile, which originated as early as around 700 and eventually became a thriving trading town. After a destructive attack by the horsemen of Nupe to its north around 1535, Oyo acquired horses and formed its own cavalry army similar to those of the Sahelian empires. As a result, during the late 1500s, Oyo expanded its control of the nearby savanna, including the Yoruba state of Ilorin, and moved west into the coastal forest gap where horses provided mobility in wars fought in the semi-open environment. On the other hand, Oyo's attempts to push south proved unsuccessful given the unsuitability of horses in the dense forest and resistance by the potent kingdom of Benin. The tropical environment meant that Oyo had to constantly replenish its supply of horses by sending enslaved people north to the Sahel and Sahara. As such, Oyo became a key intermediary in trade between the Hausa states to its north and coastal communities to the south. During the 1600s, as the trans-Saharan trade declined, Oyo became increasingly involved in the emerging coastal trade with Europeans.

As early as 900, the **Benin kingdom** was pioneered by Edo-speaking farmers living in the forest between the Yoruba states and the Niger Delta. Within Benin, town-dwelling merchants and artisans engaged in the trans-Saharan trade, exporting agricultural products, crafts and enslaved people for imported copper and salt. Around 1200, a new dynasty linked to the Yoruba city of Ife came to power in Benin, initiating a period of state centralization and territorial expansion. During the 1250s, King Ewedo reduced the power of Benin's nobles and reformed the army by introducing new weapons like improved swords and bows, and more efficient military organization. In the 1440s, King Ewuare "the Great" further centralized the government and the army under his command, ordered the construction of earthwork fortifications, and adopted canoes for warfare on the Lagos Lagoon to the west and Niger Delta to the east. Famously conquering 201 towns, Ewuare led the eastward expansion of Benin, which subdued Igbo groups on the west bank of the Niger, and one of his sons embarked on a southward campaign to establish the vassal state of Itsekiri close to the Atlantic. After a brief period of civil war, Benin's

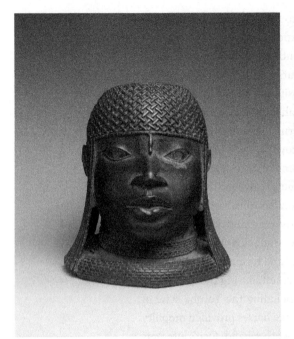 

☰ **The Benin Kingdom.** *Left:* This brass sculpture from the sixteenth century depicts the idealized likeness of an oba, or king, wearing a woven cap of coral beads. *Right:* A brass sculpture from the eighteenth century shows an *iyoba,* or queen mother of an oba. Queen mothers occupied an important place in Benin's political hierarchy.

Ozolua "the Conquerer" came to power in the 1480s and directed numerous aggressive campaigns that installed his sons as rulers of neighboring communities and subjugated the Yoruba state of Ijebu-Ode, which extended Benin's influence far to the west. By the time Portuguese mariners arrived on its coast at the end of the 1400s and start of the 1500s, Benin comprised a sizable forest empire.

Interior West Africa in the Eighteenth Century

During the 1700s, the absence of a large territorial empire in the Sahel and Savanna and frequent civil wars in the smaller states empowered highly mobile nomadic raiders like the Tuareg. In 1737, the Tuareg expanded south to seize the town of Timbuktu, contributing to the decline of this economic and intellectual center and they dominated the Niger Bend. With drought and famine weakening Kanem-Borno in the early 1700s, the Tuareg state at Aïr re-established its autonomy and in 1750 it seized the salt producing oasis of Bilma. By this time, however, the redirection of West Africa's economy toward the oceanic trade of the Atlantic coast had led to the diminishing of the trans-Saharan network and its associated trading towns like Gao and Djenne.

The eighteenth century also witnessed the beginning of a series of Muslim revivalist movements in the West African hinterland that were led by **Fulani** religious scholars. Between the 1000s and 1500s, Fulani pastoralists settled throughout West Africa's Sahel and savanna, living among but remaining separate from agricultural communities. Through links with Tuareg desert nomads and Arab traders in the towns, the Fulani adopted Islam, which encouraged the development of their common identity and provided them with their own legal system. In the 1500s, Fulani herdsmen began to move into Futa Jalon in present-day Guinea, where taxation was imposed on them by local farmers. Supported by Muslim merchants, the Fulani launched a jihad against the traditionalist farmers in 1725 and established an Islamic state in Futa Jalon in 1750.

During the tenth and eleventh centuries, the area of Futa Toro, located along the middle Senegal River, had been governed by the Takrur kingdom, which subsequently declined because of competition over resources and internal conflicts, and was conquered by the Mali Empire in the late 1200s. Futa Toro became part of the revived Jolof state in the late 1300s but then was taken over by a nominally Muslim Fulani Denianke dynasty that created the "Great Fulo Empire" at the start of the 1500s. From the 1500s to 1700s, the Great Fulo rulers of Futa Toro exported enslaved people to first the Portuguese and then the French along the coast, and their communities became targets of overland Moroccan raids aimed at seizing gold and captives. During the 1670s, Nasr el Din, a Muslim scholar from what is now Mauritania, led a jihad in Futa Toro against nomads to the north and the Jolof to the south and was supported by people who wanted protection from slave raiding. While this jihad was defeated with the help of the French based at the enclave of Saint Louis on the coast, Nasr el Din's followers established the Bundu state on the upper Senegal River and inspired future Muslim revitalization in the area. Between 1769 and 1776, Fulani and Tukolor people, motivated by earlier Muslim struggles in Futa Jalon and buoyed by people frustrated with the inability of the Denianke rulers to protect them from raids by desert nomads, fought a jihad in Futa Toro that founded a new Muslim state. This jihad was led by Muslim scholar Sulayman Bal, who did not live to see it succeed. The jihadist state of Futa Toro expanded west and southeast until around 1797, when it was defeated by the Jolof kingdom of Kajoor.

Conclusion

Between about 800 and 1600, the trans-Saharan trade represented a vibrant long-distance economic system that had a profound impact on West Africa. It led to the expansion of territorial empires on the Sahel, the most enormous of which were Mali in the 1300s and 1400s and Songhai in the 1500s. Furthermore, the flourishing trade stimulated the growth of cities such as Timbuktu, Gao, Djenne, and Kano, where

Timeline

300–400 (maybe earlier)—Introduction of the camel to the Sahara

630–710—Muslim Arab conquest of North Africa

700–800—Beginning of Ghana Empire

1076—Possible conquest of Ghana by the Almoravids

c. 1100—Rulers of Ghana convert to Islam

1224–25—Sosso invasion of Ghana; fall of Ghana

1235—Sundiata Keita defeats Sosso kingdom and establishes Mali Empire

1270–1300—Expansion of Mali Empire under Mansa Sakura including conquest of Takrur state and Takedda

1324–25—Pilgrimage of Mansa Musa Keita

1300s—Rise of Timbuktu as trading and intellectual center

1300s—Rulers of Hausa states convert to Islam

1360s—Jolof kingdom regains independence from Mali

1440s—Beginning of Portuguese raids on the coast of West Africa

1500s—Division of Mali Empire

1468—Beginning of Songhai expansion under Sonni Ali; Songhai seizes Timbuktu

1480—Songhai Empires captures Djenne

1492—Askia the Great takes power in Songhai Empire

Early 1500s—Further expansion by Songhai

Late 1500s—Military campaigns of Queen Amina of Zazzua

1591—Morocco invades and occupies Songhai—collapse of Songhai

End of 1500s–early 1600s—Idris Aloma comes to power in Kanem-Borno

1600s—Decline of trans-Saharan trade

1725—Start of Fulani jihad in Futa Jalon

1737—Tuaregs occupy Timbuktu

1750—Tuareg kingdom of Aïr seizes Bilma oasis

1750—Creation of Fulani jihadist state in Futa Jalon

1769–76—Fulani-led jihad in Futa Toro; creation of Bundu state

an urban culture developed with markets, schools, and mosques as well as artisans, merchants, and intellectuals. The most enduring impact, though, was the southward spread of Islam into West Africa along the Saharan trade routes from North Africa. On the Sahel, West African urban elites and others became part of the wider Muslim world, sharing a common faith and identity that brought literature to the region. This religious change also resulted in new tensions and divisions in West Africa, as some conscientious Muslims disapproved of people who had only partly accepted Islam or who had not accepted it at all. Besides the export of gold, the Saharan trade involved slave raiding and trading that was justified on the basis that its victims were non-Muslims or bad Muslims. During this period Islam came to dominate much of the West African hinterland and the far western coastal areas of Senegambia where the Sahara and Sahel met the Atlantic, but the new religion did not penetrate south into the coastal forest. The arrival of European ships along West Africa's coast and the opening of a transatlantic trade in the late 1400s and 1500s would ultimately cause the decline of the trans-Saharan network, though it continued to operate in a reduced manner. With the decline of the great empires of the Sahel, parts of the area became the scene of conflict that resulted in the rise of Fulani jihadist states during the 1700s. These developments set the stage for the modern division of many West African countries into a predominantly Muslim north or interior and a predominantly Christian/traditionalist south near the Atlantic.

KEY TERMS

Benin kingdom 93	jihad 90	trans-Saharan trade 83
Fulani 95	Kanem-Borno 91	trypanosomiasis 85
Ghana 87	Mali 88	
Hausa 90	Songhai 89	

STUDY QUESTIONS

1. How was the Sahara Desert both an obstacle and a highway for commerce and trade? Why was the camel such an important part of trans-Saharan trade? What were the most important commodities that were traded? Why did the trans-Saharan trade gradually move east?

2. What factors contributed to the growth and decline of Ghana? What were its major trade goods? What were the religious and military characteristics of Mali? What were some of the cultural contributions and centers of learning in the Songhai Empire? Why did Songhai fall?

3. How did the eastward shift of the trans-Saharan trade impact the Hausa? What were the slave trading tactics of Kanem-Borno?

4. What were the geographical features and resources of the coastal forest zone? What factors spurred the growth of centralized states like Benin and those of the Yoruba in this region?

5. What factors led to the decline of the trans-Saharan trade? What impact did Muslim revivalist movements have on trade and law? Why did interior West African kingdoms launch jihads?

Please see page FR-2 for the Further Readings for this chapter.
For additional digital learning resources please go to
https://www.oup.com/he/falola-stapleton1e

5

Ottoman North Africa, c. 1500–1800

During the 1500s, North Africa became the target of two expansionist forces moving in from different directions. From southwestern Europe, the Christian Iberian kingdoms of Portugal and Spain took their previous religious struggles against Muslims on the Iberian Peninsula to North Africa. At the same time, they were engaged in overseas empire-building in the Americas and initiating the transatlantic slave trade from West Africa. To facilitate these endeavors, the Portuguese and Spanish used their naval power to seize a chain of enclaves along the Atlantic and Mediterranean coastlines of northwest Africa from Morocco to Libya. From the east, the Muslim-ruled but essentially multicultural Ottoman Empire based in what is now Turkey swept across much of North Africa from Egypt to Algeria, pushing back the Iberian presence. As a result, Turkish language, culture, and military and state organization were introduced to North Africa, adding to the cosmopolitan nature of the region. The only part of North Africa to remain independent of the Ottoman Empire was Morocco, which endured as a Muslim sultanate under several dynasties as it staved off incursions by Iberians and Ottomans. In the 1700s, the Ottoman territories of North Africa asserted autonomy from the imperial center, with a military regime taking charge in Algiers, quasi-national royal dynasties emerging in Tripoli and Tunisia, and Mamluk soldiers attempting to resume their control of Egypt setting the stage for the establishment of an autonomous ruling dynasty there in the early nineteenth century. This fragmentation of Ottoman North Africa, though still under nominal imperial authority, represents the foundation of the modern states of Algeria, Tunisia, Libya, and Egypt.

Veiled women in the Casbah of Algiers.

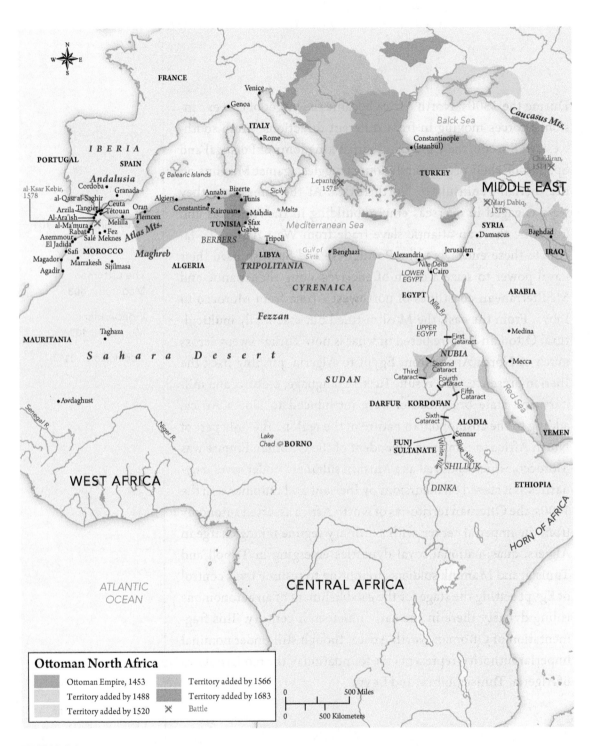

Ottoman North Africa

- Ottoman Empire, 1453
- Territory added by 1488
- Territory added by 1520
- Territory added by 1566
- Territory added by 1683
- ✕ Battle

0   500 Miles
0   500 Kilometers

≡ **MAP 5.1**

Ottoman Egypt

At the start of the 1500s, the Ottoman Empire steadily expanded. The Ottoman seizure of Constantinople (now Istanbul) in 1453, which collapsed the Byzantine Empire, facilitated further conquests in Eastern Europe, and their defeat of Persia's Safavid Empire at the 1514 Battle of Chaldiran set the stage of an Ottoman takeover in the Middle East and North Africa. Although its rulers were Muslims and initially Turks, the Ottoman Empire became transcultural, with Christians attaining high office and Christian boys captured in raids converting to Islam and training as professional soldiers and administrators. In 1516, at the Battle of Marj Dabiq in Syria, an Ottoman army skillfully used firearms and mobile artillery to defeat a Mamluk-led Egyptian force that relied on cavalry armed with swords and bows and arrows. Consequently, the Ottomans invaded Egypt again defeating Mamluk armies in several battles and occupying Cairo in January 1517. Egypt became an Ottoman province administered by an appointed Ottoman governor or pasha, though Mamluk emirs continued to govern the districts and Mamluks remained owners of vast lands. Although the Ottomans continued the practice of enslaving people from the Caucasus region who were turned into Mamluk soldiers for the Egyptian army, the Mamluks, together with some Arab allies, staged a series of rebellions against Ottoman rule in Egypt during the early 1520s. These revolts prompted Ottoman reforms to Egypt's legal and military system in which peasants were excluded from the army and were protected from the usual extortion by soldiers in exchange for paying a tax to support the military. A profitable territory, Egypt provided the Ottoman Empire with fruit, sugar, textiles, and grain as well as money from taxation and customs payments. While Egypt's Muslim scholars gained influence by mediating disputes between Ottomans and Mamluks, Christians and Jews enjoyed tolerant Ottoman rule. Since Ottoman pashas were posted to Egypt for short periods and assigned limited funds, they did not engage in ambitious long-term building projects. However, under the Ottomans Egypt experienced an expansion of literacy, and culturally there was a proliferation of Turkish coffee houses that also served as venues for musical and theatrical performances.

At the start of the 1600s, attempts by the Ottoman pashas to prevent the army from extorting civilians led to a series of military mutinies and civil wars. In 1610, in a conflict of such intensity that it has been called the second Ottoman conquest of Egypt, rebel soldiers seized Cairo and declared a new sultan but an Ottoman force recaptured the capital and executed or banished the mutineers. Despite this, local elites continued to exercise considerable authority. In 1623, for instance, at Alexandria newly arrived Ottoman governor Cesteci Ali Pasha refused to pay a customary gratuity to Egyptian officers who then organized a military attack that compelled him to flee by ship. In turn, the Ottoman government in Constantinople (Istanbul) reappointed Egypt's outgoing governor Kara Mustafa Pasha, whom it had previously dismissed. Furthermore, in 1631, Constantinople retroactively approved the Egyptian army's overthrow of newly appointed but brutal Ottoman governor Koca Musa Pasha. The weakness and corruption of the Ottoman governors allowed a Mamluk emir, Ridwan Bey al-Fiqari, to rule Egypt for a quarter century between 1631 and 1656. After Ridwan's death, the Ottoman governors re-established some authority by playing Mamluk factions against each other and gaining more control over the army. As Mamluk influence declined, the power of the Ottoman slave soldiers, the **Janissaries**, increased as they allied and intermarried with the Egyptian artisan class and protected them from excessive government taxation. At the end of the 1600s and start of the 1700s,

Ottoman Janissary. After conquering Egypt in 1517, the Ottoman Empire garrisoned the territory with enslaved soldiers called janissaries.

Egypt experienced a series of army mutinies and civil wars involving rival Janissary officers. After a major civil internal conflict in the 1710s, the death of many Janissary leaders allowed the Mamluk beys to re-establish their supremacy over Egypt for the rest of the century. In 1768, the Ottoman governor of Egypt was deposed by Mamluk leader Ali Bey al-Kabir, who declared the country's independence by halting regular tribute payments to Constantinople and having his own name inscribed on Egyptian coins. Egypt returned to the status of an independent Mamluk kingdom. While Ali Bey attempted state centralization and technological modernization and his armies occupied Syria and western Arabia, Ottoman agents sowed dissent among his commanders and in 1772 he was overthrown and killed. At the end of the eighteenth century, Egypt was governed by shifting coalitions of Mamluk leaders who preyed upon ordinary people. Furthermore, the economy was undermined as coffee exports from the Americas weakened Egypt's position as an intermediary in the coffee trade, and a series of low Nile floods hindered agriculture and caused widespread starvation.

Sudan

South of Egypt, in what is now Sudan, a group of nomadic and pastoral horsemen called the Funj moved from somewhere between the floodplains of the Upper Nile and the eastern foothills of the Ethiopian highlands during the 1500s to conquer part of Nubia along the Blue Nile as far north as its junction with the White Nile. The Funj eliminated the kingdom of Alodia, which was the last Christian state in Nubia.

≡ **Sennar, capital of the Funj Sultanate.** Around 1600, the Funj sultanate established its capital of Sennar on the Blue Nile in what is now Sudan.

By 1600, the Funj had become Muslims, amassed large herds of cattle, established towns with their capital at Sennar on the Blue Nile and collected tribute from Arabs and Nubians who were left under their own leaders. Additionally, the Funj sultanate built forts throughout the area and maintained an army with a core of armored, sword-wielding cavalry. To the north, in the 1580s, the Funj secured the Nile's third cataract as their frontier by defeating an Ottoman force moving south from Egypt. To the south, the Funj initially fought the Shilluk people for control of trade on the White Nile, but in the 1630s, they made peace to counter the arrival of pastoral Dinka groups from further south. To the east, the Funj allied with the Ethiopians against the Ottomans, but when that common threat disappeared Funj and Ethiopia fought a series of engagements in the early 1600s. Later, in 1744, the Funj defeated a large Ethiopian army that invaded their country. To the west, the Funj frequently battled the Darfur sultanate, founded in the mid-1600s, over trade in the Kordofan area that lay between them. During the early and mid-1700s, Funj experienced conflict between its sultan, who attempted to develop his own slave army to enforce royal authority, and local nobles who resisted centralization. These civil wars led to the decline of Funj and the rise in power of the Shilluk to the south. As a result, the region of present-day Sudan became vulnerable to invasion by Egypt during the early nineteenth century.

The Ottoman Maghreb

At the start of the 1500s, Christian Spain became more aggressive toward western North Africa. After the last Muslim enclave in Spain—Granada—was conquered in 1492, the Christian Spanish wanted to extend their campaign against Islam to North Africa. Around the same time, the weakening of the Zayyanid and Hafsid kingdoms meant that North African cities like Algiers and Tripoli became independent and served as operational bases for Muslim pirates or corsairs in the Mediterranean. In 1503, some of these Muslim corsairs supported a Muslim revolt in Spain further prompting Christian Spanish intervention along the coast of the Maghreb. As a result, Spanish privateer Pedro Navarro led an expeditionary campaign that seized Oran in 1509 and Algiers, Tripoli, and Tlemcen in 1510. Beleaguered Muslim rulers then requested assistance from the Greco-Turkish corsairs Aruj (Oruc), Khayr al-Din (Hayridden), and Ishaq, also known as the Barbarossa (red beard) brothers. In 1516, after fighting the Spanish along the North African coast, Aruj took over Algiers for himself leaving the Spanish in possession of the nearby island of Penon. The next year, on the invitation of Aruj, the Ottoman Empire annexed Algiers, appointing its corsair ruler as governor of the new province and dispatching Ottoman soldiers to help in the war against Spain. After Aruj led an army that seized the hinterland trans-Saharan trade center of Tlemcen, he was killed when a large Spanish force besieged and recaptured the city in 1518. Though forced to flee Algiers, Khayr al-Din received additional Ottoman military support which enabled him to recapture the city in 1525 and expand his realm to include the eastern Algerian cities of Annaba and Constantine. In 1529, he led an attack that finally removed the Spanish from Penon Island and he then ordered the construction of a causeway, dramatically increasing the size of Algiers harbor which became a major center for Ottoman naval operations in the western Mediterranean. As his brother Aruj had done, Khayr al-Din led naval raids on the Spanish coast which rescued tens of thousands of oppressed Muslim Iberians and resettled them in North Africa. Promoted to admiral of the Ottoman fleet in 1533, Khayr al-Din led naval operations that expanded Ottoman authority eastward along the North African coast seizing the cities of Tunis, Bizerte, and Kairouan from the declining Hafsid kingdom. The next year a Spanish fleet of 250 ships captured Tunis and reinstated the rule of the Hafsids, who became Spanish clients. Just as the Muslim Hafsids allied with the Christian Spanish, the Christian French cooperated with the Muslim Ottomans, including the naval forces led by Khayr al-Din. In 1541, in a determined attempt to eliminate Khayr al-Din's operational base, a massive Spanish fleet of 500 vessels commanded by Admiral Andrea Doria, and which also included Hernán Cortés who had conquered the Aztec Empire in Mexico, attacked Algiers but failed because of bad weather.

During the 1500s, the Ottomans established three **regencies** in western North Africa: Algiers, Tunis, and Tripoli. Initiated by the corsair leader Khayr al-Din, the first regency was established in Algiers and served as a base for the subsequent

☰ **Pirates and Captives.** *Left:* Khayr al-Din Barbarossa's naval victories helped secure Ottoman dominance in the Mediterranean in the early sixteenth century. *Right:* In this detail from a tapestry from about 1535, a representative of the Spanish Empire buys freedom for two female Christian slaves.

founding of the other two. Nominally headed by appointed Ottoman governors, these regencies remained largely autonomous from Constantinople given the power of local soldiers and corsairs. In the 1550s, the corsair successors of Khayr al-Din extended the supremacy of Algiers inland, taking control of economically important Tlemcen. Algiers became a significant naval resource for the Ottoman Empire, with a fleet from the city taking part in the massive Battle of Lepanto fought off the coast of Greece in 1571. The Algiers regency reached the height of its power in the 1600s as its corsairs ventured out into the Atlantic raiding the coast of Western Europe and reaching as far as Ireland and Iceland. While privateering, including ransoming captives and selling enslaved people taken during raids, represented a major part of economy of Algiers, the regency also became productive in agriculture and manufacturing. During the seventeenth century, Ottoman Algiers became an important and highly cosmopolitan Mediterranean port with a population of around 125,000 people, and the city's famous citadel, or **Casbah**, and new large mosques were constructed. By that time, after struggles between pirate captains and Turkish Janissaries in the late 1600s, Algiers had become a semi-independent military republic ruled by an official called a **dey** who retained symbolic links to Constantinople. The dey's military regime ruled the towns while local chiefs and religious leaders who acknowledged the nominal supremacy of Algiers governed the countryside. Given the raiding and pirate activities of its corsairs,

Algiers became the periodic target of retaliatory bombardments and attacks by European navies such as the French in 1682–83 and 1688, the Danes in 1770, and the Spanish in 1775 and 1783.

In 1574, eager to recover from their defeat by Christian forces at the Battle of Lepanto, the Ottomans assembled in Algiers and other places a huge fleet and army that captured Tunis and overthrew the Hafsid dynasty and its Spanish allies. This was a strategic victory that secured Ottoman dominance in the central and eastern Maghreb. The new Ottoman regency in Tunis was modeled on that of Algiers. The Ottomans appointed a **pasha** (governor) and a military commander called a **bey**, who was responsible for administering and taxing the interior. In 1591, however, Ottoman soldiers in Tunis rebelled and put one of their officers (also called a "dey") in power in the city, turning the governor into a figurehead. During the 1600s, the dey headed a military regime in Tunis while the bey became a hereditary position held by the Murad family controlling the hinterland. In 1705, Husayn bin Ali, a new bey of mixed Greco-Turkish and Tunisian origin, mobilized a large army to fend off an invasion from Algiers and then used his soldiers to take control of Tunis from the dey, who was downgraded to the capital's police chief. Although Tunisia remained a nominal part of the Ottoman Empire and its army continued to employ Turkish troops, Husayn established a quasi-national ruling dynasty that lasted until 1957. Eighteenth-century Tunis continued to serve as a base for some pirate activities, while its economy centered on producing wool and silk traded to European merchants. Active in urban society and cultural life in eighteenth-century Tunisia, elite women created endowments to build schools, mosques, and gardens, and conducted charity work for the poor.

Seized by the Spanish in 1510, Tripoli became a fortified Christian outpost surrounded by Muslim enemies, and in 1535 the city was taken by a Malta-based Christian crusader group called the Knights of Saint John, who maintained a navy in the Mediterranean. Though the Ottomans unsuccessfully besieged Tripoli in 1536, an Ottoman fleet finally captured the city in 1551 and turned it into another North African regency. The first Ottoman governor of Tripoli, the Greco-Turkish corsair Turghut (Gragut) who was later killed in an attack on Malta, made the port a base for privateer actions including raids on the Italian coast and used gun-armed Ottoman soldiers to force communities in the hinterland of Tripolitania to pay tribute, though they remained autonomous. Rebellions against Ottoman rule in the late 1500s and early 1600s failed as the Ottomans were able to turn local communities against each other. Tripoli was governed by an Ottoman pasha, but the most powerful position became the bey, who was a military officer commanding the Turkish Janissary troops. In 1577, an Ottoman force from Tripoli ventured far south into the Fezzan area in an unsuccessful attempt to control the trans-Saharan trade, though the Ottomans were able to force the local Banu Muhammad community to pay them tribute. While the Ottomans in Tripoli rejected a request for military assistance from Idris Alooma, ruler of the Borno state at Lake Chad, Turkish mercenary gunmen traveled south to enlist in his army. Furthermore, in 1578 Ottoman Tripoli extended its authority east over the port of Benghazi in Cyrenaica. In 1711, Ahmad Qaramanli, an Ottoman cavalry officer, staged a coup in Tripoli that established a quasi-national ruling dynasty that was recognized by the Ottomans and retained symbolic links to the empire. Ahmad Qaramanli sponsored pirates to gain wealth and standing in the Muslim world and sent expeditions south that imposed direct rule over Fezzan. In the mid-1700s, Tripoli's pirate captains became publicly celebrated heroes and European governments paid extortion money to the Qaramanli family to safeguard their merchant vessels. In 1793, the Ottomans, taking advantage of a dispute among the Qaramanlis, seized Tripoli attempting to re-impose imperial rule, but a military intervention by Tunisia, concerned about growing Ottoman ambitions in the region, reinstated the Qaramanli dynasty.

Independent Morocco

As most of North Africa came under Ottoman influence in the 1500s, Morocco remained independent. At the start of the 1500s, it appeared that Morocco would be taken over by Christian Iberians who wished to continue their long struggle against Muslims by warring against them in North Africa. In 1497, for instance, Christian Spain occupied the Moroccan Mediterranean port of Melilla. Taking advantage of the conflict between the Marinids and Wattasids, the Christian Portuguese seized ports along Morocco's side of the Strait of Gibraltar and down the Atlantic coast, such as Ceuta in 1415, al-Qasr al-Saghir in 1458, Arzila and Tangier in 1471, Safi in 1488, El Jadida in 1502, Agadir in 1505, Mogador in 1506, Agouz in 1507, and Azemmour in 1513. The Portuguese along with Moroccan Arab and Berber allies began to advance inland, threatening the city of Marrakesh. As a result, the Arabs of the Banu Sa'd or Saadi clan from southern Morocco, who claimed descent from the Prophet Mohammed's daughter Fatima, responded to calls by Muslim religious leaders and launched a jihad against the Portuguese invaders and their partners. After defeating a Portuguese-led army on the outskirts of Marrakesh in 1515, the Saadians pushed the Iberians back to the coast and eventually seized their enclaves, including Agadir, Safi, and Azemmour in 1541 and al-Qasr al-Saghir and Arzila in 1550, which restored Moroccan oceanic trade with West Africa. The Saadians, based in Marrakesh, also waged war against the Moroccan Wattasid dynasty with its capital at Fez. At this time Aisha Rashid or Sayyida al-Hurra (a title meaning "independent noble lady"), who as a little girl had fled the Christian conquest of Granada in 1492, inherited the governorship of Tétouan from her late first husband, became a leader of Tétouan-based corsairs allied with those of Algiers operating in the western Mediterranean, and married one of the last Wattasid sultans in 1541. Since the Wattasids received military support from the newly established Ottoman regency in nearby Algiers, the Saadians allied with the Christian Spanish who were battling the Ottomans for control of the Mediterranean. The Saadians occupied Fez in 1549, fought the Ottomans from Algiers for control of Tlemcen, and in 1558 defeated an invasion of Morocco by the Ottomans who were distracted by Spanish forces based in the enclave of Oran. With their elimination of the Wattasids and defeat of the Ottomans, the Saadians established a ruling dynasty over Morocco, ensuring that it remained outside the Ottoman Empire. Given the vulnerability of Fez to attack from Ottoman Algiers, the Saadians re-established Marrakesh as the capital of Morocco. The first Saadian Sultan of Morocco was Muhammad al-Shaykh, who saw himself as the Mahdi or divinely appointed leader and was assassinated by Ottoman agents in 1557. He was succeeded by Sultan al-Ghalib, who secured Saadian dominance by suppressing Muslim religious leaders and brotherhoods, and maintaining the clan's alliance with Spain. On the other hand, Al-Ghalib directed the construction of the Ben Yussef Madrasa, which became the largest center for Islamic learning in Morocco.

Sultan al-Ghalib's death in 1574 prompted a succession dispute that resulted in renewed foreign intervention in Morocco. Since Sultan Abd al-Malik came to power in Morocco with the support of the Ottomans, the Portuguese became concerned that these enemies would use Moroccan ports to disrupt Lisbon's growing Atlantic trade. The young King Sebastian of Portugal, who also became interested in renewing Christian religious struggles against Muslims in North Africa, backed the exiled Abu Abdallah Mohammed II, who claimed the Moroccan throne. In 1578, a Portuguese fleet of 500 ships landed a large Portuguese army at Arzila on the coast of Morocco, and they were soon joined by Moroccan allies loyal to Abdallah Mohammed. In response, Sultan Abd al-Malik raised a massive army including Moroccan cavalry and Ottoman allies with firearms and artillery. At the subsequent Battle of al-Ksar Kebir, also known as the **Battle of the Three Kings**, the Moroccan-Ottoman coalition decisively defeated the Portuguese and their partners, who suffered horrific casualties. None of the faction leaders survived the engagement. Sebastian and almost all Portugal's nobility were killed in the fighting, Abdallah Mohammed drowned trying to flee across a river and Al-Malik passed away suddenly, probably from heart attack.

Ahmad al-Mansur, Al-Malik's brother, became sultan in the wake of this famous battle and he went on to become one of Morocco's greatest rulers. Al-Mansur initiated a series of reforms including establishing an efficient central government and remodeling the Moroccan army along Ottoman lines, including the use of

firearms. The new sultan encouraged the employment of
foreign artisans, technicians
and scholars, both Muslim
and Christian, and his personal doctors originated from
France. Using the ransoms
received for Portuguese noble
captives taken at the Battle of
the Three Kings, Al-Mansur
commissioned the 15-year
construction of Marrakesh's
fabulous El Badi Palace (Palace of Wonder), with some
360 rooms decorated with
gold, onyx, and marble. To
counter Spain, which had
grown extremely wealthy
from New World gold and

Battle of the Three Kings. This image shows a detail of the only known representation of the 1578 battle. Portuguese forces are on the left, Moroccan forces are arrayed on the right.

now also ruled Portugal, Al-Mansur entered an alliance with England, suggesting in letters to Queen Elizabeth I that Morocco could colonize America and re-
conquer Iberia. The destruction of the Spanish Armada in the English Channel in
1588 presented Al-Mansur with an opportunity, as it reduced the Iberian threat.
As such, in 1591, he dispatched a Moroccan expeditionary force that included
English mercenaries south across the Sahara to conquer the Songhai Empire, with
a view to obtaining enslaved people and gold. Although Muslim religious leaders
objected to warring against Muslim co-religionists in Songhai, Al-Mansur justified the invasion on the basis that Morocco needed extra resources to regain lost
Muslim lands in Spain. However, while the Moroccan force defeated Songhai and
occupied its trans-Saharan trading towns along the Niger River, continued resistance and the decline of local gold exports meant that the conquest was never profitable. After Al-Mansur died from plague in 1603, Morocco lapsed into civil war
between rival powers in Fez and Marrakesh, and corsairs began using ports such
Rabat and Salé to raid Western Europe, including England and Ireland.

   Moroccan unity was re-established by a new dynasty. In 1659, Mawlay al-Rashid,
leader of the Alawi clan, which claimed descent from the Prophet Mohammed's
grandson, led a military campaign that overthrew the last Saadian ruler. Rallying
an army of disaffected Arab groups, al-Rashid took Fez in 1666 and Marrakesh in
1669, establishing a new Alawite royal dynasty. Mawlay Ismail, who ruled from
1672 to 1727, founded a new capital at Miknasa (Meknes) as he did not want to be

seen as favoring any of the other cities. He created a national army paid by taxation and established large **Abid** regiments consisting of Black enslaved people and free men trained in civilian trades and military skills and encouraged to marry and have children to replenish the force. Ismail stationed the army's Arab troops at new frontier forts to keep them away from the centers of power that were garrisoned by his loyal Abid units. After suppressing a number of rebellions sponsored by the Ottomans, Ismail sent retaliatory expeditions into their Algerian territory in 1679, 1682, and 1695. Turning south, the Moroccan leader attempted to revive the western trans-Saharan trade by sending a force to seize salt-producing Taghaza in 1694 and helping the Emirate of Trarza, in what is now Mauritania, to attack the French on the Senegal River in 1724. Struggling to eliminate the European presence from Morocco's coast, his armies expelled the Spanish from al-Ma'mura in 1681, Al-Ara'ish in 1689, and Arzila in 1691, and compelled the English to abandon Tangier in 1684. Pirates based at Moroccan ports harassed European shipping and Ismail, who owned about half the pirate vessels, took 60 percent of their loot as tax. Since Ismael oppressed the Muslim scholars who criticized his use of an enslaved army to impose absolute rule, his reign was not characterized by educational developments. While Ismail built impressive palaces, pavilions, and gates at his imperial capital of Miknasa (Meknes), he failed to prepare for an orderly succession. Following Ismail's death, the Abid regiments became kingmakers, deposing seven of his sons from 1727 to 1757. During the 1740s, Mawlay Abdullah used the Arab part of the army and Berber allies to exercise control over the Abid soldiers, who began to lose their political influence. His son, Mawlay Muhammad III, came to power in 1757 by using the Abid soldiers to eliminate rebellious Arab troops but then dispersing

≡ **Ahmad al-Mansur.** *Left:* Ruling Morocco from 1578 to 1603, Ahmad al-Mansur initiated numerous reforms, forged an alliance with England, and directed an invasion of the Songhai Empire. *Right:* Located in Marrakesh, El Badi Palace was commissioned by Ahmad al-Mansur in the late 1500s.

the Abid units around the country to dilute their influence. While this prompted a rebellion and famine that lasted from 1779 to 1782 and reduced Morocco's population from five to three million people, Muhammad III eventually defeated the Abid soldiers by recruiting an army from among Arab groups. Eager to improve relations with European countries and the newly independent United States, Muhammad III took steps to reduce the use of Moroccan ports by pirates. He also attempted to end the European presence along the Moroccan coast, with the Portuguese withdrawing their last outpost of Mazagan in 1769 but the Spanish fighting to retain Melilla in 1775. With Muhammad III's death in 1790, civil war resumed until Mawlay Sulayman imposed his authority in the mid-1790s with the support of Berbers and Abid soldiers. Given continued conflict with Spain, the new ruler halted trade with Europe, which isolated Morocco at a critical time and would have negative consequences for the country's future.

Abid troops. This nineteenth-century French painting shows a Moroccan sultan accompanied by his Abid troops.

Conclusion

From the sixteenth century, the extension of Ottoman influence from Egypt to Algeria furthered the cultural and religious differences between North Africa and Europe. During this time, the Mediterranean Sea was losing its strategic and economic importance as European powers built colonial empires in the Americas and developed transatlantic commerce including slave exports from West Africa to New World plantations. North African powers continued to trade with the rest of the Mediterranean, the Middle East, and Asia, and across the Sahara, but these networks were in relative decline and could not compete with the rise of European Atlantic empires. The decentralized nature of the Ottoman Empire in North Africa gave rise to quasi-national regimes in Egypt, Libya, Tunisia, and Algeria, and Morocco became defined by its exclusion from this system; but this also meant that the region became divided, and infighting plagued its royal dynasties. By the end of the 1700s, the previous balance of power in the Mediterranean between Muslim North Africa and Christian Europe had shifted to the latter. North Africa became vulnerable, and it subsequently experienced intensified European intrusion and conquest.

Timeline

1415—Portuguese seize Moroccan port of Ceuta

1471—Portuguese seize Moroccan ports of Arzila and Tangier

1492—Christian Spanish seize Granada, the last Muslim enclave in Iberia

1497—Christian Spanish take Moroccan port of Melilla

c. 1500—Foundation of the Funj sultanate in Nubia (Sudan)

1502–06—Portuguese seize Moroccan ports of Mazagan (El Jadida), Agadir, and Mogador

1509—Spanish seize Oran in Algeria

1510—Spanish seize Algiers and Tripoli

1513—Portuguese seize Moroccan port of Azemmour

1515—Saadians defeat Portuguese outside Marrakesh

1516—The corsair Aruj takes Algiers, which becomes an Ottoman regency

1517—Ottoman Empire occupies Egypt

1541—Failed Spanish attack on Algiers

1541—Saadians seize Moroccan ports of Agadir, Safi, and Azemmour from Portuguese

1549—Saadians capture Fez, founding the Saadian dynasty of Morocco

1550—Saadians seize Moroccan ports of al-Qasr, al-Saghir, and Arzila from Portuguese

1551—Ottomans seize Tripoli, making it a regency

1571—Battle of Lepanto, defeat of Ottoman navy by Christian fleet

1574—Ottoman seizure of Tunis, which becomes an Ottoman regency—end of Hafsid dynasty

1577—Ottoman force from Tripoli ventures south into Fezzan

1578—Battle of the Three Kings in Morocco

1591—Moroccan invasion of Songhay

1610—Major rebellion in Egypt against Ottoman rule

1630s—Peace between Funj and Shilluk in Sudan, and arrival of Dinka

1640—Ceuta becomes a Spanish enclave

1669—Fall of the Saadian dynasty and rise of Alawid dynasty in Morocco

1684—English abandon Tangier, which is taken by Morocco

1705—Tunis, under Husaynid dynasty, becomes an autonomous part of the Ottoman Empire

1711—Tripoli, under the Qaramanli dynasty, becomes an autonomous part of the Ottoman Empire

1744—Ethiopian invasion of Funj sultanate

1768–72—Egyptian independence under Mamluk leader Ali Bey al-Kabir

1769—Portuguese withdraw from Mazagan, their last outpost in Morocco

1779–82—Civil war and famine in Morocco

1792—Spain withdraws from Oran in Algeria

1793—Ottomans attempt to impose direct rule on Tripoli but are foiled by Tunisian intervention

KEY TERMS

Abid 110

Battle of the Three
     Kings 108

bey 106

Casbah 105

dey 105

Janissaries 102

pasha 106

regencies 104

STUDY QUESTIONS

1. What features made Ottoman society multicultural? What methods did the Ottomans use to control Egypt, and why did its rule increasingly become unstable?

2. What were the chief characteristics of the Funj sultanate?

3. How would you describe Christian–Muslim interactions after 1492? What role did corsairs play in the economies and politics of the Mediterranean in the sixteenth century? How successful were the Ottoman regencies in Algiers, Tunis, and Tripoli?

4. How was Morocco able to maintain independence? What type of interactions existed between Morocco and Portugal during this period? How did Al-Mansur and the Alawi rulers attempt to maintain Moroccan unity during their reigns?

Please see page FR-3 for the Further Readings for this chapter.
For additional digital learning resources please go to
https://www.oup.com/he/falola-stapleton1e

6

West Africa and the Transatlantic Slave Trade, c. 1500–1800

From the early 1500s to the middle 1800s, millions of West Africans were abducted by local powers, shipped across the Atlantic by European and colonial American slavers, and forced to work on plantations in South America, Central America, the Caribbean, and southern North America. This process is now called the **transatlantic slave trade**. Although modern historians debated the total number of enslaved Africans who landed in the Americas in this period, with some putting the figure at nine million and others at 20 million, a consensus emerged around an estimate of 12 million. As a central event in the history of the global African diaspora, the transatlantic slave trade resulted in large communities of people of West African descent living in many parts of the Americas such as, but not limited to, Brazil, numerous Caribbean islands, and the United States. Two factors were central to the emergence of the transatlantic slave trade: the existing institution of slavery in Africa and the Portuguese overseas expansion. While some scholars claimed that no slavery existed in West African societies before the coming of slave trading Europeans, there is ample evidence that West Africans had long been enslaved and sent north as part of the older trans-Saharan trade system. Historians have also debated the extent to which African systems of slavery were meant to assimilate new people into the slave-holding society or were simply economically exploitive. From the 1400s, the Portuguese pioneered a combination of oceanic trade, overseas plantation production, and African slave labor that would be copied by other emerging European powers in the 1600s and 1700s. West Africa had been at the southern fringe of the overland trans-Saharan trade for centuries (see Chapter 4) but now it also found itself involved in an entirely new and oceanic intercontinental network.

Re-creating Africa in the New World. Enslaved Africans socialize on a plantation in Suriname, on the northeast coast of South America, c. 1707

Portuguese Origins

Portugal was the first power to ship enslaved Africans across the Atlantic to the Americas. The Christian kingdom of Portugal emerged in the twelfth century out of the violent struggle between Christian and Muslim forces over the Iberian Peninsula that took place during the medieval era and that is generally known as the **Reconquista**. With limited agricultural potential but a long Atlantic coast, medieval Portugal focused on fishing and oceanic trade between southern and western Europe and North Africa. While Portugal often fought the neighboring Christian kingdom of Castile, the greater struggle between Christians and Muslims brought Portuguese vessels into frequent naval battles with Muslim ships; Portuguese ships also repeatedly raided Muslim communities on the North African coast.

King Afonso IV (r. 1325–1357) was the first Portuguese monarch to sponsor seagoing explorations, and in 1341 a Portuguese-led expedition arrived at the Canary Islands, located off the coast of southern Morocco; the islands were later seized by Castile. In 1415, a 45,000-strong Portuguese army transported in 200 ships and personally led by King John I seized the North African port of Ceuta, hitherto under Morocco's Marinid dynasty, located at the strategic Strait of Gibraltar that connects the Mediterranean Sea and Atlantic Ocean. The seizure of Ceuta gave Portugal access to the trans-Saharan gold trade, enabled it to threaten its rival of Castile on the Iberian Peninsula, and provided young Portuguese nobles with an opportunity to win wealth and glory in battles against North African Muslims.

Portugal's Prince Henry, King John's son who participated in the capture of Ceuta and later called **Henry the Navigator**, used his position as head of a Christian military order to support Portuguese oceanic exploration during the early and middle 1400s. Henry's royal connections were also important, as his brother King Edward, in 1433, granted him all the profits from trading in areas his expeditions discovered and the sole right to authorize exploration south of Morocco's Cape Bojador, beyond which no European had yet sailed. Based in the southern Portuguese port of Lagos, Henry's ships began sailing out into the Atlantic and south down the northwest African coastline. In 1419, they came upon the Madeira archipelago, which the Portuguese colonized in the 1420s, and then, perhaps in 1427, they landed on the Azores Islands in the North Atlantic, which they also settled. Both island chains served as staging areas for further Portuguese seagoing exploration. Exploring southward along Africa's Atlantic coast, Henry's expeditions reached Cape Bojador in 1431 and proceeded along the Mauritanian coast, reaching Cape Blanco in 1441 and Arguin Bay in 1443. In 1444, Portuguese sea captain Dinis Dias sailed 500 miles south of Arguin Bay, reaching the mouth of the Senegal River and rounding the Cape Verde Peninsula, Africa's most westerly point, therefore

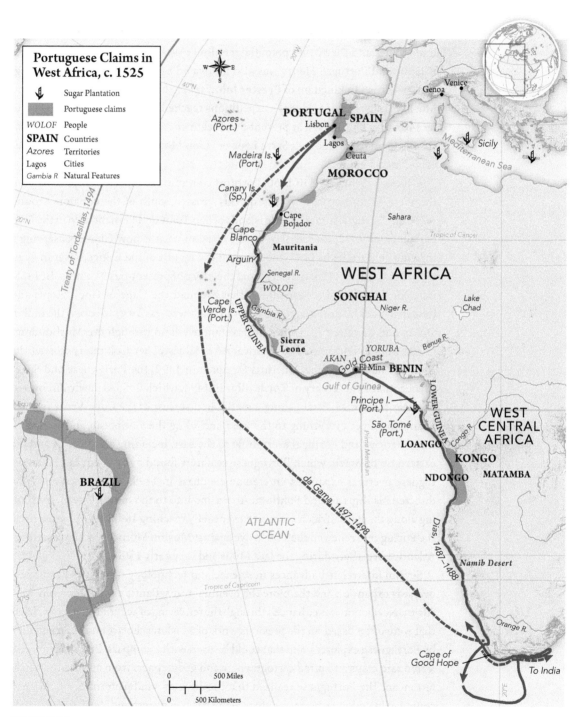

Portuguese Claims in West Africa, c. 1525

- Sugar Plantation
- Portuguese claims
- *WOLOF* People
- **SPAIN** Countries
- *Azores* Territories
- Lagos Cities
- *Gambia R* Natural Features

≡ **MAP 6.1**

passing the southern extent of the Sahara Desert. This was a major achievement for Prince Henry, as his ships had outflanked the Muslim-controlled trans-Saharan trade routes and they could potentially redirect West African gold exports to the Atlantic and Portugal. Henry was also motivated by the hope of finding the legendary Christian kingdom of **Prester John**, said to be located somewhere beyond Muslim lands. In 1456, Henry's expeditions reached the Cape Verde Islands, and by 1462 they had arrived at present-day Freetown, with the surrounding hills inspiring them to call the area Serra Lyoa or "Lion Mountain," which eventually became Sierra Leone.

Although Henry died in 1460, Portugal continued to dispatch ships to explore the West African coast and they quickly crossed south of the equator. Around 1470, the Portuguese reached the islands of São Tomé and Fernando Po in the Gulf of Guinea; in 1471, they arrived on the coast of what is now Ghana, observing a thriving gold trade; in 1482, they located the mouth of the Congo River in Central Africa, and in 1486, they explored the coast of present-day Namibia. In 1488, Bartolomeu Dias led an expedition that rounded the Cape of Good Hope, and though it quickly turned back, this proved that there was a way to access the Indian Ocean and therefore Asia without traveling overland through the Muslim-dominated Middle East and North Africa. After Christopher Columbus crossed the Atlantic and claimed the Americas for Spain in 1492, the Portuguese and Spanish negotiated the **Treaty of Tordesillas** in 1494, which divided newly discovered overseas territories. Establishing a meridian just west of the Cape Verde Islands, Spain would get everything to the west, including the Caribbean and almost all the Americas, and Portugal everything to the east, including all of Africa and the eastern tip of Brazil, which Portuguese seafarers found by accident in 1500. Portuguese overseas expansion entered a new phase in 1498, when Vasco de Gama directed his ships around Southern Africa and into to the Indian Ocean, continuing along the East African coast and eventually reaching India. At the same time, the Portuguese renewed their offensive against Muslim Morocco, taking a series of Atlantic ports there during the late 1400s and very early 1500s.

Several interrelated advances in science and technology facilitated Portuguese overseas expansion and therefore the eventual transatlantic slave trade from West Africa. Navigation was enhanced through the rendering of accurate maps and charts that were often based on the previous work of Muslim scholars and supplemented by Portuguese explorers, and that could be used with a compass. Prince Henry collected rare maps and hired cartographers and geographers from around the Mediterranean. The Portuguese realized that the circular wind patterns of the Atlantic could facilitate long voyages, as ships along the Northwest and West African coast could use the prevailing eastward wind to head out into the ocean and then travel

PORTUGUESE EXPLORATION OF THE WEST COAST OF AFRICA

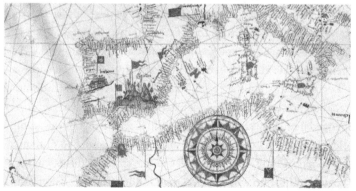

Top left: Henry the Navigator, who spearheaded Portuguese explorations of the West African coast in the first half of the fifteenth century; *Top right:* A Portuguese caravel, which was developed specifically by the Portuguese to explore the African coastline; *Bottom left:* A portolan, or marine chart, that shows sailing directions between various ports along the Mediterranean and North African coasts. *Bottom right:* Elmina ("the mine"), founded in 1482. Located in present-day Ghana, it was Portugal's most important trading post in West Africa until it was captured by the Dutch in 1637.

north to catch westward winds to bring them home to Europe. Furthermore, the Portuguese developed a new type of ship called a **caravel** which was small and maneuverable, and used triangular or lateen sails to travel in the direction of the wind.

From the beginning of their overseas expansion, the Portuguese captured and traded African enslaved people. Portuguese wars against Muslims in North Africa resulted in prisoners, and the earliest Portuguese ocean-going explorers along the West African coast brought back captives to Portugal. With its low population, Portugal needed labor particularly to support new sugar-growing operations in the southern part of the country. While sugar plantations had been operated in the eastern Mediterranean by Muslims and then Christian Crusaders during the medieval era, the Portuguese expanded this system to the Atlantic. In 1441, ten captives taken by an exploratory expedition under Nuno Tristão along the coast of Western Sahara became the first African enslaved people shipped to Europe by the Portuguese. In 1444, the Portuguese launched their first planned slave raid on West Africa with a fleet of six caravels under the command of Lançarote de Freitas, taking captives from fishing communities on islands in Mauritania's Arguin Bay. The 235 captives were shipped to Lagos in Portugal where they were sold under the personal supervision of Prince Henry who took 46 of the best enslaved people as his share of the plunder and knighted de Freitas. However, several subsequent expeditions to the Senegal coast in 1446 were unsuccessful due to resistance by local Wolof communities, and Tristão, one of Henry's favorite captains, was killed in an ambush. More African enslaved people were shipped to Portugal as the Portuguese explored the West African coast. Just over 900 enslaved people arrived in Portugal between 1441 and 1448, some 1,000 more arrived annually after 1448, with this number increasing to 2,000 per year after 1490. Nevertheless, it became clear to the Portuguese that it was much better and safer for them to acquire enslaved people from West African rulers and traders than to mount their own slave raids.

As the Portuguese established an empire of conquest and trade along the West African coast, their economic pursuits became increasingly intertwined with slavery. In 1445, the Portuguese established a trading factory on Arguin Island, and in 1461, they secured their presence there by constructing a small fort. On Arguin, the Portuguese exchanged items like clothing, honey, and flax for fish, but the amount of hinterland gold available was disappointing and it proved easier to obtain enslaved people for export. In 1482, the Portuguese monarchy took direct charge of the Portuguese coastal outpost in what is now Ghana and, with permission from a local ruler, constructed a castle called **Elmina** or "the mine" in expression of their hope to tap into the local gold trade originating from Akan in the interior. Europeans eventually called this area the "Gold Coast." Since the Portuguese did not have goods that the Akan people wanted in exchange for gold, the former became involved in the regional slave trade. The Akan needed enslaved people to work as porters for their growing gold mining industry. By 1500, the Portuguese were procuring around 500 enslaved people per year from the kingdom of Benin in what is now Nigeria and bringing them by ship to Elmina, from where they were marched to the Akan area in return for gold. By 1487, Elmina was shipping about 8,000 ounces of gold per year to Lisbon and by 1500 the amount had increased to 25,000 ounces annually. The Portuguese island of São Tomé became an assembly point for enslaved people acquired on the mainland in places like Benin, the kingdom of Kongo, and Angola, and who were then shipped to Elmina. From 1504 to 1536, the Portuguese transported at least 3,000 enslaved people from São Tomé to Elmina. Almost simultaneously, the Portuguese developed sugar plantations on São Tomé utilizing mainland enslaved people as a workforce, and by 1522 the island had become a major supplier of sugar for Europe. The successful combination of sugar production and slave labor on São Tomé was copied and expanded by the Portuguese in Brazil as the search for precious metals there proved a failure. Sugar production in Brazil was well established by the middle 1500s, and from 1575 to 1650 Brazil provided Europe with most of its sugar. Beginning in 1532 with its first transatlantic slave shipment, São Tomé became a major supplier of African enslaved people to the new Brazilian sugar plantations. After around 1540, the island's regional slave shipments to Elmina declined as the gold trade there became less profitable with the flood of American gold to Europe, and São Tomé's own sugar industry collapsed because of slave rebellions and competition from Brazil. During the second half of the 1500s, Portuguese slaving operations shifted south to the kingdom of Kongo and Angola in West-Central Africa.

Slavery and Conflict in West-Central Africa

In 1483, a Portuguese expedition led by Diogo Cão sailed up the Congo River and made contact with the centralized kingdom of Kongo, located in what is now western Democratic Republic of Congo (DRC) and northern Angola. The Portuguese and the rulers of Kongo quickly developed cordial relations with Portuguese priests and soldiers arriving in the kingdom, Kongo nobles visiting Portugal, and Kongo's King Nzinga a Nkuwu converting to Christianity taking the name João I. In 1506, after João's death, a civil war between Christian and traditionalist factions of Kongo's royal family ended with the rise to power of Christian ruler Afonso I, who closely allied his state with Portugal. With Roman Catholicism as a royal cult complete with its own priests and schools, the kingdom of Kongo tried to extend its regional influence by monopolizing trade with the Portuguese. As such, Kongo became an increasingly important supplier of enslaved people for the Portuguese, who shipped them to São Tomé, Elmina, and eventually the Americas. In 1526, Afonso I wrote a letter to Portugal's King João III, complaining that Portuguese in Kongo were acquiring enslaved people from sources other than the Kongo state, therefore undermining its monopoly. Although Portuguese support enabled Kongo to expand east to the Kwango River, with two of its kings being killed in battle against local communities there, a major setback for the kingdom happened in 1569 when a group called the Jaga invaded and sacked its capital forcing King Alvaro I to flee to an island on the Congo River. While many historians agree that the Jaga were people from east of Kongo displaced by warfare associated with slave raiding, one scholar claimed that the story of their invasion had been invented by Alvaro or the Portuguese to cover up a local rebellion. In 1571, a Portuguese expedition from São Tomé arrived in Kongo and defeated the Jaga, and a grateful Alvaro rewarded them with permission to settle on the island of Luanda to the south of his kingdom. In addition, Alvaro strengthened his grip on power by importing more Portuguese firearms for his army, retaining Portuguese mercenaries and founding a royal bodyguard of slave soldiers.

In 1575, the Portuguese founded a colony at Luanda and became determined to pursue rumors of silver in the hinterland kingdom of Ndongo that had rebuffed previous attempts by Portugal to establish relations. Since the title of the ruler of Ndongo was "ngola," the Portuguese came to call this region Angola. The Portuguese pushed inland, prompting Ndongo, in 1579, to send an army to attack a Portuguese fort. In turn, from 1580 to 1585, Portuguese forces invaded Ndongo, but stiff resistance and tropical disease compelled them to withdraw to a fortified settlement at Massangano on the Kwanza River. During the 1590s and 1610s, the Portuguese fought a number of grueling wars against Ndongo, eventually destroying its capital. Although the silver mines proved a myth, the Portuguese expanded their control of territory, and the displacement of people during these wars enabled slave raiding and turned Luanda into the most important exporter of enslaved people to Brazil. In 1617, the Portuguese at Luanda established another coastal enclave further south along the Angolan coast at Benguela, which also became a slave exporter. Such destabilization led to the founding of a new society called the **Imbangala** in which displaced people rejected kinship ties, built their group by incorporating captives who had to prove themselves in battle, elected their best fighters as leaders, and cultivated a fearsome warrior reputation. Refraining from agriculture, the Imbangala constantly moved around and survived by slave raiding and slave trading, and working as mercenaries for the Portuguese or local states.

The career of seventeenth-century Queen **Njinga** (or Nzinga) illustrates the complexities of expanding European intrusion and slave trading in what is now Angola. In the early 1620s, the Portuguese at Luanda and the kingdom of Ndongo made peace and cooperated in the slave exporting business. In 1621, Njinga, sister of the king of Ndongo, undertook a diplomatic visit to Luanda, where she converted to Christianity and met the Portuguese governor. Emphasizing her desire to negotiate with the Portuguese on equal terms, Njinga refused to sit on the floor and instead sat on the back of her kneeling servant so as to be at eye level with the governor, who sat in a chair. With the death of Ndongo's ruler in 1624, Njinga became the kingdom's regent and quickly took formal power when the late king's young son died under mysterious circumstances. Plagued by African and European questions about her legitimacy as a female ruler, Njinga married a series of husbands who served as puppet kings, and she adopted a number of male characteristics, including dressing as a

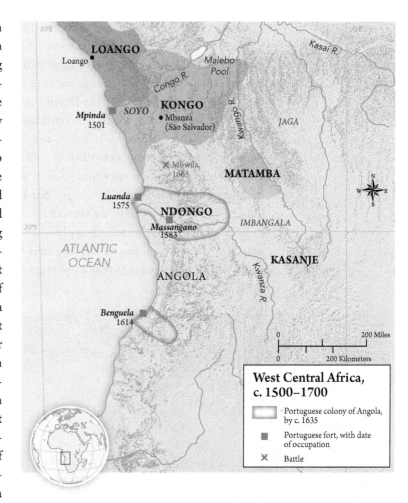

≡ MAP 6.2

man and keeping concubines who were men dressed as women. With an all-female bodyguard, Njinga became an expert warrior and personally led her army in battle. Njinga's relations with the Portuguese deteriorated as she supported local leaders who refused Portuguese demands for them to provide enslaved people as tribute. In 1626, consequently, the Portuguese invaded Ndongo, where they installed a puppet ruler and Christian convert called Ari Kiluanji, who agreed to send 100 enslaved people per year to Luanda and reopen slave markets. The exiled Njinga allied with an Imbangala group, adopted Imbangala organizational and fighting methods, and led raids that attempted to disrupt the Portuguese dominated slave routes and markets. Between 1630 and 1635, she conquered the interior state of Matamba, using it as a base for further warfare against the Portuguese and their client state of Ndongo.

The 1641 seizure of Luanda and Benguela by the Dutch, emerging rivals of the Portuguese, presented Njinga with an opportunity as these two European powers and their local African allies fought a war in Angola. Njinga supported the Dutch and sent them captives in exchange for firearms. However, in 1648 a Portuguese expedition from Brazil evicted the Dutch from Angola and then pushed Njinga's forces back to Matamba, which she continued to rule. In 1655, Njinga entered a treaty with the Portuguese in which the queen opened her area to Portuguese trade, agreed to assist the Portuguese militarily, and accepted a Portuguese mission. She also provided the Portuguese with 130 enslaved people to ransom her captive sister. Njinga died in 1663. While Njinga's long history of wars with the Portuguese prompted later writers and filmmakers to celebrate her as an early anticolonial African resistance leader and antislavery heroine, her actions reveal a pragmatic ruler who engaged in slave raiding and trading when it suited her interests. Her main goal seems to have been recognition as a sovereign ruler by Europeans and Africans.

≡ **Queen Njinga.** This engraving from about 1622 shows Queen Njinga negotiating with Portuguese emissaries. She sits on a slave's back to avoid standing in the presence of men of lower rank than herself.

During the 1600s, the Christian-ruled kingdom of Kongo and the Portuguese colony of Luanda engaged in conflict over control of small states located between the two powers. While these communities had been tributaries of Kongo, the Portuguese demanded that they hand over escaped enslaved people that had taken refuge there. In 1622, this situation led to a battle in which a Portuguese and Imbangala army defeated a force from Kongo, the Portuguese shipped prisoners taken in the battle to Brazil, and within Kongo some Portuguese traders were killed in revenge. This prompted Kongo to ally with the Dutch, with whom they planned a joint attack on Luanda in 1623, but this did not transpire given a change of regime in Kongo. During the 1640s, Kongo supported the Dutch invasion of Angola, but when the Portuguese prevailed, Kongo entered a treaty with Luanda. However, tensions renewed in the late 1650s and early 1660s when Luanda began sending military expeditions north into the disputed area, where they seized enslaved people for export and imposed their local allies as chiefs. This led to the October 1665 **Battle of Mbwila**, probably the largest military engagement in the precolo-

≡ **St. Anthony Cross.** Made by Kongo artists in the eighteenth century, this cross includes a small pendant in the middle that shows St. Anthony of Padua, who was claimed as the emblem of a Kongo religious reform movement led by the young noblewoman Beatriz Kimpa Vita (1684–1706).

nial history of West-Central Africa, in which a Portuguese army and its African allies routed a huge expedition from Kongo. Around 500 Kongo nobles were killed, including King Antonio I, whose severed head was brought to Luanda as a trophy. Some of the many prisoners from the battle whom the Portuguese shipped to Brazil subsequently led a rebellion there and helped establish an independent community of escaped enslaved people called Palmares. After the disaster of Mbwila, where many potential successors to the kingship had been killed, Kongo experienced a terrible civil war during which the capital of São Salvador was destroyed and many captives were enslaved and exported. Taking advantage of the turmoil, Kongo's province of Soyo declared independence, fending off a Portuguese expedition and establishing contact with the Dutch. At the start of the 1700s, a young woman called **Beatriz Kimpa Vita** claimed to be possessed by the spirit of the Christian Saint Anthony and started an indigenous Kongo Christian church that reoccupied the old capital and tried to reunify Kongo. Nevertheless, she was captured by the forces of one of Kongo's rival kings, and in 1706 she was condemned as a witch and heretic and burned to death with the approval of several European Catholic missionaries. Whereas it became common for modern historians to cite Kongo's collapse as an example of the devastating impact of the slave trade on West-Central Africa, research has shown that most of the kingdom's slave raids were directed outside its borders and that its breakdown was caused by internal rebellion.

Expansion of the Transatlantic Slave Trade

During the seventeenth and eighteenth centuries, other European powers built Atlantic empires and ended the Portuguese monopoly on the slave trade from West Africa. At the same time, colonial sugar production expanded from Brazil to the Caribbean, dramatically increasing the demand for slave labor. As such, the price of enslaved people steadily increased, meaning that there were huge profits to be made in the slave trade. While around 340,000 enslaved people had been exported from West Africa to the Americas during the Portuguese era of the 1500s, the number increased to almost two million during the 1600s.

During the 1600s, more emerging European maritime powers began to develop plantation colonies in the Americas and send ships to trade along the West African coast, where they built outposts or forts and visited African coastal towns to obtain enslaved people. As previously mentioned, in the early and middle 1600s, the Dutch established a colonial empire and gained a share in the transatlantic slave trade by seizing Portuguese outposts in the Americas, Africa, and Asia. This was connected to conflict in Europe and the context of religious tension between the Catholic Portuguese and the Protestant Dutch. In West Africa, the Dutch captured the Portuguese Gold Coast enclaves of Elmina in 1637 and Axim in 1642, and São Tomé, Luanda, and Benguela in 1641. However, the 1648 Portuguese counter-attack from Brazil recovered all these territories except Elmina and Axim, which remained under Dutch rule until the late nineteenth century. Dutch attempts to occupy Brazil began in the 1620s and continued until the 1650s. In 1652, the Dutch established an outpost at the strategic Cape of Good Hope on the southern tip of Africa, and their successful colonial expansion in Asia secured control of the oceanic spice trade. In 1639, the French established the enclave of Saint Louis at the mouth of the Senegal River, and in 1677 they seized the strategically important island of Gorée, previously claimed by the Portuguese, Dutch, and English. Britain's involvement in the transatlantic slave trade started in the 1560s when the English mariner John Hawkins led slave raiding and trading expeditions to the coast of Sierra Leone and shipped captives to the Caribbean. During the

1600s, England's monarchy granted a monopoly on West African trade in enslaved people, gold, and other products to a succession of English companies that began seizing enclaves along the West African coast. In 1664, the English captured James Island (now called Kunta Kinteh Island) near the mouth of the Gambia River, an outpost originally created by a Polish tributary state of Lithuania, and Cape Coast castle, a fortification on the shore of what is now Ghana that had been established by the Swedes and claimed by Danes and Dutch. Cape Coast became the main base of operations for England's Royal Africa Company, which, by the end of the 1600s, derived about 60 percent of its income from selling enslaved people. The independent slave trading port of Ouidah, on the coast of the present-day Republic of Benin, simultaneously hosted three European powers: the French founded an outpost in 1671, the English built a fort in the 1680s, and the Portuguese did the same in 1721. By the start of the 1700s, there were dozens of European enclaves and forts dotted along the West African coast and they were all involved in the growing slave trade.

During the eighteenth century, well over six million African captives were shipped to the Americas, representing over half the total number of people transported during the entire history of the transatlantic slave trade. In the 1700s, the British and French, as the major naval and colonial powers of that time, dominated the Atlantic world with their plantations, slave labor, and trade in enslaved people. In this century, Britain transported the most enslaved people from Africa to the Americas, followed closely by Portugal and then France. By this time, the production of sugar and other agricultural products in New World plantations, which depended on African slave labor, had become extremely profitable and comprised a central feature of European colonial empires. In that context, and from the European and colonial American perspective, West Africa became primarily a place to obtain enslaved labor, and the European quest for African gold, ivory, and other precious commodities declined. Unlike the Portuguese of the 1500s and 1600s, the eighteenth-century Europeans who maintained coastal enclaves in West Africa and visited the region in ships did not venture into the interior and tended to avoid direct involvement in local conflicts. Waiting on the coast, European and American ships obtained African enslaved people from African intermediaries who acquired them from hinterland kingdoms. Central to this process was the **gun–slave cycle**, whereby West African states became dependent on the importation of European firearms in exchange for enslaved people. While the early European firearms of the late 1400s and 1500s did not work well in the wet conditions of West Africa, the advent in the 1650s of more reliable flintlock muskets that West Africans called "Dane guns" made guns a desirable import. Lacking the technology to manufacture firearms, African communities could obtain them only by engaging in the

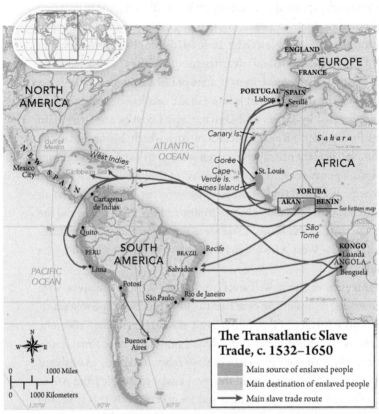

The Transatlantic Slave Trade, c. 1532–1650

▮	Main source of enslaved people
▮	Main destination of enslaved people
→	Main slave trade route

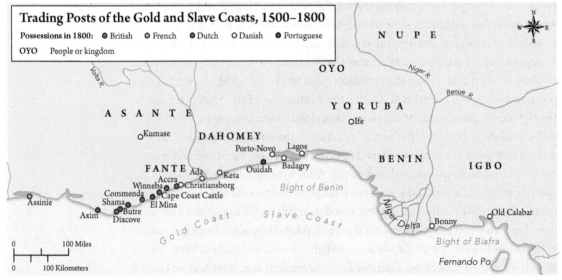

Trading Posts of the Gold and Slave Coasts, 1500–1800

Possessions in 1800: ● British ◐ French ● Dutch ○ Danish ● Portuguese

OYO   People or kingdom

≡ MAP 6.3

slave trade with Europeans, and without guns Africans became vulnerable to slave raiding. The Portuguese, as they were involved in wars in the interior, sometimes hesitated to trade guns to Africans, but the British and French of the eighteenth century had no such reservations. On the other side of the Atlantic, it was more profitable for plantation owners to work their enslaved people to death rather than provide an environment for them to reproduce, which meant that there was a constant demand for newly enslaved people from Africa.

Involvement in the transatlantic slave trade spread along the West African coast during the late 1600s and 1700s, but it was not always consistent. West-Central Africa, the area of Kongo and Angola, had been the first major exporter of enslaved people to the Americas, and it continued as the largest supplier throughout most of the history of the transatlantic slave trade. In this region the Portuguese, unlike Europeans in other parts of West Africa, continued military incursions into the interior, prompting wars that fueled the slave trade and led to the ports of Loango, Luanda, and Benguela exporting thousands of enslaved people every year during the 1700s. The region's continued importance as a source of enslaved people was reinforced by the arrival of British and French slavers at Loango in the eighteenth century, with the former obtaining around 20 percent of all their enslaved people from West-Central Africa.

The Bight of Benin, a portion of the West African coast comprising what is now Togo, Benin, and western Nigeria, had exported a limited number of enslaved people to the Portuguese during the 1500s and early 1600s, with the kingdom of Benin strictly regulating the trade. However, Benin lost its regional influence as a result of a long civil war from 1689 to 1721. Slave exports from this region increased significantly after around 1650 due to the establishment of many slave trading outlets such as Ouidah, Porto-Novo, Badagry, and Lagos along the coastal lagoons and the rise of the hinterland states of Dahomey located near the coast and Oyo further inland, both of which became heavily involved in the coastal slave trade and fought wars to gain better access to it. The gunmen of Dahomey and the cavalry of Oyo warred against each other in 1726–30 and 1742–48. Europeans visiting this region's slave ports called it the "Slave Coast." Ouidah alone exported a total of over one million captives from the late 1600s to 1800.

To the west, the Gold Coast had been an importer of enslaved people during the 1500s and early 1600s, and Europeans had built castles there to secure their position in the gold trade. From the early 1700s, slave exports from these castles increased as a result of warfare among the Akan of the interior, which resulted in the expansion of the Asante kingdom under its warrior-king Opoku Ware. In the late 1700s, Asante constructed a road network that improved commerce, including the slave trade, and allowed the kingdom to suppress rebellions. On their way to the

THE TRANSATLANTIC SLAVE TRADE

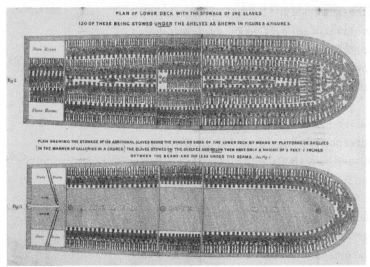

Top left: Slave traders lead a coffle of slaves in Senegal, 1780s. *Top right:* A detail from a 1662 map of Pernambuco, Brazil, shows a sugar plantation owner transported in a hammock while enslaved Africans toil in the mill. *Bottom left:* A 1787 diagram of the British slave ship *Brookes* showing over 450 enslaved Africans crammed into its stowage. *Bottom right:* Slave traders on Gorée Island off the coast of Senegal, 1797.

Americas, slave ships that had not obtained enough captives at the Bight of Benin dropped off at Gold Coast castles like Elmina and Cape Coast to fill up their holds.

East of the Bight of Benin, the densely populated Bight of Biafra, centered on the Niger Delta, had supplied enslaved people to visiting European ships during the 1600s, but these exports multiplied tremendously during the 1700s, with most enslaved people coming through the trading towns of Old and New Calabar and Bonny. British merchants from Bristol and Liverpool acquired around 85 percent of all enslaved people from this area, bringing them to British colonies across the Atlantic, including the colonies that would eventually become the United States. The slave trade in the Bight of Biafra differed from the other regions. The prevalence of tropical disease in the area meant that Europeans did not establish enclaves; the decentralized nature of African communities there meant that captives were generally not acquired during large wars but through many small raids on villages and individual abductions, and the riverine environment meant that riverboats played an important role in transporting enslaved people to the coast.

In the most westerly parts of West Africa—the Upper Guinea coast, which comprises today's Liberia, Sierra Leone, and Guinea, and Senegambia—the trans-Saharan and transatlantic slave trades overlapped. While slave exports from this region increased in the 1700s because of Muslim jihads fought in the interior in Futa Jalon and Futa Toro, the number did not come close to those of the Gold Coast, the Bights of Benin and Biafra, and West-Central Africa.

West Africa was incorporated into the "**triangular trade**," a term used to describe the three main vectors of the cyclical Atlantic economy. First, Europe exported goods such as metal ware, cloth, guns, and gun powder to West Africa, where they were exchanged for enslaved people. Second, West African enslaved people were shipped across the Atlantic to the Americas, where they worked on plantations growing sugar, cotton, or other agricultural products. Third, these agricultural products were shipped to Europe to feed a growing population.

The journey of African captives to the Americas has been described in terms of three passages. During the First Passage, prisoners taken in the West African interior were marched or transported in canoes to coastal ports where they were imprisoned in wooden stockades or castle dungeons and eventually loaded onto visiting European or American slave ships. Many captives died during this ordeal as they were abused by guards or were killed trying to escape. The **Middle Passage** represents the experience of African captives onboard slave ships bound for the Americas. Designed to transport as many enslaved people as possible to maximize profit, the holds of slave ships contained rows of long wooden shelves that chained and densely packed captives were forced to lie down on for most the transatlantic voyage. Fed barely enough to survive, the prisoners endured horrifically squalid

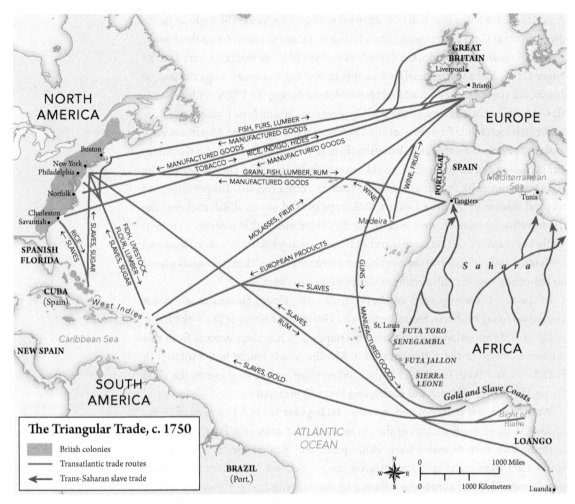

The Triangular Trade, c. 1750

- British colonies
- Transatlantic trade routes
- Trans-Saharan slave trade

≡ MAP 6.4

conditions that caused disease and psychological trauma, and many suffered abuse by ships' crews. Between 15 and 20 percent of captives, or around two million people, died during the Middle Passage. Prisoners who became sick were thrown overboard to prevent the spread of illness that might spoil the human cargo, some prisoners committed suicide, some were killed while staging rebellions, and many died of disease, hunger, or dehydration. Initially, these transatlantic voyages took around three or more months, but by the 1700s better sailing technology reduced the travel time to around six weeks. Once landed at ports in the Americas, the captives endured the Final Passage, in which they were cleaned for sale as enslaved people at humiliating public auctions and then transported to plantations for forced labor in conditions that usually led to death.

Timeline

1341—Portuguese arrive in Canary Islands

1415—Portuguese seize Ceuta in Morocco

1419—Portuguese arrive in Madeira Islands

1427—Portuguese arrive in Azores

1431—Portuguese reach Cape Bojador

1441—Portuguese take West African captives to Portugal

1444—Portuguese arrive at mouth of the Senegal River

1444—First planned Portuguese slave raid in West Africa

1445—Portuguese establish outpost on Arguin Island off the coast of Mauritania

1456—Portuguese reach Cape Verde Islands

1462—Portuguese at Sierra Leone

1470—Portuguese arrive at islands of São Tomé and Fernando Po

1471—Portuguese arrive on the Gold Coast

1482—Portuguese find the mouth of the Congo River

1483—Portuguese contact kingdom of Kongo

1482—Portuguese build Elmina castle on the Gold Coast

1488—Portuguese round the Cape of Good Hope

1492—Beginning of Spanish colonization in Americans

1494—Treaty of Tordesillas between Portugal and Spain

1498—Portuguese go around Africa and enter the Indian Ocean

1500—Portuguese arrive in Brazil

1506—Pro-Portuguese Christian faction wins Kongo civil war

1532—First Portuguese slave shipment to Brazil

1560s—First English slave trading in West Africa

1569—Jaga invasion of Kongo

1575—Portuguese found Luanda on coast of Angola

1580s–1610s—Warfare between Portuguese at Luanda and kingdom of Ndongo

Early 1600s—Emergence of Imbangala raiders in Angola

1617—Portuguese found Benguela on coast of Angola

1622—Conflict between Portuguese and Kongo

1624—Queen Njinga takes power in Ndongo

1626—Portuguese occupy Ndongo and exile Njinga, who eventually takes power in Matamba

1637—Dutch take Elmina

1639—French establish Saint Louis at mouth of Senegal River

1641—Dutch seize São Tomé, Luanda, and Benguela; Njinga and Kongo ally with Dutch against Portuguese

1648—Portuguese recapture São Tomé and Angola

1652—Dutch found outpost at Cape of Good Hope

1655—Queen Njinga enters a treaty with the Portuguese

1663—Death of Njinga

1664—English take James Island in Gambia River and Cape Coast Castle on the Gold Coast

1665—Portuguese defeat Kongo at the Battle of Mbwila; results in Kongo civil war

1677—French seize Gorée Island

1689–1721—Kingdom of Benin civil war

1706—Death of Dona Beatrix Kimpa Vita

1720s—Beginning of Asante expansion

1726–30 and 1742–48—Wars between Dahomey and Oyo

Conclusion

Historians have long debated what effect the growth of the transatlantic slave trade had on the societies of West Africa. Some scholars maintain that this trade deprived West Africa of the labor and resourcefulness of millions of its people who, as enslaved plantation workers, contributed to the growth of an Atlantic economy that enriched Western Europe and enabled it to embark on industrialization at the end of the eighteenth century. As a recipient of European goods and a source of enslaved people, West Africa became a marginal and comparatively undeveloped part of this Atlantic world and was eventually colonized by European powers in the late nineteenth century. While some historians criticize this view by pointing out that European and West African slavers operated as equals during this period, other scholars counter by highlighting that this equality only applied to what happened in West Africa and those West African leaders had no impact on the broader developments of the transatlantic slave trade that happened outside their region. Some historians see the slave trade as having a profoundly transformative impact on West African history, while others theorize that the value and scale of slave exports, when compared to the entire West African population and economy over several centuries, were not large enough to have this result. Nevertheless, some impacts seem obvious. Enslaving people was an inherently violent business, and as this business expanded so did warfare in West Africa. While not all wars in seventeenth- and eighteenth-century West and West-Central Africa were fought purely to obtain enslaved people, many conflicts were related to local states attempting to secure control of profitable slave trade routes. The slave trade also resulted in the advent of guns in the region. Within the region, power shifted from the old and large territorial empires of the hinterland Sahel, such as Songhai, that had dominated the north–south Saharan trade to the more compact coastal forest kingdoms such as Asante and Dahomey. To defend themselves, decentralized communities became more militarized, building stockades and watchtowers, obtaining weapons, and posting sentries to watch over agricultural workers. There were also cultural impacts. Since the majority of enslaved people exported across the Atlantic were young men, the gender balance of West Africa's population became skewed, therefore increasing the prevalence of polygyny. Furthermore, the need to readily identify fellow community members, so as not to enslave them, probably popularized the practice of facial scarification in the region.

KEY TERMS

Battle of Mbwila 125

Beatriz Kimpa Vita 125

caravel 120

Elmina 120

gun–slave cycle 127

Henry the
  Navigator 116

Imbangala 122

Middle Passage 131

Njinga 122

Prester John 118

Reconquista 116

transatlantic slave
  trade 115

Treaty of
  Tordesillas 118

triangular trade 131

STUDY QUESTIONS

1. How did the Reconquista shape the kingdom of Portugal? What were the central aims of Portugal's maritime activities in the fifteenth century? What role did Portugal play in the African slave trade?

2. How did Christianity factor into Portuguese–Kongo relations? What were the forces and motives behind the expansion of Portuguese colonies and the slave trade in West-Central Africa? How did Queen Njinga use diplomacy and warfare to play European powers off each other?

3. Beginning in the seventeenth century, why did the transatlantic slave trade grow exponentially? How did the gun–slave cycle and the triangular trade affect West African societies? What were the experiences of enslaved Africans during the Middle Passage?

Please see page FR-3 for the Further Readings for this chapter.
For additional digital learning resources please go to
https://www.oup.com/he/falola-stapleton1e

East Africa to c. 1800: Kingdoms, Pastoralists and Indian Ocean Trade

Historical knowledge about precolonial East Africa is extremely uneven. Given fairly rich archaeological and documentary sources, many aspects of the history of Ethiopia and East Africa's Red Sea and Indian Ocean coasts can be reconstructed going back over 1,000 years. On the other hand, contradictions between archaeology and oral traditions, combined with the lack of written accounts, mean that historians know much less about the history of the East African interior, including the Great Lakes region and the plains of the Great Rift valley. For most of the hinterland of what is now Kenya and Tanzania, and for present-day Uganda, Rwanda, and Burundi, it is difficult to discuss specific historical events and processes earlier than the last 200 or 300 years. Despite these limitations of historical knowledge, it is clear that one of the most important overall factors in East African history before 1800 was the region's involvement in the Indian Ocean trade network. Just as the trans-Saharan trade connected West Africa with North Africa and the rest of the Mediterranean region, the people of precolonial East Africa engaged in trade across the Indian Ocean, linking them with Arabia, India, and China.

Axum

Located in the Horn of Africa, near what is now Eritrea and northern Ethiopia, Axum was the earliest known East African kingdom. Although there is limited evidence its early history, a first-century CE Greco-Roman guidebook for Indian Ocean traders mentioned the kingdom, and by around 270 it minted its own coins, which circulated beyond the region. Inscriptions dating to the 300s indicate that powerful kings ruled Axum and engaged in military conquest and tribute collection, but historians know little about the details of their government, with some

Arab dhow manned by African sailors, from the *al-Maqāmāt al-ḥarīriyah*, c. 1237.

evidence that there may have been a dual monarchy and hereditary succession. Commanding a large work force that probably included enslaved people, the kings and elites of Axum constructed stone buildings and walls at their capital city of Axum and marked royal tombs using huge stone stelae with one surviving example standing 23 meters tall and weighing 150 tons. Differences in architecture, funerary monuments, and grave goods illustrate that Axum was a highly stratified society. Local agriculture was central to Axum's prosperity and involved raising cattle and growing cereal crops such as millet, wheat, barley, and sorghum, and possibly grapes and cotton.

Ancient Axum benefited from the growth of maritime trade between the Mediterranean-based Roman Empire and the Indian Ocean via the Red Sea. Through its Red Sea port of Adulis, Axum exported gold, ivory, and enslaved people, and imported glassware, metals, beads, wine, and textiles from the eastern Roman/Byzantine Empire, including Egypt, as well as the Middle East and India. Axum minted gold coins with Greek inscriptions for international trade and silver and copper coins with local Ge'ez inscriptions for the domestic economy. Based on the study of Axum's coinage, it is likely that its people practiced polytheistic beliefs until around 340, when King Ezana converted to Christianity, making it the state religion and imprinting the Christian cross on the kingdom's money. In the city of Axum, Ezana or perhaps one of his successors ordered the construction of the Cathedral of Mary of Zion, which was subsequently destroyed and rebuilt several times and which continues to serve as the central point of Ethiopian Christianity, reputedly housing the Biblical Ark of the Covenant. Given ties to the Christian church in Egypt, the Ethiopian Christian church adopted the doctrine of **Miaphysitism**, which emphasized the unified nature of Christ, whereas Western Christianity proclaimed a belief that both divine and human natures exist within Christ. International Christian influences also affected Axum's Ge'ez script with the introduction of vowels and the pattern of writing lines from left to right.

≡ **A stone stela** used to mark royal tombs in the kingdom of Aksum during the fourth century CE.

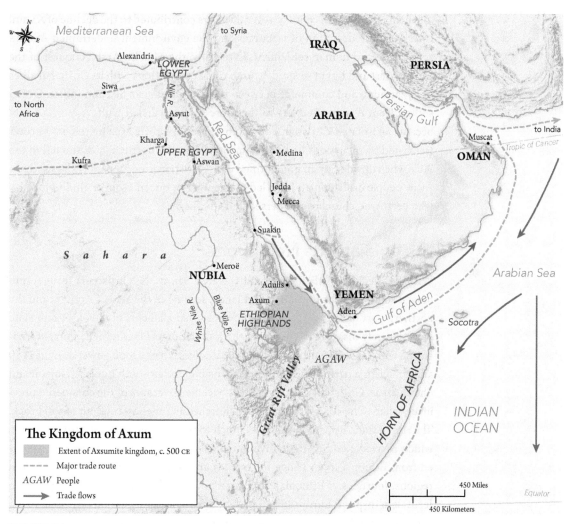

≡ **MAP 7.1**

From the 300s to 500s CE, Axum expanded west toward the Nile and east across the Red Sea to Yemen. While many histories maintain that Axum's King Ezana sent an army to destroy the kingdom of Kush's capital of Meroë and erected a stela on the site to celebrate his victory, some scholars dispute this claim, highlighting a lack of archaeological evidence for conquest and claiming that the inscriptions on the monument indicate Axumite military assistance to Meroë. Axum's King Kaleb sent an expeditionary force to conquer Yemen in the 520s, but the Sassanid Persian Empire dispatched an army that expelled the Axumites from the Arabian Peninsula during the 570s. Axum's navy continued to raid the Arabian coastline until around 700.

During the seventh century, several factors contributed to the decline of Axum. Internally, the depletion of resources and the environment undermined Axum's agriculture and human settlement. Externally, the Muslim Arab conquest of the Middle East and Egypt severed Axum's trade connections with its Christian allies in Byzantium, and commerce between the Mediterranean Sea and Indian Ocean shifted from Axum's Red Sea to the more distant Persian Gulf. As such, Axum became an isolated Christian outpost in a predominantly Muslim region. Further weakened by incursions by the Beja people from the northwest, Axum fell in the 900s when invaded by an unidentified non-Christian group, possibly the southern Agaw people or Ethiopian Jews, led by the warrior queen Esata or Gudit (Judith), who destroyed churches and persecuted Christians.

Ethiopia and Its Neighbors

With the decline of their state and the Red Sea trade, Christians from Axum moved south into the Ethiopian highlands, settling in the area of Amhara and the northern part of Shewa. It appears, however, that elements of the old Axum state never entirely disappeared, forming the foundations of medieval Ethiopia. Originating with Christian military elites, the Zagwe dynasty took power around 1150 and launched a period of Ethiopian expansion further south into the Gojjam and Shewa areas. Christian military leaders became governors of the conquered provinces, where Christian settlers carved churches and monasteries out of solid rock. The rise of the Zagwe dynasty owed much to the independence of Fatimid Egypt, which revived Red Sea trade involving enslaved people, gold, and ivory exported from Ethiopia in exchange for textiles and other luxury goods from Muslim regions. Journeys of Ethiopian Christian pilgrims through Egypt to holy sites in Jerusalem inspired European rumors about a rich and mysterious Christian king called **Prester John** located somewhere in Africa. It was in the Zagwe period that Ethiopian Christianity developed distinct features, including an emphasis on the Old Testament of the Bible and the idea that Ethiopian Christians constituted God's chosen people encircled by infidels. Concurrently, Islam spread throughout the rest of the Horn of Africa. The people of coastal Eritrea became Muslims by around 1000, many Somalis converted to Islam and a number of Muslim states emerged in the Ethiopian Highlands in the 1200s, and a series of Muslim outposts appeared along trade routes from the Red Sea and Somali coasts to the interior in this era.

By the mid-thirteenth century, internal conflicts and succession crises weakened Ethiopia's Zagwe dynasty. In 1268, the Christians of Shewa, bolstered by their involvement in revived external trade and supported by the church, rebelled against

≡ **Church of St. George, Lalibela, Ethiopia.** Designed in the shape of a cross, the Church of Saint George at Lalibela, Ethiopia was carved out of solid rock in the late twelfth or early thirteenth century.

the Zagwe rulers, leading to a series of battles and sieges. With the killing of the last Zagwe king in 1270, Shewa's leader Yekumo Amlak declared himself head of a new royal dynasty that gained religious legitimacy by claiming descent from the biblical Israelite King Solomon and Queen of Sheba, supposedly originators of the first Christian Ethiopian kingdom. Ethiopia's new **Solomonid** dynasty portrayed itself as restoring the glory of the old kingdom of Axum allegedly usurped by the previous Zagwe regime. Although a series of succession disputes plagued Ethiopia at the end of the thirteenth century, Amda Tsiyon, grandson of Yekumo Amlak, consolidated the kingdom from 1312 to 1342. Furthermore, Tsiyon embarked on aggressive empire-building attempting to control the trade routes to the coast of the Red Sea and the Gulf of Aden, and extending Ethiopian authority south to the top of the Great Rift Valley. As a result, conflict broke out between Ethiopia and the Muslim states to its south and east, and this led to the rise of the sultanate of Adal, based at the town of Harar and which mobilized many Somali converts to Islam. Although an Ethiopian invasion in 1403 drove Adal's royal family across the Red Sea to Yemen, the sultanate's rulers returned and strengthened trade with the Ottoman Empire, acquiring firearms in the process. From 1434 to 1468, Ethiopian ruler Zara Yaqob centralized his state, building a permanent capital at Debra Berham in Shewa and brutally suppressing opposition, and continued Ethiopia's southward expansion constructing new Christian monasteries and controlling trade routes. In 1450, Zara Yaqob summoned a religious council that settled a long-standing theological dispute within Ethiopian Christianity by declaring two Sabbaths, and initiated church reforms aimed at eliminating syncretic beliefs that combined older traditional religious practices with Christianity in remote areas. This prompted an Ethiopian Christian revival that defined the Ethiopian church

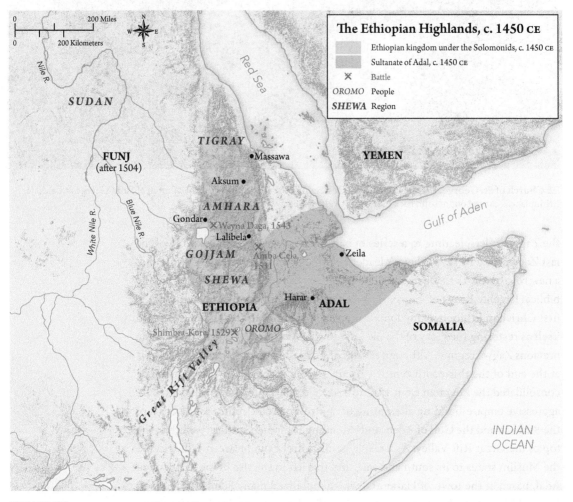

≡ MAP 7.2

well into the future, closely associated the church and the monarchy, and produced a body of Ethiopian literature including the national epic entitled **Kebra Negast** ("Glory of Kings").

During the late 1400s and early 1500s, a series of child kings weakened Christian Ethiopia, providing space for the rise of Muslim Adal as a regional power. Starting in the 1490s, the Adal religious and military leader Imam Mahfuz organized annual raids into Ethiopia that enslaved people for export to Arabia and took cattle. Ethiopian ruler Lebna Dengal, in 1517, led a retaliatory attack against Adal, capturing and decapitating Mahfuz. In 1526, the new Adal leader Ahmad ibn Ibrahim, called Gragn or "the left handed" by the Ethiopians, declared jihad against Ethiopia and ordered Adal's border towns to end tribute payments to the Christian kingdom. His Somali fighters were equipped with Ottoman firearms and artillery with which the Ethiopians had no experience, and Ahmad launched an invasion of Ethiopia, defeating its army at the battles of Shimbra-Kure in 1529 and Amba Cela in 1531. As Adal's forces occupied almost all of Ethiopia, looted churches, and gained support from communities recently conquered by the Christian kingdom, Lebna Dengal and the remnants of his Ethiopian army retreated and desperately tried to rally Christian resistance. In turn, Lebna Dengal appealed to the fellow Christian Portuguese who had made contract with Ethiopia earlier in the 1500s and who were clashing with the Ottoman Empire over control of the Red Sea. In 1541, a small but well-armed Portuguese expedition landed at Massawa on the Red Sea coast and marched into Ethiopia, where they joined Ethiopian fighters and defeated Ahmad's army in a series of engagements over the next two years. Although Ottoman musketeers arrived to buttress Ahmad's army, his forces were badly overstretched and many Somali fighters had returned home. After the 1543 Battle of Wayna Daga, where an Ethiopian-Portuguese force led by the new Ethiopian Emperor Galawdewos inflicted a crushing defeat on Adal killing Ahmad, Adal's forces withdrew from Ethiopia. While Galawdewos recovered much of Shewa, he found that the recent war had allowed Oromo pastoralists to occupy the southern highlands, where they adopted settled agriculture, converted to Christianity, and continued to expand. While periodic fighting continued between Ethiopia and Adal from the 1550s to 1570s, both powers now contended with the expanding Oromo, and civil war caused the collapse of the Adal Sultanate in the late sixteenth century.

Although Christian Ethiopia survived the Muslim Adal invasion of the 1530s and 1540s, the growing Portuguese influence represented a new threat. During the early 1500s, Portuguese Catholic priests arrived in Ethiopia and formal missionary activities began in 1557 with the appointment of a Portuguese Catholic bishop of Ethiopia. To secure Portuguese military support against the expanding Oromo and the Muslim Ottomans who took over Massawa in 1557, Ethiopian rulers

≡ **First female ruler of Ethiopia.** Empress Mentewab (1706–1773) served as the first female co-ruler of Ethiopia from 1730 to 1755.

warmed to the Catholic faith. Competition from the Catholics incited the Ethiopian Church to shift from the obscure Ge'ez language to the more popularly known **Amharic**, and to write works defending their religious doctrine and celebrating Ethiopian history. In 1622, Ethiopian Emperor Susneyos converted to Catholicism and ordered the suppression of the Ethiopian Church and its replacement by the Catholic Church led by Portuguese Jesuit priests. While many Ethiopians converted to Catholicism, a series of bloody rebellions by supporters of Ethiopian Christianity broke out across the country, convincing Susneyos to reverse his decision and abdicate in 1632. Subsequently, the new Emperor Fasiladas quickly reinstated Ethiopian Christianity, expelled the Portuguese and Jesuits, and persecuted Catholic converts. In 1635, Fasiladas founded the city of Gondar, where he built an impressive castle, making it the new permanent capital of Ethiopia. He also organized the construction of stone churches and bridges across the empire. During the late 1600s, simultaneous with the European Enlightenment, a distinct Ethiopian philosophy emerged through the writing of Zera Yacob and his protégé Walda Heywat, who explored ideas around rationalism, morality, and religion.

Imperial Ethiopia gradually declined during the eighteenth century. In the late 1600s and early 1700s, Ethiopia used firearms acquired from coastal trade to fight a series of wars that incorporated many Oromo people into the empire. More Oromo converted to Christianity, many served in the Ethiopian army, and some became key members of the imperial court. In 1705, Emperor Iyaso I led a large military expedition south of the Blue Nile, where he attempted to reassert Ethiopian control over this important slave collection point that had been taken over by the Oromo, but the failure of the campaign led to his assassination. From 1730 to 1755, following a period of internal conflict, Empress Mentewab became the first woman to serve as co-ruler of Ethiopia during the reign of her son Iyaso II. It was during this period, in 1744, that the Ethiopian army suffered a terrible defeat when it attempted to invade the Funj Sultanate in what is now Sudan. The 1755 death of

Iyaso II and rise of his son Iyoas I led to a civil war between supporters of Empress Mentewab, the new emperor's grandmother, who was of noble origin and wanted to continue as co-ruler, and those of Wubit (Welete Bersabe), who was the Oromo mother of the new emperor. Mikael Sehul, **Tigray**'s provincial ruler who controlled firearms imports and raised an army of 6,000 gunmen, took advantage of the chaos to dominate the imperial government, and in 1769 he killed Emperor Iyoas I and his successor. This began a long period of instability, known as the "Era of the Princes," in Ethiopia where regional nobles imposed and then usurped a succession of weak and short-lived emperors. Between 1779 and 1800, for instance, Tekle Giyorgis I served as emperor six times, constantly deposed, reinstated, and deposed by regional leaders. By 1800, Ethiopia consisted of three autonomous regions. In the north, Tigray dominated Red Sea trade, including firearms imports through the Ottoman enclave of Massawa; in the west, Amhara represented an important agricultural center and transit point for gold, ivory, and slave exports; and in the south, Shewa experienced Oromo expansion and traded with ports in the Gulf of Aden.

The Swahili Coast

Several factors facilitated oceanic travel between coastal East Africa and Asia across the Indian Ocean. First, **monsoon** wind patterns became central. From November to March, sailing ships used prevailing southwesterly winds to travel from China or India to East Africa and then from April to October the winds

≡ **Indian Ocean Maritime Technology** *Left:* Around 2,000 years ago, sailing vessels like this dhow began carrying trade goods across the Indian Ocean between Arabia, South Asia, and East Africa. *Right:* This exquisite astrolabe, made of brass and inlaid with silver, was made in Yemen in the late thirteenth century.

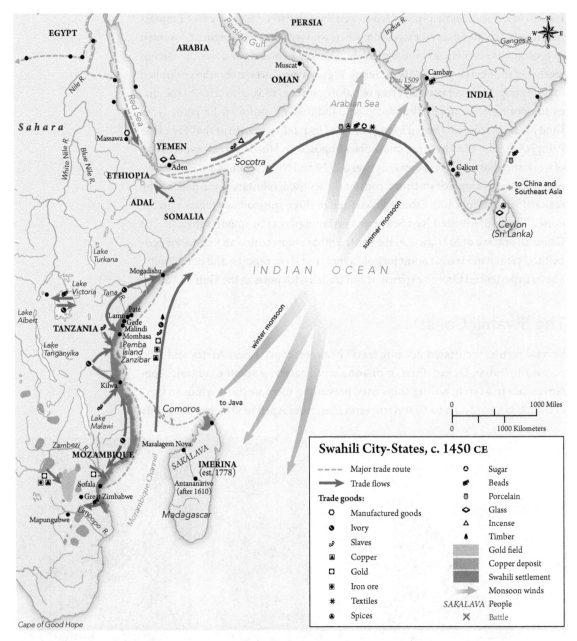

MAP 7.3

changed to the opposite direction allowing a return journey. Second, transportation technologies existed from ancient times. Perhaps 2000 years ago, Arab or Indian sailors developed the **dhow**, a type of small wooden-hull ship with a lateen sail that could sail against the wind that became the main trading vessel of the Indian Ocean. Other types of ships were used including outrigger canoes originating in Malaya and a flexible wooden boat with a square sail called *mtepe* that was used by East Africa's coastal Swahili people. By at least 1000 CE, Indian Ocean sailors navigated using the **astrolabe** invented by the ancient Greeks and the magnetic compass developed by the Chinese. Third, the East African coast contained numerous suitable harbors, local trees provided timber for ship building, and the environment contained fresh water, fertile soil, and sources of fish all of which supported local populations who engaged in trade and supplied ships.

In the context of this Indian Ocean trade system, the Swahili culture developed along the East African coast stretching almost 2,000 miles from present-day Somalia in the north to what is now Mozambique in the south. Living in many independent East African coastal towns, the Swahili people became the commercial intermediaries between the African communities living in the hinterland and Arab and South Asian traders arriving by ship. While the Swahili language (Kiswahili) is part of Africa's large Bantu linguistic group, it developed some Arabic influences given interaction with seagoing Arab traders. Indeed, the word Swahili derives from Arabic for "people of the coast." Between around 100 BCE and 300 CE, as archaeological evidence indicates, Swahili settlements along the coast of present-day Kenya and Tanzania practiced farming and fishing, used iron tools probably acquired in trade and received trade goods such as glassware, pottery, and ceramics from Egypt, Greece, and Rome. The same first-century CE Greco-Roman travel guide that mentioned Axum also discussed the East African coast, which it called Azania. From around 300 to 1000 CE, East Africa's involvement in the Indian Ocean trade increased as goods such as textiles, silk, beads, glass, and ceramics arrived from China, India, Iran, and Egypt. Exports from the African interior included gold, animal skins, ivory, rhinoceros horn, rock crystal, timber, and oils and resins used in perfumes and medicine. Besides serving as commercial middlemen, the coastal Swahili also produced their own export goods, such as high quality iron that they smelted and forged into knives and nails highly sought after in the Arab world, copper items, grain, tortoise shells, cloth, salt, and jewelry. It was in this period that Arab merchants, who referred to East Africa as **Zanj**, meaning "the land of Black people," brought the new religion of Islam to the Swahili trading centers. As with the trans-Saharan trade system in West Africa, the spread of Islam facilitated East Africa's involvement in the Indian Ocean trade by creating a common religious identity among the Swahili coastal dwellers and Arab merchants, providing uniform business practices and ethical standards, and enabling communication and record keeping, with Swahili adoptingArabic script. Involvement in the flourishing Indian Ocean trade enabled the Swahili city-states to experience what is widely believed to be their "Golden Era" between around 1000 and 1500 CE. Key imports included glassware from Egypt, silk from China, textiles from India, beads from Iran and Sri Lanka, and pottery and ceramics from various places throughout the Indian Ocean, such as Thailand and Vietnam. The Swahili exported timber to Yemen; ivory to Arabia; iron, copper, fruit, and grain to India; and finished products such as cooking and serving pots to the Persian Gulf and Red Sea. Symbolized by the visits of the Chinese imperial navy to East Africa in 1405–06, 1417, and 1421–22, trade with China increased as Chinese lacquerware and porcelain became popular among the Swahili and in the hinterland. Nevertheless, Chinese voyages to the Indian Ocean stopped as a result of changes in policy and power structures at home. During this period, exports of enslaved people from the East African interior increased, with most captives sent to Arabia, the Persian Gulf, and south Asia. By 1400, the largest Swahili ports included Mombasa, Pate, Malindi, Kilwa, and Lamu; these cities established merchant fleets on the Indian Ocean, and Kilwa and Mogadishu minted copper and silver coins. Developing a diverse urban culture, Swahili towns consisted of a stone-built center housing elite Swahili families who practiced Islam and spoke refined Kiswahili, and a distinct neighborhood for Arab and Indian merchants. Circling the town center, an intermediate layer of mud-and-wattle houses and workshops accommodated local artisans, shipwrights, and fishers, and a peripheral layer of rough dwellings lodged mainland hunters, farmers, fishers, and traders who brought goods from the interior. From the East African coast, Swahili merchants entered into business agreements with hinterland rulers, founded interior trading posts along the Zambezi and Tana rivers, and monopolized the sale of seashells used as currency in the interior as well as salt. Trade routes penetrated deeper into the interior, with south-central Africa exporting around 20 million ounces of gold through Swahili ports between roughly 800 and 1600 CE, thus becoming a crucial element of the entire Indian Ocean economy.

≡ **Kilwa** *Left:* The thirteenth-century Great Mosque was constructed on the island of Kilwa, a Swahili port on the coast of what is now Tanzania. *Right:* A print from 1572 showing Kilwa (Quiloa) and its harbor.

From around 1500, the expansion of Portuguese maritime power in the Indian Ocean led directly to the decline of the Swahili city-states on the East African coast. In 1498, a Portuguese seagoing expedition led by **Vasco da Gama** continued Portugal's exploration and conquest along the Atlantic coast of West and West-Central Africa by rounding the Cape of Good Hope and entering the Indian Ocean. Da Gama embarked on a second expedition to the Indian Ocean in 1502, and more Portuguese ships followed.

Vasco da Gama. A statue of the explorer located at Sines in Portugal.

The Portuguese quickly dominated the East African coast, as their ships were bigger, more maneuverable, and better armed with cannon than Indian Ocean vessels. Bombarded or threatened with bombardment by Portuguese ships, many Swahili ports agreed to pay tribute to the new arrivals during the first decade of the sixteenth century. The Swahili were unable to resist as they fought among themselves and their coastal defenses usually faced the hinterland, which had previously represented the only threat. After their navy defeated a combined fleet from Mamluk Egypt, India, and Persia at the 1509 Battle of Diu in India, the Portuguese established a chain of coastal enclaves and fortifications along the Indian Ocean rim, including the ports of Mozambique and Sofala along the southern part of the East African coast. From the 1530s, the Portuguese began to move inland along the Zambezi River, searching for gold and ivory to pay for spices from India. Once they took over Egypt in 1517, the Ottomans sent warships into the Red Sea and Indian Ocean to challenge the Portuguese, but this offensive was delayed by the Ottoman defeat at the great naval battle of Lepanto fought off the coast of Greece in 1571. Subsequently, during the 1580s, the Ottomans conducted several naval raids along the East African coast that prompted unsuccessful Swahili rebellions against the Portuguese. This convinced the Portuguese that they needed to bolster their presence along the northern portion of the East African coast, and, in turn, they built a strong naval base and fortress at Mombasa in present-day Kenya in the 1590s and installed a local Swahili ally as ruler of the port. In 1650, the Arab sultanate of Oman on the southern Arabian Peninsula expelled the Portuguese and began using its emerging naval power to push them

Madagassen.

≡ **Malagasy men and women.** The man in the center wears a *lamba*, a shawl-like garment worn by both men and women. Lambas are still widely worn today throughout Madagascar.

out of the northern East Africa coast. In 1698, the Omanis seized the key locations of Mombasa and Zanzibar, confining the Portuguese to the coast of Mozambique.

Despite its proximity to the East African coast, the large island of Madagascar was originally settled by people from Malaya around 2,000 years ago. Eventually, and as a result of the growth of the Indian Ocean trade network from around 1000 CE, immigrants from East Africa, South Asia, and Arabia arrived on the island. Because of this interaction, the **Malagasy language**, a Malayo-Polynesian language related to languages spoken in Indonesia and the Philippines, absorbed some Bantu and Arabic elements, and by the 1400s a writing system emerged, adopting Arabic script. For many years, Madagascar's many small states maintained involvement in the Indian Ocean trade, with those on the island's western coast developing close contacts with the East African mainland. The arrival of the Portuguese at the start of the 1500s, and the Dutch, French, English, and colonial Americans in the 1600s, prompted the rise of an external slave trade with Malagasy captives shipped to the Americas. As in West Africa, the increased slave trade stimulated political centralization, with the new Sakalava kingdoms, from the mid-1600s, using imported firearms to dominate the western and northern parts of the island. Among the most powerful of these was the kingdom of Boina that controlled the slave port of Mazalagem Nova in northwestern Madagascar. From the 1690s to 1720s, European pirates expelled from the Caribbean made northern Madagascar their staging area for attacks on ships carrying Muslim pilgrims from Asia to holy sites in Arabia. Although the British navy drove away the pirates, one of these renegades formed the Betsimisaraka kingdom on the east side of the island. From the mid-1700s, Betsimisaraka benefited from the shift in slaving operations to eastern Madagascar, as this area was closer to French plantations opening on the Indian Ocean islands of Reunion and Mauritius. Established in 1778, the kingdom of

Imerina used an alliance with Boina and imported firearms to subjugate the small states of the central highlands and impose a monopoly on slaving on the eastern side of the island. By 1800, Imerina was Madagascar's wealthiest and most powerful state, with its capital of Antananarivo, inhabited by 25,000 people, the island's largest town. Excluded from Madagascar's main slave trade, Betsimisaraka rulers began dispatching huge fleets of war canoes to the East African coast and the Comoros Islands to take captives.

The East African Interior

Compared to the Horn of Africa and East Africa's Indian Ocean coast, historians know much less about the East African interior comprising the Great Lakes region and the Great Rift Valley. Indeed, it is difficult to reconstruct the history of some parts of the hinterland before 1700 or even before 1800. In some parts of the interior, the first literate observers arrived only in the late nineteenth century on the eve of the European colonial conquest. For the study of precolonial East Africa, archaeology and oral history often reveal contradictory information; historians remain uncertain if some aspects of oral tradition are mythical or real; and for some areas, there is almost no evidence at all.

Archaeological excavations tell us that people in the East African hinterland practiced settled agriculture and metallurgy for at least 2,000 years. For the Great Lakes area, the arrival of the banana from Asia about 2,000 years ago represented a key agricultural change, as this crop improved food supplies and contributed to population growth. In addition, it appears that about 1,000 years ago, cattle raising became popular, and the relatively sudden change in pottery style across the area suggests that this development resulted from the arrival of newcomers. Nevertheless, the lack of impact on local Bantu languages indicates that this group of new arrivals was somewhat small and that it was ultimately absorbed into local communities. In a separate process, between roughly 200 BCE and 1000 CE, Nilo-Saharan-speaking (often called Nilotic) pastoral people from what is now South Sudan and southern Ethiopia, gradually relocated southward into the Great Lakes region. This movement accelerated during the 1400s and 1500s CE as other groups of Nilotic pastoralists of similar origin, probably fleeing drought at home, also shifted south. Moving east around Lake Victoria, some of these Nilotic pastoralists formed the basis of well-known East African pastoralist communities such as the Karamojong of Uganda and the Maasai of Kenya and Tanzania. Lacking centralized state structures, these pure pastoral groups organized themselves through age-sets and councils of elders. With an aggressive martial identity, they displaced pre-existing communities such as the Sirikwa from the grasslands to the highlands of the Great Rift Valley. Other Nilotic pastoralists, Luo speakers from present-day South Sudan, also traveled south around the same time and divided into small groups, with some settling northeast of Lake Victoria to found Luo communities in what is now western Kenya. Others marched west around Lake Victoria down into the area around Lakes Albert and Kivu, formed pastoral minorities that came to dominate the area's cultivators, and very likely constituted the nucleus for a series of centralized states that developed there during the 1500s and 1600s.

East African oral traditions claim that a mysterious group called the Chwezi ruled an empire called Bunyoro-Kitara that spanned much of the Great Lakes region including parts of present day Uganda, Rwanda, Burundi, Kenya, and Tanzania. Some scholars have dated this state to between roughly 1350 and 1500 CE, after which the Chwezi and their empire seemed to disappear without explanation. Lack of evidence for a powerful monarchy at archaeological sites associated with the Chwezi legend in western Uganda has led many archaeologists and historians to question if the group existed, and it seems possible that subsequent royal dynasties invented them to provide a sense of historical continuity and legitimacy. However, other scholars maintain the authenticity of the Chwezi, citing linguistic evidence for the existence of kingship in the area before around 1500 and the continued veneration of ritual centers associated with the Chwezi. Whether or not the Chwezi really existed, the period after around 1500 saw the emergence of a network of relatively small, centralized states located in East Africa's Great Lakes region.

Presenting themselves as the heirs of the Chwezi, the Bito clan of western Uganda originated with Luo immigrants and established the Bunyoro kingdom probably sometime in the late 1500s. A loose confederation, Bunyoro practiced cattle raising, which became central to royal power, but also engaged in farming, hunting, and production of salt and iron. Shortly after its foundation, Bunyoro launched a series of expansionist wars and raids against neighboring communities and imposed Bito princes as rulers of conquered areas. During the 1700s, Bunyoro's power declined as neighboring states like Nkore, Rwanda, and Buganda became more centralized, forming armies that defeated Bunyoro incursions, and Bunyoro's provincial rulers rebelled against the kingdom's central authority.

The kingdom of Buganda was founded in the 1300s by the semi-mythical hero Kintu, who originated somewhere around Mount Elgon and conquered communities around the northern shore of Lake Victoria. Perhaps prompted by Bunyoro raids, Buganda developed a highly centralized state, and in the 1600s and 1700s, it embarked on military campaigns that recovered lands lost to Bunyoro and subjugated new territories. Buganda became a highly organized state with a powerful king and royal court. Unlike neighboring kingdoms, Buganda made an exception to its patrilineal social system by not recognizing a royal clan and having kings adopt their mothers' clans, therefore ensuring that no single clan dominated the monarchy. While this promoted national unity, Buganda lacked clear rules of succession, with all royal princes having a claim to the kingship, and this caused factionalism and civil wars. Within Buganda, the queen mother wielded enormous power, maintaining a separate palace and royal court near that of king. With a strong agricultural foundation, Buganda formed a powerful army and a large navy of war canoes on Lake Victoria, and constructed a series of roads that

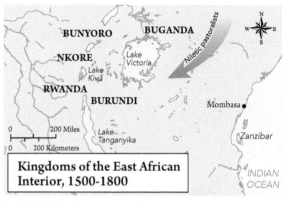

Kingdoms of the East African Interior, 1500-1800

≡ MAP 7.4

promoted communication, state administration, and military activities. By 1800, Buganda had replaced Bunyoro as the pre-eminent power of the Great Lakes.

Around Lake Kivu and the north end of Lake Tanganyika, the kingdoms of Nkore, Rwanda, and Burundi developed socioeconomic class systems. The origins of these states very likely started with the arrival of Nilotic-speaking Luo pastoralists who, through loaning their cattle and collecting tribute, developed client relationships with pre-existing populations of cultivators and hunter-gatherers. Eventually, the pastoralists formed centralized states in which those families focusing on cattle formed a distinct identity classed Hima in Nkore and Tutsi in Rwanda and Burundi, and farmers formed another class called Iru in Nkore and Hutu in Rwanda and Burundi. At the same time, a marginalized class of hunter-gatherers and potters called Twa also emerged in these kingdoms. Although kings leaned toward the supposedly superior pastoral lifestyle, they considered themselves above the herder-farmer division and adopted symbols of both socioeconomic classes. Along the East African Great Lakes, kings maintained herds of royal long-horned cattle and conducted regular fertility ceremonies; their souls were said to reside in a venerated royal drum, and their regalia included a blacksmith's hammer connecting them to the magical realm of metallurgy. Sometimes their bodyguards and executioners comprised men from the despised Twa class, unlikely to seize power. As in Buganda, queen mothers exercised significant authority in these Great Lakes states, and royal wives often became involved in palace intrigues and civil wars meant to install their sons as king.

Located in what is now southern Uganda, the rulers of the Nkore kingdom claimed historical links to the legendary Chwezi. During the mid-1700s, attacks by Bunyoro stimulated tighter political centralization and military reforms in Nkore. While Nkore usually raised ad hoc armies for defense or raiding, King Ntare

Missions des Pères Blancs
RUANDA — Vache sacrée, Reine du Troupeau

☰ **Royal cattle.** This postcard from 1910 shows one of the sacred cattle of the Rwanda monarchy.

IV founded permanent units of warriors drawn from Hima pastoral families and specializing in the use of bows and arrows and spears. This new army enabled Nkore to expand its territory and fostered social dominance of the Hima group. Though this military system generally excluded Iru farmers, a few became famous army commanders and some adopted cattle raising and dropped their Iru identity.

Founded in the 1600s by a conquering pastoral hero called Ndori, the kingdom of Rwanda developed a martial culture with a permanent army comprising pastoral warriors and support personnel drawn from agricultural communities. Some historians believe that the pastoral Tutsi and agricultural Hutu identities originally formed within the Rwanda army and then spread to the rest of the kingdom. National unity grew through the common Kinyarwanda language and a system of 18 clans, each comprising Tutsi, Hutu, and Twa members, including the royal Nyiginya clan. During the 1700s, Rwanda used its powerful army to fight a near-constant series of wars that resulted in the state's expansion across much of present-day Rwanda plus the volcano zone in the northwest and part of what is now southern Uganda. In the 1770s, Rwanda repulsed an invasion by the kingdom of Burundi, its main rival located to the south; warfare between these two states continued well into the next century. Rwanda's wars further divided its socioeconomic classes, as Tutsi pastoralists often benefited by capturing cattle and attaining glory on the battlefield while Hutu agriculturalists suffered disruptions to farming. During the 1790s, Rwanda experienced a terrible civil war between royal factions that reached a climax with a major battle fought in 1802 near present-day Butare (also called Huye) that greatly weakened the monarchy, giving power to elite families at court.

Compared to Rwanda, the early history of the Burundi kingdom is much less known. While the area was initially an extension of the Congo rain forest inhabited by hunters and fishers, the advent of iron use around 500 BCE led to the clearing of trees in some places and the advent of cultivation and livestock raising.

Living in distinct environmental pockets, the population differentiated into communities of specialist hunters, farmers, and herders, and it is possible that pastoralists arrived from the north. Sometime after 1000, the numerous small states of the area combined into two kingdoms, Nyaburunga in the south and Ntare Naremera in the north. A heroic and possibly mythical leader called Ntare Rushatsi (Shaggy Lion), according to oral tradition, unified these two states and founded the kingdom of Burundi, perhaps during the 1500s or 1600s. Besides its wars with neighboring Rwanda, Burundi's eighteenth-century history remains somewhat obscure. Like Rwanda, it developed pastoral (Tutsi/Hima), agricultural (Hutu), and hunter-gatherer (Twa) identities tied together by a common culture and language (Kirundi).

Conclusion

Originating with ancient Axum, the Christian state of Ethiopia emerged and expanded in the Horn of Africa, eventually engaging in conflict and commerce with neighboring Muslim powers. Along East Africa's Indian Ocean coast, a series of independent Swahili ports became intermediaries in the oceanic trade that linked the East African interior with Arabia and parts of Asia. A vibrant Swahili society developed with a distinct language and architecture, and the religion of Islam. From around 1500, Portuguese mariners entered the Indian Ocean, subduing the Swahili towns, taking control of the oceanic trade from Arab sailors, and intervening to save Christian Ethiopia from a Muslim offensive. In response to the Portuguese invasion of the Indian Ocean, the Ottomans established a permanent presence on the Red Sea coast of Eritrea and the Omani Arabs launched a counter-offensive in the late 1600s that took over the northern part of the East African coast, confining the Portuguese to what is now Mozambique. For a very long time, the expansion of pastoral communities represented a consistent element of East African precolonial history, with the Oromo challenging Ethiopia and other specialist cattle-keepers such as the Maasai evicting farmers from the East African plains. During the 1600s and 1700s, political centralization took place in the interior Great Lakes zone and on the island of Madagascar. Along the Great Lakes, a number of compact and highly organized kingdoms like Bunyoro and Buganda emerged, and some of these, like Rwanda and Burundi, developed distinct social classes of pastoralists and cultivators. Around the same time, and reflecting similar trends in West Africa, the arrival of Europeans led to the expansion of the slave trade and the importation of firearms in Madagascar, prompting the rise of new and larger Malagasy kingdoms like Imerina.

Timeline

200 BCE–1000 CE—Southward movement of Nilotic-speaking pastoralists

100 BCE–300 CE—Swahili coastal towns in East Africa begin to engage in Indian Ocean trade; people from Malaya arrive in Madagascar

First century CE—Foundation of Axum

c. 270—Axum mints coins

c. 340—King Ezana of Axum converts to Christianity

300–1000—Expansion of Indian Ocean trade

520s–570s—Axum sends an army to Yemen

600s—Rise of Islam in Arabia

800s—Arrival of Islam along East African coast

900s—Fall of Axum

1000–1500—"Golden Age" of Indian Ocean trade; strengthening of Islam along East African coast

c. 1150—Rise of Zagwe dynasty in Ethiopia

1270—Establishment of Solomonid dynasty in Ethiopia

1300s—Possible origins of Buganda kingdom

1350–1500—Kingdom of Bunyoro-Kitara ruled by legendary Chwezi

1400s–1500s—Acceleration of southward movement of pastoralists into Great Rift Valley

1500s—Rise of Bunyoro kingdom in Great Lakes region

1405–06, 1417—Chinese navy visits East African coast

1434–68—Ethiopia centralizes and expands under Zara Yaqob; conflict with Muslim neighbors

1498—Vasco Da Gama leads Portuguese expedition around Cape of Good Hope and into Indian Ocean

1506—Portuguese arrive in Madagascar

1507—Portuguese occupy Mozambique Island

1509—Battle of Diu—Portuguese defeat naval coalition of Persia, India, and Ottomans to dominate Indian Ocean; Portuguese subjugate Swahili ports

1526–31—Muslim Adal invades and defeats Christian Ethiopia

1541—Portuguese intervention in support of Ethiopia

1543—Battle of Wayna Daga; Ethiopia/Portuguese defeat Adal

1557—Ottoman Empire occupies Massawa on the Red Sea

1590s—Portuguese build fort at Mombasa

1600s—Rise of Buganda, Nkore, Rwanda, and Burundi

1622—Ethiopian Emperor Susneyos converts to Catholicism

1633—Emperor Fasiladas restores Ethiopian Christianity and expels Portuguese

1635—Founding of the Ethiopian city of Gondar

1650—Sultanate of Oman expels Portuguese

c. 1650s—Founding of Sakalava kingdoms in Madagascar

1690s–1720s—Pirates use Madagascar as a base

1698—Oman seizes Mombasa and Zanzibar

1700s—Decline of Bunyoro

1720s—Rise of Betsimisaraka kingdom in Madagascar

1730–55—Empress Mentewab serves as co-ruler of Ethiopia

1750s—Military reforms in Nkore

1769—Beginning of long period of instability in Ethiopia

1770—Rwanda repels invasion by Burundi

1778—Rise of Imerina kingdom in Madagascar

1790s—Civil war in Rwanda

KEY TERMS

Amharic 144

astrolabe 147

Axum 137

dhow 146

Kebra Negast 143

Malagasy language 150

Miaphysitism 138

monsoon 145

Prester John 140

Solomonid 141

Tigray 145

Vasco da Gama 149

Zanj 147

STUDY QUESTIONS

1. Which factors prompted the growth and led to the decline of ancient Axum? What was the role of Christianity as a state religion?

2. What were the distinctive features of Ethiopian Christianity? What factors led to the rise of Adal as a regional Muslim power in the Horn of Africa?

3. How did environmental factors determine trade rhythms across the Indian Ocean? Which forces fueled the growth of Swahili coastal trade? What kinds of products were traded? How did Portuguese expansion in the Indian Ocean impact Swahili and Malagasy cultures?

4. Define Nilotic pastoralism and explain the origins of early East African states. Ascertain the value of ceremony and mythical origin narratives for East African kings. Compare the kingdoms of Bunyoro, Buganda, Nkore, Rwanda and Burundi.

Please see page FR-3 for the Further Readings for this chapter.
For additional digital learning resources please go to
https://www.oup.com/he/falola-stapleton1e

Central Africa to c. 1870: Kings and Farmers, Hunters and Raiders

Although difficult to define, Central Africa generally comprises the region from the Zambezi River in the south to the Congo and Ubangi rivers in the north, and from the Great Lakes in the east to the Atlantic coast in the west. The great Central African rainforest in the north and the mixed trees and grassland of the savanna in the south characterize the region's environment. Located in the middle of the continent, Central Africa borders all the other regions of Africa—north, west, south, and east—and this situation has influenced its history. Depending on their location, and at different times, people in parts of Central Africa engaged in the Indian Ocean trade on the east coast, experienced the transatlantic slave trade occurring in the west, and encountered aggressive newcomers from the south, east, and north who moved into the region in the nineteenth century. Compared to these other regions of Africa, the precolonial history of Central Africa is perhaps the most difficult to reconstruct, relying heavily on linguistic studies and oral traditions. Archaeological research has been important, particularly for the early periods, but it remains relatively limited, and few literate visitors ventured into the region before the mid-1800s. Historians' knowledge of Central African before c. 1500 remains vague. It is clear, however, that people living on the region's southern savanna became involved in expanded trade, especially with the Indian Ocean coast, and the formation of large centralized states from at least around 1600. The history of the decentralized communities in the northern rainforest is more difficult to determine. Much more is known about the history of Central Africa after around 1800, when outsiders penetrated the region seeking people raw materials and people to enslave, destabilizing many societies.

Mbudye officials displaying emblems of office, including two lukasa memory boards and staff of office. Luba artist, Democratic Republic of the Congo. Photo by Mary Nooter Roberts.

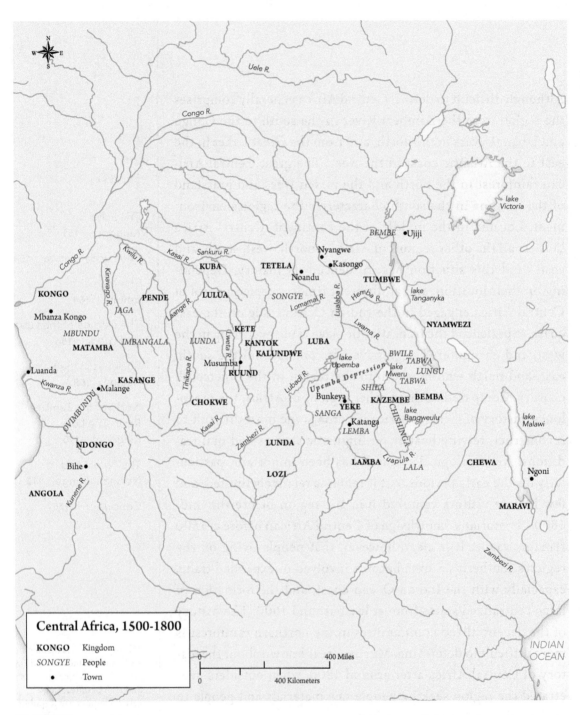

Central Africa, 1500-1800

KONGO	Kingdom
SONGYE	People
•	Town

≡ **MAP 8.1**

The Luba Kingdom

A series of centralized states emerged on Central Africa's southern savanna during the precolonial era. The **Upemba Depression**, a wetland area containing many rivers and lakes in the southern part of present-day Democratic Republic of Congo (DRC), became the home of a thriving precolonial African civilization. Almost everything that is known about the early history of the area comes from archaeological excavation. Around 500 CE, people established villages along the shores of Lake Kisale and the Lualaba River, where they lived by fishing, farming, and hunting. As the earliest Iron Age communities in the region, they made iron tools and weapons such as axes, barbed arrowheads, spear heads, knives, and hoes. Between around 700 and 900 CE, these communities grew as more people were attracted to the area's fishing resources. Regional trade developed as people from the Upemba Depression carried dried fish about 125 miles south to exchange with other communities for copper, and their artisans began making decorative bangles out of imported copper as well as more complex pottery. In turn, a hierarchical society emerged and small states formed. From around 900 to 1200 CE, the area's artisans became highly specialized, producing an extremely sophisticated style of pottery unique in sub-Saharan Africa as well as many iron objects, copper ornaments like bangles, necklaces, and belts, and copper tools such as knives and spearheads. After 1200, the area's local trade network connected with the long-distance intercontinental trade of the Indian Ocean coast. As local pottery became less complex, more copper arrived from the south in the form of copper crosses specifically made for trade, which became a type of regional currency, and glass beads and **cowrie** shells came in from the coast. This intensification of trade formed the context for the growth of the area's **Luba kingdom**, the first known centralized state in Central Africa.

Oral traditions relate the founding of the Luba kingdom. While a mysterious outsider called Kongola (the Rainbow) initially established the embryonic Luba organization, he was overthrown and killed by his nephew Kalala Ilunga, a great warrior, who created the Luba system of divine kingship that eventually spread throughout the region. Some historians believe that this story should not be taken literally but that it represents a political charter legitimizing the Luba monarchy. Re-enacted during the installation of Luba kings, the origin legend portrays a story of how a supposedly cruel and unjust regime was overturned by a great hero who initiated an age of prosperity. Historians once thought that Luba expansion involved the growth of a territorial empire, but more recently scholars have seen it as a cultural enlargement. The establishment of the Luba kingdom likely took place in the 1600s or before, and may

≡ **Memory board.** A lukasa memory board, from the late nineteenth century.

have taken place around the Luvua River. The Luba capital moved regularly because of the practice that upon a king's death, his center became a memorial site inhabited by a female medium possessed by his spirit and the incoming king moved the royal court to a new location. During the 1700s, the capitals moved around the area of the Luvua, the Upper Luvidyo, and the Upper Lusanza rivers, which contained important iron and salt deposits. With communities on the fringe sending these products as tribute to the kingdom's heartland, the Luba state controlled a regional trade network that stretched from the bottom of the Central African rainforest south to the **Copperbelt** in what is now Zambia and west to the Lualaba River. The Luba kingdom entered into marriage alliances and cultivated its capital as the region's primary ritual center, where provincial chiefs obtained symbols of power such as carvings and sacred fire, and undertook installation ceremonies that linked them to the spirit world.

The Luba kingdom expanded during the eighteenth and early nineteenth centuries. In the early 1700s, Luba directed military campaigns against the Songye people to the northwest; in the mid-to-late 1700s, it expanded northeast toward the Lualaba River; and around the turn of the nineteenth century, its capital shifted south to the salt-producing Mashyo area that remained the core of the state. In the late 1700s and early 1800s, the unification of the Kanyok people thwarted westward Luba expansion, but the latter pushed east of the Lualaba River, reaching the western shore of Lake Tanganyika. In conquered areas, some compliant local leaders remained in office, but at times the Luba imposed their own rulers while the Luba secret society called **mbudye** spread their ideology of sacred kingship. Luba expansion continued until the mid-nineteenth century.

The Lunda Empire

The **Lunda Empire** became the largest state in precolonial Central Africa. It originated with the iron-using agricultural Ruund people of the Upper Mbuji-Mayi River in present-day DRC. According to oral tradition, a local queen called Ruwej, who could not have children, married the traveling hunter Yirung. Yirung and a female servant had a son called Yaav, who became the official heir and founder of the Lunda state. All Lunda kings became known as Mwaat Yaav or "Lord of the Viper." While some scholars interpreted this story as symbolic of conquest by the Luba kingdom, others believe that linguistic evidence shows a gradual interaction between the Ruund and Luba. Several factors facilitated the success of the Lunda state. First, the broad and amorphous nature of Ruund extended families meant that these institutions struggled to solve conflicts, and therefore the Lunda state, which adopted a tight kinship-style structure, filled that role. Second, Lunda rulers practiced positional succession in that a new king inherited not only the position of his predecessor but his name, wives, and children, which enabled the state to more easily assimilate conquered communities than Luba. It appears that the foundations of the Lunda state among the Ruund began during the 1600s and early 1700s, and then expanded to other areas and peoples. Third, the arrival of the American crops maize and cassava through transatlantic trade contacts boosted food production and increased the population.

During the 1700s, the Lunda state expanded west and east due to the facility of moving across the Central African Savanah as well as the attraction of trade connections with the Atlantic and Indian Ocean coasts. Resistance by the decentralized Kete people and the unifying Kanyok prevented Lunda expansion to the more densely populated and forested north. As it grew, the Lunda Empire franchised ambitious local rulers as Lunda lords and assimilated others who became ritual owners of the land. By the mid-eighteenth century, Lunda had expanded west to the Kwango River, which constitutes the modern border of Angola and DRC, and into what is now northcentral Angola. The wars of Lunda expansion produced enslaved people exported west to the Angolan coast, from where they were shipped to Brazil by the Portuguese. This trade prompted Lunda to send a diplomatic mission to the Portuguese at Luanda in 1807. In the early 1700s, Lunda sent an army east to secure sources of salt around the Lualaba River. Around 1740, this force expanded further east to the Luapula River between Lakes Mweru and Bangweula, subduing local Shila and Bisa people and creating a Lunda satellite state under a ruler called Mwata Kazembe. In the late eighteenth century, Kazembe's Lunda pushed further east, establishing trade contacts with the Yao around Lake Malawi and to a lesser extent the Portuguese on the Zambezi River. Linked to the Indian Ocean trade system to the east, Kazembe exported ivory and copper and imported glass beads and cloth.

≡ **Kazembe.** A late-nineteenth-century depiction of Kazembe, title of the ruler of the Kazembe kingdom located in what is now eastern Zambia.

Since Kazembe's Lunda maintained commercial and tributary ties with the original Lunda to the west, the broad Lunda complex of the late eighteenth and early nineteenth century conducted trade with both the Atlantic and Indian Ocean coasts. Although a succession of rulers called Kazembe acknowledged the ceremonial supremacy of Mwaat Yaav, Kazembe's Lunda functioned as an autonomous power as it was located in present-day eastern Zambia some 600 miles from the parent state.

The Maravi Empire

Sometime during the 1400s and 1500s, between the Zambezi River and Lake Malawi, Chewa-speaking people established centralized states ruled by the Phiri clan that may have originated from Luba country, and collectively these communities acquired the name **Maravi**, meaning "flame." The three primary Chewa kingdoms of the period were Kalonga, Undi, and Lundu, and they became involved in exporting ivory to the growing east coast trade. Originally the names of the founding leaders of these states, the terms Kalonga, Undi, and Lundu became the titles of subsequent rulers. Starting in the 1530s, the Portuguese moved from the coast of present-day Mozambique up the Zambezi River, founding the outposts of Sena and Tete, and began to interact with the Maravi states to their north. At the end of the 1500s, a mysterious group called the Zimba appeared in this area and allied with the local Lundu kingdom in an effort to control the Shire Valley south of Lake Malawi. This resulted in a conflict between the Portuguese and the Zimba, who continued their expansion to the Indian Ocean coast. Historians have debated the identity of the Zimba, with some seeing them as a distinct and new power in the region and others claiming that Zimba was simply a name used by the Portuguese for any local group they were fighting. Curiously, the Zimba seemed to disappear from the historical record after around 1600.

At the start of the 1600s, a Maravi leader called Musura or Masula used an alliance with the Portuguese on the Zambezi to expand his power on the south end of Lake Malawi. Masula took the tile Kalonga, though his actual relation to the historic Kalonga state remains uncertain. Kalonga Masula sent some of his fighters south of the Zambezi to help the Portuguese in their efforts to subdue the Mutapa kingdom, and in 1622 the Portuguese assisted Masula to defeat the Lundu state on the north side of the river. However, Masula then switched allegiances, joining an anti-Portuguese regional coalition led by the exiled Mutapa ruler Kapararidze. During the early 1630s, Kapararidze failed in his attempt to oust the Portuguese from Mutapa on the south side of the Zambezi, while Kalonga Masula led a successful military campaign on the north side that conquered a large swath of territory between the Luangwa River and the coast of Mozambique. Masula's domain became known as the Maravi Empire. Within a few years, Masula re-established relations with the Portuguese, providing them with ivory in exchange for guns, gunpowder, and cloth. In the late 1600s, after the death of its founding military strongman Kalonga Masula, the Maravi Empire fragmented and pulled back from the coast.

Lacking the protection of a strong centralized state, communities around Lake Malawi became targets for different types of raiders. During the eighteenth century, decentralization following the breakup of the Maravi Empire prompted Yao groups from the east side of the lake to emerge to control the area's Indian Ocean coastal trade through which they acquired Islam and guns. In the context of the growth of the East African slave trade during the nineteenth century (see Chapter 13), fishing and farming villages around the lake became targets for increased slave raiding by bands of Yao and Swahili-Arab gunmen. Beginning in the 1830s, the arrival of the aggressive **Ngoni** groups from the south further destabilized the Chewa-speaking societies living around Lake Malawi. The Ngoni did not use firearms, but their emphasis on close combat and age-regiment military organization gave them an advantage over local societies. Crossing north of the Zambezi in 1835, the Ngoni of Zwangendaba settled on the Fipa Plateau south of Lake Tanganyika, but after their leader's death in 1848, they split into different groups and moved to new locations. Among these, the Tuta Ngoni moved far north to the

≡ **Ngoni warriors.** Taken in 1895, this picture shows Ngoni warriors in what is now northern Malawi.

southern end of Lake Victoria in what is now Tanzania, the Ngoni of Mpezeni challenged the Bemba in present-day eastern Zambia, and the Ngoni of Mombera conquered the northern end of Lake Malawi. Separate from Zwangendaba's original group, the Maseko Ngoni ventured up the east side of Lake Malawi into present-day southern Tanzania, ravaging Yao communities along the way, but they clashed with other Ngoni and eventually settled southwest of the lake in the 1850s. This Ngoni expansion resulted in the pockets of Ngoni communities that exist today in eastern Zambia, Malawi, and southern Tanzania. With the arrival of Yao, Swahili-Arab, and Ngoni raiders during the nineteenth century, communities around Lake Malawi tried to protect themselves by building stockades and watchtowers and setting traps.

The Decline of Luba and Lunda

During the nineteenth century, the arrival, in Central Africa, of new aggressive raiders with guns led to the decline of the Luba and Lunda states. Inhabiting a thinly populated and remote part of present-day eastern Angola, the Chokwe specialized in gathering beeswax and hunting elephants for ivory. The Chokwe were not involved in the Portuguese slave trade in Angola as their homeland was isolated. With the decline of the transatlantic slave trade in the mid-1800s, the Chokwe experienced a surge in demand for their wax and ivory by coastal European merchants who provided them with guns. Lacking a centralized state, large bands of Chokwe hunters and their families followed elephant herds, and when a hunting band became too large, it divided into several new groups. With expanded hunting, elephants became scarce in eastern Angola, prompting the Chokwe to move east into the realm of Mwaat Yaav's Lunda. While the Lunda Empire initially permitted transient Chokwe to hunt elephants in return for a portion of the harvested ivory, the latter began to build permanent settlements in Lunda territory and intermarry with local communities, thereby expanding the Chokwe presence and identity. Given their limited experience with firearms, the Lunda army proved unable to resist the expansion of gun-equipped Chokwe hunters. Subsequently, as elephants disappeared in Lunda, Chokwe hunters moved northeast into the Luba kingdom, where, because the local people already hunted elephants, they became intermediaries in the ivory trade with the coast. In the late nineteenth century, as elephant populations diminished and ivory ran out, the Chokwe and Ovimbundu people of Angola shifted to exporting rubber to meet a new international demand.

With the growth of ivory and slave exports from the Indian Ocean coast during the 1800s, East African traders and gunmen such as Swahili-Arabs and Nyamwezi moved into Central Africa. Swahili-Arab merchants arrived on the eastern frontier of Kazembe's Lunda, where they used their firearms to gain power, and in the 1850s, they became involved in a series of civil wars that weakened the kingdom. Around the same time, the Nyamwezi took control of trade routes through what is now Tanzania, and this facilitated their expansion further inland. During the 1850s, a Nyamwezi group called the Yeke, led by the up-and-coming warlord Msiri and equipped with guns, advanced into the Central African interi-

≡ **The ivory trade.** This engraving shows ivory being transported in a village in Central Africa in the 1860s.

or and conquered a copper-rich territory formerly comprising the western section of Kazembe's Lunda, the southern region of Luba, and the eastern reaches of Mwaat Yaav's Lunda. Constructing a fortified capital called Bunkeya and a network of strongholds, Msiri adopted Lunda-style administration, with provincial governors sending him ivory and enslaved people. Although Msiri's primary trade relationship was with the East African coast, he cultivated contacts with the Ovimbundu of southern Angola in the 1870s and sent caravans to the Atlantic port of Benguela.

Known as **Tippu Tip**, the Swahili-Arab warlord Hamed bin Muhammed established a raiding state on the Lualaba River west of Lake Tanganyika in the 1860s and sent ivory and enslaved people east to the island of Zanzibar in exchange for firearms. Tippu Tip's trading empire stretched from the westward bend of the Congo River in the north to the Luba kingdom in the south, which he significantly weakened. With the sudden arrival of flintlock muskets in this part of Central Africa in the 1860s and 1870s, local powers like Luba and Lunda did not have time to learn how to use them in warfare, giving the invaders a major advantage.

The nineteenth-century growth of ivory and slave exports from Central Africa also contributed to the rise of the **Bemba** states in what is now eastern Zambia. During the late eighteenth century, the Bemba inhabited an area with limited resources between the northern part of Lake Malawi and the southern part of Lake

Tanganyika, and they began to raid neighboring peoples like the Bisa, taking trade goods and cattle. These activities led to the formation and expansion of several small Bemba states under a nominal senior ruler. With the decline of the nearby Lunda of Kazembe in the early 1800s, the Bemba imposed greater authority over ivory and slave exports to the East African coast, establishing fortified posts along trade routes and at major river crossings. The arrival of Swahili-Arab traders in the area in the mid-nineteenth century encouraged the Bemba to mount more raids to obtain enslaved people and ivory. During the 1850s, the influx of Ngoni raiders from the south posed a major challenge to the Bemba states. Responding to this threat, the Bemba leader Chitapankwa rallied a coalition of Bemba groups supported by some Swahili-Arab gunmen, and around 1870 they drove the Ngoni east toward Lake Malawi. While Ngoni raids against the Bemba stopped, their presence had weakened regional communities, therefore facilitating further Bemba expansion. Under the centralizing influence of Chitapankwa, the Bemba kingdom continued to export enslaved people and ivory to the east coast in return for textiles, liquor, and guns.

Societies in the Kasai Region

Located on the southern fringe of the Central African rainforest, the Kasai region of present-day southern DRC contains the Kasai and Sankuru rivers, which flow together and merge with the Congo River. While people living in the northern part of this region settled across the diverse environment, including forests and clearings, communities in the southern section clustered around rivers as farming was difficult on the savanna. After around 1700, some communities in this densely populated region formed states while others remained decentralized. Though agriculture in the northern area focused on bananas and farmers in the south grew sorghum and millet, the introduction of American crops maize and cassava during the 1600s increased the food supply, reducing the impact of periodic droughts but intensifying labor demands on women. Trade increased. This first happened with fish, enslaved people, and raffia from the forest to the north being exchanged for meat, salt, and copper from the Savanna in the south. From the late 1700s, east–west riverine and overland trade expanded, with enslaved people and ivory sent to the Atlantic coast in exchange for metal ware, cloth, liquor, and firearms. During the 1600s and 1700s, as a result of these changes, leaders began to emerge, gathering followers and acquiring clients and enslaved people. Some of these leaders founded enduring kingdoms.

During the mid-1600s, in the Kasai region's northwest, a long-distance trader called Shyaam aMbul aNgoong founded the **Kuba kingdom** as a multiethnic federation ruled by Bush-ong-speaking elites, and over the next few decades it developed into a highly centralized and hierarchical state. While Kuba kings of the 1700s could order the execution or exile of subordinate rulers, a royal council with veto power supervised their decisions. The introduction of American crops via the transatlantic trade and the practice of coercing labor increased Kuba food production, enabling the state to engage in external trade and to support a class of administrators, warriors, and highly skilled artists. Kuba artists produced sophisticated carvings and decorated masks for court rituals and initiations, and elaborate raffia textiles for funerals and trade. Their work remains highly prized among today's international art collectors.

≡ **Kuba mask.** In precolonial Central Africa, Kuba society became famous for producing great works of art like this royal mask.

Located in southeastern Kasai, the Kanyok people began to form states during the 1600s and 1700s in response to Luba and Lunda expansion. Mounting warfare prompted the male Kanyok warrior society to overtake hitherto dominant matrilineal clans and create patrilineal ruling dynasties. Around the end of the 1700s, these states amalgamated into a single Kanyok kingdom that broke ties with the aggressive Luba and built huge earthwork fortifications to defend against Luba and Lunda incursions. Around 1810 the Kanyok ruler Ilung a Chibang led his army to victory in a great battle with the Luba, who vowed never to return. According to tradition, a giant snake emerged from the Lubilash River during the fighting to assist the Kanyok ("little snake") army. During the early and mid-nineteenth century, the Kanyok kingdom engaged in extensive slave raiding against nearby stateless communities and exported captives along with ivory. Kanyok power waned in the second half of the nineteenth century as a civil war broke out in the 1850s and the Luba slave and ivory trader Kasonge Cinyama, leading a gun-equipped army, attacked Kanyok in 1875. Elsewhere in Kasai, south of Kuba and west of Kanyok, the Kete and Lele societies remained decentralized, emphasizing village elders and local shrines, but during the 1700s and 1800s they suffered raids by their better-organized and wealthier neighbors.

North of the Zambezi River: The Lozi Kingdom

North of the Zambezi River in what is now Zambia, iron-age farmers who raised small stock like sheep and goats lived in decentralized and egalitarian communities from around the middle 500s. Practicing what archaeologists call the Luangwa pottery tradition, these people very likely spoke a variety of Bantu languages and were beginning to use iron implements. Changing pottery styles seem to indicate that the matrilineal communities of the Luangwa tradition assimilated other patrilineal people who possessed cattle. Located on the northern bank of the Zambezi River, the archaeological site of Ingombe Ilede ("the place where the cow sleeps") illustrates important changes that took place among the communities of this part of Central Africa. During the 1400s, the residents of Ingombe Ilede possessed iron tools and weapons, and engaged in farming, raising cattle and goats, hunting, and fishing. As a center for burgeoning trade, the people at Ingombe Ilede exported salt and ivory in exchange for gold mined south of the Zambezi, copper from the north around today's Copper Belt, and glass beads from the Indian Ocean coast to the east. The style of pottery found at the site links it to the modern Tonga people of the same area, and the presence of valuable goods such as gold in some graves means that this was a hierarchical society and likely a centralized state. While the rise of Ingombe Ilede reflected the growth of trade along the Zambezi Valley directed toward the east coast, the center declined over the next several centuries as commerce shifted from copper and gold to ivory and enslaved people.

During the 1600s and 1700s, along the upper Zambezi River, the Lozi people built a centralized kingdom perhaps influenced by the Lunda Empire to the north. The **Lozi kingdom** developed an administrative system, with the king appointing officials based on merit and ability rather than hereditary status. The king rewarded successful officials with land and dismissed ineffective ones. These officials included administrators based at the royal court, provincial governors who acted as judges, and community leaders responsible for tribute collection, labor recruitment, and military mobilization. While the Lozi kingdom did not export enslaved people to the Angolan coast, it raided nearby Tonga and Ila communities for prisoners and cattle, and subordinate rulers sent captives to the Lozi king as tribute. The kingdom employed enslaved people internally to construct a sophisticated water management system that included mounds to elevate villages above floodwaters, and a network of dams and canals along the Zambezi floodplain that enabled intensive agriculture. Within the context of this sys-

≡ **Kuomboka festival.** The royal barge used to relocate the Lozi queen during the Kuomboka festival in western Zambia. The queen's barge carries the symbol of a bird while the king's carries that of an elephant.

tem, the annual **Kuomboka** festival developed, whereby the Lozi king moved his capital to high ground to avoid the regular Zambezi floods that irrigated the plains. Involved in regional trade, Lozi exported fish, grain, and baskets in exchange for iron, wood, and bark-cloth. In the mid-1700s, the Lozi kingdom conquered its less organized neighbors, such as the Mbukushu to the west and the Subiya and Toka to the southeast. In these areas, local rulers remained in office, though under the supervision of Lozi officials who guaranteed the supply of tribute and labor to the royal court. As a result, the Lozi kingdom evolved a highly centralized heartland and a periphery of loosely controlled non-Lozi subordinate groups.

During the 1830s, the Sesotho-speaking Kololo people, having fled violence on the Highveld in present-day South Africa, moved north through what is now Botswana and crossed the Zambezi River to enter western present-day Zambia. Led by Sebetwane, they probed eastward, seizing cattle from Tonga and Ila peoples. Around 1840, the Ndebele kingdom, another group originating in South Africa but now based in southwestern Zimbabwe, raided across the Zambezi River, prompting the Kololo to move west toward the Lozi kingdom. The Kololo defeated the Lozi kingdom, weakened by a recent civil war, and took over the southern part of the Zambezi floodplain. Shortly thereafter, the Kololo defeated the Ngoni of Nxaba who had similarly moved into this area from the far south. In the late 1840s, the Kololo completed their conquest of the Lozi kingdom by expelling the Lozi royals from the northern section of their territory. As the Lozi royals went into exile among neighboring groups, where they organized a resistance movement, the charismatic Sebetwane became a more popular ruler than the former and aloof Lozi kings, and he curried favor among Lozi commoners by distributing cattle, appointing some Lozi to key state positions and taking Lozi wives. While staving off continued Ndebele incursions from the south, Sebetwane engaged with African intermediaries in the Angolan slave trade, exporting Ila and other captives in exchange for firearms. With Sebetwane's death in 1851, his son Sekeletu took over, moving the Lozi capital to the south, where the Chobe River swamps limited Ndebele raids, and trying but mostly failing to open direct trade with Europeans far to the south and the Portuguese on the Angolan coast to obtain more guns. Under Kololo occupation, the Lozi kingdom organized a more effective army that expanded the state to the west and east, hunted elephants, and constantly raided the Ila. Since Sekeletu imposed heavy taxes, treated the Lozi as enslaved agricultural workers, and exported some of them to the Angolan slave trade, discontent toward Kololo rule grew. Another major problem for the Kololo was that as they originated from cooler areas in the south, they had little immunity to malaria, which is common in the tropical and wet environment of western Zambia. Following the 1863 death of Sekeletu, a Kololo succession struggle provided the Lozi with an opportunity to rebel, and during the next year an exiled Lozi army invaded the kingdom, reinstating the Lozi royal dynasty under the new king Sepopa. Although Kololo rule of the Lozi kingdom lasted for only about 20 years, the occupation influenced the long-term development of the Lozi language as it incorporated elements of Sesotho spoken by the Kololo occupiers. In 1878, with the overthrow of Sepopa as a result of continued internal conflicts, Lewanika became Lozi king and contended with ongoing rebellion and Ndebele incursions from the south. During the 1880s, with the onset of the European "Scramble for Africa," these pressures encouraged Lewanika to cultivate friendly relations with newly arrived British officials and missionaries.

The Forest and Its Northern Fringe

In the dense Central African rainforest, where the decentralized nature of many societies presents difficulties for historical reconstruction, the human population remained sparse and change occurred slowly. Beginning perhaps 3,000 or more years ago, Bantu-speaking communities of farmers and fishers from around what is now Cameroon entered sections of the equatorial forest and adopted methods of living in that environment. Their eventual mastery of ironworking helped in this process, allowing them to cut clearings and paths more easily. Expanding throughout the forest, these Bantu speakers either incorporated the existing bands of **Twa** hunter-gatherers or cultivated a symbiotic relationship with them. Based on studies of the area's many languages, it appears that the earliest Bantu-speaking settlers formed the foundation

≡ **Peoples of the Central African Rainforest** *Left:* A Baka man and woman hunt in the Congo rainforest using nets, sticks, and vines. The woman also carries a machete for butchering the catch and a basket for carrying the meat. *Right:* A late-nineteenth century depiction of a rope bridge traversing a river in Central Africa. Communities in the Central African forest built many such bridges to facilitate trade, communication, warfare, and hunting.

for a shared equatorial cultural and political tradition that developed and spread. At the center of this tradition was the organizational concept of a "house" of relatives and dependents led by a wealthy and charismatic "big man." Although the scale of organization increased and some groups became dominant by mobilizing more people to fight wars, equatorial forest communities generally remained decentralized and small scale in comparison to their neighbors on the southern savanna.

More is known about the history of communities in the western forest after around 1600 because of the spread of the transatlantic slave trade to that area and the creation of written accounts. By the middle of the 1500s, Bantu-speaking Teke groups inhabiting the junction of the Congo and Kasai Rivers began to move eastward into the forest to avoid slave raiding by the Kongo kingdom or to search for victims of their own. In the Loango region, along the Atlantic coast north of the Congo River, the Bantu speakers of the Vili kingdoms exchanged their salt for ivory hunted by Twa deeper in the forest. During the late 1600s, the Dutch initiated a slave trade along the Loango coast and acquired captives from the Vili states in return for ironware, tobacco, liquor, cloth, and guns. The Bobangi people of the middle Congo River and the southern Teke, already involved in the Angolan slave trade, supplied most of the captives exported from the Loango coast. Among the Vili states, engagement in the slave trade initially reinforced the dominance of the Loango kingdom, but over time the Ngoyo and Kakongo kingdoms increased their power by opening their own slave ports and importing guns. As happened in West Africa, the nineteenth-century suppression of the transatlantic slave trade and the new Western demand for raw materials inspired the Vili to employ enslaved people on their own plantations.

The thickly forested and thinly populated coast of present-day Gabon, which also lacked good harbors, did not attract much oceanic trade until the early 1800s, when slave ships were looking for new sources of captives. During the mid-nineteenth century, the French tried to suppress slave trading in this area, founding a small settlement of freed enslaved people at Libreville in 1848 and promoting raw materials export. Around the same time, raiders from the northern savanna, such as the Fulani of Adamawa, ventured south into present-day eastern Cameroon, causing many small and independent groups of Fang people to flee south into the coastal forests of Cameroon and Gabon. By the 1840s, Fang hunters arrived at the Gabon estuary, where they exerted control over the ivory trade and procured firearms. In the 1860s and 1870s, the hunting out of elephants and antislavery naval operations meant that Gabon's exports shifted from ivory and enslaved people to rubber, which French merchants obtained by moving deeper into the interior. Local economic intermediaries like the Mpongwe people became trapped between Fang and European expansion.

On the northern edge of the forest, along the Ubangi River, state formation began after around 1600 as a response to raids by savanna horsemen from the north who captured and enslaved people for export across the Sahara. In the northeastern corner of what is now DRC, along the Uele River, the Mangbetu people developed agriculture centered on growing maize, cassava, and plantain, and their skilled ironworkers manufactured spears and swords prized throughout the region. While the Mangbetu leader Nabiembali forged a united Mangbetu kingdom during the 1820s, his sons fought among themselves, founding several separate and expansionist Mangbetu states in the 1860s. This process also led to the formation of a state among the nearby Bangba people. In the late eighteenth century, Azande states expanded east toward the northern Congo River and Nile watershed on the modern-day border of South Sudan and DRC. Although the Azande expanded rapidly in search of new subjects, land, and hunting areas, they avoided centralization and constantly founded new and often rival groups. Utilizing psychological warfare, the Azande cultivated a reputation for themselves as cannibals, chanting "Niam Niam" (meat, meat) before a battle to instill fear in their enemies. In this warrior society, unmarried Azande men took boys as lovers and apprentices, giving their parents spears as bride-wealth. During the 1860s and 1870s, gun-armed Arab enslavers and ivory traders from Khartoum arrived at the Uele River and became embroiled in local conflicts between the Mangbetu and Bangba. Various Azande groups were usually at war with the Khartoum traders while at the same time acquiring guns from them.

Timeline

c. 500 CE—Advent of Early Iron Age settlements in the Upemba Depression

1400s–1500s—Formation of Maravi states (Kalonga, Undi, and Lundu)

1500s—Teke people become embroiled in transatlantic slave trade

1530s—Portuguese begin expansion up the Zambezi River

1500s–1600s—Establishment of Luba kingdom

1620s–30s—Creation of Maravi Empire

c. 1650s—Establishment of the Kuba kingdom

Late 1600s—Decline of Maravi Empire; involvement of Vili states in transatlantic slave trade

1600s–1700s—Establishment and expansion of Lunda Empire of Mwaat Yaav; rise of Kanyok states; rise and expansion of Lozi kingdom

1700s–early 1800s—Expansion of Luba kingdom; unification of Kanyok kingdom; rise of Mangbetu and Azande states

1740s—Foundation of Kazembe's Lunda

1807—Lunda embassy sent to Luanda in Angola

1810—Kanyok army defeats Luba army near the Lubilash River

Early 1800s—Rise of the Bemba states in what is now eastern Zambia

Late 1830s—Arrival of Ngoni around Lake Malawi

1840s—Kololo conquest of Lozi kingdom; Fang begin moving southwest toward Gabon Estuary

1850s—Expansion of Chokwe elephant hunters; involvement of Swahili Arabs in Kazembe's Lunda—creation of Msiri's Yeke state at the expense of Lunda and Luba; civil war in Kanyok kingdom

1850–1870—Conflict between the Bemba and Ngoni

1860s—Establishment of Tippu Tip's raiding state on the west side of Lake Tanganyika

1864—Lozi overthrow Kololo rule

1860s–70s—Decline of Lunda and Luba; expansion of slave trade from East Africa; French merchants begin to press into the interior of Gabon in search of raw materials; Khartoum slave raids penetrate northern forest fringe

1874–77—Anglo-American explorer Henry Stanley uses Congo River system to cross Africa from east to west

1875—Slavers armed with guns attack Kanyok kingdom

Conclusion

During 1876 and 1877, Anglo-American explorer Henry Morton Stanley led an expedition that originated in East Africa and navigated the Lualaba and Congo Rivers to cross the continent from east to west. This event occurred in the context of a growing nineteenth-century European and American fascination with discovering geographic information about the African interior that set the stage for subsequent colonial conquest. Although most people living in Central Africa at the time never saw or perhaps even heard of Stanley, his expedition signaled the beginning of a new era for the region. The era of the large savanna kingdoms and empires such as Luba, Lunda, Maravi, and Lozi had ended. While Central African states emerged and expanded in relation to the growth of regional trade and the introduction of American crops during the 1600s and 1700s, they struggled to cope with the arrival of external forces linked to the international slave and ivory trades during the nineteenth century. These new arrivals included Swahili-Arabs and Nyamwezi gunmen from East Africa who established themselves west and south of Lake Tanganyika, Arab enslavers from Khartoum in the north who ventured into the forest fringe, and Sotho (Kololo) and Ngoni warriors from the south who crossed the Zambezi River. Though some Central African societies like the Bemba in the south and the Azande in the north seemed to thrive in this new context, many communities like those around Lake Malawi suffered greatly from raiding, and some areas became depopulated as people fled. For Central Africans, the timing of Stanley's transit could not have been worse. Weakened by division, warfare, and enslavement, the region was unprepared for the European penetration and conquest that would start within a few years.

KEY TERMS

Bemba 167	Lozi kingdom 170	Ngoni 165
Copperbelt 162	Luba kingdom 161	Tippu Tip 167
cowrie 161	Lunda Empire 163	Twa 172
Kuba kingdom 168	Maravi 164	Upemba Depression 161
Kuomboka 171	mbudye 162	

STUDY QUESTIONS

1. What is the archeological evidence for precolonial civilization in the Upemba Depression? How did the Luba kingdom expand, control trade, and centralize power? What were its main trade goods?

2. Which main factors promoted the growth of the Lunda Empire? What was its system of rule?

3. What were the consequence of Portuguese interactions with the Maravi Empire?

4. What factors led to the decline of the Luba and Lunda kingdoms? What explains the rise of the Bemba states and their reliance on ivory and slave exports?

5. How does the study of pottery styles provide information about changes in Lozi society?

6. What obstacles prevent a clear picture of the history of early forest communities, such as the Twa? How did geography impact trade and culture in the Vili, Gabon, and Mangbetu groups?

Please see page FR-4 for the Further Readings for this chapter. For additional digital learning resources please go to https://www.oup.com/he/falola-stapleton1e

Southern Africa to c. 1800: Herders, Traders and Settlers

The Cape of Good Hope.

Usually defined as the region between the Zambezi River in the north and the Cape of Good Hope in the south, Southern Africa possesses Atlantic and Indian Ocean coastlines. The central part of the region consists of the high elevation open plains of what is now Zimbabwe, central South Africa, north and eastern Botswana, and northern Namibia. The extremely arid western half of the region contains the Kalahari Desert of present-day Botswana and Namibia and the Namib Desert of Namibia's Atlantic coast. Indeed, the entire region is dry, with no natural lakes and only a few major rivers such as the Limpopo, Vaal, and Orange. On the eastern side of the region, a series of mountain ranges—Zimbabwe's Eastern Highlands and the Drakensberg Mountains—runs parallel with the Indian Ocean and separates the Indian Ocean coastal belt from the interior Zimbabwe Plateau and Highveld. In the far south, the Western Cape has a Mediterranean climate, and its pattern of a dry summers and wet winters is the opposite of the rest of Southern Africa. As a result of this geography and climate, the somewhat wetter eastern half of the region has supported a larger population than the very dry west.

Southern African indigenous languages comprise two broad linguistic categories. The region's Bantu languages, linguistically related to other Bantu languages spoken in Central and East Africa, include Shona, Tonga, Kalanga, Sotho, Tswana, and mutually intelligible Nguni languages such as Xhosa, Zulu, Ndebele, and Swati. Southern Africa's other broad linguistic category is **Khoisan**, encompassing languages such as Nama and !Kung, characterized by distinctive click sounds. In Southern African history, in general, speakers of Bantu languages were associated with settled communities of ironworking herders and farmers who formed kingdoms, whereas Khoisan language speakers were often hunter-gatherers and herders organized into relatively small groups. Over many centuries, Bantu speakers and Khoisan speakers interacted with each other, though it is clear that the former communities expanded at the expense of the later. Some of the most important themes in Southern

The Cape of Good Hope, showing British and Dutch ships moored with Table Mountain in the background, 1731.

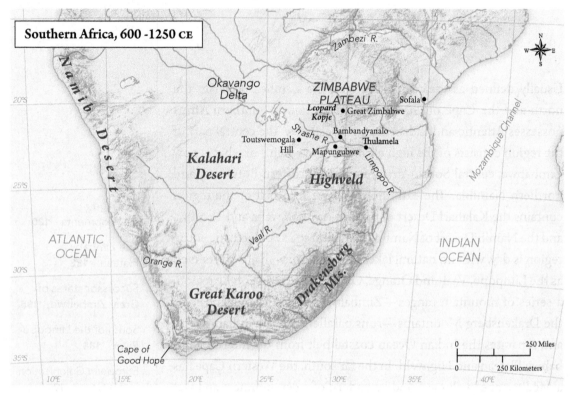

Southern Africa, 600 -1250 CE

≡ **MAP 9.1**

African history before 1800 include state formation, growing involvement in the Indian Ocean trade system and early European colonial intrusion into the Zambezi Valley and at the Cape.

Iron Age Developments

From around 200 CE, iron-using communities of farmers and herders inhabited Southern Africa during what archaeologists call the **Early Iron Age**. These societies were probably egalitarian and somewhat self-sufficient, and their settlements were located in valleys near sources of water. While scholars once believed that Iron Age Bantu-speaking people moved into Southern Africa from the north, there is no evidence of major population movement into the region, and developments occurred mostly among people already living there. Around 1000 CE, Southern African societies experienced significant change involving the rise of social stratification, movement to hilltop settlements, new pottery styles, increased cattle raising, and engagement in external trade to the Indian Ocean coast. Historians and archaeologists of Southern Africa often describe these transformed communities as belonging to the **Later Iron Age**, though the term can present an overly simplistic image of complex change. In these patrilineal societies, some men amassed large herds of cattle that they used to build political and economic power through lending livestock to poorer people who became their clients, and by using cattle as **bride price** to marry several wives who had children and added to the labor force. As such, control of cattle formed the basis of state formation in Later Iron Age Southern Africa.

The evidence for Later Iron Age developments in Southern Africa relates to a series of well-studied archaeological sites. In what is now eastern Botswana, **Toutswemogala Hill** represented the center of a network of iron-using communities that originated in the seventh century. The people of this society built large fenced structures on hilltops to accommodate herds of cattle, and there is evidence that they grew and stored cereal crops like millet and sorghum. While the discovery of shells from the Indian Ocean and Arabian beads at Toutswemogala indicate that its inhabitants were connected to trade networks that stretched to the east coast, their involvement in long-distance commerce seemed secondary to their focus on herding cattle. Eventually, over-grazing led to environmental decline, with people abandoning the Toutswemogala area and moving to other parts of the region, where they likely influenced the emerging cattle-raising culture.

Located in the southwest of present-day Zimbabwe and dating to the late 900s CE, the **Leopard's Kopje** site yielded some of the earliest archaeological evidence for local people mining gold and exporting it to the coast of what is now Mozambique. Around 1000, people from Leopard's Kopje crossed south of the Limpopo River into what is now northern South Africa and settled at a site called Bambandyanalo, where they raised cattle, produced specialized crafts such as ivory bracelets, and conducted trade with the east coast from where they acquired glass beads. As this society became more hierarchical, wealthy elites moved to the top of nearby Mapungubwe Hill but cattle and ordinary people remained at the bottom of the feature. Located at the junction of the Shashe and Limpopo Rivers, **Mapungubwe** served as a trade center from the 1000s to 1200s, exporting ivory and gold to the Indian Ocean. At Mapungubwe, hilltop stone walls and elaborate burials for elites who were interred with gold grave goods, including a gold-plated carving of a rhinoceros, represent evidence of some of the earliest known social distinctions in Southern Africa. It is very likely that Mapungubwe lay at the epicenter of a large state, as remnants of similar smaller hilltop settlements dating to the same period have been discovered across Zimbabwe, Botswana, and northern South Africa. For instance, a similar stratified community existed at Thulamela, located in the northern part of present-day South Africa's Kruger National Park, between around 1250 and 1700. At Thulamela, rulers lived in a stone-built enclosure and exported gold and ivory to the Mozambican coast in exchange for glass beads and porcelain from Asia. Mapungubwe declined during the 1200s as the gold trade shifted north to the Zimbabwe plateau and a new and larger center called Great Zimbabwe.

≡ **Mapungubwe** *Left:* A golden rhinoceros figurine discovered at Mapungubwe in 1932, in northern South Africa. *Right:* Mapungubwe Hill viewed from the north. From around the 1000s to 1200s, communities on and around Mapungubwe Hill engaged in intercontinental trade with the Indian Ocean coast.

The Zimbabwe Plateau

The name "Great Zimbabwe" comes from the Shona phrase "dzimba dza mabwe" meaning "houses of stone." The ruin of an impressive stone-built town, Great Zimbabwe represents the largest archaeological site in Africa south of Egypt's pyramids. Located north of the Limpopo River, in what is now the Republic of Zimbabwe, which is named in honor of the site, **Great Zimbabwe** sits at the center of a regional complex of smaller stone-constructed settlements. With three component parts, Great Zimbabwe consists of a hilltop settlement where stone walls link to natural rock formations, believed to be the oldest part of the site; a valley complex containing many roughly waist-high stone enclosures; and the "Great Enclosure," with 20-foot-high stone walls and a 30-foot-tall stone conical tower. Within the stone walls, the inhabitants lived in less-durable houses made from mud, animal dung, and wood with thatched roofs. The nature of the historical evidence related to Great Zimbabwe has led to numerous debates over its origins, purpose, and demise. Written a few decades after the abandonment of the site, a Portuguese account from the 1500s briefly mentioned Great Zimbabwe. Otherwise, there is no documentary evidence related to the settlement during its occupation. In addition, the site was inhabited too long ago for accurate oral traditions to have survived, with, for instance, local legends claiming inaccurately that the town was destroyed in the nineteenth century. Almost everything that scholars know about Great Zimbabwe derives from archaeological excavations and surveys. As a result, scholars know a great deal about some aspects of life at Great Zimbabwe, such as food production and trade, because of the discovery of physical remnants of these activities, but almost nothing about the town's political history. Scholars believe that Great Zimbabwe comprised the capital of a centralized state, speculating that the sophisticated construction techniques required coordination, and stone carvings of fish eagles and crocodiles signified royal totems. However, the names of Great Zimbabwe's rulers and specific events of their reigns remain unknown.

The first academic debate about Great Zimbabwe concerned who built it. The first Europeans to visit the site in the late nineteenth century, during the colonial conquest of Africa, could not conceive that supposedly primitive Africans could have built such a large and awe-inspiring set of structures. Establishing an oppressive white supremacist state that they called Southern Rhodesia (now the Republic of Zimbabwe), white settlers imagined that Great Zimbabwe had been built by foreign visitors to Africa such as the biblical King Solomon, ancient Phoenicians, or medieval Arabs. In the early twentieth century, some of the collapsed entrances of the Great Enclosure were reconstructed in Middle Eastern style to correspond with this theory. However, during the early twentieth century, some archaeologists challenged the claim of foreign provenance, pointing to a complete lack of evidence and noting that the existing evidence, including the design of the structure, indicated that local Africans, probably the ancestors of the region's Shona people, had constructed it. Refuting some of the theories of ancient origin, radio carbon dating puts the occupation of the site between roughly 1200 and 1450 CE. Although scholars now widely credit local people with constructing Great Zimbabwe, the myth of foreign origins sometimes returns in modern adventure novels and movies.

≡ **Great Zimbabwe** *Left:* The part of Great Zimbabwe known as the Great Enclosure contains a 30-foot-tall Conical Tower. *Right:* An aerial view of the Great Enclosure.

In the late twentieth century, archaeologists and historians debated the purpose of Great Zimbabwe's tall and thick walls. The lack of battlements at the top of the walls seems to indicate that the site was not meant as a fortification. Some scholars emphasize the possibility that the town grew around a religious site, a nearby cave, where they believed people assembled to hear ancestral voices spoken by spirit mediums. This corresponds with well-known traditional religious practices among Shona people. In the same vein, some scholars see the Great Enclosure as a venue for ritual initiation into adulthood. Although the design of the Great Enclosure appears to mirror initiation ceremonies used among the Venda people who live to the south, there is no evidence that Shona communities ever conducted initiations. Presenting a materialist interpretation, other scholars stress that the stone walls served as symbols of wealth and power. With the abundance of trade goods discovered at Great Zimbabwe, including tens of thousands of glass beads, it is obvious that the site functioned as a major center for regional and intercontinental commerce. Involved in the Indian Ocean trade network during its "Golden Age" in the 1300s and 1400s, the people of Great Zimbabwe exported gold and ivory to Swahili ports on the East African coast, and imported glass beads and porcelain items from Asia. It is possible that the town's stone walls may have initially served as privacy and security screens for trade deals, and that over time they became status symbols, growing in height and constructed in more elaborate styles.

Scholars have also debated why Great Zimbabwe was abandoned sometime around 1450. Evidence of widespread fires could indicate the settlement's destruction during a war, but can also be explained by local funerary practices whereby a recently deceased person's hut was burned. Another possibility is that local gold mines, located to the west of Great Zimbabwe and providing the town with its main export, became exhausted and the gold trade shifted north to new sources in the Mazowe Valley, giving rise to the Mutapa kingdom of that area. Furthermore, environmental degradation likely contributed to the fall of Great Zimbabwe. The town's inhabitants lived from raising livestock such as cattle and growing crops, and they cooked their food over open fires. With around 20,000 people living at Great Zimbabwe by around 1400, the surrounding lands suffered erosion caused by overgrazing of domesticated animals and harvesting of firewood, and fields became exhausted by repeated planting in the same place. The Great Zimbabwe settlement became unsustainable, as people had to walk further and further away to grow crops, graze herds, collect wood, and engage in hunting and gathering. After a while, they established new settlements in more productive lands, and while they continued to construct some small-scale stone walls, the massive walls of Great Zimbabwe were not copied elsewhere in the area.

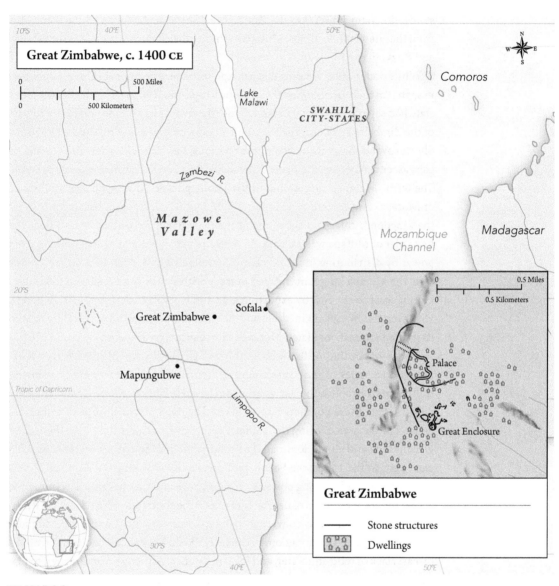

≡ **MAP 9.2**

Successor States of Great Zimbabwe

Much more is known about the successor states of Great Zimbabwe that existed on the Zimbabwe Plateau from around 1500. The historical reconstructions of these Shona kingdoms are based on a combination of oral tradition, archaeological excavations, and historical documents authored by visiting Portuguese missionaries and conquerors. While the Shona and Kalanga peoples of this area organized many states, the main powers on the Zimbabwe Plateau were Torwa in the southwest from the late 1400s to 1680s, Mutapa in the northeast during the 1500s and 1600s, and Rozvi in the 1700s and early 1800s.

While oral tradition claims that an expedition sent north from Great Zimbabwe in search of rock salt founded the **Mutapa kingdom**, it appears likely that the latter state had separate origins. Located in the Mazowe Valley on the northeastern part of the Zimbabwe Plateau, the Mutapa kingdom emerged around the 1400s, with a Shona royal dynasty using economic relations, marriage alliances, and warfare to gain ascendency over the decentralized Tarava/Tonga communities of that area. The term "Mutapa," originating in the Shona phrase "Mwenemutapa" or "prince of Mutapa" and revised as "Monomutapa" by the Portuguese, became a title for the kingdom's ruler and the name of the state itself. According to tradition, the first ruler of Mutapa was Mutota. As the state expanded, the Mutapa ruler gained power by distributing land and claiming divine right of rule. Like Great Zimbabwe, the Mutapa kingdom engaged in trade with Swahili and Arabs on the Indian Ocean coast to the east by exporting gold and ivory in exchange for Asian goods. However, the Manyika kingdom, another Shona state, located in the highlands to its immediate east, mediated Mutapa's direct access to the coast.

At the end of the 1400s and beginning of the 1500s, the Mutapa kingdom experienced a series of civil wars and rebellions that likely led to a faction moving southwest to establish the Torwa kingdom based at Khami, where stone walls were constructed. These conflicts also weakened Mutapa just as European colonizers arrived in the area. During the 1500s, Portuguese mariners took over the Indian Ocean trade and either dominated or conquered trading centers on the East African coast. In the 1530s, the Portuguese pressed inland along the Zambezi Valley, seizing the Swahili trading posts of Sena and Tete, and they became determined to access the gold resources of nearby Mutapa on the south side of the Zambezi River. After a failed attempt to convert the Mutapa ruler to Christianity, a Portuguese expedition invaded the kingdom in the early 1570s, but it failed because of tropical disease, lack of food and water, and local resistance. Although Mutapa tried to placate the Portuguese by granting them some marginal gold mines, the Portuguese invaded neighboring Manyika in the mid-1570s, but they once again failed to secure profitable resources.

The Portuguese eventually gained greater access to Mutapa. In the late 1590s, the Mutapa ruler Gatsi Rusere employed Portuguese military allies against raiders from the Maravi Empire located on the north side of the Zambezi River. Subsequently, Portuguese gunmen played a key role in securing Gatsi Rusere's victory in a Mutapa civil war during the first decade of the 1600s, and, as a result, the ruler expanded their access to gold mines and land in the kingdom. During the 1620s, following the death of Gatsi Rusere, another Mutapa civil war broke out in which the Portuguese intervened to install the Christian convert Mavhura as the new ruler. Signing a treaty that made Mutapa a vassal of Portugal, Mavhura granted the Portuguese control over the kingdom's gold mines and exemption from local laws, and he expelled Muslim traders who competed with the Portuguese. As a result, Portuguese settlers seized land inside and outside Mutapa, built forts, raised their own local armies, and enslaved people to work their mines and plantations. Although Mutapa traditionalists led by Kapararidze staged a rebellion in the early 1630s that drove the Portuguese back to Sena and Tete on the Zambezi River, Portuguese reinforcements from the coast counterattacked, reinstalling the Christian ruler Mavhura in Mutapa as well as subjugating the Manyika kingdom. During the rest of the 1600s, Mutapa continued as a Portuguese puppet state as Portuguese settlements called **prazos** expanded on the south side of the Zambezi River.

The decline of Portuguese-dominated Mutapa as a regional power, along with a corresponding increase in violence in the area during the late 1600s, prompted local Shona leaders to mobilize their own armies by offering cattle to young men in exchange for military service. During the 1670s, one of these leaders, called Dombo, earned the Shona title Changamire (lord) by using his army called the Rozvi (destroyers) to expand his control of the northeast Zimbabwe Plateau. In the early 1680s, the Rozvi expanded southwest to conquer the Torwa kingdom, where they made the center their capital and absorbed many of the locality's Kalanga-speaking people. As several resurgent Mutapa leaders staged rebellions against the Portuguese in the 1670s and 1680s, Dombo turned to the northeast. During the mid-1680s and 1690s, he led a series of military campaigns that expelled the Portuguese from both Mutapa and Manyika. Although Dombo's death in 1696 delayed the Rozvi war against the Portuguese, the continued Rozvi threat and civil war in Mutapa prompted most Portuguese settlers to abandon the Zimbabwe Plateau and move down into the Zambezi Valley. In the eighteenth century, as Mutapa continued to suffer internal strife, the **Rozvi Empire** under the descendants of Dombo, all called by the title Changamire, expanded across the Zimbabwe Plateau creating a large federation of tributary states. Around this time, a Rozvi section moved south of the Limpopo River, into what is now northern South Africa, and founded the Singo state among the Venda people. Mindful of the fate of Mutapa, the Rozvi Empire banned the Portuguese from entering its territory but continued to trade with them at Sena and Tete in order to access the Indian Ocean economy. As a result, lack of Portuguese written sources about Rozvi means that less is known about the internal dynamics of this eighteenth-century Zimbabwean empire than about the earlier history of Mutapa. The Rozvi Empire represented the main power on the Zimbabwe Plateau, and the largest polity known to have existed there, until the early to mid-nineteenth century.

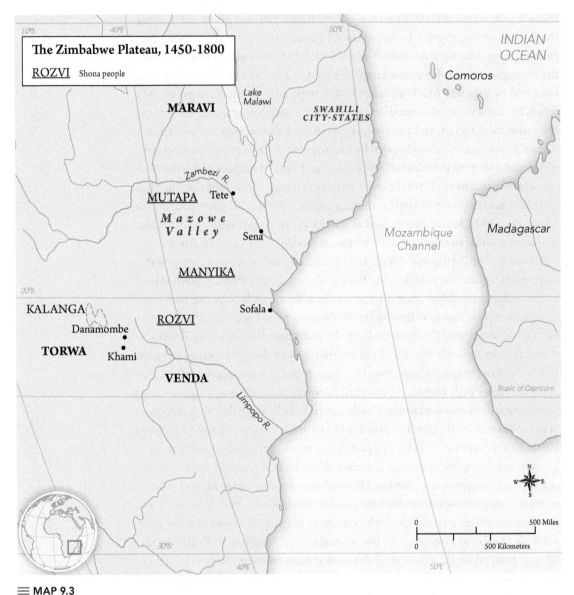

The Zimbabwe Plateau, 1450-1800

ROZVI Shona people

≡ MAP 9.3

South of the Limpopo River

It is difficult to reconstruct the history of societies that inhabited what is now South Africa, Botswana, southern Mozambique, eSwatini (Swaziland), and Lesotho before the eighteenth century. Early Iron Age farmers and herders tended to avoid the **Highveld**, a high-altitude plateau and grassland in the middle of South Africa, as the area's soil was not conducive to their cultivation techniques. Since the

Highveld offered good grazing land, the expansion of cattle raising by Later Iron Age societies prompted them to move onto the northern Highveld in the 1100s and then the southern Highveld during the 1400s. In this area, the ancestors of today's Tswana and Sotho people built homesteads from stone because of the lack of trees and lived in a relatively small number of large, densely populated towns that grew around the Highveld's few reliable water sources. Highveld communities engaged in herding, farming, and hunting, and did not smelt iron but acquired it from communities to the east in exchange for cattle. Simultaneously, hierarchies emerged centered on the control and distribution of cattle. Among the Tswana-speaking people living on the eastern fringe of the Kalahari Desert, large kingdoms developed, such as the Hurutshe and Kwena in the 1600s and the Ngwaketse and Ngwato in the 1700s. At the start of the nineteenth century, the capital town of the Tlhaping consisted of over 10,000 inhabitants, making it the same size as colonial Cape Town. By the late 1700s, the Tswana states engaged in long-distance trade, exporting cattle to the Portuguese at Delagoa Bay to the east and the Dutch Cape Colony to the south.

Between the Drakensberg Mountains and the Indian Ocean coast, numerous small rivers supported a somewhat evenly distributed Later Iron Age population living in a network of many small settlements. A few written accounts by European sailors shipwrecked along what is now the coast of southern Mozambique and eastern South Africa during the 1500s and 1600s reveal the existence of complex centralized states in the area. During the 1700s, the expansion of international trade at Delagoa Bay stimulated state formation among Later Iron Age communities located in present-day southern Mozambique, northeastern South Africa, and eSwatini (Swaziland). While Portuguese seagoing traders had been active in the bay from the 1600s, the availability of foreign goods increased as European and South Asia merchants began acquiring increasing amounts of ivory from Delagoa Bay during the 1760s and American whalers began obtaining cattle there in the 1790s. Among African societies in the bay hinterland, competition over this amplified trade led to more conflict, territorial expansion, and political centralization. This gave rise to the Pedi kingdom some 180 miles to the northwest and the Maputo kingdom just south of Delagoa Bay. Further to the south, among speakers of Nguni languages, these dynamics contributed to the emergence of the Ndwandwe, Mthethwa, Hlubi, Qwabe, and Ngwane kingdoms. Later, warfare among these states formed the context for the creation of the Zulu kingdom in the early nineteenth century. Even further to the south, in what is now the Eastern Cape Province of South Africa, Nguni-speakers formed the **Xhosa kingdom** in the 1600s, and this entity split into the Gcaleka and Rharhabe states, which expanded west in the 1700s. Throughout Southern Africa, small communities of decentralized specialist hunters and gatherers, usually speaking Khoisan languages, lived on the margins of Later Iron Age societies of Bantu speakers like the Tswana, Sotho, and Nguni, providing them with game meat and wildlife products. Over time, the larger Bantu-speaking groups absorbed some of the Khoisan, resulting in the incorporation of distinctive Khoisan click sounds into the Nguni and Sotho languages.

In the Western Cape, Khoisan communities remained somewhat isolated from the rest of the region because of their area's different climate and the obstacle represented by the Great Karoo Desert. As such, Khoisan groups survived through raising livestock as well as hunting and gathering, and did not develop metallurgy, agriculture, or the large centralized states that appeared elsewhere in the region. Of all the peoples of Southern Africa, they were some of the first to experience European colonial conquest and the least prepared to resist it.

European Colonization in the Cape

After 1500, the Cape Peninsula became an important point for Portuguese and eventually other European ships to stop over on their voyages around the southern tip of Africa, traveling between the Atlantic and Indian oceans. European sailors visiting the Cape sought supplies such as fresh water and meat. However, while the indigenous Khoisan groups traded with the newcomers who brought precious iron knives and tools, the former became hesitant to part with large numbers of the livestock on which their survival depended. In addition, as pastoralists and hunter-gatherers, the Khoisan did not grow crops that they could trade with European seafarers. All this meant that it was difficult for European ships to acquire supplies at the Cape, and at times violence broke out between visiting sailors and local Khoisan. Consequently, in 1652, as the Dutch challenged the Portuguese in Angola and Brazil, **the Dutch East India Company** established a permanent post on the Cape Peninsula, under the command of Jan Van Riebeeck, to engage in sustained trade with the Khoisan in the hope of providing a sustainable source of supplies for visiting Dutch ships. However, the same problems continued, with the Khoisan unable to offer the Dutch the amount of livestock they demanded. This prompted the Dutch, in the late 1650s, to found a settlement of former company employees who raised livestock and grew crops to resupply ships. The original Dutch outpost eventually became the port of Cape Town and the center of an expanding Dutch **Cape Colony**, where lack of tropical disease such as malaria facilitated European settlement.

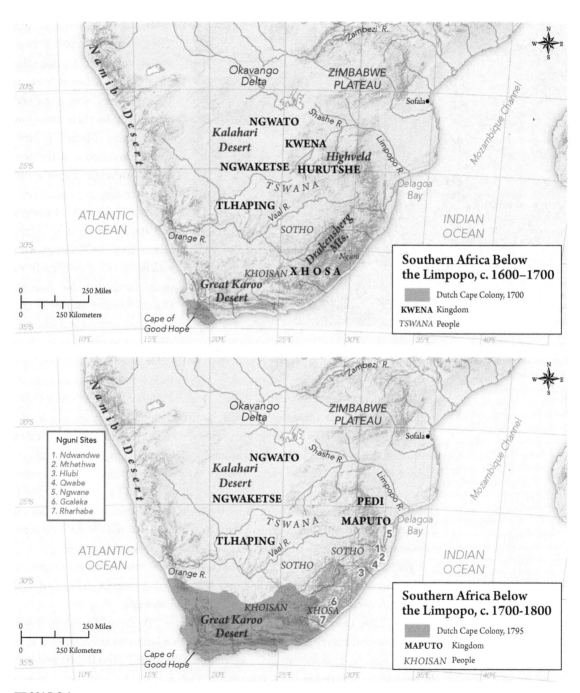

Southern Africa Below the Limpopo, c. 1600–1700

Dutch Cape Colony, 1700

KWENA Kingdom

TSWANA People

Southern Africa Below the Limpopo, c. 1700–1800

Dutch Cape Colony, 1795

MAPUTO Kingdom

KHOISAN People

Nguni Sites
1. Ndwandwe
2. Mthethwa
3. Hlubi
4. Qwabe
5. Ngwane
6. Gcaleka
7. Rharhabe

☰ **MAP 9.4**

≡ **Encounter of different cultures.** This nineteenth-century painting shows a romantic depiction of the first encounter between Jan van Riebeeck and the Khoisan in 1652.

The Dutch settlers and Khoisan quickly clashed over access to land. During the First Dutch–Khoisan War of 1659–60, the Khoisan trapped the Dutch in their fort, but the Khoisan alliance eventually deteriorated and the war ended through negotiation. Subsequently, the Dutch constructed a network of hedges and fences to separate themselves from the Khoisan, who suffered gradual eviction from their land. In the Second Dutch–Khoisan War of 1673–77, Dutch settlers and Khoisan allies seized cattle from other Khoisan communities and defeated the prominent Cochoqua Khoisan group in the Saldanha Bay and Boland regions of the Western Cape. In the late 1600s, the Cape's embryonic European settler society grew with the arrival of French Protestants called Huguenots, who fled religious persecution in Europe and mixed with the Dutch. During the eighteenth century, European settlement expanded north and east. As they ventured beyond the farms and vineyards of the Cape Peninsula, and the authority of the Dutch East India Company, Dutch settlers known as **Trekboers** adopted the pastoral economy of the Khoisan and clung to a form of Calvinist Protestant Christianity that reinforced their separate identity. The term Trekboer originated in the Dutch words for pulling (Trek) a wagon and farmer (Boer). Lacking a standing army, the Trekboers organized temporary military formations called "commandos" that formed, disbanded, and reformed as necessary and included armed Khoisan servants.

In the 1730s, Dutch settlers advanced north of the Piketberg Mountains, inciting stiff Khoisan guerrilla resistance in that area that lasted for the rest of the century. The eastward movement of Dutch settlers across the Karoo Desert and into the grazing land between the Gamtoos and Fish rivers led to violence between them and Khoisan communities from the 1770s to 1790s. At the same time, in the northeastern Cape, particularly the Sneeuwberg region, there was almost continuous warfare between incoming European settlers and local Khoisan. Europeans frequently saw the Khoisan as subhuman, with several Khoisan captives shipped to Europe, where they were exhibited as circus freaks. These included a Khoisan woman called **Sarah Baartman**, whose genitals and prominent buttocks attracted public attention at shows in Britain and France in the early 1800s, and whose bones and body cast were on display in a Paris museum until the 1970s.

Several interrelated factors facilitated Dutch success in conflicts with the Khoisan. Technologically, the Khoisan did not produce iron weapons, and the Dutch quickly banned the trade of iron and firearms with them. Dutch guns and horses gave them advantages in firepower and mobility. While the Khoisan acquired some firearms and developed hit-and-run tactics to counter colonial firepower, they could never match the military power of the Cape. Politically, the Dutch exploited the small scale of Khoisan organization, playing rival groups off against one another and enlisting the help of Khoisan allies in wars against other Khoisan. Importantly, the Khoisan population declined partly because of the impact of imported European diseases for which they had limited immunity, like smallpox, which became an epidemic in 1713. Furthermore, Dutch policies of extermination blocked Khoisan access to water sources, and a bounty on dead Khoisan encouraged settlers to kill them indiscriminately. Due to European settler expansion, many Khoisan fled the Cape, going north to found new trans-frontier communities such as the **Griqua**, which became a major force in the late 1700s and early 1800s, and east, where they often amalgamated with the larger Xhosa society.

A colonial society developed in the Cape Colony. Cape Town became a prominent port surrounded by settler plantations, producing wine, fruit, and grain, and further inland frontier settlers focused on raising livestock. Beginning in 1654 and continuing throughout the 1700s,

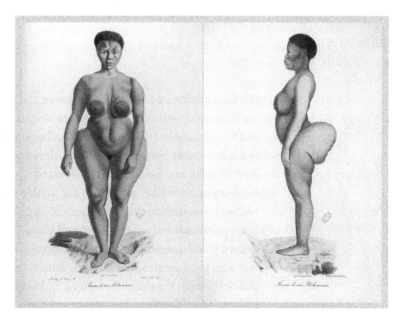

☰ **Saartjie (or Sarah) Baartman** was a Khoisan woman from the Cape put on display in Europe in the early nineteenth century.

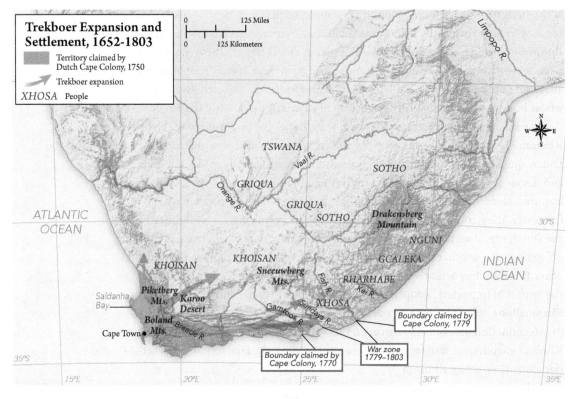

Trekboer Expansion and Settlement, 1652-1803

■ Territory claimed by Dutch Cape Colony, 1750

→ Trekboer expansion

XHOSA   People

≡ MAP 9.5

the Dutch bolstered their labor force in the Cape by importing enslaved people from other parts of Africa, such as Mozambique and Madagascar, and South and Southeast Asia. During the 1750s, the population of Cape Town consisted of about 5,000 free people and 6,000 enslaved people. As Dutch colonial frontiers pushed north and east, many dispossessed Khoisan became indentured servants working in slave-like conditions for settler farmers. Gradually, most distinct Khoisan communities and languages disappeared in the Cape as the Khoisan became absorbed into a larger creolized **Cape Coloured** identity that adopted localized Dutch language and Dutch colonial culture. With diverse African, Asian, and European origins, the Cape Coloured community occupied a subordinate position within the racially stratified and white-ruled society of the Dutch Cape Colony. Most people within the broad Cape Coloured identity became Christians, but one segment, called the Cape Malay, who were descended from Southeast Asian enslaved people and exiles sent to Cape Town by the Dutch, retained their Muslim faith.

In the late 1700s, eastward-moving Trekboers entered the grassland between the Sundays and Fish Rivers, the **Zuurveld (sour grass)**, where they encountered the more numerous Xhosa people for the first time. Expanding westward, the agricultural, pastoral, and iron-using Xhosa were already absorbing smaller Khoisan communities living on the Zuurveld and presented a much tougher obstacle to colonial expansion. Although the Trekboers and Xhosa conducted trade, they fought each other over land and livestock. During the First Cape–Xhosa War of 1779–81, the Trekboers expelled Xhosa groups east of the Fish River and Cape governor Baron Van Plettenberg declared this the eastern border of the colony. Nevertheless, with the disbanding of the Trekboer commandos after the war, many Xhosa returned to their lands on the west side of the unguarded Fish River frontier. In 1793, during the Second Cape–Xhosa War, the

≡ **Frontier life.** A nineteenth-century depiction of a Trekboer, a group of Khoisan, and an ox-wagon.

Trekboers attempted to exploit divisions among the Xhosa states by allying with the Rharhabe Xhosa on the east side of the Fish against other Xhosa groups west of the Fish. However, this Cape–Rharhabe alliance broke down, inciting a major but ultimately inconclusive conflict between the Trekboers and western Xhosa over the Zuurveld. Over the next few years, a civil war within the Rharhabe kingdom resulted in more Xhosa moving west of the Fish, confining the Trekboers to the western part of the Zuurveld along the Sundays River.

In 1795, the British seized the Cape Colony to prevent Revolutionary France, which had occupied the Netherlands base of the Dutch East India Company, from using the southern tip of Africa as a naval base to block their shipping to and from India. Attempting to stabilize the eastern frontier of their new colony, the British, in 1799, sent a military expedition to the Zuurveld, where it tried but failed to expel the Xhosa east of the Fish River. At the same time, Khoisan indentured servants rebelled against their abusive Trekboer masters and joined with Xhosa groups in the Zuurveld. Although British governor Francis Dundas negotiated peace whereby the Khoisan returned to work and the Xhosa gained permission to live west of the Fish, violence flared again when Trekboers attacked the Xhosa and objected to the Khoisan attending Christian missionary schools and churches. In 1802, the Khoisan and Xhosa launched an intensive westward offensive that drove the Trekboers off the Zuurveld just as the British, because of a lull in tensions with France, withdrew from the Cape Colony in early 1803. Lacking military power, the new Cape administration of the Dutch Batavian Republic ended this Third Cape–Xhosa War (1799–1803) through negotiation granting the Khoisan rebels land and allowing the Xhosa to remain west of the Fish as Trekboers slowly returned to the Zuurveld. These late-eighteenth and very-early-nineteenth-century conflicts in the Eastern Cape ended in stalemate as the Trekboers possessed horses and guns but the Xhosa enjoyed the advantage of numbers. In addition, both sides could not fight protracted wars as they lacked standing armies, and therefore Trekboer and Xhosa combatants had to return home to attend livestock and agriculture.

Conclusion

It is difficult to reconstruct the history of most of Southern Africa before c. 1700. Archaeological evidence reveals that the region's Iron Age societies underwent significant change beginning around the 1000s, with the expansion of cattle raising, movement into new areas such as the Highveld, increased trade to the Indian Ocean coast, greater socioeconomic stratification, and the expansion of

Timeline

c. 200 CE—Beginning of Early Iron Age in Southern Africa

c. 600s—Start of settlement at Toutsewemogala Hill

c. 900s—Start of Leopard's Kopje culture

c. 1000 CE—Beginning of Later Iron Age in Southern Africa

c. 1000s—1200s—Occupation of Mapungubwe Hill

c. 1100s—Later Iron Age herders and farmers move onto the Highveld

c. 1200–1450—Rise and decline of Great Zimbabwe

c. 1250—Origins of Thulamela settlement

1530s—Portuguese enter the Zambezi Valley

1570s—Portuguese invasion of Mutapa kingdom fails

1600s—Rise of the Tswana kingdoms of Hurutshe and Kwena, and the Xhosa kingdoms in the Eastern Cape

1620s—Portuguese gain control of the Mutapa kingdom

1652—Dutch East India Company establishes Cape Colony

1654—Dutch bring first enslaved people to the Cape

1659–60—First Dutch–Khoisan War in the Cape

1673–77—Second Dutch–Khoisan War in the Cape

1670s–80s—Rise of the Rozvi Empire on the Zimbabwe Plateau

1713—Smallpox epidemic among Khoisan in the Cape

1700s—Rise of the Tswana kingdoms of Ngwaketse and Ngwato; expansion of the Xhosa kingdoms in the Eastern Cape; Dutch conquest of Khoisan in the Western Cape

1760s; start of increased oceanic trade at Delagoa Bay and state formation among Nguni-speaking people

1760s—Dutch settlers encounter Xhosa people

1779–81—First Cape–Xhosa War

1793—Second Cape–Xhosa War

1795—British occupy the Cape Colony

1799–1803—Third Cape–Xhosa War

1803—British give back the Cape Colony to the Dutch

centralized states. With information derived from archaeology, oral tradition, and a few documents authored by visiting outsiders, it is clear that kingdoms of various sizes existed in much of the region during the 1500s and 1600s. By 1800, Southern African states included the large Rozvi Empire on the Zimbabwe Plateau, Tswana kingdoms centered on great towns on the Highveld, and a series of Nguni polities (the forbearers of today's Swazi, Zulu, and Xhosa people) between the Drakensberg Mountains and the Indian Ocean coast. The historical record is much clearer for the parts of Southern Africa where early European colonization took place as the colonizers produced documentary records. During the late 1500s and 1600s, Portuguese from the East Coast moved inland along the Zambesi River, subjugated the Mutapa and Manyika kingdoms, and were eventually expelled from the Zimbabwe Plateau by the rising Rozvi Empire. From the 1650s and throughout the 1700s, Dutch colonization at the Cape proved more successful because of the absence of tropical disease in the area and weak resistance by the Khoisan, who lacked iron and large state structures. However, Dutch expansion stopped in the late 1700s when the settlers encountered the more populous and well-organized Iron Age Xhosa people of the Eastern Cape. Throughout Southern Africa, as a result of the expansion of Dutch settlement at the Cape and kingdoms of Bantu speakers elsewhere, many Khoisan groups disappeared or retreated into marginal lands like the Kalahari Desert.

KEY TERMS

bride price 181

Cape Colony 190

Cape Coloured 194

Dutch East India Company 190

Early Iron Age 180

Great Zimbabwe 182

Griqua 193

Highveld 188

Khoisan 179

Later Iron Age 181

Leopard's Kopje 181

Mapungubwe 181

Mutapa kingdom 186

prazos 187

Rozvi Empire 187

Sarah Baartman 193

Toutswemogala Hill 181

Trekboers 192

Xhosa kingdom 189

Zuurveld 195

STUDY QUESTIONS

1. What are the most important themes in Southern African history up to c. 1800? What were the main changes that had occurred in Southern African society by 1000 CE? What is the archaeological evidence for the early Limpopo River populations?

2. What are the main questions in the debates concerning Great Zimbabwe? What were the main factors behind the expansion of the Mutapa kingdom? What type of interactions did the kingdom have with the Portuguese?

3. What were the benefits and drawbacks of living on the Highveld? What were the main features of the societies that flourished south of the Limpopo River?

4. What were the motives for the Dutch settlement of Cape Town? Why did the Dutch settlers clash with Khoisan communities? How did the Dutch control the Khoisan? Who were the Cape Coloureds? The Trekboerrs? What impact did imperial rivalries between the British and French have on South Africa?

Please see page FR-4 for the Further Readings for this chapter. For additional digital learning resources please go to https://www.oup.com/he/falola-stapleton1e

10

North Africa, c. 1800–1880: Modernization and Colonialism

By the 1700s, what had begun several centuries earlier as a power struggle between Europe and Ottoman Turkey for dominance in the Mediterranean had turned into a pattern whereby North African–based pirates of transcultural origin preyed on European and American merchant vessels. This provided the context, and sometimes the pretext, for European and US intervention in North Africa in the early 1800s. At this time, industrializing northwestern Europe, and to some extent the United States, were seeking sources of raw materials to feed their factories and overseas markets for their mass produced exports. As a result, they began to intervene in other parts of the world, building global empires. Seeing their region left behind in this process and recognizing its vulnerability to Western domination, North African leaders attempted to modernize their economies, states, and militaries during the nineteenth century. However, these Westernization programs generally failed, partly because of foreign interference, and resulted in North African governments incurring huge debts to European powers, inviting further foreign intervention in the region. During the early and mid-1800s, France conquered Algeria, France and Spain bullied Morocco, the troubled Ottoman Empire reintegrated Libya, and Tunisia and Egypt surrendered their economic independence to European officials.

Egypt

At the end of the eighteenth century, Egypt became susceptible to invasion as it suffered famine, plague, and Mamluk rebellions against the Ottomans. While an Ottoman fleet and army arrived in 1786 and subjugated the Mamluks, the Turks were distracted by war with Russia, thus allowing the Mamluks to regain power at the start of the 1790s. Egypt then became the scene for struggles between Britain and Revolutionary France.

Napoleon in Egypt.
The French general contemplates the mysteries of the Sphinx in this late nineteenth century orientalist painting.

Napoleon Bonaparte, a popular French general, convinced his superiors that a military occupation of Egypt would undermine Britain by cutting off its commercial contact with India. The French regime seemed oblivious to the possibility that this would result in war with the Ottoman Empire. In July 1798, a French fleet slipped past the British navy in the Mediterranean and landed 36,000 French troops near Alexandria. Occupying the city, Napoleon issued a statement declaring his support for Islam and criticizing the ruling Mamluks. In late July, Napoleon's army defeated a Mamluk force at the **Battle of the Pyramids** and then seized Cairo. However, the British navy discovered and annihilated the French fleet just off the Egyptian coast, which stranded Napoleon's expeditionary force. In 1799, Napoleon, fancying himself a latter-day Alexander the Great, led his troops into Syria to oppose an Ottoman army that was approaching Egypt, and then the French returned to the Egyptian coast, where they defeated another Ottoman force that had landed by sea. Napoleon planned to make Egypt and the Middle East a French colony and to dig a canal at Suez that would link the Mediterranean and Red Sea. After Napoleon returned to France in August 1799, the French expeditionary force fought on against the Ottomans, British, and Egyptians but surrendered in August 1801. Although Napoleon's military adventure in Egypt failed, it provided European powers with a demonstration of the Ottoman Empire's weakness and inspired subsequent European imperialism in North Africa. It also partly stimulated what modern scholars have called **orientalism**, whereby Europeans began to see North Africa and the Middle East as home to exotic though inferior societies in need of Western civilization.

≡ **The Battle of the Pyramids.** Painted 10 years after the great battle, this painting shows French forces on the right holding their ground against Mamluk cavalry charges.

The Ottoman army that reoccupied Egypt in 1801 included the Macedonian-born **Muhammed Ali**, who led a military unit from Albania. In 1805, after he directed a siege that overcame the Mamluk stronghold of Minya, Ali gained appointment as Ottoman viceroy of Egypt. Ali also led Egyptian resistance to an 1807 British military intervention that aimed to reinstall the Mamluks, and he subdued an 1810 Mamluk rebellion. To eliminate the Mamluk threat, he invited Mamluk leaders to a celebration in Cairo but then had all of them killed. In addition, Ali confiscated the lands of Muslim scholars, who lost their economic power and became subordinate to the state. Initiating reforms aimed at turning Egypt into a modern state with a professional civil service, Ali ended the system in which Mamluk leaders raised and commanded military contingents in return for landed estates where they taxed peasants. With the estates taken over by the central government, peasants paid taxes to the Egyptian state and became subject to conscription for the army. In addition, all goods had to be initially sold to the state, which resold them for profit. The revenues accrued from these activities supported the expansion of a central government with specific departments, and stimulated the manufacturing of textiles and ammunition, though lack of natural resources thwarted Egyptian plans to industrialize. Since Ali recognized that Western European technology was surging ahead of the Muslim world, he expanded Western-style education through the establishment of new technical schools, the translation of European books into Arabic, and the founding of a printing press, and he sent Egyptians to study in Europe. Rifa'a al-Tahtawi, a student at Cairo's Al-Azhar University, studied in Paris from 1826 to 1831 and returned home, where he founded a language school, supervised the translation of 2,000 books into Arabic, and wrote his own works that introduced Egyptians to the concept of citizenship, encouraging them to accept modernization and remain united. Although Ali's reforms challenged traditional Muslim gender segregation in Egypt as some women became involved in the new schools and hospitals, the growing industrial textile production focused on male labor and displaced female craft workers.

The new Egyptian regime became involved in numerous military campaigns. During the 1810s, Ali orchestrated the construction of an Egyptian navy that ferried troops across the Red Sea to Arabia, where they joined Ottoman campaigns against the rebel Saud clan that had recently converted to a Muslim fundamentalist movement called **Wahhabism**. In 1820–21, Ali launched an Egyptian invasion of Sudan to secure gold to pay for his continued reforms and to acquire enslaved Sudanese soldiers who would be loyal to him. After using firearms and artillery to defeat the cavalry of the Sudanese Arabs, the Egyptian army established the city of Khartoum as a new administrative center at the confluence of the Blue and White Nile rivers. The Egyptian military also occupied Sennar, the capital of the

≡ **Egyptian Modernizers** *Left:* Ruling Egypt from 1805 to 1848, Mohammed Ali initiated a series of important government and military reforms, making the country autonomous from the Ottoman Empire. *Right:* Egyptian scholar Rifa'a al-Tahtawi (1801–1873) studied in Paris and returned to Cairo, where he founded a language school and supervised the translation of over 2,000 books into Arabic.

failing Funj kingdom, and turned west to defeat the kingdom of Darfur. While the Egyptians were disappointed with the lack of gold available in Sudan, they directed expeditions southward to obtain ivory and captives for enslavement, prompting tenacious resistance by the Shilluk and Dinka peoples. Nevertheless, Ali's development of a large army of enslaved soldiers was hampered by the fact that Egypt's Sudanese troops had to remain in Sudan to secure Egyptian control there. As such, Ali embarked on the creation of a new army composed of Egyptian peasant conscripts, who were paid and fed by the state and led by Mamluk officers who attended new military schools with European instructors.

Although Ali sent Egyptian troops to support failed Ottoman attempts to suppress rebellion in Greece during the 1820s, he launched an invasion of Syria during the 1830s that wrested control of the area from Constantinople. In addition, Egyptian military expeditions in Yemen and the Arabian coast of the Persian Gulf prompted the British to seize Aden in 1839 to protect their oceanic trade with

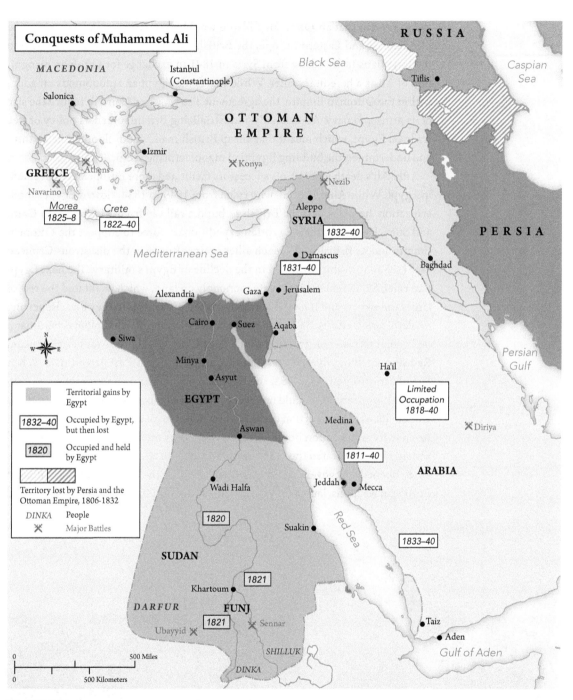

Conquests of Muhammed Ali

MACEDONIA

Istanbul
(Constantinople)

Black Sea

RUSSIA

Caspian Sea

Tiflis

Salonica

OTTOMAN
EMPIRE

Izmir

✖ Konya

✖ Nezib

Aleppo

SYRIA

1832–40

PERSIA

GREECE

✖ Athens

Navarino

Morea
1825–8

Crete
1822–40

Mediterranean Sea

Damascus

1831–40

Baghdad

Alexandria

Gaza ● Jerusalem

Cairo ● Suez

Aqaba

Siwa

Ha'il

Persian Gulf

Minya

Asyut

EGYPT

Medina

Limited Occupation
1818–40

✖ Diriya

Aswan

1811–40

ARABIA

Wadi Halfa

Jeddah ● Mecca

	Territorial gains by Egypt
1832–40	Occupied by Egypt, but then lost
1820	Occupied and held by Egypt

Territory lost by Persia and the
Ottoman Empire, 1806-1832

DINKA   People

✖   Major Battles

Suakin

Red Sea

1833–40

SUDAN

1820

DARFUR

Khartoum

1821

FUNJ

1821

Ubayyid ✖

✖ Sennar

SHILLUK

DINKA

Taiz

Aden

Gulf of Aden

0   500 Miles

0   500 Kilometers

≡ **MAP 10.1**

India. Fearful that an Ottoman collapse would allow Russia to advance into the Middle East and Eastern Europe, the British with their powerful navy pressured the Egyptians to withdraw from Syria in 1841 in exchange for Ottoman recognition of Ali as a hereditary ruler. While this made Egypt an autonomous kingdom within the Ottoman Empire, the agreement also required Cairo to reduce the size of its army and navy. Additionally, industrializing Britain forced its policy of free trade on Egypt, which meant that cheap British-made goods flooded the country and undermined the budding Egyptian manufacturing sector.

After Ali's death in 1849, his successors facilitated more European involvement in Egypt. While Abbas Hilmi, who ruled from 1849 to 1854, slowed Egypt's modernization, he permitted the British to build a railway from Alexandria to Cairo and Suez. He also sent an Egyptian expeditionary force to support the Ottoman Empire and its British and French allies against Russia in the disastrous Crimean War (1853–56), which resulted in the decline of Egypt's military. The next Egyptian ruler, Sa'id, removed the state monopoly on land, which facilitated the rise of large landowners and the rush of impoverished peasants into the cities. Renewing modernization efforts, Sa'id also gave a concession to French diplomat Ferdinand de Lesseps to plan construction of the Suez Canal to join the Mediterranean and Red seas, enabling ships to travel more quickly between Europe and Asia. When Ismail came to power in 1863, the Egyptian economy was booming from cotton sales to Europeans who could not access their traditional suppliers in the southern United States because of that country's civil war. Ismail used the extra government revenue from the cotton boom to speed up Egypt's modernization and Westernization. He orchestrated the building of railways and telegraphs, improved Egypt's cities, opened new government departments, rebuilt the Egyptian military, bought European weapons, launched military adventures in Crete and along Africa's Red

≡ **The Suze Canal** *Left:* The grand opening of the Suez Canal in 1869. *Right:* Boat traffic on the canal in 1890.

Sea coast, and financed the digging of the **Suez Canal**, which opened in 1869 amid grand celebrations. However, the end of the American Civil War in 1865 also meant the end of Egypt's economic prosperity, and Ismail's projects resulted in overspending and debts to European countries. In 1875, with the canal turning Egypt into a much more strategically important country, the indebted Ismail sold his shares in the Suez Canal Company to the British government. As the major shareholders in the canal, Britain and France subsequently imposed "dual control" over Egypt's mismanaged state finances, which undermined Egypt's autonomy and set the stage for future European intervention.

Algeria

At the start of the nineteenth century, Algeria comprised a military republic under a ruler called the "dey," who acknowledged nominal Ottoman supremacy (see Chapter 5). While Algerian piracy declined in the late 1700s, and the Spanish withdrew from their Oran enclave in 1792, the preoccupation of European powers with the Napoleonic Wars in the early 1800s prompted an increase in piracy based out of Algiers. In 1815, in response to Algerian piracy against American merchant vessels in the Mediterranean, a United States naval squadron was dispatched to Algiers, forcing Dey Omar bin Muhammad to pay compensation and grant American ships free passage. The next year, in the Second Barbary War, British and Dutch warships bombarded Algiers, compelling the dey to outlaw the taking and ransoming of Christian captives. After the Napoleonic Wars, the European powers remained at peace with each other and therefore concentrated on using their navies to suppress North African piracy. In turn, the deys of Algiers attempted to make up for the loss of their piracy income by increasing local taxes, but this stimulated rebellions, often led by Muslim Sufi brotherhoods. This made Algeria vulnerable to foreign invasion. In the 1820s, a dispute developed between Paris and Algiers over the former's failure to pay Algerian Jewish merchants for grain shipments to France during the French Revolution. At the time, France's conservative King Charles X was looking for a military adventure to politically weaken his liberal critics, and French merchants wished greater access to the Algerian market. In July 1830, the French navy bombarded Algiers and landed a large army that defeated the dey's Ottoman-Algerian force and occupied the city. Although Charles X abdicated later the same month when the liberals won elections in France, the new government decided to maintain control of Algiers to suppress piracy and slavery. Algeria was transferred from Ottoman to French authority.

While the French initially exercised limited occupation of Algeria, controlling the main towns but leaving other parts of the country to local rulers, this policy changed with the ambitions of French settlers and Algerian resistance. In 1837, French forces seized the city of Constantine, where a quasi-autonomous Ottoman ruler had become a symbol of Muslim defiance. West of Algiers, Muslim scholar Abd al-Qadir rallied an Algerian army with the assistance of neighboring Morocco and waged a war against French occupation that prompted Paris to impose full control. During the 1840s, the French army under Marshal Thomas-Robert Bugeaud pursued a vicious war against Abd al-Qadir's resistance fighters, burning villages, destroying crops, cutting down fruit trees, looting markets, and sometimes burning Algerians who were hiding in caves. Embroiled in a conflict with the sultan of Morocco, Abd al-Qadir surrendered to the French in 1847 and was imprisoned in France but later released to live in exile in Syria. By 1847, the population of French settlers in Algeria numbered 109,000 and they clashed with the local French military administration as they wanted more land and political rights. As a result of the 1848 French Revolution, Algeria was placed under a dual administration in which French settlers enjoyed the rights of French citizens, and they elected representatives to the civilian government in Paris, which effectively made Algeria part of France, while Algerian Muslims became colonial subjects under military rule.

The loss of Muslim land to settlers and the co-opting of Muslim leaders by the French colonial state prompted a number of Muslim rebellions in Algeria from the 1840s to 1870s that were brutally suppressed. Although Emperor Louis Napoleon III took steps to liberalize the colonial system in Algeria in the 1860s, his regime ended with France's defeat by Prussia in 1870–71, and the new French republic renewed the exploitative colonial state. Under French settlers, the Algerian economy shifted to viticulture at the expense of food production, causing hunger and resentment among Algerian Muslims, who were religiously prohibited from drinking alcohol. French Catholic missionaries arrived and founded hospitals, schools, and orphanages, but their attempts to convert Muslim Algerians largely failed. At the same time, many Algerians and French settlers were recruited by the French as soldiers, participating in all France's major military campaigns including the Crimean War (1853–56), the Franco-Austrian War (1859), the French intervention in Mexico (1861–67), the Franco-Prussian War (1870–71), and many later conflicts.

Tunisia

In the late eighteenth and early nineteenth centuries, the quasi-autonomous ruler of Tunisia, Hammuda Bey, used the threat of piracy to extract payments from European powers wishing to protect their merchant ships in the Mediterranean. Economic disagreements caused the neighboring Ottoman regencies of Tunisia and Algeria to fight each other during the first decade of the nineteenth century.

≡ **The French Invasion of Algeria** *Left:* During the 1840s, Marshal Thomas Robert Bugeaud (1784–1849) led the French military campaign that suppressed resistance to the occupation of Algeria. *Right:* Abd al-Qadir (1808–1883) led Algerian resistance against the French invaders.

Following Hammuda's death in 1815, conflict within Tunisia's ruling family facilitated European intrusion. In 1819, European naval power reduced piracy from Tunis, and in 1830, Husayn Bey entered a treaty with France in which he agreed to suppress piracy and gave economic and legal privileges to Europeans in Tunisia. Furthermore, Husayn supported the 1830 French invasion of Algeria as it removed an old enemy, provided business opportunities in supplying the French army, and held out the possibility that Tunisia might gain some Algerian territory. Trying to balance relations with the French in Algeria and the Ottomans in Libya, Tunisia appointed French instructors for its military and hosted visiting French warships while dispatching a Tunisian contingent to support the Ottomans in the Crimean War. Ahmed Bey, who ruled from 1837 to 1855, remodeled the Tunisian army by reducing its historic reliance on Turkish-Ottoman soldiers and creating a Western-style Tunisian force, with officers trained at a local military academy. In the early 1860s, as part of its modernization process, Tunisia temporarily created the first constitutional monarchy in the Muslim world. Nevertheless, military reforms, an ambitious construction program, and the failure of a new taxation system put Tunisia into considerable debt to Europeans, who were increasingly active in its economy. Consequently, in 1868–69 an international financial commission headed by a French official took control of the Tunisian economy. During the 1870s, Prime Minister Khayr al-Din improved the tax system, founded a Western-style college, and promoted olive production, but influential European diplomats opposed his efforts to impose tariffs that would encourage Tunisian industrialization. Tunisia increasingly became the target of European Great Power politics. In 1871, given France's weakness after its defeat by Prussia and Britain's desire to limit the French presence in North Africa, European powers recognized Tunisia as part of the Ottoman Empire. However, this policy changed in 1878 as newly unified Germany, wanting to distract France from affairs in Europe, arranged for the Congress of Berlin to declare Tunisia within the French sphere of influence. This led to the French colonial occupation of Tunisia in 1881.

Libya

Like other North African rulers of the turn of the eighteenth and nineteenth centuries, Tripoli's Yusuf Qaramanli used piracy and hostage taking to extort money from European powers and the United States. Many of the Libyan-based pirates were actually Ottomans or renegade Europeans. In 1803–04, given that Yusuf had declared war on the United States for failing to pay him ransom for a captured American vessel, the United States Navy blockaded Tripoli, but the blockade failed when pirates seized a large American warship. Defeated in this First Barbary War, the United States withdrew its forces from Libya, released Libyan prisoners, and paid Yusuf a substantial ransom for American captives. Bolstered by this success, Yusuf enlarged his army, using it to extend direct control over Cyrenaica in the east and Fezzan in the south, which meant that trans-Saharan trade caravans were funneled to Tripoli. Since the British navy forced Tripoli to abandon piracy in the 1810s, Yusuf tried to compensate for this loss of revenue by dispatching expeditions south to enslave people from the area around Lake Chad. However, in the 1820s Yusuf's trans-Saharan military operations were foiled by the denial of loans from antislavery-minded Britain, and therefore he returned to piracy in the Mediterranean. As a result, in 1830 a French fleet visited Tripoli and compelled Yusuf to sign a treaty whereby he agreed to halt piracy, reduce the size of Libya's navy, and refrain from supporting Algerian forces resisting the French invasion. Yusuf's 1832 abdication led to a civil war in Libya in which the French and British backed rival factions from the ruling Qaramanli family. Reacting to increased European intervention in North Africa, particularly the French invasion of Algeria, the Ottomans acted decisively to end the instability in Libya and bolster their flagging power in the region. In 1835, an Ottoman fleet landed an army in Tripoli, overthrew the Qaramanli dynasty without a fight, and imposed direct Ottoman rule. While Turkish troops controlled Libyan towns, an emerging Muslim purification movement founded by Algerian scholar Muhammad al-Sanusi, who was also called the Grand Sanusi, opposed their rule in the countryside and gained popularity among the nomadic Arabs of Cyrenaica. Tripoli then became a major source of enslaved Africans for the Ottoman Empire. Due to the abolition of the slave trade in Tunisia in 1846 and French Algeria in 1848, exports of enslaved people from Tripoli to the Ottoman Middle East expanded and continued after Constantinople (Istanbul) ordered them stopped in 1857. The loss of Ottoman territory after the empire's defeat by Russia in 1878 prompted European powers to become interested in Libya, and Italian investment in the territory increased. However, Libya remained part of the Ottoman Empire until the early twentieth century.

Morocco

In Morocco, where the ruling Alawite dynasty remained separate from Ottoman North Africa, a return to state-sponsored piracy in the early nineteenth century was halted by an 1828 Austrian naval bombardment of the port of Larache on the Atlantic coast. The 1830 French invasion of Algeria cut off Morocco from the rest of Muslim North Africa, and Moroccan support of Algerian insurgents led to Morocco's defeat in an 1844 war with France. In the subsequent Treaty of Tangier, France withdrew from the Moroccan frontier town of Oudja and Morocco agreed to what would become its modern border with Algeria. This inspired Moroccan ruler Mawlay Abderrahman to oppose Algerians fighting the French, tighten relations with Britain, and modernize his army by importing European weapons and constructing coastal defences. However, in 1859, a weak government in Spain sought to reinforce its domestic position by going to war with Morocco over the Spanish enclave of Ceuta. Despite Spanish military incompetence and the outbreak of cholera among their soldiers, the Spanish

≡ **The Barbary Wars.** Fighting between Libyan pirates and United States sailors during the First Barbary War (1803–1804).

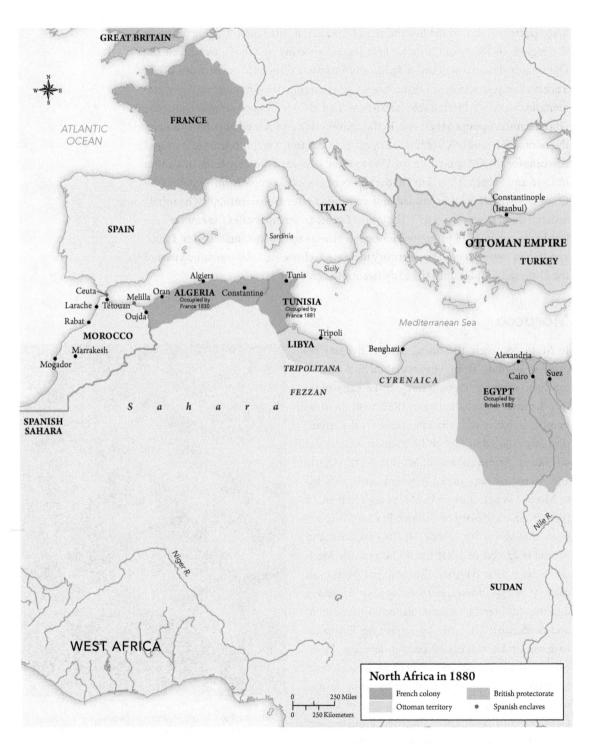

GREAT BRITAIN

FRANCE

ATLANTIC
OCEAN

SPAIN

ITALY

Sardinia

Constantinople
(Istanbul)

OTTOMAN EMPIRE

TURKEY

Algiers

Tunis

Sicily

Ceuta

Oran

ALGERIA
Occupied by
France 1830

Constantine

TUNISIA
Occupied by
France 1881

Melilla

Mediterranean Sea

Larache   Tétouan

Oujda

Rabat

Tripoli

LIBYA

Benghazi

Alexandria

MOROCCO

Marrakesh

TRIPOLITANA

CYRENAICA

Cairo

Suez

Mogador

EGYPT
Occupied by
Britain 1882

SPANISH
SAHARA

S   a   h   a   r   a

FEZZAN

Niger R.

Nile R.

SUDAN

WEST AFRICA

| 0 | | 250 Miles |
| 0 | | 250 Kilometers |

North Africa in 1880

| | French colony | | British protectorate |
| | Ottoman territory | ● | Spanish enclaves |

≡ **MAP 10.2**

expeditionary force occupied the Moroccan town of Tétouan. The conflict ended with a British-mediated treaty that expanded the Spanish outposts of Ceuta and Melilla, imposed Spanish rule in southern Morocco, and obliged the Moroccan government to pay the Spaniards a large indemnity to recover Tétouan. Coming to power in 1859, Moroccan ruler Sidi Muhammed IV paid the indemnity and continued military reforms by taking out loans from European powers. From 1873 to 1894, Mawlay Hassan Westernized and expanded the army, which he used to suppress rebellions and impose authority over remote parts of Morocco. While the Moroccan government balanced diplomatic relations with Europe by importing military instructors from Britain, France, Germany, Belgium, and Spain, these officers worked more for the interests of their home states than for those of Morocco, and as a result the expensive Moroccan army became ineffective. While the European powers recognized the independence of Morocco in the 1880 Treaty of Madrid, France gained increasing influence in the country, though this would eventually be challenged by Germany.

Conclusion

By 1880, the stage was set for a thorough European takeover of North Africa. The region had become a pawn in the "great game" played by European powers seeking to secure points of global strategic and economic importance, such as the new Suez Canal in Egypt. Simultaneously, North African powers grew weak and indebted, unable to fend off foreign intervention. Confident of their superiority, nineteenth-century Europeans staged large international exhibitions that demonstrated their technological achievements and portrayed North Africa, as well as other parts of Asia and Africa, as exotic and primitive. When Egyptian ruler Ismail visited the 1867 Paris Exhibition, he was incorporated like an actor into a display of a medieval Cairo palace, and Egyptians visiting the 1889 Paris Exhibition expressed disgust that the reconstruction of contemporary Cairo was modeled on the old dirty part of the city and featured the façade of a mosque that led into a café. At the same time, growing Western dominance and intrusion inspired some nineteenth-century North African Muslim scholars to formulate **Islamic Modernism**, an intellectual movement that attempted to reconcile Islam with factors that had emerged from Europe's "Enlightenment," such as nationalism, rationalism, and equality. While the Western concept of nationalism may have been imported to North Africa by Napoleon, continued European intrusion also prompted the growth of nationalism in the region. For example, in Egypt, Mohammad Ali tried to protect the country's antiquities from foreign looting, and Egyptian scholars wrote books highlighting the glories of ancient Egyptian civilization to inspire national pride and encourage modernization to restore Egyptian greatness.

Timeline

KEY TERMS

STUDY QUESTIONS

1. What were the legacies of the French military occupation of Egypt, 1798–1803? What do we mean by orientalism? What modernization programs did Muhammed Ali pursue? What impact did the opening of the Suze Canal have on Egypt's position in world affairs?

2. What made Algeria vulnerable to foreign invasion? In what stages did the French occupation of Algeria

proceed? What were the pros and cons of Tunisia's modernization process?

3. Which countries and parties were involved in the Barbary Wars? What were the outcomes? Which European countries sought influence over Morocco?

Please see page FR-5 for the Further Readings for this chapter. For additional digital learning resources please go to https://www.oup.com/he/falola-stapleton1e

11

West Africa, c. 1800–1880:
Abolition and Jihad

In 1800, West Africa was on the verge of an important transformation. Over the previous three centuries, the relationship between West Africans, and Europeans and colonial Americans arriving on the coast had been characterized by an increasing involvement in the Transatlantic slave trade (see Chapter 6). The export of enslaved people from West Africa peaked in the eighteenth century and fueled the success of plantation economies in the colonial Americas. During the early and mid-nineteenth century, however, the export of enslaved people from West Africa's Atlantic coast was phased out in favor of the export of West African raw materials and agricultural products needed to feed the growing industries and populations of Western Europe and North America. This economic transition had tremendous consequences for West Africa. Simultaneously, while the gradual decline of the trans-Saharan trade in the 1700s had reduced the economic and political vitality of West Africa's Sahel hinterland, a series of Muslim holy wars fought in the first half of the nineteenth century rejuvenated this zone.

Abolition of the Slave Trade

An almost century-long process ended the transatlantic slave trade. As the preeminent world power of the 1800s, Britain took the lead in abolishing the oceanic trade in enslaved people and ending slavery in the Atlantic. However, the British political process to end slavery was highly contentious and gradual, as it pitted established British elites with stakes in slave labor plantations in the Caribbean against other emerging leaders from the abolitionist movement. France had been the first major European power of the era to abolish slavery in 1794, during the French Revolution, but objections by French colonial plantation owners prompted the new regime of Napoleon to restore the institution in 1802. Within the British Empire, after political

A market in Freetown, Sierra Leone, late nineteenth century.

≡ **Abolitionist bestseller.** The frontispiece to the *Interesting Narrative of the Life of Olaudah Equiano* (1789).

disputes in the late 1700s, slave trading was outlawed in 1807, and a gradual process to emancipate enslaved people began in 1833 and was complete by the end of that decade. Throughout the 1800s, Britain used diplomatic and military pressure to convince other states in Europe, the Americas, and the Middle East to end slave trading. Among these powers was France, which banned slave trading in its empire in 1835 and freed enslaved people in 1848. Although the American Revolution of the 1770s and 1780s led to the abolition of slavery in the northern United States and a prohibition on the importation of enslaved people into the entire country in 1808, legal enslavement of people of African descent persisted in the American South until the 1863 Emancipation Proclamation during the American Civil War. In Latin America, many countries ended slavery when they gained independence from Spain in the 1810s and 1820s, but the practice continued in Cuba until 1886, and in 1888 Brazil became the last state in the Americas to free its enslaved people.

A combination of factors contributed to the end of slave trading and slavery by European and American powers. First, a major economic transformation gradually rendered slavery obsolete. Beginning with Britain in the late 1700s, the **Industrial Revolution** meant that wealth generation began to shift from colonial plantations that relied on slave labor to urban factories in the metropole that employed low-paid wageworkers. Exporting huge amounts of cheap factory-made textiles produced in cities like Birmingham and Manchester, Britain began to promote a system of international free trade in which free wage earners who could use their money to buy products represented a much more profitable market than unpaid enslaved people. That said, the expansion of factory production in Britain, and eventually elsewhere, created short-term opportunities for slaveholding plantation owners who produced products used by industries, which is why slavery persisted for a while in places like the cotton-growing American South. Second, while there had long been ethical objections to slavery in the Western world, an organized **abolitionist movement** developed in Britain in the late 1700s and spread to other countries, motivated by Christian religious morality often emphasized by new

Protestant denominations such as Methodists and Quakers, and by new Enlightenment political ideas about the equality of human beings. Abolitionists became activists who published newspapers and books and organized speaking tours, including by formerly enslaved people, to spread public awareness of the injustice and horrors of the institution.

Among the leading late-eighteenth-century British abolitionists were **William Wilberforce**, who led the movement within the British parliament, and formerly enslaved people **Ottobah Cugoana** and **Gustavus Vassa** (Olaudah Equiano), who styled themselves the "Sons of Africa." While Vassa wrote what became a famous account of his enslavement in West Africa and transportation to the Americas on a slave ship, modern scholars have debated the narrative's veracity because of evidence that he had been born in the Carolinas. With increased public support, and in the context of the spread of limited democracy in Britain, abolitionists put pressure on the British and other governments, successfully convincing them to take legislative action against the slave trade and slavery. Third, resistance by enslaved people played an important role in ending slavery, as uprisings made investment in slave ships and colonial plantations a risky business, and news of these struggles also highlighted the inherent violence and oppression of the slave system. Although there had long been slave rebellions in the Americas, including the long struggle of the Palmares community of escaped enslaved people in Brazil during the 1600s, the increased arrival of West African captives in the Americas during the eighteenth-century sugar boom led to more resistance. In the Caribbean, captives from what is now Ghana

≡ **Slave Revolts.** *Top:* A battle during the Haitian Revolution (1791–1804). *Bottom:* African slaves, led by Joseph Cinqué, kill Captain Ramon Ferrer during an insurrection on board the Spanish slave ship *Amistad* off the coast of Cuba in July 1839.

staged major uprisings on the Danish-controlled island of Saint John in 1733 and on the British island of Jamaica in 1760, and although these uprisings were suppressed, fugitive enslaved people called **maroons** escaped to remote areas and continued guerrilla warfare against colonial forces. In 1739, in the British colony of South Carolina, enslaved people who may have been from the kingdom of Kongo staged what became called the **Stono Rebellion**—the largest slave uprising in the British mainland colonies—and tried to march to Spanish Florida. Influenced by the French Revolution, the most successful slave rebellion occurred in the Caribbean French colony of Saint Domingue in the 1790s and led to the independence of the **Republic of Haiti** in 1804.

Abolitionist powers used force to suppress transatlantic slave shipments. Britain and, to a lesser extent, the United States prosecuted naval campaigns against slaving ships in West African waters. In 1819, given the end of the Napoleonic Wars a few years earlier, Britain established the **West Africa Squadron** of the Royal Navy, which grew from an initial complement of 6 ships to 36 vessels during the 1840s. Britain's antislavery naval operations grew increasingly aggressive, as, for instance, in 1840, when the warship HMS *Wanderer* blockaded the Spanish slaving enclave of Gallinas in Sierra Leone/Liberia, seizing 15 slave ships and staging an amphibious raid that destroyed slave pens and freed 800 prisoners intended for shipment to Cuba. Although Britain concluded diplomatic agreements allowing its navy to search and seize vessels from other maritime powers and banning ships from carrying items related to the slave trade, such as shackles and chains, some slavers used legal action to impede these antislavery operations. Britain also imposed antislavery agreements on West African coastal powers, such as in 1851, when the Royal Navy bombarded Lagos and replaced its ruler with another who agreed to stop slave trading. From the 1810s to late 1860s, Britain's West Africa Squadron intercepted about 1,500 slave ships, representing perhaps one in five, and liberated about 160,000 out of 2.7 million enslaved people exported from West Africa during that time.

As part of its treaty with Britain that ended the War of 1812, the United States mounted limited antislavery naval patrols off the coast of West Africa between 1818 and 1821, but the policy was discontinued because of lawsuits launched by slave traders and Washington's anger over British interception of American vessels suspected of carrying enslaved people. In 1842, the US government reinstated antislavery naval operations because of pressure from the British government and domestic abolitionists. Initially based in the Cape Verde Islands and then in Luanda, Angola, the US navy antislavery squadron or Africa Squadron seized 36 slave vessels before it was disbanded in 1861 with the start of the American Civil War.

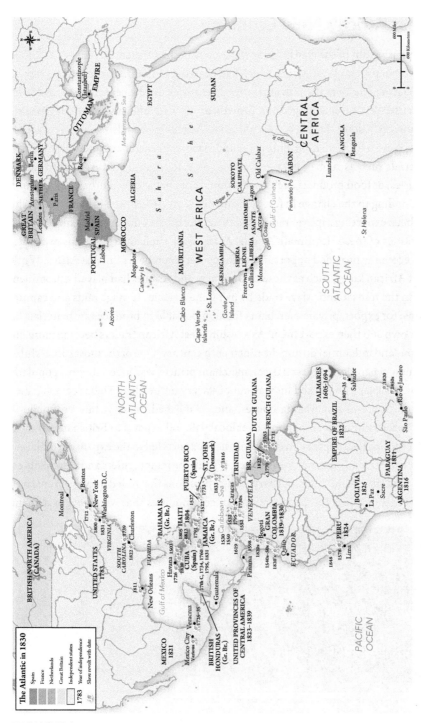

The Atlantic in 1830

Spain
France
Netherlands
Great Britain
Independent states

1783   Year of independence
        Slave revolt with date

≡ MAP 11.1

West Africa's New Economy

The phasing out of the transatlantic slave trade in the nineteenth century had a significant impact on West Africa, which had been the source of most captives shipped to the Americas over the previous several centuries. At the center of the abolitionist cause, Britain encouraged the growth of what its officials called "**legitimate commerce**" along the West African coast. Instead of acquiring enslaved people from West Africa, visiting European and American merchants now wanted raw materials such as rubber, palm oil, cotton, or acacia gum (gum Arabic) to supply factories, or food products such as groundnuts or cocoa to feed urban populations. Responding to the change in foreign demand, West African rulers and traders who had been exporting captives redirected their efforts to producing and exporting vast quantities of these "legitimate" goods. At the same time, the rise of this raw materials economy provided opportunities for new entrepreneurs in West Africa. While West African kings, such as those of Dahomey and Asante, had played a prominent role in the transatlantic slave trade by using their armies to stage raids and capture people for export, private merchants found it possible to produce raw materials on their own and then export them. As a result, West African traders became more numerous and influential during the nineteenth century. One of the most successful of this new generation of West African merchant princes was Jubo Jubogha, popularly known as Jaja, who worked his way out of slavery in the Niger Delta region, gained control of prominent trading houses, and established the city-state of Opobo in 1869, exercising a near monopoly over local palm oil exports to British merchants.

Ironically, the suppression of oceanic slave exports led to the expansion of slavery within nineteenth-century West Africa. Within the region, rulers and merchants established large plantations and harvesting operations that relied heavily on enslaved workers to produce the large amounts of commodities that were now in demand

PALAVER BETWEEN JA-JA AND THE ENGLISH CONSUL AT OPOBO

≡ **Jaja of Opobo.** In 1869 King Jaja (1821–1891) established the city-state of Opobo in the Niger Delta. In this scene, Jaja, seated on the left, negotiates trade terms with British officials.

along the coast. Slave raids and slave trading continued within nineteenth-century West Africa, though now focusing on a regional slave market. One aspect of West African slavery that changed at this time was that more women than men were enslaved. Whereas the gender preferences of European and American slavers meant that more male than female captives were exported during the transatlantic slave trade of the 1600s and 1700s, West African slave owners preferred to enslave women, reflecting the regional practice of women working in agriculture.

The Spread of Christianity

The abolition of the transatlantic slave trade also encouraged the spread of Christianity along the West African coast. In Europe and the Americas, the abolitionist movement emerged simultaneously with the growth of evangelical movements whereby Christian churches established **missionary societies** engaged in energetic efforts to spread their religion to other parts of the world. Leading abolitionists like Wilberforce were involved in the founding of missionary societies. Many Christian missionaries saw West Africa as a region desperately in need of redemption given its history of slave trading, and as a fertile field for religious conversion. Recognizing Islam's long history in the region and seeing that it was undergoing revitalization in the hinterland, nineteenth-century missionaries felt some urgency to advance Christianity in West Africa. Sustained Christian missionary activity in West Africa began at the start of the nineteenth century among settlements of freed enslaved people such as Freetown (see below) being established along the coast. Displaced from their home societies, captives liberated from slave vessels by the British navy and settled along the coast presented as ready converts for Christian missionaries. From freed slave colonial enclaves, missionaries and new West African Christians moved to independent African communities along the coast and ventured further inland to continue their evangelizing efforts. While the number of people who converted to the new religion remained small, pockets of Christianity developed along coastal West Africa. Some formerly enslaved people who converted to Christianity in places like Freetown eventually returned to their homes in other parts of West Africa, bringing their new religion with them. For example, on the urging of freed slave converts who had returned to what is now western Nigeria, the Anglican **Church Missionary Society** (CMS) founded a mission at the coastal settlement of Badagry in 1842 and then moved a short distance inland to establish another mission at Abeokuta among the Yoruba people in 1845. These were the first Christian missions in Nigeria. At this time, European missionaries aimed to found a self-governing, self-propagating, and self-financing African church. They could not foresee later colonial conquest in the region.

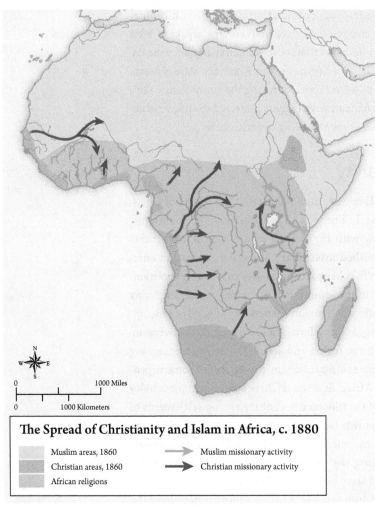

The Spread of Christianity and Islam in Africa, c. 1880

Muslim areas, 1860

Christian areas, 1860

African religions

→ Muslim missionary activity

→ Christian missionary activity

≡ **MAP 11.2**

Another central activity in spreading Christianity in West Africa, and in which the liberated slave converts played a key role, was that missionaries undertook the long process of establishing written scripts for West African languages so that they could print local versions of the Bible. Missionaries and their supporters viewed the translation of the Bible into local languages as foundational to the building of West African Christianity. Although Arabic script was already used to write some West African languages, European missionaries decided to employ the Latin characters with which they were familiar and which would tie West African Christianity to the Western world. An important figure in the creation of West African missionary literature was **Samuel Ajayi Crowther**, who, as a child originating from what is now western Nigeria, was rescued from a slave port by the British navy and then resettled in Sierra Leone, where he converted to Christianity. Educated in Freetown and London, Crowther became an Anglican minister and joined the missions in Badagry and Abeokuta in the 1840s, where he worked on creating a Latin script for the local Yoruba language, which was also his own first language. Crowther published a Yoruba dictionary and grammar book and initiated and supervised the Yoruba translation of the Bible completed in the 1880s. A skilled linguist, he was also instrumental in the creation of written texts for the Igbo and Nupe languages of Nigeria, and in 1864 he became the Anglican Church's first African bishop. Similar processes happened across the region. In 1835, the Basel Evangelical Missionary Society, a Protestant nondenominational group based in Switzerland, established a mission at Akropong in the Gold Coast (today's Ghana), where Danish and German missionaries studied the Twi version of Akan language. With the help of local Christian converts like David Asante, who had worked as a domestic servant for the missionaries and then studied in Switzerland where he was ordained, the Basel mission created a Latin script for Twi and published Twi literature during the 1850s and 1860s, culminating in the first Twi Bible in 1871.

European Exploration of the West African Interior

At the same time that European missionaries arrived along the coast, European explorers became interested in finding out more about the geography of the West African interior, particularly the course of the great **Niger River**, which allowed access to the region. In 1788, in the context of Europe's age of scientific discov-

ery, a group of British elites formed the Association for Promoting the Discovery of the Interior Parts of Africa, otherwise known as the **African Association**. Cooperating with the British government, the African Association sponsored British expeditions that sought to make geographic discoveries in West Africa to enhance British commercial activities. Several British explorers tried to use the Gambia River to work their way eastward into the interior and toward the Niger River. Intending to reach Timbuktu, British officer Daniel Houghton began his journey at the mouth of the Gambia River in 1790 but was robbed several times and eventually died of starvation in the Sahara. Scottish explorer Mungo Park led two expeditions into the West African hinterland. From 1794 to 1796, and starting at the Gambia, Park reached Ségou on the Niger River and returned to Britain to publish an account of his expedition entitled *Travels in the Interior of Africa*, which stimulated public interest in West Africa. In 1805, Park returned to the Gambia at the head of a British government expedition tasked with testing the theory that the Niger and Congo rivers were connected. Since he refused to pay passage tax to local powers and used firearms to force his way down the Niger, Park's group fell

≡ **Samuel Ajayi Crowther** Bishop Samuel Ajayi Crowther, originally from western Nigeria, played a key role in the spread of Christianity across West Africa during the nineteenth century.

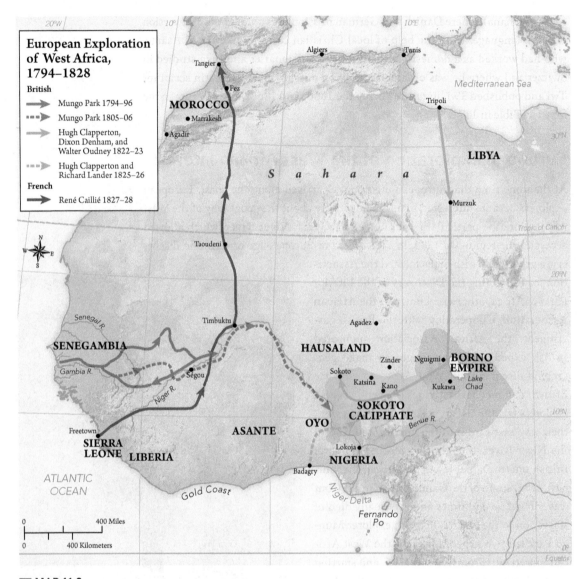

European Exploration of West Africa, 1794–1828

British

→ Mungo Park 1794–96

┈▶ Mungo Park 1805–06

→ Hugh Clapperton, Dixon Denham, and Walter Oudney 1822–23

┈▶ Hugh Clapperton and Richard Lander 1825–26

French

→ René Caillié 1827–28

≡ **MAP 11.3**

into an ambush and he drowned in what is now Nigeria. Other British expeditions started on the coast of Libya and marched south across the Sahara toward the Niger. In 1818, a small British expedition attempted this journey, but illness forced them to turn back at Murzuk in southern Libya. In 1822–23, another British expedition, led by naval officer Hugh Clapperton, set out from Tripoli and reached Lake Chad and the Borno Empire. During a second expedition in 1825–26, Clapperton landed at the West African port of Badagry and marched north across the Niger to the Sokoto Caliphate, where he died of disease. Attempting to promote Christianity and commerce in West Africa, the British government organized an 1841 Niger expedition that used three iron steamboats to transport 150 Europeans from the coast upriver to the confluence of the Niger and Benue rivers at Lokoja, where they intended to establish an outpost. However, the expedition suffered greatly from tropical disease and quickly withdrew to the island of Fernando Po in the Gulf of Guinea. Samuel Ajayi Crowther accompanied the expedition as an interpreter. The British government, supported by Anglican missionaries, launched subsequent Niger expeditions in 1854 and 1857, which established outposts along the Niger at Aboh, Onitsha, and Lokoja, and led to the CMS founding the Niger Mission.

Warfare and European Intervention

During the early and mid-nineteenth century, as slave exports were giving way to the raw materials trade, West Africa became the scene of continued and sometimes increased warfare and more aggressive European intervention. In what is now the Gambia and Senegal, European intrusion became acute. After the Napoleonic Wars, Britain sought a new outpost along the coast of Senegambia from which to mount antislavery naval patrols and encourage "legitimate commerce." Since the British returned captured French enclaves like Gorée Island off the coast of Senegal in 1814, the former sought to expand their presence along the nearby Gambia River. In 1816, a British officer acquired Banjul Island, located at the river's mouth, from a local ruler called the King of Kombo, and in 1821 this enclave, renamed Bathurst, became the center of the new British colony of Gambia. From the 1820s to 1850s, through a combination of treaties and warfare, the British gradually obtained more islands up the Gambia River and portions of the river shoreline from local rulers. The arrival of formerly enslaved people taken from captured slaving vessels and West Indian veterans of the British military fostered the creation of a small Christian creole community in Bathurst, though the people of the hinterland were overwhelming Muslim. Based at their colony of Saint Louis, the French sought to control the Senegal River, which was a major source of acacia gum, important as a dye in the Western textile industry. In 1825, a French military expedition defeated the Emirate of Trarza, on the north side of the Senegal River mouth, as it had begun exporting acacia gum to British merchants further up the Atlantic coast. The French also objected to Trarza cultivating an alliance with the Waalo Kingdom, located on the south side of the river mouth, as it represented the main source of this product for French merchants. During the 1840s and 1850s, the French began building a chain of forts inland along the Senegal River. In 1855,

≡ **Asante Soldiers.** Asante cavalryman and foot soldier with musket.

French forces led by Governor Louis Faidherbe subdued the combined forces of Trarza and Waalo and absorbed these territories into the expanding colony of Senegal. Further French expansion up the Senegal River during the late 1850s and 1860s led to conflict with the new Tukolor Empire (see page 238) in the hinterland.

At the start of the 1800s, the **kingdom of Asante**, which had expanded in the interior of the Gold Coast during the heyday of the slave trade in the previous century, seized control of the coastal Fante communities that served as intermediaries in the transatlantic trade. Since the British encouraged the Fante to act independently, Asante imposed a trade blockade on British outposts like Cape Coast Castle along the Gold Coast. At the start of 1824, a British force invaded Asante but was defeated at the Battle of Nsamankow on the banks of the Pra River, where General Charles MacCarthy, the British commander and governor of Sierra Leone, was killed and his decapitated head taken to the Asante capital of Kumasi. An Asante army then counterattacked Cape Coast Castle but was driven away. However, in 1826, a coalition of coastal communities and the British inflicted a decisive defeat on the Asante at the Battle of Katamanso, fought on the coastal plain a few miles from Accra. Although the Asante army had used firearms for a long time, they panicked when confronted with the sound and flash of British rockets with which they had no experience. As a result, the Fante gained independence and Asante lost control of the coast, with the kingdom's southern frontier fixed at the Pra River. In the early 1860s, tensions flared again as the British granted asylum to Asante dissidents. This led to an abortive war in 1863–64 in which the Asante raided the coast but pulled back and the British sent troops to the Pra River but tropical disease compelled them to withdraw. This British setback emboldened the pro-war party within the Asante kingdom paving the way for future conflict over the Gold Coast. In 1873–74, the British mounted a major military expedition that invaded Asante and burned Kumasi, forcing the kingdom to renounce claims to the coast and open the area to free trade.

In the early 1800s, the fall of the Oyo Empire set off a series of wars that continued for the rest of the century among the Yoruba states of what is now western

Nigeria. These conflicts are called the **Yoruba Wars**. Gaining military support from the new and expanding Muslim Sokoto Caliphate to its north, the Yoruba state of Ilorin broke from the Oyo Empire in the early 1820s. However, Sokoto then incorporated Ilorin into its caliphate by overthrowing the local Yoruba ruler and imposing a Muslim Fulani emir. To the north, Oyo also experienced defeats by the armies of Borgu and Nupe, with the latter incorporated into the Sokoto Caliphate as the Bida Emirate in the 1840s. In the south, Oyo suffered many problems, including rebellions by the Egba in the 1790s, and Ijebu and Ife in 1822, and the reassertion of autonomy by Dahomey in the 1820s and 1830s. Oyo collapsed in the early 1830s as Dahomey blocked its access to the coastal slave trade and the Sokoto Caliphate in the north prevented it from acquiring new horses for its cavalry army. Consequently, many Yoruba people moved south into the forest, where they established new states like New Oyo, Ibadan, and Ijayi, and in the south the Egba created the town of Abeokuta. As the new Yoruba states fought among themselves to fill the power vacuum, they abandoned cavalry warfare as unsuitable for the forest environment and quickly adopted firearms imported through coastal trade. While the Yoruba were relatively late in taking up firearms compared to some of their coastal neighbors in West Africa, guns proliferated across Yorubaland in the

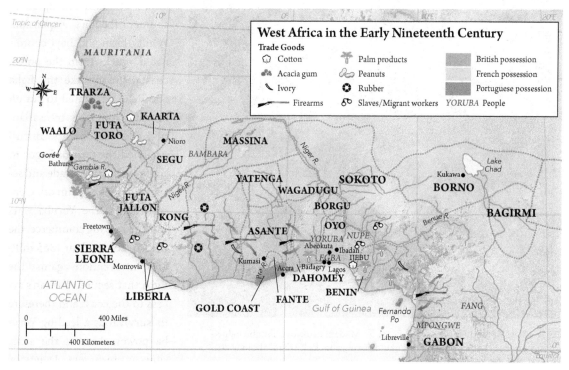

≡ MAP 11.4

mid-nineteenth century. While few Yoruba possessed firearms in the 1840s, these weapons became widespread in the 1850s, and almost every Yoruba fighter of the 1870s carried one.

By the 1840s, **Ibadan** had become a major Yoruba power. Whereas the other Yoruba states were hereditary monarchies, Ibadan developed as a military meritocracy in which leaders emerged based on their skill in war, and they attracted followings of men who advanced by proving themselves in combat. While Yoruba men moved to Ibadan to take advantage of these new opportunities, the state had to constantly engage in warfare as leaders had to display their military prowess and procure enslaved people to exchange for guns along the coast. Around 1840, at the Battle of Osogbo, the forces of Ibadan halted the southward advance of Muslim jihadists from Ilorin associated with the Sokoto Caliphate. This was perhaps the most important military engagement of the nineteenth-century Yoruba wars, as it checked the southward expansion of Sokoto, and hence Islam, and secured Ibadan's place as a new dominant power in the area. During the 1850s, Ibadan expanded by taking control of some neighboring Yoruba communities, and it constructed a network of defensive outposts along its northern frontier to guard against further jihadist attacks from Ilorin. Subsequently, shifting coalitions of states attempted to counter Ibadan's expansion. While Ilorin and Ijayi coordinated attacks from the north, coastal groups like the Egba and Ijebu attempted to cut off Ibadan from the transatlantic trade. In 1861, the British occupied the port of Lagos to suppress the slave trade and secure supplies of palm oil. Concerned that the Yoruba wars were disrupting commerce, the British launched an 1865 military intervention against the Egba that secured Ibadan's access to the coast and therefore its survival as a leading Yoruba power. Around the same time, a resurgent Dahomey

≡ **Madam Tinubu.** The female slave trader Madam Efunroye Tinubu helped supply guns to the defenders of Abeokuta during attacks by the Dahomey army in 1851 and 1864.

took advantage of these conflicts and pushed eastward into Yoruba country. In 1851 and 1864, the Dahomey army, with its core of elite female warriors, attacked the fortified Egba town of Abeokuta but was repelled both times. The female slave trader Madam Efunroye Tinubu, exiled from Lagos, and British missionaries supplied the defenders of Abeokuta with guns and ammunition. The Yoruba wars of the mid-1800s increased the number of enslaved people exported from this area, and since these conflicts happened at the end of the transatlantic slave trade era, Yoruba captives became some of the last to arrive in Brazil and Cuba, where they retained a distinct identity.

Freed Slave Settlements on the Coast

In the late eighteenth and early nineteenth century, external powers founded settlements of once enslaved people along the West African coast. The efforts to establish these colonies were informed not only by an abolitionist desire to repatriate formerly enslaved people to their ancestral continent but also by white racist fears that freed Black people constituted a danger to white society in Europe and the Americas. This trend began in London where, by the end of the 1700s, a community called the **Black Poor** had developed, composed of people who had arrived on slave or naval vessels, formerly enslaved people or servants from the Caribbean, and some **Black Loyalists** who had fled the rebellious British colonies that became the United States during the American Revolution. In 1787, the Committee for the Relief of the Black Poor, a British civic organization concerned about human suffering but that also disapproved of Black men marrying white women, organized the shipment of about 300 Black residents of London to Sierra Leone with the support of the British government. The group also included around 70 white women married to Black men. However, the settlement scheme was generally unpopular among Black Londoners as the committee and the government coerced people into joining it. The settlers established Granville Town, named after British abolitionist Granville Sharpe, near the mouth of the Sierra Leone River in what was imagined as the Province of Freedom. However, the settlers were harassed by British slavers based at Bunce Island about 20 miles upriver, many died from tropical disease, and in 1789 the settlement was attacked and destroyed by an indigenous Temne group that had originally permitted the colony on their land but probably did not understand that it was meant to be permanent. In 1792, the **Sierra Leone Company**, formed by British abolitionists and approved by the British government over the objections of British slave owners, shipped 1,200 Black Loyalists from the British colony of Nova Scotia in North America, where they were suffering from racial discrimination, across the Atlantic to Sierra Leone, where they founded Freetown. Around the same time, British abolitionists rallied some of the surviving settlers from Granville Town and re-established this community, which was absorbed into the new Freetown project. In 1794, during the war between Britain and Revolutionary France, the French navy destroyed Freetown, but the settlers rebuilt. Resentful over lack of access to freehold land, some of the Nova Scotian settlers staged a rebellion in 1800, but the British brought in Jamaican maroons who suppressed the uprising and gained farms in the colony as a reward. In 1808, the British government took over Freetown, which became the crown colony of Sierra Leone, and the Sierra Leone Company transformed into the African Institution, which included Wilberforce and other abolitionists among its leaders, and which aimed to cultivate the colony as a haven for liberated enslaved people and a regional center for Christianity. Once London outlawed the slave trade in 1807, British warships landed freed enslaved people at Freetown and these "re-captives" were then effectively sold as apprentices to missionaries, merchants, or farmers and experienced conditions reminiscent of slavery, with some conscripted into the army or navy. Villages for re-captives were created around the Sierra Leone colony and some were resettled in the Gambia and Liberia. With Freetown as the regional headquarters of Britain's West Africa Squadron, about 50,000 re-captives arrived in Sierra Leone from 1808 to the 1850s. Eventually, the descendants of the Nova Scotians, maroons, re-captives, and discharged soldiers from the Caribbean formed the Creole or **Krio** society of Sierra Leone that adopted Christianity and Western culture and spoke a new language based on English and a mixture of West African languages. Many Krio also eventually became intermediaries in the raw materials trade between the interior and the coast. The Sierra Leone colony became the epicenter of Christian missionary religious and educational operations in West Africa. In 1827, Anglican clergy in Freetown founded Fourah Bay College, which became Africa's first Western-style university. Between 1825 and the early 1860s, simultaneous with missionary endeavors, British military forces made up of convict troops from Britain and re-captive militiamen expanded the Sierra Leone colony by attacking Temne and other indigenous communities.

≡ **Paul Cuffee.** African-American sea captain and merchant Paul Cuffee (1759–1817) lobbied the United States government to establish a settlement of freed slaves in West Africa, and this eventually led to the foundation of Liberia.

The United States copied the Sierra Leone colony. After visiting Sierra Leone during the 1810s, African-American sea captain Paul Cuffee advocated for the US government to embark on a program to resettle free Blacks in Sierra Leone and Haiti. In 1821, the **American Colonization Society** (ACS), an organization formed by white abolitionists and slave owners in the United States, began settling free African-Americans on West Africa's "Grain Coast," which had long supplied malagueta peppers, palm oil, and enslaved people to visiting ships. While America's increasingly wealthy southern white slave owners wanted to deport free Blacks, who they feared would provoke slave rebellions, northern Black abolitionists opposed the resettlement scheme as it seemed like a way to avoid granting civil rights to Blacks. Distressed by the blatant racism of some of the ACS leaders, Cuffee withdrew his support for the project, as he feared that the planned colony would become a dumping ground for unwanted African-Americans and not the Christian society he hoped to create. Land for the settlement at Cape Mesurado was acquired when US Navy Captain Robert Stockton, accompanied by an ACS official, put a pistol to the head of indigenous Dei leader King Peter and threatened to pull the trigger unless he signed a treaty. The original settlement was named Monrovia after US president James Monroe, who was an important supporter of the ACS. From the 1820s to 1840s, the ACS settlement expanded as African-American militias fought wars against the area's many small-scale indigenous communities. Although more than half of the 4,500 African-American settlers who arrived in the colony during its first two decades died from tropical disease, the ACS kept recruiting volunteers and shipping them to West Africa.

In 1847, partly to avoid annexation by Britain or France, which did not recognize the ACS as a sovereign power, the African-American settlers declared their independence as the Republic of Liberia, with its capital at Monrovia and a government and flag modeled on those of the United States. The republic's first president was Joseph Jenkins Roberts, who had been freed as a child in Virginia by his owner, who was also his father, and who became a merchant and militia leader in Liberia and the colony's first Black governor. The African-American settlers and their descendants, called **Americo-Liberians**, founded a society inspired by the American south, with themselves in the dominant role as traders and plantation owners and indigenous Liberians exploited as cheap labor with no rights. From 1846 to 1867, the United States Navy brought 5,700 African re-captives taken from slave ships to Liberia, where they experienced partial integration into Americo-Liberian society but were called "Congoes" to indicate a direct African origin. After its independence, and under the guise of suppressing the slave trade, Liberia expanded steadily, with President Roberts personally leading wars against the Kru (Kroo) people. In 1857, Liberia annexed the nearby Republic of Maryland, a similar African-American settlement founded at Cape Palmas in the 1830s, after an expedition led by Roberts helped it conquer the local Grebo. While the United States Navy assisted Liberia in its expansionist wars, southern slave-owning politicians delayed formal American recognition of the West African republic. In 1862, in the context of southern succession and the American Civil War, the United States recognized Liberia and subsequently provided it with formal diplomatic and military support. With funding from the United States, Liberia founded educational institutions, including Liberia College in Monrovia in 1862 and Cuttington Collegiate and Divinity School in Maryland in 1889. Americo-Liberian politics was characterized by **colorism**, whereby light-skinned Monrovia merchants such as Roberts, who formed the Republican Party in 1848, initially controlled the government, but the darker-skinned upriver traders who founded the True Whig Party in 1869 challenged them. Economically, Liberia exported West African raw materials and agricultural products to the United States and Europe. By the 1880s, however, the Liberian economy was in trouble as large European firms, particularly from Germany, dominated the local market, competition from neighboring British and French territories undercut Liberian exports, and the Liberian government became heavily indebted to foreign banks.

France developed a small settlement of freed African enslaved people in West Africa. In 1839, a French naval officer acquired a small piece of land on the Gabon estuary from a local Mpongwe leader who received French protection as a reward. During the early 1840s, American and French missionaries arrived to work among

≡ **Early Liberia.** *Top:* Born in the United States, Joseph Jenkins Roberts (1809–1876) served as the first president of Liberia from 1848 to 1856 and returned for another presidential term from 1872 to 1876. *Bottom:* This watercolor shows an assembly of the Liberian Senate in in 1856.

the indigenous people, and the enclave became a base for French naval operations to suppress the oceanic slave trade and to challenge British supremacy in the region. In 1849, following France's emancipation of enslaved people, the small colony became the home for around 260 Africans whom the French navy had taken from a slave vessel intercepted on its way to Brazil. In turn, the settlement was dubbed Libreville or "Freetown." Since French antislavery naval operations were never very aggressive, few former captives were settled in Libreville, which did not see the emergence of a distinct creole society as in Sierra Leone or Liberia. Instead, from the 1840s to 1880s, Libreville served as a jumping-off point for a series of French expeditions that gradually ventured into the interior of Gabon, expanding French authority by entering into treaties with local peoples like the Fang, who were simultaneously moving down from the north to become intermediaries in the coastal trade. This process culminated in the late 1870s with several French expeditions led by Pierre Savorgnan de Brazza and in his establishment of the hinterland outpost of Franceville in 1880. This solidified Gabon as a French sphere of influence.

Some freed enslaved people in nineteenth-century Brazil returned to Africa on their own. This began in 1835 in the wake of a Muslim-inspired slave revolt in the Brazilian city of Salvador, where authorities deported around 200 rebel enslaved people to West Africa. This was the second time some of these deportees crossed the Atlantic. After this, enslaved people in Brazil and Cuba began saving money to buy their freedom and charter vessels to bring them to the coast of what is now Nigeria, the area where many of them or their parents had originated, and they established distinct communities in Badagry and Lagos. This process accelerated after the emancipation of enslaved people in Cuba and Brazil and continued until the early twentieth century. The Brazilian returnees constituted an important Westernized group in Lagos, with many practicing Catholicism; becoming merchants involved in the trade with Brazil or skilled artisans; sending their children to study in Brazil, Cuba, or Europe; and building Brazilian-style houses. Some of the returnees maintained their pre-enslavement Islamic faith and comprised the nucleus of Lagos's Muslim community.

Jihads in the Hinterland

A number of Muslim revitalization movements occurred in the Sahel and Savanna hinterland of West Africa during the eighteenth and nineteenth centuries. The process started in the 1700s when Fulani pastoralists led Muslim jihads or holy wars in Futa Jalon in what is now Guinea and Futa Toro on the present-day border of Senegal and Mauritania, creating Muslim **theocratic** states. In the 1800s, similar jihads led to the founding of a series of Islamist states across West Africa, including two large territorial empires: Sokoto and Tukolor. The size of these new empires was reminiscent of medieval Mali and sixteenth-century Songhai.

By the end of the 1700s, the nominally Muslim rulers of the Hausa states of northern Nigeria had elicited resentment by heavily taxing their subjects and enslaving fellow Muslims. At the turn of the eighteenth and nineteenth centuries, Muslim Fulani scholar Usman dan Fodio toured Hausaland, building a network of supporters for his movement to revitalize Islam in the region. From 1804 to 1808, dan Fodio orchestrated a jihad that began with a rebellion against the Hausa ruler of Gobir and ended with his forces taking over all the Hausa kingdoms. The jihad began with small infantry forces conducting guerrilla attacks on the large Hausa cavalry armies, but gradually the movement attracted more Fulani and Tuaregs motivated by religious zeal and Hausa peasants angry over taxation. Dan Fodio established an Islamic caliphate based at the city of Sokoto, and by 1812 he had replaced the Hausa rulers with Fulani emirs loyal to him. Under his son Mohammad Bello, who took over after dan Fodio's death in 1817, rebellions were suppressed and warfare among the now subordinate Hausa states declined, allowing the caliphate to expand into neighboring territories. The largest African empire since Songhai, the **Sokoto Caliphate** stretched from what is now Burkina Faso in the west, across northern Nigeria, to present-day Cameroon in the east. Although the original Fulani jihadists had fought on foot, the caliphate copied the cavalry military tradition of the conquered Hausa states. Sokoto did not maintain a standing army but relied on the semi-autonomous emirs to send contingents of elite cavalry and peasant infantry when called upon. In 1826, a British explorer observed that Sokoto could assemble an army of around 50,000 or 60,000 troops, a tenth of whom were mounted on horses. Importantly, limited trade connections with the coast meant that Sokoto did not import many firearms.

The Sokoto Caliphate's economy focused on waging almost constant jihadist warfare to acquire huge numbers of captives who became slave laborers on a network of plantations established around walled towns and fortresses. These plantations produced a wide range of agricultural goods such as sorghum, millet, and cotton for the regional market. Sokoto's plantation system emerged because of a combination of vast lands and scarce labor, and the desire to stop the export of enslaved Muslims to the Atlantic coast. Historians have debated whether Sokoto's leaders justified slavery on the basis of perceived racial or religious differences. By the late nineteenth century, enslaved people constituted around half of Sokoto's total population of ten million, and their exploitation was justified on the basis of encouraging conversion to Islam with provisions for them to earn freedom.

The creation of the Sokoto Caliphate inspired other jihads in West Africa. To the east of Sokoto, around Lake Chad, a similar jihad began in 1808 in Borno and resulted in the takeover of that kingdom by Muslim religious leader

Muhammad al Kanemi, who originated among Saharan nomads. He reformed Borno's administrative and legal systems along Muslim lines, founded a new capital at Kukawa, and reorganized the army to include many more horsemen from the Sahara. During the early 1800s, Borno successfully defended itself from invasion by the expansionist Sokoto Caliphate, with al-Kanemi writing to the Sokoto rulers questioning the morale legitimacy of their attack on a fellow Muslim state. By the 1850s, however, Borno had lost a considerable amount of its western lands to Sokoto, which also cut off Borno from the trans-Saharan trade. West of Sokoto, dan Fodio's success inspired a Fulani jihad led by Seku Ahmadu that defeated

≣ Sokoto Caliphate horseman. Cavalry remained important in the Sokoto Caliphate throughout the nineteenth century.

the traditionalist Bambara people and established the Massina state along the Upper Niger in 1818. The Massina state conquered the historic Niger trading town of Djenne and created a new capital at Hamdullahi ("praise to God").

During the 1840s, Muslim scholar Umar Tal led a jihad in Futa Jalon, located in what is now Guinea. Originating from the Tukolor community in Futa Toro on the present-day border between Senegal and Mauritania, Tal had lived in Sokoto and recently returned from pilgrimage to the Islamic holy sites in Arabia. Tal's jihad first targeted the Kaarta state established in the 1700s and ruled by traditionalist kings who controlled the area's engagement in the trans-Saharan trade. In the 1850s, the jihadists seized the gold-producing Bambuk area and then the Kaarta capital of Nioro. Unlike Sokoto, the success of Tal's jihad centered on acquiring guns from coastal traders in exchange for non-Muslim enslaved people, and he ordered the construction of fortresses to secure conquered lands. Once Futa Jalon was under his authority, Tal launched an offensive into his Futa Toro homeland,

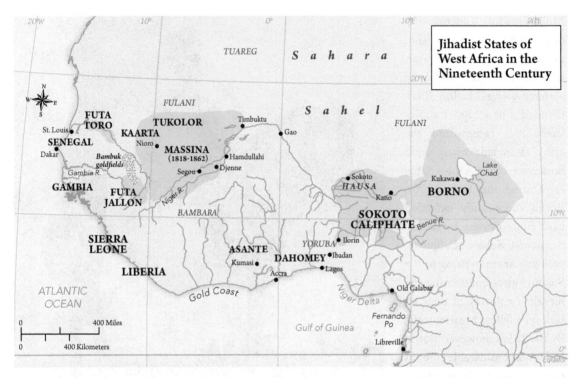

≡ MAP 11.5

where his fighters clashed with the French, who, from their base in Saint Louis, had established a chain of forts along the Senegal River. After several disastrous battles against the French in the west, including a failed siege of the French fort at Medina in what is now Mali in 1857, Tal redirected his expansion eastward toward the trading towns of the Upper Niger River. In the early 1860s, his forces captured the town of Segou, which Tal made his capital, and then they defeated the Massina state, itself the product of an earlier Fulani jihad, destroying its capital of Hamdullahi and occupying Djenne. After Tal was killed in 1864 during a rebellion led by the former rulers of Massina, his nephew Tidiani Tal took over what became known as the Tukolor Empire, which became a Muslim military theocracy and dominated the vast territory between the Senegal River and the Niger River Bend.

Conclusion

During the nineteenth century, West Africa shifted from exporting enslaved people to exporting raw materials to Europeans and Americans on the Atlantic coast. Within West Africa, this led to the expansion of a class of local intermediaries in the

Timeline

1700   1733—Slave rebellion in Dutch West Indies

1739—Stono Rebellion in South Carolina

1760—Slave rebellion in Jamaica

1787—Granville Town established in Sierra Leone

1792—Settlement of "Black Loyalists" from Nova Scotia in Sierra Leone

1794—Revolutionary France abolishes slavery

1800   1800—Rebellion by Nova Scotian settlers in Sierra Leone

1802—France reinstates slavery

1804—Establishment of the Republic of Haiti

1804–08 Fulani jihad creates Sokoto Caliphate

1807—Britain outlaws slave trade within British Empire

1808—Beginning of British naval campaign to suppress slave trade along West African coast

1808—United States bans slave trade

1808—Britain establishes colony of Sierra Leone

1816—British acquire what becomes Bathurst in the Gambia

1818—Fulani jihad creates Massina state on Upper Niger

1818–21—United States mounts antislavery naval patrols off coast of West Africa

1819—Britain established West Africa Squadron to suppress slave trade

1820s—early 1830s; fall of Oyo Empire-start of Yoruba Wars

1821—British create the colony of Gambia

1821—American Colonization Society begins, settling free African-Americans in Liberia

1824—Battle of Nsamankow; Asante defeat British in the Gold Coast

1825—First Franco-Trarza War in Senegal

1826—Battle of Katamanso; British and Fante defeat Asante in the Gold Coast

1827—Founding of Fourah Bay College in Sierra Leone

1833—Britain emancipates enslaved people within its empire

1835—France outlaws slave trade

1835—Basel Evangelical Missionary Society establishes a mission at Akropong, Gold Coast

1840—British navy blockades slave outpost of Gallinas in Sierra Leone/Liberia

1840—Battle of Osogbo; Ibadan defeats Ilorin and limits southward expansion of Sokoto Caliphate

1840s—Rise of Ibadan; rise of Tukolor Empire

1842—United States reinstates antislavery naval patrols

1842—British missionaries arrive in Badagry, Nigeria

1845—British missionaries arrive in Abeokuta, Nigeria

1847—Declaration of Republic of Liberia

1848—France emancipates enslaved people

1849—France settles liberated African enslaved people in Libreville, Gabon

1851—British navy bombards Lagos

1851—Dahomey attack on Abeokuta

1855—Second Franco-Trarza War in Senegal

1857—Tukolor Empire besieges French at Fort Medina

1861—British occupation of Lagos

1862—United States government recognizes Liberia

1863—Emancipation of enslaved people within the United States

1863–64—Tensions between British and Asante in Gold Coast

1864—Dahomey attack on Abeokuta

1864—Samuel Ajayi Crowther becomes first African bishop of the Anglican Church

1865—British intervention in Yoruba wars

1869—Jaja establishes city-state of Opobo in
what is now south-eastern Nigeria

1871—Bible published in Twi language

1873—Anglo-Asante War

1886—End of slavery in Cuba

1888—End of slavery in Brazil

coastal trade; the spread of missionary Christianity, which produced enclaves of Christian converts and a literature in local languages; and the founding of colonies of Westernized and Christianized formerly enslaved people. The economic transition of the 1800s also led to the increased use of slave labor within West Africa and continued warfare between African states seeking to control coastal trade with violence fueled by firearm imports. One of the most important changes of this period involved the nature of foreign engagement with West Africa. European and American slavers of the 1700s had mostly waited on the Atlantic shoreline for deliveries of enslaved people by African intermediaries. However, the British and French of the early to middle 1800s began to intrude more robustly within West Africa, expanding their small coastal colonies inland and fighting wars against African powers to secure trade routes and sources of raw materials. Concurrently, a series of Islamist movements in the West African hinterland established several large and expansionist Muslim empires fully engaged in slave raiding and the employment of slave labor in plantation agriculture. The nineteenth-century growth of European colonialism and Christianity from the coast, and Muslim revitalization in the interior, represent foundational trends in the shaping of contemporary West Africa. Christianity began to spread across the southern coastal belt, Islam revived in the hinterland, the French and British began expanding their colonial holdings, and the economy emphasized export of commodities.

KEY TERMS

abolitionist movement 218

African Association 225

American Colonization
Society 233

Americo-Liberians 233

Black Loyalists 231

Black Poor 231

Church Missionary Society 223

colorism 234

Gustavus Vassa 219

Ibadan 230

Industrial Revolution 218

Kingdom of Asante 228

Krio 232

Legitimate Commerce 222

STUDY QUESTIONS

1. What were the economic, practical, and ethical reasons in favor of abolition? Who were some of the leaders of the abolition movement?

2. What was "legitimate commerce"? What impact did this new type of economy have on West African societies? How did the nature of West African slavery change after the abolition of the transatlantic slave trade?

3. Which factors contributed to the growth of Christianity in West Africa? What impulses drove the growth of missionary societies in the nineteenth century? Why were many Europeans eager to explore West Africa?

4. What promoted an increase in wars and conflicts in West Africa in the nineteenth century? Which state emerged as a dominant power as a result of the Yoruba Wars?

5. Why were coastal settlements like Granville Town and Freetown founded in the late eighteenth and early nineteenth centuries? Who were the Americo-Liberians?

6. Which large empires were founded by jihadists in the interior of West Africa in the nineteenth century?

Please see page FR-5 for the Further Readings for this chapter. For additional digital learning resources please go to https://www.oup.com/he/falola-stapleton1e

East Africa, c. 1800–1880: Expansion of the Slave Trade

Slave exports from the East African coast increased dramatically during the nineteenth century. Starting in the late 1700s, the increased price of enslaved people and eventually British antislavery naval operations in West Africa led to some European and colonial American slaving ships travelling the long distance around the Cape of Good Hope to East Africa or Madagascar, where they acquired captives and brought them to the Caribbean, Brazil, Cuba, and the United States. From the 1790s, given trade disruptions in the Atlantic associated with the American and Haitian revolutions, sugar production and export expanded on France's Indian Ocean island colonies of Réunion and Mauritius. These colonial sugar plantations relied on the labor of an increasing number of enslaved people from East Africa, with most coming from Mozambique and Madagascar. On Mauritius, the number of enslaved people almost doubled, from around 34,000 in 1787 to around 65,000 in 1807. Although Revolutionary France banned slavery in 1794, the French plantations owners of Réunion and Mauritius ignored this injunction and governed themselves until the re-establishment of slavery by Napoleon. With the British occupation of Mauritius in 1810, the island's sugar exports entered the British market, causing a further expansion of plantations and associated slave labor. The importation of East African enslaved people continued on Réunion well into the late nineteenth century. By the mid-1800s, Madagascar was transformed from a slave exporter into an importer of East African enslaved people, adding to regional demand.

A Malagasy woman
dressed in European
fashion, Tamatave, late
nineteenth century.

While Kilwa and Mozambique Island became the primary coastal assembling points for enslaved people brought by caravans from the East African hinterland, the pattern of monsoon winds made it difficult for large sailing ships to access these ports. As a result, small vessels transported enslaved people from these centers north to the island of **Zanzibar**, from where slave ships brought them to Réunion and Mauritius. This turned Zanzibar into a major trade hub, and the Omani Arabs who ruled the island became the main intermediaries in the expanding East African slave trade of the nineteenth century. In 1822, the abolitionist British pressured the sultan of Oman, Sayyid Sa'id, to outlaw slave trading. This prompted the Omanis, who wanted to make up for their loss in revenue, to establish clove plantations on Zanzibar, but this in fact created more demand for enslaved workers. With the British busy suppressing the transatlantic slave trade out of West Africa, the Omani Arabs easily ignored the prohibition on slaving. During the 1830s and 1840s, Zanzibar imported around 10,000 to 15,000 enslaved people per year, with some retained for local plantation work and others re-exported to the Indian Ocean markets. Furthermore, beginning in the 1820s, Zanzibar became the transit point for the export of East African ivory used to make ornaments, piano keys, and billiard balls increasingly fashionable among the growing elite of Western Europe and North America. From the 1840s, Zanzibar dispatched its own trade caravans into the East African hinterland to acquire ivory and captives, and to attempt to impose a monopoly on this trade. In 1840, recognizing the importance of the East African trade, Sultan Sayyid Sa'id

≣ **Zanzibar** *Left:* A slave market on the island of Zanzibar c. 1860. *Right:* Freed slaves on the steps of a Christian mission in Zanzibar, c. 1880.

transferred the Omani capital from Muscat to Zanzibar. From 1859 to 1872, Zanzibar imported between 20,000 and 25,000 enslaved people per year. Around the same time, an increasing number of Indian entrepreneurs arrived on Zanzibar and became the main financiers of the Swahili-Arab caravans that began to reach the interior Great Lakes region. As the British mounted naval anti-slavery patrols in the Indian Ocean in the late nineteenth century, the slave trade decentralized, with enslaved people exported from many small ports along the coast of Mozambique.

The impact of the expanded nineteenth-century slave trade on East Africa was similar to that of the earlier transatlantic slave trade on West Africa. Across much of the East African interior, violence increased, guns proliferated, communities became militarized, wooden stockades surrounded villages, people experienced displacement, and some areas became depop-

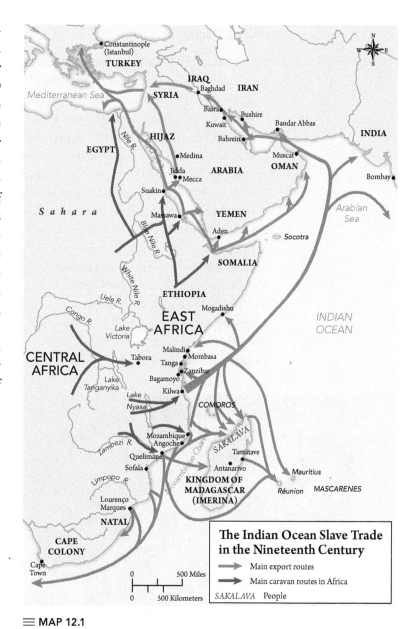

≡ MAP 12.1

ulated. Simultaneously, the new context provided an opportunity for some older states to centralize and expand, and for new leaders and powers to emerge.

Madagascar

On the island of Madagascar, the kingdom of **Imerina** emerged in the late 1700s and engaged in slave raiding and exporting. Coming to power in 1809, Radama I continued to expand the kingdom, and, in response to a prohibition on enslaving Imerina's subjects, he stretched the state's resources by dispatching slave raids further and further from its borders. In 1817, Radama entered an alliance with the abolitionist British, who provided firearms, ammunition, and military advisors, and, in turn, Imerina banned slave exports and accepted British missionaries. With British assistance, Radama created a permanent army with an officer class comprised of the Imerina nobility, soldiers conscripted from the peasantry, and labor provided by enslaved captives no longer exported. In turn, Radama used this army to conquer most of the island, and by 1825 he ruled the kingdom of Madagascar. In 1828, army officers installed Queen Ranavalona I, wife of the recently deceased Radama, and then became involved in politics and business, neglecting the kingdom's military. As such, the Sakalava states of western Madagascar reasserted their autonomy and began exporting enslaved people to Zanzibar. During the 1830s and 1840s, Ranavalona I sought to reduce foreign domination by breaking the alliance with Britain and attempting to establish a local firearms manufacturing industry. In 1845, French and British warships bombarded the port of Tamatave on the island's east coast in retaliation for the queen threatening European missionaries and **Malagasy** Christian converts. Later, in 1869, Queen Ranavalona II adopted a different policy, making Christianity the official religion, ordering the burning of traditional religious symbols, and accepting British missionaries and soldiers. Ruling until 1883, she also attempted to curb deforestation by encouraging construction with brick instead of wood and banning slash-and-burn agriculture and charcoal

≡ **Queen Ranavalona II** ruled the Kingdom of Madagascar from 1868 to 1883.

making in forest areas. At the same time, Prime Minister Rainilaiarivony, also the queen's husband, reformed the army and imported weapons from Britain and the United States. During the 1800s, the centralization and expansion of Imerina led to Madagascar transforming from an exporter of enslaved Malagasy people to an importer of enslaved East Africans who worked in large-scale agricultural projects. In the 1870s, the number of enslaved people imported to Madagascar per year increased from 11,000 to 17,000, and this practice continued into the 1880s.

Ethiopia

Nineteenth-century Ethiopia experienced a resurgence of imperial power. At the start of the nineteenth century, the provincial rulers of Tigray, Shewa, and Amhara dominated the Ethiopian emperor. Egypt's invasion of nearby Sudan in the 1820s and the con-

Ethiopia in the Nineteenth Century

≡ **MAP 12.2**

tinued Ottoman presence at Massawa on the Red Sea coast prompted Ethiopia's regional leaders to seek military assistance from fellow Christian powers Britain and France, but these requests went unheeded. In the mid-1800s, frontier clashes between the modernized Egyptian army in Sudan and Ethiopian forces demonstrated the ineffectiveness of the latter. During an Ethiopian civil war in the early 1850s, Kasa Haylu, a minor member of the royal family, gained control of Amhara and the Ethiopian capital city of Gondar. In 1855, Kasa captured the ruler of

Tigray, who intended to take the Ethiopian throne, and then had himself installed as Emperor Tewodros in reference to a prophesied king who would defeat Islam and retake Jerusalem. Moving the Ethiopian capital to the strategically located Debre Tabor and turning the natural stronghold of Maqdala into his headquarters, Tewodros organized military expeditions that subjugated Tigray, Shewa, and the rebellious province of Wollo, and he married into Tigray's ruling family. Centralizing the state, Tewodros replaced feudal regional lords with military leaders loyal to the emperor and constructed a series of roads from his capital to the provinces.

However, a lack of resources undermined Tewodros's desire to create a permanent and modernized army paid by the central government, and this meant he had to continue relying on soldiers who robbed the peasantry, alienating them from the imperial court. Given his failure to import modern weapons, Tewodros forced Western missionaries working in Ethiopia to construct artillery for his army. In the early 1860s, threats from the Egyptians in Sudan and a trade blockade by the Ottomans on the Red Sea coast compelled Tewodros to appeal to Britain for assistance. However, London rejected this appeal as it had become dependent on supplies of Egyptian cotton, and the Ottoman Empire served as an ally against possible Russian expansion into British-ruled India. Tewodros responded by detaining British diplomats in Ethiopia. As a result, in 1867–68, a British-Indian expeditionary force from India landed on the coast of what is now Eritrea and marched inland, defeating the poorly equipped Ethiopian army at Maqdala, freeing the British hostages, and prompting Tewodros to commit suicide. Although the British force withdrew, they left behind modern weapons for the regional ruler of Tigray, Kasa Mercha, who had supported their operation. Subsequently, Kasa used these arms to defeat the ruler of Amhara, who claimed the emperorship, and in 1871 he seized the throne, taking the name Emperor Yohannes IV. At the same time, Shewa remained autonomous under the provincial ruler Menelik, who would later become emperor.

Great Lakes Kingdoms

At the turn of the eighteenth and nineteenth century, **Buganda** represented the primary power of the northern part of the Great Lakes region, eclipsing the nearby state of Bunyoro. While Buganda conquered new territory and reached its largest size in the 1820s, its army became too large and hierarchical and therefore vulnerable to guerrilla attacks by small communities defending their independence. Since Arab traders brought the first firearms to Buganda in 1844 and these made a huge impression by contributing to a battlefield defeat against Bunyoro, Buganda shifted its approach to warfare from close combat with spear and shield to shooting with flintlock muskets. However, despite its new weapons, Buganda struggled to retain its declining regional power during the mid- and late nineteenth century. In the early 1850s, Buganda's King Suna founded a series of military chieftaincies that answered to the central court, and he expanded the number of men liable for military service. Responding to the arrival of more coastal traders south of Lake Victoria, Suna used Buganda's canoe navy to try to impose greater control over the northern half of the lake, but island communities resisted tenaciously. Coming to power in 1856, King Mutesa orchestrated numerous military campaigns during the 1860s and 1870s to reinforce Buganda's regional authority, but many of them experienced defeat or logistical problems. Unable to expand any further, Buganda launched long-distance raids such as an 1879 expedition to Rwanda that was badly defeated. While these reverses on land prompted Mutesa to further expand the canoe navy and renew efforts to control Lake Victoria, Buganda's inland warriors were unprepared to fight on the water and did not work well with the socially marginalized islanders who paddled the canoes. As such, Buganda's large navy struggled to subdue the expert canoeists of the island fishing communities who mounted hit-and-run attacks on the lake. Under Mutesa, influence in Buganda shifted from experienced war leaders to a royal bodyguard equipped with imported firearms and rewarded for loyalty to the king rather than military effectiveness. Around this time, some Baganda (people of Buganda) began to convert to Islam and Christianity, prompted by the arrival of Arab traders and European missionaries. During the second half of the nineteenth century, Buganda became the largest exporter of enslaved people in the northern Great Lakes.

THEODOROS II
ROI D'ABYSSINIE

≡ **Emperor Tewodros II** ruled Ethiopia from 1855 to 1868. He committed suicide after British forces defeated the Ethiopians at the Battle of Maqdala.

Emerging from a period of civil war at the end of the eighteenth century, the kingdom of **Rwanda** continued its expansion west toward Lake Kivu and northwest into the volcano area, almost doubling in size between 1800 and 1870. Throughout the first half of the nineteenth century, Rwanda clashed with an

≡ **Mutesa I** ruled the Kingdom of Buganda for nearly 30 years, from 1856 to 1884.

emergent Burundi, though neither state could overwhelm the other. In the 1850s, Rwanda began trading with caravans from the coast, but they were banned from entering the kingdom due to anxiety over Swahili-Arab guns. In 1871, an Arab caravan was annihilated when it violated this prohibition. During a civil war in the late 1860s, a royal wife called Muronrunkwere installed her young son Rwabugiri as king of Rwanda. Coming of age in 1875, Rwabugiri embarked on an almost continuous series of expansionist wars and placed newly conquered areas under the supervision of a royal wife and military commander. These military operations included a major raid on Burundi in 1879–80, several expeditions to rebellious Ijwi Island in Lake Kivu in the late 1880s and 1890s, and other invasions south and west of Lake Kivu to obtain ivory and enslaved people for export. Rwanda's defeat of invading Swahili-Arabs in 1888 and 1891 likely promoted a false confidence in its armies' ability to combat firearm-equipped enemies, and, as such, the kingdom did not incorporate guns into its military system. Given the demands of feeding constantly mobilized armies, Rwanda's peasantry staged three major provincial rebellions and many small uprisings during the late nineteenth century. Simultaneously, Rwabugiri's centralization of the state promoted further polarization among the kingdom's Tutsi pastoralists and Hutu farmers.

During the nineteenth century, **Burundi** became a prominent power in the southern Great Lakes region, competing with nearby Rwanda. Under Ntare Rugamba (Battle Lion), who ruled from around 1800 to 1850, Burundi established a core of professional warriors and created a new administrative system whereby royal princes, royal wives, or court officials governed subjugated areas and they continued expansion. Nevertheless, Burundi remained less centralized than Rwanda, with conflict emerging among royal princes (Baganwa) and between the king and the princes. In the 1850s, Mwezi Gisabo, the youngest son of the late ruler, came to power in a civil war, and in the late 1860s he fought another conflict to wrest power from his older brother, who had served as regent. From the late 1860s to 1880s, Mwezi Gisabo used Burundi's formidable military to fend off incursions by Swahili-Arab and Nyamwezi slave raiders spreading throughout the region.

The arrival of **Maasai** pastoralists during the eighteenth century stimulated centralization among the Shambaa farmers of the Usambara highlands of what is now northern Tanzania. The Shambaa abandoned vulnerable villages on the lower slopes and moved to higher ground, establishing large defensive towns that also attracted refugees from further afield. While a legendary hunter named Mbegha founded the original **Shambaa** kingdom, a civil war in the late 1700s led to its division into two states centered on the towns of Mshihwi and Vugha. During the early and mid-nineteenth century, the Shambaa kingdom of Vugha clashed with gun-armed Zigua people engaged in the ivory and slave trade with the coast. In the 1870s and 1880s, rival Shambaa leaders acquired guns by exporting enslaved people to the coast and received backing from the antagonistic rulers of Mombasa and Zanzibar. By this time, power in the Usambara area shifted from the highlands to the lowlands because of proximity to coastal trade routes.

The **Pare** people, living between the Usambara Mountains and Mount Kilimanjaro along the current Kenya–Tanzania border, transformed their small states into a number of larger kingdoms during the eighteenth century. While the northern Pare formed the single state of Ugweno, united by the common language of Kingweno, the southern Pare established six separate states and spoke the Chasa language. In these Pare kingdoms, rainmakers became important ritual and military leaders. Some Pare clans specialized in iron production and exported iron to the Chagga people around Mount Kilimanjaro, the Maasai on the plains, and south to the Shambaa in return for livestock and hides. By around 1800, increased trade with the coastal centers of Mombasa and Pangani led to increased warfare along the Pangani River. This initially represented an opportunity for Para ironworkers, who began the large-scale production and export of weapons such as spearheads and axe blades. By the 1860s, Swahili-Arab traders from the coast allied themselves to specific Pare rulers and supplied them with firearms used to take captives from neighboring groups. From the south, Shambaa and Zigua gunmen entered the Pare highlands and became intermediaries in the ivory and slave trade. Although Ugweno's ruler, Ghendewa, attempted to stabilize the kingdom in the mid-1800s, the state fragmented as upstart commoners with firearms usurped traditional elites with ritual powers, and previously subordinate leaders became independent slavers supplying the coastal trade. During the 1880s, as a result of the increase in slave raids, agricultural collapse caused famine and armed guards accompanied women to market.

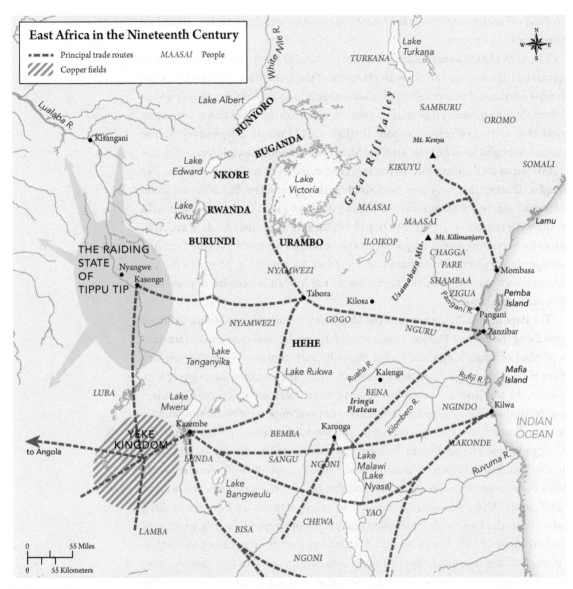

East Africa in the Nineteenth Century

- – – – Principal trade routes   *MAASAI*   People
- ///// Copper fields

≡ **MAP 12.3**

While the people of present-day central Tanzania lived in many small farming communities at the start of the nineteen century, the arrival of Swahili-Arabs from the east coast and the Ngoni from the south in the 1840s stimulated political centralization in this area. As such, in the mid-1800s, the Sangu leader Munyigumba subjugated other Sangu groups on the Ruaha Plain and established a large Sangu state that raided neighboring groups and trade caravans. Founding a capital at Ilamba on the Ruaha River, Munyigumba's Sangu copied Ngoni military methods such as age-regimental organization, encirclement tactics, and the use of short stabbing spears and large cowhide shields. In the same area, another leader called Munyigumba, perhaps named after the Sangu ruler, launched a series of conflicts from the 1850s to 1870s that led to the amalgamation of the Hehe Kingdom. The name Hehe stems from a war cry "Hee, Hee, Hee, we are fighting the enemy, ahee!" Like the Sangu, the Hehe adopted Ngoni fighting techniques. Emerging as the dominant power on Tanzania's southern highlands, Munyigumba's Hehe drove the Sangu off the Ruaha Plain and into nearby hills and pushed the Bena people from the forests of the Iringa Plateau into the open Kilombero Valley. Furthermore, the Hehe expanded north into the land of the Gogo people, where they clashed with southward-moving Maasai pastoralists and east toward what is now the city of Kilosa, where they sometimes attacked and sometimes traded with Swahili-Arab caravans. Although firearms were proliferating in East Africa during the mid-to-late nineteenth century, Hehe expansion relied not on guns but on Munyigumba's leadership and strategic alliances. In addition, most of the people the Hehe fought had not widely adopted firearms. After Munyigumba's death in 1878, a Hehe civil war broke out, pitting the late ruler's son Mkwawa against a Nyamwezi rival called Mwambambe, who recruited Ruga Ruga gunmen from the warlord Nyungu ya Mawe (see below). Around 1881, Mkwawa's army slaughtered his rival's force at the Battle of Ilundamatwe ("the place where many heads are piled up"). As leader of the Hehe, Mkwawa continued the policy of expansion during the 1880s, fighting the Maasai and Sangu, clashing with the Ngoni but then making peace with them, and raiding Swahili-Arab caravans. Inspired by a stone fort built by the Sangu that the Hehe unsuccessfully attacked several times, Mkwawa ordered the construction of a similar stone fortification at his capital of Kalenga.

Hinterland Warlords

In the parts of East Africa not governed by established kingdoms, the expansion of the slave and ivory trades in the 1800s led to the rise of powerful warlords who organized raiding parties consisting of displaced young men generally called **"Ruga Ruga"** armed with imported firearms. Central to this process were the Nyamwezi people who lived in what is now western Tanzania and who had already become specialist caravan carriers and guards. In the 1850s, the Nyamwezi leader, Msiri, led his people into the central African interior and carved out their new **Yeke** kingdom in a copper-rich territory taken from the pre-existing Lunda and

Luba states. While Msiri primarily exported enslaved people to the East African coast, he began sending caravans west to Benguela on the Atlantic coast of Angola in the 1870s. Beginning around 1860, a man called Mbula Mtelya took the name **Mirambo**—which means "corpses" and signified his martial prowess—and united several Nyamwezi communities. Mirambo's new and larger state of Urambo dominated trade east of Lake Tanganyika and south of Lake Victoria. Building a permanent army under his personnel command, Mirambo embarked on a series of conquests that enlarged his territory and compelled subjugated communities to supply him with young men who became his Ruga Ruga fighters. Around the same time, coastal Arabs based at the commercial center of Tabora took over the nearby Nyamwezi state of Unyanyembe, using it as a base from which to control regional trade. From 1871 to 1875, Mirambo and the Tabora Arabs fought a war over trade routes between the Indian Ocean coast and the port of Ujiji on the eastern shore of Lake Tanganyika. While the Arabs received some reinforcements from Zanzibar and blocked the Nyamwezi from acquiring gunpowder, the divided Arab leaders failed to contain Mirambo's guerrilla attacks that disrupted trade. Ultimately, Mirambo agreed to the passage of Arab caravans through his territory as long as they paid a tax. During the 1870s, Nyungu ya Mawe (pot of stone), an exiled Nyamwezi leader from Unyanyembe, forged a new conquest state south of Tabora and east of Lake Rukwa, subduing a number of small Kimbu kingdoms engaged in ivory exports to the coast. Copying Mirambo's methods, Nyungu ya Mawe extracted enslaved people and ivory from conquered districts governed by his military leaders. Further south, around Lake Malawi, gun-armed Yao raiders attacked decentralized Chewa farming and fishing communities, taking captives to the coast of Mozambique. In the 1860s, a man named Hamed bin Muhammad, born in Zanzibar and popularly known as **Tippu Tip**, founded a raiding state on the west side of Lake Tanganyika along the Lualaba River. With his Swahili-Arab and Nyamwezi gunmen, Tippu Tip exported enslaved people and ivory east to Zanzibar where he also founded his own clove plantations. Since they had little experience with firearms, the people of Central Africa struggled to resist gun-armed invaders from East Africa.

≣ **Ruga Ruga.** This 1890 engraving shows a band of Ruga Ruga warriors

Pastoralist Expansion

During the late 1700s and early 1800s, on the grass-lands of present-day Kenya and northern Tanzania, the hitherto decentralized Maasai herders began to rally around prophets who attracted warriors from across the society, directed large raiding operations, and amassed huge personal herds from shares of captured cattle. As a result, the moderating influence of the Maasai elders declined and the warriors became more aggressive, which led to a series of nineteenth-century wars between the Maasai and the various Iloikop groups of the region. In the early nineteenth century, a prophet, or **laibon**, called Supet led warriors from several Maasai groups in a southward push into what is now northern Tanzania. During the 1810s, Supet led his alliance of Maasai pure pastoralists against the Iloogolala, an Iloikop group who lived by farming, herding, and raiding. The Maasai, in what is remembered as the first significant war in their history, scattered and absorbed Iloogolala communities. In the early 1860s, after a period of drought and cattle raiding, the now elderly Supet directed another major Maasai campaign that displaced the Ilosekelai, anoth-

≡ **Slave trader.** Tippu Tip (1832–1905), whose real name was Hamed bin Muhammad, founded and led a slave raiding state on the west side of Lake Tanganyika during the late nineteenth century.

er Iloikop group west of Lake Nakuru. By the 1870s, a new prophet called Mbatiany, Supet's son, united a dozen Maasai groups into the Purko-Kisongo confederation. In the early 1870s, in the last Maasai-Iloikop war, Mbatiany rallied a huge Maasai army that defeated the Ilaikipiak in a series of bloody battles on the east side of Lake Nakuru and evicted them from the Rift Valley grassland. Maasai attempts to expand further south into central Tanzania were frustrated by the Gogo in the 1830s and the Hehe from the 1860s to 1880s. From the 1840s, the increased number of Swahili-Arab caravans entering the East African hinterland avoided the Maasai area as it was arid, and the Maasai cultivated a fearsome reputation and developed courageous charging tactics to counter slow-firing muskets. While in the first half of the 1800s warfare among East African pastoralists like the Maasai strove to secure resources for a growing population, in the second half of the century it was about feeding starving people suffering from drought and new human and cattle diseases introduced by increased links with the coast.

In the early 1800s, the pure pastoralist and decentralized **Turkana** people moved east from present-day northern Uganda to Lake Turkana in northwestern

Kenya. With a breed of cattle well suited to arid conditions and trade links that gave them iron weapons, the Turkana expelled or absorbed the earlier inhabitants of the Lake Turkana area such the Siger and Kor people. Like the Maasai, the Turkana organized their society around councils of elders and age grades. However, the Turkana expansion weakened the authority of elders as Turkana groups spread out over a large area. Furthermore, increased warfare and contact with the Maasai inspired the Turkana to change from generational age grades in which all of a man's brothers had to be initiated into adulthood before any of his sons, to biological age grades in which all the society's young men became adult warriors. In turn, the Turkana age grades increasingly served as cohesive military units in which young men proved themselves and then gained status through achievements in warfare, particularly cattle raiding. Due to Maasai resistance, Turkana expansion slowed in the 1820s and 1830s, but it picked up again in the 1850s with the rise of a popular diviner called Lokerio who mobilized armies and encouraged widespread raiding from which he gained a share of the captured cattle. During the 1870s, Maasai attacks and the outbreak of a cattle disease called lung sickness, which did not affect Turkana cattle, facilitated Turkana expansion south of Lake Turkana. Unlike the Maasai and Turkana, centralizing prophets did not emerge among the Samburu, a similar group of pastoralists in present-day northern Kenya, because they had to move their herds around much more frequently in the very dry environment and therefore did not have opportunities for large gatherings of warriors.

European Explorers

The expansion of the East African slave and ivory trade during the nineteenth century attracted more Europeans to the region, including elephant hunters, abolitionists, missionaries, diplomats and explorers. As happened with West Africa a few years earlier, European explorers of the mid- to late nineteenth century took an interest in mapping the interior of East Africa. Founded in 1830, the **Royal Geographical Society** in Britain supported exploratory expeditions to various parts of the world, including Africa, and spread the results of these ventures through lectures and the publications of journals and books. This group absorbed the older African Association, which had sponsored expeditions to explore the Niger River in West Africa. By the middle 1800s, European explorers' interests shifted to East Africa, and they became obsessed with finding the source of the famous Nile River. Many of these expeditions used Zanzibar as a staging area to hire African guides and porters, and prepare supplies, and they then traveled inland on established caravan routes, giving trade goods to local rulers to secure their passage and suffering terribly from tropical disease. Though East Africa's geographic features were familiar to the local people who lived around them, the explorers gave these lakes and

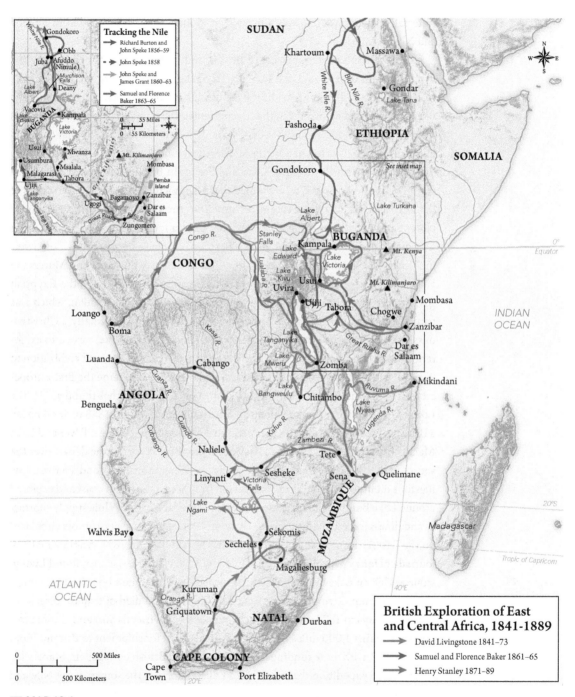

Tracking the Nile

→ Richard Burton and John Speke 1856–59

- - → John Speke 1858

→ John Speke and James Grant 1860–63

→ Samuel and Florence Baker 1863–65

0   55 Miles
0   55 Kilometers

British Exploration of East and Central Africa, 1841-1889

→ David Livingstone 1841–73

→ Samuel and Florence Baker 1861–65

→ Henry Stanley 1871–89

≡ **MAP 12.4**

waterfalls new names that were formalized in maps and books printed in Europe and North America.

In 1858, British explorers Richard Burton and John Hanning Speke became the first Europeans to arrive at Lake Tanganyika. Speke continued north to Lake Victoria (called Nyanza and other names by the region's inhabitants), which he named after the British queen, and he suspected that it represented the Nile's source. To confirm this theory, Speke conducted another expedition between 1860 and 1863 that marched inland from Zanzibar to Lake Victoria, where he found the mouth of the White Nile that he followed north through Sudan and Egypt. In Britain, a public disagreement played out between Speke, who claimed that Lake Victoria constituted the source of the Nile, and Burton, who expressed skepticism. Around the same time, British explorer Samuel Baker and his wife Florence Baker, a formerly enslaved person from Ottoman-ruled Eastern Europe, used Khartoum as a base of operations, "discovering" Lake Albert, which was named after Queen Victoria's husband, and Murchison Falls, named after the head of the Royal Geographic Society. In 1869, the Egyptian government hired Baker to extend Egyptian rule over southern Sudan, which was named Equatoria, and to suppress the slave trade in that area. Originally, a Christian missionary working in what is now Botswana, **David Livingstone**, turned to exploration as he thought that bringing British commerce, Christianity, and civilization to Africa was the only way to end the slave trade. In 1855, he became the first European to see Victoria Falls (called Mosi-oa-Tunya or "the smoke that thunders" by the Lozi people), which he named after the British queen, and from 1858 to 1864 he led a British government–funded expedition that explored the Zambezi River and Lake Malawi (then called Lake Nyasa). In 1866, attempting to resolve the debate over the source of the Nile by searching the area south of lakes Tanganyika and Victoria, Livingstone mounted an expedition that set out from the East African coast and explored around Lake Bangweulu, Lake Mweru, and the Lualaba River. While supply shortages and illness forced Livingstone to rely on assistance from slavers, rumors circulated on the East African coast and in Britain that he had died. In 1871, Anglo-American journalist **Henry Morton Stanley**, funded by a New York newspaper, found Livingstone at Ujiji on Lake Tanganyika and returned home to write a book and gain international acclaim. Livingstone continued his journey and died of tropical disease in eastern Zambia in 1873, but his African employees and friends Susi and Chuma carried his remains 1,000 miles to the East African coast for shipment to Britain. From 1874 to 1877, with more funding from American and British newspapers, Stanley led a well-armed expedition that established Lake Victoria as the source of the Nile and used the Congo River system to cross Africa from East to West. Published in New York in 1878, Stanley's two-volume account of the journey, *Through Darkest Africa*, earned him more fame and wealth and firmly established the stereotype of the **Dark Continent**. Although explorers like Burton and Livingstone had little impact on East

and Central Africa at the time they visited these regions, and they could not foresee future European colonial conquest, their stories of travel and adventure popularized Africa in Western Europe and North America and revealed the existence of navigable rivers and valuable natural resources in the African hinterland. In part, this set the stage for the European "Scramble for Africa" that began in the 1880s.

≡ **European Exploration of East Africa** *Left:* Murchison Falls, sighted by Samuel Baker and Florence Baker in 1864. *Center:* Victoria Falls—"The Smoke that Thunders"—is one of the largest waterfalls in the world. *Right:* The 1871 meeting of explorers David Livingstone and Henry Morton Stanley at Ujiji, in what is now Tanzania.

Conclusion

Nineteenth-century East Africa experienced a dramatic expansion of the slave trade. The causes of this included new labor demands from plantations on Indian Ocean islands and the shifting of transatlantic slave ships to East Africa as a result of British efforts to suppress the West African slave trade. In East Africa, the escalation of the slave trade intertwined with the concurrent increase in ivory exports to satisfy new markets in Europe and North America. As Swahili-Arab caravans penetrated the East African interior, Omani-ruled Zanzibar became the main collection and transit point for enslaved people and ivory. On the East African mainland, the slave and ivory trade brought increased warfare as guns proliferated and people fortified their communities. Among the region's existing states, Buganda struggled to maintain its dominance in the northern Great Lakes and became a chief exporter of enslaved people, and Rwanda and Burundi centralized and embarked on wars of conquest. On the other hand, the Shambaa and Pare states, which had emerged in the previous century, fragmented as a result of their encounters with slave and ivory traders armed with guns. Taking advantage of this new situation, warlords such as Mirambo and Tippu Tip organized and armed displaced young men to dominate areas where they extracted enslaved people and ivory. Decentralized specialist pastoral groups, such as the Maasai and Turkana, rallied around prophets and continued their expansion into what is now Kenya and Tanzania. Simultaneously, European explorers ventured into East Africa and returned home to generate public interest in the region.

Timeline

1790s—Expansion of sugar production and increased importation of enslaved people on French islands of Réunion and Mauritius; slave ships from the Atlantic begin to sail to the East African coast

c. 1800–50—Reign of Ntare Rugamba in Burundi; conflict between Burundi and Rwanda—Buganda defends its position as the most powerful state in northern Great Lakes

early 1800—expansion of pastoralists—Turkana pastoralists move to Lake Turkana; Maasai move south into southern Kenya and northern Tanzania

1810s—War between Maasai led by the prophet Supet and Iloogolala

1817—Madagascar's Imerina Kingdon allies with the British

1830—Formation of the Royal Geographic Society

1840—Sultan of Oman moves capital to Zanzibar

1840s+—Increase in Swahili-Arab caravans moving into East African interior for enslaved people and ivory; proliferation of firearms

1845—British and French warships bombard Tamatave in eastern Madagascar

1850s—Rise of the Hehe kingdom

1850s—Establishment of Yeke state by Msiri; expansion of Turkana led by prophet Lokerio

1855—Installation of Emperor Tewodros in Ethiopia

1856—King Mutesa comes to power in Buganda

1858—British explorers Burton and Speke arrive at Lake Tanganyika and Speke names Lake Victoria

1858–64—Livingstone leads Zambezi Expedition and explores Lake Malawi

c. 1860s—Rise of the warlords Mirambo in central Tanzania and Tippu Tip west of Lake Tanganyika

1860–63—Speke's expedition to Lake Victoria

early 1860s—War between Supet's Maasai and Ilosekelai around Lake Nakuru; drought and diseases plague the Maasai

1866—Livingstone sets out to investigate source of the Nile

1868—British military expedition to Ethiopia; death of Emperor Tewodros

1869—Queen Ranavalona II declares Christianity the official religion of Imerina; Madagascar is now an importer rather than exporter of enslaved people

1869—Egyptian government hires Samuel Baker to suppress the slave trade in southern Sudan

Late 1860s—coming of age of Mwezi Gisabo in Burundi

1871—Stanley finds Livingstone at Ujiji on Lake Tanganyika

c. 1870s—Rise of the warlord Nyungu ya Mawe in present-day Tanzania; conflict between Maasai led by the prophet Mbatiany and the Ilaikipiak around Lake Nakuru

1871—Installation of Emperor Yohannes IV in Ethiopia

1873—Death of Livingstone in eastern Zambia

1871–75—War between Mirambo and Swahili-Arabs in central Tanzania

1874–77—Stanley crosses Africa from east to west

1875—King Rwabugiri of Rwanda comes of age and initiates military expansion

1878—Rise of Mkwawa as Hehe ruler

1879—Failed raid by Buganda against Rwanda

1879–80—War between Rwanda and Burundi

KEY TERMS

Buganda 248

Burundi 250

Dark Continent 258

David Livingstone 258

Henry Morton
  Stanley 258

Imerina 246

laibon 255

Maasai 251

Malagasy 246

Mirambo 254

Pare 251

Royal Geographical
  Society 256

Ruga Ruga 253

Rwanda 249

Shambaa 251

Tippu Tip 254

Turkana 255

Yeke 253

Zanzibar 244

STUDY QUESTIONS

1. Why did slave exports from the East African coast increase dramatically during the nineteenth century? What was Zanzibar's position in this trade? How did the increase in the slave trade effect East African societies the way the earlier transatlantic slave trade impacted West African peoples?

2. How did Radama I rise to power in Imerina? What was the style of his rule? What were Malagasy attitudes toward slavery?

3. How did Ethiopia enjoy an imperial resurgence in the nineteenth century? What role did religion play?

4. Which states competed for power in the Great Lakes region in the nineteenth century? What impact did the arrival of Maasai pastoralists have on the peoples of northern Tanzania?

5. What effect did powerful men like Tippu Tip and Mirambo have on East African politics and societies in the late nineteenth century? Who were the Ruga Ruga?

6. How did the expansion of the East African slave and ivory trade during the nineteenth century attract elephant hunters, abolitionists, missionaries, diplomats, and explorers?

7. Why did the Maasai rally around prophets in the late 1700s and early 1800s?

Please see page FR-5 for the Further Readings for this chapter.
For additional digital learning resources please go to
https://www.oup.com/he/falola-stapleton1e

13

Southern Africa, c. 1800–1870: Expansion of Settler Colonialism

Southern Africa experienced European **colonialism** earlier than most parts of Africa with the relative lack of tropical disease facilitating the arrival of European settlers or **settler colonialism** that became rare in the rest of the continent. Nevertheless, at the start of the nineteenth century indigenous African states and societies still controlled most of the region, though they were becoming more involved in international trade. In 1800, the Cape Colony comprised the southwestern tip of Africa and was home to a well-established and racially hierarchical settler society that exploited African and Asian slave labor in agricultural production. On the Cape's arid northern frontier, Griqua horsemen of European and African origin raided African communities such as the Sotho and Tswana, taking livestock and captives to trade with the settlers of the colony. On the Cape's eastern frontier, pastoral Dutch-speaking Boer settlers struggled with the indigenous Xhosa and Khoisan over control of grazing land. However, most Xhosa-speaking people, living further east along the Indian Ocean coast, had little direct contact with colonialists. On the interior Highveld and on the east side of the Drakensberg Mountains, a series of African states competed with each other over access to expanding international trade centered on Delagoa Bay in what is now southern Mozambique. In the north, across the Limpopo River, the large Rozvi Empire dominated the Zimbabwe Plateau and included Shona and Kalanga people. Over the next few decades, Southern Africa experienced profound change as some new and larger African states emerged and settler colonialism expanded across most of present-day South Africa.

Commemorating the Xhosa cattle killing. This is a detail from the Keiskamma Tapestry, created by weavers in the Eastern Cape Province of South Africa to commemorate the "cattle killing" episode of 1856–57. This particular panel depicts the aftermath of the slaughter of living cattle and the hope for return of ancestral cattle.

State Expansion and Conflict in the Southeast

In the early 1800s, Southeastern Africa became the scene of the expansion of African states, increased warfare, and long-distance movements of people. For many years, during the late nineteenth century and most of the twentieth century, historians attributed this tumult solely to the rise and expansion of the Zulu kingdom under its founder King Shaka, a great military leader who supposedly revolutionized warfare in the region. According to this traditional interpretation, Zulu aggression compelled people to seek protection in mountain strongholds, such as those in Lesotho and Swaziland, or to undertake dramatic relocations, such as that accomplished by the Ndebele, who moved from the southeastern coast to the Highveld and eventually to what is now Zimbabwe. Considered part of an internal African revolution called the **mfecane** or "crushing," scholars saw these events as separate from the expansion of European colonialism overtaking other parts of Southern Africa at the same time. Views of Shaka varied, with colonial historians vilifying him as a tyrant and African nationalists celebrating him as a visionary leader. In the late twentieth century, historians seeking to explain this early-nineteenth-century process began to look beyond the singular figure of **Shaka** as a great man of history and gave more credit to broader factors such as regional droughts and increasing external trade, particularly via Delagoa Bay, in stimulating change in the region. The most controversial view of the subject involved looking at the role of different forms of colonial aggression and intrusion in stimulating African state formation, warfare, and movement. According to this interpretation, early-nineteenth-century African societies in the region were caught between pressures from Portuguese slaving from Delagoa Bay, raiding from the independent colonial outlet of Port Natal, military expeditions mounted from the Cape Colony, and Griqua slave and cattle raids on the Highveld. Furthermore, revisionist historians maintained that these different colonial forces had caused violence within African societies and then took the focus off themselves by blaming African leaders like Shaka for the instability. It is important to understand that this revisionist history emerged at the end of Apartheid in South Africa during the late 1980s and early 1990s. This transition was marred by violence between Zulu nationalists claiming special status as the heirs of Skaka (egged on by elements of the outgoing white minority state) and African nationalists promoting equality and unity. During the simultaneous academic debate about early-nineteenth-century Southern Africa, revisionists received accusations of racism in that they allegedly sought to ignore the agency of historic African leaders and attribute the development of African societies to colonialists, and supporters of the traditional view suffered charges of repeating colonial propaganda. More substantially, there were also disagreements over evidence

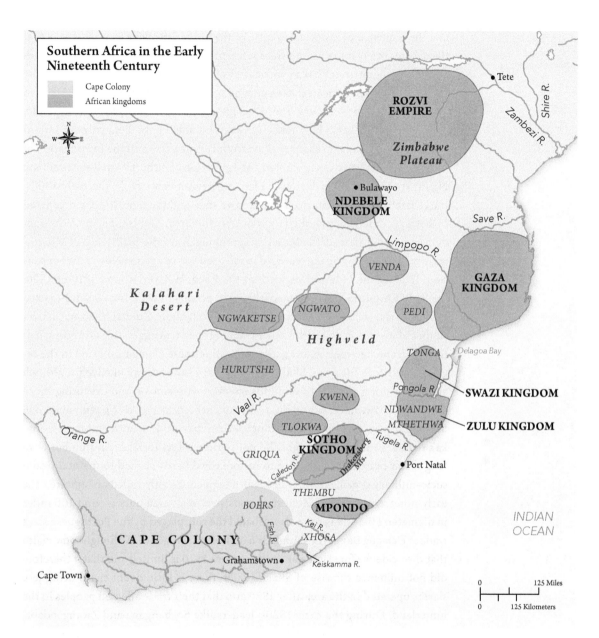

Southern Africa in the Early Nineteenth Century

Cape Colony

African kingdoms

≡ MAP 13.1

and the sequence of historical events. While limited primary sources means that the debate largely remains unresolved, few historians of Southern Africa maintain the old Zulu-centric or Shaka-centric view of these events.

A series of large African states emerged or expanded in Southeastern Africa in the early nineteenth century. These included the Zulu, Swazi, Ndebele, Mpondo, Sotho, and Ngwaketse kingdoms. On the east side of the Drakensberg Mountains, the expansion of seagoing trade from Delagoa Bay and the introduction of maize from the Americas prompted amalgamation of hitherto small states among Nguni-speaking people during the late eighteenth century. In the early 1800s, the centralized and militarized Ndwandwe state and the more loosely organized Mthethwa confederacy clashed for control of this area. At this time, the Zulu kingdom comprised a part of the Mthethwa grouping. After the 1818 defeat of Mthethwa, the Zulu of King Shaka emerged to rally resistance against Ndwandwe expansion. Driving the Ndwandwe north of the Pongola River around 1819 or 1820, the **Zulu kingdom** became one of the main powers in what is now southeastern South Africa. While traditionalist historians attribute Zulu success to Shaka's supposed invention of a lethal short-stabbing spear, an aggressive encircling battle tactic, and age-regiment organization, all of these elements existed in the region well before his time. Shaka's real military innovations involved nighttime attacks, burning villages to blind his enemies with smoke, and executing those accused of cowardice. Since Zulu warriors served in the king's regiments due to the prospect of eventually gaining cattle to pay pride wealth and marry, Shaka's regular military campaigns did not represent territorial expansion but were long-distance cattle raids meant to restore royal herds needed to maintain Zulu socio-military organization. Indeed, although commonly called an "empire," the early-nineteenth-century Zulu state consisted of an area only around 100 miles in diameter. Historians have also debated the role played by the Portuguese slave trade at Delagoa Bay in the foundation of the Zulu kingdom. Although some claim that the evidence for slaving at the bay before 1820 is limited and that it therefore did not influence the rise of Shaka's Zulu, there is little doubt that Portuguese slavers operated in the area after 1820 and that their trade affected peoples in the hinterland. During the early 1820s, leaders like Soshangane and Zwangendaba, former allies of the defeated Ndwandwe, moved their groups closer to Delagoa Bay, where they vanquished the existing Tembe and Tsonga communities and engaged in slave trading. Shortly thereafter, Soshangane and Zwangendaba led their followers northward away from the bay. In the early 1820s, possibly to get away from the increased slaving around the Delagoa Bay, Shaka moved his Zulu kingdom further south, making contact with independent British slave and ivory traders who were establishing themselves at the new outpost of Port Natal. During several military campaigns in the late 1820s, Shaka enlisted the support of these firearm-equipped colonial privateers and their African entourage. In 1828, Shaka was assassinated during a coup that brought his half-brother Dingane to power.

Around 1815, the Ndwandwe expanded their agricultural land by expelling the Ngwane people into mountains north of the Pongola River. Under King Sobhuza I, this mountain state became the Swazi kingdom, absorbed pre-existing communities, and specialized in exporting cattle to nearby Delagoa Bay. After the defeat of the Ndwandwe by the Zulu, Sobhuza tried to enter an alliance or tributary relationship with Shaka in the early 1820s, but this did not last and the Zulu mounted raids against the Swazi state for the next few decades.

At the turn of the eighteenth and nineteenth centuries, the Orange River area in central South Africa was home to a number of groups generally called **Griqua**, who were descended from Khoisan refugees, escaped enslaved people and fugitive Europeans from the Cape Colony. Using horses and guns acquired through colonial trade, the Griqua raided Tswana and Sotho communities on the southwestern Highveld, seizing captives and livestock exported south to the Cape settlers. Since the Griqua had adopted Christianity and Dutch language through their ties to the Cape, British missionaries arrived in the early 1800s, seeing them as the key to spreading Christianity in the region and therefore ignored their predatory habits. Further north, during the 1810s, the Ngwaketse Tswana Kingdom of Makaba II emerged victorious in a series of wars with the Griqua and other Tswana groups such as the Hurutshe, and gained control of western Highveld trade routes south to the Cape, east to Delagoa Bay, and north to the Zimbabwe Plateau.

In the early 1820s, the Ndwandwe–Zulu conflict in southeastern South Africa led to the departure of Mzilikazi and his Khumalo clan from the Pongola River area. They moved inland onto the Highveld around present-day Pretoria, where they absorbed Sotho and Tswana people into what became the **Ndebele kingdom**.

CHAKA KING OF THE ZOOLUS.

London. Published by E.Churton, 26 Holles St.

≡ **Zulu king.** A British depiction from 1836 of Zulu king Shaka.

≡ **Moshoeshoe** founded the kingdom of Lesotho in the 1820s and ruled until his death in 1870.

The impact of this development on the Pedi kingdom of the area is not clear, but it survived until the late nineteenth century. During the early 1830s, Mzilikazi's Ndebele shifted to the western Highveld, where they sought to dominate north–south trade between the Cape and the Zimbabwe Plateau. The Ndebele subjugated the Hurutshe Tswana and pushed the Ngwaketse Tswana further west toward the Kalahari Desert. They also raided south into the Caledon Valley. While the Ndebele constantly fought with small bands of mounted Griqua gunmen, the former did not seem to appreciate the potential destructive power of firearms and neglected acquiring them.

During the 1820s, the Caledon River, with its water and defensive flat-topped mountains, became the scene of conflict between local Sotho groups and people arriving from nearby drought-stricken areas. Among the leaders in this area was the Sotho warrior-queen Mantatisi, whom sensationalist colonial sources characterized as a giant with one eye, and the newly arrived Ngwane leader, Matiwane, who had been involved in the Ndwandwe–Zulu War. Within the Caledon's violent context, and particularly after an Ndebele incursion drove out Matiwane's Ngwane around 1827 or 1828, the Sotho leaders Sekonyela of the Tlokwa and Moshoeshoe of the Kwena established rival kingdoms based on different mountain strongholds. Subsequently, Moshoeshoe's acceptance of European Christian missionaries in the 1830s gave him colonial contacts through which his people acquired firearms and horses that gave them an advantage in local conflicts. In 1852, **Moshoeshoe** finally subdued the Tlokwa, becoming ruler of a centralized **Sotho Kingdom** or Lesotho.

Further south along the Indian Ocean coast, below the Zulu kingdom, the long-existing Mpondo state led by Faku became an aggressive power during the 1810 and 1820s, raiding and imposing tributary relations on neighboring communities. The Mpondo decisively defeated a Zulu incursion in 1824, but another Zulu attack in 1828, this time supplemented by colonial gunmen from Port Natal, was more successful in seizing cattle, though it did not displace Faku's people. In 1828, after the second Zulu raid, Faku's Mpondo joined forces with the nearby Thembu and a British expeditionary force from the Cape Colony to destroy the recently arrived Ngwane of Matiwane at the Battle of Mbolompo. While traditional historians portrayed the Mpondo of the 1820s as hapless victims of Zulu aggression, oral and documentary evidence presents a very different picture.

British Expansion

In 1806, the British seized the Cape Colony for the second and last time, as renewed hostilities with France meant London once again secured the strategically important shipping route around Southern Africa. Although the British Empire outlawed the international slave trade in 1807, the economy of the British ruled Cape Colony still depended on enslaved people and various other types of coercive labor. As with previous Dutch regimes, the British sought to impose stability on the colony's eastern frontier, where violence continued between Dutch settlers called **Boers** and more numerous Xhosa groups. In the Eastern Cape, the arrival of this second British regime tipped the local balance of power sharply to the colonial side and inspired a steady eastward expansion of the Cape Colony that continued throughout the rest of the nineteenth century. In 1811, a powerful British military expedition traveled to the Eastern Cape and violently evicted all the Xhosa communities to the eastern side of the Fish River, declaring it, as the Dutch did, the eastern border of the colony. The British total approach to warfare involving wholesale destruction of villages and crops, and the indiscriminate slaughter of men, women, and children, shocked the Xhosa, who had previously fought limited conflicts and refrained from targeting noncombatants. To guard the frontier, the British erected a series of forts and border posts, at the center of which was Grahamstown, which became the capital town of the Cape's eastern districts. Supported by British colonial policy, frontier settlers conducted livestock raids across the Fish River on the pretext of pursuing Xhosa cattle rustlers. Continued colonial aggression prompted an ambitious though ultimately disastrous Xhosa attack on Grahamstown in 1819. As a result, the British created a buffer zone along the colonial border by pushing the Xhosa yet further east over the Keiskamma River. In 1820, the arrival of British settlers bolstered the Eastern Cape's embryonic colonial towns and supplemented the region's existing Boer settler population.

The continuation of colonial incursions into Xhosa territory during the 1820s and early 1830s led to the Cape–Xhosa War of 1834–35. While this conflict began with limited Xhosa retaliatory attacks into the Cape Colony, local British officials exaggerated these raids to create a pretext for a massive colonial invasion and conquest of the land between the Keiskamma and Kei rivers. This territory became the Cape Colony's Queen Adelaide Province, where, for the first time, Xhosa communities came under colonial rule. However, in this instance, the views of British officials in the Cape did not align with those of the imperial government in London. Humanitarians in the imperial government objected to the actions of the colonial administration in the Cape and compelled them to withdraw from the newly conquered province, which reverted to independent Xhosa control. In the

Eastern Cape, expansionist settlers deeply resented this retrocession, blaming it on meddling missionaries and humanitarians who sympathized with the Xhosa.

Another important development began during the 1834–35 Cape–Xhosa War. British forces raided east of the Kei River from where they seized livestock and relocated Xhosa people into colonial territory. While British officials and missionaries called this group the **Fingo** (later Mfengu) and claimed that they were refugees from the wars of Shaka further up the coast, most were actually local Xhosa people redefined as a pro-colonial African community. At this point, given the abolitionist ethos in Britain, the imperial government would have disapproved of resettling thousands of Xhosa laborers into the Cape Colony, and therefore it was more

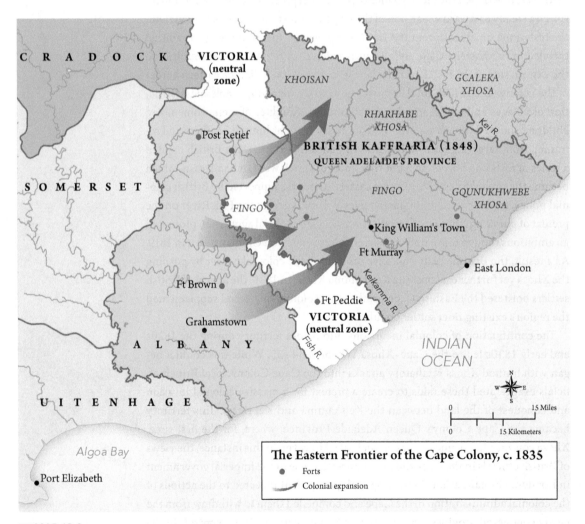

The Eastern Frontier of the Cape Colony, c. 1835

- Forts
- Colonial expansion

≡ MAP 13.2

acceptable to portray them as refugees from another area. In the Eastern Cape, the Fingo became converts to missionary Christianity and provided labor for the colonial economy. Over the subsequent years, as the Xhosa groups lost their land and cattle to settler expansion and suffered colonial attacks, the Fingo population swelled as more people sought the relative safety of their colonial reserves.

In response to settler lobbying and newspaper propaganda depicting the Xhosa as predatory savages constantly violating the colonial border, the British imperial government eventually approved a more aggressive approach along the Cape's eastern frontier. In 1846–47, during another Cape–Xhosa War, British and colonial forces again invaded and conquered the territory between the Keiskamma and Kei rivers. This area became British Kaffraria, technically a separate British territory from the Cape Colony, and contained numerous subjugated Xhosa communities. From 1850 to 1853, in the second longest war in South African history, many Xhosa groups within British Kaffraria, as well as some Khoisan, rebelled against colonial domination and oppression. While Xhosa leaders like Maqoma and Sandile developed a type of guerrilla warfare to counter the superior firepower of British forces, colonial troops destroyed Xhosa food supplies and took their cattle, starving the rebels into submission. The increasing recruitment of African allies, particularly from Fingo reserves, represented another important factor driving colonial victory in these wars. After the Cape–Xhosa War of 1850–53, the colonial state stripped Xhosa and Khoisan of more of their land, giving it to settlers including newly arrived German veterans of the British army.

Several cataclysmic events in the 1850s fatally undermined Xhosa independence and resistance to colonial expansion. The first was the regional outbreak of a cattle disease called lung sickness in the early 1850s that seriously damaged Xhosa herds. The second was the **Xhosa cattle-killing movement** of 1856–57, in which several young women, the most prominent of whom was **Nongqawuse**, prophesied that the killing of cattle and a ban on cultivation would stimulate a Xhosa national rebirth and the disappearance of the Europeans. While previous prophets had mobilized the Xhosa during wars against the Cape Colony, in this instance there were no calls for attacks on settlers. On both sides of the colonial border, the prophecies of the late 1850s resulted in starvation and displacement, and in violence between Xhosa who followed the predictions and those who remained unconvinced. In turn, opportunistic colonial officials took advantage by coercing starving Xhosa into becoming laborers within the Cape Colony, transferring land from destabilized Xhosa communities to settlers and imprisoning important Xhosa leaders like Maqoma on trumped-up charges. Debating the causes of the Xhosa cattle killing, historians have seen it variously as a traditionalist religious reaction against colonial conquest, a result of religious syncretism involving Christian and

≡ **Xhosa Leaders of the Nineteenth Century** *Left:* Nongqawuse and Nonkosi, both teenage girls, made prophesies associated with the Xhosa cattle killing of 1856–57. *Middle:* Tiyo Soga (1829–1871) became the first Xhosa person ordained as a Christian minister. *Right:* During the nineteenth century, King Sandile (1820–1878) of the Rharhabe Xhosa fought several wars against the British in the Eastern Cape. He was killed in the Cape–Xhosa War of 1877–78.

traditional concepts, a women's uprising against male sexual abuse, and an uprising by commoner Xhosa against their failed leaders. In 1865, after the Xhosa collapse, the Cape Colony annexed British Kaffraria and colonizers began to extend their influence east of the Kei River into the area of the Gcaleka Xhosa, Thembu, Mpondomise, and Mpondo peoples.

At the same time as the British Cape Colony expanded eastward during the early and mid-1800s, European Protestant Christian missionaries began to evangelize among the Xhosa. The missionaries created a written script for Xhosa language, enabling a Bible translation, and they built a series of schools, churches, and stations across the Eastern Cape region. This resulted in a social division among the Xhosa between Westernized Christian converts and traditionalists. During the 1810s, two Xhosa prophets characterized this separation: the traditionalist Makana (also called Makhanda or Nxele), who led the disastrous attack on Grahamstown, and the Christian prophet Ntsikana, who preached cooperation with Europeans. Prominent among later Xhosa Christians was Tiyo Soga, who traveled for theological education to Scotland, where, in 1856, he became the first Xhosa person ordained as Christian clergy. Accompanied by his Scottish wife, Janet Burnside, Tiyo Soga returned to the Eastern Cape, where he continued missionary work, translated religious texts into Xhosa, wrote Xhosa hymns, and authored anonymous letters to colonial newspapers defending his Xhosa people. Eventually, in the late nineteenth century, Xhosa Christians founded Xhosa-language newspapers and organized Western-style self-help organizations in the Eastern Cape, working within the exiting colonial regime to advance their interests.

Boer Expansion

Beginning in the late 1830s, thousands of Boers left their homes in the Cape Colony and used ox-wagons and horses to move into the interior of what is now South Africa, where they militarily defeated African states and founded independent republics. Subsequent historians, depending on their backgrounds, put forth different explanations of this event. In early-twentieth-century South Africa, as Boers started calling themselves **Afrikaners** to emphasize their imagined claim on the country, Afrikaner nationalist historians celebrated this **Great Trek** as the central event in the creation of the South African nation. To them, the nineteenth-century Boers had suffered oppression by the British rulers of the Cape Colony and therefore left that territory to seek freedom and self-determination. In the process, according to this view, the Boers brought the "light" of Christianity and civilization to the interior of a "dark continent."

In contrast, twentieth-century English-speaking white South African historians saw the nineteenth-century Boers as backward people who had left Europe before the Enlightenment of the 1700s and therefore missed the emergence of ideas about freedom and equality. As such, according to this liberal portrayal, the Boers left the Cape Colony because they objected to the British emancipation of enslaved people in 1833, and they ventured into the interior to continue their oppressive labor practices with regard to Africans. The common theme in both interpretations is that the Boers departed the Cape to get away from the British. However, it is clear that the Boers were also attracted by opportunities available in the South African hinterland. Like their eighteenth-century Trekboer ancestors who had moved into the Eastern Cape and the Griqua who moved to the Orange River frontier, the Boer trekkers of the late 1830s and 1840s undertook expansion to obtain land, labor, and livestock, and they did so without the support of a colonial power. The timing of their departure was largely determined by the outcome of the Cape–Xhosa War of 1834–35, after which the British imperial government forced the Cape administration to withdraw from newly conquered lands. While the frustrated Boers realized that the British government would not support their expansion, the former knew they had the firepower and mobility to conquer African communities in the interior and that they could establish global trade links through Portuguese Delagoa Bay and the independent community of British traders at Port Natal. Furthermore, the Boer leaders were encouraged by the knowledge that other European settlers were engaging in the same type of independent conquests in parts of North America

≡ **Battle of Veg Kop.** In 1836, Boers moving into the interior of what is now South Africa defeated the Ndebele at the Battle of Veg Kop.

and Australia. The Boers were not just running away from the British, they were continuing an established process of settler expansion and moving toward what they saw as opportunities in the interior.

Upon leaving the Cape Colony, the Boers divided into two large groups. The first, led by Andries Potgieter, trekked north onto the Highveld grasslands beyond the Vaal River, where they targeted the main power in that region, the Ndebele kingdom. During several key battles in 1836 and 1837, Potgieter's Boers, along with Griqua and local Tswana allies, defeated Mzilikazi's Ndebele, forcing them to withdraw north of the Limpopo River into what is now southwestern Zimbabwe. During this conflict, a large cattle raid conducted by the Zulu kingdom to the southeast seriously weakened the Ndebele state. With the departure of the Ndebele, the Boers became the dominant force on the Highveld, imposing tributary relations on many of the resident Tswana and Sotho communities. Under Piet Retief, the second major Boer group that moved into the interior turned south to cross the Drakensberg Mountains and enter the Indian Ocean coast of what is now the South African province of Kwa-Zulu/Natal, where they encountered the Zulu kingdom. Although the Zulu king **Dingane** had Retief and his Boer entourage killed during negotiations, the remaining Boers in the area received reinforcements from those on the Highveld and defeated the Zulu kingdom at the 1838 Battle of Blood River. Subsequently, the Boers formed

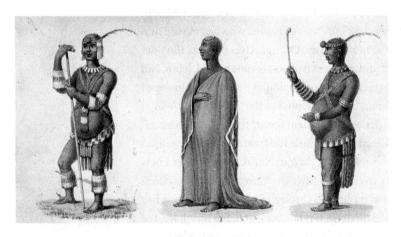

≡ **King Dingane**, who ruled the Zulu Kingdom from 1828 to 1840, is shown here wearing different types of attire.

their Republic of Natalia out of a huge chunk of land taken from the Zulu kingdom. Dingane attempted to lead his people north away from the Boers, as Mzilikazi had done, but was blocked by the Swazi kingdom. As a result, in early 1840, the Zulu fought a civil war that ended in the death of Dingane and the rise of Mpande, who made peace with the Boers of Natalia.

During the 1840s, the British government tried to exert control over the Boers who had left the Cape, as they remained British subjects. In 1843, the British military occupied the Republic of Natalia, as an independent Boer state on the Southern African coast potentially threatened British shipping, especially if it allied with a rival naval power. As this territory became the British colony of **Natal** in which Port Natal eventually became the city of Durban, many Boers moved inland to the Highveld and Zulu king Mpande shifted his allegiance to the British. Over the next few years, British settlers and Indian indentured workers arrived building a colonial economy based on sugar production and export. Between the Orange and Vaal Rivers, some Boer communities tried but failed to resist an 1848 British take-over and the creation of Britain's new Orange River Colony. After fighting a pro-tracted war against Xhosa and Khoi rebels in the Eastern Cape from 1850 to 1853, and dispatching a failed military expedition to Lesotho in 1852 in support of Boer claims, the British government decided to withdraw from the interior of Southern Africa, perceiving the area as lacking economic or strategic importance. Retaining control of the strategically important coastline of the Cape and Natal, the British granted autonomy to the interior Boers, who amalgamated their small states into two larger republics. In the 1852 Sand River Convention, the British recognized the Transvaal or **South African Republic** north of the Vaal River and in the 1854 Bloemfontein Convention, Britain's Orange River Colony transformed into the Boer republic of the **Orange Free State**.

The two independent Boer republics continued expansion at the expense of African societies. In 1858, the Boers of the Orange Free State invaded neighboring Lesotho from which they had already taken land. While the Sotho defended their mountain strongholds and used their horsemen to raid Boer farms, the Boers de-stroyed the kingdom's crops and food supplies. This First Free State–Lesotho War ended through British mediation as both sides accepted a treaty recognizing a for-mal border between their states. Although distracted by internal struggles during the first half of the 1860s, the Free State Boers again invaded Lesotho in 1865–66 in what came to be called "the War of Cannon's Boom" (the Second Free State–Lesotho War) as both sides used some artillery. Besieged in his mountain strong-hold by the Boers, Lesotho's elderly king Moshoeshoe accepted a peace agreement in which he surrendered thousands of cattle and gave huge tracts of land to the Free State. In early 1868, Moshoeshoe staved off yet another Boer offensive by agreeing to make Lesotho a British protectorate. Subsequently, the British and the Free State Boers, without consulting anyone from Lesotho, negotiated new borders for the kingdom, in which it lost more land to the Boers. These remain the modern borders of Lesotho.

While the Boers who moved north of the Vaal in the 1830s and 1840s primarily engaged in elephant hunting, they established farms in the 1850s and 1860s and acquired labor by enslaving people from local African communities, which led to conflict. During the 1850s, the Boers in the northwestern Transvaal attacked Kekana and Langa people who hid in caves and on top of mountains. In the eastern Transvaal, Boer encroachment impelled the Pedi kingdom to found a new mountaintop fortification at Mosego, while the Swazi kingdom formed an alliance with

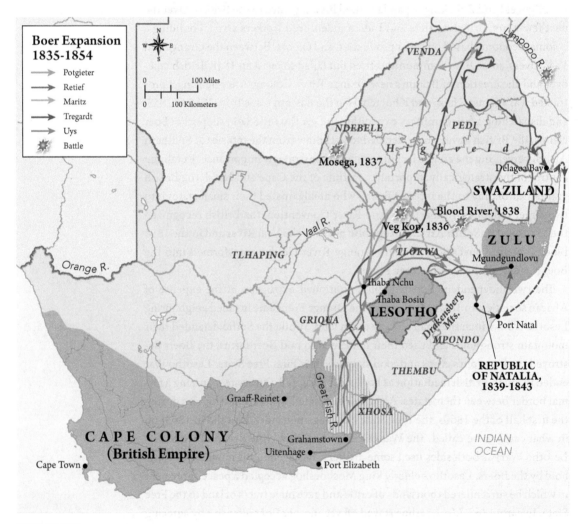

≡ MAP 13.3

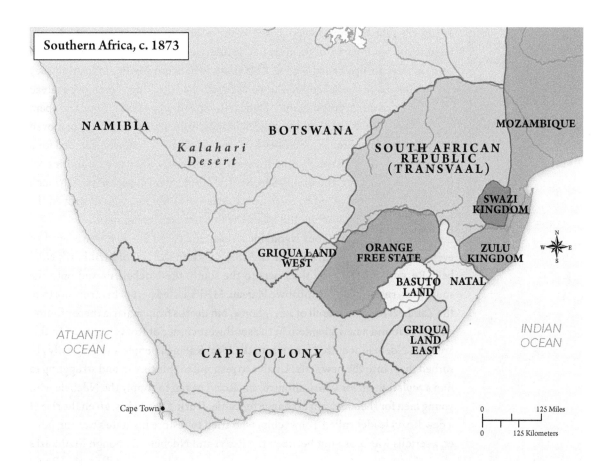

Southern Africa, c. 1873

≡ **MAP 13.4**

the Boers, providing them with enslaved people. In the arid western Transvaal, Boer slave and cattle raids in the 1850s pushed some Tswana groups, such as the Kwena, further west into what is now Botswana, while other Tswana groups, like the Hurutshe, accepted republican authority. On the Transvaal's northern frontier, in the Zoutpansberg Mountains, the Venda leader Makhado led effective resistance to Boer intrusion that expelled them from the area in 1867. The Boers would not return to that region for 30 years.

The Zimbabwe Plateau

At the start of the nineteenth century, the large Rozvi Empire dominated much of the Zimbabwe Plateau between the Limpopo and Zambezi Rivers. During the 1830s, a series of groups displaced by conflicts in what is now South Africa moved north across the Limpopo and destabilized the Rozvi Empire. Arriving in the early

1830s, the first such group comprised Sotho people from the Highveld who entered Rozvi territory from the west but were defeated and escaped southward. In turn, several groups called Ngoni, a version of the word Nguni, indicating they spoke a language similar to the Zulu and Swazi, transited the Zimbabwe Plateau and continued north crossing the Zambezi River. Some of these groups had spent time around the Delagoa Bay area but left in the late 1820s. Maseko's Ngoni moved through the Rozvi Empire, followed by Zwangendaba's Ngoni, who camped for a year on the Mazowe River raiding livestock from nearby Shona communities before they crossed the Zambezi in 1835. Several other Ngoni groups passed through the area, including one led by the warrior-queen Nyamazana, who destroyed the Rozvi capital of Danamombe and killed the Rozvi ruler Chirisamhuru.

Weakened by the previous Ngoni incursions, the Rozvi Shona Empire faced an even more serious challenge in the late 1830s with the arrival of Mzilikazi's Ndebele. Recently defeated by the Boers to the south, the Ndebele moved onto the southwestern part of the Zimbabwe Plateau. Mzilikazi led part of his army north to the Zambezi River in search of a new home, but deaths from malaria there prompted him to found a new kingdom in the southwest corner of Rozvi territory. In this area, the Ndebele acquired grain from the local Kalanga people and gradually absorbed them into the new state. Unable to respond to this threat, and struggling to find a replacement for Chirisamhuru, the Rozvi began to supply the Ndebele with young men for their army in exchange for cattle. During the 1850s, given the rise of a new Rozvi leader called Tohwechipi who tried to restore his state's waning power, a serious war broke out between the Rozvi and Ndebele. Although Mzilikazi's Ndebele expelled the Rozvi from the southwest, they could not overcome the Rozvi hilltop strongholds with those in the east defended by gunmen who had acquired their weapons by trading with the Portuguese on the east coast. The Ndebele continued raiding Shona communities to their east and in 1866, they inflicted a final defeat on the Rozvi, signaling the end of their empire. In 1870, the Ndebele kingdom, based at its capital of Bulawayo, was at the

≡ **Ndebele** warriors around 1835.

height of its power, absorbing Kalanga and Shona people in the southwest, collecting tribute from Shona groups on its eastern frontier, and dominating trade on the plateau. Although only the kingdom's elite originated from southeastern South Africa near the Zulu and Swazi states, their Nguni language spread among the various Sotho, Tswana, Kalanga, and Shona people they assimilated, and this variant of Nguni eventually became known as Sindebele (the language of the Ndebele). On the Zimbabwe Plateau, the Ndebele identity came to dominate the southwest, while the Shona identity and language remained widespread in the east.

In the highlands on the eastern edge of the Zimbabwe Plateau, around the modern border of Zimbabwe and Mozambique, another Nguni group, led by Soshangane, arrived around 1836. Following a similar pattern to Mzilikazi, Soshangane founded the Gaza kingdom in what is now southern Mozambique by absorbing local people. It also exported cattle and enslaved people to the Portuguese at Delagoa Bay. However, the Gaza state moved around during the middle to late 1800s, suffered from tropical disease affecting people and livestock, and therefore failed to stabilize to the same extent as the Ndebele kingdom. Nevertheless, the descendants of Soshangane's subjects remained in the area, where they became known as Shangaan or Tsonga.

Conclusion

At the end of the 1860s, settler colonialism dominated much of Southern Africa. British colonial territories comprised most of the coast, with the old Cape Colony having expanded east subjugating Xhosa communities, and the newer colony of Natal representing an outpost on the Indian Ocean. The independent Boer republics of the Orange Free State and Transvaal controlled the interior Highveld and conquered or evicted many African groups. The kingdom of Lesotho accepted British rule to avoid complete dispossession by the neighboring Free State Boers. Independent African kingdoms remained but on the margins of this complex of settler powers. The Zulu kingdom existed as a tributary of British Natal, the Swazi kingdom survived by cooperating with the Boers, the Pedi kingdom held out in its mountain fortress, Tswana states like the Ngwaketse and Ngwato moved west into the fringes of the Kalahari Desert, and the Venda expelled the Boers from their mountainous homeland. Having moved north of the Limpopo River to escape Boer expansion, the Ndebele kingdom carved out part of the Zimbabwe Plateau, destroying the older Rozvi Empire. While settler colonialism expanded dramatically in early- and mid-nineteenth-century Southern Africa, the economy of the region remained agricultural. This changed with the discovery of diamonds in the late 1860s and gold in the late 1880s.

Timeline

1795—First British occupation of the Cape Colony

1803—British withdraw from the Cape Colony

1806—Second British occupation of the Cape Colony

1807—British Empire outlaws slave trade

1810s—Ngwaketse kingdom achieves control of trade in western Highveld

1811—British expel the Xhosa east of the Fish River

1818—Defeat of Mthethwa by Ndwandwe—rise of Zulu kingdom under Shaka

1819—Xhosa attack on Grahamstown in the Eastern Cape

1820—Arrival of British settlers in the Eastern Cape

1820s—Expansion of Portuguese slaving from Delagoa Bay

Early 1820s—Rise of Swazi kingdom under Sobhuza I and Lesotho under Moshoeshoe; Zulu–Ndwandwe conflict; Ndebele of Mzilikazi move onto the Highveld; establishment of Port Natal

1824—Mpondo defeat Zulu incursion

1828—Battle of Mbolompo; Zulu and Port Natal traders attack Mpondo kingdom; Assassination of Zulu king Shaka and rise of Dingane as Zulu king

Early 1830s—Ndebele kingdom moves to the western Highveld

1830s—Groups from the south, such as the Ngoni, cross through the Rozvi Empire, weakening it

1833–34—British Empire emancipates enslaved people; coercive labor continues

1834–35—Cape–Xhosa War—Zwangendaba's Ngoni cross through the Rozvi Empire on their way north

1836—British withdraw from conquered territory in the eastern Cape

1836+—Boers begin to move from the Cape Colony into the interior; Soshangane begins to establish Gaza kingdom in southern Mozambique

1836–37—Boers defeat the Ndebele kingdom, which moves further north into present-day Zimbabwe

1838—Boers defeat Zulu at the Battle of Blood River; creation of Boer Republic of Natalia

Late 1830s—Ndebele kingdom established in southwestern Zimbabwe Plateau

1840—Zulu Civil War results in rise of Mpande and death of Dingane

1843—British occupy Republic of Natalia, which becomes Colony of Natal

1846–47—Cape–Xhosa War results in conquest of British Kaffraria

1848—British impose Orange River Colony on the Boers between the Orange and Vaal Rivers

1850s—Expansion of the Boer Transvaal Republic; Ndebele and Rozvi states clash on the Zimbabwe Plateau

1850–53—Cape–Xhosa War

1852—British attack Lesotho; Sand River Convention recognizes Transvaal Republic

1854—Bloemfontein Convention recognizes the Boer republic of the Orange Free State (formerly Orange River Colony)

1856—Ordination of Tiyo Soga in Scotland

1856–57—Xhosa cattle-killing movement

1858—Free State–Lesotho War

1865—Cape Colony annexes British Kaffraria

1865–66—Free State–Lesotho War (War of Cannon's Boom)

1866—Demise of Rozvi Empire following defeat by the Ndebele

1867—Venda expel Boers from Zoutpansberg (northern Transvaal)

1868—Moshoeshoe agrees to make Lesotho a British protectorate

KEY TERMS

Afrikaners 273

Boers 269

Dingane 274

Fingo 270

Great Trek 273

Griqua 267

mfecane 264

Moshoeshoe 268

Natal 275

Ndebele kingdom 267

Nongqawuse 271

Orange Free State 275

settler colonialism 263

Shaka 264

Sotho kingdom 268

South African Republic (Transvaal) 275

Xhosa cattle-killing movement 271

Zulu kingdom 266

STUDY QUESTIONS

1. Why do historians hold different views on Shaka and his legacy? How were conflicts between southern African peoples in the nineteenth century both separate and interrelated with encroaching European settler colonialism?

2. Why did the British seize the Cape Colony? What were the outcomes of the Cape–Xhosa Wars? Why were the Xhosa unable to mount a defense against British invasion?

3. What role did women play in the cattle-killing movement of 1856–57? What conditions facilitated the emergence of prophetesses in Xhosa society?

4. Why are there different historical interpretations of Boer expansion? How would you characterize Boer-African interactions in the Transvaal?

5. What similar patterns of expansion and collapse did the Ngoni, Rozvi, and Gaza kingdoms experience in the nineteenth century?

Please see page FR-6 for the Further Readings for this chapter.
For additional digital learning resources please go to
https://www.oup.com/he/falola-stapleton1e

Thematic Conclusion to Part One

Agg. al Cost. Vol. II.   6 5 4 1   Ouest   2   Tav. 35.

Veduta della Città di Temboctiu

Despite Africa's great diversity of language and culture, the continent's precolonial history reflected common themes centered on communalism, trade, politics, the family, and religion and spirituality. It is helpful to review these themes before moving on to the dramatic changes that took place during the colonial and postcolonial eras.

Communalism

Although definitions vary, **communalism** connotes a society organized around collective ownership, in which goods are shared equally among members of the commune and in which social stratification is absent. The extent to which communalism could be said to be absolute in precolonial Africa has remained a subject of debate among scholars. Despite the existence of large and hierarchical precolonial empires like Mali, Songhay, Oyo, Benin, and Lunda, ordinary communities operated largely though a system that can be called African communalism, in which economic production and prosperity was shared. This does not mean that all properties and lands were communally owned, and in some places, royal families, as descendants of the community's founders, maintained authority to allocate resources. People owned their homes and other properties, which the community as a whole maintained through collective efforts. Furthermore, in the communal spirit, anyone could eat anywhere in the community, as food was offered to all. In the hospitality of African communalism, food was prepared in excess of the numbers of the family members expected to participate in the meal so as to accommodate unexpected visitors. In the same manner, the house door was open to all to pass the night, provided that visitors maintained good behavior. This basic value system is expressed in the Zulu saying *Umuntu ngumuntu ngabantu* meaning "a person is a person because of other people," and this is connected to the concept of *Ubuntu* or "humanity."

Whereas land was owned and cultivated by the individual and his family members, this essential commodity, which was often plentiful in the

Timbuktu in the early nineteenth century

precolonial era, could be revoked by the royal family representing the community, or in the case of an acephalous community, by the ancestral owners of the land. Common reasons for revoking land privileges included serious violations of community customs and laws, and relocation to another area. Not bought and sold as a commodity, land remained under the jurisdiction of a royal family or ancestral inhabitants who could reallocate it to others as long as they respected this relationship. In some cases, land might be exchanged for livestock, with rituals performed to seek ancestral approval. Generally, land was sacred, as it was believed to be owned by the ancestors and to be in the control of the spiritual forces among which the ancestors resided. Accordingly, the only way to transfer or use a piece of landade, successfully, was through loyalty to these forces through the descendants of those to whom the spirits had handed over the property.

During wars, the landholders were expected to side with the royal family or their hosts/landlords, because their livelihood had been tied to the existence and stability of this family and the geographical entity they established. Of course, betrayal of this loyalty was not uncommon in the face of better opportunities or greediness. During peacetime, landholders were expected to display and renew their loyalty to the first family by paying tribute in forms such as farm produce, working on the farmlands of this family, and assisting in all the projects of the family that required labor. The relationship between the landlords and the landholders was, however, dependent on the political structure of that particular society. As communal practices involved reciprocity, a family worked on their neighbor's farmland so as to gain the same support from the neighbor over time. Since farming and other agrarian activities represented the mainstay of the precolonial economy of many African societies, labor was thus drawn from the family and, by extension, the entire community. This arrangement became the foundation for the economic life of most societies. In such a cashless society, services were obtained through mutually supporting relationships and goods bartered for their equivalent.

Since some studies show that the relatively small size of precolonial African communities facilitated communalism, it appears that communities that grew to a large size struggled to maintain this system. In precolonial Africa, societies with larger populations experienced more internal competition and tended to develop hierarchical structures. Equality and reciprocity existed as important concepts but were not total. For instance, a stranger could be well taken care of and respected, but as the saying goes among the Yoruba people of Southwestern Nigeria, *Oko ole je ti baba ati omo ki oma ni ala*—"there is a limit to every relationship." This limit boils down to protecting one's interests. Within some precolonial societies, this is what spurred the use and classification of some people as slaves or pawns. It is telling that the possession of slaves became a marker of social status.

≡ **Kuba raffia cloth.** In raffia cloth-making, men weave the base of the cloth and women embroider designs onto it. This example is from Katanga Province, Democratic Republic of the Congo.

Within such a communal setting, the raising of children became a community responsibility. This is reflected in the Yoruba saying *Oju kan ni o bi omo, igba oju ni'ba wo*, which means "a child is born into a single family, but s/he is trained by multitudes." In other words, a child cannot be properly trained solely within his or her household because of the emotional attachment of parents who might overlook some acts considered insolent by the culture or community. Since a child would have to relate with others in the society, older community members would help the parents of the child in grooming him or her for the social expectations of the culture. Given their economic structure and the importance of agricultural labor, precolonial society adopted the communal doctrine in which children and childbirth were essential factors in attainment of high social status. As a primary source of labor for the community, children were considered the primary social investment of the family. To maintain order, the communal system limited the individual and ensured that social hierarchies were acknowledged and maintained, thus giving the individual a sense of place within society. Supporting this structure was a system of extended families that also helped raise children.

While many factors informed the emergence of African communalism, security concerns and the agricultural nature of society were very important. Similar factors inspired the development of other communal cultures in Europe, Asia, and the Americas during different historical periods. Although African societies have experienced many changes since precolonial times, aspects of African communalism remain vibrant throughout the continent. In sum, understanding African communalism is as complex as understanding African culture itself.

Trade and Commerce

As we have discussed in this first part of the book, the major economic engagement of the people of Africa during this period was agriculture, including farming, herding, and fishing, depending on the geographical features of the region in which each group was located. Even though the pattern of their farming activities is commonly described as subsistence—in other words, within the limit of self-consumption—families often did not consume all that they produced. After harvesting crops, which took place at different times in different areas, families carefully stored their farm produce in safe places, where their value could be sustained until the next harvest season. Considering that an individual family could not produce all it needed for the year round, excess farm produce would be traded with neighbors for other essential needs of the family. The herder exchanged his livestock for farm produce, while the farmer exchanged part of his farm produce for an equivalent amount of fish from the fisher. Since it was difficult to ascertain the exact equivalence of the goods in exchange, agreement on such was the preoccupation of the trading parties, thereby making this trading system a flexible one. In most cases, the worth of the goods was determined by the level of their demand and scarcity, which meant that some goods were considered luxury items. As trade expanded, designated items like cowries, gold, and copper became acceptable standard means of exchange across parts of Africa. Yet, the barter system remained dominant until the colonial incursion.

Insofar as people's survival depended largely on economic activities, trade and commerce in Africa is likely as old as the evolution of the society into clusters and communities. During people's transition from nomadic to sedentary, security and economic viability represented major factors in selecting a place to live. With security concerns including possible attacks by warlords or bandits, and dangers from wild animals, sedentary communities commonly constructed some type of fortification or defenses. Economic viability also included proximity to a

☰ **Cowrie shells.** For centuries, cowrie shells have been used as currency throughout Africa, especially in the Indian Ocean region.

trade center or market, or involved the establishment of a new point of exchange that would attract merchants. Trade items varied according to a region's resources and the emerging specializations of certain communities, and could include agricultural produce, livestock, fish, leather, cloth, salt, copper, gold, and eventually iron tools and weapons. In some areas, people captured and enslaved by warlords became a commodity for exchange, and their possession became a status symbol. Host communities organized markets and collected market taxes, while those near trade routes collected tolls from travelers. These tax-collecting entities, which evolved into kingdoms and empires, were responsible for the maintenance and security of the trade routes. Depending on the business of a particular trading route, the collection of tolls sometimes served as the major source of the wealth for a kingdom. The size and operating days of markets varied considerably, and traders also conducted business with communities along trade routes. Markets also served as places of cultural exchange involving language, religion, dress, food, and other factors, as well as the building of social relations among people of diverse cultural groups. During the precolonial era, the flourishing of regional trade led to the expansion of trade languages such as Hausa in West Africa and Kiswahili in East Africa.

In precolonial Africa, people became involved in several intercontinental trade systems. After the Arab Muslim conquest of North Africa from around 630 to

710 CE, Arabs became involved in Africa's overland trans-Saharan and maritime Indian Ocean trade networks. While both these systems dated back to ancient times, they flourished from around 1000 to 1500 CE. In both networks, African exports such as gold, hides, salt, agricultural products, and enslaved people were exchanged for imported luxury items such as textiles, porcelain items, weapons, and books. From the 1400s and 1500s, European seafarers developed trade along West Africa's Atlantic coast, which eventually turned into the transatlantic slave trade, and they eventually took over the Indian Ocean system from Arab sailors. In association with these economic networks, great trading towns developed in Africa, such as Timbuktu, Djenne, and Agadez in the West African hinterland; Sofala, Kilwa, and Mombasa on the east coast; and Lagos, Badagry, and Ouidah on the coast of West Africa. The cultural exchange associated with these trade systems resulted in the introduction of new religions to parts of precolonial Africa. Trade along the Red Sea and Nile River resulted in the spread of Christianity to Ethiopia and Nubia. Arabs introduced Islam to West and East Africa, and later Europeans brought Christianity to the West and West-Central African coast. While tropical disease kept Europeans mostly confined to the coast of West and East Africa, their influence became more aggressive and intrusive from the start of the 1800s. Overall, the attraction of foreigners to the resources of Africa has long remained a constant feature in the history of the continent.

Political Organization

While the earliest African societies were decentralized, the development of settled communities led to a consequent organization of both centralized and decentralized political systems. Africa's first centralized states emerged during ancient times in North Africa, particularly along the Nile in Egypt and Nubia. Subsequently, south of the Sahara, other centralized states developed over time, related to the expansion of trade and wars of conquest. Economically successful and politically stable states attracted migrants who contributed to these developments and stimulated change. A monarch claiming descent from a founding hero, usually a great warrior or hunter, ruled many centralized states in precolonial Africa. The monarch's absolute power was justified by association with spiritual forces and signified by ornate costume, a large entourage, and a glorious palace. In reality, however, the involvement of a governing or advisory council and systems of checks-and-balances inherent in customs and traditions limited a ruler's personal authority. Systems of royal succession varied widely over time and place, with some states rotating new rulers from among different royal houses and others following more direct lines of inheritance. At times, established traditions of governance and succession broke down as precolonial states experienced violent internal struggles for power. While scholars have debated if **matriarchy** (rule by women) ever existed in African history, all known precolonial states represented patriarchies, though women held important titles, queen mothers exercised great influence, and there were some female rulers. Even **matrilineal** societies, such as those in parts of West and much of Central Africa, where inheritance was/is traced through the maternal line were/are mostly ruled by men. Examples of prominent centralized states in precolonial Africa include Oyo and Benin in present-day Nigeria, Kongo in what is now northern Angola and western Democratic Republic of the Congo (DRC), Luba and Lunda in what is now southern DRC, Mutapa in modern Zimbabwe, and Buganda in contemporary Uganda. The spread of Islam through trans-Saharan and Indian Ocean trade introduced Muslim concepts of monarchy and government, demonstrated through the Mali and Songhai empires of West Africa's Sahel, the Sokoto Caliphate in northern Nigeria, and the Sultanate of Adal in the horn of Africa. Islam also brought the concept of jihad or holy war, which informed the growth of states like Sokoto and Tukolor in nineteenth-century West Africa.

Many precolonial African societies developed decentralized political structures. This was sometimes informed by geography, as, for example, the hilly and mountainous terrain of the Benue area of Central Nigeria likely made it difficult for the Tiv people and other inhabitants to form a centralized kingdom. Frequently, decentralized communities relied on leadership by councils of elders and distinguished personalities, and sometimes these societies were organized into a system of age grades, meaning people of a certain age belonged to a broad corporate entity with a specific identity. The importance of elders in such a system led to its description as gerontocracy. Often called "stateless" or **acephalous** (headless), these societies lacked monarchs and relied much more on democratic traditions and on reaching consensus at a community level. Such decentralized societies united around shared cultural values, religious beliefs, age grade systems, and

≡ **Queen-mother mask from Benin.** This graceful and serene mask, carved from ivory in the sixteenth century, depicts an *iyoba*, or queen-mother.

language. Examples of well-known decentralized African peoples include the Ewe of Ghana, the Igbo of eastern Nigeria, the Fang of Gabon, the Kikuyu of Kenya, and all the pure pastoral societies of East Africa, such as the Maasai and Turkana.

Family

The family, dwelling in a compound or homestead, formed the foundation of precolonial African societies. At the center of family life was marriage and child birth, both which were greatly celebrated as they guaranteed the continuation of the family in the future. Marriage practices varied significantly in precolonial Africa. In almost all **patrilineal** societies, and a few matrilineal ones, a prospective husband provided his future bride's family with some form of wealth, such as agricultural products, livestock, trade goods, or a period of labor, depending on the main economic activities of the area. Known as **bride price** or "bride wealth," this practice showed respect to the bride's family, cemented a new relationship between the two families, and served as compensation of the loss of the bride's labor and other contributions to her parent's family. The provision of bride wealth also confirmed that the groom had not stolen his bride or taken her in a dishonorable way, and that the bride's family had not abandoned her. Intermediaries acting on behalf of the groom would usually negotiate marriage arrangements and bride wealth. Within the context of patrilineal societies, and after the delivery of bride wealth, the bride usually left her parent's home to live as a "stranger wife" among her husband's family. In this situation, a new wife enhanced her status among her in-laws by having children who would provide labor and continue the family line. In this situation, women who did not produce children risked ostracism and even outright exile. In matrilineal societies, such as among the Bemba and Yao peoples of eastern Zambia and Malawi, respectively, it was common for new husbands to go to live with their bride's family as "stranger husbands" who experienced marginalization and became subject to labor demands by their parents-in-law. In general, the frequency of divorce varied from society to society, but in some cases, it involved the return of bride wealth to the husband's family. Disputes between married couples were often resolved by the intervention of other family members, emphasizing the importance of the extended family in African culture.

In many African societies, particularly patrilineal ones, **polygamy** was encouraged as more wives and children constituted a larger work force for the family. High rates of child mortality in precolonial times may have also contributed to the drive to produce more children. The instance of polygamy also varied a great deal over time and place as, in some instances, only men from well-off families could afford to provide bride wealth for multiple wives, and therefore polygamy became a status symbol. Many factors affected precolonial family structure as, for example, scholars believe that the extraction of many young men from West Africa during the transatlantic slave trade increased the frequency of polygamy in that region. In precolonial Southern Africa, the importance of cattle-raising meant that only cattle-wealthy families could afford bride wealth, and therefore they engaged in polygamy, increasing their labor force and reinforcing their wealth, prestige, and authority, and this may have contributed to the rise of the region's kingdoms. Within families, gender divisions of labor also varied considerably across regions. While West African societies involved men in agricultural work, Southern African communities generally expected men to engage in raising livestock and women to focus on cultivation.

Religion and African Spirituality

While traditional African religions show enormous variation, they also share some common features. In general, African religious beliefs evolved as people in the distant past attempted to explain what they saw and experienced in their environment. Southern Africa's Khoisan hunter-gathers, practicing perhaps Africa's oldest set of spiritual beliefs, pray to the moon and sun, narrate legends of god-like beings and heroes who often take the form of animals, and enter trances through hunting specific animals and/or through dance to experience the world of the spirits. Beliefs around ancestral spirits and greater divine beings seem to have developed further among settled agricultural and pastoral communities. Among Nigeria's Yoruba people, traditional religion focuses on a complex pantheon of gods with different genders and jurisdictions, such as the male gods Ogun for iron and war and Sango for thunder and lightning, and the female gods Osun for beauty, love, diplomacy, and wealth and Oya for wind, fire, fertility, and magic. On the other hand, many societies in East, Central, and Southern Africa usually subscribe to a belief in one creator god called, for example, Mwari by the Shona of Zimbabwe and Ngai among the Kikuyu and Maasai of Kenya.

A common feature of African traditional religion involves a belief that the spirits of departed ancestors influence the world of the living, and this prompts **ancestral reverence** expressed through various rituals. In West Africa, masquerades represent an important activity in which ancestors visit the living during set celebrations or festivals often tied to the agricultural season. Across the continent, many peoples believed/believe that ancestral spirits possess the body of a living spirit medium and speak through that person. Among the Shona people, some prominent ancestors like Nehanda maintain consistent contact with the world of the living by possessing a series of spirit mediums that live and die over centuries.

☰ **Obatala priests** pray in their temple in Ile-Ife, in present-day Nigeria.

In general, African traditional beliefs about ancestors tie these spirits to specific lands, meaning that it is considered very important for a recently departed person to be buried in his or her home area, among his or her ancestors. Furthermore, African societies understood that they could be affected by both good and evil supernatural forces. While mainstream religious practices involve ancestral reverence aimed at stimulating helpful results for the living, such as a good harvest or personal health, deviant spiritual practices such as curses and spells that sought to harness malignant forces for harmful acts could also be deployed surreptitiously. A range of spiritual specialists existed and still exists within most African precolonial religions, and includes priests, guardians of sacred shrines, spirit mediums, soothsayers, and healers.

With the arrival of Islam and Christianity in parts of Africa during the precolonial era, aspects of older traditional spiritual beliefs merged with the new faiths. There are many examples of this trend, which scholars call religious syncretism. Among Hausa-speaking people in northern Nigeria and Niger, the Bori spirit possession cult in which marginalized women predominate as spirit mediums coexists with the region's predominant Muslim faith. Although Western missionaries converted many African people to Christianity, those converts often did not abandon their traditional ancestral reverence and other spiritual beliefs. Indeed, African beliefs about ancestors became highly compatible with newly arrived world religions. Additionally, African captives transported across the Atlantic during the slave-trade era brought their traditional religions to the Americas, where these beliefs combined in different ways, with Christianity introduced there by European colonizers. In Cuba, for example, Yoruba religion merged with Christianity to produce Santeria. Of course, religious **syncretism** could lead to conflict: European Catholic priests persecuted adherents to the localized Christian movement in the kingdom of Kongo during the eighteenth century, and Arab-Sudanese Muslim extremists attacked syncretic Muslims in the western Sudan area of Darfur during the early twenty-first century.

KEY TERMS

acephalous 289	communalism 283	patrilineal 290
ancestral reverence 291	matriarchy 289	polygamy 290
bride price 290	matrilineal 289	syncretism 293

Part Two

Africa since 1870

Bustling Metropolis. Lagos, Nigeria is the most populous city in Africa, with over 20 million people living in its greater metropolitan zone. This photo shows a bustling scene in the center of the city. Over half the people of Africa live in an urban area.

14

Introduction: Africa in 1870

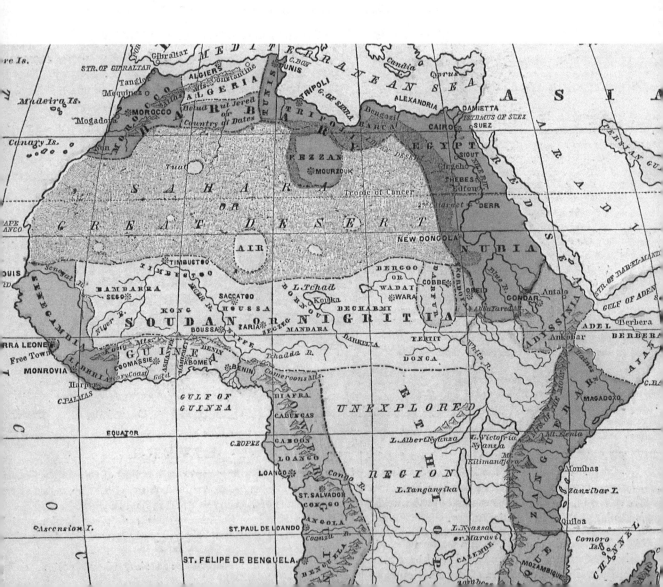

During the 1870s, Africa was on the verge of a major transition. This was the last decade before the start of the thorough and rapid European conquest of the continent that would mark the beginning of Africa's era of colonial rule. In 1870, a variety of independent and dynamic African societies inhabited the vast interior, ranging from compact highly centralized kingdoms to vast territorial empires to decentralized communities, connected to each other and the outside world through different trade networks. Whereas the over three centuries of slave exports from West Africa to the Americas had recently been stopped, the internal African use of slave labor was increasing, and slave raiding and international slave trading had expanded to new areas such as East Africa. At that time, the European colonial presence in Africa consisted of a series of small enclaves spread all along the continent's coastline, and more substantial settler colonies in parts of the north and south where tropical disease was less prevalent. While many of these coastal colonial holdings had existed for a long time, their influence was spreading inland, and they were beginning to serve as bases for more aggressive European actions in nearby parts of the interior. By 1870, Africa represented an increasingly important source of raw materials for European and North American industries, and the location of several strategically vital choke points for international shipping—the Cape of Good Hope in the south and the Suez Canal in the north. Nevertheless, in the 1870s, most Africans in the hinterland had never seen a European and Europeans still had very little knowledge about the people and geography of the African interior.

In the early 1870s, the **Ottoman Empire**, centered in what is now Turkey, vied with Western European powers for control of North Africa's Mediterranean coast. France had conquered Algeria in the mid-1800s and created

Africa in 1872. A map of Africa from a geography textbook published in the United States in 1872.

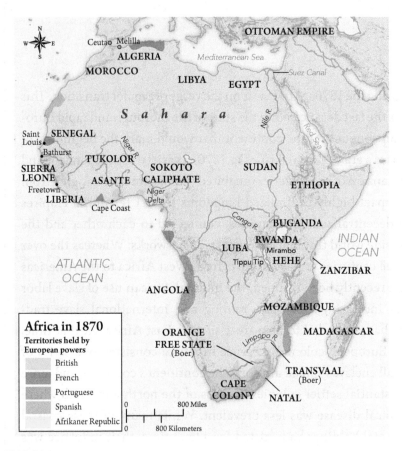

≡ MAP 14.1

a system where French settlers enjoyed the rights of French citizenship, including voting in French elections, while Algeria's Muslim majority became colonial subjects without civil rights. The defeat of France in the Franco-Prussian War of 1870–71 led to the replacement of French military administration with civilian settler rule in Algeria and the arrival of more French settlers. These factors prompted a major Muslim rebellion in 1871 that was suppressed but inspired French settlers to impose more oppressive policies. During the 1830s, just after the initial French invasion of Algeria, the Ottoman Empire re-established direct rule over Libya, but local resistance meant that Ottoman officials were restricted to towns. Given the ban of the slave trade in Algeria and Tunisia in the 1840s, Ottoman Libya continued to acquire African enslaved people through the **trans-Saharan slave trade**, and they were exported to the Middle East well into the late nineteenth century. Technically part of the Ottoman Empire, the semi-autonomous Tunisian government of the mid-1800s tried to balance relations with French Algeria to the west and a resurgent Ottoman Libya to the east and embarked on a modernization program that incurred a huge debt with European powers. In 1871, because of France's recent defeat by Prussia and Britain's aim to weaken French control in North Africa, European states recognized Tunisia as an Ottoman province. Around the same time, the independent sultanate of Morocco was desperately trying to placate various Western European powers as it had been cut off from the rest of North Africa by the French conquest of Algeria and had recently lost territory to Spanish invasion. In 1869, a French company in Egypt, nominally part of the Ottoman Empire, completed a decade-long project to dig a canal through the Isthmus of Suez, linking the Mediterranean and Red seas, which dramatically reduced the length of voyages between Europe and the Americas and Asia and had a profound impact on world shipping. The **Suez Canal** suddenly became one of the world's most strategically important points. Debts incurred by the Egyptian government's modernization programs had formed the context for its involvement in the construction of the canal, and in 1875 continuing financial problems prompted it to sell a major interest in the canal to Britain. With the French and British in control of the canal, many Egyptians came to resent increasing foreign intrusion in their country.

While Sudan had long been a source of enslaved people for Egypt, the Egyptian occupation of that territory and the establishment of Khartoum in the 1820s had accelerated this process. By the early 1870s, Arab slavers from Khartoum were raiding communities as far south as the Ubangi and Uele rivers on the fringe of the Central African forest in what is now South Sudan and the Democratic Republic of the Congo (DRC). Boosted by the opening of the Suez Canal and encouraged by abolitionist Britain, Egypt reasserted its authority over Sudan, where its failed attempts to eliminate the slave trade only alienated local Arab elites. As part of a campaign to expand southward in the 1870s, Egypt dispatched contracted British officials to establish its rule over the Equatoria region of southern Sudan, where they also struggled against the slave trade and made contact with Great Lakes kingdoms like Buganda.

In the Horn of Africa, in the late 1860s and early 1870s, the Christian kingdom of **Ethiopia** was challenged by Muslim powers such as the Egyptians in Sudan and both the Egyptians and Ottomans on the Red Sea coast. Though Emperor Tewodros tried to centralize Ethiopia's government and deal with these threats, his detention of British missionaries led to a British punitive expedition in 1867–68 that ended with his suicide. As a reward for facilitating the British intervention, the ruler of Ethiopia's Tigray region acquired modern weapons that he used to defeat local rivals and install himself as Emperor Yohannes IV in 1872. During the mid-1870s, Yohannes led successful Ethiopian resistance against the Egyptians, who expanded their holding on the Red Sea coast and invaded northern Ethiopia. At the same time, a regional ruler called Menelik rose to power in the semi-autonomous region of Shewa, and he would later become one of the most famous Ethiopian emperors.

In 1870, the coast of West Africa was the location of a network of European colonial outposts, while the hinterland was controlled by African states and societies. Though some of the coastal enclaves had been established by the Portuguese and Dutch centuries before to service the **transatlantic slave trade**, the main European powers in West Africa were now the British and French. France's primary West African outpost was Saint Louis, located near the mouth of the Senegal River, and from where the French colonial military was gradually expanding inland. Britain maintained a number of important enclaves including Bathurst at the mouth of the Gambia River; Cape Coast Castle, from where they launched a major punitive expedition against the interior Asante Kingdom in 1873; and Lagos Island, which was occupied by the British in 1861 and served as a base for their intervention in conflicts among the neighboring Yoruba states. British officials and merchants also began to assert more influence over the competitive trading houses of the Niger Delta. Furthermore, Africa's west coast was the location of two major settlements of freed enslaved people from North America and their descendants: **Sierra Leone** was a British colony created at the start of the nineteenth century, and **Liberia** was an independent republic with close ties to the United States. During the nineteenth century, West Africa was experiencing a transition from an economy focused on exporting enslaved people to the plantations of the New World to the production and export of raw materials such as palm oil and rubber destined to support industrial production in Britain and North America. By the end of the 1860s, British naval and diplomatic efforts to suppress the Atlantic slave trade had stopped slave ships from operating along the West African coast. Ironically, the shift to raw material export, called **legitimate commerce** by the British, resulted in an increased use of enslaved workers to produce or harvest these commodities within West Africa. This change also contributed to a series of nineteenth-century trade wars among, for example, the Yoruba states of what is now western Nigeria and in the Sierra Leone hinterland. Simultaneous with the growth of a colonial presence along the West African coast, foreign and local missionaries stepped up their efforts to spread Christianity along with Western-style education systems. By 1870, Freetown was home to Africa's first Western-style university, and Samuel Ajayi Crowther, freed from slavery by the British navy and educated in Sierra Leone, had translated the Bible into Nigeria's Yoruba language and become the Anglican church's first African bishop. Simultaneously, two large Muslim empires established by successful jihads earlier in the century dominated West Africa's interior Sahel zone. The **Sokoto Caliphate** was located in what is now northern Nigeria, and its southward expansion had been stopped by the Yoruba states, and the **Tukulor Empire** controlled the upper Niger River in an area that now comprises parts of Mali and Guinea, and it had already clashed with the French, expanding east up the Senegal River. These inland empires engaged in slave raiding and slave trading, and used slave labor on huge plantations.

At the beginning of the 1870s, large sections of the East African interior had been plagued by the violence and destabilization of the slave trade for a few decades. Although slave trading was not new to Central and East Africa, slave raiding and the export of captives to the Indian Ocean coast expanded significantly in the nineteenth century. The abolition of the West African slave trade in the early to middle 1800s prompted ocean-going slavers from places like Brazil and Cuba to undertake long voyages to East Africa, and the French and Arabs established slave-labor plantations on islands in the Indian Ocean. The main intermediaries in the nineteenth-century East Africa slave trade were Omani Arabs based on the island of Zanzibar, and Swahili-Arab traders located along the coast and in parts of the interior and who operated regular trade caravans. This East African slave trade was also closely linked to an increase in ivory exports resulting from new demand in Europe, and these interrelated trades resulted in a proliferation of firearms in the hinterland. During the 1870s, parts of the East African interior were dominated by local warlords such as **Mirambo**, who operated east of Lake Tanganyika in what is now central Tanzania, and **Tippu Tip**, who controlled a vast area on the west side of the same lake in what is now eastern DRC. These leaders' slave raiding and elephant hunting activities depended on armies of displaced, gun-toting young men who preyed upon decentralized societies such as those around Lake Malawi, which were hard-hit in this period. During the 1860s and 1870s, these raiders also seriously weakened the established Lunda and Luba kingdoms of Central Africa's southern savanna, as these states did not have many firearms. Not all hinterland states were devastated by slave raiding, as Rwanda remained somewhat isolated; Buganda used new trade opportunities to acquire modern weapons; and new aggressive powers arose, such as the Hehe Kingdom in central Tanzania, the Bemba in what is now eastern Zambia, and the Ngoni around Lake Malawi. Indeed, the decentralized and pastoral Maasai of the East African grasslands cultivated such a fearsome warrior reputation that slave raiders avoided them. As the slave trade expanded, East Africa also became the subject of fascination among European explorers seeking to map the area and solve geographic puzzles such as the location of the source of the Nile. The travel writings and adventure stories of these explorers attracted considerable media attention in Europe and North America, and chief among them was Henry Morton Stanley, who discovered the supposedly lost David Livingstone on the east bank of Lake Tanganyika in 1871 and then used the Congo River system to cross Central Africa from East to West in 1874–77.

Colonial conquest in Southern Africa had started much earlier than the rest of the continent. It also involved, because of the absence of tropical disease in the far south, the arrival of European settlers who subjugated Africans dispossessing them of their land and exploiting them as cheap agricultural labor. By around 1870, the British colonial territories of the Cape Colony and Natal comprised much of the coast of what would later become South Africa and represented a historically important point in controlling shipping between Europe and Asia. The **Cape Colony**, initially established by the Dutch some 200 years earlier, had expanded eastward along the coast during the early and mid-nineteenth century, and in 1872 London granted its settler society a form of internal autonomy called **responsible government**. Up to this point, the British Empire had not been interested in conquering the interior of Southern Africa, but this was about to change given the discovery of diamonds in the northern Cape in the late 1860s. In the hinterland of this region, during the 1870s, descendants of earlier Dutch settlers called **Boers** controlled two independent republics, the Transvaal and Orange Free State, which they had founded three decades before by moving from the coast and defeating African states like the **Ndebele** and **Zulu**. On the fringes of Southern Africa's British and Boer settler states, a few African societies remained independent, such as various Xhosa-speaking communities east of the Cape Colony, the Zulu Kingdom adjacent to Natal, and the Pedi, Swazi, and Tswana kingdoms that bordered the Transvaal. At the end of the 1860s, the mountain kingdom of **Lesotho** volunteered to come under indirect British authority to preserve its remaining territory from conquest by the expansionist Boers of the Orange Free State. Further north, between the Limpopo and Zambezi rivers, the migrant Ndebele kingdom had arrived a few decades previous and carved out a territory for itself abutting a network of Shona states. While colonial rule did not extend that far north in the 1870s, white hunters and missionaries were beginning to arrive from the Cape by traveling the north–south trade road that skirted the eastern edge of the Kalahari Desert through what is now Botswana.

KEY TERMS

15

The Scramble for Africa, c. 1880–1910

Between about 1880 and 1910, almost all of Africa was conquered by European powers in a process so rapid that it was called the "Scramble for Africa." Only two African countries remained independent: Liberia and Ethiopia. Located in West Africa, Liberia had become a republic of formerly enslaved African Americans in 1847 and, as such, it came under the protection of the United States. Ethiopia, in East Africa, was the only African state to successfully defend itself from European invasion in this period, as it defeated an Italian army at the 1896 Battle of Adwa. While the Scramble involved very many bloody wars of colonial invasion and conquest in every region of Africa, many African societies did not resist and came under European rule through treaty.

Europeans and Africans had very different perceptions of the Scramble. For Europeans, the defining event of the partition of Africa was the **Berlin Conference**, which was conducted from November 1884 to February 1885. German chancellor Otto von Bismarck convened the international meeting, and hosting it symbolized newly unified Germany's emergence as a colonial power. The European governments were in regular diplomatic contact with each other and had an established history of holding international conferences to discuss specific issues. The Berlin Conference initially sought to deal with Belgian King Leopold II's private empire building in the Congo, which is discussed later in this chapter, but it expanded its deliberations to cover all of Africa. Representatives of 13 European states and the United States were present at the event, but no one from Africa was invited. While the conference resolved to end slavery within Africa, it also divided the continent into areas claimed by the various European powers. Since most of these areas had never been visited by Europeans, the principle of **effective occupation** was established, which meant that European territorial claims in Africa had to be ratified by some kind of physical presence. This set off a race by the European powers to send colonial officials and agents to the various parts of Africa they had claimed. Although this was a competitive process and there were some tense incidents during the Scramble between

Fierce Combat. Hehe warriors battle German troops during an engagement in central Tanzania in 1891.

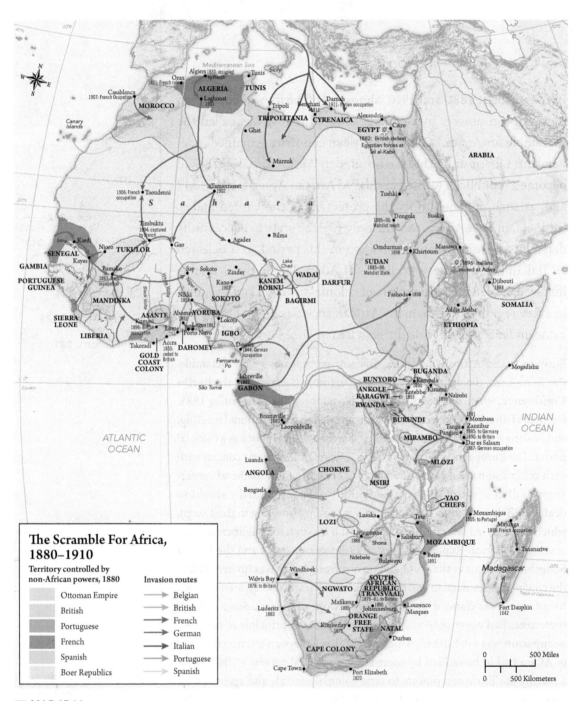

The Scramble For Africa, 1880–1910

Territory controlled by
non-African powers, 1880

- Ottoman Empire
- British
- Portuguese
- French
- Spanish
- Boer Republics

Invasion routes

- Belgian
- British
- French
- German
- Italian
- Portuguese
- Spanish

≡ MAP 15.1A

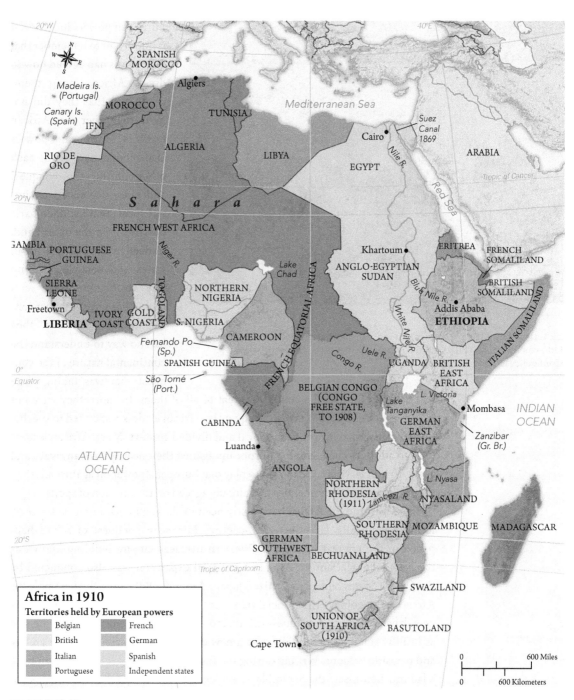

Africa in 1910

Territories held by European powers

- Belgian
- British
- Italian
- Portuguese
- French
- German
- Spanish
- Independent states

MORROCCO · SPANISH MOROCCO · Algiers · TUNISIA · Madeira Is. (Portugal) · Canary Is. (Spain) · IFNI · RIO DE ORO · ALGERIA · LIBYA · Mediterranean Sea · Suez Canal 1869 · Cairo · EGYPT · ARABIA · Tropic of Cancer · Red Sea · Nile R.

Sahara

FRENCH WEST AFRICA · Niger R. · Lake Chad · GAMBIA · PORTUGUESE GUINEA · SIERRA LEONE · Freetown · LIBERIA · IVORY COAST · GOLD COAST · TOGOLAND · NORTHERN NIGERIA · S. NIGERIA · CAMEROON · Khartoum · ANGLO-EGYPTIAN SUDAN · ERITREA · FRENCH SOMALILAND · BRITISH SOMALILAND · Addis Ababa · ETHIOPIA · ITALIAN SOMALILAND · Blue Nile R.

FRENCH EQUATORIAL AFRICA · Fernando Po (Sp.) · SPANISH GUINEA · São Tomé (Port.) · *Equator* · 0° · Uele R. · Congo R. · White Nile R. · UGANDA · BRITISH EAST AFRICA · L. Victoria · Lake Tanganyika · Mombasa · INDIAN OCEAN · CABINDA · Luanda · BELGIAN CONGO (CONGO FREE STATE, TO 1908) · GERMAN EAST AFRICA · Zanzibar (Gr. Br.)

ATLANTIC OCEAN · ANGOLA · NORTHERN RHODESIA (1911) · Zambezi R. · L. Nyasa · NYASALAND · SOUTHERN RHODESIA · MOZAMBIQUE · MADAGASCAR · GERMAN SOUTHWEST AFRICA · BECHUANALAND · SWAZILAND · Tropic of Capricorn · UNION OF SOUTH AFRICA (1910) · BASUTOLAND · Cape Town

0   600 Miles
0   600 Kilometers

≡ **MAP 15.1B**

≡ **Carving up Africa.** Representatives of European states, including Germany's Otto von Bismarck (seated at the center right), met at the 1884–85 Berlin Conference to claim territory in Africa.

European powers in Africa, it is important to remember that Europeans had agreed how to divide Africa among themselves and that they did not fight each other over African territory. European powers also cooperated with each other during the conquest and often negotiated territorial swaps that included parts of Africa. On the other hand, leaders in the many African states and societies had no way to communicate with each other across the vast continent, and, therefore, they had no way to understand the continental nature of the conquest that was taking place and how it represented a common threat to all of them. In short, they were not fully aware of the big picture. Consequently, African leaders responded to specific European colonial invasions in a local and divided context. Many African leaders tried to ally with the incoming Europeans against their nearby African rivals, and a few African leaders tried in vain to play one European power off against another, not realizing that their enemies had already agreed on the division of spoils.

The **Scramble for Africa** has mostly been explained in economic or strategic terms. Specifically, late-nineteenth-century European conquest of Africa happened in the context of renewed Western overseas empire building known as the **New Imperialism**. In Asia, this imperial expansion was also conducted by the United States and a modernized Japan. Around 1900, when the Scramble for Africa was ongoing, British social reformer Thomas Hobson maintained that the new drive for colonial conquest originated with the replacement of what he saw as healthy small-scale capitalism by a new economy dominated by a few greedy and parasitic tycoons. Writing during the First World War, Russian revolutionary Vladimir Lenin saw the Scramble as evidence that the capitalist system was beginning to tear itself apart as large-scale industrial capitalists raced to occupy new areas to invest their excess capital. As a Marxist and soon-to-be leader of the 1917 Bolshevik Revolution, Lenin saw the Scramble within the framework of his belief that a working-class revolution would topple capitalism and usher in new and more equitable socialist and then communist stages of history. Although Lenin recognized the acquisition of raw materials for Western industries as one reason for colonial conquest, he gave primacy to investment opportunities, which ultimately proved wrong as European powers invested very little in their African colonies, which were ruled as inexpensively as possible. Cold War–era British historians Ronald Robinson and John Gallagher, rejecting economic theories associated with Marxism, conceived the Scramble as having been driven by the perceived strategic interests of the European powers. In this view, several key conquests, beginning with the 1882 British occupation of Egypt to secure the strategically vital Suez Canal, set off a domino effect of territorial seizures across Africa by European powers. In 1885, for instance, the British signed treaties with Tswana rulers in Southern Africa to create the Bechuanaland Protectorate, today's Botswana, to block interaction between the recently arrived Germans in South West Africa (Namibia) and the nearby Boers of the Transvaal and Orange Free State republics who were resisting British domination in what would later become South Africa. In the 1970s and 1980s, however, materialist historian A.G. Hopkins highlighted that European powers had no major strategic interests in West Africa, yet they rushed to conquer this region during the late nineteenth century. European merchants had long acquired raw materials along the West African coast, but an economic depression in the 1870s, as Hopkins explains, motivated them to cut costs by conquering the area so as to eliminate the African middlemen in the trade and gain direct control over the producers in the interior. Some of the same events can be understood through the lenses of both strategic and economic theories. While some historians see the Second Anglo-Boer War (1899–1902) as caused by the British need to protect the strategically important Cape shipping route from the growing Boer republics, others explain it as resulting from the British ambition to control the Transvaal's gold mines as a major economic asset.

Many factors facilitated the Scramble. Europeans possessed new technologies, products of the **Second Industrial Revolution** of the mid-nineteenth century, that helped them conquer Africa. While many African armies possessed firearms, they were usually obsolete muzzle-loaders acquired through trade over many years. These old weapons were slow to load and had a very short range. On the other hand, the European-led armies that invaded Africa were armed with new rapid-firing, accurate, and long-range guns such as breech-loading rifles; the **Maxim gun**, which was the first modern machine-gun; and artillery with explosive shells. This overwhelming advantage in firepower inspired British writer Hilaire Belloc to pen the satirical line, "Whatever happens, we have got the Maxim gun, and they have not." Indeed, the Maxim gun was so new that it was first used in warfare during the "Scramble for Africa." Africans had not had a chance to acquire these new inventions, and the **Brussels Agreement** of 1890, the product of another meeting of European powers, banned the export of modern weapons to Africa. Transportation and communications technology was also important. Ocean-going steam-driven, steel-hulled ships reduced travel time between Europe and Africa; steam trains and riverboats enabled Europeans to access the African interior and extract its natural resources; and the telegraph sped up European communications and enabled them to react quickly to developments in the colonies. In most areas, the construction of railways from the coast into the interior took place at the same time as colonial conquest. Accurate maps provided the European invaders with information on routes and resources and legitimized the conquest by demarcating new borders. Lastly, medical improvements such as the development of **quinine** as a prophylaxis against malaria reduced the deadliness of tropical disease that had long restricted European activities in tropical Africa. During the late nineteenth and early twentieth century, European plantations of cinchona trees, indigenous to South America, were established in India and South East Asia, where the bark was used to mass produce quinine. While almost half of the European troops sent to the West African coast died during the early 1800s, this mortality rate fell to less than 10 percent during the 1880s and 1890s.

A particularly extreme version of European racism developed in the late nineteenth century and provided justification for the colonial conquest of Africa. The pseudo-science of **Social Darwinism**, which tried to apply the evolutionary biology of Charles Darwin to human societies, placed white northern Europeans at the top and Black Africans at the bottom of an imagined racial hierarchy. As a result of this feeling of racial supremacy, some Europeans believed that they had a natural right to conquer and exploit Africans, and others thought that they had a moral obligation—called **the white man's burden**—to elevate supposedly less fortunate beings. Jingoist European nationalism and competition was also important. Newly unified Germany wanted to create a worldwide empire so that it would have the same imperial status as Great Britain. Likewise, France conquered much of the immense but largely unprofitable Sahara Desert partly to compensate for its loss in the Franco-Prussian War, fought in Europe in 1870–71, and the consequent rise of Germany as a new European power. Several groups of Europeans with interests in Africa pressed their home governments to extend colonial rule. Christian missionaries had been active in Africa for a long time before the Scramble, but their frustrations with the slow pace of Africa's religious conversion and influence from the rising white racism of the time convinced many evangelicals of the need for direct

THE TOOLS OF EMPIRE

Top left: A drawing of the Maxim gun brought to Africa by Henry Stanley's Emin Pasha Relief expedition of 1886–89. *Top right*: A British nurse, aided by African medical assistants, administers quinine to villagers in East Africa, c. 1930. *Bottom left*: A steamboat moored on the Nile River, c. 1890. *Bottom right*: This detail from a 1911 map of Africa shows the demarcation of borders by European imperialists.

European intervention. Seeking more profits from the extraction of resources, European businessmen gained charters that allowed their companies to form armies and conquer and administer African territory on behalf of their imperial governments. **Chartered companies** became one of the main institutions that prosecuted the Scramble. While these factors informed the overall progress of the European conquest, the Scramble occurred slightly differently in each region of Africa.

North Africa

As part of the Mediterranean Rim, North Africa is geographically close to southern Europe and therefore experienced earlier and more direct European invasion. France had colonized Algeria in the 1830s and 1840s. Russia's 1877–78 military defeat of the Ottoman Empire, the so-called "Sick Man of Europe," prompted European powers to invade parts of North Africa hitherto under the nominal authority of Istanbul. By around 1870, Tunisia had modernized its administration but in the process became indebted to France. In April 1881, France invaded Tunisia, sending an army overland from neighboring Algeria and landing troops on the coast. After Tunisian ruler Sadik Bey accepted a French protectorate under which he became a puppet, French warships bombarded Tunisian rebels at the port of Sfax and French troops occupied the inland city of Kairouan. Other European powers accepted the French invasion of Tunisia. Britain agreed to the French occupation in exchange for the Mediterranean island of Cyprus, which had belonged to the Ottomans; Germany thought the conquest would forestall French claims in Europe; and Italy objected as it had business interests in Tunisia, but it lacked the military power to challenge France.

Opened in 1869, the **Suez Canal** dramatically increased the strategic importance of Egypt as it linked the Red and Mediterranean seas, thereby creating a shorter shipping route between Europe and Asia. By this time the Egyptian government had become seriously indebted to Britain and France. In May 1882, given a nationalist uprising in Egypt that threatened access to the canal, a multinational naval force comprising ships from Britain, France, the United States, Greece, Italy, Germany, and Russia arrived off the Mediterranean coast of Egypt. In July, British warships bombarded coastal defense batteries at Alexandria, where anti-foreign riots were breaking out, and British marines occupied the city. British forces took control of both ends of the Suez Canal and brought in reinforcements, including many from India. At the Battle of Tell el-Kebir, fought in September 1882, a 25,000-strong British army led by Garnet Wolseley decisively defeated an Egyptian nationalist force under Urabi Pasha, who was exiled to Ceylon. Egypt remained technically part of the Ottoman Empire and had its own ruler called the **khedive**, but it was occupied by Britain and a British officer commanded the Egyptian army.

By the start of the twentieth century, Morocco was plagued by civil war and indebted to European powers. France renounced its claims to Egypt in 1903 in return for the British agreeing not to get involved in Morocco. In 1907, with anti-European violence in Morocco, French forces were landed by ship at Casablanca and French soldiers marched across the border from Algeria. In 1911, after the French occupied the city of Fez, a German gunboat arrived at Agadir on the Atlantic coast to support Moroccan independence. However, the warship withdrew when the French gave Germany some territory along the Congo River. The next year Moroccan ruler Mawlay Abd al-Hafiz, who had recently come to power in a civil war, accepted a French protectorate. Morocco remained nominally independent but was administered by France. Subsequently, France and Spain agreed that the latter would have control over the far south and far north of Morocco. French firepower suppressed rebellions in Fez and Marrakech. In the interior, particularly in the mountainous Rif region, resistance against Spanish and French occupation continued into the 1920s.

≡ **The Battle of Tell el-Kebir.** British and Egyptian forces engage at the Battle of Tell el-Kebir. Garnet Wolseley (1833–1913), who commanded British forces, had previously led British invasions of the Asante Empire in 1873–74 and the Pedi Kingdom in 1879.

In October 1911, responding to domestic public pressure for colonial expansion and a desire to make up for the 1896 defeat by Ethiopia, Italy invaded Libya which was under Ottoman administration. Italian warships bombarded Tripoli, and Italian soldiers came ashore and pushed Ottoman and local Arab forces into the interior. With Italian naval dominance in the Mediterranean, the Ottomans could only support their forces by smuggling supplies overland through British-occupied Egypt. While around 100,000 Italian troops were brought to Libya, they were poorly trained and could not move inland beyond the range of naval guns. In Libya, the Italians made the first use of aircraft in warfare. In the broader naval campaign of this Italo-Turkish War, the Italian fleet sank Ottoman ships near Beirut, bombarded coastal Yemen and the Dardanelles, and grabbed Aegean islands. The outbreak of another war in the Balkans prompted the Ottomans, in October 1912, to make peace by accepting the Italian occupation of Libya in exchange for the return of islands in the Aegean. Arab guerrilla resistance in the Libyan interior continued throughout the 1920s and early 1930s.

Northeast Africa

In the 1820s, Egypt, under the modernizing leader Muhammad Ali, had conquered Sudan to acquire gold and enslaved people for the Egyptian army. During the 1860s and 1870s the Egyptian administration, under pressure from abolitionist Britain, tried to end slavery in Sudan, but this threatened local economic interests. As a result, in 1881 the Muslim religious leader Muhammad Ahmed proclaimed himself the **Mahdi**, a savior chosen by God to restore a pure form of Islam. The Mahdi mobilized a large Sudanese army to wage holy war against Egyptian control. The rebels seized Egyptian forts and captured firearms from the defeated Egyptian army. After occupying Egypt in 1882, Britain was drawn into the conflict in Sudan as control of the Nile River was seen as the key to controlling Egypt. In late 1883, a British-led Egyptian army marched into Sudan, but the Mahdists annihilated it at the Battle of Shaykan. While the British government decided to abandon Sudan and sent General Charles Gordon there to organize the withdrawal, he delayed and was trapped by Mahdist forces that besieged Khartoum. The British sent a relief expedition, led by Wolseley, from Egypt, but it failed to reach Khartoum before the Mahdists took the city and killed Gordon in January 1885. The British and Egyptians then abandoned Sudan, leaving it under the rule of the Mahdi, who died in June and was succeeded by Abdallahi al-Taaisha, known as the Khalifa (successor), who imposed strict Islamic law and pursued jihad against non-believers, including

≡ **Mahdist Resistance in Sudan** *Left:* Muhammad Ahmed (1844–85), popularly known as the Mahdi, led an Islamist uprising against Anglo-Egyptian rule in Sudan during the 1880s. *Right:* General Charles Gordon, who was killed by Mahdist forces in Khartoum in 1885.

invading neighboring countries. In 1889, the Mahdists
invaded Christian-ruled Ethiopia, where they killed Ethiopian Emperor Yohannes IV
in battle, and in the same year
they moved north into southern Egypt but were driven
back across the frontier by the
British-led Egyptian army. In
1895, they clashed with Italian colonial forces in western
Eritrea.

In 1896, the British became
concerned about French and
Belgian ambitions in Sudan,
and the defeat of the Italians
at the Battle of Adwa raised
the possibility of an alliance
between the Mahdist state
and Ethiopia. If another Eu-

≡ **Death by machinery.** A contemporary print showing the Battle of Omdurman.
British forces hold their line against the charging Mahdists. Winston Churchill
participated in the engagement as a newspaper correspondent and afterward wrote
that the British army "fed out death by machinery." Although this illustration
depicts the British wearing red uniforms, they in fact wore khaki during the battle.

ropean power were to occupy Sudan, then it could cut off the flow of the Nile River to Egypt, which would destabilize that country and therefore threaten British
control of the strategically vital Suez Canal. In March 1896 a British-Egyptian
army led by General Horatio Kitchener began a slow invasion of Sudan, working
its way up the Nile supported by gunboats on the river and the building of a railway. In April 1898, Kitchener's growing force defeated the Mahdists at Atbara,
an important crossing point on the Nile, and proceeded to the Mahdist capital
of Omdurman, where in September a massive Mahdist army was devastated by
British firepower, including Maxim guns and artillery fired from river boats. At
this decisive **Battle of Omdurman**, some 10,000 Mahdist fighters were killed
while the Anglo-Egyptian army lost just 48 men. The Khalifa escaped but was
killed by a British column the next year. An Anglo-Egyptian colonial state was
imposed on Sudan.

Immediately after the Battle of Omdurman, Kitchener led a British-Egyptian
force further south along the Nile to confront a French expedition at Fashoda
in what is now South Sudan. The **Fashoda Incident** of September 1898 was the
closest that two European powers came to fighting each other over part of Africa during the Scramble. Beginning in 1896, at the same time Kitchener's force

had been pushing up the Nile from Egypt, a small French force under Major Jean-Baptiste Marchand marched inland from the Atlantic coast of French colonial Gabon, took a Belgian steamer up the Ubangi River across Central Africa and then walked to southern Sudan, arriving at Fashoda in July 1898. After their 14-month long journey, Marchand's group was supposed to link up with a French-Ethiopian expedition, but that expedition was aborted because of hunger and disease, and French hopes to ally with the Mahdists were dashed when the latter attacked them. On September 18, 1898, Kitchener's Anglo-Egyptian force of 1,500 soldiers arrived by riverboat at Fashoda to confront the French expedition, which consisted of only 12 Europeans and 140 Senegalese troops. Badly outnumbered, the French conceded to British demands and withdrew in November. More broadly, the French government backed down because of a political scandal at home and fear of British naval might. Ultimately, the Fashoda Incident led to better relations between France and Britain with the two powers agreeing on their colonial borders in Africa in 1899 and entering into a formal alliance against Germany in 1904.

The opening of the Suez Canal meant that the Horn of Africa, which dominated approaches to the Red Sea, became of greater strategic importance to world powers. As such, in the 1870s Egypt tried to expand its control over the Red Sea and the Horn of Africa, which led to conflict with Ethiopia. Egypt took over a series of ports in the Horn of Africa, Massawa and Zulla in what is now Eritrea along the Red Sea coast and Berbera and Zayla on the Gulf of Aden, and imposed an arms embargo on Ethiopia which was the chief regional power. The 1884–85 Anglo-Egyptian withdrawal from Sudan weakened the Egyptian presence in the Horn of Africa, and Italy exploited Egypt's weakness in the area. In 1883, Italian colonial forces landed on the Red Sea coast of what would become their colony of Eritrea, and two years later they took Massawa from the departing Egyptians. Moving inland, the Italians saw Ethiopia as a threat and renewed the existing arms embargo against it. Although the Ethiopians had assisted the British during their retreat from Sudan, Britain supported Italian ambitions in the Horn of Africa to counter the French presence at Djibouti. Defeated by Ethiopian forces along the Eritrean frontier in 1887, the Italians expanded their military presence in Eritrea, built a railway inland from Massawa, and imposed a full trade blockade on Ethiopia. The Mahdist threat from Sudan distracted Ethiopian emperor Yohannes IV from dealing with the Italians in Eritrea, who took advantage of the situation by moving into parts of Ethiopia's Tigray region. Since he became emperor with the help of Italian weapons, Menelik I signed the 1889 Treaty of Wuchale, in which Ethiopia ceded to Italy the territory it had already taken and Italy recognized the new emperor. Given his agreement with the Italians in

Eritrea, Menelik then directed Ethiopia's expansion southward to acquire enslaved people, gold, and ivory. During the early 1890s Menelik purchased up-to-date weapons from the French, British, and Italians who saw Ethiopia as a foil against Mahdism in Sudan.

Conflict between Ethiopia and Italy was prompted by differing versions of the Treaty of Wuchale; the

≡ **Turning back the invaders.** Equipped with repeating rifles, machine guns, and cannon, the Ethiopian army under Menelik II routed an Italian invasion force at the battle of Adwa. The *Times of London* complained that "the prestige of European arms as a whole has been greatly impaired."

Italian text obliged Ethiopia to conduct all foreign relations through Italy, while the Amharic version made this optional. Menelik renounced the treaty in 1893, and the next year Italian forces started to invade parts of Tigray. In January 1896, Ethiopian troops besieged an Italian fort at Mekele, and Menelik, hoping for a negotiated settlement, let the defenders withdraw to Eritrea with their weapons. In turn, the Italians mounted a concerted invasion of Ethiopia, intending to attack the Ethiopian army camped at Adwa. Advancing on the Ethiopian camp during the night, the Italian brigades became separated and were poorly positioned for the battle that took place the next morning of March 1, 1896, when they were routed by Ethiopian forces. Although the Italian army comprised 20,000 men, the Ethiopians totaled over 100,000 and they were equipped with modern rifles and some artillery. Over half the Italian army was killed or wounded, and the Ethiopians captured many of their weapons. After his victory at the **Battle of Adwa**, Menelik declined to advance into Eritrea as his massive army had no food and the Italian colony was well fortified. In Italy, the defeat at Adwa caused rioting in some cities and the collapse of the government, and was viewed as a national humiliation. A new Italian administration signed the Treaty of Addis Ababa, which formalized the Ethiopian–Eritrean border and renounced Italian claims over Ethiopia. Although some Ethiopian nationalist historians have explained Ethiopia's victory in terms of its long national history and strong identity, the Battle of Adwa pitted one of Europe's weakest colonial powers against Africa's strongest state. Had the British or French invaded Ethiopia, the conflict likely would have turned out differently.

West Africa

During the 1850s and 1860s, the French, based at the West African ports of Dakar and Saint Louis, advanced inland up the Senegal River to dominate trade and prevent the westward expansion of the Tukolor Empire. While the French defeat by Prussia in Europe in 1871 spurred French colonial expansion in Africa, it was conducted mostly by the locally recruited **Tirailleurs Sénégalais** so as not to deprive France of soldiers and therefore weaken its defense. Furthermore, French military officers in late-nineteenth-century West Africa extended French authority on their own and sometimes blatantly defied instructions from the disorganized civilian government in Paris. Between 1879 and 1883, the French expanded down the Niger River, building a series of forts and constructing a railway from Senegal to Bamako, capital of today's Mali. Pushing into the southern part of the Tukolor Empire, the French used artillery to bombard Tukolor forts, and they encouraged the subject Bambara population to rebel. From 1885 to 1887, French and Tukolor forces cooperated in suppressing Mahmadu Lamine's Muslim state of Futa Bondu between the Gambia and Senegal rivers. After the destruction of Futa Bondu, the French continued their offensive against Tukolor and manipulated conflicts between Tukolor regional leaders. In April 1890, the French captured the Tukolor center of Ségou on the Niger, which pushed Tukolor forces east, undermining their efforts to cooperate with Samori Toure's Mandinka Empire to the south. After a failed Tukolor counteroffensive that tried to mobilize a broader anti-French alliance, the French seized the important Niger trading towns of Djenne and Mopti in April 1893 as Tukolor ruler Ahmadu Seku fled to the Sokoto Caliphate in what is now northern Nigeria.

From 1865 to 1875, Samori Toure founded the Mandinka Empire near the Upper Niger Basin, around what is now the Republic of Guinea, and used firearms imported through the British colony of Sierra Leone to take control of the local gold trade. This became West Africa's third-largest empire after Tukolor and Sokoto. In the early 1880s, French attempts to move south of the Tukolor Empire and link up with colonial enclaves in Côte d'Ivoire (Ivory Coast) led to conflict with Samori's state. In January 1882, the French occupied Bamako and used it as a staging area for attacks that drove the Mandinka Empire south and east. While the French and Samori signed the Treaty of Bissandugu in 1887, which formalized the Niger River as the Mandinka northeastern border, the French encouraged dissident leaders within the empire. In 1891, the French discarded the treaty and sent an invasion force south of the Niger, which was countered by Samori's fighters, well-armed with imported up-to-date rifles, who conducted a guerrilla war. As part of his army fought delaying actions against the French, Samori tried to escape colonial conquest by moving his state east to the northern part of what is now Côte d'Ivoire and Ghana. In 1893, a French column pushed Samori's forces further east to prevent them from assisting the Tukolor Empire, and several other French expeditions cut off the Mandinka supply of firearms from Sierra Leone and Liberia. More French actions against Samori were delayed by Tuareg resistance to the French occupation of Timbuktu on the Niger Bend, which took place at the end of 1894 and the start of 1895. In early 1895, a French expedition landed at Côte d'Ivoire and marched inland to the state of Kong, which had accepted French protection, but the colonial troops suffered

≡ **Resister to French colonialism.** Samori Toure, leader of West Africa's Mandinka Empire, surrendered to French colonial forces in 1898.

heavy casualties fighting Samori's forces and had to turn back. The Asante kingdom, which came under British authority in 1896, halted the eastward movement of the Mandinka Empire. Since the Mandinka massacred a French mission sent to offer Samori terms under which he could capitulate but retain control of some areas, another French expedition invaded his remaining territory in 1898. By this time, the British and French had agreed on the borders of their West African territories, which gave the latter a free hand to deal with the Mandinka leader. Captured by the French in August 1898, Samori was exiled to Gabon, where he died in 1900.

From the 1860s to 1880s, in what is now the Republic of Benin, the inland kingdom of Dahomey and the French vied for control of the Atlantic trading ports of Porto Novo and Cotonou. In March 1890, Dahomey armies attacked the French presence at these ports but were repelled by colonial firepower. In October 1890, this First Franco–Dahomey War ended when Dahomey's ruler, Behanzin, accepted French authority over Porto Novo and Cotonou. Acquiring modern firearms from German traders in nearby Togo, Behanzin attempted to reassert Dahomey's control over the coast in 1892, which led to the Second Franco–Dahomey War. The French blocked further arms imports, and French officials justified military action against Dahomey to end slavery and ritual human sacrifice. A large French expedition invaded Dahomey, and after a series of grueling battles French colonial troops occupied the Dahomey capital of Abomey in November 1892. Dahomey's elite corps of female warriors, called **Amazons** by Europeans, were prominent in the fighting but were defeated by better-armed French forces. Behanzin surrendered in January 1894, and he was banished to Martinique and eventually Algeria, where he died in 1906. As a result of the 1894 conflict, French rule was extended further north, French merchants took over the palm oil trade from the Dahomey kingdom, and in 1904 the French colonial territory of Dahomey was incorporated into the larger French West Africa.

In 1861, the British took control of the West African port of Lagos, which became a staging area for subsequent colonial expansion into what would become Nigeria. British colonialism in the area was spurred on by the arrival of French and German agents in the 1880s. After an 1886 British intervention that ended a long war between Ibadan and a coalition of other Yoruba states in the Lagos hinterland, Yoruba rulers agreed to submit their disputes to the British governor in Lagos and to open the area to free trade and British merchants. In 1892, a British military expedition subjugated the Yoruba state of Ijebu, which had refused to negotiate trade with the Lagos governor. By 1893, almost all the Yoruba leaders, intimidated by British firepower, had signed away their sovereignty and their states became part of an expanded Lagos colony. In 1894, New Oyo was bombarded by the British and became the last Yoruba state to come under British control.

From the 1850s, the British consul in the Bight of Biafra and Niger Delta, located east of Lagos, gained greater power by imposing treaties that promoted free trade, suppressed the slave trade and supported missionaries. After the arrival of French and German competitors in the mid-1880s, the British consul secured treaties of protection with all the area's rulers including Jaja who had founded the powerful trading center of Opobo about 15 years earlier. On the basis of these treaties, the British declared the Oil Rivers Protectorate in 1885 and renamed the territory the Niger Coast Protectorate in 1893. In 1887, Jaja, who had refused to grant British traders free access to Opobo, was tricked into attending negotiations with the British who then arrested him and sent him to the Gold Coast (Ghana), London, and eventually Saint Vincent in the Caribbean. In 1891, he died, possibly from poisoning, while traveling back to Opobo. In 1897, a British expedition conquered the kingdom of Benin, which had rejected British treaty offers and massacred a British diplomatic mission. Benin City was looted and burned, and its rich art works sold to subsidize the cost of the military operation.

By 1881, George Goldie had amalgamated the three largest British trading firms operating along the Niger River into the National African Company. In 1886, Goldie's company was granted a charter from the British government to gain control over the Niger and Benue rivers by making treaties and suppressing the slave trade. While the Oil Rivers Protectorate had secured British domination of the coast and Niger Delta, Goldie's renamed Royal Niger Company (RNC) was to secure the navigable rivers of the Nigerian interior and prevent French and German encroachment. Forming its own army called the Royal Niger Constabulary, the RNC made treaties with local rulers who did not always understand that they were signing away their sovereignty. In addition, the RNC imposed high import duties that undermined other European and African merchants. Prevented from accessing their historic trading area up the Niger and importing food, the delta trading town of Brass clashed with the RNC, and in 1894 it was bombed into submission by forces from the Niger Coast Protectorate. The establishment of a French presence on the Niger River prompted the RNC, in 1897, to conquer Nupe and Ilorin which were tributary states of the large Sokoto Caliphate to the north. In 1898, the British government purchased the RNC from Goldie and sent army officer Frederick Lugard to transform its constabulary into the West African Frontier Force (WAFF), which conquered Borgu the next year. French forces abandoned the area and moved west into Dahomey. In 1900, the former RNC's territory south of the Niger and Benue was joined with the Niger Coast Protectorate to create the Protectorate of Southern Nigeria. The Lagos Colony was absorbed into the Protectorate of Southern Nigeria in 1906. The conquest of the decentralized Igbo people of south eastern Nigeria continued into the 1900s and 1910s.

In 1900 the former RNC territory north of the Niger River, along with Ilorin, became the Protectorate of Northern Nigeria under the leadership of Lugard. The British worried that the neighboring Sokoto Caliphate would encourage resistance in places like Ilorin and serve as an avenue for French expansion. Since Sokoto had rejected overtures from the RNC, Lugard embarked on military conquest justified on the basis that the caliphate practiced slavery and was portrayed as representing a threat to regional security. Lugard mounted a series of military expeditions that steadily seized the semi-autonomous emirates that comprised the Sokoto Caliphate. By 1902, the British controlled Bida, Kontagora, Yola, Gombe, Bauchi, and Zaria. British machine guns cut down the emirs' traditional cavalry and British artillery bombed town walls. In 1903, Lugard's force took the market city of Kano without a fight and then defeated an army led by Caliph Attahiru II outside Sokoto. At the end of July 1903, Attahiru and the remnants of his army made a last stand at Burmi, where the caliph, his two sons, and some 600 followers were killed. Lugard found replacements for the defeated emirs, and the former caliphate

≡ **Female Leaders in Late Nineteenth-Century West Africa** *Left:* In 1900, Queen Mother Yaa Asantewaa led a rebellion by the Asante against British rule in what is now Ghana. *Right:* A modern depiction of Madam Yoko (c. 1849–1906), leader of the Kpaa Mende Confederacy in Sierra Leone, who allied with the British during the late nineteenth century.

was incorporated into Northern Nigeria. In 1904, the Lake Chad state of Borno, suffering from civil war and recent invasion, was annexed, becoming the north-eastern portion of Northern Nigeria. In 1914, the British combined Northern and Southern Nigeria to create the single colonial territory of Nigeria, with Lugard as its first governor.

During most of the nineteenth century, the British and the interior kingdom of Asante had vied for control of Fante trading communities along the Gold Coast. The 1871 British purchase of Dutch forts on the coast threatened Asante's sup-ply of imported firearms. As a result, in 1873 an Asante army invaded the coast and besieged a small British garrison at Cape Coast castle. In late 1873 and early 1874, a British punitive expedition under Wolseley fought its way into the Asante kingdom, where it burned the capital of Kumasi. The Asante resisted tenaciously, but their obsolete muskets were no match for British breech-loading rifles. In the subsequent Treaty of Fomena, the Asante renounced claims to the coast, agreed to pay an indemnity to Britain, and guaranteed free trade in their area. Recovering during the 1880s, Asante spurned a British offer to become a protectorate in 1890 and sent a delegation to London to try to avert war in 1895. Worried that the French to the west in Côte d'Ivoire or the Germans to the east in Togo would move into Asante, the British invaded in 1896 and occupied the kingdom without a fight. The Asante ruler Prempeh was banished to the Seychelles Islands in the Indian Ocean. In March 1900, after the British governor demanded the surrender of the sacred **golden stool**, the Asante besieged the British fort at Kumasi, where many defenders died of hunger and disease. Queen Mother **Yaa Asantewaa** led the Asante rebels. A colonial relief force from the coast, the organization of which had been delayed by the Second Anglo-Boer War (1899–1902) in South Africa, arrived at Kumasi in September. While more Asante leaders were exiled to the Seychelles, where the queen mother died in 1921, the British quietly dropped the demand for the golden stool and in 1902 Asante was merged with the Gold Coast Protectorate. In 1925 Prempeh was returned home and in 1935 the British allowed the monarchy to be reinstated under Prempeh II within the context of colonial rule.

During the 1880s, British and Creole (Krio) merchants from Freetown, which Britain had established as a naval base for antislavery operations and a settlement for formerly enslaved people in the early 1800s, began to push into the interior of what is now Sierra Leone. This led to a series of "trade wars," and the Freetown traders demanded that Britain extend its authority over the hinterland. Samori Toure, who was busy fighting the French, promised the British that he would not enter Sierra Leone as long as he continued to receive guns from Freetown. In 1887, a British expedition destroyed a number of towns of the Yoni Temne who had been at war with Britain's ally Madam Yoko, leader of the Kpaa Mende Confederacy. In 1890, with the French advancing against Samori, who vainly sought an alliance with Britain, the British signed treaties with rulers in the Sierra Leone interior and created the Frontier Police to enforce their rule. British efforts to drive Samori's people out of Sierra Leone led to an accidental skirmish between British and French troops in 1893. In 1896, the British declared a protectorate over Sierra Leone, which was administered from the adjacent colony of Freetown. The imposition of British taxation prompted a widespread rebellion in Sierra Leone in 1898, which is discussed in Chapter 4.

Like Freetown, the British founded Bathurst at the mouth of the Gambia River in the early 1800s and used it as a trading outpost and base for naval operations against the transatlantic slave trade. Since the French controlled the hinterland, the British had tried to exchange the Gambia with France for Côte d'Ivoire, but the deal fell through. In 1887, the French occupied towns along the Gambia River, where they assisted traditionalist leaders in an ongoing struggle against expansionist Muslim powers. After the British made treaties with rulers up the river, the French withdrew and negotiated borders between the Gambia and Senegal. In 1891, the British completed their occupation of the small territory (14 miles wide and 200 miles long) that became the Gambia, and many of the area's Soninke states, drained by long internal wars, were too exhausted to resist. Several Muslim leaders stubbornly fought the British takeover. Fode Silla was defeated in 1894, and Fode Kabba slipped in and out of French territory until 1900.

East Africa

Up to the mid-1880s, British policy toward East Africa had centered on recognizing the sultan of Zanzibar's claim over the mainland coast of what is now Kenya and Tanzania which enabled British merchants, explorers and missionaries to access the hinterland. This changed in 1885, when Germany declared a protectorate over the mainland of present-day Tanzania, which prompted Britain to drop its support for Zanzibar and impose its own authority from the coast of Kenya inland to agriculturally rich southern Uganda. In 1888, the British government granted a charter to William MacKinnon's **Imperial British East Africa Company (IBEAC)**, which established itself near Mombasa on the Kenyan coast, from where it would attempt to extend British rule inland to Lake Victoria. At this time, the kingdom of Buganda was the leading power around Lake Victoria, but it was embroiled in a religious civil war in which Muslim converts were aligned with Arab traders, Catholic converts were associated with French missionaries, and Protestant converts were linked to British missionaries. The three factions had each acquired firearms from their foreign sponsors. In 1889, a Christian alliance defeated the Muslim faction and reinstalled Mwanga, originally a traditionalist, as the king, and a short time later he signed a treaty with German empire-builder Carl Peters. However, this agreement was invalidated by an 1890 agreement whereby Germany gave up claims to Uganda in exchange for the strategically important island of Heligoland in the North Sea. In December 1890, an IBEAC expedition led by Frederick Lugard arrived in Buganda and extorted Mwanga into signing away his sovereignty to Britain. When violence broke out between Buganda's Protestants and Catholics in 1892, Lugard's machine guns ensured the former's victory. Consequently, a Protestant elite came to dominate Buganda, and Mwanga, who had initially backed the Catholics, converted to Protestantism. In 1893, the British government took over the administration of East Africa from the IBEAC, which was struggling financially, and three years later London bought the company from MacKinnon. During the same year the British and their Protestant allies in Buganda suppressed a Muslim rebellion and then mounted an offensive against neighboring Bunyoro, which had long been a regional rival of Buganda. In 1897, Mwanga, resentful over British limitations on this authority, fled the capital and mobilized a rebellion by Muslims and Catholics, which was defeated by colonial machine guns. The British replaced Mwanga with his one-year-old son Daudi Chwa, who was guided by a regency of two Protestants and one Catholic. Mwanga and similarly deposed Bunyoro leader Kabarega fought a guerrilla war against the British and their Baganda (people of Buganda) allies until 1899, when both fugitive kings were captured and sent to the Seychelles. In 1900, the British and Baganda Protestant elites signed the Uganda Agreement, under which Buganda received former Bunyoro lands and became the center of British expansion across the larger Protectorate of Uganda.

During the late 1880s and early 1890s, the IBEAC had seen present-day Kenya as a corridor through which to reach the richer territory of Uganda. In 1895, the British government assumed administration of the East Africa Protectorate from the IBEAC, and eventually, in 1920, the territory was renamed Kenya. During 1895–96, the new British administration, supported by Royal Navy landing parties, crushed a rebellion by coastal Swahili and inland Giriama communities. Between 1895 and 1905, the pastoral and decentralized

≡ **Signing away their land.** The Kikuyu people in what is today Kenya negotiate a treaty with officials from the Imperial British East Africa Association.

☰ **German ally.** King Musinga (1883–1944) of Rwanda poses with the German flag in 1912.

Nandi people around Mount Elgon tenaciously resisted British efforts to build a road and then a railway, meant to connect the port of Mombasa with Uganda, through their territory. The British responded with a series of brutal punitive expeditions, supported by Luo, Maasai, and Somali allies, which destroyed Nandi homes and seized their livestock. In late 1905, the British invited the Nandi spiritual and war leader, Koitalel, to negotiations, where he was shot dead by British captain Richard Meinertzhagen.

Leasing the coast of East Africa for 50 years from the sultan of Zanzibar in 1888, Carl Peters's German East Africa Company pushed inland and used modern firearms to gun down the pastoral Maasai. The imposition of German control prompted an 1888–89 rebellion by coastal Swahili-Arabs that was put down by an expeditionary force under Captain Hermann von Wissman, who had been dispatched by Berlin. The cost of suppressing the rebellion incited the German government to take over control of East Africa from Peters's company. From 1891 to 1898, the expanding Hehe state of interior central Tanzania fought the encroachment of German colonial rule from the coast. Hehe resistance ended because of hunger, disease, and war-weariness, and in 1898, the Hehe leader Mkwawa shot himself to avoid capture by the Germans. In post-independence Tanzania, nationalists would remember Mkwawa as a great hero of anti-colonial resistance. In 1895, German colonialists arrived in the inland centralized state of Rwanda around the same time that the death of King Rwabugiri had caused an internal power struggle. After Rwandan warriors were slaughtered while attacking a Belgian outpost at Shangi on the south end of Lake Kivu in 1896, a faction led by Queen Mother Kanjogera supporting the young Musinga as the new ruler emerged and gained supremacy by allying with the newly arrived Germans. With German military support, Musinga expanded his control into the mountainous north of present-day Rwanda, where local resistance was crushed. In 1896, the Germans established an outpost at the trading center of Bujumbura on the north end of Lake Tanganyika, which was used as a staging area for expeditions into the nearby kingdom of Burundi. A 1902 German expedition that included allies from nearby Rwanda burned Burundi's capital and forced its ruler, Mwezi Gisabo, to accept German authority. Mwezi Gisabo then cooperated with the Germans, using their firepower to extend his rule over neighboring communities. Rwanda, Burundi, and the mainland of today's Tanzania became German East Africa.

In the early 1880s, the French decided to strengthen their position in the Indian Ocean, where they already had several small island colonies, by subjugating the island kingdom of Madagascar, where there were brewing tensions between a westernized Christian monarchy and traditionalist commoners. After French warships bombarded coastal towns, some of which were then seized by French marines, Madagascar's Queen Ranavalona III signed a treaty whereby she agreed to accept a French resident in her capital of Antananarivo and to pay an indemnity to France. While the treaty did not use the term "protectorate," the French thought that they had imposed this status on Madagascar. In 1890, the British and French agreed to divide the western Indian Ocean, which confirmed the latter's claim over Zanzibar and the former over Madagascar. Since Ranavalona III

≡ **The French Conquest of Madagascar** *Left:* Queen Ranavalona III (1861–1917) was ruler of Madagascar during the French invasion of 1895 and was exiled to Algeria. *Right:* A French poster from 1895 celebrates the French conquest of the island.

rejected French claims over the island, the French navy once again bombed coastal towns, and in 1895 a French invasion force was landed. Although the French troops suffered greatly from malaria and heavy rains, the resistance of the Malagasy army was undermined by colonial firepower and a local rebellion against the kingdom's forced labor and Christianization. The French army occupied Antananarivo, and Ranavalona III capitulated by accepting a French protectorate whereby the colonial power would rule indirectly through the existing monarchy. At the end of 1895, a popular rebellion against both the French and the monarchy broke out across the island. Wearing the red togas that symbolized traditional Malagasy warriors, the rebels targeted Christian missionaries and churches as well as foreign businesses. In 1896, France annexed the island, abolished the monarchy, and banished Ranavalona III to Algeria. Under General Joseph-Simon Gallieni, who had been active in the colonization of Indochina, French forces consisting largely of colonial troops from West Africa and Algeria conducted a systematic counterinsurgency campaign until 1905. The French administration paid for these operations by selling 900,000 hectares of land in Madagascar to French settlers and chartered companies.

Central Africa

During the 1890s, Rabih ibn Fadl Allah, a Sudanese slaver who led a well-armed private army and claimed to be a follower of the Mahdi, conquered the Bagirimi and Borno states around Lake Chad. While Rabih tried unsuccessfully to acquire firearms from Britain's RNC in what is now Nigeria, the French sent an expedition up the Congo and Ubangi rivers to establish a base in what became southern Chad. At the end of the 1890s, the French attempted to unify their African territories by having three columns converge on Lake Chad. One expedition traveled up the Congo River by steamboat, a second started in North Africa and marched south across the Sahara Desert, and a third originated in Dakar, Senegal, and trekked across what is now Mali, Burkina Faso, and Niger. The Dakar expedition, led by the psychopathic Captain Paul Voulet, massacred villages along its path and was pursued for 1,200 miles by another French force from Timbuktu that was sent to stop it. Voulet's expedition mutinied, and his own men killed him. In April 1900, elements of the three expeditions rendezvoused near Lake Chad, defeated Rabih's army, and displayed his decapitated head to mark their victory. An administration center called Fort Lamy (today's Ndjamena), named after Major Amédée-François

Lamy, who had led the column from North Africa and who was killed in the battle with Rabih, was created to oversee control of French colonial Chad. This conquest geographically united French possessions in West, Central, and North Africa.

As the constitutional monarch of Belgium during the late nineteenth century, Leopold II could not convince the government of his small country to engage in overseas empire building. In 1876, he established the International Africa Association (IAA), and during the 1880s it orchestrated the private colonial conquest of the Congo River Basin, which became the Congo Free State. The stated aims of the IAA were to abolish the slave trade and conduct scientific research, but in practice Leopold's regime ruthlessly extracted rubber and ivory from the Congo. Leopold, who never visited the Congo, hired the famous explorer Henry Stanley to begin the process of taking control of the Congo River. In 1881, Stanley organized local people to carry a disassembled steamboat 250 miles from the Congo's Atlantic coast, bypassing rapids and waterfalls, inland to the site of future Leopoldville (today's Kinshasa), where it was assembled and used to travel further up river. During the 1880s and 1890s, the Congo Free State used half its revenue to construct a fleet of steamboats at Leopoldville that extended colonial rule 870 miles northeast up the Congo River to what became Stanleyville (now Kisangani) and another 500 miles south up the Lualaba River to mineral rich Katanga. From 1890 to 1898, a railway was built to connect the Atlantic coast with Leopoldville. In 1891, Leopold, worried that the British would push north from Northern Rhodesia (Zambia), hired British-Canadian mercenary William Stairs to lead an expedition that set out from the East African coast, marched to Katanga, and subdued the Yeke state, which had dominated the area. To enforce its rule, the Congo Free State created an army called the **Force Publique**, initially recruited from other parts of Africa but eventually comprised of Congolese, which gained a reputation for extreme cruelty and lack of discipline. If Congolese communities failed to produce quotas of rubber for export, they were punished by flogging, and hostages had their hands or feet cut off.

With the British and Germans advancing inland from East Africa, the Swahili-Arab warlord Tippu Tip allied with Leopold in 1887 and became governor of the eastern Congo Free State. However, when Tippu Tip retired to Zanzibar in 1891, the Congo Free State clashed with the remaining Swahili-Arab leaders, who resisted taxation of their ivory exports and attempts to curtail their slave trading. Between 1892 and 1894, in what the Belgians called the "Arab War," the Force

☰ **Belgian Atrocities in the Congo** *Left:* A photo from 1907 depicts Congolese men and women whose hands have been cut off because they failed to meet rubber-collection quotas. *Right:* Painting, from about 1970 by the artist Tshibumba Kanda-Matulu, shows members of the Force Publique brutalizing Congolese citizens.

Publique used the mobility of its riverboats to defeat the Swahili-Arabs in eastern Congo. During the late 1890s, the most serious challenge to the Congo Free State came from Force Publique soldiers who mutinied over abuse by their Belgian officers.

Stories of atrocities by Leopold's regime, considered extreme even by the standards of the time, prompted the 1904 establishment of the Congo Reform Association, which mounted a publicity campaign in North America and Europe against the Congo Free State. Celebrity authors Joseph Conrad, Arthur Conan Doyle, and Mark Twain were involved in the movement, which called for Leopold to be put on trial for his horrific crimes. British diplomat Roger Casement visited the Congo in 1904 and wrote a critical report that was later confirmed by an official Belgian investigation. Given the scandal, the Belgian government purchased the Congo Free State from Leopold in 1908, and the territory became the Belgian Congo. Many historians claim that between five and ten million Congolese, or half the area's total population, perished during the reign of the Congo Free State (1885–1908). This has led to characterizations of Leopold's regime as genocidal and to comparisons with the Holocaust of the Second World War. However, there is no indication that Leopold's state intended to exterminate the Congolese, a key element of the international legal definition of **genocide**. In addition, a recent Belgian scholar argues that the Congo's total population, and hence the number of deaths, has been exaggerated, and points out that the first census there was not conducted in 1924.

Conclusion

The contemporary political map of Africa is largely a product of the European colonial conquest. Countries like Nigeria, Kenya, and Democratic Republic of Congo (DRC) did not exist before the late nineteenth and early twentieth century's "Scramble for Africa." European colonial invaders, usually ignoring the human and physical geography, imposed new borders and state structures on the African territories and peoples they subjugated. As such, the new colonial territories sometimes lumped together communities that had been historic rivals and divided some peoples with a common history and culture. For example, colonial Nigeria included both the formerly jihadist Muslim emirates in the north and Christian communities in the south, and the Tonga people were divided between Northern Rhodesia (Zambia) and Southern Rhodesia (Zimbabwe) as their Zambezi River home became an international border. When the European rulers withdrew during the decolonization era of the late 1950s and 1960s, Africa did not revert to its pre-conquest political status, but the existing colonies were simply transformed into independent states with largely the same borders that had been negotiated by European officials in Berlin in 1884. Of course, borders were not all that the European colonialists imposed on Africa. As discussed in Chapter 4, new administrative and economic systems came with colonial rule.

Timeline

1800
1869—Opening of Suez Canal

1870–71—Franco-Prussian War

1874—British invasion of Asante kingdom

1876—Establishment of International Africa Association

1879–93—French conquest of Tukolor Empire

1881—French Invasion of Tunisia

1881—Establishment of the Congo Free State

1881—Establishment of Royal Niger Company

1881—Start of Mahdi's rebellion in Sudan

1882—British occupation of Egypt

1882–98—Samori Toure resists French colonialism in West Africa

1883—Italians arrive in Eritrea

1884—Berlin Conference

1885—Death of Charles Gordon and British-Egyptian withdrawal from Sudan

1888—Imperial British East Africa Company

1889—Anti-German Rebellion on the East African Coast

1890—Brussels Convention

1890—British intervention in Buganda Civil War

1891–98—German–Hehe Wars in Central Tanzania

1892–94—"Arab War" in Eastern Congo

1895—French Invasion of Madagascar

1895—First German Expedition Arrives in Rwanda

1895–96—Rebellion in coastal Kenya

1896—British establish protectorate over Asante kingdom

1896—Battle of Adwa

1898—Battle of Omdurman and the Fashoda Incident

1900
1900—Rebellion of Asante kingdom

1900—British Establishment of Protectorates of Southern Nigeria and Northern Nigeria

1900—French conquest of area around Lake Chad

1902—German expedition conquers Burundi

1903—British defeat of Sokoto Caliphate

1904—Congo Reform Association established

1908—Belgian Congo acquired from Leopold II

1911—Italian conquest of Libya

1912—French protectorate over Morocco

1914—Unification of Nigeria as a single British territory

KEY TERMS

Amazons 320

Battle of Adwa 317

Battle of Omdurman 315

Berlin Conference 305

Brussels Agreement 310

Chartered companies 311

Effective occupation 305

Fashoda Incident 315

Force Publique 329

Genocide 330

Golden stool 323

Imperial British East Africa Company (IBEAC) 324

Khedive 312

Mahdi 314

Maxim gun 309

New imperialism 308

STUDY QUESTIONS

1. What factors facilitated the Scramble for Africa? What are some of the different interpretations historians have used to explain the Scramble?

2. What strategies did European countries use in their efforts to colonize Morocco and Libya?

3. What was the Mahdist uprising? How did the British respond? What role did the Suez Canal play in this conflict?

4. Why is the Battle of Adwa important?

5. How did France expand into Tukolor, Mandinka, and Dahomey? How did the British expand into Yoruba states, the Niger River area, Sierra Leone, and the Gambia?

6. What role did religion play in the Ugandan discord of the late nineteenth century?

7. Compare Belgian colonialism to that of other European countries. How was it similar? How was it different?

Please see page FR-6 for the Further Readings for this chapter.
For additional digital learning resources please go to
https://www.oup.com/he/falola-stapleton1e

Southern Africa's Mineral Revolution, c. 1870–1910

In the late nineteenth century, as the Scramble for Africa was unfolding across the continent, Southern Africa experienced a **mineral revolution** with the discovery of diamonds in the late 1860s and gold in the late 1880s. As discussed previously, European colonial conquest had begun earlier in the tip of Southern Africa than the rest of the continent, and the lack of tropical disease facilitated the establishment of settlements by the Dutch (eventually called Boers) and British, beginning in the seventeenth century. By the 1870s, the region was divided between the British colonies of the Cape and Natal on the coast, the Boer republics of the Orange Free State and Transvaal in the interior, and a few independent African states that had survived the colonial conquest of the previous few decades. Up to the late nineteenth century, Southern Africa had an agrarian economy, and the British Empire controlled the strategically important coastline but was disinterested in the impoverished interior. This changed dramatically with the discovery of valuable minerals that led to the rise of a capitalist industrial mining economy subsidized by low-paid African migrant labor, the extension of colonial rule over the remaining independent African communities, and European expansion into the hinterland and beyond the Zambezi River.

Diamond Discovery

In the late 1860s, diamonds were discovered in a frontier area that is now part of the Northern Cape Province of South Africa. People flocked to the diamond fields, where the mining town of **Kimberley** grew rapidly. There were conflicting claims to the diamond diggings. Although the Tlhaping Tswana had lived in the area for a very long time, the diamond fields were claimed by the self-governing British Cape Colony to the south, the Boer

Mineral revolution.
Diamond miners at the bottom of a great shaft at the Wesselton Mines, Kimberley, South Africa, c. 1910.

☰ **Griqua leader.** Nicolaas Waterboer was granted ownership of the diamond fields in the northern Cape in 1871 and then agreed to come under British rule.

republics of the Orange Free State and Transvaal to the east and northeast, and the trans-frontier Griqua of Nicolaas Waterboer, who also lived in the area. In 1871, the British government appointed R.W. Keate—the lieutenant-governor of Natal, which had no claim to the diamond fields—to arbitrate the dispute. He found in favor of the Griqua leader Waterboer, who then agreed to come under British authority within the new territory of Griqualand West. Boer leaders felt cheated and became hostile to brewing British plans to create a British-dominated federation of colonial territories in Southern Africa. Tswana claims to the diamond fields were ignored, and they struggled to get mining permits from the colonial administration. In 1878, some Griqua and Tswana who had lost land to white settlers rebelled against British rule in Griqualand West, but they were suppressed by colonial forces sent up from the Cape. The Cape Colony absorbed Griqualand West in 1881.

A network of African migrant labor had been developing around Southern Africa's settler commercial farms for a few decades. The advent of diamond mining expanded and institutionalized this system. African people across the region flocked to Kimberley to work in the diamond mines for a few months and return home with trade goods, including guns, bought with their wages. This initially occurred without colonial coercion with migrant workers originating from independent African communities, such as the Shona in what is now Zimbabwe, the Pedi kingdom in the eastern Transvaal, and the Zulu kingdom in the southeast. From 1871 to 1875, between 50,000 and 80,000 Africans traveled to and from Kimberley annually. At that time white "diggers" with mining permits employed African workers who were accommodated in tents or shacks and who could move around freely after working hours. In the mid-1880s, diamond mining companies around Kimberley introduced a **compound system** whereby African mine workers on six-month contracts were required to live entirely in fenced, prison-like compounds patrolled by mine police. These enclosures were meant to reduce the theft of diamonds and to discipline the African workforce to facilitate the transition from surface digging to underground mining. By 1889, the Kimberley diamond fields had been monopolized by Cecil Rhodes's De Beers Consolidated Mines, which accommodated some 10,000 African miners in its compounds. In this system, African miners were subjected to degrading strip searches, and poor and cramped living conditions in the compounds promoted the spread of infectious diseases like tuberculosis. This system of migrant labor and mine compounds, discussed further in Chapter 17, was subsequently extended to the gold mines in the Transvaal.

In 1877, the imperial British government, eager to expand its influence in the region given diamond discovery, imposed a federation of colonial territories on Southern Africa. The plan had been inspired by the successful 1867 Canadian confederation, but unlike that model, which had been generated from within the British North American territories, London sought to impose federation on unwilling participants in South Africa. The administration of the self-governing Cape Colony was interested in federation but worried that, as the region's largest economy, it would have to absorb most of the costs, and there was concern in Cape Town that the tumultuous region was not yet ready. Alienated from Britain by the diamond field dispute and looking for other economic partners, the Transvaal Boer republic was making plans to build a railway east to the Indian Ocean coast of Portuguese-ruled Mozambique.

London annexed the Transvaal in 1877, and the penniless Boer republic, which had lost a war against the Pedi kingdom the previous year, did not resist. The British government appointed Sir Henry Bartle Frere as governor of the Cape and high commissioner of Southern Africa, with a mandate to turn the federation into a reality. This would be accomplished, it was believed, by subduing the last independent African states in the region, which would bolster the confidence of white settlers, especially the Boers, and provide more African land and labor for the colonial economy. As a result, during the late 1870s the British army, along with settler and African allies, fought a series of wars to conquer African states in Southern Africa. During the Cape–Xhosa War of 1877–78, the Cape Colony subdued a rebellion by the Rharhabe Xhosa, who had been under colonial rule since the 1850s, and advanced Cape control eastward across the Kei River and over the previously independent Gcaleka Xhosa. While Rharhabe Xhosa leaders Sandile and Siyolo fought a desperate struggle in the bush of the Amatola Mountains, they were eventually hunted down and killed by African colonial allies. Inhabiting an open area across the Kei, the Gcaleka were devastated by colonial firepower.

During the 1860s and most of the 1870s, the British in Natal had supported the Zulu kingdom in its disputes with the Transvaal Boers, and in 1873 a British colonial official had crowned **Cetshwayo** as the new Zulu king. The confederation scheme prompted a sudden reversal in British policy, and British officials began portraying the Zulu kingdom as a threat to regional security. In 1878,

☰ **Diamond mining.** *Left:* Open-pit mining at the Premier Mine in South Africa, c. 1910. The Cullinan Diamond—the largest rough diamond of gem quality ever found—was discovered there in 1905. *Right:* Mine workers in a compound in Kimberley, c. 1900.

the British government issued Cetshwayo with the impossible demand that he should disband the Zulu military, which was an integral part of Zulu society. In January 1879, the British invaded the Zulu kingdom with three separate forces that crossed the border at different points. Underestimating Zulu military capabilities, the British had divided their forces. As such, the southern and northern British columns were besieged by the Zulu army, and the middle column was caught off guard at Isandlwana and annihilated by Zulu warriors. At the **Battle of Isandlwana**, fought on January 22, 1879, over 1,300 British soldiers and African allies were killed, which represented the worst military defeat inflicted on Britain by indigenous people. For Cetshwayo, however, Isandlwana was not to be celebrated as over 1,000 Zulu had been killed by British firepower, and his hopes of a negotiated settlement were dashed as the British became intent on revenge. Subsequently, British forces regrouped, reinvaded the Zulu kingdom with a single large force, and defeated the Zulu army at the Zulu capital of Ulundi in early July 1879. After this Anglo-Zulu War of 1879, the British abolished the Zulu monarchy; appointed 13 pro-British Zulu chiefs, including one white trader, to govern Zululand; and captured Cetshwayo, who was sent to Britain, where he visited Queen Victoria. At the start of 1883, Cetshwayo was returned to Zululand, which turned ongoing violence between Zulu royalists and supporters of the 13 appointed chiefs into a vicious civil war. After Cetshwayo's sudden and mysterious death in early 1884, his son Dinuzulu led monarchist forces and gained the support from some Transvaal Boers in exchange for giving them land, where they proclaimed the New Republic. British forces supported the 13 chiefs, and in 1887, after fighting had temporarily subsided, Britain annexed Zululand except the land that had been given to the Boers. The next year, a rebellion by Zulu royalists led by Dinuzulu was suppressed by the British. Convicted of treason by a colonial court, Dinuzulu was imprisoned on the island of Saint Helena until 1898, when he was returned to Zululand, which had been added to the colony of Natal the previous year.

Located in the eastern part of the Transvaal, the Pedi kingdom used its mountain stronghold and guns acquired in trade and wage labor on the diamond fields to resist encroachment by the Boer republic, which lacked a standing army. In 1876, the Transvaal Boers had mounted a large expedition against the Pedi, but it was unsuccessful, mostly because the Boers' Swazi allies returned home early once they had captured a large amount of livestock. In 1878, after British annexation of the Transvaal, the new British colonial administration organized another attack by mostly local Boer and African forces on the Pedi stronghold, but this also failed. After the defeat of the Zulu in 1879, British General Garnet Wolseley and a large force of British soldiers were sent to the Transvaal and prepared for another but much larger assault on the Pedi. With a force twice as large as the one assembled by the Boers in 1876, and which included 8,000 mercenaries from the Swazi kingdom, the British overwhelmed the Pedi stronghold. The Pedi kingdom was incorporated into the Transvaal, and Pedi ruler Sekhukhune was imprisoned until 1881, when he was released and then poisoned by a rival Pedi leader.

At the start of the 1880s, British plans for a South African federation were wrecked by a series of rebellions. The kingdom of Lesotho had volunteered to come under British authority in the late 1860s to avoid complete dispossession by the Orange Free State Boers, who had been expanding for several decades. Lesotho had survived because of its mountainous terrain and military use of horses and guns. However, the

≡ **Zulu leader.** Cetshwayo (1826–1884) was king of the Zulu during the 1879 British invasion.

British imperial government placed the administration of colonial Basutoland (Lesotho) under the self-governing Cape Colony, which facilitated the arrival of white settlers and made it illegal for Africans to own guns. During the 1880–81 "Gun War," the people of Lesotho successfully defended their mountain communities from Cape colonial forces, which led to a diplomatic intervention by imperial Britain and a negotiated settlement. Rebel leaders received amnesty, residents of Basutoland were allowed to retain their guns under license, and the territory once again came under the administration of London, though with considerable autonomy given to Sotho traditional leaders. This arrangement meant that, in the future, Basutoland would not join South Africa, and it became the independent and landlocked country of Lesotho in 1966. Located in the Transkei area in the eastern part of the Cape Colony, the Mpondomise and some Thembu people had come under colonial rule through treaty in the 1870s. These communities eventually became dissatisfied with loss of land to settlers from the Cape and the undermining of their chiefs' authority. Seeing the war in Basutoland as an opportunity, the Mpondomise and Thembu rebelled in late 1880. By the end of the year, Cape forces had crushed the Transkei rebellion because the rebels' lack of experience and the area's open terrain facilitated colonial firepower. Rebel leaders were deposed and their land given to Africans who had remained loyal to the Cape.

In the Transvaal, the conquest of the Pedi enabled the Boers to unify against the British occupation. The Boers objected to the arrival of British soldiers, clergy, and businessmen, but they were most aggrieved by British taxation and they had never paid tax before. At the end of 1880, Boer leaders proclaimed the restoration of the independent Transvaal Republic as armed Boers surrounded British garrisons within the Transvaal and blocked the mountain passes through which British relief forces would have to travel once they were landed on the Natal coast. Although the Boers lacked formal military training, they inflicted a stunning defeat on the British army in February 1881 at Majuba Hill, which overlooks a key mountain pass from Natal. The new British high commissioner, George Pomeroy Colley, was killed in the battle. The British government negotiated with the Transvaal Boers since the war was unpopular in Britain, there were troubles brewing in Ireland, and it was possible that the Orange Free State Boers would join the war in support of their Transvaal colleagues. In any case, the diamond fields of the Northern Cape, the region's key economic asset, remained under British control. In August 1881, British soldiers withdrew from the Transvaal, which regained internal self-government, and in 1884 Britain withdrew sovereignty over the republic. The result of the 1880–81 Transvaal Rebellion (also called the First Anglo-Boer War) was that Britain, for the time being, abandoned its plan to create a large federal state in what would eventually become South Africa.

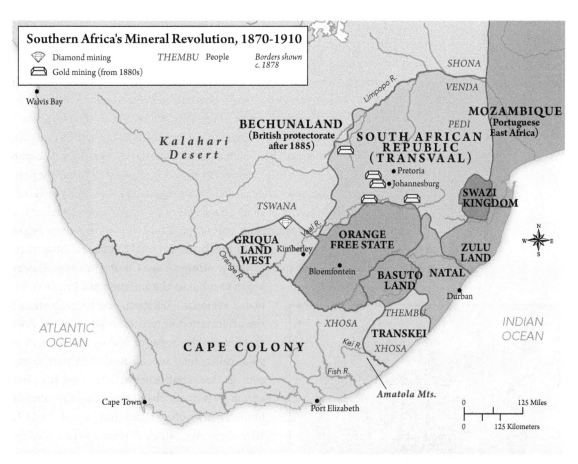

Southern Africa's Mineral Revolution, 1870–1910

Diamond mining   *THEMBU* People   Borders shown
Gold mining (from 1880s)   c. 1878

≡ MAP 16.1

Gold Discovery

In 1886, gold was discovered in the Transvaal. This caused a dramatic shift in regional economic power from the British controlled coast to the Boer republics of the interior. As a gold rush brought many people from around the world to the Witwatersrand (White Water Ridge), the area in the southern Transvaal where gold had been discovered, a new city called Johannesburg sprang up very quickly on the Highveld. The region rapidly became the world's largest producer of gold. With revenue from taxing the expanding gold mining industry, the hitherto bankrupt Boer republics began to import modern weapons. During the 1890s, the better armed Transvaal Boers subdued African communities on their periphery, such as the Gananwa in the northwest and the Venda in the north. For Britain, this raised the possibility of the Boers making an alliance with another major European power, particularly Germany, which had begun the colonization of neighboring South West Africa (Namibia) in 1884. Indeed, Britain had made treaties with the Tswana chiefs, themselves afraid of westward Boer expansion, in 1885, and created the British territory of the Bechuanaland Protectorate (Botswana) so as to forestall contact between German South West Africa and the Boer republics. The mostly British businessmen who owned the mining industry in the Transvaal, including **Cecil Rhodes** who had made a fortune on the diamond fields, began to resent what they saw as restrictive and inefficient Transvaal government policies. For example, as the miners dug deeper, they needed explosives, but the Transvaal government retained a monopoly on the sale of dynamite and compelled the mine industry to buy overpriced and inferior products. The mine owners began to think that a new administration in the Transvaal might better facilitate their industry. Elected as premier of the self-governing Cape Colony in 1890, Rhodes began to rekindle the ambition of a British-dominated regional federation, and he orchestrated the colonization of territories north of the Boer republics in the hopes of finding new sources of gold, called the "Second Rand." In part to encourage Boer confidence in federation, Rhodes's administration in the Cape weakened already limited black voting rights and passed the 1894 Glen Grey Act, which deprived Africans of agricultural land and pushed them into migrant labor. Although Rhodes initially tried to encourage the Boers to accept federation by building a railway from the Cape to Johannesburg and Pretoria in the Transvaal and proposing a customs union, he lost patience with continued Boer opposition and the lack of gold discoveries in newly colonized Southern Rhodesia (Zimbabwe) north of the Boer republics. In 1895, Rhodes organized an armed incursion, called the **Jameson Raid**, into the Transvaal, aimed at stimulating an uprising among foreign mine workers called **uitlanders** (outlanders) and overthrowing the republican government of President Paul Kruger. The plot failed as the uitlanders did not rebel and the Boers captured Rhodes's armed

THE RHODES COLOSSUS
STRIDING FROM CAPE TOWN TO CAIRO.

.*. Mr. Rhodes had announced his intention to continue the telegraph northwards across the Zambezi to Uganda, then, crossing the Soudan, to complete the overland telegraph line from Cape Town to Cairo.

☰ **Colossus.** This iconic cartoon was published in *Punch* magazine in 1892 when Rhodes was promoting the construction of a telegraph line from Cape Town to Cairo.

party. This caused a political scandal that ended Rhodes's premiership in the Cape and the apparent involvement of British imperial authorities in the conspiracy greatly enflamed relations between Britain and the Boer republics.

The Scramble in Southern Africa

The development of industrial gold mining in the Transvaal in the late nineteenth century provided the context for the Scramble in much of Southern and South-Central Africa. In 1888, Rhodes, seeking in vain for gold discoveries north of the Boer republics and dreaming of extending British rule from the Cape in the south to Cairo in the north, sent agents to the Ndebele kingdom in the southwest of what is now Zimbabwe. Promised money, 1,000 modern firearms, ammunition, and a gunboat for the Zambezi River by Rhodes's agents, the Ndebele king, Lobengula, signed the **Rudd Concession**, which gave the British exclusive mineral rights in his territory. Lobengula only received 500 of the promised rifles. When he heard that Cape newspapers were reporting that he had sold his country to Britain, Lobengula believed he had been tricked and tried in vain to suspend the concession. Since Rhodes and his associates mistakenly believed that the Ndebele kingdom ruled the neighboring Shona communities to its east, the Rudd Concession was interpreted as extending over the eastern half of present-day Zimbabwe. On the strength of the concession, Rhodes received a royal charter from London and formed the **British South Africa Company (BSAC)** to facilitate the colonial conquest of the area between the Limpopo and Zambezi rivers. In 1890, the BSAC sent an armed expedition called the Pioneer Column north through Bechuanaland (Botswana), around the Ndebele kingdom and into the territory of the Shona. The column established posts at Fort Victoria (today's Masvingo) and Salisbury (today's Harare) and these later became colonial towns, but at this early stage the colonial occupation did not have much impact on the Shona people of these areas. After it became obvious that the Shona lands did not contain vast gold resources, the BSAC used an Ndebele raid on a Shona community near Fort Victoria as an excuse to invade the Ndebele kingdom in the hope that it might contain minerals. In late 1893, several BSAC military columns, armed with Maxim guns, artillery, and searchlights mounted on wagons, moved into Ndebele territory and defeated Ndebele armies sent against them. The Ndebele did not make effective use of the firearms they possessed and were gunned down in charges on colonial wagon laagers. The Ngwato Tswana ruler, Khama, a firm British ally who lived in Bechuanaland and a longtime enemy of Lobengula, sent his warriors to help in the invasion. Lobengula fled north toward the Zambezi and died from fever, possibly malaria, in

LOBENGULA
From an authentic early photograph

≡ **King of the Ndebele.** Lobengula was king of the Ndebele in what is now Zimbabwe from 1868 until he was overthrown and died during the 1893–94 British invasion.

early 1894. In the wake of the war, the victorious BSAC abolished the Ndebele monarchy, the Ndebele capital of Bulawayo became a colonial town and a regional railway hub, and Ndebele land and cattle were seized. The territories of Mashonaland (the Shona homeland) and Matabeleland (the Ndebele area) were combined into BSAC-administered Southern Rhodesia, named after Rhodes, whom settlers celebrated as the founder. As discussed in Chapter 17, violent abuse and taxation by the BSAC led to uprisings by some of the Ndebele and Shona during 1896 and 1897. In the late nineteenth and early twentieth centuries, white settlers from what would become South Africa and some from Britain moved to Southern Rhodesia, where they took most of the agriculturally productive land and established large commercial farms. The relatively cool environment of the Zimbabwe Plateau, where tropical diseases like malaria were less prevalent than in neighboring areas, enabled white settlement. Although some mining developed in colonial Southern Rhodesia, Rhodes's dreams of a "Second Rand" did not come to fruition.

In 1890, Lewanika, ruler of the Lozi kingdom on the Upper Zambezi River in what is now western Zambia, agreed to come under the authority of the British government, but at the time he was not aware that the agents that he had negotiated with were actually from the BSAC. Lewanika wanted British protection from Ndebele raids and the BSAC were hesitant to fight the powerful Lozi state, which possessed firearms. As such, the Lozi kingdom came under British rule voluntarily and the Lozi monarchy continued to function throughout the colonial era. In 1899, the British imperial government formalized the Protectorate of Barotseland–North-Western Rhodesia, which was administered by the BSAC. Rhodes was interested in pushing further north into Katanga, but this was hindered by the 1891 arrival of the William Stairs expedition, which placed the area under the authority of Leopold II's Congo Free State. In the east of what is now Zambia, the BSAC bought mineral rights from a Portuguese company and established a subsidiary called the North Charterland Exploration Company (NCEC) in 1895. The NCEC challenged the dominance of the Ngoni state of

Mpeseni for control of the zone just west of Lake Nyasa. At the end of the 1890s, instability among the Bemba of the area led to their appointment of a French missionary as king and he submitted to British colonial rule. In 1900, Britain established the Protectorate of North-Eastern Rhodesia, which was also under BSAC administration. In 1911, the territories of Barotseland–North-Western Rhodesia and North-Eastern Rhodesia were combined as Northern Rhodesia (today's Zambia), which became the scene of a large copper-mining industry and was governed by the BSAC until 1924. In one of the numerous geographic anomalies created by colonial partition of Africa, the southern protrusion of Belgian-ruled Katanga (the southern part of the Belgian Congo) meant that a very narrow band of territory joined the two halves of Northern Rhodesia.

By 1880, British and Scottish merchants and missionaries had been operating around Lake Nyasa (Lake Malawi) for a few years. In 1888, the financially struggling African Lakes Company, based south of the lake at Blantyre, clashed with Swahili-Arab ivory and slave traders for control of the north part of the lake. With a few British officers such as Frederick Lugard, who would later lead the conquest of Uganda and northern Nigeria, the company recruited a local militia from Tonga, Nkonde, and Mambwe communities that had been victimized by Swahili-Arab slave raids. With the failure of the African Lakes Company to gain a royal charter and the Portuguese expanding from Mozambique, the British government sent Harry Johnson to the Lake Nyasa area in 1889. Johnson, who was also an associate of Rhodes, gradually claimed territory west and south of the lake for Britain, and in 1891 he proclaimed the Central Africa Protectorate, which was later renamed Nyasaland (today's Malawi). In 1891, Rhodes's BSAC bought a controlling interest in the African Lakes Company, which continued to operate in the new British territory. The British use of steamboats, which served as gun platforms and ferried troops, was central to their gaining control over the many African communities around Lake Nyasa. Between 1891 and 1895, the Blantyre-based colonial administration used troops from India to gradually destroy the numerous fortifications of the Yao slavers who dominated the southern portion of the lake. Although the Swahili-Arab slavers at the north end of the lake had entered into a treaty with Johnson in 1889, they repudiated it in 1895, which prompted British forces to destroy their stockades. During the second half of the 1890s the British in Nyasaland subdued the Ngoni groups, who did not use guns, around the lake and in North-Eastern Rhodesia. The last British military operation against the Ngoni took place in late 1900 and involved the destruction of 300 villages which pushed displaced people into the regional migrant labor system.

During the 1880s, the Portuguese hope of joining their colonies of Angola on the Atlantic coast and Mozambique on the Indian Ocean coast by conquering south-central Africa (today's Zambia and Zimbabwe) conflicted with Britain's dream of controlling Africa from Cape to Cairo. In 1885, a Portuguese expedition marched some 3000 miles from Moçâmedes on the coast of Angola to the Mozambican port of Quelimane. However, in early 1890 Lisbon conceded to an ultimatum from the much more powerful Britain to withdraw Portuguese forces from south-central Africa, and in the same year both

≡ **Exiled leader.** Gungunhana (far left) was king of the Gaza state in what is now Mozambique until the Portuguese invasion of 1895, after which he was exiled to the Azores.

powers concluded a treaty that finalized the borders of their colonial territories. In Portugal, this was considered a national disgrace and caused the government to collapse. This loss made Portugal determined to expand its control over the interior of southern Mozambique which was dominated by the Gaza kingdom. Predicting conflict with the Portuguese, the Gaza ruler, Gungunhana, requested British protection, but this was refused as the colonial powers had already agreed on their borders. In 1895, Portugal organized its largest colonial military expedition of the late nineteenth century to invade the Gaza state. After Gaza warriors were gunned down by Portuguese rifles and machine guns, Gungunhana became a prisoner and was shipped off to Portugal. He died in the Azores in 1906.

Though the Portuguese had conquered parts of Angola in the 1500s and 1600s, their efforts to control the southern interior began in the late nineteenth century. Following the arrival of Boers from the south and Portuguese settlers from Madeira, the Humbe people of the Moçâmedes hinterland rebelled against Portuguese taxation in 1885–86. Portuguese forces defeated the rebels in several engagements but were too weak to complete their subjugation. When the Humbe rebelled again in 1891, Portuguese forces pursued them east of the Cunene River, where they clashed with the Ovambo. The last Humbe rebellion took place in 1898 and was suppressed by Portuguese forces that seized livestock. In 1904, in response to

Ovambo raids against the Humbe, a Portuguese expedition crossed the Cunene but was almost immediately ambushed, took heavy casualties, and fled back into Angola. In 1907, a much larger Portuguese column rampaged through Ovambo territory in southeastern Angola. Further north, the Portuguese at the port of Benguela pushed inland into central Angola during the 1890s and encountered resistance from the Ovimbundu people. In 1902, Portuguese firepower defeated a major Ovimbundu alliance with limited guerrilla warfare continuing until 1904.

In 1884, Germany declared a protectorate over Southern Africa's Atlantic coast from the Orange River in the south to the Cunene River in the north, which became German South West Africa (present-day Namibia). The new German colony did not include the enclave of Walvis Bay, one of that coast's only deep-water harbors, which the British had claimed in 1878. By the 1880s, there had been years of conflict in the area between northward-moving Nama pastoralists from the Cape, where they had acquired horses and guns from European settlers, and the Herero of central Namibia, who had obtained firearms from European traders seeking cattle to feed workers in the region's diamond mines. The Herero leader, Maherero, quickly accepted German protection, but he renounced it in 1888 as Nama attacks against his people continued. In 1890, Maherero, on his deathbed, renewed his deal with the Germans when they constructed a post in his territory at Windhoek, which became the colonial capital. The Nama leader, Hendrik Witbooi, inspired by Christian prophecies, rejected German authority. As such, the Nama fought a guerrilla war against the Germans during 1893 and 1894 and surrendered when the Germans seized important waterholes and turned other African groups against them. In 1896, the Germans intervened in a Herero civil war in favor of Samuel Maherero (son of Maherero), who, once he gained power, conceded to German settlement on his lands. In the late 1890s, the spread of **rinderpest**, a deadly cattle disease, across the region greatly undermined Herero and Nama society. In turn, they were recruited as migrant workers for the gold mines of the Transvaal. With its arid environment and limited tropical disease, South West Africa was seen by the German government as a colony for European settlement along the lines of neighboring British and Boer territories. As discussed in Chapter 17, the Herero and Nama rebelled against German colonial rule in 1904.

The South African War

After the 1895 Jameson Raid, in which mining magnate Rhodes failed to overthrow the Boer government in the Transvaal, tensions between imperial Britain and the Transvaal's Kruger administration revolved around the uitlander issue. The uitlanders were white foreign mine workers, including many British subjects, who were living in the Transvaal,

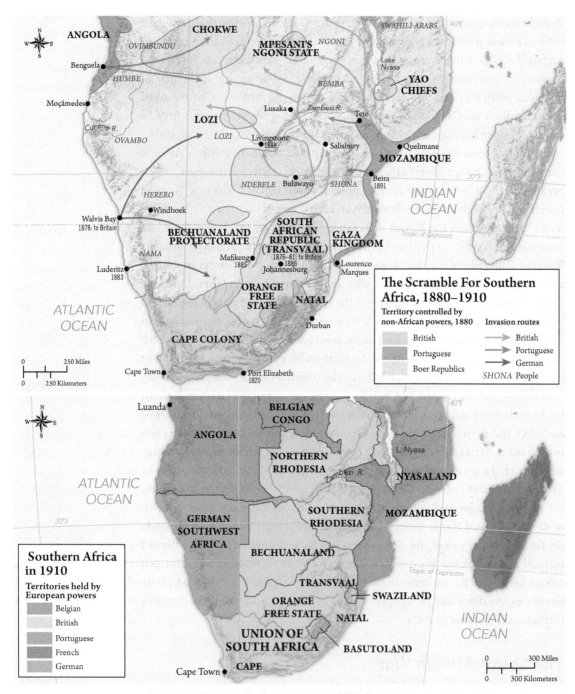

The Scramble For Southern Africa, 1880–1910

Territory controlled by non-African powers, 1880

British
Portuguese
Boer Republics

Invasion routes
British
Portuguese
German
SHONA People

Southern Africa in 1910

Territories held by European powers

Belgian
British
Portuguese
French
German

≡ MAP 16.2

where they were subject to compulsory military service but could not vote in the republic's elections. The British government demanded that the uitlanders be given the vote so that they would elect a pro-British government in the republic, which would be sympathetic to joining a British-dominated regional federation. However, President Kruger resisted these pressures as he did not want to surrender Boer independence. To defend themselves, the Boer republics imported over one million pounds worth of modern weapons, mostly from Germany, including 50,000 rifles and 100 artillery pieces. As it seemed war was inevitable, the Boer republics of the Transvaal and Orange Free State planned a pre-emptive strike on the neighboring British territories before the British could ship in large military forces. The Boers hoped to occupy all of the British colony of Natal to prevent British forces from landing on the coast and to seize the railway centers of the Northern Cape to stop them being used by the British to mount an invasion of the republics. The Boer republics also sought international diplomatic support against Britain, though this was never a realistic possibility. If the Boers could accomplish all this, so they thought, the British might negotiate a settlement as they had done in 1881. The war began in October 1899 when a Boer force ambushed a British ammunition train just outside the railway center of Mafeking in the Northern Cape. However, the subsequent Boer invasions of British territory became bogged down in the sieges of Mafeking and Kimberley in the Northern Cape and Ladysmith in Natal. The British then dispatched overwhelming numbers of troops to South Africa to end Boer independence.

Boer and British forces were very different. The Boers were well armed, but their supply of ammunition was limited as they could not manufacture artillery shells, and once the war began British naval power prevented further imports. The republics did not have standing armies and relied on a system in which every Boer man was obliged to perform unpaid military service when called upon by the state, and to provide his own weapon, horse, and food. On the plus side, Boer military units called **commandos** were highly mobile, and the Boer fighters were familiar with the local environment, were skilled marksmen, and employed numerous African spies. On the negative side, the commandos lacked logistical support, and they elected their own leaders from among local elites and held war councils where battle plans were discussed and voted on, which often led to disagreements. Because of the small Boer populations in the republics, only about 70,000 Boer men fought in the conflict. Around 2,000 foreign volunteers mostly from Germany, Holland, Russia, and Ireland supplemented them. The British enjoyed massive numerical superiority. From October 1899 to January 1900, some 112,000 British soldiers were shipped to South Africa, and by the end of the war Britain had deployed about 450,000 troops, including many from the settler dominions of Canada, Australia, and New Zealand. Although the British army was well equipped, professional, and hierarchical, British officers who had fought relatively small colonial campaigns had no experience in supplying or leading such huge forces. In addition, they lacked

≡ **British defeat.** Dead British soldiers litter the battlefield of Spion Kop, January 24, 1900.

accurate maps of the region and had no local intelligence network. Black South Africans served both sides. Although a myth developed that this was a "white man's war," some 10,000 Black "after-riders" accompanied the Boer commandos during the start of the conflict, and the British military in South Africa eventually employed 100,000 Black personnel, including 40,000 who were armed. Many Black South Africans thought, vainly as it turned out, that a British victory against the Boers would result in the expansion of Black political rights throughout the white settler–dominated region.

The **South African War** or Second Anglo-Boer War (1899–1902) unfolded in two phases: the conventional war and the guerrilla war. At the start of the conventional war, the Boer pre-emptive strikes did not penetrate British territory far enough to prevent the arrival of British forces and the launching of British counteroffensives. Furthermore, the protracted sieges led to frustrated Boer fighters returning home to work their farms. Toward the end of 1899, British forces in the Cape and Natal, led by Redvers Buller, moved straight up the railways to try to lift the Boer sieges. In one week in mid-December 1899, dubbed "Black Week," advancing British forces were defeated by the Boers at the battles of Magersfontein and Stormberg in the Cape and Colenso in Natal. In January 1900, the continued British attack on the Natal front led to another British military disaster at Spion Kop, where 1,100 British troops were killed or wounded. Present at the battle were future South African prime minister Louis Botha leading Transvaal forces, future British prime minister Winston Churchill serving as a British military journalist, and future Indian independence leader Mohandas Gandhi working as a stretcher bearer in the British military. Given these battlefield catastrophes, the British regrouped for a second offensive against the Boers. Under a new overall commander, Frederick Sleigh Roberts, British forces in South Africa created accurate maps, gathered intelligence, built a logistical system to supply their troops, imported hundreds of thousands of horses to make their army more mobile, and brought in tens of thousands more soldiers. During the second British offensive, which began in

February 1900, the British again advanced against the Boers in the Cape and Natal but tried to outflank and encircle their forces. At the Battle of Paardeberg, fought in late February, the British trapped a large Boer force, killing or wounding 4,000 Boers and capturing 4,000 more. Over the next few months the Boer commandos withdrew, and British forces lifted the sieges and invaded the Boer republics, occupying Bloemfontein, capital of the Orange Free State, and then Pretoria, capital of the Transvaal. Roberts declared that the republics were now British colonies, and thousands of Boer fighters surrendered and took an oath of loyalty to Britain. Another major military disaster for the Boers took place in July when around 4,500 of them were trapped by the British and surrendered at Brandwater Basin in the Orange Free State.

The guerrilla phase of the war began in June 1900. Called **bittereinders** because they vowed to fight to the "bitter end," some Boers broke into small groups and conducted hit-and-run attacks against the British. The constantly moving *bittereinders* ambushed British trains, cut telegraph wires, raided storage facilities, briefly occupied towns, and executed or flogged Africans found working for the British. Many Boers who had taken loyalty oaths returned to the commandos. President Kruger fled to Portuguese Mozambique and then Europe, where he passed away in 1904. While the Boer leaders in South Africa found it increasingly difficult to coordinate their actions, they hoped to make the war very costly for the British to prompt them to negotiate. Now commanded by Horatio Kitchener, British forces conducted a brutal counterinsurgency campaign that involved destroying Boer farms as they were supplying the guerrilla fighters and herding 116,000 Boer elders, women, and children and their African servants into squalid **concentration camps**. In these camps, some 28,000 Boer non-combatants and 20,000 Africans died from disease. British welfare

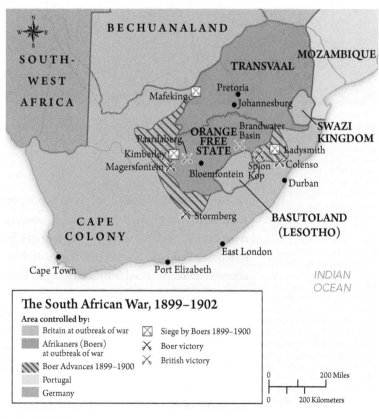

The South African War, 1899–1902

Area controlled by:
- Britain at outbreak of war
- Afrikaners (Boers) at outbreak of war
- Boer Advances 1899–1900
- Portugal
- Germany

- Siege by Boers 1899–1900
- Boer victory
- British victory

0   200 Miles
0   200 Kilometers

≡ **MAP 16.3**

☰ **Concentration Camps.** *Left:* Emily Hobhouse (1860–1926), a British activist and feminist, protested the British internment of Boer women and children in concentration camps during the South African War. *Right:* A French lithograph from 1901 shows the squalid conditions inside a concentration camp.

activist **Emily Hobhouse** traveled to South Africa to visit the camps and published scathing reports about them in British newspapers. The British divided the former republics into small areas that were separated by barbed wire fences and small fortifications called blockhouses, and were patrolled by fast-moving British columns and armored trains mounted with search lights. Furthermore, the British employed more local troops who knew the environment, including Boers who had changed sides, and armed Africans. To some extent, the conflict turned into a Boer civil war, with the *bittereinders* largely coming from the former landowning elite who had lost everything, and lower-class Boers derisively called "joiners" siding with the British.

By the beginning of 1902, both sides wanted the terrible conflict to end. The British government endured criticism at home for its conduct of the war, and it feared that more destruction would hinder the chances of gaining Boer cooperation in a future pro-British administration. On the Boer side, many of the *bittereinders* began to wonder if the "bitter end" actually meant the elimination of Boer society, though a few Boer leaders wanted to continue the struggle under any circumstances. For the Boers, at that time, the military situation appeared hopeless as around 15,000 Boer fighters opposed 250,000 British troops. The war had caused the deaths of about 75,000 people. A key factor in pushing the Boer guerrilla leaders to negotiate was that African people in the former republics were beginning to occupy abandoned Boer farms and African communities were actively resisting the Boer commandos. In late May 1902, at peace talks held at Vereeniging in the southern Transvaal, 54 out of 60 Boer delegates voted to concede independence. In the subsequent Treaty of Vereeniging, the British granted generous terms, including amnesty to all Boer fighters, protection of their property rights and the Dutch language, funds for reconstruction, and promises that the colonies would be self-governed and that Black voting would never be extended beyond the Cape Colony. In 1907, the former Boer republics turned British colonies were granted responsible government, a form of internal self-government. In 1910, the Union of South Africa, with former Boer military leader Louis Botha as prime minister, was created as a self-governing country within the British Empire, with the same quasi-autonomous status as Canada, New Zealand, and Australia. The Union comprised the older British colonies of the Cape and Natal, and the two former republics of the Transvaal and Orange Free State, all of which became provinces within the new country. The Union government was elected by South Africa's white minority, and the Cape's historic qualified nonracial franchise became a provincial anomaly that was phased out in the 1930s. With reference to the South African War, the Boer control of the ensuing Union government inspired the saying that "the Boers lost the war but won the peace." However, the British burning of Boer farms and the concentration camp deaths were gravely resented by many Boers and influenced the 1914 formation of the Nationalist Party, which sought to distance South Africa from imperial Britain and impose even greater racial segregation.

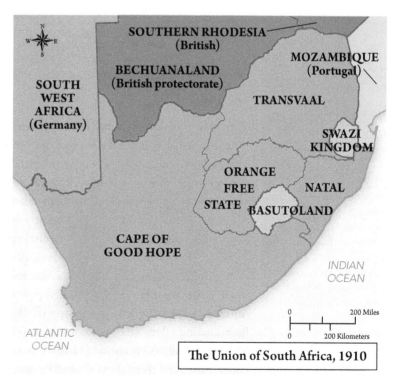

≡ **MAP 16.4**   The Union of South Africa, 1910

Timeline

1867—Diamond discovery in the Northern Cape

1871—Diamond fields dispute

1877—British annexation of Transvaal

1877–78—Cape–Xhosa War

1879—Anglo-Zulu War

1879—Anglo-Pedi War

1880—Transkei Rebellion

1880–81—First Anglo-Boer War or Transvaal Rebellion

1880–81—Gun War in Lesotho

1884—German occupation of South West Africa

1885—British establishment of Bechuanaland Protectorate

1886—Gold discovery in Transvaal

1888—Rudd Concession

1890—BSAC occupation of Mashonaland

1890—Lozi Kingdom accepts British protection

1891—British proclaim Central African Protectorate (Nyasaland)

1893—BSAC invasion of Ndebele kingdom

1893–94—German–Nama War

1895—Jameson Raid

1895—Portuguese–Gaza War in Mozambique

1899–1902—South African War (Second Anglo-Boer War)

1900—British defeat of the Ngoni in Nyasaland

1902—Portuguese defeat of the Ovimbundu in Angola

1910—Union of South Africa

1911—British creation of Protectorate of Northern Rhodesia

Conclusion

The discovery of diamonds and gold in the late nineteenth century meant that Southern Africa developed in different ways from the rest of the continent. During the twentieth century, South Africa became a quasi-independent regional power with an industrial mining economy and a white-minority government. Dispossessed of the country's best agricultural land and denied civil rights, the Black majority was transformed into a class of low-paid migrant workers whose poverty subsidized white economic prosperity. Within this context, South Africa became the largest economy on the continent, a status it held until very recently. Proximity to South Africa also influenced the growth of smaller settler societies in Southern Rhodesia (Zimbabwe) and South West Africa (Namibia), where white-minority states also denied power to the Black majorities. In Southern Africa, a regional migrant labor system developed, with colonial territories such as Bechuanaland (Botswana), Basutoland (Lesotho), Swaziland (Eswatini), Northern Rhodesia (Zambia), Nyasaland (Malawi), and Mozambique becoming neglected and impoverished and therefore economically dependent on sending temporary workers to earn cash in the mines of South Africa. This dependence on South Africa continued even after these countries became politically autonomous in the 1960s and 1970s. Within this context, settler colonialism in Southern Africa survived much longer than European colonial rule in the rest of Africa, with white-minority regimes lasting up until 1980 in Zimbabwe, 1990 in Namibia, and 1994 in South Africa. The evolution of these regimes and their eventual collapse is the subject of Chapter 23

KEY TERMS

Battle of Isandlwana 338

bittereinders 351

British South Africa Company (BSAC) 343

Cecil Rhodes 342

Cetshwayo 337

commandos 349

compound system 336

concentration camps 352

Emily Hobhouse 352

Jameson Raid 342

Kimberley 335

mineral revolution 335

rinderpest 347

Rudd Concession 343

South African War 350

uitlanders 342

STUDY QUESTIONS

1. How was the Scramble in Southern Africa different from the Scramble in other parts of Africa?

2. How did the discovery of diamonds expand and institutionalize South African migrant labor? What were the political and colonial ramifications of the diamond industry?

3. What was the gold rush? How did Cecil Rhodes's actions impact British–Boer relations?

4. Why is the discovery of gold and diamonds in Southern Africa in the late nineteenth century characterized as a "mineral revolution"?

5. What events sparked the South African War? What tactics were employed by the British and Boer military forces?

Please see page FR-7 for the Further Readings for this chapter.
For additional digital learning resources please go to
https://www.oup.com/he/falola-stapleton1e

17

Colonial Rule in Africa: The State and the Economy, c. 1900–1939

In most of Africa, the period of European colonial rule was relatively short, lasting from around 1900 to 1960. Many people who were born just before or around the time of colonial conquest lived to see independence. Despite its brevity, the experience of European colonial rule reinvented Africa and Africans in many ways, particularly in terms of the state and economy. Entirely new political structures, including territorial borders and administrative and legal systems, were imposed by colonial rule and then inherited by African states when they achieved independence. The colonial state structure was undemocratic, predatory, and violent, and created a political tradition that the Ugandan scholar Mahmood Mamdani has called "**decentralized despotism**," in which a weak central government depends on a network of local strongmen who rule communities for their own interests. Within the arbitrarily imposed borders of Africa, colonial rule encouraged regionalism, stronger ethnic identities, and religious differences. New economic systems were imposed to extract Africa's wealth for the benefit of colonial and global business interests. Though colonial rule ended in the 1960s for most Africans, the same economic system continues, with African countries exporting cheap raw materials, the value of which increases when these are processed or used in manufacturing outside of Africa. As such, one of the most enduring legacies of colonial rule is that African economies do not fully benefit from the resources they produce. In addition, colonial environmental policies ignored many centuries of African experience on the land and had negative effects on communities, some of which were evicted from their homes in the name of wildlife conservation or poorly conceived public health programs.

Colonial city. The port of Algiers, c. 1900.

The Early Years of Colonial Rule

After the European conquest of the late nineteenth century, the initial two or three decades of colonial rule in Africa were characterized by military occupation and the use of blatant extortion to begin the process of creating the colonial state and economy. Under threat of punitive expeditions that would seize livestock and destroy homes, African communities were compelled to pay tax to the colonial government and provide unpaid labor for the building of infrastructure such as telegraphs, bridges, roads, and railways to facilitate extraction of resources and colonial control. Some areas such as Southern Rhodesia (Zimbabwe), Northern Rhodesia (Zambia), and parts of the Belgian Congo (DRC) and Portuguese Mozambique were administered by Concessionary Companies that tried to profit from extracting resources without much consideration for the inhabitants. These shocking abuses often provoked violent African rebellions that were usually more widespread than previous African attempts to defend their sovereignty from European invasion during the Scramble. While the initial colonial invasions impacted African rulers and other elites who responded in a divided manner, the subsequent imposition of colonial taxation and forced labor provoked ordinary people to resist. The objective and organization of these African rebellions later became the subject of debate among historians. Although colonial historians of the first half of the 1900s saw them as impulsive negative reactions to the supposed progress brought by Europeans, nationalist historians inspired by the struggle for independence in the 1950s and 1960s tended to exaggerate and glorify early anti-colonial revolts. More recent historians have tried to move away from these polarized views.

In 1896–97, some Ndebele and Shona groups in Southern Rhodesia rose up against the taxation and oppression of Cecil Rhodes's British South Africa Company (BSAC). The absence of many colonial police, who had gone to the Boer republic of the Transvaal to participate in the failed Jameson Raid in 1895, provided an opportunity for the rebels. Starting with a mutiny by colonial African police, the Ndebele in the southwest rebelled first and were then followed by Shona communities in the east. Settler farms were attacked and colonialists besieged in the town of Bulawayo, formerly the capital of the Ndebele kingdom, until the arrival of a relief force from the south. After making a separate peace with the Ndebele, who were given some concessions, Rhodes turned his forces against the Shona, many of whom were dynamited in caves, and the spirit mediums Nehanda and Kaguvi were hanged. The colonialists were particularly surprised and vindictive about the Shona uprising as they believed that colonial rule had protected the Shona from Ndebele raids. Trying to take the focus off colonial maladministration, the colonial view of the rebellion was that it represented a plot by primitive and malevolent witchdoctors who duped supposedly superstitious people into rebelling against the Europeans. Nationalist historians of the 1960s, however, demonstrated the importance of colonial oppression in prompting the uprising, which they saw as a unified pan-ethnic movement called the **First Chimurenga** (independence struggle) led by a new revolutionary leadership composed of traditional spirit mediums. Later scholars, while agreeing on the causes of the conflict, demonstrated that the Ndebele and Shona rebelled separately, that only a minority of each group participated in the revolt, and that their existing political leaders led them with the spirit mediums playing their usual supportive role of mobilizing people for war. After Zimbabwe gained independence in 1980 with an African nationalist government, the nationalist portrayal of the First Chimurenga became the official history celebrated in public events and monuments and taught in schools. As such, it remains a very powerful and well-known view of Zimbabwean history.

In 1898, a rebellion broke out among the Temne and Mende peoples, who were the largest ethnic groups in the newly colonized hinterland of British-ruled Sierra Leone. The uprising was motivated by the imposition of a new tax, and so the event became called the Hut Tax War, but it was also inspired by the abolition of the internal slave trade, loss of authority among chiefs, and abuse by colonial police. The rebels fought a grueling guerrilla campaign that the British countered by assaulting Temne and Mende stockades one by one. The Temne rebel leader Bai Bureh, who had fought as an ally of the British a few years earlier, was captured and exiled to the Gold Coast (Ghana) until 1905, and long after his death in 1908 he would be celebrated as an early nationalist hero.

The **Herero and Nama Rebellion** of 1904–07 in German South West Africa (Namibia) was prompted by German railway construction, debt collection, and labor recruitment. Samuel Maherero, the Herero leader who had received German support in the civil war that had brought him to power in the 1890s, led his people in the conflict but ordered them not to attack European women, children, or missionaries. The Herero enemy was the German colonial state. Commanded by General Lothar von Trotha, the Germans responded with an intentional campaign of genocide in which around 80 percent of the Herero

Plate 1   Charwe, the medium of Nehanda (left), with the medium of Kagubi in prison, 1897.

≡ **Spirit mediums.** In 1896–97, Shona spirit mediums Nehanda and Kaguvi were involved in a rebellion against British colonial rule in what is now Zimbabwe and hanged.

and 60 percent of the Nama were exterminated. They were driven into the desert, where they died of thirst. Others were transported by train to a death camp on Shark Island in Luderitz Bay, where they worked as slave labor and became the subject of unethical medical experiments. Many Herero escaped to British-ruled Bechuanaland (Botswana), where their descendants still live. Lacking African labor for their putative settler colony, the Germans then extended their rule north over the Ovambo people on the Angolan border. Historians have debated whether or not the German campaign represented a genocide, an international legal term coined years later in the wake of the Holocaust of the Second World War (1939–45). While a few historians have portrayed Von Trotha as a rogue general, many acknowledge that German actions in colonial Namibia correspond retroactively to the international legal definition of genocide and could be described as the first genocide of the twentieth century. From 1990, when Germany was unified and Namibia gained independence from South Africa, there were calls from descendants of the survivors for Germany to pay them reparations. In 2016, the German government, which had long acknowledged responsibility for the Holocaust, made a formal apology for the genocide committed in colonial Namibia. In 2021, with mounting domestic and foreign political pressure, the German government formally acknowledged responsibility for genocide in Namibia promising to provide the country with US$1.3 billion over three years to support the development of infrastructure.

In 1905–06, the **Maji Maji Rebellion** erupted in the central and southern regions of German East Africa (Tanzania) and was prompted by restrictive German policies, such as compulsory cotton growing, that jeopardized food production and restrictions on hunting. The uprising was named after water, called "maji" in Kiswahili, that the prophet Kijikitile Ngwale administered to the rebels promising that it would protect them from colonial bullets. After unsuccessfully attacking colonial outposts, the rebels fought a guerrilla war that the Germans suppressed with a brutal scorched earth campaign. While the Germans admitted to killing 26,000 people, between 250,000 and 300,000 died in the war-related famine. Although nationalist historians of the 1960s believed that Maji Maji represented the emergence of proto-nationalism among Tanzania's diverse peoples, recent scholars maintain that it was a set of rebellions that broke out for different reasons and that it represented part of a protracted series of wars that had begun prior to the arrival of the Germans.

In 1906, in the British colony of Natal that would soon become part of South Africa, a violent incident related to the imposition of a new poll tax on individual men, in addition to the existing "hut tax" on homesteads (see page 369), incited an aggressive response by colonial forces that pushed many Zulu people into rebellion. The settler

☰ **Defiance and defeat.** Herero prisoners in German South West Africa c. 1904.

minority saw the conflict as a chance to finalize the colonial conquest of the African majority of Natal, who had never been defeated in a war. While the neighboring Zulu kingdom had been subjugated in 1879, the African population within Natal had never been conquered in the same way. During the 1906 violence, several thousand Africans were killed, hundreds were convicted of treason and sentenced to hard labor and floggings, and the severed head of rebel leader Bambatha was toured around the area to intimidate the population.

In northern Nigeria, the 1906 Satiru Rebellion represented a Muslim-inspired attempt to overthrow the new British colonial regime that had recently conquered the Sokoto Caliphate. This incident made the British concerned about future Muslim resistance and informed the type of colonial administration imposed on the area, which is discussed below.

Although these revolts of the 1890s and 1900s were usually larger and deadlier conflicts than those fought during the initial European invasions, the rebellions were all eventually suppressed by colonial firepower and divide-and-rule strategies.

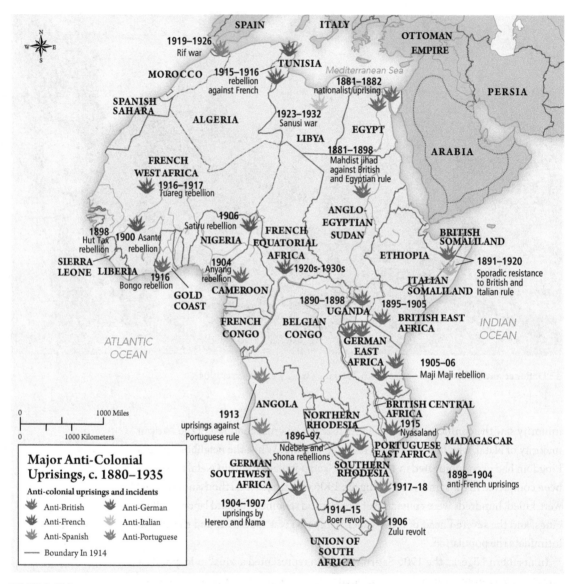

SPAIN ITALY OTTOMAN EMPIRE

1919–1926
Rif war

TUNISIA Mediterranean Sea

MOROCCO **1915–1916**
rebellion
against French

1881–1882
nationalist uprising

PERSIA

SPANISH
SAHARA

ALGERIA **1923–1932**
Sanusi war

EGYPT

LIBYA

ARABIA

FRENCH
WEST AFRICA **1916–1917**
Tuareg rebellion

1881–1898
Mahdist jihad
against British
and Egyptian rule

1906
Satiru rebellion

ANGLO-
EGYPTIAN
SUDAN

BRITISH
SOMALILAND

1898
Hut Tax
rebellion

1900 Asante
rebellion

NIGERIA

FRENCH
EQUATORIAL
AFRICA

ETHIOPIA

1891–1920
Sporadic resistance
to British and
Italian rule

SIERRA
LEONE LIBERIA

1916
Bongo rebellion

1904
Anyang
rebellion

1920s-1930s

ITALIAN
SOMALILAND

GOLD
COAST

CAMEROON

1890–1898
UGANDA

1895–1905

FRENCH
CONGO

BELGIAN
CONGO

BRITISH EAST
AFRICA

INDIAN
OCEAN

ATLANTIC
OCEAN

GERMAN
EAST
AFRICA

1905–06
Maji Maji rebellion

0   1000 Miles

0   1000 Kilometers

1913
uprisings against
Portuguese rule

ANGOLA

NORTHERN
RHODESIA

BRITISH CENTRAL
AFRICA
1915
Nyasaland

1896–97
Ndebele and
Shona rebellions

PORTUGUESE
EAST AFRICA

MADAGASCAR

**Major Anti-Colonial
Uprisings, c. 1880–1935**

Anti-colonial uprisings and incidents

GERMAN
SOUTHWEST
AFRICA

SOUTHERN
RHODESIA

1898–1904
anti-French uprisings

Anti-British   Anti-German

Anti-French   Anti-Italian

Anti-Spanish   Anti-Portuguese

—— Boundary In 1914

1904–1907
uprisings by
Herero and Nama

1914–15
Boer revolt

1917–18

1906
Zulu revolt

UNION OF
SOUTH
AFRICA

≡ **MAP 17.1**

Similar African rebellions took place during the First World War and were related to a combination of increased colonial demands for manpower and production, and the simultaneous weakening of the colonial state as officials, police, and soldiers went off to war. These uprisings will be discussed in more detail in Chapter 20, on the world wars. After the First World War (1914–18), with the colonies of defeated Germany given over to the victorious powers and African resistance defeated, colonial administrations became institutionalized as direct threats and regular violence were usually no longer needed to enforce the day-to-day realities of colonial rule. In addition to wars of conquest and the campaigns of the First World War, African societies were traumatized by the impact of the **influenza pandemic of 1918–19**, which killed over two million Africans and led to widespread hunger. Furthermore, there were some attempts to reform colonial rule to make it more efficient, which meant that concessionary companies, also facing financial problems, withdrew from administration. The period between the world wars, 1919 to 1939, is often referred to as the **high tide of colonial rule**, as it was then that the colonial state and economy stabilized and episodes of serious African armed resistance decreased.

Colonial States

By around 1920, each European colonial power had developed a different approach to governing its African colonies. The British employed a system that they called **indirect rule**. Originating in British-controlled India, which had been colonized much earlier, this system was pioneered in Africa by British officer Frederick Lugard, who had been involved in the colonial conquest of Nyasaland (Malawi) in the 1880s, Uganda in the 1890s, and northern Nigeria in the early 1900s. Lugard became the first governor of Nigeria in 1914, and in 1922 he published a book entitled *The Dual Mandate in Tropical Africa,* which outlined the indirect rule system and justified British imperialism, which he claimed would facilitate the expansion of Christianity and civilization. In colonial Africa, indirect rule involved a small number of aloof British officials supervising a hierarchy of African rulers who governed through existing African political structures such as kingdoms and chiefdoms, and who were guided by the "customary law" of local societies. One of the central principles of indirect rule was that Africans in the British colonies would always be different from the British, and as members of supposedly inferior societies they needed **paternalistic** guidance. The purpose of the indirect rule system was to limit African resistance by making it seem to African people as if not much had changed under British colonial rule, and to cut costs as it reduced African rebellions that were expensive to suppress. Further, African functionaries of the colonial state were paid much less than British officials. This apparent lack of change was mostly an illusion since the British, during the conquest period, had often removed the legitimate rulers of African states and replaced them with more compliant local partners who could be and often were removed if they upset the colonial status quo. Additionally, in writing down and creating systematic codes of "customary law" for different ethnic groups, British colonial officials and anthropologists changed local African legal systems to better reflect colonial priorities and values. They also made these systems much less flexible.

☰ **Indirect rule.** British officials and the royal court of Buganda in 1913. King Daudi Cwa (1896–1939) is the child seated on the left.

British indirect rule usually worked well in places where there was a long history of centralized government, such as in northern Nigeria, which had been the location of the Sokoto Caliphate and was now dominated by a network of Muslim emirs, and in East Africa's highly centralized Buganda kingdom, which had allied with the British in the 1890s. No longer functioning as sovereign rulers, these "traditional" leaders became symbols of ethnic identity, and the primary organizational element of the British colonial state in Africa became the "tribe," which was imagined as a primordial concept. The indirect rule system, however, struggled to gain legitimacy among historically decentralized peoples such as the Igbo of southeastern Nigeria and the Maasai of Kenya, who continued to struggle against colonial control. In southeastern Nigeria, British officials tried to impose this system by arbitrarily appointing some men as "warrant chiefs," but the Igbo people generally saw them as glorified tax collectors and opportunists. Indirect rule was often imposed by force. For example, in southwestern Nigeria, in 1914, where Lugard's soldiers violently suppressed protest among the Egba people of Ijemo (part of Abeokuta) so as to cancel their previous independence agreement with the British and incorporate them into the newly amalgamated colonial entity of Nigeria under an indirect-rule system already practiced in the north. In the long term, indirect rule created many problems for Africa as it fostered regionalism and ethnic identities, and its conservatism and traditionalism were at odds with the ambitions of the emerging class of westernized Africans who were products of missionary education.

The official French policy of administration in Africa was **direct rule**, which imposed European bureaucratic organization and the French legal system on the colonies. This was related to the French ideal of assimilation of African people, which meant that they would adopt French language, culture, and identity. Africans would become French. As such, there were two distinct classes of African inhabitants of France's African territories. The African products of this **assimilationist** program became "citizens" of France and theoretically had the same rights and responsibilities as citizens in the mother country, while other Africans were considered "subjects" and lived under a dictatorial colonial regime. With considerable French economic, cultural, and educational influences, the **Four Communes** of coastal Senegal (Gorée, Dakar, Rufisque, and Saint Louis) became the center of the much celebrated assimilationist system in French colonial Africa. In 1914, the French citizens of the Four Communes elected Blaise Diagne, a Senegalese man who had studied in France and worked as a French colonial official throughout Africa, to represent them in the National Assembly in Paris. He was the first Black African to achieve that status and became a symbol of the ideals of assimilation and citizenship. However, in the vast interior of French Africa the resources necessary for assimilation, particularly schools, were very limited and African communities resisted aspects of assimilation. As such, the overwhelming majority of people in the French territories remained colonial subjects with few rights. In remote areas the French quietly employed the same indirect-rule administrative system as the British, and in the early twentieth century French rhetoric shifted away from assimilation, which was clearly not feasible in most places, to ruling in partnership or association with Africans.

The Belgian and Portuguese colonial regimes in Africa also employed an assimilationist rhetoric, but it

≡ **Assimilation and citizenship.** In 1914, Blaise Diagne (1872–1934) became the first Black African elected to the French National Assembly.

was more superficial than that of the French. Portuguese officials advanced a theory, called **Lusotropicalism**, that had originated in the former Portuguese colony of Brazil in South America. According to this theory, the Portuguese regime in Africa was more beneficial to Africans than that of other colonial powers, the Portuguese were less racist than other European colonizers and mixed more freely with African people, and the centuries-long history of Portuguese presence on the continent meant that Lisbon's African territories were not foreign colonies but integral parts of Portugal. In Portuguese-ruled Mozambique, Angola, and Guinea-Bissau, an African who adopted Portuguese language and culture and Christianity gained the status of an "assimilado," which was similar to becoming a citizen of Portugal. In reality, very few Africans gained this distinction. Portuguese colonial rule remained extremely oppressive and violent throughout much of the twentieth century, and educational resources were very limited. The reason for the stark difference between rhetoric and reality in Portuguese Africa was that Portugal itself was under the fascist dictatorship of the "New State," led by Antonio Salazar and his successor Marcello Caetano from 1922 to 1974. While most European powers had democratic governments at home and therefore had to respond to domestic public opinion about abuses in the colonies, this was not the case in Portugal.

The Belgian Congo, which had been purchased from King Leopold II by the Belgian government in 1908, was divided into a pyramidal hierarchy of provinces and districts governed by a large number of Belgian colonial officials who supervised African "traditional chiefs" who managed the daily affairs of their communities. The Belgian Congo had the largest proportion of European officials to African population of any colony in Africa. No Congolese gained experience administering the colonial state and access to anything beyond rudimentary Western education was extremely rare. Although the Belgians introduced a paternalistic assimilationist system in the 1940s as part of colonial reforms, pitifully few Africans benefitted. In the former German territories of Rwanda and Burundi, the new Belgian administration imposed a combination of racial segregation and indirect rule in the 1920s. Under Belgian supervision, and reflecting colonial Social Darwinist ideology, a supposedly racially superior Tutsi minority became an administrative and intellectual elite reigning over an allegedly inferior Hutu majority. The precolonial governance system in which each hill was administered by three chiefs with different responsibilities, usually two Tutsi and one Hutu, was centralized into one chief who would always be a Tutsi. Tutsi gained preferential access to Western education and the Tutsi kings of Rwanda and Burundi were transformed from substantive traditionalist rulers to symbols of Christianity and westernization. In 1931, in Rwanda, the Belgians replaced the traditionalist king Musinga with the Catholic convert Mutara Rudahigwa, who became popularly known as the "king of the whites." At the same time, the Belgians used Tutsi officials to supervise intensified taxation and compulsory labor among Hutu peasant farmers.

A security force establishment upheld colonial rule. It would have been too expensive to occupy Africa with large European armies. Therefore, colonial administrators created local police and military units that were led by a small number of European officers and composed of a locally recruited African rank-and-file. Most of these forces were founded during the conquest era and then transitioned into regular features of the colonial state. In most cases, colonial African police and soldiers were recruited from remote areas where there were few economic or educational opportunities, and among allegedly martial races or martial tribes which were ethnic groups that colonial officials thought possessed inherent military characteristics. Other ethnic groups perceived as lacking martial attributes were often excluded from the colonial security forces. The British colonial military in Nigeria, Gold Coast (Ghana), and Uganda became dominated by supposedly martial northerners, in Kenya the Kamba ethnic group was overrepresented in the King's African Rifles (KAR), in the Belgian Congo men from the north were recruited into the Force Publique, and

≡ **Colonial security forces.** *Left:* An African soldier of France's Tirailleurs Sénégalais, c. 1905. *Right:* Members of the King's African Rifles, in Uganda, in 1916.

the French preferred to recruit among the Bambara people of the interior Sahel. Colonial security forces were not, therefore, national institutions but elements of an ethnic divide-and-rule strategy. They were also expected to be cheap, as salaries were low, the forces were small, and they often used obsolete weapons and equipment. That said, the primarily African membership of these police and military forces illustrates that European colonial rule could not have survived without African cooperation.

The British settler colonies in Southern Africa developed racially exclusive white-minority governments that used legislation to further subjugate and exploit the African majority. When Britain's Cape Colony gained internal self-government (known as "responsible government") in 1872, its constitution set up a nonracial qualified franchise based on individual property ownership. As a result of existing socioeconomic discrimination and the recent colonial conquest, there were more white voters than Black ones even though the Black population was in the overwhelming majority. As more Black residents of the Cape qualified to vote, the white-dominated Cape governments of the late nineteenth century increased the franchise requirements to keep Black voters in a minority. The neighboring British settler colony of Natal, which gained responsible government in 1892, and the region's Boer republics of the Orange Free State and the Transvaal had exclusively white voting systems. In 1910, after the South African War (1899–1902), the Cape, Natal, and former Boer republics were combined into the Union of South Africa, which was a self-governing **dominion** within the British Empire along the lines of Canada and Australia. At this time the white population of South Africa amounted to around 1.3 million people and comprised perhaps 20 percent of the total population. The union government was composed of and elected by the white minority and the Cape Province's nonracial franchise was gradually phased out by the 1930s. In 1913, the all-white union government passed the **Natives Land Act**, which undermined African ownership of agricultural land and pushed more Africans into low-paid migrant labor in South Africa's mines.

In 1923, Southern Rhodesia, previously administered by the BSAC, gained responsible government with a technically nonracial franchise that greatly favored the **white settler** minority. Seeing themselves as a particularly British frontier society, white Rhodesian voters decided against joining the Union of South Africa, which was

☰ **Colonial authority.** Government House in Nairobi, c. 1935. It was built in 1907 to serve as the official residence of the governor of British East Africa and is now the official residence of the president of Kenya.

dominated by Boer or Afrikaner politicians. At this time, there was around 40,000 white settlers living in Southern Rhodesia compared to about a million Africans. Copying neighboring South Africa, the Southern Rhodesian white settler government passed a series of laws, particularly the 1931 Land Apportionment Act, which restricted African agriculture, impoverished African communities, and promoted the growth of white commercial farming. The internal stability of this exclusionist state is illustrated by the fact that Godfrey Huggins, who led its government from the 1930s to 1950s, became the longest-serving prime minister in British Commonwealth history.

In both South Africa and Southern Rhodesia, the rise of white-minority states and racially discriminatory legislation prompted the simultaneous growth of the African nationalist movement that pursued civil rights during the early twentieth century. The white minority in Kenya, wealthy and influential, wanted to obtain white minority rule, but their numbers were small and their political ambitions were opposed by the Indian minority, who feared loss of rights. During the early 1920s, there were around 10,000 white settlers in Kenya, compared to 23,000 Indians and three million Africans. In 1923, the British government declared that the territory would be governed according to a policy of "African paramountcy," though the meaning of this remained unclear. This created an ambiguous situation in colonial Kenya where white settlers were at the top of a colonial racial hierarchy, but their formal political role amounted to dominating a weak legislative council that advised the British governor.

Colonial Economies

For the most part, the aim of European colonial rule in Africa was extraction of wealth. The exact methods employed to achieve this varied from place to place and depended largely on available resources. In general, though, African people were forced into this new colonial capitalist economy through the requirement that they pay a variety of taxes to the colonial state. The most common form of taxation in colonial Africa was the **hut tax**, which required a male household head to pay a set amount of money for each hut in his homestead or compound. It was thought that households with more huts were larger and therefore wealthier, and thus could pay more tax. There were other kinds of taxes, such poll taxes on individual workers, and even a tax on dog ownership that was imposed in Southern Rhodesia. Tax revenue subsidized the running of the colonial state, but it had another more important purpose. Since Africans now had to acquire money to pay their taxes and increasingly to buy other commodities that were gaining popularity, they had to either produce something to sell on the international market or work for wages in places like large commercial farms, mines, or ports.

In short, taxation was the motor of the capitalist colonial economy in Africa. Furthermore, the transportation infrastructure built in colonial times did not link different parts of Africa but simply facilitated the export of raw materials. Minerals and crops produced in the interior were moved by railway or road to the coastal ports, where they were loaded on ships bound for other parts of the world.

The few colonial territories with known valuable minerals became the scene of mining economies that were very profitable from a colonial perspective yet produced horrible suffering for African people. The primary mining economies of colonial Africa were the tin mines of Nigeria's Jos Plateau, the Copper Belt of neighboring Northern Rhodesia (Zambia) and the Belgian Congo's southern region of Katanga, and the diamond and gold mines of South Africa. A mixed mining economy based on extraction of coal, gold, and other minerals also developed in Southern Rhodesia. Colonial profits from mining were maximized by systems of migrant labor that undercut African wages. For migrant labor to develop, the colonial state had to impose two interrelated policies: taxation and land alienation. All African people were subject to taxation, but widespread dispossession of land happened in only a few places and primarily in settler-dominated Southern Africa. Stripped of their productive land and crowded into small reserves, African people could not readily engage in commercial agriculture to pay their compulsory taxes. A system of colonial labor recruitment organized the transportation of men from these impoverished areas to the mines, where they were employed on temporary contracts. Colonial laws often forbade migrant workers from moving their families from the rural reserves to areas closer to the mines, which meant that the migrant workers remained temporary and transitory and thus low paid. This also discouraged the formation of an African urban working-class consciousness that might have begun to organize demands for higher salaries. In Southern Africa, a regional migrant labor system developed in which densely populated and poor territories like Nyasaland (Malawi) supplied African workers who were recruited by colonial labor bureaus and transported by rail to and from the gold mines around Johannesburg in South Africa. Migrant workers from Northern Rhodesia, Nyasaland, and Mozambique often passed through Southern Rhodesia, working for very low pay and in very dangerous mines, with their ultimate destination being the South African gold mines, where salaries were slightly higher. For many, Johannesburg was imagined as a city of gold where fortunes could be made. In reality, migrant workers in South Africa were crammed into overcrowded and squalid hostels and forced to toil for low wages in poor conditions, and mining companies operated beer halls and company stores to recoup some of the salaries. Many migrant workers, either from other parts of South Africa or neighboring territories, returned home with work-related health issues, such as silicosis, caused by inhaling small dust particles, or tuberculosis, which is an infectious disease that spread in the mine compounds. In many parts of Southern Africa, engagement in

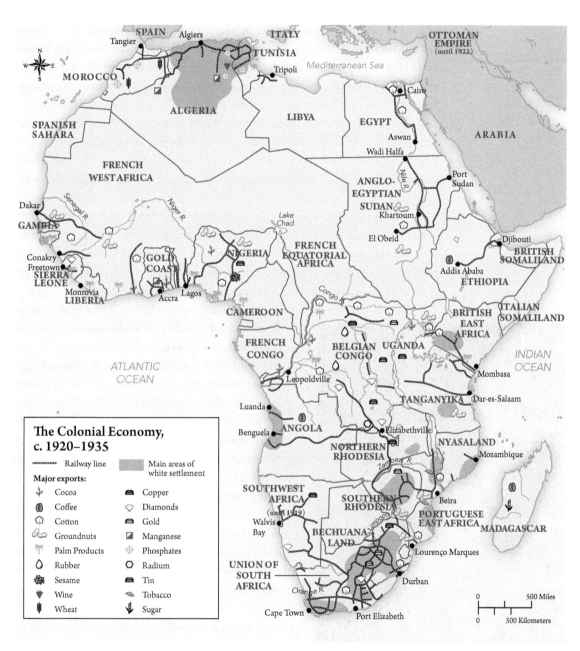

SPAIN
Tangier Algiers ITALY
MOROCCO TUNISIA Mediterranean Sea
Tripoli
ALGERIA LIBYA EGYPT OTTOMAN EMPIRE (until 1922)
SPANISH SAHARA Cairo
Aswan ARABIA
Wadi Halfa Nile R.
FRENCH WEST AFRICA ANGLO-EGYPTIAN SUDAN Port Sudan
Dakar Senegal R. Niger R. Lake Chad Khartoum
GAMBIA El Obeid BRITISH SOMALILAND
Conakry NIGERIA FRENCH EQUATORIAL AFRICA Addis Ababa Djibouti
Freetown GOLD COAST ETHIOPIA
SIERRA LEONE ITALIAN SOMALILAND
Monrovia Accra Lagos BRITISH EAST AFRICA
LIBERIA CAMEROON Congo R.
ATLANTIC OCEAN FRENCH CONGO BELGIAN CONGO UGANDA INDIAN OCEAN
Leopoldville Mombasa
Luanda TANGANYIKA Dar-es-Salaam
Benguela ANGOLA Elizabethville
NORTHERN RHODESIA NYASALAND Mozambique
Zambezi R.
SOUTHWEST AFRICA (until 1919) SOUTHERN RHODESIA Beira MADAGASCAR
Walvis Bay BECHUANA LAND Limpopo R. PORTUGUESE EAST AFRICA
UNION OF SOUTH AFRICA Lourenço Marques
Orange R. Durban
Cape Town Port Elizabeth

The Colonial Economy, c. 1920–1935

- - - - - - Railway line

Main areas of white settlement

Major exports:

Cocoa	Copper
Coffee	Diamonds
Cotton	Gold
Groundnuts	Manganese
Palm Products	Phosphates
Rubber	Radium
Sesame	Tin
Wine	Tobacco
Wheat	Sugar

0   500 Miles
0   500 Kilometers

≡ **MAP 17.2**

migrant labor came to represent a symbol of manhood, especially as precolonial warrior cultures became less significant. Migrant labor reconfigured social structure as women left behind in rural communities took on greater workloads and new roles in the family, and male mine hostel dwellers sometimes entered homosexual relations with younger men, who became **mine wives**.

Colonial Africa was the scene of several types of large-scale commercial agricultural production. In some areas, international companies set up plantations to mass produce crops for the world market. In parts of the Belgian Congo the Anglo-Dutch conglomerate Unilever operated plantations to produce palm oil, and in Liberia the American tire manufacturer Firestone created the world's largest rubber plantation in 1926. Liberia was an independent republic ruled by a minority Americo-Liberian elite, but its economy developed along similar lines to that of neighboring European colonies. Since plantation production involved eviction of Africans from their land and the employment of exploited migrant workers similar to the mining industry, these types of colonial economies sometimes provoked African protests that were costly to suppress and politically embarrassing. As such, plantations were not widely favored by colonial administrations, and in many areas, they were considered impractical.

In South Africa, Southern Rhodesia, Kenya, and Algeria, white settlers set up large commercial farms on land stolen from African communities. The difference between plantation production and this **settler production** was that the latter involved the development of a white settler society in Africa that lived on the land and passed down their farms to their offspring. Some white commercial farms produced maize sold to nearby mines to feed migrant workers, and other settlers grew export crops, such as tobacco, for Europe and North America. From a colonial perspective, some of the perceived advantages of settler production proved mythological. While it was thought that European settlers would remain loyal to European colonial governments, local settler societies in parts of Africa developed their own interests, usually related to control of land and African labor, and these were sometimes at odds with the broader imperial agenda. For instance, and as discussed later, the white settler society in Southern Rhodesia saw itself as distinctly British, yet its government illegally broke from Britain in 1965 to avoid political reforms that would have granted civil rights to the Black majority. Furthermore, the technologically

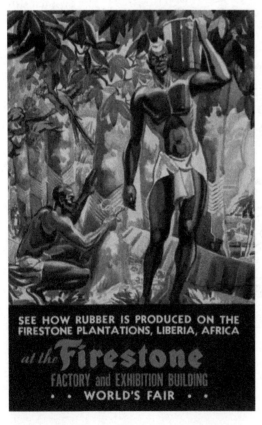

SEE HOW RUBBER IS PRODUCED ON THE FIRESTONE PLANTATIONS, LIBERIA, AFRICA

at the **Firestone**

FACTORY and EXHIBITION BUILDING

· · **WORLD'S FAIR** · ·

≡ **Commercial agriculture.** A 1930s advertisement for Firestone's rubber plantation in Liberia.

more advanced settler farmers were not always as productive as some thought they would be. The white farmers of Kenya, primarily located in the White Highlands near Nairobi, were always out-produced by the African small-scale farmers of neighboring Tanganyika (Tanzania). In Southern Rhodesia and South Africa, settler farming was bolstered by discriminatory legislation that undercut Black agricultural competition and restricted Black land ownership. A similar process took place in French Algeria, where white commercial farms benefited from Muslim dispossession and cheap labor. Finally, the prevalence of tropical disease meant that much of Africa was not attractive to white settlers, and in the few areas they settled, largely in Southern Africa, there was widespread resistance to their land-grabbing and oppression.

The most common form of economy in colonial Africa involved African peasants engaged in small-scale farming to produce **cash crops**. Including groundnuts, cocoa, and cotton, these were crops that were meant to be sold for money and exported to the world market. Superficially, and like indirect rule, peasant farming made it seem as if colonialism had not caused much change in Africa, as African people were working their lands using what was imagined as "age old" methods. This cut down on instances of violent resistance, which were extremely expensive and disconcerting for colonial regimes to counter. In some areas, of course, there was resistance to the imposition of this type of peasant farming. For example, in the early twentieth century, British attempts to force the Dinka and Shilluk people of South Sudan to grow cotton was seen as threatening food production. On closer inspection, though, African agriculture was changing as communal access to land was being partly replaced by Western-style individual land tenure, and farmers had to balance growing food for their own consumption with growing "cash crops" to get money for taxes and other mounting expenses such as children's school fees and imported consumer goods. Eventually, a system of **marketing boards** was set up to decrease prices paid to African farmers for their products and therefore make money for the colonial regimes and increase the profits made by international buyers. In many places, a farmer had to sell crops to a government marketing board, which set prices as low as possible and then sold the products on to the international market at a higher rate.

Another impact of peasant production and colonial management of this system was that African farmers were encouraged to specialize in producing certain crops. In Senegal the preferred crop was groundnuts, in Gold Coast (Ghana) it was cocoa, and in Rwanda it was coffee and tea. This monoculture facilitated export as international buyers could centralize their logistics, but it made African farmers vulnerable to the international fluctuation of prices for the single commodity they produced. If, for instance, the price of cocoa collapsed, then Gold Coast farmers would have a very rough year. In such circumstances, the colonial administration still collected taxes, but would do very little to support African farmers. who were thought to survive through precolonial subsistence

THE COLONIAL ECONOMY

Top left: Women in the Gold Coast carry bales of cocoa on their heads in the early 1900s. *Top right:* A white settler supervises workers on his tobacco farm in Rhodesia in the 1920s. *Bottom left:* African, white, and Chinese gold miners in South Africa, c. 1900. *Bottom right:* A column of men transport bushels of tea leaves on a plantation in Nyasaland (Malawi) in 1940.

agriculture. For the colonizers, this was a cheap and efficient economic system that worked well in many places. Although practiced throughout the continent, African "peasant production" was commonly associated with colonial West Africa, where the tropical environment had kept out white settlers and where there were few mining economies.

People and the Environment

The imposition of the colonial state and economy often alienated African people from the environment. Under colonial rule, Africans were stereotyped as enemies of nature who, if left on their own, would hunt animals to extinction and cut down every tree. As such, colonial regimes created laws that criminalized African hunting, an important economic and social activity in precolonial times. Anyone caught breaking these rules could be prosecuted and punished as a poacher. Government wildlife departments were, like the police and military, racially hierarchical organizations. Armed white rangers commanding usually unarmed Black security guards enforced these game laws. In the early days of colonial rule the concept of wildlife conservation emerged, but it was meant to preserve certain species of animals so that white elites could have the enjoyment of hunting them. During the late nineteenth and early twentieth century, within this context, large parts of Africa were officially demarcated as **game reserves**. Influenced by North American practices, the colonial approach to wildlife conservation in Africa began to change in the early twentieth century as the idea of total conservation within state managed national parks gained ground. Africa's first national parks were Virunga National Park, created in 1925 in eastern Belgian Congo to preserve the mountain gorillas, and Kruger National Park, previously a game reserve, which was founded in 1927 in northeastern South Africa. Many other national parks were established across colonial Africa immediately following the Second World War, including Tsavo National Park in Kenya in 1948 and the Serengeti National Park in Tanganyika in 1951. African communities were evicted and excluded from these vast national parks, which became attractions for foreign white tourists who paid to see exotic African wildlife. Outside these parks, particularly in parts of Eastern and Southern Africa, big game hunting became a tourism industry controlled by white-owned safari companies and professional hunters.

Efforts by the colonial state to combat tropical diseases like **malaria**, which is carried by anopheles mosquitos, and **sleeping sickness** (trypanosomiasis), which is carried by tsetse flies, often proved counterproductive. Seeing African approaches to disease as primitive and ineffective, colonial experts thought that Western science and technology could eliminate these insect-born parasites that were seen as a threat to colonial economic and social development. Colonial campaigns against these diseases involved

≡ **Safari.** Former US president Teddy Roosevelt on a hunting trip in East Africa, c. 1909.

relocating and concentrating African communities to supposedly healthier areas where they could more easily receive medical treatment, education, and clean water, and be mobilized for work within the colonial economy. Ironically, without people engaging in agriculture and hunting, the supposedly unhealthy areas that were evacuated reverted to bush with more wildlife and therefore became a more conducive environment for tsetse flies. In the early twentieth century, the amount of tsetse-infested areas in Tanzania increased, despite concentrated German and then British anti-tsetse measures. Similar expansion of tsetse ecologies took place in Uganda and Zambia, where people were relocated and concentrated, and depopulated areas became overgrown. The creation of huge game reserves and national parks also increased tsetse ecologies.

In East and Southern Africa settler dispossession often forced African people into smaller areas that became overcrowded which in turn led to health problems and environmental degradation such as erosion and desertification caused by deforestation and overgrazing. Colonial authorities often blamed these problems on inefficient or wasteful African agricultural methods. In fact, many colonial experts ignored indigenous knowledge and innovation that promoted sustainable use and sometimes rehabilitation of the environment. In some areas colonial soil conservation policies, such as controlling grass fires and restricting livestock grazing, provoked African resentment and limited resistance, often among women, whose traditional role as agricultural experts was ignored. In Kenya, settler control of the "White Highlands" cut off many African communities from their historical pasturelands, and grazing livestock in this area was criminalized as trespassing. In some places, Africans were prevented from accessing forests that were sources of firewood and building material.

Colonial economic projects changed environments and created new health problems. In German Cameroon, plantations were developed in coastal lowlands that were hot and wet, which exposed migrant workers from the drier interior to malaria and

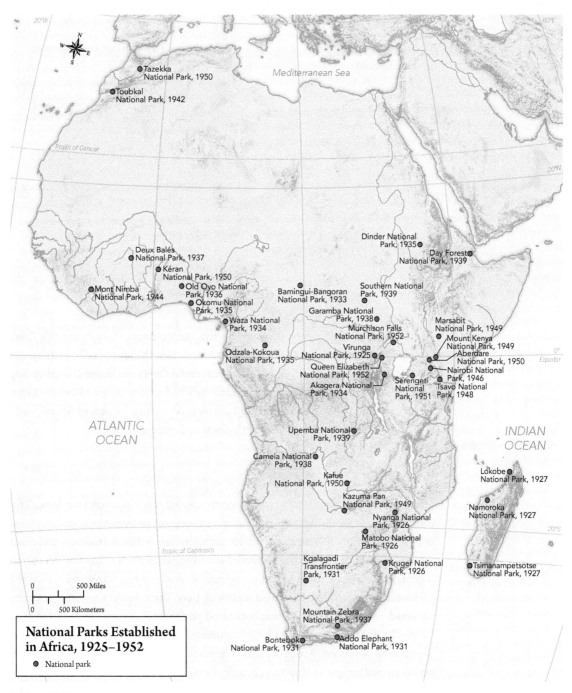

National Parks Established in Africa, 1925–1952
● National park

≡ MAP 17.3

Timeline

other diseases. In Egypt, the enlargement of irrigated cotton fields along the Nile River led to an increase in malaria, bilharzia, and cholera. Health concerns also justified the racial segregation of colonial cities, as Africans and Asians were blamed for spreading disease like plague and cholera, and therefore they had to be kept apart from the European community. The overcrowded and poorly serviced Black slums of Africa's colonial cities became places associated with illness and disease.

Conclusion

The nature of the colonial state and economy created many problems for Africa's future. Despite some differences in rhetoric by European powers, the state structures imposed on colonial Africa created an authoritarian political tradition and used divide-and-rule strategies that promoted ethno-regional rivalry. The few democratic governments were minority settler regimes determined to control and exploit the African majority which was denied representation. The colonial economies extracted wealth from Africa in ways that optimized profits for European governments and international business interests by minimizing the compensation given to African workers and producers. Africa became an exporter of raw materials for the world market but gained almost no long-term benefit. Arrogant colonial regimes created a range of policies that assumed that African people were enemies of nature conservation and entirely ignorant of local health issues and appropriate agricultural methods. Such attitudes persisted well into the postcolonial era.

KEY TERMS

assimilationist 365

cash crops 373

decentralized
  despotism 357

direct rule 365

dominion 368

First Chimurenga 359

Four Communes 365

game reserves 375

Herero and Nama
  Rebellion 359

high tide of colonial rule 363

hut tax 369

Indirect rule 363

influenza pandemic of
  1918–19 363

Lusotropicalism 366

Maji Maji Rebellion 360

malaria 375

marketing boards 373

mine wives 372

Natives Land Act 368

settler production 372

sleeping sickness 375

white settler 368

STUDY QUESTIONS

1. How would you characterize the European treatment of Africans in the early phase of colonial rule? What were some of the major causes for the rebellions and resistance movements that Africans levied against colonizing companies and governments?

2. Compare British indirect rule and French direct rule. How were French and Portuguese agendas of assimilation similar? How do they contrast with Belgian administrative models? What forms of racism, discrimination, and oppression resulted from these methods of control?

3. How did tax collection by colonial authorities facilitate the creation of a colonial capitalist economy in Africa? How did the colonial economy impact migrant labor, family dynamics, and wealth disparities among Africans?

4. How did colonial rule alienate African people from their environment? How did colonial policies about nature conservation and tropical disease lead to increasingly oppressive conditions for Africans living under colonial rule?

Please see page FR-7 for the Further Readings for this chapter.
For additional digital learning resources please go to
https://www.oup.com/he/falola-stapleton1e

Colonial Rule in Africa: Social and Cultural Change, c. 1900–1950

Many aspects of African society and culture changed significantly during the era of European colonial rule. African people did not simply and uncritically copy European social or cultural trends, but nonetheless, external influences from different sources accelerated in this period and helped shape today's African society. While Christianity and Islam had arrived in parts of Africa long before the late-nineteenth-century Scramble, both these world religions gained very many new African adherents from around 1900 to 1960. Western Christianity expanded more dramatically in colonial Africa, but it was also changed and adapted by African congregations. The development of colonial economies also led to the formation of new classes of African people such as westernized elites and urban workers, and in this context, the traditional socioeconomic roles of men and women changed a great deal. At the same time, colonial divide-and-rule strategies and the movement of people from different rural areas to colonial cities gave new importance to African ethnic identities. Popular culture was also changing with the arrival of new sports such as football (soccer), which became prevalent across the continent, and the development of creative new regional music styles combining various imported and local instruments and genres. Of course, it is important to remember that these shifting social and cultural factors were interrelated in different ways. For example, in the growing cities of colonial Africa, men worked jobs in places like docks or railway facilities and some women sold vegetables or beer, and they used the money gained from wages or sales to buy food and pay rent and children's school fees. In their spare time, they attended football matches, dance parties, and Christian or Muslim religious services. This was very different from the typical rural lifestyle of the previous century.

Changing social patterns. Couples in the Belgian Congo, 1910.

Religion

Some of the most significant social change that occurred in colonial Africa concerned religion. During this period the two great world religions of Christianity and Islam both expanded in many parts of Africa. As discussed in a previous chapter, European Christian missionaries had been working in parts of Africa for many years prior to colonial conquest, but the number of Africans who converted to Christianity was relatively small and they were mostly confined to coastal areas. The process of conversion accelerated dramatically during the early twentieth century, with Christianity spreading across much of colonial Africa, particularly in areas where Islam had not already taken hold. There are several possible explanations for this sudden success of Christianity. In practical terms, colonial rule facilitated the activities of European and African missionaries in parts of the interior that they had not previously accessed, and with the loss of African sovereignty local traditional authorities found it difficult to oppose their work. By 1910, there were 10,000 white missionaries working in Africa, and by the 1920s missions owned huge amounts of land, including an astonishing 400,000 acres in Southern Rhodesia (Zimbabwe). Christian missionaries operated most of the emerging Western-style education systems in colonial Africa, and access was generally restricted to Christian converts. In 1945, for instance, over 96 percent of students in Britain's African colonies were enrolled in mission schools. Since gaining literacy and Western educational qualifications became a key to social and economic success within the European dominated colonial system, there were strong motivations for African people to convert to Christianity. A similar dynamic may have been at work in healthcare, which was another field dominated by missionaries. Of course, not all Africans in this period converted to Christianity for opportunistic reasons, as very many Africans became devoted Christians and Christianity continues to be extremely important in African society. On a psychological level, perhaps, Christianity seemed more attractive within the context of colonial rule by Christian European powers. At the same time, many traditional African beliefs, such as reverence for ancestors, were compatible with Christianity, though some missionaries did not approve of religious **syncretism**.

With the spread of missionary Christianity, the divisions of Western Christian denominations such as Catholicism and various types of Protestantism become entrenched in colonial Africa. The different colonial regimes tended to favor mission denominations from the colonial metropole, which meant, for example, that Catholicism became widespread in the French and Belgian territories and Protestantism became popular in British colonies. This division was not absolute as, for

≡ **Mission Christianity** *Left:* European missionaries conduct a baptism ceremony in the French Congo, c. 1914. *Right:* A Catholic nun teaches reading and writing to Zulu girls at a mission school in Natal, South Africa, c. 1910.

instance, Catholicism became prominent in British-ruled southeastern Nigeria. In the Belgian and Portuguese colonies, the Catholic Church worked closely with colonial administrators.

In addition to mission Christianity, which was connected to established churches in Europe and North America, African independent Christian churches were formed and became tremendously popular during the colonial era and after. A number of causes account for the formation of African independent churches. Influenced by the extreme racism of the late nineteenth and early twentieth centuries, white missionaries limited advancement of Black clergy within the church and showed a lack of tolerance for African cultural expression, such as the performance of African music or dancing during religious services. Another major obstacle to some Africans joining missionary churches was that the churches rejected **polygamy**, an important African social institution, though not all independent churches accepted the practice. African independent churches were also influenced by the growth of revivalism within mission churches in the early twentieth century and by counter-establishment mission churches that preached Adventism or belief in the imminent second coming of Jesus Christ. Originating from the United States, the Jehovah's Witness or Watch Tower movement arrived in Nyasaland (Malawi) and Northern Rhodesia (Zambia) in the early twentieth century, and eventually inspired an independent branch in 1937, and the Seventh Day Adventist Church sent missionaries to South Africa in the late 1880s and quickly spread north into Southern Rhodesia, Northern Rhodesia, and the Belgian Congo. In some areas, the massive number of Christian conversions could not keep pace with the

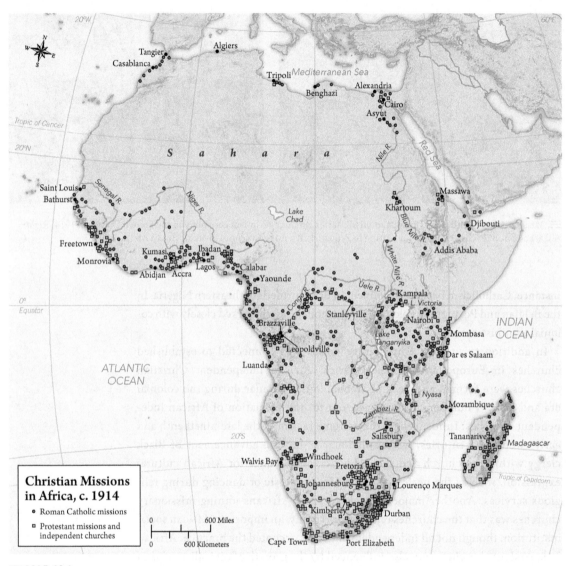

Christian Missions in Africa, c. 1914

- Roman Catholic missions
- Protestant missions and independent churches

0   600 Miles

0   600 Kilometers

≡ **MAP 18.1**

number of missionaries available, which meant that African religious leaders emerged and interpreted Christianity in their own way which led to breakaway movements.

Although thousands of independent Christian churches developed across Africa, they can be divided into two very general categories: Ethiopian and Zionist. **Ethiopian churches** had nothing to do with Ethiopia per se, but sometimes they used the name of Ethiopia, the only African country to have successfully defended itself from colonial invasion during the Scramble, to symbolize their independence from foreign missionary churches. Ethiopian churches often originated as splinter groups from missionary churches, and, as such, their doctrines and services were very similar to the parent institution. Some of the first "Ethiopian" type churches were the Native Baptist Church established in Lagos, Nigeria, in 1888 and South Africa's Ethiopian Church that split from the missionary Wesleyan movement in Pretoria in 1892. **Zionist churches**, the other very broad category of African independent Christianity, tended to emerge on their own or with some influence from revivalist or counter-establishment millenarian mission churches, particularly from North America. The term "Zionist," in this case, refers to the town of Zion, Illinois, in the United States, which was the home of an early-twentieth-century evangelical movement that sent representatives to South Africa in 1904. Although diverse, African "Zionist" churches tended to share a number of characteristics, such as charismatic and prophetic leadership; emphasis on the Old Testament of the Bible; the practice of faith healing; programs to eradicate witchcraft, which was seen as evil; and an African interpretation of Christianity. Although independent, these movements were still inspired to some extent by mission churches, and some of the founders of these groups had first experienced Christianity in a mission church. Founded in the 1930s, the Apostolic (Vapostori) churches in Zimbabwe and the Aladura churches in Nigeria were partly motivated by missionary revivalism, which was gaining popularity at that time, and the white robes members wear originated from those worn by Catholic and/or Anglican clergy.

Independent churches were very important in the spread of Christianity throughout colonial Africa. For example, during 1913 and 1914 a Liberian man called William Wade Harris, dressed in a white robe and turban and carrying a bamboo cross and a Bible, walked from Liberia to the Gold Coast (Ghana) on a great mission to spread Christianity and encourage the burning of traditional fetishes. Called the **Prophet Harris**, he baptized 100,000 people, many of whom later joined Catholic and Protestant mission churches in the region. Similarly, **Simon Kimbangu**, who had been converted to Christianity by Baptist missionaries, became a wildly popular faith healer in the Belgian Congo and attracted thousands of followers who abandoned their work to seek out the prophet. Like the Prophet Harris in West Africa, Kimbangu encouraged his followers to destroy traditional fetishes and renounce witchcraft. He did not advocate violence or resistance to taxation, but he did quote passages from the Bible to decry colonial oppression and exploitation. While the Belgians were fearful of a rebellion

≡ **Independent church.** A Kimbanguist church in Nkamba, Democratic Republic of the Congo, 2013. Over 22 million believers worldwide ascribe to Kimbanguism.

and imprisoned Kimbangu from 1921 until his death in 1951, Kimbanguism flourished as an underground independent Christian church in the Congo and it was legalized in 1959. It also spread to the nearby French territories of Congo-Brazzaville and Gabon, and Portuguese Angola. Marie Muilu, Kimbangu's wife, led the movement after her husband's imprisonment, and eventually their sons assumed leadership of the church. Although colonial officials often worried that African independent churches would encourage resistance to colonial rule, very few of them became involved in such actions, and followers of these movements generally sought spiritual relief. Independent churches of all types continue to be incredibly successful in many African countries. A prominent example is South Africa's Zion Christian Church, which was founded in 1924 and had around five million members by 2001. It is the largest African independent church in the Southern Africa region.

Islam expanded in parts of colonial Africa despite the fact that the European colonial rulers were generally Christians. Colonial regimes recognized that Islam had a long history in areas such as North Africa, the West African Sahel, and coastal East Africa. Aware of the recent history of Muslim jihads in parts of Africa now under their control, colonial officials worried that Islam had the potential to mobilize Africans across ethnic lines and in opposition to European rule. Colonial officials also respected the fact that Islam, like Christianity but unlike African traditional religions, is a faith based on literacy, with the Qur'an as a central text. In northern Nigeria, the British colonial state restricted the activities of Christian missionaries so as to avoid alienating the Muslim emirs upon whom the indirect rule system relied. In return for colonial support, the emirs in northern Nigeria prevented the rise of prophetic Muslim movements that so concerned the British. At the same time, southern Nigeria was being vigorously Christianized, which meant that the country became divided between a largely Christian south and a predominantly Muslim north. Furthermore, the missionary dominance of Western education meant that southern Nigerians would have much greater access to this type of schooling. A similar situation developed in British-ruled Sudan. While British officials in northern Sudan cooperated with Muslim elites to protect Islam and Arabic language, the British in southern Sudan specifically kept out Muslim influences and facilitated the spread of missionary Christianity and English language. These religious regional differences would lead to grave problems for future Nigeria and Sudan.

French colonial officials, perhaps partly because of the French government's secular tradition, sometimes had a troubled relationship with Muslim elites in Africa, especially in the conquest era of the nineteenth and early twentieth centuries. Indeed, a paranoia about Muslim conspiracy continued among French colonial officials throughout the colonial era. However, after the First World War, during which there was not as much Muslim-inspired resistance to French rule as anticipated, the French administration became more tolerant toward Islam, which was widespread across their African colonial territories. Though they did not develop the same formal relationship with Muslim elites that the British did in northern Nigeria, the French cooperated with some Muslim brotherhoods and merchant networks in West Africa. While the French colonial regime tried to create Franco-Arab **madrasas** (Muslim schools) to develop an educated Muslim elite in Africa, the madrasas were generally unsuccessful as Muslim parents did not want their children educated by infidels. Similarly, French attempts to create a "Black Muslim" or "French Muslim" identity, as opposed to a broader Muslim identity, in their sub-Saharan African colonies also failed. In the 1920s, the French, much like the British in Nigeria, recognized the Sahel as a Muslim area and limited the activities of Christian missionaries there, but the spread of Islam into the savannah and coastal forest was discouraged.

≡ **Islam in West Africa.** The Great Mosque of Touba, Senegal. Construction started in 1883. It is one of the largest mosques in Africa.

With the decline of trade in the Sahel and Sahara during the colonial era, Muslim merchants across West Africa refocused their activities southward, which led to the growth of Muslim communities in coastal towns such as Lagos in Nigeria, Freetown in Sierra Leone, and Conakry in Guinea. For some Africans, Islam became attractive because, unlike mission Christianity, it permitted polygamy.

Class, Gender, and Ethnicity

Several new classes of African people emerged within colonial society. One of these classes was the small but prominent **African westernized elite**. The members of this class succeeded within the missionary education system, mastered the relevant colonial language, and became literate in European and African languages. They also adopted some Western habits of living, including dress, food, and types of housing. They engaged in monogamous marriage, became more individually oriented, focused on the nuclear rather than the extended family, and converted to Christianity. Within the colonial system, the new westernized elite were usually employed in relatively well-paid jobs such as clerks, interpreters, teachers, journalists, and clergy. They sought to replicate European or American middle-class life in Africa. A new type of social stratification emerged as the literate and individualistic westernized elite separated themselves from and often looked down upon the illiterate and communal masses. The westernized elites also saw themselves as civilized people and loyal colonial subjects. In British territories they formed Boy Scout and Girl Guide troops. In French territories, given the assimilationist system, they were often citizens of France. Racist European colonials often viewed the emerging westernized African elites as upstarts and troublemakers. In Southern Rhodesia and other places, one of the most prominent symbols of this elite status was the "white wedding," including an elaborate white bridal gown, wedding rings, church ceremony, printed invitations, and a reception with speeches given by family and friends. The westernized elites did not reject all African customs. For example, despite the disproval of missionaries, they stuck with the traditional marriage practice of having the groom provide bride-wealth or dowry to the bride's family. The colonial capitalist economy, however, changed the form of bride-wealth from livestock or agricultural produce to cash.

A new urban working class developed in the growing cities of colonial Africa. Cities had long existed in precolonial Africa, such as in West Africa, where interior urban centers were associated with the trans-Saharan trade, and in East Africa, where Swahili ports were engaged in Indian Ocean commerce. While some of these older cities became important to the European colonial conquerors for strategic of economic reasons, many new urban centers were founded and expanded during the colonial era, including ports to export raw materials like Conakry in Guinea, administrative capitals like Leopoldville (Kinshasa) in the Belgian Congo, railway hubs like Nairobi in Kenya, and mining towns like Johannesburg in South Africa. As people from the countryside moved to these cities to engage in wage labor for employers or open their own small businesses, a permanent urban population developed. This urbanization also took place in the mining centers of Southern Africa despite restrictions related to the migrant labor system. Colonial cities were racially segregated, with well-serviced and prosperous European sections and large neglected slums for Africans. Unlike people in rural areas, city dwellers did not work the land to survive but used money earned by work or entrepreneurship to pay for food, accommodation, and other goods and services.

Under colonial rule, gender roles in African societies were both altered and reinforced. For men, the loss of African sovereignty meant that their precolonial military role as defenders and raiders was replaced by new roles within the colonial economy as peasant producers or wage-earning workers. Although colonial rule opened up some new opportunities for African women, which enabled them to challenge male dominance in their societies, they were now subject to another level of male control, that of the racist white male colonial official.

≡ **Westernized elite** *Left*: A wedding party in Windhoek, South West Africa, 1926. *Right:* Boy Scouts in the Gold Coast (Ghana), 1937.

In many places, women tried to escape some aspects of traditional patriarchal society, such as arranged marriages, polygamy, or female genital mutilation/cutting, by going to live in colonial towns or at mission stations. In urban areas, African women could live independently and support relatives back home in the rural areas by engaging in the capitalist colonial economy as, for example, street vendors, domestic servants, beer brewers, or sex workers. They could usually not access the regular salaried jobs reserved for African men, such as dock hands, construction workers, railway employees, drivers, general laborers, or mine workers. The exodus of women from rural areas also prompted rural-based male African traditional leaders, within the context of the indirect rule system, to call for intervention by male European colonial officials, who enacted laws that tried to restrict African women's movement to urban areas. In rural reserves immersed in migrant labor, the absence of adult men for long periods meant that women had to do the jobs women had always done plus the work previously done by men. While women continued to perform much of the agricultural work across Africa, men benefited more from the adoption of cash cropping as they took ownership of farming land under individual land tenure, and therefore they became the ones selling produce and collecting the money. Colonialism and Christianity also undermined African women's involvement in entrepreneurship and traditional spirituality, and matrilineal-descent systems practiced in some societies were sidelined. In terms of sexuality, colonial officials imagined Africans to be uniformly heterosexual. British colonial officials, in particular, imposed laws that criminalized same-sex relationships.

Historians have debated the origins of ethnicity in Africa. It is clear that in present-day Africa, ethnic identities and affiliations are very important and have become a principal feature of politics in many countries. Colonial observers considered African people to be members of primordial ethnic groups called "tribes" that possessed inherent and distinct characteristics and were naturally antagonistic to each other. This belief was used to justify colonial rule as imposing peace on people who otherwise would engage in ancient and irrational "tribal warfare." In the postcolonial era, materialist historians began to rethink this assumption and maintained that strong ethnic affiliations and conflicts in Africa were a product of the colonial era. In this view, colonial officials, missionaries, and African elites manipulated ethnic identity as a way to mobilize African people given that the precolonial African states had become irrelevant. Urban areas were crucibles for the prioritization of ethnic identity as people moving there from different rural regions settled in ethnolinguistic neighborhoods where ethnic brokers emerged to advance the interests of their groups within the context of intense competition for jobs, services, and housing. As explained above, the imposition of the indirect rule system also encouraged ethnic loyalties, as different ethnic groups were subject to different conditions and the divide-and-rule strategy of colonial officials meant that some ethnicities were favored and others marginalized. In recent years, however, some scholars have questioned the role of colonial manipulation in emphasizing ethnicity in Africa and have pointed to the fact that Africans possessed ethnic identities related to language and culture before the late nineteenth century and that these affiliations continued to be relevant after colonial conquest.

Popular Culture

New forms of popular culture developed in colonial Africa, usually starting in the growing cities and spreading out to the countryside. This process is well illustrated by the examples of music and sport, but it also involved dance, clothing, theater, and film. One of the most important features in propagating these new cultural expressions, and which made them much more than just local entertainments, was that they were turned into successful businesses within the colonial economy. At the same time, the popularity of new types of music and sports shows that despite the day-to-day hardships that resulted from colonial rule, African people remained inventive and managed to enjoy themselves.

Music

During the colonial era, African people were exposed to numerous new musical influences. Missionaries brought Christian hymns and choirs, colonial police and militaries introduced marching bands with new instruments such as brass horns, and sailors and colonialists imported African-American jazz. During earlier times, specifically the transatlantic slave trade era, elements of African music had been brought to the Americas, where they formed the basis of new African-American styles that were then disseminated back to Africa in the late nineteenth and early twentieth centuries. Merchants in Africa imported and sold instruments like harmonicas, accordions, banjos, and guitars, and eventually gramophones, records, and radios. African people began to incorporate these styles and instruments into their own musical traditions in ways that creatively expressed their new experiences. The styles became popular not just through musicians performing at social events or clubs, but also through the birth of an African music industry with records and radio broadcasts. As such, a series of new African musical styles, including West African highlife, Congolese rumba, and South African jazz, developed and became popular during the colonial era.

The famous **highlife** music of West Africa developed from three sources. The first was "palm wine" music, which, by the late nineteenth century, had spread across coastal West Africa, growing out of the palm wine bars where local musicians mixed with visiting sailors and stevedores, including African-Americans who introduced ragtime, and Liberians who pioneered a special type of two-fingered guitar playing. Originating in ports like Lagos in Nigeria and Accra in the Gold Coast (Ghana), palm wine music spread into the interior of West Africa, where it was Africanized through the use of indigenous languages and local instruments and rhythms. During the 1930s, about 200,000 gramophone records of palm wine music, also called "African Blues," were sold every year in West Africa. The second source of highlife music were the colonial military brass and fife bands that arrived in the conquest era, particularly the musicians of Britain's West Indian Regiment who served in the Gold Coast and Sierra Leone and performed Caribbean calypso music during their off-duty hours. Combining military-style bass drums and bugles with local instruments and singing in vernacular languages, civilian brass bands became popular in the Gold Coast during the 1920s and spread to Nigeria in the 1930s. Representing the third source of highlife, dance orchestras became popular among the coastal elite of West Africa during the early twentieth century and played European and American dance music such as polkas, waltzes, ragtime, tangos, sambas, and rumbas. In the 1920s, Sierra Leone had the Dapa Dan Jazz Band, Nigeria had the Lagos City Orchestra, and the Gold Coast had the Cape Coast Sugar Babies. The term "highlife" was coined in the 1920s in the Gold Coast, where local people began to assemble outside prohibitively expensive clubs from where they heard elite dance bands playing familiar palm wine music. By the 1940s, highlife music had evolved into two types: dance band highlife, which was popular in the cities, and guitar band highlife, which spread to rural areas where smaller groups built on existing expertise with stringed instruments and sang in indigenous language. During the Second World War, the West African dance bands began to play swing music, which was popular with the many visiting British and American servicemen. In the late 1940s and 1950s, a style of highlife that incorporated swing and Caribbean influences was pioneered in Accra, from where it spread to other West African cities. E.T. Mensah, a saxophone player who had entertained American troops in the Gold Coast during the war and then led the influential Tempos Band in the 1950s, became known as the "King of Highlife."

Congolese rumba, or "soukous," which is taken from the French word *secouer* ("to shake"), is another famous genre of African music that emerged during the colonial era. Located on opposite sides of a wide part of the Congo River known as the Malebo Pool, the French colonial city of Brazzaville and the Belgian colonial capital of Leopoldville (Kinshasa) attracted people from across Central Africa who brought various musical styles and traditional instruments with them. In the 1880s and 1890s, colonial explorers, officials, missionaries, and traders imported Western instruments, and in the 1920s migrant workers from countries on the West African coast, such as Dahomey, Sierra Leone, and the Gold Coast, began performing the music that was popular in their home region. Congolese musicians

≡ **"King of Highlife."** Ghanaian musician E.T. Mensah (1919–1996) emerged as a popular entertainer in the 1940s and 1950s. Here he is shown playing in the Netherlands in 1987.

began copying their West African colleagues by hanging out at West African clubs and repeatedly playing imported records. The Congolese musicians replaced English or Spanish lyrics they did not understand with their own Kikongo or Lingala versions and incorporated local methods and instruments such as the almost ubiquitous African thumb piano (called "likembe" or "sanza" in Congo) made from metal keys mounted on a wooden board. During the 1920s, Congolese musicians became the focus for new types of multiethnic dance such as agbaya, which involved a group of men and women dancing in a circle, with each person taking a turn to dance in the center; maringa, which was a partnered dance emphasizing side-to-side hip motion; and kebo, which involved women and girls dancing in single-file and singing. In the 1920s and 1930s, dancehalls that charged admission fees and sold food and drinks were opened in cities and rural areas. European and American dances such as the one-step, foxtrot, waltz, and cakewalk were also popular in the dancehalls, where people gathered to show-off their imported fashionable clothing. Missionaries on both sides of the Congo River disapproved of this interwar-era dance craze, as they saw maringa as too sensual, and dancehalls and dance parties were also places where Africans consumed large quantities of alcohol. In Leopoldville, most dancing happened between 4 p.m. and 7 p.m., as Belgian colonial authorities imposed a nighttime curfew on African residents of the city. The first radio stations were opened in Brazzaville in 1935 and in Leopoldville in 1937, and during the Second World

War, the exiled French and Belgian governments used these sites from which to broadcast radio propaganda to German-occupied Europe. During the 1940s, one Leopoldville radio station erected loudspeakers in the African part of town so that people without radios could listen to the music broadcasts. These early radio stations played records of Latin American dance music such as the rumba, which was already gaining local and international popularity. On both sides of the Congo River, the most popular type of Latin American music was the Cuban "son" (sound), which had familiar transatlantic African roots and which Congolese mistakenly called rumba. Congolese bands singing in French and Lingala began developing their own version of this genre, which became called "Congolese rumba" and which, beginning in the late 1940s, was captured on gramophone records by three Leopoldville recording studios opened by Greek businessmen. These records were distributed across Central Africa and made their way to other parts of Africa and overseas. In the late 1940s and 1950s, the young ferryman, boxer, and singer Antoine Wendo Kolosoy or Papa Wendo, who formed the group Victoria Kin in Leopoldville during the Second World War, became the first big star of Congolese rumba, with radio performances, record deals, and tours in Africa, Europe, and the United States. A rumor that one of Wendo's songs could wake the dead led to his arrest by colonial police and excommunication from the Catholic Church.

South African jazz emerged in the early twentieth century from a variety of influences. While church choirs and military bands introduced new approaches to music, African-American influences were centrally important in the growth of South African jazz. African-American music was first performed in South Africa by the Black crewmembers of a Civil War–era Confederate warship that docked in Cape Town in 1863. It was continued by visiting minstrel shows from the United States, which began with white actors engaging in racist impersonations of African Americans in the mid-1800s but evolved into polished musical performances by African Americans during the late nineteenth and early twentieth centuries. One of the most prominent of these African-American groups was the Virginia Jubilee Singers led by Orpheus McAdoo, who visited Cape Town, Kimberley, and Johannesburg in the 1890s and who were excused from the restrictive and racist pass law regulations as authorities considered them "honourary whites." These American minstrel shows became popular with mixed-race ("Coloured") workers in Cape Town and partly inspired the growth of the city's famous New Year's minstrel festival that began in the early 1900s. During the 1920s, Zulu mineworkers around Johannesburg began combining elements of minstrel performances with traditional Zulu songs and high-kicking dance. In the early twentieth century, African-American missionaries, such as

those of the American Methodist Episcopal (AME) Church, were also important in bringing jazz to South Africa. Listening to New Orleans jazz records
imported from the United States, South African musicians tried to copy African-American performers but also improvised their songs. From the 1920s to
1940s, the growing slums of Johannesburg, where migrant workers from across
the region brought various musical styles and combined them with foreign influences like minstrel shows, were the scene of the emergence of marabi music
and lifestyle. Played in illegal drinking establishments called "shebeens" and
at weekend slum-yard parties, this Black working-class music involved African
songs and rhythms performed with Western instruments. With the further
American influence of post–Second World War "bebop" music, modern South
African jazz developed during the 1950s at a time when the strict racial segregation and oppression of apartheid began to drive Black musicians out of the
country. In the 1940s and 1950s, Sophiatown, one of the oldest Black sections
of Johannesburg, became a center for the development of South African jazz.

≡ **South African Jazz** *Left:* Orpheus McAdoo, in 1900. His Virginia Jubilee Singers was an important influence on the
development of South African jazz. *Right:* First coming to prominence in the jazz musical *King Kong*, South African singer
Miriam Makeba (1932–2008) became an international celebrity in the 1960s. She is shown here in 1980 with trumpeter
Hugh Masekela, known as "the father of South African jazz."

In 1959, the Epistles, a "bebop" jazz band including Cape Town pianist Dollar Brand and trumpeter Hugh Masekela, became the first Black South African band to record an album. That same year, the jazz-inspired musical theater production *King Kong*, which had an all-Black cast including singer Miriam Makeba—whose first solo recording was already successful in the United States—portrayed life in a Black South African township and became a hit in Johannesburg and then played in London. In subsequent decades, Masekela and Makeba would become internationally renowned artists who were also involved in the anti-apartheid struggle.

Sports

Precolonial Africa enjoyed a vibrant sporting culture involving activities such as running, wrestling, dancing, and canoe, horse, or camel racing. However, colonial officials, soldiers, missionaries, and settlers did not appreciate these African sports and imported their own. The first recorded football (soccer) matches in Africa took place among white settlers in South Africa in the 1860s, at a time when soccer and rugby were just beginning to evolve into separate games in Britain. French settlers in Algeria formed football clubs in the 1890s, with the first known soccer game in Nigeria played at an elite colonial school in Calabar in 1904. Belgians working in the Congo began organizing soccer teams in the 1910s. Following the construction of railways from ports into the hinterland, soccer clubs were formed in places like Southern and Northern Rhodesia, Uganda, and the Belgian Congo by the 1920s. Within mission schools, mine compounds, and colonial military and police barracks, sports like soccer, cricket, and sometimes polo were encouraged as they promoted physical fitness and teamwork. Despite the racial segregation that characterized the watching and playing of sport in colonial times, African people became incredibly interested in soccer, with teams and leagues formed across the continent before the Second World War. In the 1920s and 1930s, football leagues became an important element of urban life in colonial Africa, and some teams became rallying points for African urban identities, such as Orlando Pirates in South Africa's Soweto township, Matabeleland Highlanders Football Club in Bulawayo in Southern Rhodesia, and Queens (later Simba) Sports Club in Dar es Salaam, Tanganyika. Football clubs also came to symbolize ethnic-regional identities, such as in contemporary Zimbabwe where the Matabeleland Highlanders of Bulawayo, formed in 1926, represent the Ndebele identity of the west and the Dynamos Football Club of Harare, formed in 1963, represent the Shona ethnicity of the east. Illustrating how various elements of popular culture influenced each other, the name Orlando Pirates was inspired when Soweto residents viewed the 1940 Hollywood pirate movie *The Sea Hawk*. The rise of new sports was related to masculine identity as westernized African elites saw them as a way to display middle-class gentlemanliness and sportsmanship while working-class fans sometimes tried to demonstrate their manhood by engaging in soccer hooliganism. In South Africa, by the 1920s, sports had become racially divided, with soccer seen as a Black working-class interest and rugby and cricket popular among whites.

Local communities, the colonial state, and mission churches contested control of African sport. While Frenchmen and Belgians at the start of the twentieth century played the first football matches in Brazzaville, 11 independent African teams formed into the Native Sports Federation there in 1929. In 1931, the Native Sports Federation, hoping to gain more resources, agreed to be taken over by the French colonial administration, which prompted the Catholic Church, in 1933, to form its own rival sporting organization as a way to attract converts. These organizations greatly popularized football, and in early 1936 some 25 teams participated in a Brazzaville-Leopoldville tournament. However, the state-sponsored Native Sports Federation collapsed in 1937 as African players suspected that they were not getting a fair share of sporting resources paid for by game admission fees and senior players objected to new rules that they play without shoes. This left the Catholic Church largely in control of Brazzaville football, but just after the Second World War, when the expansion of the urban population resulted in an another upsurge in the popularity of football, many players again felt exploited by lack of pay and insurance and broke with the church organization to form independent and popular clubs. These included Diables Noirs (Black Devils—inspired by the Belgian national Red Devils team) in 1950 and Renaissance (renamed L'Etoile or the Star) in 1951, both of which continue to exist as prominent Congolese football clubs.

≡ **African sport.** A 1939 soccer match in Leopoldville, the Belgian Congo.

Timeline

1800 1888—Native Baptist Church established in Lagos, Nigeria

1892—Ethiopian Church established in South Africa

1900 1904—First known football (soccer) match played in Nigeria

1913–14—Journey of Prophet Harris in West Africa

1921—Simon Kimbangu imprisoned in the Belgian Congo

1924—Zion Christian Church founded in South Africa

1926—Formation of Matabeleland Highlanders football club in Southern Rhodesia (Zimbabwe)

1931—Formation of Native Sports Federation in Brazzaville

1935—First radio station opened in Brazzaville

1937—First radio station opened in Leopoldville

1937—Independent Watch Tower movements established in Nyasaland (Malawi) and Northern Rhodesia (Zambia)

1940—Formation of Orlando Pirates football club in South Africa

Late 1940s—Recording industry begins in Leopoldville

1950–51—Formation of Diables Noir and Renaissance football clubs in Brazzaville

1959—Musical *King Kong* opens in South Africa

Conclusion

Many of the most prominent features of contemporary African society and culture were profoundly shaped by the colonial experience. This was the era in which Africa became sharply divided between predominantly Muslim and predominantly Christian regions. A new westernized African elite emerged from the mission schools, and people moved from rural areas to colonial cities where they found new ways of life. People began to think of themselves primarily as belonging to broad ethno-regional identities and associated less with narrow affiliations that had been more relevant in precolonial times. The colonial economy led to changing gender roles, and women explored opportunities to escape aspects of male-dominated societies. A new popular culture emerged that had transatlantic influences but was still distinctly African. New musical styles combined imported and domestic elements, including American influences that were originally African, and were popularized through nightclubs, dance crazes, a recording industry and radio broadcasts. While a number of European sports were brought to Africa by colonialists and missionaries, football (soccer) became wildly successful across the continent before the Second World War.

KEY TERMS

African westernized elite 388

Congolese rumba 392

Ethiopian churches 384

highlife 392

madrasas 387

polygamy 383

Prophet Harris 385

Simon Kimbangu 385

South African jazz 394

syncretism 382

Zionist churches 385

STUDY QUESTIONS

1. What explains the sudden success of Christian missionary efforts in Africa in the early twentieth century? Why did independent churches become popular during this same period? Why did Islam attract many new adherents even though colonial rulers were generally Christian?

2. What new social classes developed under colonial rule? What are the main outlines of the historical debate concerning the origins of the concept of "ethnicity" in Africa?

3. How did colonial-era African music develop? Why did soccer appeal to many Africans?

Please see page FR-8 for the Further Readings for this chapter.
For additional digital learning resources please go to
https://www.oup.com/he/falola-stapleton1e

New Forms of Protest between the World Wars, 1919–1939

The rise of colonial economies and subsequent social change influenced the growth of new forms of African protest against colonialism. While African military resistance to colonial rule never completely ended, armed insurgency became less frequent between the two world wars, which is also called the **interwar period**. During the 1920s and 1930s, African people adopted new aims, ideologies, and methods to deal with grievances created by colonial rule. Within this context, most protest was geared toward advancing African interests within the existing colonial system rather than overthrowing it and re-establishing independent states. At the same time, these new protest movements, influenced by ideas from abroad and changing international developments, gradually became more radical and anti-colonial. Their pleas for human rights and self-governance were ignored by stubborn colonial regimes.

Armed Resistance

A series of violent rebellions against colonial rule took place during the First World War, when the colonial rulers demanded that African communities provide more manpower and resources for the war effort yet sent soldiers and police, those who enforced colonial occupation, away to the theaters of fighting. The uprisings that took place in South Africa, Nyasaland (Malawi), the Gold Coast (Ghana), Nigeria, Mozambique, Angola, and French West Africa during the First World War will be discussed in Chapter 20. The colonial suppression of these movements did not end armed resistance, which, in a few places, continued into the 1920s and 1930s. The new technologies of motor vehicles and aircraft were central in colonial military success in these conflicts. In 1920, the British in Somaliland used airplanes to bomb the strongholds of Muslim Somali rebel leader Sayyid Mohammed Abdullah Hassan, whom the British called the "Mad Mullah." This ended 20 years of resistance to colonial rule in the territory and inspired British official plans to use airpower as a cheap and efficient way to control their

Rural protesters. A group of women from Aba, Nigeria, c. 1930. In the Women's War of 1929, women such as these protested the colonial imposition of male warrant chiefs and new direct taxation that undermined women's roles in local government and entrepreneurship.

401

empire. During the 1920s in Morocco, the Spanish military fought the followers of Abd el-Karim el-Khattabi, who had created an Islamist state in the Rif Mountains. By 1927, combined Spanish and French offensives had defeated the Rif rebels. While the French had governed only what they considered the economically useful parts of Morocco, in the early 1930s they fought a grueling military campaign to take control of the Atlas Mountains and environs from Berber rebels who had controlled these areas for many years. This military effort had been prompted by rising tensions in Europe, which made the French government eager to decisively end resistance in Morocco so that colonial occupation troops could be transferred to defend France from a resurgent Germany. Within France, left-wing activists protested these military operations. Italy's fascist regime of Benito Mussolini began to extend its control of Libya during the 1920s from the coast, which it had occupied in 1911, to the interior, which led to tenacious guerrilla resistance by Sanusi (or Senussi) Arab communities. The Italians employed extreme measures to end this resistance. They constructed a 185-mile barbed wire fence along the Egyptian border to cut off the insurgent supply route, used motor vehicles and airplanes to hunt down the rebels, imprisoned almost the entire civilian population of eastern Libya in concentration camps, destroyed livestock and settlements, and massacred thousands of people. Resistance concluded in 1931 when captured rebel leader Omar Mukhtar, after a 30-minute trial, was hanged in front of a crowd of 20,000 camp inmates.

In the late 1920s and early 1930s in French Equatorial Africa, in what is now eastern Cameroon and western Central African Republic, people refused to pay

≡ **Resistance fighters** *Left:* Sanusi followers of Omar Mukhtar march in resistance to Italian rule near Libya's border with Egypt, 1915. *Right:* Emperor Haile Selassie, astride a mule and shaded by a parasol, leads resistance fighters during the Second Italo-Ethiopian War (1935–36.)

taxes and perform unpaid labor on the construction of a colonial railway. The rebels were encouraged by the prophet Barka Ngainoumbey, called Karnu, meaning "roller up of earth," who gave out magical hoe handles that were supposed to offer protection from French bullets. During this "War of the Hoe Handles," the French colonial army pursued a scorched earth campaign, herded people into prison camps, and smoked rebels out of caves so they could be machine-gunned in the open. Barka Ngainoumbey was killed during a French attack on his village and his corpse was displayed around the territory as proof that his magic did not work.

Seeking revenge for Italy's defeat at the 1896 Battle of Adwa and intent on expanding its empire in the Horn of Africa, the Mussolini regime invaded independent Ethiopia in 1935–36 in the **Second Italo-Ethiopian War**. Although the Ethiopian army could muster hundreds of thousands of men, it was poorly equipped by the standards of the 1930s and was supported by just a dozen airplanes with only four pilots and a few obsolete armored vehicles. The Italian colonial army in East Africa comprised around half a million troops, mostly locally recruited Eritreans and Somalis, and they were augmented by 600 aircraft and 800 tanks. Although the Ethiopians put up stubborn resistance, the Italian air force ignited the Ethiopian countryside with incendiary bombs and dropped poison gas on Ethiopian soldiers and civilians. The League of Nations imposed ineffective sanctions of Italy, and these were withdrawn just days after fugitive Ethiopian Emperor Haile Selassie addressed the organization in Geneva. European Great Power politics worked against Ethiopia. Although Nazi Germany had supplied weapons and ammunition to Ethiopia during the war in order to keep Italy distracted from Hitler's occupation of Austria, France and Britain tolerated Italy's invasion of Ethiopia out of fear of pushing Rome closer to Berlin. Subsequently, Mussolini added Ethiopia to Italy's East African empire and quickly made an alliance with Nazi Germany, and eventually militarist Japan, that would lead to the Second World War. The Italian conquest of Ethiopia, a country that had become a symbol of African hope due to its status as one of the last two independent African nations, outraged emergent nationalist leaders on the continent and African-American leaders in the diaspora. To some extent, it contributed to the increasing militancy of the new types of African protest that surfaced in the 1920s and 1930s.

New Ideas: Pan-Africanism and Communism

During the interwar period, new ideologies from outside Africa began to gain traction among African people. Emerging among African Americans in reaction to racist oppression, Pan-Africanism advanced the goals of uniting all people of

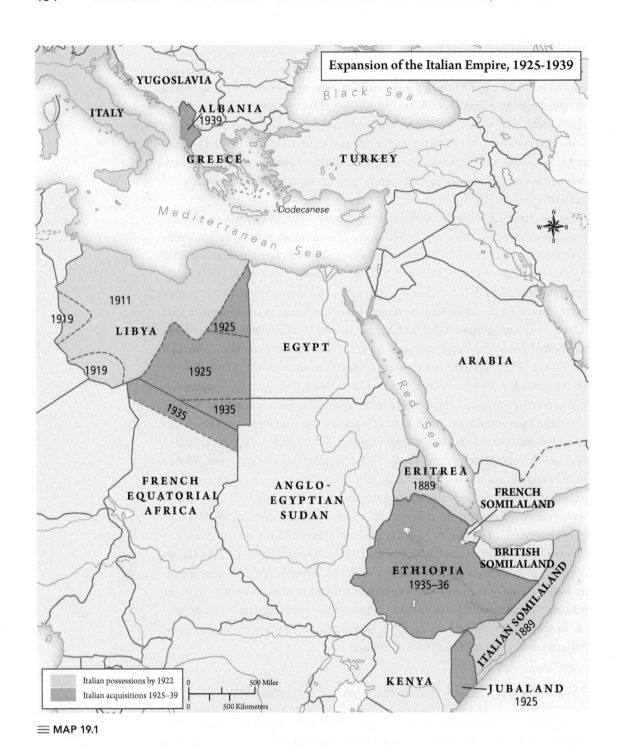

Expansion of the Italian Empire, 1925-1939

≡ MAP 19.1

African descent and having African Americans return to their ancestral home in Africa. A pioneer of this ideology was **Edward Wilmot Blyden**, who was born in the Caribbean, lived briefly in the United States, and became a journalist and educator in Liberia and Sierra Leone in the late nineteenth and early twentieth centuries. Inspired by the Zionist movement, which advocated the creation of a Jewish homeland, Blyden's writings encouraged African Americans to resettle in Africa, and later he maintained that Islam was more authentically African than Christianity, which had been imported by Western missionaries. In the early twentieth century, American academic and civil rights activist W.E.B. du Bois, who was a co-founder of the National Association for the Advancement of Colored People (NAACP) in 1909, and Jamaican journalist and activist Marcus Garvey, who lived in the United States during the 1910s and 1920s, further developed and popularized **Pan-Africanism**. Another important figure in the history of Pan-Africanism was Dusé Mohamed Ali, an Egyptian-born actor and playwright in London, who founded the newspaper *African Times and Orient Review* in 1912. Held in London in 1900, the First Pan-African Conference urged European powers and the United States to respect the sovereignty of the Black-ruled states of Ethiopia, Liberia, and Haiti, and petitioned the British government to investigate racial discrimination and exploitation in white-minority dominated South Africa and Southern Rhodesia. A series of **Pan-African Congresses** was held between the world wars. The 1919 Congress was held in Paris and mainly lobbied the **Versailles Peace Conference**, a meeting of the victorious powers of the First World War, to grant African colonies internal self-government, and the 1921 Congress in London sharply criticized the British Empire for its abuse of African people. Attending the 1921 Congress, Senegalese politician and member of the French government Blaise Diagne (see Chapter 17) objected to what he considered overly radical statements, and he subsequently broke with the Pan-African movement to pursue African equality within the context of French citizenship. Other Pan-African congresses were held in London in 1923 and New York City in 1927, none were held during the 1930s, and they continued after the Second World War. While delegates at the first few Pan-Africanist meetings were primarily from the Americas, there was increasing African participation and interest over the years.

Marcus Garvey's variant of Pan-Africanism, called **Garveyism**, became a more radical Black Nationalist movement and advocated the expulsion of Europeans from Africa. Although Du Bois and other Pan-Africanist leaders criticized Garvey's Black separatism as surrendering to white supremacy and endangering the

PAN-AFRICANISM

Top left: Born in the Caribbean, Edward Wilmot Blyden (1832–1912) became an educator and journalist in West Africa and a founder of the Pan-African ideology. *Top right:* American academic, writer, editor, and civil rights activist W.E.B. du Bois (1868–1963), who co-founded the National Association for the Advancement of Colored People (NAACP) in 1909. *Bottom left:* Born in Jamaica, Marcus Garvey (1887–1940) was an African-American journalist and pioneer of a radical stream of Pan-Africanism. *Bottom right:* Dusé Mohamed Ali (1866–1945), an Egyptian-born actor and playwright, who founded the newspaper *African Times and Orient Review* in London, 1912.

movement for equal rights in the United States, it became attractive to many Africans living under colonial rule and so gravely worried European colonial officials. During the 1920s, copies of Garvey's *Negro World* newspaper, founded in New York in 1918 and circulated by Garvey's Black Star shipping line, were being read in West and Southern Africa, and in 1920 a branch of Garvey's **Universal Negro Improvement Association** (UNIA) was founded in Lagos, Nigeria. Colonial officials in Africa were horrified by Garveyism. In 1922, colonial regimes in French West Africa, and the British territories like the Gambia, Nigeria, the Gold Coast, and Nyasaland banned the *Negro World* newspaper. In Senegal, UNIA organizers, many of whom came from Freetown in Sierra Leone, were harassed and constantly watched by French authorities. Although Garvey's movement organized African-American settlement in the "Black republic" of Liberia and planned to lease land there for an agricultural project, the Liberian government broke with Garvey in 1924 after Firestone Corporation agreed to open a massive rubber plantation in the country. Although Garveyism waned in the Americas after the 1925 imprisonment of its founder in the United States, the broad ideals of the movement continued to resonate in colonial Africa.

During the colonial era Africans also became aware of the ideologies of **socialism**, which advocated for public ownership of economic assets, and **communism**, which sought to establish a classless and stateless society along the lines advocated by nineteenth-century German philosopher Karl Marx. With the Bolshevik Revolution of 1917, these principles were seemingly being put into practice in the newly formed Soviet Union and spread by an international communist movement that was strongly anti-imperialist. The Communist Party of South Africa (CPSA) was established in 1921 to pursue white working-class interests, but during the mid-1920s it shifted its aim to creating a nonracial South Africa, and by the end of the decade most party members were Black. In 1927, the South African trade unionist and CPSA leader James La Guma and African National Congress activist Josiah Gumede attended the first conference of the communist-initiated League against Imperialism in Brussels, Belgium, and then visited the Soviet Union, where they participated in the tenth-anniversary celebrations of the revolution. Although Gumede had been critical of communism a few years earlier, he returned to South Africa claiming that racism did not exist in the Soviet Union. During the early 1930s, several Black South African leaders of the CPSA, such as Moses Kotane and Albert Nzula, studied communism in the Soviet Union. However, during the Second World War, the Soviet Union softened its anti-colonial stance and reduced its role in the international communist movement as it had allied with the imperial powers Britain and France against Nazi Germany.

Elite Associations

The small number of westernized Africans, mostly graduates of missionary schools and including some who had studied overseas, began to form elite associations to pursue their goals, which usually involved expanding African access to Western education, opening up higher paying and more prestigious jobs for Africans, and moderately opposing racist and oppressive colonial policies. Organized along Western-style constitutional lines, these groups pursued their agenda through restrained measures such as holding meetings, publishing newspapers, and sending letters and petitions to the colonial governments. When these methods failed to convince local colonial officials, the elite associations would sometimes send deputations to Europe to appeal directly to the imperial government. The first elite organizations were based on narrow ethnic and regional affiliations, but often they eventually merged into colony-wide or national groups. All the while, and despite repeated disappointments, the African members of these associations saw themselves as good imperial citizens, and they usually remained steadfastly loyal to the colonial government. For example, the South African Native National Congress (SANNC—later renamed the African National Congress), formed in 1912 as South Africa's first nation-wide African political group and aimed at opposing white minority rule in the new country, patriotically suspended its protest against the newly passed and highly discriminatory Natives Land Act during the First World War. This loyalty was not rewarded, and after the war racial oppression intensified in South Africa. By the end of the 1930s, given the influence of Pan-Africanism and anger over the Italian conquest of Ethiopia, the demands of some elite associations had become more stridently anti-colonial and their leaders began to express desires for African independence that would develop more fully and gain increased popular support after the Second World War.

There were many examples of elite associations across colonial Africa, and with more being established in the British colonies, where there tended to be greater access to Western education. This was particularly the case in the coastal parts of British West Africa, which had long been the scene of missionary endeavors. As early as the late nineteenth century, mission-educated African elites in places like the Gold Coast (Ghana) and Sierra Leone became frustrated that the British administration seemed to be moving away from involving westernized Africans in local governance and toward the system of indirect rule through African traditional leaders. One of the first such elite organizations in West Africa was the Gold Coast Aborigines Rights Protection Society (GCARPS), which was formed in 1897 and was successful in convincing the British government to cancel proposed legislation that would jeopardize African land ownership in the southern part of the Gold Coast. Named after the older Aborigines Protection Society in Britain, the GCARPS was inspired by the new Pan-Africanist movement in the Americas and by reports of recent anti-colonial military achievements such as Ethiopia's 1896 defeat of Italy and Japan's 1905 defeat of Russia. **Joseph E. Casely Hayford**, a teacher, lawyer, and journalist, was among the founders of the GCARPS and was then central in creating a new regional West African political grouping. The **National Congress of British West Africa** (NCBWA) was formed in Accra, Gold Coast, in 1917, with representatives from the Gold Coast, Nigeria, Sierra Leone, and the Gambia. With a regional vision, its westernized elite members wanted to move away from the dominance of traditional leaders under the indirect rule system to a more British-style and democratic representative administrative. The NCBWA also advocated for freedom of the press, the establishment of cooperative economic projects, the expulsion of Middle Eastern merchants from the region, and the creation of a West African university. Branches of the NCBWA were established in Accra, Bathurst, Freetown, and Lagos, and in 1920 it sent a small delegation to London to present its objectives to the British government but the secretary of state for the colonies would not meet with them as the governors of West Africa had deemed the organization unrepresentative of the broader West African population. During the 1920s the NCBWA competed for members with Garvey's more radical UNIA from the United States. In this competition, the NCBWA stressed that it was a pro-British organization seeking not African independence but greater indigenous representation in the colonial government. While the regional NCBWA declined during the 1920s and did not last long after Casely Hayford's death in 1930, the territorial branches remained active into the 1930s. From that point, the Western-style political associations in the four British West African territories developed separately.

≡ **Elite Association.** Members of the Gold Coast Aborigines Rights Protection Society meet with the Prince of Wales in 1925.

In Sierra Leone, in 1924, the NCBWA branch in Freetown and the slightly newer Committee of Educated Aborigines (CEA) in the interior were influential in convincing the colonial state to establish a legislative council. The new and mostly advisory body would be composed of some representatives elected by the educated and business elite of Freetown, and traditional leaders from the interior. Several prominent NCBWA leaders were elected to the new legislative council. These were Edinburgh-trained medical doctor Herbert Bankole-Bright, who had launched the *Aurora* newspaper in 1918, and London-educated lawyer Ernest Beoku-Betts, who also served as mayor of Freetown in 1925–26. Within the council, the elected African members criticized the colonial state for increasing the salaries of European civil servants and for the low pay and slow rate of promotion for their African counterparts. Bankole-Bright and Beoku-Betts dominated African elite politics in Sierra Leone during the 1920s and early 1930s.

In Nigeria, elite associations emerged around the bustling port city of Lagos. Although the Lagos branch of the NCBWA immediately became dysfunctional due to internal squabbles and a hostile governor who saw it as unrepresentative of the African majority, its ideas and some of its members were influential in founding other Western-style political groups in Nigeria. In 1923, the Nigerian National Democratic Party (NNDP), Nigeria's first political party, was formed and dominated elections for the Lagos legislative council until the late 1930s. The NNDP advocated for greater democracy in Nigeria as well as for more social, educational, and economic development in which Nigerians could participate. The founding leader of the NNDP was Herbert Macaulay, who was the originator of the Nigerian *Daily News* and who was a grandson of the famous Bishop Samuel Ajayi Crowther, who had translated the Bible into Yoruba and became the first bishop of the Niger Delta in the nineteenth century. Macaulay criticized the British colonial administration for taxing Nigerians without giving them representation in government. The NNDP was eventually eclipsed by the more radical **Nigerian Youth Movement** (NYM), which was formed in 1934 to advocate for higher levels of education. By the late 1930s, it was working toward the independence of Nigeria within the British Empire. Several key leaders of the NYM had studied abroad, such as Eyo Ito and Nnamdi Azikiwe, both of whom had gone to the United States, and Adeyemo Alakija and H.O. Davis, who had spent time in Britain. They introduced Pan-Africanism to Nigerian elite politics. As discussed in Chapter 21, Azikiwe would go on to play a central role in Nigerian nationalism and decolonization after the Second World War and became independent Nigeria's first governor-general and then president in the early 1960s.

Colonial Kenya serves as a good example of the historical trajectory and some of the problems of African elite associations in the interwar years. The colonial city of Nairobi became the center of the emerging Kenyan political movement. Nairobi was located in the heartland of the Kikuyu people, who had experienced greater access to missionary education than other Kenyan ethnic groups but who had also lost more of their land to white settlers. Formed around 1920, the first Western-style political group in Kenya was the Kikuyu Association, but in 1921 the failure of its conservative leaders to confront the colonial government over a reduction in the wages of African workers promoted a split in the movement. A telephone operator called Harry Thuku and others formed the Young Kikuyu Association (KYA) to more ambitiously engage the colonial state. Finding the Kikuyu ethnic label too narrow and wishing to address the problems of all Kenya's African people, the KYA changed its name to the East Africa Association (EAA) and sought to protect existing African land ownership and oppose settler domination. Though it was Kenya's first multiethnic African political organization, the core of EAA membership remained Kikuyu. Women were prominent in this movement.

In March 1922, the arrest of Thuku prompted a crowd of Kenyan women to protest at the Nairobi police station where he was being detained, and security forces fired on them, killing at least 21 including prominent women's rights activist Mary Muthoni Nyanjiru. The EAA declined after Thuku's exile to Italian Somaliland.

Formed in the mid-1920s, the Kikuyu Central Association (KCA) took up the same struggle, with **Jomo Kenyatta** becoming its general secretary in 1927 and Thuku becoming president after he was released in 1931. Kenyatta became the founding editor of the KCA newspaper *Muiguithania* (the Reconciler), which was Kenya's first African nationalist publication. From 1929 to 1932, the KCA gained prominence by opposing an ultimately unsuccessful campaign by Christian missionaries to have the colonial government outlaw the Kikuyu traditional initiation through **female genital modification** (FGM). While white female missionaries led the struggle against what they saw as barbaric mutilation, disgruntled

≡ **Victim of protest.** An American missionary in early-twentieth-century Kenya, Hulda Stumpf (bottom left) was murdered in 1930 amid the controversy over female genital modification (FGM).

Kenyan female Christians left the mission churches and organized protest gatherings where they sang songs ridiculing the missionaries. During the crisis, American female missionary Hulda Stumpf, an opponent of FGM, was murdered and her genitalia mutilated. Though much remains unknown about the murder and Kenyan women's thoughts on the FGM controversy, historians see the event as sharpening protest against colonial rule in Kenya.

Living and studying in London from 1931 to 1946, Kenyatta was strongly influenced by Caribbean Pan-Africanist and communist George Padmore, and both men travelled together to the Soviet Union in 1933. Incensed by the 1935–36 Italian conquest of Ethiopia, Kenyatta gave anti-colonial lectures throughout Britain and helped form a Pan-Africanist group called the International African Service Bureau. With the outbreak of the Second World War, the KCA was banned in 1940, but two years later a more radical group called the Kenya African Union (KAU), which demanded independence, was formed and Kenyatta became its president when he returned home. At the same time, another ethnic-regional political movement was taking shape. During the 1930s and 1940s, Luo labor migrants from western Kenya who were working in other parts of the country such as Nairobi formed the Luo Union. The group's main aims were to organize the transportation of the bodies of dead Luo back to their home area for burial, which was culturally very important, and to promote education and unity among their ethnic group. The leadership of the Luo Union came from the mission-educated elite, including **Oginga Odinga**, who taught at a mission school. After the Second World War, and within the context of violent anti-colonial insurgency in the 1950s, Kenyan politics would become polarized between Kikuyu and Luo movements and leaders. After independence, Jomo Kenyatta became president of Kenya and Oginga Odinga became a leading critic of his regime, and years later their sons, respectively Uhuru Kenyatta and Raila Odinga, repeated the same roles.

≡ **Luo leader.** A Kenyan teacher and traditional leader, Oginga Odinga (1911–1994) was active in Luo politics in the 1940s and in Kenya's independence movement in the 1950s. He became a political opposition leader after independence.

The interwar-era African elite associations of Southern Africa shared similar trends. In Southern Rhodesia (Zimbabwe), the Southern Rhodesia Native Association (SRNA) was created in 1919 and based itself around the city of Salisbury and the Shona ethnic group of that eastern region, while the Rhodesia Bantu Voters Association (RBVA) was launched in 1923 and focused on the city of Bulawayo and the Ndebele ethnicity of that area. Dominated by African westernized elites, both groups represented the tiny number of Black voters in the white-minority-ruled territory, and they advocated for an expansion of the qualified franchise and removal of various types of racial discrimination. In 1925, the RBVA, which was slightly more radical than its counterpart, demanded the state provide free and compulsory education for African children. While this policy was implemented for white children in the 1930s, the fact that education formed one of the qualifications for voting meant that the settler state did not want to expand the educated African elite and claimed that it would be too expensive to extend this measure to the Black majority. As discussed below, the rise of the more radical and mass-based African trade union movement in Southern Rhodesia in the 1920s greatly challenged these narrow and conservative elite groups.

Most of French colonial Africa did not experience the same growth of African protest politics during the interwar era as in the British territories. In France, during the 1920s, a few westernized Africans, like Lamine Senghor from Senegal and Tiemoko Garan Kouyaté from what is now Mali, worked with left-wing French political activists in protesting colonial rule, but their impact back home was minimal. Given a lack of educational facilities, most French territories had a tiny number of westernized Africans and the French colonial state was much less tolerant of African political organizations and newspapers. In the exceptional Four Communes of Senegal, assimilated African politicians worked in the political context of France. In the 1920s and 1930s, Blaise Diagne, who defended French forced labor in Africa to the International Labour Organization (ILO), dominated these compliant francophone West African elites. However, in French-ruled Cameroon and Madagascar, African movements demanded independence during the interwar era, doing this before their counterparts in the British colonies.

Initially a German colony, Cameroon was taken over by France after the First World War and ruled as a League of Nations mandate. In 1929, leaders of Cameroon's Duala community sent two petitions to the League of Nations. The first petition asked that the League intervene in a land dispute that the Dualas were having with the French colonial administration. The second, which was more radical, requested that the League remove the French mandate and appoint a League administration that would prepare Cameroon for independence. The Duala community was unusual in that it had a high level of Western education, and as such many of its members worked as junior civil servants in the French administration and many Duala were also economically successful as they owned cocoa and palm oil plantations. Duala leaders believed that the 1884 treaty that had brought them under German colonial rule during the Scramble had expired when the Germans were evicted and that no new agreement had been entered into, which meant that the French presence was illegitimate. In addition, the Duala understood that there was a legal difference between a colony and a League of Nations mandate, which was technically meant to be prepared for independence. In 1931, French police fired on a large demonstration by Cameroonian women protesting the extension of colonial taxation to women and children. This resulted in more complaints to the League of Nations. Although these petitions did not change the nature of French rule in Cameroon, they articulated a desire for African independence that would be realized after the Second World War.

Protest politics in Madagascar was the most radical of Africa's interwar period. During 1919–20, some Malagasy living in Paris, many of whom had recently fought in the French army during the First World War, formed an association that campaigned for the granting of French citizenship to all Malagasy without the usual conditions that were part of the French assimilationist system. This did not happen as granting full civil rights to all the people of Madagascar would have ended forced labor and other forms of economic exploitation on the island. **Jean Ralaimongo**, a teacher and war veteran, and other members of the Paris-based Malagasy group returned to Madagascar, and in 1927 they launched an anticolonial newspaper called *L'Opinion*, which criticized French policies on forced labor and land ownership. Ralaimongo was arrested along with other activists, but he continued to write newspaper pieces from prison. In 1929, his newspaper published a petition demanding full French citizenship for all Malagasy people. This led to a large public gathering in Tananarive (Antananarivo), the capital, where a similar pronouncement was made and there were demands that Malagasy representatives join the French government in Paris. Subsequent public demonstrations were banned. In 1931, Malagasy nationalist leaders like Ralaimongo, though now banished to remote communities, began to demand freedom and independence. The French colonial rulers responded with more repression.

Organized Labor

In the 1920s and 1930s, the international labor movement spread to colonial Africa. The basic idea was that workers, united by their common interests, would band together in unions to negotiate with their employers for better working conditions such as increased salaries and benefits. In this process, the power of workers rested in their ability to stage strikes in which they would refuse to work and therefore shutdown their industry. During the interwar years, foreign union organizers, including from Britain, travelled to parts of colonial Africa to advise workers on how to form a labor movement. As in Europe and North America at this time, trade unionism in colonial Africa was fiercely and often violently opposed by the state and business. Unions particularly worried colonial officials in Africa given the potential of working-class consciousness to smooth over the ethnic divisions that were exploited by colonial rule.

The first trade union in Southern Africa was formed among Black and mixed-race dockworkers in Cape Town in 1919. Called the Industrial and Commercial Workers' Union of Africa (ICU), it was led by **Clements Kadalie**, who was originally from Nyasaland (Malawi), and was involved in an unsuccessful Cape Town dockworkers' strike in the same year. During the 1920s, the ICU expanded to include workers in other economic sectors and it spread across South Africa and to neighboring territories such as South West Africa (Namibia), Southern Rhodesia (Zimbabwe), and Northern Rhodesia (Zambia). However, it struggled to organize the region's mineworkers because of the closed and controlling nature of the mine compound system. The ICU was much more radical than the region's African elite associations, such as the SANNC, and gained more support from African working-class people. The union wanted the elimination of the **pass laws** in South Africa, which required Africans to carry identity documents endorsed by employers and which represented the method by which the migrant labor system controlled and exploited African workers. By the late 1920s, the ICU collapsed due to financial problems, internal conflicts between communists and followers of Garveyism, and state repression.

≡ **Labor leader.** Clements Kadalie (1896–1951—second from right) was the leader of the Industrial and Commercial Workers Union (ICU) in South Africa during the 1920s.

In Northern Rhodesia, the Copperbelt Strike of 1935, during which the police killed six protestors, was prompted by the sudden implementation of a new tax that reinforced the migrant labor system. African miners also felt aggrieved by making less money than their European colleagues, being barred from high-paying jobs, and suffering workplace harassment. This event marked the first labor action and the first serious incident of anti-colonial protest in Northern Rhodesia after the conquest period. Although the workers' demands were not met, the strike resulted in some colonial reforms, including the government paying for the healthcare of mineworkers' relatives and the beginning of a transition from migrant to permanent labor in the copper mines. Furthermore, since the Watch Tower Movement was partly blamed for inciting the strike, Protestant missionaries encouraged by the mine industry focused their spiritual and educational efforts on the Copperbelt to woo African workers away from independent churches. Colonial and mine officials also suspected that Beni dance societies that mimicked military drills and became popular in Southern and Central African mine compounds after the First World War were behind the 1935 strike. While later nationalist historians took up this view, portraying Beni societies as embryonic nationalist movements, the official investigation into the labor action dismissed these claims, and there is little evidence that they did much to mobilize African workers in the same way as trade unions. In 1940, the Copperbelt's white miners went on strike and were successful in gaining increased pay and an agreement that lower-paid Black workers would not be allowed to take their jobs. Later the same year, African mine workers went on strike demanding a pay raise, but the military was sent to force them back to work, and just over a dozen strikers were killed. Because of the increased production needed for the Second World War, the colonial state convinced the mine owners to increase wages for African workers and there was a gradual phasing out of the racial restrictions on higher paid jobs.

A labor movement also developed in British West Africa. In 1919, railway workers in Freetown, Sierra Leone, went on strike to protest significant rises in food prices and the delay in pay to government workers. In the context of increasing unemployment, the strike ignited popular attacks on Syrian merchants, who were blamed for the price increases, and their property across the territory. Within a few days, police and military units suppressed the disturbance and the railway strikers returned to work. In 1925, the Railway Workers' Union was formed in Freetown, and in January of the next year it staged another strike over the requirement that Black railway employees had to take special tests while white ones did not. The strikers inspired popular support among the people of

Freetown, who collected money for them. However, the colonial governor once again used the military to crush the strike, and many strikers were dismissed or had their salaries cut, and the union was outlawed. Since prominent legislative council members Bankole-Bright and Beoku-Betts had supported the strike, the British governor took revenge on the educated African elite by scrapping the Freetown city council.

African civil servants formed the first labor union in Nigeria in 1912, and the Nigerian Teachers' Union and Railway Workers' Union were established in 1931. Some early strikes in Nigeria were successful, such as a 1921 labor action by railway mechanics and a 1929 strike by coal industry workers, which both prevented planned wage reductions. At the start of the 1930s, **I.T.A. Wallace-Johnson**, a former clerk and sailor from Freetown who was influenced by communism and Pan-Africanism, became active in promoting the emerging trade union movement in Nigeria. In 1930, he traveled to Hamburg, Germany, to attend the International Trade Union Conference of Negro Workers, which had been organized by the Soviet-sponsored Communist International (Comintern). Wallace-Johnson then began to write for the *Negro Worker*, a journal established by the Hamburg conference that encouraged Black workers to become more proactive and that was banned by colonial administrations in Africa. In 1933, Wallace-Johnson visited Moscow to attend another international labor conference, where he interacted with George Padmore and Jomo Kenyatta who were also visiting the Soviet Union at the time. Deported from Nigeria because of his trade union activities, Wallace-Johnson moved to the Gold Coast, where, in 1935, he established the West African Youth League (WAYL), which pressed for colonial representation in the British government and campaigned for improved safety conditions and salaries for African workers. He was convicted of sedition for a newspaper article he wrote that condemned Christianity and imperialism, but he travelled to Britain and appealed to the Privy Council, which overturned the ruling. Back in the Gold Coast, the WAYL dissolved due to its leader's absence and the fact that high cocoa prices

≡ **Union organizer.** I.T.A. Wallace-Johnson (1894–1965)—West African workers' leader, journalist, activist, and politician.

in the mid-1930s made the organization less attractive to cocoa farmers. In 1938, Wallace-Johnson returned to Sierra Leone, where he founded another branch of the WAYL, which became instrumental in creating unions among government employees, seamen, and diamond miners. In Sierra Leone, the WAYL quickly expanded to 30,000 members. It was the first Western-style political group in West Africa to fully include women, such as **Constance Agatha Cummings-John**, who had studied in both Britain and the United States and who successfully ran as a WAYL candidate in the 1938 Freetown municipal council election. Indeed, the rise of the WAYL, which attempted to bridge the gap between African elites and workers, deposed the more conservative and elitist NCBWA of Bankole-Bright from its dominant position in Sierra Leone politics. The WAYL collapsed during the Second World War as Wallace-Johnson and other leaders were imprisoned for sedition.

Rural Protest

Several types of rural protest took place in colonial Africa during the interwar period. Many of these happened in 1929 and during the early 1930s as the onset of the Great Depression reduced prices gained from sales of cash crops. In 1924, and again in 1930–31, cocoa farmers in the Gold Coast organized themselves and refused to sell their products in objection to the low prices they were being offered by overseas buyers. These boycotts were undermined when poorer cocoa producers broke ranks when offered slightly more money for their product. The most serious attempt to hold up cocoa supplies took place in 1937–38, and though it was supplemented by an African boycott on the purchase of imported European goods, it had little impact on prices. These events prompted the colonial regime to set up a marketing board that would buy all cocoa at a set price and then sell it on to international buyers. The situation with cocoa farming in Nigeria was very different. In southwest Nigeria, where there was considerable anti-tax protest during the First World War, cocoa farmers formed cooperative societies during the interwar period and the colonial government supported these since they focused on increasing production and creating financial self-sufficiency. Members of a cooperative could vote on its activities and take out loans from the society's account to make agricultural improvements. These societies were successful, and by the late 1940s they had spread across all of Nigeria.

Some rural protests turned violent. The **Women's War of 1929**, a violent uprising by Igbo rural women in southeastern Nigeria, was inspired by the fact that the colonial imposition of male warrant chiefs and new direct taxation had undermined women's roles in local government and entrepreneurship. These riots built on the traditional practice of "sitting on a man," whereby women punished a man who they thought had committed an injustice by surrounding his house, singing and dancing, and harassing him. In 1929, female protestors took this action a step further by attacking the homes of warrant chiefs (some of whom resigned), blocking roads, and disrupting markets. In suppressing the protest, colonial security forces killed about 55 women. A colonial commission did implement some colonial reforms in response to the disturbances, including more involvement of women in local administration, but people in southeastern Nigeria continued to resist tax collection throughout the 1930s.

In the Belgian Congo, the Pende people of the Kwilu area rose up against colonial rule in 1931. It appears that they were not trying to re-establish sovereignty but were reacting against a series of grievances, including coercive labor recruitment, forceful extraction of agricultural products, falling prices for their products and rising colonial taxes, forced resettlement of communities in the name of combating sleeping sickness, and sexual abuse by colonial officials. Colonial security forces employed machine guns to suppress the revolt, killing around 550 people, many of whom believed that traditional magic would protect them from bullets. In 1932, shortly after the Pende Rebellion, the Mpeve movement emerged in the Belgian Congo and prophesized that a talking serpent would chase away the whites. Believing that a magic potion would grant them special powers, adherents of the sect refused to pay colonial tax. Around the same time, followers of the Kimbanguist religious movement were also involved in resistance to taxation (see Chapter 18).

At times, independent Christian churches were associated with protest. In 1921, in South Africa's Eastern Cape, members of the Church of God and the Saints of Christ, popularly known as the **Israelites**, settled on state land at Bulhoek to await the fulfillment of a prophecy that the world would end. Local whites complained that the Israelites were stealing livestock, and their boycott of white businesses also provoked complaints. Israelite leader Enoch Mgijima had previously broken with the pacifist African-American missionaries who had started the church, and during the First World War he had violent apocalyptic visions. At Bulhoek, several thousand Israelites, many of whom had been dispossessed by the racist South African government, dressed in Biblical costumes, which included men carrying spears and swords, and constructed their own Ark of the Covenant containing the Ten Commandments written in Xhosa. They were confronted by a force of 1,000 armed police with several machine guns. A clash ensued; some 200 Israelites were shot dead, 100 were wounded, and 141 were arrested and subsequently sentenced to terms of imprisonment with hard labor. No police were killed and only several were injured during the incident. This was the first massacre of Black protestors in South Africa since the formation of the union in 1910. While Mgijima was released from prison in 1924 and died in 1929, the Israelite church continued to exist in the Eastern Cape. In Nyasaland and Northern Rhodesia, the American-inspired though independent **Watch Tower** movement (later known as Jehovah's Witnesses), which preached that all governments not led by Christ would collapse, inspired great concern among British colonial officials before and after the First World War. As such, Watch Tower prophet Elliot Kamwana was arrested in 1910 in Nyasaland and kept in exile on the Indian Ocean islands of Mauritius and Seychelles from 1914 to 1937.

Conclusion

The 1920s and 1930s are often referred to as the "high tide" of colonialism in Africa as it was during this time that European rule seemed at its most stable. It is also worth noting that this period corresponded with the Great Depression, which meant that the financially troubled colonial powers tended to rule their African territories as cheaply as possible and therefore did not make very great demands on their African subjects. During this period, new African protest movements emerged, each one aspiring to improve conditions for particular segments of African society within the existing colonial system. Elite associations wrote petitions asking for better educational and economic opportunities and more Western-style democratic governance, trade unions staged strikes in pursuit of higher wages and better working conditions, and rural farmers generally wanted better prices for their cash crops and relief from colonial oppression. Although very few of these movements demanded that the colonial rulers depart, the responses of colonial regimes ranged from unfriendliness to modest requests for political reform to the use of deadly repression against strikers and rural protestors. Within this context, and due to influence of Garvyeism, communism, and other ideologies, the modest protest movements of the interwar years gradually became more radical in their objectives. This was important in setting the stage for the events of the Second World War, when colonial regimes made dramatic new demands on African subjects, creating grievances and new conditions that allowed for the growth, in the late 1940s and 1950s, of mass nationalist movements that demanded full independence.

Timeline

1800 1897—Formation of Gold Coast Aborigines Rights Protection Society

1900 1900—Pan-African Conference in London

1909—Formation of National Association for the Advancement of Colored People (NAACP) in the United States by W.E.B. du Bois and others

1910—Arrest of Watch Tower leader Elliot Kamwana in Nyasaland

1910—Union of South Africa

1912—Formation of South African Native National Congress (SANNC—later African National Congress ANC)

1912—First labor union formed in Nigeria

1914—Marcus Garvey forms the Universal Negro Improvement Association (UNIA) in the United States

1917—Formation of National Congress of British West Africa (NCBWA) in Accra, Gold Coast

1918—Marcus Garvey founds *Negro World* newspaper in New York

1919—First Pan-African Congress in Paris

1919—Formation of Southern Rhodesia Native Association (SRNA)

1919—Formation of Industrial and Commercial Workers' Union (ICU) in South Africa

1919—Railway workers' strike in Freetown, Sierra Leone

1920—Branches of NCBWA open in Lagos, Freetown, and Bathurst

1920—Use of airplanes to bomb rebels in British Somaliland

1920—Branch of Garvey's UNIA formed in Lagos, Nigeria

1921—Formation of the Communist Party of South Africa (CPSA)

1921—Second Pan-African Congress in London, Brussels, and Paris

1921—Formation of East Africa Association (EAA) in Kenya

1921—Bulhoek Massacre in South Africa

1921–27—Rif Wars in Spanish Morocco

1923—Formation of Nigerian National Democratic Party (NNDP) in Lagos

1923—Third Pan-African Congress in London and Lisbon

1923—Formation of Rhodesia Bantu Voters Association (RBVA) in Southern Rhodesia

1923–31—Italian subjugation of the interior of Libya

1924—Cocoa Boycott in Gold Coast

1924 or 1925—Formation of Kikuyu Central Association (KCA) in Kenya

1925—Imprisonment of Marcus Garvey in the United States

1925—Railway workers' strike in Freetown, Sierra Leone

1927—Fourth Pan-African Congress in New York City

1927—Black South African communists visit the Soviet Union

1927–32—Rebellion in French Equatorial Africa

1929—Women's War in Southeastern Nigeria

1929—Duala communities in Cameroon send petitions to League of Nations

1929—Demands for French citizenship for all Malagasy people

1930s—Formation of Luo Union in Kenya

1930—Blaise Diagne defends forced labor in the French colonies

1930–31—Cocoa boycott in the Gold Coast

1931—Women's Protest in Cameroon

1931—Pende Rebellion in Belgian Congo

1931—Railway Workers' Union established in Nigeria

1930–34—French conquest of Atlas Mountains in Morocco

1933—Jomo Kenyatta visits the Soviet Union

1934—Formation of Nigerian Youth Movement (NYM)

1935—Copperbelt Strike in Northern Rhodesia

1935—West African Youth League (WAYL) formed in the Gold Coast but is short lived

1935–36—Italian invasion of Ethiopia

1937–38—Cocoa boycott in the Gold Coast

1938—WAYL formed in Sierra Leone

1940—Strikes by white and then Black miners in the Copperbelt of Northern Rhodesia

1942—Kenya African Union (KAU) formed

1945—Fifth Pan-African Congress in Manchester

KEY TERMS

Clements Kadalie 415

communism 407

Constance Agatha Cummings-John 418

Edward Wilmot Blyden 405

female genital modification 411

Garveyism 405

I.T.A. Wallace-Johnson 417

interwar period 401

Israelites 419

Jean Ralaimongo 414

Jomo Kenyatta 411

Joseph E. Casely Hayford 409

National Congress of British West Africa 409

Nigerian Youth Movement 410

Oginga Odinga 412

Pan-African Congresses 405

Pan-Africanism 405

pass laws 415

Second Italo-Ethiopian War 403

socialism 407

Universal Negro Improvement Association 407

Versailles Peace Conference 405

Watch Tower 420

Women's War of 1929 418

STUDY QUESTIONS

1. What new forms of protest were expressed by Africans in the interwar period? What were the principal aims of these protest movements? How did colonial authorities suppress both armed and peaceful resistance to their rule?

2. What are the main objectives of Pan-Africanism? Who were its main proponents? What were some of the early efforts to promote Pan-Africanism? Why and how did communism gain the attention of some African activists?

3. How did elite associations develop in Africa in the early twentieth century? Which groups of people did they comprise? What were the overarching philosophies and goals of elite associations?

4. Why did labor movements arise in the interwar period? How effective were strikes? What role did women play in rural protests? How did the types of protest in rural areas compare with other forms of protest discussed in this chapter?

Please see page FR-8 for the Further Readings for this chapter.
For additional digital learning resources please go to
https://www.oup.com/he/falola-stapleton1e

20

Africa and the World Wars, 1914–1945

The era of European colonial rule in Africa also corresponded with the First and Second World Wars. Although these global conflicts began in Europe and Asia, they had profound impacts on Africa and Africans. Since European colonial powers ended up on opposite sides of both world wars, destructive and deadly fighting spread to their territories in Africa. Furthermore, in both conflicts the European powers mobilized African manpower and resources in support of the war effort. That said, in many ways each world war had a different impact on Africa. The First World War (1914–18) resulted in the last major reworking of the colonial map of Africa. Victorious powers like Britain and France seized Germany's colonies, and during the conflict some of the last major African rebellions against colonial rule were defeated, which generally served to strengthen colonial powers in the interwar period. In contrast, the Second World War (1939–45) weakened European colonial rule in Africa and created the circumstances for the rise of African independence movements in the 1950s. These circumstances included mounting expectations for self-determination, increased African grievances related to renewed colonial oppression, the expansion of African cities, and a changing international context.

The First World War in Africa

South of the Sahara, the First World War in Africa pitted Britain, France, Belgium, and eventually Portugal against Germany. When the war started in August 1914, the German colonies of Togoland (Togo), Kamerun (Cameroon), South West Africa (Namibia), and German East Africa (the mainland part of today's Tanzania plus Rwanda and Burundi) were all surrounded by enemy territories. Eventually, each German colony was invaded and became the scene of terrible fighting and suffering. Some European officials did not want to fight the war in Africa. For instance, British secretary

Combatants. Two African sailors of the Free French naval force, 1942.

425

of state for war Herbert Horatio Kitchener, who had led several major campaigns of colonial conquest in Africa, thought it best to focus on defeating Germany in the main war theater in Europe and to force Berlin to surrender its African colonies in subsequent peace negotiations. Kitchener did not get his way as he died in 1916. Similarly, many colonial officials on both sides of the war believed that Africa should remain neutral as fighting would destroy recently constructed colonial infrastructure such as bridges and railways and provide recently conquered Africans with an opportunity to rebel. These opinions did not hold sway, and the war was fought in Africa. For Britain and France, it became strategically important to secure port facilities in Germany's African colonies as these could be used to support German warships in the south Atlantic and Indian Ocean. They also sought to capture communications facilities to further isolate Germany. After these initial objectives were achieved, however, the war in Africa turned into a race to acquire new territory, with France focusing on West Africa and Britain on East Africa. Smaller colonial powers also threw themselves into this new Scramble. The Belgian government, which initially wanted its large Congo colony to remain neutral, eventually occupied German territory in Africa with a view to exchanging it for parts of Belgium that had been occupied by German troops. The white-minority government of South Africa, a self-governing state within the British Empire, saw the war as an opportunity for regional territorial expansion particularly into neighboring German South West Africa. In 1915, Portugal joined the war against Germany largely to acquire land in East Africa that it had lost to Germany by diplomacy a few years earlier.

Although the German colonies were isolated and German colonial forces in Africa outnumbered, many German military officers believed they had a patriotic duty to fight in order to draw away enemy resources from the main theaters of conflict. They also hoped, vainly as it turned out, that holding on to some territory might help Germany salvage its empire in Africa in future negotiations after the war. While Germany did not have any colonies in North Africa, the war spread to that region as well because the nearby Ottoman Empire sided with Berlin. It should be remembered that the Ottoman Empire had strong historical ties with North Africa as it had once dominated the region and it had been evicted from Libya just a few years before.

The briefest campaign of the First World War in Africa took place in Togoland, a sliver of German territory between the British Gold Coast (Ghana) and France's Dahomey (Benin). In August 1914, British forces from the Gold Coast invaded Togoland to capture the port of Lomé and the large radio transmitter located inland at Kamina, which allowed Berlin to communicate with its ships in the south Atlantic and embassies in South America. The fighting only lasted a few weeks as the few German defenders put up token resistance. Notably, during the Togoland campaign, an

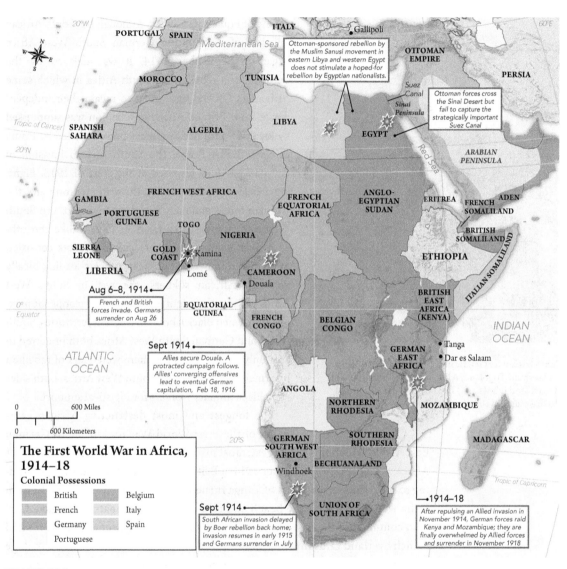

The First World War in Africa, 1914–18

Colonial Possessions

British
French
Germany
Portuguese
Belgium
Italy
Spain

Ottoman-sponsored rebellion by the Muslim Sanusi movement in eastern Libya and western Egypt does not stimulate a hoped-for rebellion by Egyptian nationalists.

Ottoman forces cross the Sinai Desert but fail to capture the strategically important Suez Canal.

Aug 6–8, 1914
French and British forces invade. Germans surrender on Aug 26

Sept 1914
Allies secure Douala. A protracted campaign follows. Allies' converging offensives lead to eventual German capitulation, Feb 18, 1916

Sept 1914
South African invasion delayed by Boer rebellion back home; invasion resumes in early 1915 and Germans surrender in July

1914–18
After repulsing an Allied invasion in November 1914, German forces raid Kenya and Mozambique; they are finally overwhelmed by Allied forces and surrender in November 1918

≡ **MAP 20.1**

African serviceman called Alhaji Grunshi from the Gold Coast Regiment became the first British soldier to fire a shot in the entire war. Fighting lasted much longer in German's other West African colony of Cameroon. In August 1914, British and French forces landed at the port of Douala and invaded overland from British Nigeria and French Gabon. The German defenders bought time by relocating inland, the invaders were slowed by the rainy season, and the British, French, and some Belgian troops failed to coordinate as they were preoccupied with seizing territory. In early 1916 the remaining German colonial troops escaped into the neutral Spanish

≡ **African serviceman.** In 1914, during fighting in German Togoland, Alhaji Grunshi from the Gold Coast (today's Ghana) became the first British soldier to fire a shot in the First World War.

colony of Equatorial Guinea. Although the South African invasion of neighboring German South West Africa began in September 1914, it was delayed by the outbreak of a rebellion in South Africa in which some Afrikaners (Boers) attempted to regain their independence from Britain. After the rebellion was suppressed by loyalist South African forces personally led by Prime Minister Louis Botha, the South African invasion of German territory resumed at the start of 1915. Fighting a delaying action across the arid environment, the German forces gradually withdrew into northern South West Africa and surrendered in July. Unlike the other African campaigns, where colonial forces consisted of a small number of European officers leading locally recruited African soldiers, the war in South West Africa was mostly fought by armed white troops supported by unarmed Black laborers. As settler territories, South Africa and German South West Africa both preferred to arm only white soldiers as there were fears of rebellion by armed Black troops. In South West Africa, both sides used Black military workers for logistical support.

The longest and most destructive African campaign of the First World War took place in German East Africa, which was the largest, most profitable, and best defended of Berlin's African colonies. In November 1914, a British plan to use an amphibious landing to seize the German port of Tanga turned disastrous as troops brought from India were trapped on the beach and fled back to their boats. This gave German commander **Paul von Lettow-Vorbeck** a chance to prepare his forces and launch overland raids into neighboring Kenya (British East Africa) to sabotage Britain's important railway that linked the Indian Ocean coast with Uganda. In the middle of 1916, German East Africa was invaded from all sides, with British forces moving south from Kenya, Belgian colonial troops advancing east from the Congo, Rhodesian and South African units marching northeast from Northern Rhodesia (Zambia) and Nyasaland (Malawi), and a Portuguese expeditionary force briefly pushing north across the Mozambique border. In turn, Von Lettow led a grueling series of delaying actions across the territory, the German colonial force invaded Mozambique in 1917, and it eventually surrendered at Abercorn, Northern Rhodesia on November 25, 1918, some two weeks after the armistice.

Long out of contact with Berlin, Von Lettow had discovered the war was over from captured British documents. While Britain initially employed mostly Indian and white South African soldiers in German East Africa, tropical disease took a heavy toll on them, and during 1917 the force was dramatically Africanized. In a territory with few railways and roads, British military operations were supported by around one million supply carriers recruited and conscripted from across the region, of whom 100,000 died from exhaustion, disease, and hunger. In total, the East Africa campaign claimed the lives of over 300,000 people, the vast majority of whom were civilians who died from starvation as their crops and livestock had been confiscated by the combatants. The impact of this famine would be felt in parts of what is now Tanzania for many generations and would permanently change social relations in some areas.

The First World War was also fought in North Africa. In January 1915 and July 1916 Ottoman forces, based in the Middle East and supported by Germany, crossed the Sinai Desert but failed in their efforts to capture the strategically important Suez Canal in British-occupied Egypt. More surreptitiously, the Ottomans also sponsored a rebellion by the Muslim Sanusi movement that began in eastern Libya and moved into western Egypt but that did not stimulate a hoped-for rebellion by Egyptian nationalists. The Ottoman sultan declared a jihad against Britain and France to encourage rebellion among the Muslim subjects of these colonial empires, but this call went mostly unheeded. Lastly, in 1916 the British used the war as an excuse to invade and conquer the Sultanate of Darfur, which was absorbed into neighboring Sudan.

During the First World War, several hundred thousand African soldiers and military laborers served in European colonial forces outside their continent. This represented the largest single exodus of Africans from Africa since the transatlantic slave trade. Several years before the start of the war, the French government had formulated a plan to make extensive use of colonial African troops to defend the motherland from an aggressive Germany. By 1918, around 450,000 African soldiers, many of them conscripts, had fought in the

≣ **Determined adversary.** Paul von Lettow-Vorbeck (1870–1964) led German forces in East Africa during the First World War and was the last German commander to surrender during the entire conflict.

≡ **Colonial troops.** Members of an Algerian spahi cavalry regiment prepare a meal after a battle in northern France in 1914. Over 200,000 men from France's North African colonies served in Europe during the war.

French army in Western Europe, and over 30,000 of them had perished. For France, these African colonial troops were extremely important as they formed shock troops for major offensives and helped suppress a widespread mutiny by metropolitan French soldiers in 1917. The French also sent African troops to fight in the 1915 Gallipoli campaign, which tried but failed to knock the Ottoman Empire out of the war, and later to the Balkans to support Serbia. Restricting armed military service to the white minority, the South African government sent several thousand white soldiers to fight in Western Europe, where they suffered shockingly heavy casualties during the Battle of the Somme in 1916. Experiencing military manpower problems related to recruiting from a minority, South Africa's racist recruiting policy was slightly relaxed to allow an infantry battalion of mixed-race men to go to East Africa in 1915 and another to the Middle East in 1918 to join a British offensive against the Ottomans. Although Britain decided not to employ armed Black African troops outside Africa, about 25,000 Black South Africans and 6,000 mixed-race South Africans worked as unarmed but uniformed military labor in France, cutting timber, maintaining railways and roads, and loading and unloading ships. Around 600 Black men from the South African Native Labour Contingent (SANLC) were drowned in February 1917 when the SS *Mendi*, a steamship transporting them across the English Channel to France, sank after an accidental collision with another vessel. Similarly, fear of rebellion in Egypt meant that the British were hesitant to send armed Egyptian troops outside their country, but 170,000 unarmed Egyptians served in the Camel Transport Corps in the Middle East and 23,000 members of the Egyptian Labour Corps worked in the Middle East and France.

During the war, African communities were subjected to constant and increasing demands for men and resources by a colonial state that was simultaneously and obviously being weakened by the departure of European officials and soldiers for military duties elsewhere. This contradictory situation led to a series of African rebellions.

In Nyasaland in 1915, the American-educated Baptist minister **John Chilembwe** objected to British conscription of local men as supply carriers for the military in East Africa. The people of Nyasaland suffered greatly during the war as the British administration forced them to sell most of their food crops to support the army, the money that was paid in return was useless as there was no food to buy, and malnutrition encouraged the spread of diseases like bubonic plague, which was thought to have been eradicated from the territory. Beginning with the killing of a white plantation manager with whom Chilembwe's congregants had a long-standing dispute, the uprising involved only around 200 people, but it was brutally suppressed by a paranoid British colonial administration. Subsequent historians have disagreed over Chilembwe's motivations. He has been seen as an early nationalist hero who was inspired by the history of the abolitionist movement in the United States and wanted to martyr himself to stir future generations, as a man pushed to the edge by psychological stress and as a scapegoat for British maladministration and overreaction.

In the Bongo area of the Gold Coast, where people had actively resisted British rule up to 1911, riots erupted in 1915 and 1916 against local police and abusive British-appointed chiefs. The British rushed in troops and crushed the rebellion. In eastern Nigeria a prophet called Elijah II rallied Igbo people disgruntled by flagging palm-oil prices, but tensions calmed when the price increased, and in western Nigeria there were several serious uprisings by Yoruba communities over colonial taxation. The Yoruba rebellions were suppressed by force, and around the town of Abeokuta some 500 people were killed. Across French West Africa, military conscription combined with the antagonism between French colonial officials and local Muslim leaders prompted widespread resistance and rebellion. In 1917, the rebellious Volta-Bani region was pacified by the largest French military campaign in Africa up to that time, which caused the deaths of 30,000 local people and 300 French troops. After the war, the French divided the bothersome area into two administrative entities that later became the independent countries of Mali and Burkina Faso. By contrast, and despite the Ottoman call for jihad, Muslims in neighboring northern Nigeria did not rebel against the British, illustrating the effectiveness of indirect rule. In Angola and Mozambique, the brutality of Portuguese rule led to major revolts.

≡ **Rebel leader.** Baptist minister John Chilembwe (1871–1915), pictured here on the left, led an uprising against British rule in Nyasaland in 1915.

Some African elites saw the First World War as an opportunity to ingratiate themselves to the colonial powers in the hope that this would result in colonial reforms. At the start of 1918 , **Blaise Diagne**, the first African elected to represent part of Africa in the French legislature in 1914, was appointed as high commissioner for the recruitment of troops in Black Africa, with a rank equivalent to governor. He was the highest ranked Black official in French colonial Africa (see Chapter 17). The French government thought that Diagne could reduce the massive resistance to recruiting, and he accepted the post as he was promised that, after the war, France would ease colonial oppression and widen African access to French citizenship. Although Diagne was a brilliantly successful military recruiter who garnered tens of thousands of enlistees from previously rebellious areas, the French government failed to honor its pledge as the reforms were never enacted. Subsequently, many people in French colonial Africa criticized Diagne for having opportunistically climbed the French colonial hierarchy by convincing his people to suffer the horrors of trench warfare, including poison gas and artillery bombardment on the Western Front. In white-ruled South Africa, moderate elite protest groups such as the Black South African Native National Congress (SANNC) and the mixed-race African Political Organization (APO) both encouraged their supporters to enlist in the military as an investment in future civil rights. In Bechuanaland (Botswana), Tswana chiefs provided military labor and cattle for the war effort as a way to ingratiate themselves to Britain and thereby prevent their territory from being handed over to adjacent white supremacist and expansionist South Africa.

In the wake of the First World War, around 2.4 million Africans died during the influenza pandemic of 1918–19, the spread of which was accelerated when the troops returned from war theaters. This led to a collapse of food production and famine in many areas that greatly weakened African societies as they entered the interwar era of the 1920s and 1930s. (See Chapter 27 for more information on epidemics and pandemics in African history.)

The reconfiguration of the map of colonial Africa following the First World War paved the way for a number of dire problems in the future. With the 1919 Treaty of Versailles, which formally ended the First World War, defeated Germany was stripped of its overseas colonies, which became **mandates** of the newly created **League of Nations**, an international organization meant to maintain world peace. Although these mandates were supposed to be prepared for eventual independence and governed for the benefit of the local people, they were given to the victorious powers as spoils of war and were administered as if they were colonies. Most of Togo was given to France, though a small slice of it was joined to Britain's Gold Coast. Similarly, the French took the majority of Cameroon, with a section along the western border tacked onto neighboring British-ruled Nigeria. Over the next few decades the different education and administrative systems of the colonial rulers meant that the British-ruled Southern Cameroons became largely anglophone while the rest of Cameroon became francophone. Later, in the independence era of the early 1960s, Southern Cameroon joined Cameroon to create a bilingual—English–French—state. Eventually, however, the dominant francophone majority marginalized the anglophone minority of the west, which led to violent protest and calls for separatism in that area. After the First World War, the administration

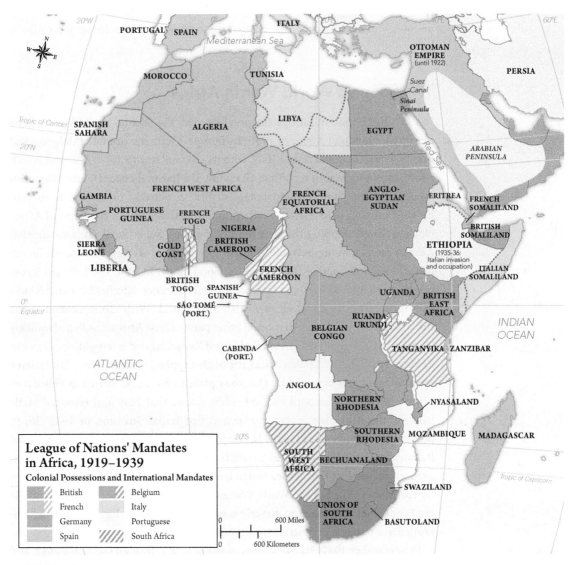

League of Nations' Mandates in Africa, 1919–1939

Colonial Possessions and International Mandates

- British
- French
- Germany
- Spain
- Belgium
- Italy
- Portuguese
- South Africa

≡ **MAP 20.2**

of South West Africa was handed over to South Africa, which imported Afrikaner settlers and ruled the mandate as if it were another South African province. This ultimately led to a protracted African nationalist insurgency against South African occupation from the 1960s to 1980s that overlapped with civil war in Angola and resulted in the independence of Namibia in 1990. While the British gained a mandate over most of German East Africa, which was renamed Tanganyika, Belgium was given control of Rwanda and Burundi, which bordered on the Belgian Congo. In Rwanda and Burundi during the 1920s and 1930s, the Belgians reinvented existing Tutsi, Hutu, and Twa sociopolitical identities as racial classifications and imposed a racial hierarchy that created the context for postcolonial genocides in both countries.

The Second World War in Africa

While it had begun in Europe the previous year, the Second World War became a reality for colonial Africa in 1940. In Europe, Germany occupied Belgium and France, which inspired fascist Italy, with its colonial territories in East and North Africa, to join the war in support of Germany. The Italian dictator **Benito Mussolini** thought that he could take advantage of British setbacks in the war to expand his colonial empire in Africa. Furthermore, Italian control of the Horn of Africa blocked Allied shipping through the Red Sea and Suez Canal. This meant that Allied vessels moving between Europe and Asia had to travel the much longer distance around South Africa's Cape of Good Hope. In June 1940, Italian forces based in Eritrea and Ethiopia advanced a short distance into British-ruled Kenya and Sudan, and occupied all of British Somaliland. With reinforcements from India, South Africa, West Africa, and other parts of East Africa, the British quickly launched a counteroffensive from Sudan and Kenya, landed an amphibious force in British Somaliland and pushed back the badly supplied Italians. When the Italians were defeated at a major battle that took place in Keren in Eritrea in February–March 1941, British troops entered Addis Ababa that May and returned Haile Selassie, the Ethiopian emperor who had fled Italian invasion in 1935–36, to power. By November, most of the Italian forces in East Africa had surrendered, and Italian naval vessels based in Eritrea on the Red Sea were either destroyed or managed to escape. This East Africa campaign represented the first major land victory for the Allies in the Second World War and allowed British supply ships to access the Suez Canal and therefore directly support their forces in Egypt, who were embroiled in a struggle of central importance to the outcome of the war.

In September 1940, Italian troops based in Libya invaded western Egypt, and although they meant to reach the Suez Canal, their advance did not progress very far because of logistical challenges. The subsequent British counterattack was stunningly successful, pressed deep inside Libya, and yielded the capture of 130,000 Italian troops and 22 Italian generals. Bolstered by the arrival of the German *Afrika Korps* in early 1941, the Italians regrouped and another Axis offensive pushed the British back eastward across the Egyptian border. Their supply lines lengthened, the advancing Axis forces were once again halted and driven westward into Libya by a series of British operations. In the middle of 1942, yet another Axis offensive, led by German general Erwin Rommel, caused the British to retreat eastward to El Alamein, only 60 miles from the major Egyptian port of Alexandria. It seemed possible that Rommel's force in North Africa might take the Suez Canal and even eventually link up with the German military, moving through the Caucasus region of the Soviet Union. After building up their forces, which could now be supplied via the Suez Canal given access to the Red Sea, the British in Egypt, commanded by General Bernard Montgomery, launched a massive offensive in October 1942 that decisively drove the Germans and Italians back westward through Libya and eventually into Tunisia. The Allied victory at this **Second Battle of El Alamein** was famously described by British prime minister Winston Churchill as the "end of the beginning" of the war.

With the November 1942 landings of American and British troops in Morocco and Algeria during Operation Torch, the Axis forces in Tunisia faced enemy advances from both west and east. Since Hitler refused to allow an Axis evacuation of North Africa, some 230,000 German and Italian troops surrendered to Allied forces in Tunis in early May 1943. The Allies then used North Africa as a base for their July 1943 invasion of Sicily and the September 1943 landings in mainland Italy, which led to the demise of the Mussolini regime. While the North Africa campaign is often described as a "war without hate" as the

≡ **Humiliating defeat.** Thousands of Italians were captured after the strategic Libyan port of Tobruk fell to British forces in January 1941. Here naval personnel march to a prison camp after their surrender.

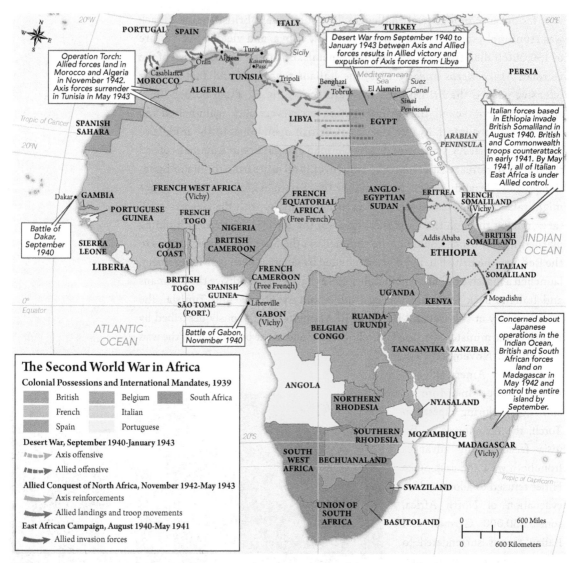

MAP 20.3

opposing armies did not commit war crimes against each other, the Holocaust of the Second World War had a North African dimension. During the fighting, Italian fascists pursued anti-Semitic policies by confining thousands of Libyan Jews in labor camps where many died of disease, and deported hundreds of Jews with British citizenship to the Bergen-Belsen concentration camp in Germany.

In France's African colonies, governors had to decide to throw in with either the **Vichy** regime in France, which had been set up as a German puppet, or the exiled Free French leaders, eventually led by **Charles de Gaulle**, who were supported by

Britain. In North Africa, French officials initially sided with Vichy but changed sides in November 1942 when Allied troops landed in Morocco and Algeria. The territories of French West Africa, with the exception of Cameroon, aligned with Vichy, while those in French Equatorial Africa gravitated to the Free French, with the exception of Gabon. The Free French position in Equatorial Africa owed much to the influence of **Felix Eboue**, the Black Guyanese governor of Chad, and the city of Brazzaville in what is now the Republic of Congo became the Free French capital. These divisions among French officials led to fighting in some of France's African territories. Although the British were not technically at war with Vichy France, the Royal Navy attacked a French fleet on the coast of Algeria in July 1940 in order to prevent the ships from assisting Germany or Italy in the Mediterranean Sea. In September 1940, the Royal Navy tried but failed to land Free French troops at Vichy-controlled Dakar, the main port of Senegal, which was an important West African harbor and held the gold reserves of German occupied Poland and France. A few weeks later, Free French forces from Cameroon, again transported by British ships, seized Libreville, Gabon, where the Vichy-aligned governor committed suicide. In early 1941, Free French forces based in Chad advanced north into Libya to distract the Italians, who were fighting the British for control of Egypt. In East Africa, French Somaliland (Djibouti) sided with Vichy, but it was occupied by the British in 1942 after they defeated Italy in the Horn of Africa. The December 1941 entry of Japan into the war on the Axis side prompted Britain and South Africa to occupy Madagascar, as there was concern that Japanese submarines might use the Vichy-ruled island to threaten Allied shipping in that part of the Indian Ocean. The importance of Africa for the Free French, especially in terms of military manpower and natural resources, led to the 1944 **Brazzaville Conference**, where Free French leaders like De Gaulle promised postwar reforms including self-government and reduced economic exploitation for the African colonies. However, the concept of independence for African territories was rejected.

Just like the 1914–18 conflict, a great number of African service personnel traveled outside Africa during the Second World War. Tens of thousands of African troops, including 75,000 from West Africa, formed part of the army that tried to defend France from German invasion in

≡ **Planning the future of postwar Africa.** Free French leaders Charles de Gaulle and Felix Eboue meet in 1940.

1940. After the fall of France, the Germans executed from 1,500 to 3,000 African prisoners-of-war, and many others became slave workers for German war production. Among these prisoners was **Léopold Sédar Senghor**, a Senegalese French citizen and a graduate of the University of Paris, who had enlisted as a private in the French colonial army in 1939 to defend France and who would become the first president of independent Senegal in 1960 (see Chapter 22). African troops formed the backbone of the Free French military, which, as part of the wider Allied war effort, fought in Italy and Western Europe from 1943 to 1945. However, once Free French forces moved into France in 1944, leaders like De Gaulle considered it embarrassing for Black African subjects to be seen as liberating white French people from German occupation. As such, a predominantly white Free French unit was chosen to liberate Paris and Black African soldiers were disarmed and sent to camps in the south of France, from where they were shipped back to Africa. Protests broke out in some of the camps because of the poor living conditions and lack of back-pay for former prisoners-of-war. In December 1944, at Thiaroye in Senegal, a protest led to some 35 ex-prisoners being shot dead by French camp guards.

Although Belgium was occupied by Germany in the summer of 1940, the exiled Belgian government still controlled the Belgian Congo, which was used to support the Allied struggle. In early 1941 a 10,000-strong contingent from the *Force Publique*, the Belgian colonial army in the Congo, traveled about 1,200 miles by river boat, railway, and road to reach southern Sudan, from where they crossed into Ethiopia to join the fight against the Italians. In 1942, a force of about 13,000 *Force Publique* soldiers was shipped to Nigeria, from where they were supposed to invade the neighboring Vichy French territory of Dahomey, but the operation was called off when the French officials in that colony changed sides. The same Congolese colonial troops were then transported, some by ship and some overland, to Egypt, where they helped secure the Suez Canal and guard prisoner-of-war camps, and in 1944 they were deployed to Palestine. Allied authorities assigned the *Force Publique* to security duties given the unit's shortage of white officers from occupied Belgium. In addition, a *Force Publique* field hospital served in East Africa, Madagascar, and Burma. Some Congolese civilians were unexpectedly caught up in the war. In 1944, Augusta Chiwy, a nurse from the Belgian Congo, treated wounded American soldiers in the besieged Belgian town of Bastogne during the Battle of the Bulge.

Britain sent many thousands of its colonial African soldiers to fight a grueling jungle war against the Japanese in Burma. In 1942, Japan invaded Burma to prevent the Allies from using it as a route to supply China, and Japanese forces in Burma also threatened the important British territory of India. Starting in 1943, British colonial forces from Africa were shipped to India, from where they participated in the protracted Allied effort to push the Japanese out of Burma. About 80,000 men from British West Africa, including Nigeria, the Gold Coast, Sierra Leone, and the

Gambia, and 46,000 men from British East and Central Africa, including Kenya, Uganda, Tanganyika (Tanzania), Nyasaland, Northern Rhodesia, and Southern Rhodesia (Zimbabwe), fought in Burma during the last stage of the Second World War. To this day, some streets and military centers in the former British colonies of Africa bear names related to the Burma campaign.

British colonial forces from Southern Africa tended to serve in the Mediterranean theater of the war. After fighting in the East African campaign, all-white South African ground and air combat units fought in North Africa in 1941 and 1942, and then were involved in the Allied push up the Italian Peninsula during 1944–45. South African naval vessels were also active in the Mediterranean and elsewhere. Further, tens of thousands of unarmed Black, mixed-race, and Indian South Africans served as uniformed military labor in North Africa and Italy. Among the many thousands of other Black South Africans taken prisoner in North Africa, Job Maseko made an improvised bomb that he used to sink a German vessel at a port in Libya. Within South Africa, these contributions to the Allied war effort were controversial as Afrikaner nationalists did not want to help Britain, their historic enemy, and some Afrikaner extremists were openly sympathetic to Nazi Germany. Jan Smuts, who had fought the British during the South African War (1899–1902) and returned for a second stint as prime minister in 1939, was central in maintaining South Africa's wartime support for Britain amid these tensions.

The leaders of the British Southern African territories of Bechuanaland (Botswana), Basutoland (Lesotho), and Swaziland (Eswatini) wished to ingratiate themselves with the British government so that their lands would not be given over to racist South Africa. They provided manpower for the African Auxiliary Pioneer Corps (AAPC). The AAPC comprised mostly unarmed soldiers who worked as engineers in North Africa, the Middle East, Sicily and Italy. The British did not send the AAPC to Burma because many of these men had enlisted specifically to fight Hitler and before Japan had entered the war.

Colonial Africa provided a massive amount of resources for the Allied war effort. While colonial economic investment in Africa had been minimal during the Great Depression of the 1930s, the Second World War saw a huge increase in production which some historians have called the **Second Colonial Occupation**. The colonial state pushed many Africans off their land to make way for large-scale plantation agriculture and forced labor was reintroduced in areas where it had not been practiced for several decades. The Belgian Congo hastened production of valuable materials for the Allies such as 160,000 tons of copper annually, 9,000 tons of rubber in 1943 and 11,300 in 1944, 12,500 tons of tin in 1943 and 17,300 in 1944, and uranium for the construction of atomic bombs in the United States. After the Japanese conquest of Southeast Asia, which had been the principal exporter of natural rubber for the world market, the Allies turned to African sources of rubber such as Liberia, Nigeria, and the Belgian Congo.

Indeed, in parts of the Belgian Congo coercive methods of rubber extraction were introduced that were reminiscent of Leopold II's Congo Free State. The Vichy regime initially exported some of its West African rubber to Germany, but this was hindered by British naval blockade, and when the Free French took over these territories they redirected rubber shipments to the Allies and imposed even more coercive measures on African rubber collectors. While Africans in many territories including French and British ones were often compelled to provide a regular quota of rubber, in some areas the increase in demand for rubber provided people with a new opportunity to earn money that they could use to purchase imported goods like bicycles. Africa's total production of rubber increased from 18,000 tons in 1941 to 50,000 tons in 1953 and 60,000 in 1944. Natural rubber was extremely important for the war effort as it was used in the construction of all ships, aircraft, and vehicles. Other resources were also vital. British authorities in Nigeria conscripted around 18,000 men to work under harsh and unsafe conditions in the tin mines of the Jos Plateau. The Free French, eager to fill their war chest, stepped up gold mining in Gabon, where workers and porters endured terrible conditions and those who deserted were tracked down by colonial police. The international price of many agricultural products rose but many African farmers did not benefit as colonial marketing boards cut prices and directed the extra profits to wartime activities. That said, some African peasant farmers selling high-priced crops such as coffee or cocoa thrived during the war and this widened the socioeconomic gap in some rural communities. To better extract these resources, networks of roads and railways were expanded, often through the toil of conscripted African workers. Such conditions provoked resistance, such as in the Belgian Congo during 1944, when disgruntled African workers and soldiers attempted to stage a rebellion.

Impacts of the Second World War

A "second colonial occupation" of Africa continued after the Second World War. In the late 1940s and 1950s, some colonial regimes embarked on massive economic development projects that had negative effects on local people and the environment. In 1946, the British government launched an ambitious project to grow groundnuts (peanuts) in Tanganyika to produce cooking oil, which was in short supply in postwar Britain. Colonial agricultural experts ignored African farming methods, which they considered primitive; they thought that supposedly more advanced Western techniques and technology would be more successful. Called the "Groundnut Army," thousands of British war veterans were sent to Tanganyika, where they wrecked tractors and bulldozers trying to clear the thick bush, and they found that the soil was unsuitable, the area lacked water, and African workers went on strike for better wages. The **Groundnut Scheme** was cancelled in 1951 after it

AFRICAN CONTRIBUTIONS TO THE ALLIED WAR EFFORT

Top left: Augusta Chiwy, a nurse from the Belgian Congo, assisted US soldiers during the Siege of Bastogne in 1944. Here she is seen as a nursing student (front row center) in Leuven, Belgium, in 1943. *Top right:* Troops of Britain's 11th East African Brigade in Burma during the Second World War. *Bottom left:* Members of the African Auxiliary Corps with Australian Army engineers in the Middle East in 1942. *Bottom right:* Harvested rubber being weighed at a trading post in French Equatorial Africa in 1943. Seated behind a desk on the left, colonial officials record the transaction.

had produced only 2,000 tons of groundnuts at a cost of £49 million, and it turned part of central Tanganyika into a virtual desert.

Beginning in the 1930s, the French colonial state created a massive irrigation project on the Upper Niger River in what is now Mali that was meant to produce 100,000 tons of cotton per year but never managed to exceed 3,500 tons annually.

Farmers were forced to move to the thinly populated arid area where they lived un-der the authoritarian regime of the *Office du Niger*. In 1945, when compulsion was ended, about 40 percent of the residents left. During the 1940s, production shifted from cotton to rice, which African farmers preferred to grow because it offered food security. In Southern Africa, postwar colonial regimes constructed huge dams on the Zambezi River to produce hydroelectric power for the region, in the process creating some of the world's biggest man-made lakes. These were the Kariba Dam, which was constructed between 1955 and 1959 on the border between Southern Rhodesia (Zimbabwe) and Northern Rhodesia (Zambia), then under a white-minority federal administration, and the Cahora Bassa Dam, which was built by the Portuguese colonial government in Mozambique between 1969 and 1973. Tens of thousands of inhabitants of the Zambezi Valley, whose riverine way of life was destroyed by the rising waters, were dislocated to remote wilderness areas where there were no services and where they were exposed to insect-born diseases like sleeping sickness and malaria. More generally, after the Second World War in much of Southern and East Africa, colonial administrations seeking to boost agricul-tural production intensified and strictly enforced soil conservation policies that were resisted by small-scale African farmers who saw them as authoritarian and op-pressive and who were forced to engage in unpaid labor on these projects (for example, in constructing terraces) and to pay for them through increased taxation. In some places, large-scale white farmers and some of the more successful African ones benefited more from these ini-tiatives and therefore supported them, further polar-izing rural populations. In the postwar era, emerging Africa nationalist leaders, for instance in Tanganyika and Kenya, gained new popularity among African peas-ants by criticizing compulsory soil conservation rules.

≡ **Second Colonial Occupation.** Construction of the Kariba Dam in the 1950s.

The rapid growth of cities represented one of the most significant impacts of the Second World War on Africa. African cities had been growing steadily be-tween the world wars, but from 1939 this urbaniza-tion intensified. In Kenya, Nairobi had a population of around 30,000 in 1928 and around 50,000 in 1936, but this jumped to almost 109,000 in 1944. Driven off their rural lands or seeking escape from labor conscription, many African people flocked to the cities to earn wages working on the construction of new harbor or airport infrastructure that would support the Allied cause. In Sierra Leone, Freetown became an important port for Allied convoys that was visited by thousands of ships during the war; the number of people employed in all sectors grew from 10,000 in early 1940 to 50,000 in 1942, and during this time the total population of the city almost doubled. There were also jobs in new industries that manufactured goods in Africa to compensate for the decrease in imported goods from war-torn Europe. Using African-produced rubber, Bata Shoe company began making footwear in Southern Rhodesia and would continue doing so for decades; plants in Mozambique and Angola made shoes, engine fan belts, and washers; and Africa's first tire-manufacturing industry developed in South Africa. During the war, South Africa's growing manufacturing sector surpassed mining as the country's largest employer. Africa's wartime cities also became scenes of conflict as people sometimes fought over scarce food and housing, and workers went on strike to demand better wages. Urban unemployment became a problem as the cities received more people than there were jobs, and this situation became much worse after the war ended and resource produc-

≡ **Urbanization.** A neighborhood in Freetown, Sierra Leone, in the 1950s.

tion and export declined. In addition, discharged soldiers returned home and competed for the decreasing number of urban jobs. The arrival of large numbers of European, American, and African servicemen, mostly young males, in Africa's cities prompted the growth of the sex trade and the spread of sexually transmitted disease. In West Africa, a wartime system of human trafficking developed whereby girls and women from Nigeria were smuggled into the Gold Coast, where they became sex workers.

Immediately after the war, larger urban populations and growing urban discontent meant that cities would provide a fertile ground for the growth of African nationalism. During the interwar years, Westernized African elite politicians had generally used moderate means to lobby for gradual colonial reforms. By the late 1930s, inspired by events like the Italian invasion of Ethiopia and ideas like Pan-Africanism and communism, some of them were becoming more radical in challenging colonial rule and were transitioning into African nationalist leaders seeking independence. The Second World War accelerated the development of the African nationalist movement, whereby the narrowly elite leadership found popular support among the enlarged and disgruntled urban population and rural people fed up with intrusion from the colonial state. African nationalist leaders like Kwame Nkrumah of the Gold Coast and Jomo Kenyatta of Kenya were inspired by the 1941 **Atlantic Charter** in which the leaders of Britain and the United States had pledged that all peoples should have a right to self-determination. The previously mentioned Brazzaville Conference of 1944 was also important in this regard. The proliferation of African newspapers during the war had spread Allied propaganda about the fight for democracy and freedom against Axis oppression, and after the war the press discussed and popularized the very similar ambitions of the rising African nationalist movements. Although African veterans of the Second World War played no greater role in the nationalist movement than any other social group, the idea that they had fought for democracy and freedom yet returned home to authoritarianism highlighted the hypocrisy and racism of the colonial system. This concept became so popular that a myth developed that greatly exaggerated the importance of disgruntled African veterans in the postwar nationalist movement. While some veterans did get involved in nationalism, it is easy to forget that there were very many Second World War veterans among the colonial police and soldiers, who would arrest, beat, and sometimes kill nationalist protestors during the late 1940s and 1950s. African war veterans found themselves on both sides of the unfolding nationalist struggle.

Conclusion

The world wars had profound effects on Africa. In both conflicts, African people fought and died in their own continent as well as overseas, and Africa provided resources for the colonial powers who were also some of the main combatant powers. The First World War in Africa represented a continuation of the Scramble for Africa, but unlike the colonial invasions of the late nineteenth century, European powers now fought each other over African territory. Colonial rule then entered into a period of relative stability in which the colonial powers developed their administrative systems and exploitive colonial economies. During the Second World War, fighting in Africa (aside from the French colonies, which experienced something of a civil war), focused on access to the strategically central Suez Canal via the Horn of Africa and North Africa. As such, military events in Africa were much more important in determining the outcome of the Second World War than they had been in the First World War. Finally, grievances created by the Second Colonial Occupation and rapid urbanization set the stage for the rise of African nationalist movements.

Timeline

KEY TERMS

STUDY QUESTIONS

1. What contributions did Africans make in the two world wars? How did European empires mobilize African manpower and resources in support of their war efforts?

2. How did Europeans view African servicemen in European forces? How was the map of colonial Africa reconfigured at the end of the First World War? In what manner did the victorious powers administer the mandates they were awarded by the Treaty of Versailles?

3. How did the Second World War weaken colonial power in Africa? What were the motives for the "second colonial occupation" of Africa? What factors promoted the rise in African nationalism after the war?

Please see page FR-9 for the Further Readings for this chapter.
For additional digital learning resources please go to
https://www.oup.com/he/falola-stapleton1e

Decolonization and African Nationalism, Part One: 1945–1970

In the late 1940s, right after the end of the Second World War, the European powers had very little interest in granting independence to their colonies in Africa. With Europe devastated by the conflict, resources and manpower from colonial Africa were seen as important in postwar reconstruction and economic recovery. As discussed in Chapter 20, the European colonial powers had accelerated their extraction of resources from Africa during the Second World War, and this continued in the immediate postwar years, including large projects such as the Groundnut Scheme in Tanganyika (Tanzania) and the construction of the Kariba Dam in between Southern and Northern Rhodesia (Zimbabwe and Zambia). Although the rise of independence movements in Asia, the achievement of India's independence from Britain in 1947, and Indochina's independence from France in 1954 inspired African nationalists with similar ambitions, the loss of these territories made European governments more determined to hang on to their African possessions. Furthermore, the European powers also saw African resources, military manpower, and military bases as increasingly important in the emerging global **Cold War** in which they were allied with the United States against the Soviet Union.

Changing Imperial Policies

Despite European determination in the late 1940s and early 1950s to retain control in Africa, between 1956 and 1968 most African colonies were transformed into independent states with their own governments. This process of **decolonization** was more rapid than the earlier Scramble for Africa. The first African countries to receive independence after the Second World War were Eritrea in 1947, though the United Nations federated it to Ethiopia in 1952, and Libya in 1951, as these were the colonies of defeated Italy. The rush toward independence started in 1956 in the north, with

Independence.
Ghanaians celebrated their independence in 1957 with festive ceremonies. This young girl's expression reflects the optimism that many Africans felt during this period, and her chest is emblazoned with a salute to her country's newly-gained freedom.

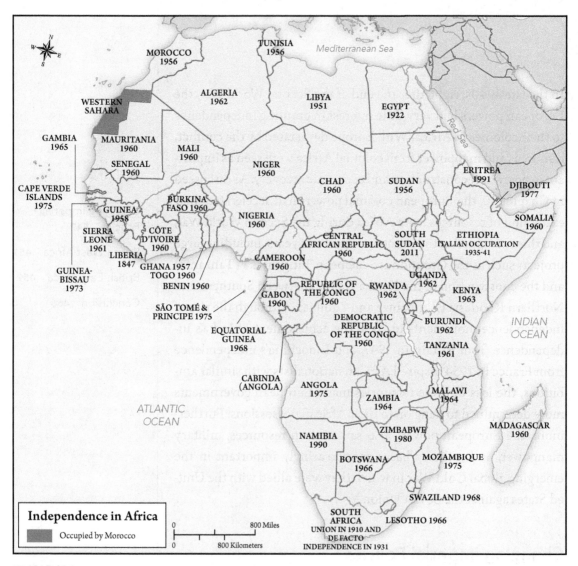

Independence in Africa

Occupied by Morocco

0 ___ 800 Miles

0 ___ 800 Kilometers

≡ **MAP 21.1**

France withdrawing from Morocco and Tunisia, and Britain granting sovereignty to Sudan. In 1957, Ghana, formerly the British-ruled Gold Coast, became the first African territory south of the Sahara Desert to attain independence. Dubbed the "Year of Africa" by British and United Nations officials, 1960 saw the number of independent African states increase from 9 to 26. The new states included many former French territories in West and Equatorial Africa as well as Madagascar, but also the large countries of Nigeria and Congo, former British and Belgian colonies respectively. Many colonial territories in East Africa became independent during the early 1960s, such as the formerly Belgian-administered Rwanda and Burundi in 1962 and the former British territories of Tanganyika in 1961, Uganda in 1962, and Kenya in 1963. Britain granted independence to the small Southern African territories of Botswana (Bechuanaland) and Lesotho (Basutoland) in 1966, and Swaziland in 1968, which was also the same year the Spanish withdrew from Equatorial Guinea.

What caused this change? Over the years, various scholars have offered contradicting theories. The liberal-nationalist view focused on the weakness of the European powers, which had been exhausted by the Second World War and therefore were not strong enough to contend with the rise of mass nationalism in Africa that demanded independence. The main problem with this approach is that if European weakness was the main factor, then decolonization happened in the wrong order. Britain, the strongest postwar European power, was the first to grant independence in sub-Saharan Africa, in 1957, while the weak colonial rulers of Spain and Portugal held out much longer. As discussed later, Portugal fought three brutal wars in the 1960s and early 1970s to hold on to its African territories, which were ultimately relinquished only in 1974. Other scholars have sought to explain decolonization by claiming that it represented a conspiracy on the part of European powers, abetted by their ally the United States, to deprive Africa of real independence as a way to continue the economic exploitation of the continent. As a way of satisfying demands for African independence, European colonial officials returned home and were replaced by westernized African politicians who were simply puppets of the former colonial rulers. This theory is called **neocolonialism**, and it has several problems. While specific European powers like France did favor such an approach to decolonization, it is impossible to prove that the different colonial rulers conspired among themselves. Additionally, there were so many changes in governments in Africa in the years immediately after independence that a simple conspiracy between outgoing colonial rulers and incoming African leaders cannot explain Africa's continued problems of economic exploitation and poverty.

Many factors broadly influenced the decolonization of Africa during the late 1950s and 1960s. The international political climate was turning against colonial empires. The two dominant superpowers of the post–Second World War era, the United States and the Soviet Union, were both officially anti-colonial but for different ideological reasons. The United States had been founded with an anti-colonial revolution against Britain in 1776, and the Soviet Union was steeped in Marxist rhetoric that decried imperialist exploitation. During the Second World War, these two powers had taken the lead in the fight against Nazi Germany and promoted the values of democracy and self-determination, sometimes to the frustration of their beleaguered imperial allies, Britain and Free France. Established at the end of the war, the **United Nations** gradually became more anti-colonial as former colonies in Asia and then the newly independent African countries joined the international organization. The UN became divided between a small but powerful Security Council that included colonial powers Britain and France as well as the superpowers, and a large but weak General Assembly, which became dominated by an anti-colonial block of member states. Within Africa, the formerly elitist and moderate African political organizations that had largely emerged between the world

☰ **No longer a great power.** UN Security Council votes on Suez Crisis: The US votes in direct opposition to Great Britain.

wars were transforming into mass nationalist movements. This had been caused by renewed colonial oppression and demands for increased production during and immediately after the Second World War and occurred within the simultaneous context of Africa's dramatically growing cities. In densely populated urban centers, people discontented by inflation and unemployment flocked to nationalist rallies where they heard speeches by westernized African politicians who had been motivated by wartime propaganda about freedom and democracy.

Among the European powers, Britain took the lead in decolonizing Africa. No other European power had considered granting independence to a sub-Saharan African territory before 1958. While the British government had been determined to remain in Africa during the late 1940s and early 1950s, in 1960 British prime minister Harold MacMillan addressed the South African parliament in Cape Town and warned that "winds of change" were blowing across the continent. Two major events in the mid- to late 1950s had informed a change in British policy. First, from 1952 to 1960, the British military fought a brutal counterinsurgency war in Kenya against a rebel group called the Land and Freedom Army. Although the British defeated this movement—which they called Mau Mau—it was a costly and politically embarrassing campaign that London did not want to repeat in other colonies (see page 460). Second, in 1956 Britain had collaborated with France and Israel to invade independent Egypt and secure the Suez Canal from an Egyptian nationalist government. With the Soviet Union threatening to intervene on behalf of Egypt and the United States unwilling to back them, Britain and France were forced to withdraw from Suez. This **Suez Crisis** taught Britain that it was no longer a great power and that it had to play a subordinate role to the United States. With the "emergency" in Kenya and the Suez affair in Egypt, Britain could not get out of Africa fast enough, and this pressured other reluctant and weaker European powers like France and Belgium to follow suit.

British West Africa

In the late 1930s, Britain had begun to move away from the policy of indirect rule in its West Africa territories and toward fostering the growth of the westernized and educated African elite that would, it was thought, eventually take the reins of self-government within the context of the British Empire. This was because Britain's West African territories had a significant, though still relatively small, number of people with Western education and the Gold Coast had the highest proportion of Western-educated people of any part of Africa. The coastal areas of British West Africa had the most developed system of higher education in colonial Africa, with Fourah Bay College, Africa's first Western-style university, opening in Freetown,

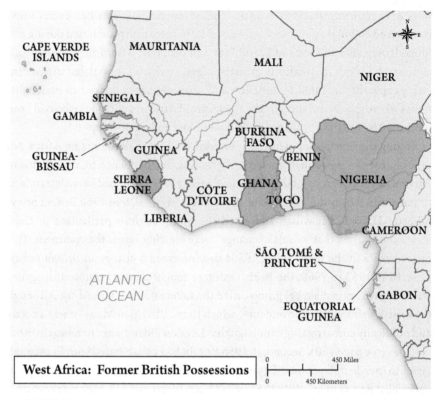

≡ MAP 21.2

Sierra Leone, in 1827, Achimota College opening in Accra, Gold Coast, in 1927, and Ibadan University, Nigeria's first university, opening in 1948. Western-style African political organizations and newspapers were also comparatively advanced in West Africa, and during the second half of the 1930s African political leaders there had called for self-government and independence. Britain's plans for political reform in West Africa were delayed by the Second World War, and by the late 1940s they had been superseded by growing African demands for independence. Similar interwar plans for colonial self-government were not put in place for British territories in East Africa because the number of Western-educated African people there was negligible and some of these territories were inhabited by white and Asian settlers.

Ghana (the Gold Coast)

In 1946, the British government granted a new constitution for the Gold Coast in which, for the first time, elected members formed a majority of the legislative council, though this body still merely advised the governor, who held the real power. The next year, Western-educated elites formed the United Gold Coast Convention (UGCC), which advocated for the attainment of self-government in the shortest possible time but stuck to using legal means of achieving this aim. Within the leadership of the UGCC was **Kwame Nkrumah**, who, having returned to the Gold Coast in 1947, had spent ten years studying in the United States (1935–45) and then two years studying in Britain (1945–47). As a Pan-Africanist, Nkrumah had been central in organizing the 5th Pan-African Congress in Manchester, Britain, in 1945, in which delegates agreed to work toward the creation of an independent United States of Africa governed through democratic and socialist principles. In February 1948, in Accra, police shot at ex-servicemen staging a demonstration over poor veterans' benefits. Three protestors were killed and 60 injured. This incited widespread rioting in Accra and other parts of the Gold Coast in which many foreign owned businesses were looted, and British authorities responded by briefly detaining the UGCC leadership, including Nkrumah. In June 1949, Nkrumah broke with the moderate and elitist UGCC and formed a new nationalist organization called the **Convention People's Party (CPP)**, which demanded immediate independence and gained popularity among ordinary people.

Reacting to the 1948 riots, the British government created a new Gold Coast constitution which increased the amount of elected representation in the legislative council but in which the governor retained executive power. Although Nkrumah was again imprisoned by the British for his leadership of anti-colonial strikes and protests, his CPP won a strong majority of the seats in the legislative council election of February 1951. Right after the election, Nkrumah, who had himself won a seat, was released from prison, and the next day he accepted an invitation from the British governor to form a government within the legislative council. Working with the British administration, Nkrumah led a political transformation between 1952 and 1954 that included the creation of the formal position of prime minister to which he was elected by the council (now called an assembly); the end of election of assembly members by traditional tribal authorities; and the expansion of the assembly, which consisted of representatives elected by equally sized constituencies. With the new constitution of 1954, the Gold Coast became an internally self-governing territory in which the British retained control of foreign relations and defense.

After winning another majority in the assembly election of June 1954, the mostly southern-based CPP began a process of centralization that was opposed by new regional political groups in the interior—the National Liberation Movement in Asante and the Northern People's Party in the far north. These organizations sought a federal political system in which each region of the Gold Coast would

≡ **First president of Ghana.** Ghanaian president Kwame Nkrumah (1912–1972) and US president John F. Kennedy in 1961.

have its own government. The Asante and northern regions had been governed by powerful traditional leaders within the context of British indirect rule, and the local elites feared political domination by the Westernized and educated southerners like Nkrumah. Supporting Nkrumah's plan for a unitary state, the British declared that they would grant independence on this basis if it was requested by a solid majority of the members of the assembly, and an election was called to test public opinion on the matter. In the July 1956 election the divided opposition meant that while the CPP won 57 percent of the popular vote, it gained a two-thirds majority in the assembly, winning constituencies across the country, including in Asante and the north. The next month, the assembly passed a resolution, boycotted by the opposition, that formally requested independence, and this was subsequently accepted by the British government. Ghana, formerly the Gold Coast, became an independent dominion within the **British Commonwealth** in March 1957, with Nkrumah continuing as prime minister and a British-appointed governor general representing the British monarch, who was still the head of state. In 1960, after a country-wide referendum, Ghana broke governmental ties with Britain and became a republic, with Nkrumah as its first president.

Nigeria

By the late 1940s, Nigerian political organizations had developed along regional lines. As explained in earlier chapters, colonial Nigeria had become divided between a predominantly Christian and relatively more prosperous south (which itself was split between the Yoruba of the west and the Igbo of the east) and a predominantly Muslim and impoverished north governed by conservative emirs. With its base of support in the eastern part of the country, the **National Congress of Nigeria and the Cameroons (NCNC)** was led by **Nnamdi Azikiwe** and advocated for the independence of Nigeria as a single nation. In western Nigeria, the **Action Group (AG)** was led by **Obafemi Awolowo** and sought to rally the Yoruba people of that area but also supported minority rights across the country. Formed in 1949, the **Northern People's Congress (NPC)** was led by the few Western-educated elites in that region, particularly **Ahmadu Bello**, who also held a prestigious traditional position as Sardauna of Sokoto. Seeking to counter southern political dominance, Bello worked to protect the integrity of northern culture and religion.

Nigeria's regional divisions were further entrenched by postwar British political reforms that introduced the federal system as a way for a large and diverse country to move toward self-government. In 1946, the British imposed a new constitution on Nigeria, which, although real power remained with the governor, expanded the partly elected legislative council to cover the entire country but also created separate legislative councils for each of the three regions. Amid increasing demands for autonomy, constitutional talks were held in Ibadan in 1950 and another new constitution created for Nigeria. While electoral politics was expanded with a larger national assembly and a national council of ministers, the federal principle was strengthened by the granting of broad powers to regional assemblies that could not be superseded by the central government. The NPC and AG supported the federal approach which was opposed by the NCNC. Yet another new constitution, enacted in 1954, entrenched the federal system and set the stage for the eventual granting of independence. By this time, the NPC formed the regional government in the north under the premiership of Ahmadu Bello, the AG formed the regional government in the west under Obafemi Awolowo, and the NCNC formed the regional government in the east. Because the south was split between the NCNC and AG, the NPC won the 1954 federal election and formed the central government with other regional representatives included in the cabinet.

Full powers of self-government were gained by the western and eastern regions in 1957 and by the less developed northern region in 1959. At the same time, a federal coalition government, including the NPC, NCNC, and AG, was formed under the leadership of the NPC's **Abubakar Balewa**, who became prime minister and

≡ **Nigerian leaders.** (left to right) Prime Minister Abubakar Tafawa Balewa (1912–66), Northern Region premier Ahmadu Bello (1910–66) and Governor General (later President) Nnamdi Azikiwe (1904–96) in 1960.

managed Nigeria's internal affairs with little interference from Britain. During this political transition, the discovery of oil in eastern Nigeria in 1956 and the start of commercial production and export in 1958 inspired much hope for the future of Nigeria's economy. However, it also launched a political struggle between the regional and central governments over control of oil revenues. Furthermore, smaller ethnic groups began to resent the dominance of the larger Hausa (north), Yoruba (west), and Igbo (east) in the new political arrangements. In central Nigeria, Tiv and Idoma communities came to develop a "middle belt" consciousness, fueling a desire to distinguish themselves from the north and the south, and there were calls for the creation of a mid-west region between west and east. In 1959, the constitution for an independent Nigeria, which had been negotiated by the regional leaders in Britain, came into effect, confirming the federal system and giving the more populous north a majority of seats in the federal parliament. The December 1959 election resulted in the NPC, which had gained the largest number of seats but still fell short of a majority, forming a coalition government with the NCNC and the AG led by Awolowo taking the role of parliamentary opposition. Nigeria became independent in October 1960, with Prime Minister Balewa leading the federal government and Azikiwe in the largely ceremonial position of governor general representing the British monarch, who was still head of state. In 1963, Nigeria de-clared itself a republic, which meant that Azikiwe became president.

Sierra Leone

When the Second World War ended, Sierra Leone was still divided in two, with the colony of Freetown enjoying some representative government through an elected legislative council and the more populous but less developed protectorate of the interior administered by traditional chiefs within the indirect rule system. In 1947, the British government, as it did in other West African territories at the time, at-tempted to impose a new constitution on Sierra Leone. In this case the proposed constitution sought to amalgamate the administration of the colony and the pro-tectorate through the creation of a single council, with a majority of members com-ing from the protectorate. Led by Dr. H.C. Bankole-Bright, the Krio inhabitants of Freetown formed the National Council of Sierra Leone (NCSL) in 1950 to oppose the constitution as they claimed that the mostly illiterate council members from the protectorate would be useless in government. Formed the next year, the **Sierra Leone People's Party (SLPP)** was led by Dr. **Milton Margai** and represented the com-paratively small group of protectorate-educated elites and the traditional chiefs who supported the new con-stitution. The elections of 1951, which were conducted on the basis of a slightly revised constitution, which still gave more council representation to the protectorate, resulted in an SLPP majority, with party leaders like Margai and Siaka Stevens eventually gaining positions on the new executive council, which functioned like a cabinet. Within the council, the NCSL's Bankole-Bright demanded independence for the Freetown colony, but this was rejected without discussion. In 1955, as the NCSL and SLPP continued to argue over constitutional arrangements, people in Freetown rioted over increased food prices caused by the rush of people to the recent-ly discovered diamond fields in the interior, and there were violent protests in the interior against tax increases and abuse by chiefs.

With another new constitution put in place in 1958, Sierra Leone gained a form of internal self-government under Prime Minister Margai of the SLPP, with the British governor continuing to control foreign affairs,

≡ **West African leader.** Prime Minister Sir Milton Margai (1895–1964) of Sierra Leone in 1963.

defense, and the civil service. Knighted by the queen in 1959, Sir Milton formed the United National Front (UNF), which included the SLPP and other small parties and sought to present a united position at the independence conference with the British government in London in April and May 1960. It was decided that in April 1961 Sierra Leone would become an independent state within the British Commonwealth. Siaka Stevens, the only UNF delegate who had refused to sign the agreement as he objected to continued defense arrangements with Britain, returned home to form the All People's Congress (APC), which put forth a socialist agenda and built up a following in the north as the conservative SLPP was dominated by the southern Mende people. Sierra Leone gained independence on schedule and Sir Milton and the SLPP were re-elected in the first post-independence election, held in 1962. The British monarch remained the ceremonial head of state of Sierra Leone until 1971, when, after much turmoil that will be discussed in Chapter 24 a new APC government under Stevens declared a republic.

The Gambia

Britain's devolution of political power to the Gambia was slower than in its other West African territories. There were questions over whether or not the Gambia, with its small size, economy, and educated elite, could function as an independent country. In addition, British officials also considered the possibility that this sliver of a British territory could eventually be absorbed by the French colony of Senegal, which gained independence in 1960 and which completely encircled the Gambia. During the decolonization process of the early 1960s, British officials favored this possibility, but at the time it was rejected by anglophone Gambian political leaders, who feared being dominated by the much larger francophone Senegal. Another important factor in the Gambia was that the administration was divided between the colony of Bathurst, where there was a significant educated elite, and the much less developed protectorate of the interior, which was ruled by chiefs and colonial officials.

From 1946 to 1954, the British imposed a series of constitutions on the Gambia that created and then enlarged a legislative council consisting of both elected and appointed representatives. These reforms stimulated the growth of small political parties around Bathurst, such as the Gambia Democratic Party (GDP). In the late 1950s, the granting of independence to Ghana and internal self-government to Sierra Leone prompted demands for self-government in the Gambia. This became a partial reality with the 1959 constitution, in which, for the first time, representatives from the protectorate would compose a majority in the House of Representatives and a council of ministers would be created. In the 1960 election, the new People's Progressive Party (PPP), led by **D.K. Jawara** and formed to provide a political voice for the protectorate, won the most seats in the house, but it did not form a government as the British governor demanded a coalition made up of all parties. This prompted Jawara and the PPP, inspired by Nigeria's independence, to circulate an "independence manifesto" that proposed full internal self-government in 1961 and independence in 1962. New elections in 1962 resulted in a strong PPP victory and Jawara became prime minister, with the Gambia granted internal self-government the next year. The center of political life had shifted from urban Bathurst to the rural countryside. Jawara convinced the British government that new elections were not necessary before the granting of independence within the British Commonwealth, which occurred in February 1965. Although Jawara was knighted by the British queen the next year, the Gambia was declared a republic in 1970.

British East Africa

Kenya

Although Kenya was the last British colony in East Africa to become independent, events there impacted the decolonization of the rest of the continent. During the colonial era, the Kikuyu people of central Kenya had been disproportionally affected by British rule as white settlers took their best land in what became called the **White Highlands**. While many Kikuyu became landless squatters or low-paid laborers on white-owned farms, or went to the nearby city of Nairobi to find other work, some became successful peasant farmers loyal to the colonial regime. With the failure of the moderate Kenya Africa Union (KAU) to end racial discrimination in the 1940s and early 1950s, discontent among trade union members and squatters became more intense. In October 1952, the British government in Kenya declared a state of emergency after a Kikuyu chief and a white woman were murdered. Thousands of British soldiers were flown into Kenya and several massive security sweeps of Nairobi resulted in tens of thousands of people

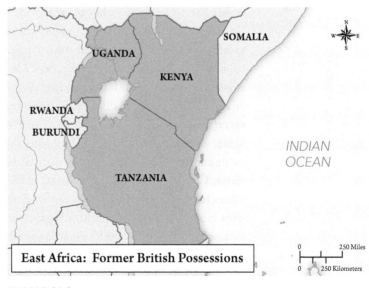

East Africa: Former British Possessions

≡ **MAP 21.3**

being detained or expelled from the city. **Jomo Kenyatta**, leader of the now out-lawed KAU, was arrested and convicted of treason, though there was no evidence implicating him in violent resistance. Militants fled to the African reserves and high-altitude forests, from where they mounted attacks on white settlers and Kikuyu, who remained loyal to the British. The rebels called themselves the Land and Free-dom Army, but the British called them **Mau Mau**, though the origin of the term is unclear. There were around 12,000 insurgents who were organized into separate and sometimes feuding groups under leaders Dedan Kimathi, Stanley Mathenge, and Waruhiu Itote, who was also called "General China." Lacking any foreign spon-sorship, the rebels were poorly armed with spears, machetes, and a few homemade or captured guns, and they did not articulate a clear ideology or agenda, with rebels bound to the movement by traditional oaths. The fighters of the Land and Freedom Army became skilled at hiding in the forest, which became their sanctuary, and they communicated by leaving messages in secret "letter boxes." Most (but not all) armed Mau Mau fighters were men, but Kenyan women were very active in providing them with intelligence and food. While British officials portrayed the Mau Mau move-ment as a type of mass psychological disorder caused by overly rapid modernization, subsequent scholars debated if it represented a Kikuyu civil war or a true national in-dependence movement. The British military campaign, often inaccurately portrayed as an example of effective "minimum force" counterinsurgency, was particularly brutal, with around 800,000 Kenyans confined to concentration camps where many were tortured, some camps were denied food, and living conditions were squalid. Special prisons were built for thousands of female inmates who were subjected to violence and humiliation while being forced to take lessons on domestic duties and Christianity. In addition to British and African colonial soldiers who were brought to Kenya, the colonial state dramatically expanded the Kenya Police and created a Kikuyu "Home Guard" to fight the rebels. After large security force sweeps failed to eliminate the small and elusive insurgent bands in the forests, the British embarked on a program of using small unit patrols that proved more effective. One particularly successful tactic involved security force members, including some former Mau Mau fighters who had changed sides, disguising themselves as rebels so that they could locate and infiltrate rebel groups. In early 1956, only about 900 insurgents remained active. General China surrendered and avoided the death penalty by encouraging others to capitulate, Kimathi was captured and eventually hanged, and Mathenge went missing. In 1956, the British began to reform the colonial system in Kenya, making more land available for the Kikuyu, allowing the African majority to engage in profitable coffee growing, raising wages for Africans working in the cities, and permitting the direct election of African members in the Legislative Assembly. The British government had realized that maintaining colonial rule in Kenya and other

≡ **Counter-insurgency.** A Kenyan suspected of participating in the Mau Mau rebellion is taken into custody by British soldiers. During the rebellion, hundreds of thousands of Africans were sent to concentration camps established by the British.

parts of Africa would require expensive and politically embarrassing military campaigns. The Hola massacre of 1959, in which 11 Kenyan prisoners were beaten to death by guards, illustrated these potential problems.

In 1960, the British ended the state of emergency in Kenya, abandoned support for the dominant white and Asian minorities, and initiated a majority-rule, one-person-one-vote political system that would lead to independence. That same year, two Kenyan political parties were formed: **Kenya African National Union (KANU)**, which had support among the Kikuyu and Luo ethnic groups and favored a unitary government, and the Kenya African Democratic Union (KADU), which championed the interests of minority ethnic groups and advocated a federal system. Kenyatta was released from prison in 1961 and he soon became the leader of KANU. During 1962, KANU and KADU jointly negotiated with the British government, creating a weak federal constitution for Kenya. Tom Mboya, a Kenyan trade union leader who had been critical of British military operations during the emergency and then joined KANU, was instrumental in this process. KANU won a strong majority in the May 1963 election, Kenya became internally self-governing with Kenyatta as prime minister in June, and the country gained full independence within the British Commonwealth in December. While the KANU government quickly abolished the weak federal system and Kenya became a republic in 1964, President Kenyatta reassured Kenyan whites that their property rights would be respected, and Kenya maintained close relations with Britain, including military cooperation. Kenyatta's regime quickly became authoritarian. In 1964, KADU was voluntarily absorbed into the ruling KANU party, and in 1969 the Kenyan People's Union (KPU), a newly formed leftist party strongly supported by the Luo of western Kenya and led by former vice president Oginga Odinga, was banned by the government. That same year, Mboya was gunned down in central Nairobi, with many suspecting that he had been the victim of a political assassination.

Tanganyika

Although the British government had done little to prepare its East African territories for independence before the late 1950s, Tanganyika's special international legal status meant that in theory it was supposed to eventually gain some form of self-government. As a former German colony, Tanganyika had become a British-administered mandate of the League of Nations after the First World War, and in 1947 this status was changed to that of a trust territory of the United Nations. During the late 1940s and early 1950s, various local cooperative unions in different parts of Tanganyika protested local grievances, such as taxation, compulsory agricultural projects and livestock culling, and dispossession of land that was earmarked for white settlers. This was also the period in which Britain's ambitious Tanganyika Groundnut Scheme became a colossal failure. In the early 1950s, the urban elite of the Tanganyika African Association (TAA), originally formed as the African Association in 1929, brought these grievances to the attention of the United Nations Trusteeship Council in New York. **Julius Nyerere**, who had studied in Makerere University in Uganda and the University of Edinburgh in Scotland, became the TAA president in 1953 and quickly emerged as a charismatic nationalist leader. In July 1954, TAA changed its name to the **Tanganyika African National Union (TANU)**, which reflected its new political goal of gaining independence. TANU also organized women's and youth wings, and arranged for local cooperatives, trade unions, and traditional groups to join the movement as affiliates. Under the leadership of **Bibi Titi Mohamed**, TANU's women's wing garnered support for the movement among Tanganyika's women. At the same time, the British colonial state sponsored the creation of a "multiracial" political system that would give equal representation to the territory's European, Asian, and African communities, despite the fact that the latter represented an overwhelming majority. In 1958, an election was held in which each voter was to cast a ballot for a representative of each of the three races to sit on the new Legislative Council. Although TANU opposed the "multiracial" system, it participated in the election, winning 13 out of 15 seats and gaining 68 percent of the popular vote.

As a result of TANU's strong political support and the broad change in British policy to Africa that had been informed by the conflict in Kenya and the Suez Crisis, the British government conceded that Tanganyika would gain internal self-government by 1964 and independence by 1970. Prompted by continuing protest, the British sped up the transition, with Tanganyika gaining responsible government in 1960, and independence followed in 1961 with a TANU government led by Prime Minister Nyerere. Tanganyika was the first British territory in East Africa to become an autonomous state and it became a republic under President Nyerere in 1962. However, at the start of 1964 Nyerere had to request British military intervention to quell a mutiny by Tanganyika's army over low pay, slow promotion, and the continued authority of British officers. As a result, Nyerere expelled British military advisors and transformed his country's military into a TANU party militia based on the example of communist Chi-

≡ **East African leaders.** (Left to right) Julius Nyerere of Tanzania, Jomo Kenyatta of Kenya, and Milton Obote of Uganda in 1967.

na. In 1964, Tanganyika united with the politically volatile island of Zanzibar to create Tanzania which became a one-party state under TANU the following year. In 1969, Bibi Titi Mohamed was arrested on charges of plotting to overthrow the government and sentenced to life imprisonment. She was released after two years and then dropped out of public life.

Uganda

British political reforms in East Africa began in Uganda, which lacked a substantial white settler population and had a significant group of Western-educated African people who were mainly from the country's southern region. Indeed, East Africa's first institution of higher education, Makerere University, had opened in Uganda in 1949 and was producing graduates for the region. In the East African interior, the British protectorate of Uganda had become divided between a marginalized north and a relatively more prosperous and agriculturally productive south. The south was also the location of the traditional Buganda kingdom, which had allied with the British in the late nineteenth century and which the British had used as a base to conquer nearby areas to form the wider colonial territory of Uganda. In 1949, Buganda became the scene of riots over colonial price controls on cotton exports, Asian control of cotton processing, and lack of political representation apart from the much-resented British-appointed chiefs. In 1952, the British reformed the economy in favor of African farmers and transformed the legislative council, previously dominated by the tiny European minority, into a body of elected representatives from across the protectorate. This meant that the privileged position of Buganda would be lost. Furthermore, the British government was considering making Uganda part of an East African federation that would be dominated by the white settlers of Kenya where the Mau Mau insurgency had just begun. In 1952, the Uganda National Congress (UNC) was formed, and while it became Uganda's first countrywide political organization and had a Pan-African agenda, it was mostly based in Buganda, which was becoming alienated from wider protectorate politics.

In 1953, Buganda's Kabaka (king) Frederick Mutesa II was forcibly exiled to Britain after he objected to Buganda's possible inclusion in an East African federation and demanded that the kingdom be separated from the rest of Uganda. The *kabaka* was repatriated in 1955 after he agreed not to oppose Buganda's independence within the larger Uganda; in return, he was transformed from a ceremonial ruler to one with the power to appoint and dismiss Buganda officials and chiefs. This led to the formation of more political parties in Uganda to contest elections for the legislative council. Since the late nineteenth century, Buganda had been divided between Protestant and Catholic factions, with the British colonial rulers favoring the former. Disappointed over the continued Protestant dominance, Catholics from Buganda formed the Democratic Party (DP) in 1956 and advocated for the Africanization of the colonial civil service. In 1960, the splintering of the UNC allowed northern politician **Milton Obote** to form the **Uganda People's Congress (UPC)**, which gained support in the rest of the protectorate, where the possible continuation of Buganda domination was resented. During the March 1961 elections that would lead to responsible government, the Kabaka's Protestant faction in Buganda boycotted the polls. This meant that the DP, led by Benedicto Kiwanuka, formed the first administration of an internally self-governing Uganda. Alarmed by the victory of their political rivals, the Kabaka Yekka (KY—"King Alone") party was formed within Buganda to press for a federal constitution for Uganda in which Buganda would enjoy internal autonomy. Promising to support the federal system and to appoint the *kabaka* as Uganda's future head of state, Obote's UPC formed a political alliance with the KY to defeat the DP in the election of April 1962. Uganda became independent in October 1962 with a coalition UPC-KY government led by Prime Minister Obote. The next year, Kabaka Mutesa II

Timeline

1946—British impose new constitutions on the Gold Coast and Nigeria

1946–54—Constitutional reforms in the Gambia

1947—Formation of United Gold Coast Convention (UGCC)

1947—Tanganyika becomes a United Nations trust territory

1948—Protests in the Gold Coast

1949—Formation of Convention People's Party (CPP), led by Kwame Nkrumah, in the Gold Coast

1949—Riots in Buganda

1951—Nkrumah's CPP wins electoral victory in the Gold Coast

1951—Legislative council elections in Sierra Leone

1952—British reforms in Uganda

1952–60—State of emergency in Kenya

1953—Julius Nyerere becomes leader of the Tanganyika African Association (TAA)

1953—Kabaka Frederick Mutesa II exiled to Britain

1954—The Gold Coast granted internal self-government under CPP, led by Nkrumah

1954—TAA changes its name to Tanganyika African National Union (TANU)

1954—New constitution entrenches federal system in Nigeria

1955—Rioting in Sierra Leone

1955—Kabaka Mutesa returns to Buganda

1956—Suez Crisis

1957—Independence for Ghana (formerly the Gold Coast)

1957—Self-government for the western and eastern regions of Nigeria

1958—Legislative council election in Tanganyika won by Nyerere's TANU—Britain abandons "multiracial" policy in Tanganyika

1958—Internal self-government for Sierra Leone under Sierra Leone People's Party (SLPP) led by Milton Margai

1959—Self-government for northern region of Nigeria

1959—New constitution in the Gambia grants electoral majority to the interior

1960—"Winds of Change" Speech

1960—Ghana become a republic

1960—Nigeria gains independence

1960—Tanganyika gains internal self-government under TANU

1960—Formation of Kenya African National Union (KANU) and Kenya African Democratic Union (KADU)

1960—Formation of Uganda People's Congress (UPC) led by Milton Obote

1961—Sierra Leone gains independence

1961—Tanganyika gains independence with TANU government under Nyerere

1961—Internal self-government for Uganda—formation of Kabaka Yekka (KY) party.

1962—Uganda gains independence with a federal system and a coalition UPC/KY government under Prime Minister Milton Obote

1963—Kenya becomes self-governing and then independent under KANU government of Jomo Kenyatta

1963—Nigeria becomes a republic

1963—The Gambia becomes internally self-governing under the People's Progressive Party (PPP) of D.K. Jawara

1963—Kabaka Mutesa II becomes president of Uganda

1964—Army mutiny in East Africa

1964—Tanganyika and Zanzibar merge as Tanzania

1965—The Gambia gains independence

1966—Mutesa II overthrown by Obote, who takes the presidency in Uganda

1971—Sierra Leone becomes a republic

became the president of Uganda. Obote dealt with the 1964 East African army mutiny, which was centered on Tanganyika but spread to Uganda and Kenya, by giving in to the demands of the mutineers, which encouraged the development of an undisciplined and predatory Ugandan military. In 1966, Obote, using his northern-dominated army, abolished the federal system and forcibly incorporated Buganda into the rest of the country. Kabaka Mutesa, his palace attacked by Ugandan troops, went into exile. Obote named himself president.

Conclusion

The decolonization of Africa began with the British territories in West Africa. Building on pre–Second World War plans, the British government enacted limited democratic reforms in the Gold Coast, Nigeria, Sierra Leone, and the Gambia in the late 1940s. At this point, the British thought that these territories could become internally self-governing within the British Empire. Full independence had not yet been envisioned. Within these West African territories, political reforms stimulated the growth of African political parties that pressed for the faster devolution of governmental power and demanded sovereignty. Along with Cold War tensions that increased hostility toward colonial empires, the key events of the Mau Mau War in Kenya and the Suez Crisis in Egypt in the mid-1950s prompted Britain to withdraw quickly from its African colonies. While British West Africa had been preparing for self-government and sovereignty for about a decade and still encountered many problems in the early years of independence, Britain's East African territories experienced a more rapid transition. In the early 1950s, Britain was considering the creation of an East African regional federation that would be dominated by the white and Asian minorities, but by the end of the 1950s it was clear that each colony would become a separate, independent state with a majority-rule government. Once Tanzania, Uganda, and Kenya became independent in the early 1960s, African political leaders who had campaigned for independence inherited political power and quickly created authoritarian regimes.

KEY TERMS

Abubakar Balewa 455

Action Group 455

Ahmadu Bello 455

Bibi Titi
  Mohamed 462

British Commonwealth 454

Cold War 447

Convention People's Party
  (CPP) 453

D.K. Jawara 458

decolonization 447

Jomo Kenyatta 460

Julius Nyerere 462

Kenyan African National
  Union (KANU) 461

STUDY QUESTIONS

1. Why were European colonial powers reluctant to grant independence to their African colonies after the Second World War? How did the Cold War influence the way European colonial powers, the United States, and the USSR viewed Africa?

2. What political changes led to African states rapidly achieving independence in the 1950s and 1960s? How did the Suez Crisis and the Mau Mau rebellion act as a catalyst for these rapid changes?

3. How did Britain transfer power to Ghana, Nigeria, Sierra Leone, and the Gambia? How did the way they achieved independence differ from the process for Kenya, Tanganyika, and Uganda?

Please see page FR-10 for the Further Readings for this chapter.
For additional digital learning resources please go to
https://www.oup.com/he/falola-stapleton1e

Decolonization and African Nationalism, Part Two: 1945–1974

KICK OUT
SOUTH AFRICAN
APARTHEID

KICK OUT
U.S. RACISM AND
IMPERIALISM

SUPPORT THE MPLA
(MOVIMENTO POPULAR DE
LIBERTAÇÃO DE ANGOLA)

Although Britain began negotiated political devolution in its West African territories in the early 1950s, the other European colonial powers resisted relinquishing control of their African empires. Despite the dramatic global changes after the Second World War, France, Belgium, and Portugal were determined to retain their profitable and strategically important African territories. For those colonial powers, loss of African empires signified relegation to second class or lower status in world affairs. Just as the Mau Mau war in Kenya during the 1950s pushed Britain to quickly decolonize East Africa, armed liberation struggles by African nationalists played an even greater role in compelling France and Portugal to grant sudden independence to their territories. While Belgium's colonies did not gain independence through warfare, Belgian attempts to retain influence in Africa led to chaotic and violent decolonization in the Congo, Rwanda, and Burundi.

French Africa

Algeria

The decolonization of France's African empire was greatly influenced by the **Algerian War of Independence**, which lasted from 1954 to 1962. During the 1920s and 1930s, an anti-colonial movement developed among Algeria's Muslim majority, who were dominated by a French settler minority. In 1945, when the Second World War ended in Europe, French security forces shot down Algerian Muslims protesting for independence in the town of Setif, and this led to retaliatory attacks by Muslims on French settlers in rural areas. The violence escalated, with French airplanes and warships bombarding Muslim communities, and gangs of settlers murdering Muslims for not wearing a white armband to symbolize loyalty to France. As a result, many Algerian Muslims became radicalized, and in 1954 a number of small pro-independence groups merged to form the **National Liberation Front (FLN)**, which launched a war to liberate the

Global fight against imperialism and racism. Armed liberation struggles in several European colonies in Africa during the 1960s and '70s brought international attention to the Cold War conflict between the United States and the Soviet Union. Angola, in particular, became a focal point in the global fight against imperialism and racism.

469

country from French occupation. Supported and armed by the Arab nationalist government in Egypt and the Soviet Union, the FLN began attacks on French civilian and military targets in Algeria at the start of November 1954. The recent French withdrawal from Indochina, where they had been militarily defeated by a nationalist movement, made the government in Paris more determined to retain Algeria, which it viewed as an integral part of France. With attacks against civilians by both the FLN and French settlers, the French administration abandoned reforms meant to placate the independence movement and embarked on an all-out war against the insurgents. In 1956 and 1957, a general strike and a series of bombings orchestrated by the FLN prompted the French military to impose a reign of terror on the Muslim population of Algiers. French security forces tortured and murdered suspected independence activists and critics of the colonial regime. The military wing of the FLN evolved from a small guerrilla force into a large and well-organized army, with 30,000 fighters based in neighboring Tunisia, which became independent in 1956, and somewhere between 6,000 and 25,000 insurgents conducting hit-and-run attacks inside Algeria. Eventually, the FLN established "liberated areas" inside Algeria, where they formed a state structure that collected taxes and enlisted new recruits. By 1956, there were 400,000 French troops in Algeria, including about 170,000 local Muslim auxiliaries. The French divided the country into sectors, each with a dedicated security force that tried to clear out insurgents. Other counter-insurgency measures included the construction of barbed wire and landmine barriers, known as the Morice Line, along Algeria's border with Tunisia to prevent infiltration, and the forced displacement of about two million Algerians into guarded camps to prevent them from aiding the rebels. Crops and livestock were also destroyed so they could not be used by the FLN. Beginning in 1958, French counterinsurgency strategy in Algeria shifted from trying to control individual sectors to mounting large search-and-destroy operations against insurgent controlled areas. While Algerian female prisoners were subjected to sexual violence by French security force personnel, during the late 1950s the French state tried to win support from Algerian Muslim women by launching health and educational projects, reforming marriage and divorce laws to give women more rights, and granting them the vote. However, a French campaign to gain support among Muslim women by encouraging them to adopt Western dress backfired as the FLN labeled those who removed their traditional veils as prostitutes.

The Algerian War greatly impacted France itself. In 1958, the French military in Algiers, fearful that the civilian government in Paris would order a withdrawal, staged a coup and demanded that former Second World War Free French leader and hero **Charles de Gaulle** set up a unity government that would preserve French

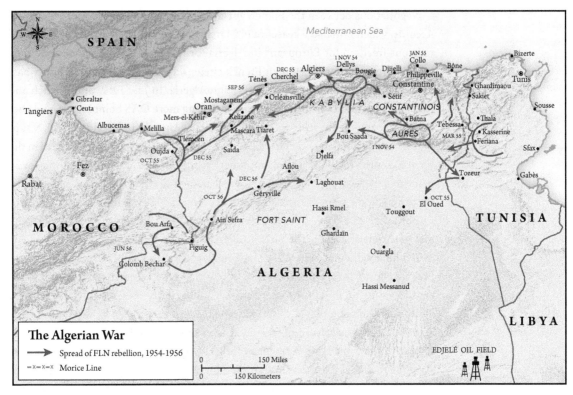

The Algerian War

→ Spread of FLN rebellion, 1954-1956
═x═x═x═ Morice Line

≡ **MAP 22.1**

rule in Algeria. In case their demands were not met, French officers planned to use military forces on the island of Corsica to take power by force in Paris. In May, just hours before the planned operation, the French civilian government conceded the military's demands and de Gaulle assumed power. De Gaulle initially declared his support for French rule in Algeria, but he quickly realized that the war was unwinnable and embarked on a series of reforms that would lead to Algerian independence. Extending a bombing campaign to France, the FLN rejected de Gaulle's attempt at a compromise that would grant Algeria a form of independence closely associated with France. In September 1959, with French public opinion turning against the war, de Gaulle acknowledged the possibility that Algeria could become a fully independent state. This angered conservative elements in France and Algeria. In January 1960, French settlers in Algeria violently rebelled against the French government during the "Week of the Barricades" and former French generals based in fascist Spain founded the Secret Army Organization (OAS), which embarked on terrorist attacks and made an unsuccessful coup attempt in France and Algeria in hope of stopping Algerian independence.

Negotiations between the French government and the FLN produced the **Evian Accords**, which initiated a ceasefire in March 1962; recognized property rights and religious freedom for Europeans in Algeria for three years, after which time they would have to opt for Algerian or French citizenship; and gave France military bases and access to oil resources in a sovereign Algeria. In July 1962, after French and Algerian voters had approved the accords despite more OAS bombings, Algeria became independent. Even before the official date of Algerian independence, FLN supporters began attacking French settlers and Algerian Muslims who had served in the French security forces. Over the subsequent year, more than 1.4 million people (or 13 percent of the total population) fled Algeria, including almost all Jewish inhabitants. Returning home from Tunisia and Morocco, the FLN's external forces imposed an authoritarian one-party state that existed for the next three decades. In 1965, the first president of Algeria, the FLN leader Ahmed Ben Bella, was overthrown by his own military. The Algerian War of Independence was incredibly lethal, with 26,500 French security force personnel and 3,000 settlers killed. French officials claimed to have killed 141,000 FLN insurgents, though most of these were probably civilians, 5,000 people died in France in terrorist incidents, and the FLN likely killed around 70,000 Algerian Muslim civilians. Estimates of the total death toll vary considerably, with the French government putting the figure at around 350,000, the FLN claiming that it was over one million, and many historians suggesting that between 700,000 and 800,000 people lost their lives. These figures do not include those who were murdered in reprisals that followed independence. Furthermore, during the war over two million Algerians were displaced from their homes; the number who died from starvation or disease in remote areas remains unknown.

Madagascar and Cameroon

There were two other violent, but less well-known, independence struggles in France's African colonies. As already discussed, a political movement demanding independence began in Madagascar during the early 1930s. During the Second World War, France's standing on the island was weakened by South African occupation and subsequent Free French extraction of resources. Immediately after the war, French settlers opposed colonial reforms, and in 1946 a Malagasy delegation in Paris demanded independence within a broad French context but this was rejected by the French government. Around the same time, the Democratic Movement for Malagasy Renewal (MDRM) was formed on the island, and in response to its repression by French settlers, members of the group began to advocate violence to overthrow colonial rule. In late March 1947, around 2,000 nationalist rebels began attacking French soldiers, officials, and settlers. Within a short span of time the violence spread across the island, though the larger cities were not affected and the number of insurgents grew to between 15,000 and 20,000. The MDRM leaders, who dissociated

THE ALGERIAN WAR

Top left: FLN soldiers at a training camp, 1958. *Top right:* French police guard a group of arrested demonstrators in Algiers, April 1956. *Bottom left:* During the "Week of the Barricades," January 24–31, 1960, dissident settlers threw up barricades to protest President de Gaulle's dismissal of General Massu, one of the leaders of an army revolt. *Bottom right:* Members of a women's section of the FLN rally in support of independence in 1962.

themselves from the violence, were arrested by French authorities and the group was outlawed. By late 1948, the French had mobilized 30,000 security force personnel on the island, and these troops gradually regained control by engaging in burning of villages, summary executions, and torture. The last rebel stronghold fell in November 1948. During the conflict, somewhere between 30,000 and 89,000 people perished, mostly from disease and hunger, out of a total Malagasy population of three and a half million. The war persuaded most Malagasy that the best form of independence was within the context of continued close association with France.

In September 1945, people in Douala, Cameroon, rioted over crippling poverty and this prompted French settlers to protect themselves by forming armed militias. Led by radical nationalist Ruben Um Nyobe and supported by the French Communist Party, the Union of the Peoples of Cameroon (UPC) was founded in 1948 and demanded independence as the French had failed to prepare the former German colony, and now UN trust territory, for independence. The UPC also supported the reunification of Cameroon with the smaller Southern Cameroons, which had been administered by Britain since the end of the First World War. With the French regime organizing conservative pro-colonial groups to attack them, the UPC embarked on a violent campaign in 1955 and the group was subsequently banned. The exiled UPC leaders were initially based in Southern Cameroons, but they were expelled by the British and then moved to Egypt and recently independent Sudan, Ghana, and Guinea. While UPC insurgents conducted a guerrilla war in southwestern Cameroon during the late 1950s, the French military responded with an intensive counterinsurgency campaign that involved relocating rural people to fortified communities from where they could not assist the rebels. In 1958, Nyobe was killed by French forces and many insurgents surrendered. In the late 1950s, French policy changed to promoting the independence and reunification of Cameroon, which prompted a split in the UPC, with one element entering the legal political process. The other faction formed a more radical movement called Cameroonian Army of National Liberation (ALNK), led by Félix-Roland Moumié, which continued the armed struggle in western Cameroon. With the independence of Cameroon in January 1960, the country's first president, Ahmadou Ahidjo, requested military assistance from France, which sent more troops to crush the rebellion. Later that year, French agents used poison to assassinate Moumie in Geneva, Switzerland. Although the anglophone people of Southern Cameroons voted in a 1961 referendum to rejoin newly independent Cameroon, many of them eventually came to regret this decision as the francophone majority dominated the country. Under Ahidjo, Cameroon became a dictatorial one-party state with military support from France. A limited ALNK insurgency continued until 1971, when the group's leader, Ernest Ouandie, was captured and executed in public.

The French Community

Immediately after the Second World War, in 1946, the French government declared its colonial empire to be a French Union, claiming that there was no longer a difference between the mother country and the overseas territories. While

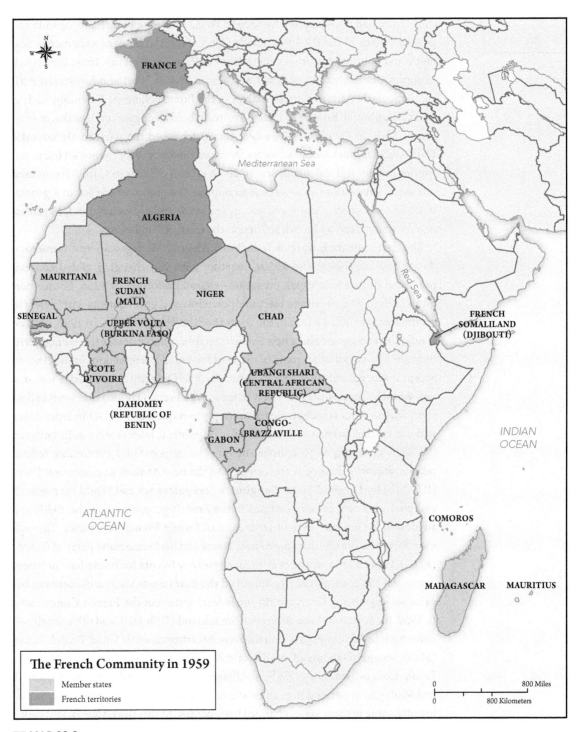

The French Community in 1959
- Member states
- French territories

FRANCE

Mediterranean Sea

ALGERIA

MAURITANIA

FRENCH SUDAN (MALI)

NIGER

SENEGAL

UPPER VOLTA (BURKINA FASO)

CHAD

FRENCH SOMALILAND (DJIBOUTI)

Red Sea

COTE D'IVOIRE

DAHOMEY (REPUBLIC OF BENIN)

UBANGI SHARI (CENTRAL AFRICAN REPUBLIC)

CONGO-BRAZZAVILLE

GABON

ATLANTIC OCEAN

INDIAN OCEAN

COMOROS

MADAGASCAR

MAURITIUS

0   800 Miles

0   800 Kilometers

≡ MAP 22.2

this reform had been inspired by Second World War Free French propaganda and promises made at the 1944 Brazzaville Conference, the changes were merely cosmetic and political power was centralized in Paris. At the same time, the French Union inspired African political leaders from French West and Equatorial Africa, particularly African representatives in the French National Assembly, such as **Félix Houphouët-Boigny** of Côte d'Ivoire, to hold a congress in Bamako, in what is now Mali, in October 1946, where they established the **African Democratic Rally** (RDA), which would advocate for greater autonomy for France's African territories but not full independence. In 1949, French officials in Côte d'Ivoire used internal RDA conflict as an excuse to oppress the group, which led to a general strike and a boycott of European goods, and at the end of January 1950, 13 protestors were shot dead by French soldiers at the town of Dimbokro.

The decolonization wars in Indochina, Algeria, Madagascar, and Cameroon during the late 1940s and 1950s, together with the changing global context, prompted France to embark on serious colonial reforms. In 1956, France permitted colonial territories to elect their own internal governments with a view to eventual independence within the context of the French Union. In 1958, with de Gaulle's rise to power and a new French republic, people across the French territories in Africa and other parts of the world voted in a referendum on whether to accept a new constitution that included their self-governing territories within a new **French Community** (the new name for the French Union) that would allow territories to request independence or simply to request immediate independence without further French assistance. African political leaders were split between the RDA grouping of Houphouët-Boigny that supported a continuing federal relationship with France at the center, and the new African Regroupment Party (RPA) led by **Léopold Sédar Senghor**, a Senegalese Second World War veteran and poet who held senior positions in the French government in the 1950s and advocated for an independent federation of former French territories. Through the efforts of trade union leader **Sékou Touré** and his Democratic Party of Guinea (PDG), Guinea became the only French territory to vote for immediate independence. All the other territories approved the new constitution and therefore became self-governing states within the federal system of the French Community. In 1959, the Comoros Islands, French Somaliland (Djibouti), and other small colonies outside Africa opted to remain French territories while Chad, French Sudan (Mali), Senegal, Dahomey, Côte d'Ivoire, Mauritania, Niger, Upper Volta (Burkina Faso), Congo-Brazzaville, Gabon, Ubangi Shari (Central African Republic), and Madagascar decided to become states within the French Community. Subsequently, some of these states changed their names. At this time Algeria, embroiled in its independence war, sent representatives to the government in France. With assistance from recently independent Ghana and Eastern Bloc socialist countries, Guinea successfully transitioned to an independent state under an authoritarian one-party rule. With Guinea serving as an example of African independence and Algeria likely to become independent in a short time, France quickly granted full independence to most of its African territories in 1960. Some territories opted to remain members of a now largely symbolic French Community and others did not. Many of these former French colonies remained linked to Paris through a series of agreements relating to economic, military, and technical assistance. Prominent African political leaders Houphouët-Boigny and Senghor became presidents of Côte d'Ivoire and Senegal, respectively, and maintained good relations with France.

≡ **West African leaders.** Felix Houphouët-Boigny (right) and Léopold Senghor.

The Belgian Territories: Congo, Rwanda, and Burundi

Congo

During the late 1940s and well into the 1950s, the Belgian government refused to acknowledge the prospect of self-government or independence for the Congo. Although Belgium had supported the principle of national self-determination in the United Nations right after the Second World War, Brussels consistently rejected international demands for it to decolonize the Congo. The vast Belgian Congo was rich in natural resources, particularly minerals in the southern region of Katanga, and many Belgians were employed in its administration and economy. While the Belgian colonial regime in the late 1940s created a system whereby westernized Congolese could gain legal equality with the white residents of the Congo, this was a cosmetic reform, as only several thousand people qualified and the promise of civil rights never materialized. As a result, westernized Congolese became frustrated with Belgian rule.

During the early to mid-1950s, the Belgian colonial state began to publicly talk about forming a new Belgian-Congolese community that would eventually gain civil rights, including the right to vote. In 1955, Belgian King Baudouin visited the Congo, where he openly supported the proposed reforms, and a Belgian professor proposed a 30-year plan for gradually transitioning the Congo to independence, including a program of enlarging the westernized Congolese population, who would replace Belgian civil servants. Such talk was opposed by elements of the Belgian government in Brussels and by many of the Belgian residents of the Congo, who did not want to lose their dominant position. Emerging Congolese political leaders, fully aware of concrete moves toward independence in British territories like the Gold Coast and Nigeria, were also critical of these plans as it meant Belgian rule would continue long into the future. In 1957, the first municipal elections in which Congolese people could vote and run for office were conducted in the urban areas of Leopoldville (Kinshasa), Jadotville (Likasi), and Elisabethville (Lubumbashi). These elections fueled popular demands for full independence in the Congo, which were also inspired by news of the 1957 independence of Ghana and the 1958 French promise of colonial self-determination.

In the rapidly changing political atmosphere of the 1950s, the few westernized Congolese began to organize embryonic political parties that attracted mass support in the cities. However, they had very different goals. Initially formed as a cultural organization in 1950, the **Association of Bakongo (ABAKO)** transformed into a political movement in the mid-1950s and opposed Belgian rule. Led by **Joseph Kasavubu**, a senior accounting clerk in the colonial administration, ABAKO advocated a federal system for a future independent Congo in which the Bakongo ethnic group of the west, around Leopoldville, would have a degree of autonomy. Indeed, ABAKO was an irredentist movement that favored the eventual reunification of the Bakongo people, who had been split between Portuguese Angola, French Equatorial Africa, and the Belgian Congo. ABAKO, which also had strong ties with the Kimbanguist Church, won the 1957 municipal elections in Leopoldville, with Kasavubu becoming mayor of a section of the city. In 1958, the **Confederation of the Tribal Associations of Katanga (CONAKAT)** was formed in the southern mining region and pressed for Congolese independence within a federal context in which Katanga would govern itself. CONAKAT was generally supported by people from the Lunda and Yeke ethnic groups, who considered themselves indigenous Katangese and resented the arrival of ethnic Luba and Lulua labor migrants from neighboring Kasai. **Moïse Tshombe**, CONAKAT's conservative and pro-Western

leader, was a businessman in Katanga who became close to Belgian mining interests. Also established in 1958, the **National Movement of the Congolese (MNC)** attempted to build a pan-ethnic political alliance that initially advocated a moderate and gradual approach to independence but quickly became more radical and leftist in orientation. By 1959, the MNC was led by the charismatic **Patrice Lumumba**, a post office clerk and part-time beer salesman, who was interested in Pan-Africanism and had attended the All-Africa People's Congress in newly independent Ghana, where he met Kwame Nkrumah. Lumumba favored a strong central government for an independent Congo, and his MNC became popular in the northeast around the city

≡ **Charismatic leader.** Patrice Lumumba (1925–1961) became the first prime minister of the Republic of the Congo (formerly the Belgian Congo and now the Democratic Republic of Congo) on independence in 1960 and was overthrown shortly thereafter and murdered at the start of 1961.

of Stanleyville (Kisangani). The political rise of Lumumba prompted a split in the MNC, with Albert Kalonji breaking off to create a federalist group called MNC-Kalonji (MNC-K), which championed self-government for the diamond-rich Kasai region. The African Solidarity Party (PSA) was formed in 1959, and under Antoine Gizenga it became popular in the western areas of Kwilu and Kwango, and campaigned for national unity and the adoption of a socialist system.

In January 1959, an anti-colonial protest in Leopoldville that had been organized by ABAKO turned into several days of rioting in which several hundred people died as the Belgian security forces restored control. This led to an almost immediate change in Belgian policy, with King Baudouin announcing on the radio that Congo would become fully independent without delay and the Belgian government would organize a staged transition over the next several years. Although many Belgian residents of the Congo opposed independence, Congolese protests continued over the next few months and caused Brussels to accelerate its independence timetable. The Belgian government thought that a rapid granting of independence would leave Congo dependent upon Belgian assistance for years to come. In January 1960, with little notice, the Belgian government brought Congolese political leaders and traditional chiefs to Brussels to participate in a round table conference on Congo's independence. Lumumba, who was serving a five-year prison sentence for leading protests in Stanleyville, was released from detention so he could join the talks. The Belgian officials conceded to Congolese demands and scheduled an election for May and the granting of independence for June of that year. In the run-up to the May elections, an alliance of regional federalist parties, chiefly ABAKO and MNC-K, campaigned against the nationalist MNC-Lumumba (MNC-L) and the PSA. Winning the most seats in parliament, the MNC-L and PSA formed a coalition, which resulted in Lumumba becoming the Congo's first prime minister. However, the regional parties had gained considerable support in the election, which resulted in ABAKO's Kasavubu being appointed as president. Furthermore, Tshombe's CONAKAT gained control of the provincial government in Katanga. On time, Belgian handed independence to Congo at the end of June 1960. At the independence ceremony in Leopoldville, King Baudouin gave a speech celebrating the achievements of Belgium's civilizing mission in the Congo, but this incensed the anti-colonial Lumumba, who, though not scheduled to speak, took the microphone and presented a blistering critique of Belgian oppression. The new country had a Pan-Africanist prime minister, an ethnic federalist president, and a separatist in charge of the richest province.

The independent Congo quickly descended into chaos. Known as the **Congo Crisis**, this tragedy represented a huge blow to the hopes for a peaceful and prosperous independent Africa. In early July 1960, one week after the independence ceremony, Belgian general Émile Janssens, who was still in command of the army, assembled his Congolese subordinates and wrote on a blackboard "Before Independence = After Independence." This immediately provoked a military mutiny in which Congolese soldiers and then Congolese civilians attacked Belgian residents. Lumumba dismissed General Janssens and other Belgian officers, appointed hastily commissioned Congolese officers such as former journalist **Joseph Mobutu** to take over the military, and promoted all soldiers by one rank. However, the violence continued and spread across the country. Within days, Belgium sent 6,000 troops to the Congo to protect Belgian civilians, which led to accusations that Brussels was trying to re-colonize the newly independent country. It was in this context, with the breakdown of the central government and the army in rebellion, that Tshombe's CONAKAT declared the independence of Katanga. This move was supported by the Belgian government and Belgian and South African mining companies. Around the same time, Kalonji proclaimed himself emperor of the autonomous region of South Kasai, though he did not declare complete independence from the Congo. Lumumba demanded UN intervention and threatened that if this was not forthcoming he would seek support from the Soviet Union, which was looking for a foothold in Africa. Although a UN peacekeeping force with troops from various countries including recently independent African states arrived in late July and replaced Belgian soldiers, the UN refused to act against Katanga secession as it was an internal affair of the Congo. In August, a frustrated Lumumba requested military assistance from the Soviets, which prompted the United States and Belgian governments, allies in the Cold War struggle against the Soviet Union, to plot his assassination. Since Lumumba had sent a Congolese military force to suppress the separatist Kalonji regime in South Kasai, where it had massacred several thousand people, UN secretary general Dag Hammarskjöld accused the Congo's prime minister of committing genocide. As a result, President Kasavubu dismissed the prime minister, but Lumumba rejected his removal and then issued his own dismissal of the president. This political impasse was broken by Colonel Mobutu, now working secretly for US intelligence, who ordered his soldiers to place Lumumba under house arrest. In January 1961, after Lumumba escaped Leopoldville but was recaptured, Mobutu had him flown to Katanga, where he was murdered by Tshombe's separatist regime. Lumumba's body was dismembered and dissolved in acid.

After Lumumba's death, the UN force in the Congo acted more aggressively against the secessionist regime in Katanga, which hired Belgian, French, and South African mercenaries to protect it. With the September 1961 death of UN secretary general Hammarskjöld in a plane crash in Northern Rhodesia (Zambia) while on his way to negotiate a ceasefire in Katanga, the UN stepped up its military campaign.

≡ **Congolese leaders.** Moïse Tshombe (left), Joseph Kasavubu (center left), and Joseph Mobutu (center right) in 1963.

It eventually forced Tshombe and many of his supporters to flee the country. During this conflict, Belgian influence in the Congo was superseded by the United States, which lost faith in the concept of an independent, pro-Western Katanga and began to support a pro-Western government for the entire Congo. Indeed, former separatist leader Tshombe returned to the Congo in 1964 to become the national prime minister under President Kasavubu just as left-wing supporters of the late Lumumba were launching a rebellion in the country's east.

Rwanda and Burundi

The small territories of Rwanda and Burundi, formerly part of German East Africa and bordering on the Belgian Congo, had become Belgian-administered mandates of the League of Nations after the First World War. As discussed in Chapter 17 during the 1920s and 1930s Belgian officials in these areas imposed a Social Darwinist racial hierarchy on the existing Tutsi, Hutu, and Twa identities. The Belgians ruled through the historic monarchies of Rwanda and Burundi but also recreated the minority Tutsi as a Western-educated administrative elite who supervised the majority Hutu, most of whom were peasant farmers. Reinforcing this hierarchy, the colonial-missionary education system taught a history that claimed that the Tutsi were a racially superior pastoral people from the Horn of Africa who had arrived in Rwanda and Burundi centuries before and had conquered the supposedly inferior Hutu farmers and Twa hunter-gatherers who already lived there. Following the Second World War, Rwanda and Burundi became UN trust territories but were still administered by Belgium. Around this time, many Tutsi, because of their greater access to Western education and the similarities they shared with Western-educated people in other parts of Africa, became interested in self-determination, nationalism, and socialism. This created a contradiction whereby the prime beneficiaries of Belgian rule, who were also a minority with pretensions of racial superiority and exotic origin, became the main critics of colonialism in Rwanda and Burundi.

During the 1950s, a small Hutu counter-elite, mainly educated in the Catholic schools, emerged in Rwanda. With the help of sympathetic European clergy, this group developed an indigenous rights agenda called **Hutu Power,** which portrayed the Tutsi as malevolent foreign invaders who had illegitimately conquered and continued to exploit the supposedly hard-working and devotedly Catholic Hutu. The leader of this emerging movement was **Grégoire Kayibanda**, who had attended a Catholic youth conference in Belgium and edited a Catholic magazine in Rwanda. In 1957, Kayibanda, along with Swiss-born Archbishop André Perraudin, published the "Hutu Manifesto," which explained the problems of Rwanda in terms of racial division between Tutsi and Hutu, and called for the emancipation of the Hutu. Later that year, with independence on track in other parts of Africa and municipal elections taking place in the adjacent Belgian Congo, Kayibanda formed the Muhutu Social Movement (MSM), which pressed for the improvement of Hutu social conditions and established links with Catholic labor leaders and politicians in Belgium. At the end of 1957, more extremist Hutu leaders formed the anti-Tutsi Association for the Promotion of the Hutu Masses (APROSOMA). In 1959, Tutsi leaders with ties to the monarchy formed the Rwandan National Union (UNAR). When the Belgian administration announced that it would hold elections for a territorial government in late 1959, these associations transformed into political parties that continued to be sharply divided along Hutu–Tutsi lines. The death of King Mutara Rudahigwa, who died suddenly in a hospital from a brain hemorrhage, causing many people to suspect that he had been murdered, prompted UNAR to demand immediate independence for Rwanda as a constitutional monarchy. Kayibanda, in October 1959, transformed MSM into the Party for the Emancipation of the Hutu (PARMEHUTU), which campaigned for the end of Tutsi colonialism and feudalism, a gradual transition to independence, and good relations with Belgium. As the Belgian government realized

☰ **Hutu leader.** Grégoire Kayibanda (1924–1976—center right) during a White House visit in 1962. Kayibanda led the Hutu Power movement that took over Rwanda in 1959 and became president of the country on independence in 1962.

that it would have to withdraw formal control of its African territories, the new and conservative Hutu political leaders who could claim majority support in a democratic system seemed like more reliable postcolonial partners than the minority Tutsi elites.

In November 1959, when violence broke out between Hutu supporters of PAR-MEHUTU and Tutsi supporters of UNAR, the Belgian administration declared a state of emergency and brought in troops from the Congo. With the tacit approval of the Belgians, PARMEHUTU gangs brutally deposed Tutsi chiefs and installed Hutu replacements. Rescheduled to June 1960, the territorial elections were conducted in an atmosphere of fear and violence. They resulted in an overwhelming victory for PARMEHUTU, which dominated the legislature. Tutsi parties like UNAR did very poorly. At this time a Rwandan military was created, which, reflecting the broader population, consisted of 14 percent Tutsi and 86 percent Hutu soldiers. In 1961, as the Belgians decided to give separate independence to Rwanda and Burundi, the new Rwandan king, Kigeli V Ndahindurwa, fled the country and the monarchy was abolished. In July 1962, Belgium, over the protests of the UN, granted independence to the Republic of Rwanda, with President Kayibanda leading a PARMEHUTU government. In what became known as the "Social Revolution," power had shifted suddenly from the Tutsi minority and monarchy to leaders from the Hutu majority who were supported by Belgium. Between 1959 and 1964, around 340,000 Rwandans, mostly Tutsi, fled their country. Exiled in neighboring Burundi, Uganda, Congo, and Tanzania, some of them formed armed groups intent on retaking control of Rwanda, an aim in which they were supported by communist China. Armed incursions into Rwanda by these Tutsi fighters during the early 1960s were repulsed by Rwanda's Belgian-equipped and -trained army and provided an excuse for the Kayibanda regime to carry out revenge massacres of Tutsi civilians in 1964. Even though somewhere between 10,000 and 20,000 Tutsi civilians were killed and all Tutsi political leaders were either killed or chased out of the country, the UN remained silent. The only state to protest was Burundi, which was still under a Tutsi regime. At the time, some foreign observers described the mass murder of Tutsi in Rwanda as genocide. Under Kayibanda, Rwanda became a Hutu majoritarian regime in which the Tutsi minority was oppressed and served as a scapegoat for the country's problems.

As the Hutu Revolution was unfolding in Rwanda during the end of the 1950s, polarized Hutu and Tutsi political parties were also formed in Burundi, where the Western-educated and dominant Tutsi minority was similarly turning against colonialism. However, Belgian policy in decolonizing Burundi was not as decisive as in Rwanda. The Union for National Progress (UPRONA), led by the charismatic **Crown Prince Louis Rwagasore**, insisted on immediate independence from

Belgium and advised Burundians to boycott Belgian businesses and stop paying colonial tax. UPRONA stressed national unity and had support from both Tutsi and Hutu. Sponsored by the local Belgian administration that wanted to see a friendly group in power, the Christian Democratic Party (PDC) was led by a competing faction of the Tutsi royal family that feared losing power in a democratic political system controlled by the Hutu majority. The Party of the People (PP) was blatantly pro-Hutu, inspired by recent events in Rwanda, and supported by some local Belgian residents and officials. Since Rwagasore was briefly imprisoned by the Belgian regime, which portrayed him as a communist, the first elections in Burundi in late 1960 were won by the PDC, which formed a transitional government. Rwagasore was released on the insistence of the UN, and in September 1961 his UPRONA party won a massive victory in the elections that were meant to create the government that would take power upon independence. However, in October, Prime Minister-Elect Rwagasore was assassinated on the orders of PDC leaders.

In July 1962, Burundi became an independent constitutional monarchy. While King Mwambutsa became increasingly authoritarian, the legislature was paralyzed by quarrelling between Hutu and Tutsi politicians. The arrival of Tutsi refugees from Rwanda served to heighten tensions in Burundi and made Tutsi leaders, including the king, worried about the rise of Hutu political leaders who were just beginning to understand their potential in a democratic system. Pierre Ngendandumwe, Burundi's first Hutu prime minister, was assassinated by a Tutsi refugee from Rwanda in January 1965, only three days after his appointment. In July 1965, the king, who had recently refused to accept elected Hutu legislators, declared an absolute monarchy, which prompted Hutu soldiers to launch a failed coup attempt. As a result, in October, Tutsi army officer Michel Micombero took power. He ordered Tutsi troops to murder 5,000 Hutu soldiers and civilians, eventually abolished the monarchy, and instituted a Tutsi military regime that lasted for many years. Micombero co-opted UPRONA, which became the only legal political party.

≣ **Nationalist hero.** In 1961, Burundi's Crown Prince Louis Rwagasore (1932– 61), a popular political leader promoting unity, was assassinated shortly after he had been elected prime minister just before the country's independence.

Portuguese Africa

While most African countries were gaining independence in the late 1950s and 1960s, the Portuguese dictatorship of **Antonio Salazar** insisted that Angola, Mozambique, and Guinea-Bissau were integral parts of Portugal and therefore could not be decolonized. In these three territories, frustrated and repressed African nationalists embarked on armed struggles for independence in the early 1960s. Given the Cold War context, Portugal was supported by its fellow North Atlantic Treaty Organization (NATO) member states and the African nationalist groups were sponsored by the Soviet Union and its allies.

In 1960, Portuguese forces massacred 500 unarmed protestors in the northern Mozambique town of Mueda. Consequently, in 1962 several Mozambican nationalist groups merged to form the **Front for the Liberation of Mozambique (FRE-LIMO)**, which was led by the US-educated **Eduardo Mondlane**. Based across the northern border in recently independent and sympathetic Tanzania, FRELIMO initiated a guerrilla war against the Portuguese in Mozambique in 1964. By the late 1960s, FRELIMO's successful campaign had established "liberated zones" in northern Mozambique and allowed it to expand its operations to independent Zambia, from where it infiltrated Tete province in central Mozambique. In 1969, after Mondlane was assassinated by the Portuguese, who sent him a parcel bomb in Tanzania, the more avidly communist Samora Machel took command of the organization. During the early 1970s, despite Portuguese offensives and an Africanization of Portuguese forces, Portugal failed to quell FRELIMO, which gained control of a third of Mozambique.

Rebellion against Portuguese rule broke out in Angola in 1961. On the central plateau, a dissident Christian group destroyed Portuguese agriculture and property but was quickly suppressed by colonial security forces. Followers of the newly formed **Popular Movement for the Liberation of Angola (MPLA)** attacked Portuguese police and prisons, and a Portuguese cruise liner was hijacked on the ocean. The most serious revolt of 1961 took place in northern Angola, where the Bakongo people resented Portuguese interference in the selection of their traditional leader. Based over the border in recently independent but chaotic Congo, the **Union of Peoples of Angola (UPA)** obtained arms from the Congolese military and infiltrated rebels into northern Angola, where they killed several hundred Portuguese settlers and more of their African supporters. Beyond cross-border ethnic identity, the rebels' link to Congo was based on the fact that UPA leader **Holden Roberto** was the brother-in-law of Congolese military commander Joseph Mobutu. Inspired by events in the former Belgian Congo, UPA leaders believed that sudden violence would induce a rapid Portuguese withdrawal from Angola, but this did not happen. Portuguese settlers and their African allies formed militias that massacred communities suspected of rebel sympathies; the Portuguese air force dropped bombs including napalm on rebel areas; the Portuguese army brought in reinforcements; and African civilians in the area were confined to guarded camps. The UPA insurgents resorted to limited hit-and-run attacks and fled back into Congo when pursued by Portuguese forces. The rebellion fizzled out within two years, but it resulted in the deaths of 2,000 Europeans and 50,000 Africans, and in the displacement of many thousands who became refugees in Congo.

During the 1960s, a divided African nationalist movement fought the Portuguese, and sometimes each other, in Angola. Merging with another organization, Roberto's UPA transformed into the **National Liberation Front of Angola (FNLA)**, which was based in Congo and which gained more support there after Mobutu formally took control of the government in 1965. Led by **Agostinho Neto**, the MPLA was most popular in Luanda but created an exile base in independent Zambia, where it received Eastern Bloc military support and sent insurgents into eastern Angola. Founded in 1966, the **National Union for the Total Independence of Angola (UNITA)** was led by **Jonas Savimbi** and was based in southern Angola among the Ovimbundu people. UNITA received some support from communist China and fought a limited guerrilla campaign. In the late 1960s, the northern-based FNLA and the southern-based UNITA formed a loose alliance to fight against MPLA. Furthermore, a number of small rebel groups in the oil-rich Cabinda area, physically disconnected from the rest of Angola, came together in 1963 to create the Front for the Liberation of the Cabinda Enclave (FLEC).

≡ **Rebellion against Portuguese rule.** *Left:* (Left to right) Holden Roberto, Jomo Kenyatta (president of Kenya), Agostinho Neto, and Jonas Savimbi in 1968. *Right:* Eduardo Mondlane (right) and Samora Machel (left); leaders of the Front for the Liberation of Mozambique (FRELIMO) that fought the Portuguese colonial regime. In 1969, Mondlane was assassinated by the Portuguese.

Portuguese counterinsurgency in Angola was more successful than in Lisbon's other African territories. As explained above, the nationalist forces were bitterly divided. In addition, the vast size of Angola hampered insurgent infiltration. MPLA fighters based in Zambia had to march for six weeks to reach inhabited parts of Angola. Because of Angola's oil resources, the Portuguese devoted a large military force to defend it, and by 1970 there were some 70,000 Portuguese and colonial troops supported by over 100 aircraft and 60 helicopters in the territory. Unlike in Mozambique, from the start of the war Portuguese forces in Angola were composed of many local African personnel who knew the geography and local languages. By 1973, one million Angolan civilians had been confined in secured camps to prevent them from providing support to the insurgents. Copying French operations in Algeria and ongoing American counterinsurgency tactics in Vietnam, Portuguese forces divided Angola into sectors, each with a dedicated garrison that constantly patrolled the countryside and the Portuguese air force sprayed defoliant that reduced bush cover for the insurgents.

The most effective anti-Portuguese armed struggle was waged in the small West African territory of Guinea-Bissau. While the **African Party for the Independence of Guinea and Cape Verde (PAIGC)** was formed in 1956 to pursue a peaceful campaign for self-determination, a massacre of striking dockworkers by Portuguese security forces in 1959 prompted the movement to cross into the newly independent Republic of Guinea, from where they embarked on an armed insurgency back home. Led by **Amilcar Cabral**, PAIGC established liberated zones in rural Guinea-Bissau as early as 1963 and used a broad socialist and democratic agenda to gain support from the people. Staging out of Guinea and eventually Senegal, PAIGC fighters were equipped and trained by the Soviet Union and Cuba, wounded insurgents were sometimes flown to Eastern Europe for medical treatment, and at times Guinean artillery fired across the border at Portuguese forces. Although Portugal initially neglected the defense of the tiny and unprofitable Guinea-Bissau, this changed in the late 1960s as Lisbon decided that losing the territory would undermine its hold on other parts of Africa. The Portuguese force in Guinea-Bissau was dramatically increased, with troops coming from Portugal and recruited in the territory; military offensives utilized helicopters and small boats in the country's vast riverine environment; and an economic development program was initiated to win back the support of rural people. In November 1970, Portuguese forces launched a daring sea-borne raid on Conakry, the capital of the Republic of Guinea, which rescued Portuguese prisoners and destroyed insurgent supply boats. However, the raid prompted international criticism and led to the dispatching of Soviet naval vessels to the region. In 1973, although Cabral was assassinated by rivals within in his own movement (though likely with the support of Portuguese agents), the larger war was going well for PAIGC as it acquired Soviet surface-to-air missiles that grounded the Portuguese air force, and Portuguese control was limited to urban areas. PAIGC declared Guinea-Bissau's independence in September 1973, and this was legitimized by UN recognition. While the death toll of Guinea-Bissau's independence war is unknown, some 12,000 insurgents, 8,000 African colonial troops, and 1,900 Portuguese personnel were killed.

Fighting three counterinsurgency wars in Africa became a massive burden for Portugal, which was not a large or wealthy country. By the early 1970s, over half of the annual budget was being spent on these conflicts, and the military conscription of young Portuguese men who were sent to fight in Africa was unpopular. In April 1974, the Portuguese military overthrew the regime of Marcello Caetano, the successor of Salazar who had passed away a few years earlier, and it embarked on a program of democratization. This led to a very sudden Portuguese withdrawal from Africa. Guinea-Bissau's independence was confirmed and Mozambique and Angola became independent in 1975. While PAIGC and FRELIMO easily took power in Guinea-Bissau and Mozambique, respectively, Angola experienced a three-way civil war between MPLA, UNITA, and FLNA that was intensified by the intervention of proxy forces fighting on either side of the Cold War struggle between the United States and the Soviet Union.

≡ **Our history did not begin in chains.** This poster in support of the armed struggle to liberate Guinea-Bissau from Portuguese control quotes both American civil rights leader Malcom X ("Our history did not begin in chains and will not end in chains.") and PAIGC leader Amilcar Cabral ("Liberation for us is to take back our history and our destiny.")

Conclusion

Trying to hold on to their African colonies after the Second World War, France, Belgium, and Portugal were eventually compelled to grant these territories sudden independence, though under different circumstances. While France tried to cosmetically reform its African empire in the late 1940s and 1950s, this plan was spoiled by armed independence movements in Madagascar, Cameroon, and particularly Algeria. Ultimately, France granted a rapid independence to most of its African territories in 1960 in a way that kept them dependent upon the former

Timeline

1946—Creation of the French Union

1947–48—Unsuccessful independence struggle in French colony of Madagascar

1954—Formation of the National Liberation Front (FLN) and start of independence war against the French in Algeria

1955—Start of insurgency in French-administered UN trust territory of Cameroon

1957—Municipal elections in the Belgian Congo

1958—Threat of military coup brings Charles de Gaulle to power in France

1958—Referendum in French territories, creation of French Community and independence of Guinea

1959—Rioting in the Belgian Congo

1959—Hutu revolution in Belgian administered Rwanda

1959—Start of independence war against Portugal in Guinea-Bissau

1960—Violent protest by French settlers in Algeria known as the "Week of the Barricades"

1960—Independence of many French territories in Africa, including Senegal, Mali, Niger, Cameroon, Dahomey, Côte d'Ivoire, Upper Volta, and Madagascar

1960—Independence of the Belgian Congo; southern region of Katanga declares secession; arrival of UN force in Congo

1960—Massacre of protestors by Portuguese forces in Mozambique

1961—Murder of Patrice Lumumba, prime minister of Congo

1961—Assassination of prime minister-elect Crown Prince Louis Rwagasore in Burundi

1961—Rebellions against Portuguese rule in Angola and start of independence war

1962—Independence of Algeria

1962—Independence of Rwanda and Burundi

1962—Front for the Liberation of Mozambique (FRELIMO) starts insurgency against Portuguese

1963—UN suppresses Katanga secession

1965—Tutsi military regime takes power in Burundi

1970—Portuguese commando raid on Conakry, Republic of Guinea

1973—African Party for the Independence of Guinea and Cape Verde (PAIGC) declares independence with UN support

1974—Military coup in Portugal

1975—Independence of Mozambique, and Angola

colonial master well into the future. The Belgians did nothing to prepare Congo for self-government until protests prompted a very fast transition to independence in 1960 that was supposed to keep the country dependent on Brussels, but the weak Congolese state almost collapsed with an army mutiny and regional secession. In contrast, the authoritarian regime in Portugal refused to contemplate decolonization, and it fought major conflicts against armed African independence movements in Mozambique, Angola, and Guinea-Bissau during the 1960s and early 1970s. Pressures created by these wars led to regime change in Lisbon in 1974 and the rapid dismantling of Portugal's empire in Africa.

KEY TERMS

STUDY QUESTIONS

1. What forces sparked the escalation of violence and radicalization that ignited in the Algerian War of Independence? How did events in Algeria impact politics in France? How did the process of decolonization in France's other African possessions compare with the Algerian experience? With Britain's approach to decolonization?

2. How did Belgium respond to Congolese independence movements and the rise of Patrice Lumumba? How did the Congo Crisis become embroiled in Cold War rivalries? Why did Hutu and Tutsi clash in Rwanda?

3. Why did wars of liberation accompany the waning years of Portuguese rule in Mozambique, Angola, and Guinea-Bissau? What were the main reasons for Portugal's withdrawal from its African colonies in 1974?

Please see page FR-10 for the Further Readings for this chapter.
For additional digital learning resources please go to
https://www.oup.com/he/falola-stapleton1e

White Supremacy and Apartheid in Southern Africa, 1948–1994

At the same time that many African colonies were engaged in a process that would lead to their independence in the 1950s and 1960s, the Southern Africa region continued to be dominated by white-minority regimes in South Africa, South West Africa (Namibia) and Southern Rhodesia (Zimbabwe), and the Portuguese colonies of Angola and Mozambique. Reacting to the threat seemingly posed by the rise of African nationalism across the continent, these settler states became more racist and reactionary in this period, with the 1948 implementation of apartheid in South Africa and the 1962 election of the Rhodesian Front in Southern Rhodesia. African nationalists in all these Southern African countries attempted to work within the existing legal framework to gain civil rights but experienced harsh state repression in which protestors were killed. As a result, by the mid-1960s activists had embarked on armed struggles to liberate their countries from minority rule. The global Cold War was superimposed on these conflicts as apartheid South Africa and white-ruled Rhodesia, despite tightening international sanctions, received some support from capitalist Western powers, and the African liberation movements enjoyed the sponsorship of the communist Eastern Bloc.

South Africa

In 1910, the Union of South Africa, combining the old British coastal colonies of the Cape and Natal with the interior former Boer republics of the Orange Free State and Transvaal, was created as a self-governing territory within the British Empire. The new country had emerged from the South African War of 1899–1902, when British military forces conquered the Boer republics to gain control of the gold mining industry that had recently developed in the Transvaal. The war had ended with the Treaty of Vereeniging (1902), which had given many concessions to the defeated Boers, including

Campaign poster for Nelson Mandela. Leader of the African National Congress, he was chosen as South Africa's first democratically elected president in 1994.

funds to reconstruct the country and a promise that qualified Black voting rights in the Cape would not be extended to the rest of the country. The constitution of the 1910 Union created a unitary state in which government positions and voting was restricted to South Africa's white settler minority. Initially, the Union government was dominated by the South African Party, which was led by former Boer republican military leaders **Louis Botha,** who was prime minister from 1910 until his death in 1919, and **Jan Smuts,** who first served as prime minister from 1919 to 1924. While it derived its core political support from Afrikaners (Boers), the South African Party was willing to cooperate with imperial Britain and the mining industry, and wished to create a broad South African white identity. In 1913, Botha's government passed the **Natives Land Act,** which significantly restricted Black land ownership across the country, undercutting the growth of small-scale commercial agriculture among Black South Africans. This forced more Black South

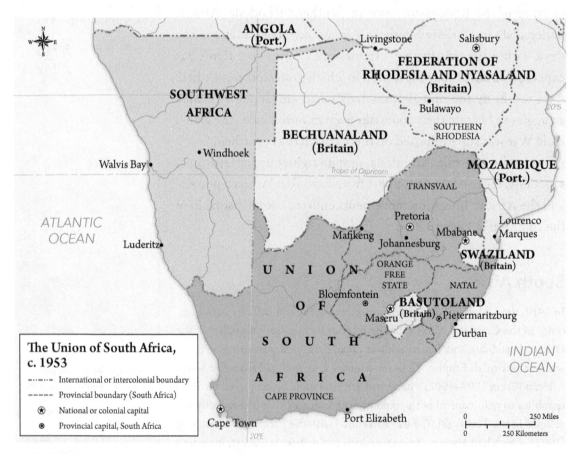

≡ MAP 23.1

Africans to accept low-paid migrant labor work in the mines and reduced economic competition for the white farming sector.

The ruling South African Party encountered opposition from several other groups within the South African parliament. Formed in 1910, the South African Labour Party represented white working-class voters. Fearful of economic competition from Black workers who might accept lower salaries than white workers, the Labour Party pressed for relatively higher-paid jobs, primarily in the mining industry, to be reserved exclusively for white employees. In 1914, more extremist Afrikaners created the **National Party**, led by **J.M.B. Hertzog**, who had also fought in the Boer forces in the 1899–1902 struggle and had briefly served as a cabinet minister under Botha. The National Party advocated greater autonomy from Britain due to lingering grievances over the South African War (1899–1902) and they wanted stricter racial segregation. During the First World War (1914–18), many Afrikaners staged an armed rebellion against the South African government, which had automatically entered the conflict on the side of Britain and was preparing for an invasion of the neighboring German colony of South West Africa (Namibia). Although it criticized South Africa's wartime cooperation with Britain, the National Party did not actively support the ultimately failed Afrikaner rebellion but sympathized with the rebels and successfully pressured for them to

≡ **Leaders of the Union of South Africa.** *Left:* Jan Smuts (1870–1950) was prime minister of South Africa from 1919 to 1924 and from 1939 to 1948. *Center:* J.B.M. Hertzog (1866–1942), founding leader of the National Party, was prime minister of South Africa from 1924 to 1939. *Right:* A founder of the purified Nationalist Party in the 1930s, D.F. Malan (1874–1959) served as prime minister of South Africa from 1948 to 1954 in the government that imposed the apartheid system.

receive light prison sentences. The Labour Party and the National Party eventually worked together against the South African Party government.

In 1922, Afrikaner and English white mine workers in and around Johannesburg, incensed by Black workers being employed in jobs supposedly reserved for whites, staged an armed uprising against the state and murdered Black people on the street. Under the banner of "Workers of the World Unite for a White South Africa," many of the rebels were veterans of the First World War and were well armed with rifles and a machine gun. Prime Minister Smuts, who as minister of mines had been forced to concede to the demands of striking white mine workers in 1913, deployed 20,000 white troops to crush the rebellion. This resulted in 200 deaths.

The **Rand Revolt** of 1922 had a profound impact on white electoral politics in South Africa. In 1924, angry white voters rejected Smuts's South African Party, which resulted in a coalition of the National Party and Labour Party coming to power. Under Prime Minister Hertzog, the new "Pact Government" of the mid-1920s passed laws that reserved higher-paying working-class jobs for whites, created social programs to lift white Afrikaners out of poverty, and favored white agriculture. In 1930, white women were given the franchise, dramatically reducing the political power of mixed-race and Black male voters in the Cape, and in 1936 the nonracial voting system in that province was phased out. During the 1920s, the Hertzog government began to create a system for administering Black South Africans, which focused on empowering traditional leaders in a patchwork of ethnically defined rural reserves. This was meant to undermine the development of a nationwide urban Black working-class identity that was being fostered by the new **Industrial and Commercial Workers' Union (ICU)**. In 1931, the passage of the **Statute of Westminster** in London, which removed the British government's veto power over legislation in the self-governing dominions such as Canada and South Africa, created a major political change among white South Africans. With South Africa now effectively independent, one of the main differences between Hertzog's National Party and Smuts's South African Party became minimal, and the two groups formed a coalition government called "Fusion" and in 1934 merged to become the United Party. Hertzog continued as prime minister, with Smuts taking a cabinet position. Frustrated by the amalgamation of these two parties, extremist supporters of the National Party, including some government ministers, broke away to create the Purified National Party in 1934. The new party was led by Dutch Reformed Church clergyman and Afrikaans newspaper editor **D.F. Malan** and opposed the United Party in parliament.

South Africa's involvement in the Second World War (1939-45) became extremely controversial. As with the other British dominions like Canada and Australia, and reflecting the autonomy gained in 1931, the South African government made its own decision to enter the war on the side of Britain. Reflecting the views of many Afrikaners, Prime Minister Hertzog did not support this policy, which led to his replacement by the pro-British Smuts, who returned for a second term as prime minister in 1939. This prompted some Afrikaners to leave the ruling United Party and join the Purified Nationalist Party, which renamed itself the Reunited National Party. In 1939, radical Afrikaners, many of them sympathetic to Nazi Germany, formed the **Ox-wagon Sentinel movement**, which opposed South Africa's wartime alliance with

≡ **South African participation in the Second World War.** A South African servicewoman with Britain's Women's Auxiliary Air Force (WAAF) fits a gas mask on a soldier.

Britain and established a paramilitary group called the *Stormjaers* (Assault Troops) that engaged in sabotage, including the destruction of telephone lines, electrical lines, and railways. Smuts's government suppressed this movement, detaining many of its members during the war.

The results of the 1948 South African election were largely informed by the domestic impact of the Second World War. Many Afrikaners resented that their country had sent troops to fight on the side of their old enemy, Britain. Perhaps more importantly, the wartime economic boom, which included the growth of local manufacturing, had led to a relaxation of racial limitations around employment, and white workers began to again feel threatened by Black economic competition. As a result, the white electorate rejected Smuts and his United Party and placed their faith in Malan's National Party, which had campaigned on the promise of imposing a system of more thorough racial segregation called **apartheid** (apartness).

The Apartheid System

During the early 1950s, Prime Minister Malan's government passed a series of laws that together came to comprise the **apartheid system**. While white supremacy and racial segregation had a long history in South Africa that predated the 1910 Union, different provinces had slightly different policies. The apartheid laws created a thorough and strict system of racial segregation that was meant to be uniform across the country and to regulate every aspect of life. Passed in 1950, the **Population Registration Act** represented a foundational apartheid law that defined a set of racial population groups and compelled every South African to be categorized as a member of one of them. Based on physical appearance and social status, the population groups were initially white, Black, and Coloured (mixed-race), and the category of Indian was added later. People with an ambiguous identity were subjected to a series of humiliating tests to determine their race, such as passing a pencil through the hair on a person's head; if the pencil passed through easily then the person was considered white, and if the pencil became stuck then the person would be considered Coloured or Black. The 1950, **Group Areas Act**, which was updated many times over the next few decades, assigned urban spaces on the basis of race, with Black residents receiving the smallest areas and usually those far away from town centers. This led to the state engaging in the forced removal of people who were living in an area designated for another race. One of the most infamous examples of this policy occurred in 1955, when the state destroyed the primarily Black but also somewhat multiracial Johannesburg suburb of **Sophiatown**, which had become a center for the development of South African popular music. Sophiatown was transformed into the exclusively white community of Triomf (Afrikaans for "triumph"). In 1952, the Native Laws Amendment Act limited the right of Black South Africans to live permanently in urban areas and the Pass Laws Act eliminated

≡ **Apartheid.** *Left:* Evicted residents of Sophiatown wait for their belongings to be loaded onto trucks in 1955. *Center:* An apartheid-era sign, c.1967. *Right:* ANC leader Nelson Mandela, who initiated armed struggle against the apartheid state in 1961 and was imprisoned for 27 years.

earlier regional laws requiring Black men to carry identity documents and created a nationwide system in which all Blacks over 16 years old had to carry these passes, which had to be endorsed by a white employer to grant permission for the holder to be in a white area. The 1953 Reservation of Separate Amenities Act legalized racial segregation of public services, facilities, and vehicles, and stipulated that equal facilities did not have to be provided for all races.

The many apartheid laws were intended to govern all aspects of life in South Africa. The Prohibition of Mixed Marriages Act of 1949 outlawed marriage between whites and people of other races, and the Immorality Act of 1950 prohibited sexual intercourse between people of different racial groups. While existing discrimination and segregation meant that these "morality" laws did not impact the majority of South Africans, they show that the National Party was serious about applying its apartheid policy in every possible way.

Apartheid laws related to education and government were more impactful. The **Bantu Education Act** of 1953 established a separate education system for Black students, which, with its lack of emphasis on science and math and its focus on African languages and Bible study, was designed to prepare them for a subordinate role in South African society as mine workers or domestic servants. Government support for missionary schools was withdrawn. In much better-funded schools, white students were subjected to Christian National Education, which indoctrinated them to National Party ideology and prepared them for a future in the dominant minority. Building on previous policies initiated in the 1920s, the **Bantu Authorities Act** of 1951 restricted Black South African political representation to a series of ethnically defined rural homelands and gave limited powers of self-government to traditional leaders within those areas. The apartheid state envisioned that these self-governing ethnic homelands would eventually become independent from South Africa in the same way, it was claimed, that European colonies in Africa were moving toward sovereignty.

During the nineteenth century, African societies in what later became South Africa had used military means to resist colonial conquest, but they were all defeated. The last instance of traditional African military resistance in South Africa was the 1906 Zulu Rebellion in the British colony of Natal. New forms of African protest emerged in the late nineteenth and early twentieth centuries. As elsewhere in colonial Africa, westernized Black elites formed Western-style political organizations to seek redress of grievances and advance their interests within the existing system. In 1909, a delegation of Black South Africans visited London to express their objections to the racist nature of the proposed constitution of the Union of South Africa and to request the intervention of the British government to change it. They were largely ignored. In 1912, after the creation of the white minority–ruled Union,

≡ **The first Black South African woman to gain a university degree.** Charlotte Maxeke (1874–1939) founded the Bantu Women's League in 1918 and this organization later became the ANC Women's League.

African westernized elites and traditional leaders formed the first nationwide Black political movement, the South African Native National Congress (SAN-NC), later renamed the **African National Congress** (ANC). From the 1910s to 1940s, this group worked within the existing system to criticize racial oppression and exploitation. During the 1920s and 1930s, many ordinary Black and mixed-race South Africans protested through the new trade union movement as well as independent churches. During the interwar years, **Charlotte Maxeke**, the first Black South African woman to gain a university degree, for which she studied in the United States, formed the **Bantu Women's League**, which was active in protesting discriminatory pass laws and later became the ANC Women's League. In the 1940s, a new generation of Black activists formed the ANC Youth League, which embarked on more radical mass protest.

Passive Resistance to Apartheid

During the 1950s, the ANC organized a passive resistance campaign against the new apartheid laws. Called the **Defiance Campaign** and partly inspired by a similar movement in India that had led to independence in 1947, this program involved large numbers of activists purposefully and peacefully breaking apartheid laws with the intention of getting arrested by the police and filling up the jails so as to stretch the coercive means of the state and widely illustrate the unjust nature of the apartheid system. Led by Albert Luthuli, a Zulu teacher and traditional chief, the ANC was a broad and diverse organization that included Black, white, Indian, and mixed-race people as well as Christian clergy, African nationalists, trade unionists, pacifists, and communists. As such, some of the group's leaders began to think that they needed to clearly articulate their objectives. In 1955, the ANC held a Conference of the People in Kliptown, near Johannesburg, at which some 3,000 delegates approved a document called the **Freedom Charter**, which stated the organization's vision for a future South Africa. The charter was influenced by the American Declaration of Independence as well as socialist literature like Marx's *Communist Manifesto*. According to the Freedom Charter, the ANC wanted to create a nonracial South Africa where the people would govern, where there would be equal rights, where the people would share in the country's wealth including its land, and where people would have work and good housing and live in peace. For some radical African nationalists, this document was too accommodating to South Africa's dominant white minority, who, it was claimed, were also exerting undue influence within the ANC, particularly among clergy and communists. Consequently, in 1959 a group led by **Robert Sobukwe** broke from the ANC to form the **Pan-Africanist Congress** (PAC), which pursued a more militant Black power agenda and became a second major anti-apartheid organization. Another important event in anti-apartheid protest was the 1956 march by 20,000 women on the Union Buildings in Pretoria, where they protested the extension of pass laws to Black women. The event was organized by the ANC Women's League, led by **Lillian Ngoyi**, and the recently formed Federation of South African Women.

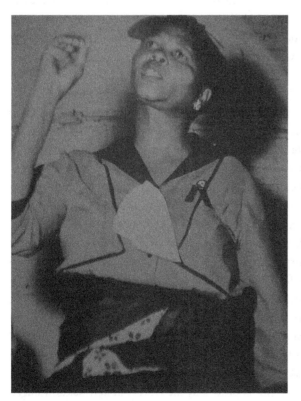 

≡ **Resisting Apartheid.** *Left:* During the 1950s, Lilian Ngoyi (1911–1980) led anti- apartheid protest by the ANC Women's League and Federation of South African Women. Arrested in 1956, she spent many years confined to her home area of Soweto near Johannesburg. *Right:* Awarded the Nobel Peace Prize in 1960, ANC president Albert Luthuli (1898–1967) pursued peaceful protest against apartheid and was unaware that other activists planned to launch an armed struggle against the white-minority regime.

The National Party government immediately cracked down on anti-apartheid protest. The 1950 Suppression of Communist Act was used to label any anti-apartheid protestor as a communist and to thereby imprison that person or limit his or her participation in public events. In response to passive resistance during the early 1950s, the apartheid regime passed other laws that enabled it to declare states of emergency in specific areas where people could be detained by the police without charges, and penalties were increased for those engaged in protest to demand the repeal of a law. In addition, the South African Police responded brutally against nonviolent anti-apartheid protestors and the movement's leaders were harassed. In 1956, the apartheid state charged 156 prominent anti-apartheid activists for treason because it was claimed that the Freedom Charter, approved the previous year, constituted a plan to overthrow the government and that some activists had discussed acquiring foreign support and weapons. Among those who were put on trial were ANC leaders Walter Sisulu, **Nelson Mandela**, and Lillian Ngoyi, and South African Communist Party (SACP) activists Joe Slovo and Ruth First. Although all the defendants were eventually acquitted by a South African court, this long **Treason Trial** hobbled the leadership of the anti-apartheid movement for several years.

The Sharpeville Massacre

On March 21, 1960, the South African Police shot into a crowd of around 6,000 protestors at Sharpeville, near Johannesburg, killing 69 and wounding 180 people. Known as the **Sharpeville Massacre**, this event became a key turning point in the history of apartheid and the struggle against it. The National Party government formally outlawed membership in the ANC and PAC, which had to operate in secret or in exile. Within the anti-apartheid movement, many leaders began to realize that passive resistance was futile as it was met with increasingly deadly violence from state security forces. They would have to fight to liberate their country from an oppressive minority regime. Members of the ANC and SACP, including Mandela and Slovo, jointly formed an armed group in July 1961 called **Umkhonto we Sizwe (Spear of the Nation)**, also known as **MK**. During the next few months, MK published a manifesto declaring war on the apartheid state and orchestrated a bombing campaign in South Africa's cities that tried to avoid loss of life, and some of its members secretly left the country for military training in Algeria and Ethiopia. Although MK's violent campaign was initially shocking for pacific ANC leaders like Luthuli, who had not approved it, the ANC publicly acknowledged its armed wing in 1962. In 1963, many MK operatives, including Mandela, who were also highly recognizable figures given their role in previous protests, were arrested, convicted of treason, and sentenced to life imprisonment. ANC leaders who had fled the country, such as Slovo and Oliver Tambo, who eventually led the organization, continued the movement's activities from exile. The PAC formed an armed movement called Poqo (Xhosa for "alone"), which engaged in unrestrained violence by groups armed with machetes and axes that attacked whites, police, and state-paid traditional leaders, mostly in the Cape. These actions fizzled out, and plans for a 1963 mass uprising were aborted after British colonial police in Basutoland (Lesotho from 1966) raided a PAC office where they seized membership lists and handed them over to South African authorities. PAC leaders were either imprisoned or went to exile.

≡ **Remembrance.** This painting commemorates the victims of the 1960 Sharpeville Massacre.

The apartheid state appeared strong during the mid- and late 1960s. The main anti-apartheid organizations had been suppressed and many of their leaders were in prison. Based abroad, and increasingly supported by the Eastern Bloc, the ANC and PAC struggled to infiltrate armed insurgents into South Africa, which was protected by a ring of friendly or dependent buffer states such as white minority–ruled Southern Rhodesia (Zimbabwe), the Portuguese colonies of Angola and Mozambique, impoverished Bechuanaland (Botswana), the conservative monarchy of Swaziland and South African–occupied South West Africa (Namibia). While the UN General Assembly became hostile to apartheid in South Africa and tried to impose diplomatic and economic sanctions, these were generally ineffective as Western powers retained their core links with Pretoria, which successfully portrayed itself as an anti-communist bastion and an island of stability in chaotic Africa. Britain withdrew much of its formal presence as South Africa became a republic in 1961 and the British High Commission territories were granted self-government and then independence, with Bechuanaland becoming Botswana and Basutoland becoming Lesotho in 1966, and Swaziland gaining sovereignty in 1968. While various South African governments had long sought to absorb these small territories, this was opposed by the African residents and influential African traditional rulers who retained considerable power after independence.

The End of Apartheid

Several events during the mid-1970s began a process of undermining the apartheid state. The 1974 military coup in Lisbon and the subsequent withdrawal of Portugal from Africa weakened the protective ring around South Africa, and Pretoria was drawn into a costly war in Angola. In June 1976, an uprising of Black youth began in Soweto, near Johannesburg, and quickly spread to all major South African urban centers. The **Soweto Uprising** had been inspired by the emergence of the **Black Consciousness movement**. Led by **Steven Biko**, it urged Black South Africans to develop self-respect and confidence in their struggle for civil rights and to distance themselves from legal white-led and paternalistic anti-apartheid organizations, such as the National Union of South African Students (NUSAS). During the late 1960s and early 1970s, the Black Consciousness movement prompted the creation of the South African Students' Organization (SASO), which recruited Black post-secondary students, and the South African Students' Movement (SASM), which mobilized high school students. Black Consciousness activists were also involved in many local development projects aimed at improving the lives of Black South Africans. The immediate cause of the 1976 youth uprising was the apartheid government announcement that Afrikaans would become the medium of instruction in Black schools, which the students, politicized by Black Consciousness, correctly interpreted as a way of further limiting their future to subordinate roles in the racist society and economy. During the protest in Soweto and elsewhere, the security

☰ **The struggle against apartheid.** *Left:* In 1976, South African Police fired on Black youth protesting the imposition of Afrikaans as a language of instruction in schools. *Right:* Steve Biko (1946–1977), a founder of South Africa's Black Consciousness Movement during the late 1960s, was arrested and murdered by police in 1977.

forces killed hundreds of Black youth, several thousand people were detained, and thousands more fled the country to join the exiled anti-apartheid liberation movements. These developments reinvigorated the struggle against apartheid.

The National Party government responded to these events in several ways. Pretoria accelerated the process of granting independence to the ethnically defined Black homelands, such as Transkei in 1976, Bophuthatswana in 1977, Venda in 1979, and Ciskei in 1981. These states had Black governments, but they were dominated by traditional leaders and they were financially and militarily dependent upon the South African government. Not recognized by any other country in the world, these puppet states were derisively called **Bantustans** and essentially deprived Black South Africans of citizenship in their own country. Externally, South Africa halted its policy of overt hostility to neigh-

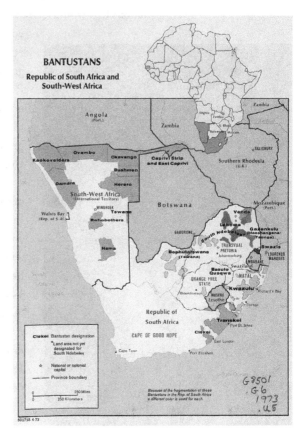

boring majority-ruled countries and pursued a policy of using its regional economic power, sometimes combined with covert military destabilization, to bully them into submission. For instance, in 1984 the FRELIMO government of Mozambique, in the Nkomati Accord, agreed to expel exiled ANC activists and Pretoria falsely promised to stop its sponsorship of the rebel Mozambique National Resistance (RENAMO). Internally, the apartheid regime created a new constitution that went into effect in 1983. A new tricameral parliament, with separate houses for whites, Coloureds, and Indians, tried to broaden the basis of support for the apartheid state, but in reality political power was centralized in the new position of state president that was assumed by the intransigent **P.W. Botha**. During the 1980s, the ANC's armed wing, MK, stepped up its military operations as it was able to infiltrate South Africa through independent Botswana and Zimbabwe, and it began to target security force members, state officials, and white farmers. More broadly, the **United Democratic Front** (UDF) emerged as a wide umbrella movement of many smaller anti-apartheid groups within South Africa that staged massive popular protests against the new constitution. In some ways the UDF

≡ **Bantustans.** Produced by the US Central Intelligence Agency in 1973, this map shows the many Bantustans in both South Africa and South-West Africa. The Bantu Authorities Act of 1951 restricted Black South African political representation to a series of ethnically defined rural homelands.

represented the return of the outlawed ANC to South Africa. Botha's government responded by declaring a state of emergency in some parts of the country, and in 1986 this was extended across the whole of South Africa. As the UDF protestors aimed to make South African ungovernable as a way to compel political change, the apartheid state began to arm criminal gangs and a Zulu nationalist movement called **Inkatha** and to pit them against the anti-apartheid activists. South Africa's Black townships became scenes of extreme violence, including the burning to death of many accused state informants. The National Party government claimed that this "Black-on-Black" violence, much of which it had orchestrated, would get much worse if the white minority surrendered political power.

In 1989, the unwell but stubborn President Botha was replaced by **F.W. de Klerk**, formerly minister of education, who initiated a process of reforms and negotiations that would lead to the end of apartheid. International sanctions mounted. The United States government in 1986 imposed economic sanctions on South Africa, with the US Congress voting to override the veto of President Ronald Reagan. This worsened an already ailing South African economy. With liberalization in the Soviet Union and the fall of the Eastern Bloc, the armed anti-apartheid groups lost their international sponsorship and the United States no longer valued apartheid South Africa as an anti-communist ally as communism was no longer a threat. In early 1990, de Klerk's government lifted the ban on the ANC, PAC, SACP, and other groups, and began releasing political prisoners such as Mandela, who embarked on a successful international tour and became ANC president the next year. During the early 1990s, ANC and NP representatives negotiated a nonracial and democratic constitution for South Africa. A number of groups attempted to use violence to derail this process. Zulu nationalists from the Inkatha Freedom Party (IFP), led by **Mangosutho Buthelezi**, demanded a federal state in which their province of KwaZulu/Natal would have self-government, the PAC accused the ANC of selling out to the ruling white minority, and white supremacists from the Afrikaner Resistance Movement (AWB) and Conservative Party accused the National Party of compromising on white interests, with some demanding a self-governing

≡ **Inkatha leader.** During the 1980s and early 1990s, Zulu nationalist Chief Mangosutho Buthelezi (b. 1928) led the Inkatha Freedom Party, which vied for a federal system in South Africa and clashed with ANC members.

homeland for Afrikaners. Furthermore, shadowy elements of the state security forces, either going rogue or acting under covert instructions from government officials, were active in fomenting trouble and were known as the "Third Force."

Despite the violence, or perhaps because of it, the negotiators quickly produced a new constitution, with South Africa holding its first democratic elections in April 1994. Although it had been previously agreed that the first post-apartheid government would include representatives from all the major parties, including the NP and IFP, the ANC had won the most votes, which meant that it led this unity government with Mandela becoming the country's first Black president. The ANC's Thabo Mbeki and the NP's de Klerk became deputy presidents, and the IFP's Buthelezi became minister of home affairs. The ANC also led the provincial governments, except for violence-wracked Kwa-Zulu/Natal, where the IFP gained power, and the Western Cape, where the relatively large white and Coloured communities voted for the NP. The previous ANC–NP talks had produced some compromises for the white minority. As a way of reducing resistance among members of the outgoing apartheid state, those who had committed crimes during the apartheid era could testify before a **Truth and Reconciliation Commission** and request amnesty. Additionally, the great inequity in land ownership would be addressed through a system of restitution, in which those who could prove that they had been dispossessed could recover their land. However, the cutoff date of 1913, the year the Natives Land Act had been passed, limited the amount of restitution that was possible as most evictions had taken place during the colonial wars of the previous century. While the Mandela administration launched a Reconstruction and Development Plan (RDP) to build houses for the poor and provide running water and electricity to shantytowns, the ANC privatized the economy and a new wealthy Black elite emerged that benefitted from connections to the ruling party. This led to accusations that the end of apartheid did not mean much for most Black South Africans, who still struggled to find jobs and continued to live in extreme poverty.

From the 1960s to 1980s, historians of South Africa debated the historical origins of apartheid, and therefore they differed on how the system would eventually come to an end. Liberal historians emphasized the much earlier historical experience of Afrikaners whose ancestors had arrived in the Cape in the mid-1600s to 1700s and, as such, had missed the European Enlightenment, where ideas about freedom and democracy had emerged. For the liberal scholars, apartheid was rooted in Afrikaner backwardness and was anathema to a liberal free enterprise economy. Apartheid would eventually collapse, the liberals anticipated, given the supposed natural integrative tendencies of capitalism. In contrast, radical historians, inspired by Marxist interpretations, claimed that capitalism in South Africa was dependent upon the apartheid system to provide cheap Black labor for white-owned mines and industries and therefore apartheid could only end with an anti-capitalist revolution. While the manner in which the apartheid system collapsed in the early 1990s seemed to vindicate the liberal view, some would say that the legacy of apartheid continued to support racial capitalism in South Africa. During the 2010s, South Africans began protesting lack of transformation in higher education and the economy, and corruption by the ruling ANC. In 2013, activists expelled from the ANC formed a new political party called the Economic Freedom Fighters (EFF) to pursue more substantial change toward an equitable society.

South West Africa (Namibia)

During the First World War, the Union of South Africa had invaded and occupied the neighboring German colony of South West Africa. Like the other former German colonies in Africa, South West Africa became a League of Nations mandate and its administration was given to the South African government, which ruled it as another province and brought in white Afrikaner settlers during the 1920s. At this time communities like the Bondelswarts and Ovambo resisted South African control but were bombed or intimidated into submission by the new South African Air Force. In 1946, the government of Jan Smuts refused to transfer authority over South West Africa to the United Nations, though South Africa did not annex the territory. With the election of the National Party in South Africa in 1948, the new apartheid policies were extended to South West Africa, where the white minority gained the right to elect representatives in the South African parliament. Many of the white settlers of South West Africa, among both the German and Afrikaner communities, became ardent National Party supporters. In 1959, the police killed 11 people who were protesting forced removals in the territorial capital of Windhoek. This prompted African nationalists from the South West African National Union (SWANU) and **South West African People's Organization** (SWAPO) to demand that the country be handed over to the UN as a trust territory that would be prepared for independence. In 1962, SWAPO resolved to fight to liberate its country and formed an exiled armed wing called the People's Liberation Army of Namibia (PLAN). Hesitant to engage in violence and lacking international support, SWANU eventually collapsed. During the late 1960s, the UN General Assembly revoked South Africa's mandate over South West Africa, recognized the new name of the territory as Namibia, and acknowledged SWAPO as the legitimate representative of the Namibian people. Although the UN General Assembly voted in 1971 to declare the South African occupation of Namibia illegal, support for South Africa among the Western powers on the UN Security Council meant that little was done.

While SWAPO gained international legitimacy, its military campaign experienced serious problems during the 1960s and early 1970s. SWAPO/PLAN acquired military support and revolutionary ideology from Eastern Bloc sponsors, but geography worked against it. Based in independent Zambia and Tanzania, it could only infiltrate guerrilla fighters into Namibia via the narrow and well-guarded **Caprivi Strip** or through Angola, where they were likely to be intercepted by Portuguese forces allied with Pretoria. The Namibian independence war began in March 1966, when South African security forces raided a PLAN insurgent base at Omgulumbashe in northern South West Africa. From this point, the PLAN campaign focused on the Caprivi Strip, where insurgents planted landmines and assassinated local officials. PLAN's fortunes changed from 1975, when, after the departure of the Portuguese, the Popular Movement for the Liberation of Angola (MPLA) came to power in Angola, in spite of a civil war and South African military intervention. As a neighboring liberation movement, and one also propped up with support from the Eastern Bloc, the MPLA government in Angola allowed SWAPO/PLAN to establish staging areas in southern Angola, from where it could more easily infiltrate fighters into northern South West Africa. As a result, the insurgency escalated in northern South West Africa, particularly the Ovamboland area, where SWAPO enjoyed considerable support and was able to create liberated zones, and guerrillas began to venture further south into the white farmlands. During the 1980s, a number of factors limited SWAPO/PLAN activities inside South West Africa. First, South African military forces began crossing into southern Angola, where they clashed with MPLA and allied Cuban troops, which pushed PLAN bases away from the border. Second, South African military support for the National Union for the Total Independence of Angola (UNITA), a rebel group fighting the MPLA state, meant that UNITA kept SWAPO/PLAN out of its haven in southeastern Angola, which further limited insurgent infiltration of northern South West Africa. Third, South African counterinsurgency forces in South West Africa pursued

≡ **SWAPO leader.** Sam Nujoma (b.1929), leader of the South West African People's Organization (SWAPO), with Romanian dictator Nicolae Ceauşescu in 1979.

more aggressive and highly mobile search-and-destroy tactics and employed more local troops who knew the languages and terrain. Since SWAPO/PLAN was confined to certain parts of Ovamboland, the future of South West Africa was determined by conventional battles fought between South Africa and Angolan/Cuban forces in southern Angola. When its forces were defeated at the 1988 Battle of Cuito Cuanavale, South Africa withdrew its troops from southern Angola, as it was unwilling to suffer more casualties among its white military conscripts. Instead, it engaged in international negotiations that resulted in the independence of Namibia in 1990. SWAPO won UN-supervised elections in Namibia, and the movement's long-time leader, **Sam Nujoma**, became the country's first president. This transition took place within the context of South Africa's ruling National Party beginning political reforms at home and negotiating with the anti-apartheid ANC.

Independence in South-Central Africa

The British territories of South-Central Africa, located on both sides of the Zambezi River and brought under British authority in the 1890s, represented two different types of colonialism. South of the Zambezi, Southern Rhodesia was dominated by a white settler minority that had gained responsible government, a form of internal self-rule within the British Empire, in 1923. The African majority had been dispossessed of much of the country's best agricultural land and a series of racially discriminatory laws had turned them into a class of low-paid wage workers on settler commercial farms or in mines. North of the Zambezi River, Northern Rhodesia and Nyasaland did not have significant settler communities and the African people there were administered by British colonial officials working indirectly through African traditional leaders. The Northern Rhodesian economy was centered on copper mining, and both these territories sent large numbers of migrant workers south to the mines of white-ruled Southern Rhodesia and South Africa.

In 1953, despite their differences, these three territories were brought together by the British government to form the Federation of the Rhodesias and Nyasaland, otherwise known as the **Central African Federation**. Given the 1948 election of the anti-British National Party in South Africa, Britain wished to create a new regional ally in Southern Africa by forging together three small territories into a much larger entity. As such, the British government invested heavily in the new federation, sending it the latest jet fighters and bombers to build up an air force and engaging in the Kariba Dam project on the Zambezi River, which would supply electricity to drive the expansion of the federal economy. The white minority of Southern Rhodesia greatly supported the federal scheme as it would give them control over the mineral and human resources of the two northern territories and

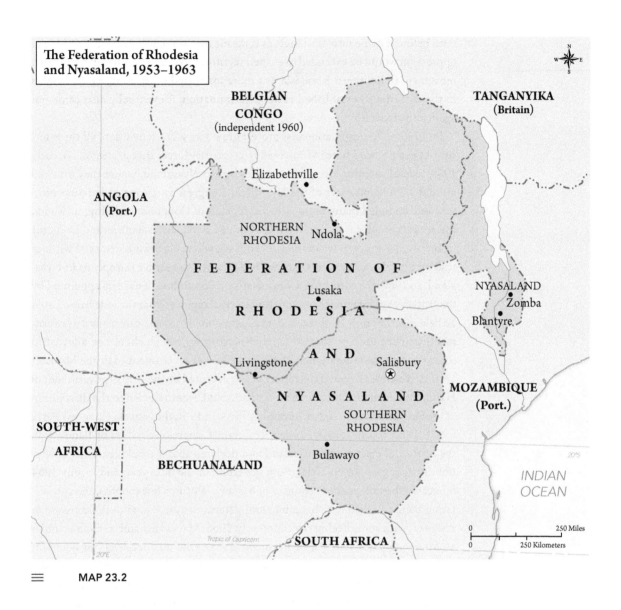

The Federation of Rhodesia
and Nyasaland, 1953–1963

BELGIAN
CONGO
(independent 1960)

TANGANYIKA
(Britain)

ANGOLA
(Port.)

Elizabethville

NORTHERN
RHODESIA Ndola

F E D E R A T I O N   O F

Lusaka

NYASALAND
Zomba

R H O D E S I A

Blantyre

Livingstone A N D Salisbury
⍟

N Y A S A L A N D

SOUTHERN
RHODESIA

MOZAMBIQUE
(Port.)

SOUTH-WEST

AFRICA

BECHUANALAND Bulawayo

INDIAN
OCEAN

20°S

Tropic of Capricorn

SOUTH AFRICA

0   250 Miles

0   250 Kilometers

20°E

MAP 23.2

it seemed to represent a way to achieve long sought-after dominion status similar
to that enjoyed by Canada, Australia, New Zealand, and South Africa. Without
federation, Southern Rhodesia was simply too small and economically weak to
be granted autonomy within the British Commonwealth. The political system of
the federation was "multiracial," which meant that the white minority would have
full political rights and Africans would gradually be granted more civil rights as
they became more westernized. However, the emerging African nationalist movements in Northern Rhodesia and Nyasaland strongly opposed the federation,

even before it came into existence, as it meant that white minority rule and racial oppression would be extended over their territories. While the African nationalist movement in Southern Rhodesia was more interested in pressing for civil rights in the face of well-established racial discrimination, it eventually also came out against the federation.

By 1960, as African nationalist protest grew across the federation, all three territories experienced states of emergency as security forces shot protestors. In early 1959, federal security forces were dispatched to Nyasaland, where they arrested around 1,300 supporters of the Nyasaland Congress Party and killed 50 protestors and wounded many more. The top officials of Congress, including its leader, the American-educated Dr. Hastings Kamuzu Banda, who had worked as doctor in Britain, were flown to Southern Rhodesia, where they were detained without trial on the false accusation that they had planned to murder Europeans in Nyasaland. In 1960, the **Monkton Commission**, a committee of experts appointed by the British government to investigate the crisis, reported that the federation could be held together only by force, and it recommended that African-majority governments be permitted in the two northern territories, which should be allowed to separate from the federation. Although the federal government of Prime Minister Sir Roy Welensky rejected the report, it was accepted by the British government of Harold MacMillan, which took steps that would eventually led to the dissolution of the federation at the end of December 1963. In 1961, the Malawi Congress Party (MCP), a new name for the banned Nyasaland Congress Party, led by Banda, won the territorial election in Nyasaland and declared that it would leave the federation. Britain granted Nyasaland self-government the next year, and in July 1964 it became the independent country of Malawi. Within a few months, the authoritarian Banda clashed with his cabinet ministers, many of whom were dismissed or resigned, with some fleeing the country. In 1966, Malawi became a republic under an MCP one-party state led by President Banda, who was declared "president for life" several years later. In Northern Rhodesia, the federation had been initially opposed by the Northern Rhodesia African National Congress (NRANC) led by Harry Nkumbula, but in the late 1950s **Kenneth Kaunda** founded a more radical splinter group called the Zambian African National Congress (ZANC). Both groups were banned, both leaders were imprisoned at different times, and by 1960 Kaunda had emerged as leader of the United National Independence Party (UNIP). In 1962, given the reforms brought about by the Monkton Commission, Kaunda's UNIP won a territorial election in Northern Rhodesia, and in 1964 it won another election with a much wider franchise in preparation for independence. In October 1964, Northern Rhodesia became the independent Republic of Zambia with a UNIP government under President Kaunda.

The 1963 breakup of the federation created an impasse between the governments of Britain and Southern Rhodesia. In 1962, given the imminent demise of the federation, the overwhelmingly white voters of Southern Rhodesia elected the **Rhodesian Front** (RF) party, which promised to support white supremacy in the territory, particularly in terms of retaining the racially discriminatory Land Apportionment Act, originally passed in 1930, which sustained white commercial farming. The RF government, first led by Premier Winston Field and then **Ian Smith** from 1964, demanded that Britain immediately grant Southern Rhodesia dominion status within the British Commonwealth. Unwilling to hand independence to a white-minority regime, the British government requested that Southern Rhodesia promise to eventually move toward a one-person-one-vote system, but this was rejected by the RF's Smith, who bragged that it would not happen in a thousand years. The impasse was broken when the RF government announced its Unilateral Declaration of Independence (UDI) on November 11, 1965. Making this proclamation on Remembrance Day, normally set aside to commemorate the sacrifice of British subjects who had died during the world wars, was meant to highlight the RF view that Southern Rhodesia had earned its dominion status by fighting for the mother country, which had now betrayed the hitherto loyal territory. While the British government objected to UDI as an illegal action and froze some Southern Rhodesian bank accounts in Britain, London hesitated to use military force to suppress the rogue regime. Within the Commonwealth, heads of newly independent African countries, particularly Julius Nyerere of Tanzania, were furious that Britain was unwilling to crush the Rhodesian rebellion. The UN declared Smith's Rhodesia an illegal racist regime and imposed a host of mandatory military and economic sanctions. During the late 1960s, consequently, Southern

≡ **The transition to independence in South-Central Africa.** *Left:* Rhodesian Prime Minister Ian Smith (1919–2007) practices shooting. *Right:* During the 1970s, Robert Mugabe (left—1924–2019) led the Zimbabwe African Nationalist Union (ZANU) and Joshua Nkomo (1917–1999) led the Zimbabwe African People's Union (ZAPU) in an armed struggle against Rhodesia's white-minority regime.

Rhodesia strengthened its military and economic relations with neighboring Portuguese-ruled Mozambique and apartheid South Africa to form a bastion of colonial and white-minority states in Southern Africa.

During the 1950s and early 1960s, the African nationalist movement in Southern Rhodesia had been subjected to state violence and its organizations were constantly banned and then reformed under new names. The Southern Rhodesia African National Congress (ANC) became the National Democratic Party (NDP), which became the **Zimbabwe African People's Union** (ZAPU). In 1963, ZAPU leaders who had fled to Northern Rhodesia fell out over strategy. While ZAPU's leader **Joshua Nkomo** favored remaining in exile to organize international sanctions against Southern Rhodesia, younger more radical activists like Ndabaningi Sithole and **Robert Mugabe** wanted to return home to lead mass protests against the RF regime and they founded a new group called the **Zimbabwe African National Union** (ZANU). From this point, ZAPU and ZANU would pursuit separate campaigns against white minority rule in Southern Rhodesia. When leaders from both groups returned home to organize protest, they were arrested by Rhodesian security forces and spent the next decade in prison. With Smith's UDI in 1965, both organizations formed armed wings to fight for the liberation of their country. ZAPU established the Zimbabwe People's Revolutionary Army (ZIPRA) and ZANU created the Zimbabwe African National Liberation Army (ZANLA), with both receiving arms and training from Eastern Bloc powers. During the late 1960s, both ZAPU and ZANU were based in independent Zambia and attempted to infiltrate insurgents across the southern border into white-ruled Rhodesia. This initial armed campaign failed because if insurgents managed to cross the border, which consisted of the Zambezi River and Lake Kariba, they would have to traverse the wilderness of the Zambezi Valley, where the partly open terrain made them vulnerable to detection by the Rhodesian Air Force, and there were few rural communities from which to draw supplies and recruits. In 1971, ZANLA leader **Josiah Tongogara** made the important decision to move his fighters to Mozambique's Tete Province, where they allied with FRELIMO, which had gained experience in guerrilla warfare against the Portuguese. From Tete, ZANLA insurgents more easily infiltrated northeastern Rhodesia, where they could hide among the forests and hills, and work on politicizing the dense rural African population. With the departure of the Portuguese in 1974 and FRELIMO's assumption of power in Mozambique, ZANLA established camps all along Rhodesia's eastern border and therefore expanded infiltration and guerrilla warfare. It was during this period that ZANU/ZANLA gained Chinese military support and adopted a Maoist guerrilla warfare doctrine that emphasized gaining support from the rural people, and it turned into a primarily ethnic Shona movement reflecting the demographics of eastern Rhodesia and the Mozambique border. Although ZANU/ZANLA claimed to be fighting against racism and sexism, they often assigned female insurgents the traditional roles of carrying supplies and cooking food, and many female recruits fell victim to sexual violence in insurgent camps in Mozambique. There were, however, female guerrilla leaders within ZANLA, such as **Joice Mujuru**, who took the war name Teurai Ropa, meaning "Spill Blood" and later became a vice president of Zimbabwe. Seeking to win over rural Africans, ZANU/ZANLA mobilized traditional spirit mediums and emphasized grievances over inequitable

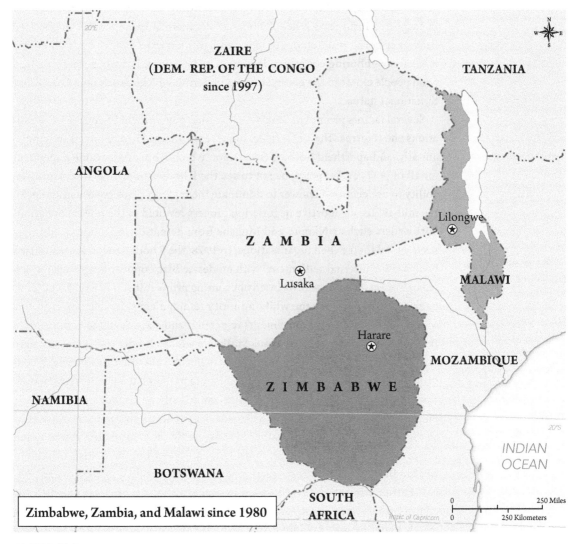

Zimbabwe, Zambia, and Malawi since 1980

≡ **MAP 23.3**

land ownership. Remaining in Zambia and expanding into Botswana in the late 1970s, ZAPU/ZIPRA received Soviet support, adopted the Leninist revolutionary theory that advocated a top-down seizure of power, and developed a conventional army that was meant to cross into Rhodesia at some key moment when the regime there had been weakened. This moment never arrived. Simultaneously, ZAPU/ZIPRA derived its support and recruitment from the Ndebele ethnic group of southwestern Zimbabwe. During the 1970s, the Rhodesian state responded to the escalating insurgency with a brutal campaign that involved resettling rural communities in squalid "protected villages" and establishing "free fire zones" where anyone became a valid military target. Measuring their success by the number of suspected insurgents killed, Rhodesian counterinsurgency forces emphasized helicopter-borne reaction operations and lightning cross-border raids on enemy bases in neighboring countries. This strategy backfired. It pushed the brutalized rural people closer to the insurgents and undermined Rhodesia's questionable international status.

Several factors prompted Smith's Rhodesian government to engage in negotiations and reforms. The 1974-75 Portuguese withdrawal had removed an important ally, and apartheid South Africa, upon which Rhodesia became dependent for all imports and exports, began to see the **Rhodesian War** as threatening its ability to use economic power to dominate the region's Black governed states. In the mid-1970s, an abortive negotiation process resulted in the release of nationalist leaders such as Nkomo and Mugabe from detention in Rhodesia and they soon joined their exiled organizations. In 1978, the Rhodesian government tried to create an "internal settlement" with moderate Black opposition groups, which led to Bishop Abel Muzorewa briefly becoming prime minster of a renamed Zimbabwe-Rhodesia. Since the white minority retained considerable power in this arrangement, the armed movements rejected it and continued the war. In 1979, Britain hosted the **Lancaster House talks,** in which all sides in the conflict were represented. The negotiations produced a majority-rule constitution, which conceded that for 10 years there would be separate parliamentary representation for the white minority and that land reform could only be conducted on the basis of a free market economy. A ceasefire was declared, Rhodesian forces withdrew to their barracks, insurgents gathered at assembly areas inside the country, and the process was monitored by a multinational force from the British Commonwealth. In February 1980, an election was held that resulted in a victory for ZANU-Patriotic Front (ZANU-PF) led by Robert Mugabe. Many whites fled the country. That April, Britain granted independence to the Republic of Zimbabwe, which would be governed by Prime Minister Mugabe and his ZANU-PF. New Zimbabwe military and police forces were created by combining elements of

Timeline

1910—Union of South Africa

1912—Creation of the South African Native National Congress (Later African National Congress or ANC)

1913—Natives Land Act in South Africa

1914—Creation of the National Party in South Africa

1922—Rand Revolt in South Africa

1923—Responsible government for Southern Rhodesia

1924—Pact Government (National Party and Labour Party coalition) in South Africa

1931—Statute of Westminster removes British veto over legislation in the dominions

1931—Land Apportionment Act in Southern Rhodesia

1948—Election of the National Party in South Africa and beginning of apartheid

1953—Creation of Central African Federation

1955—ANC adopts the Freedom Charter

1959—Pan-Africanist Congress (PAC) splits from the ANC

1959—Massacre in South West Africa

1960—Sharpeville Massacre

1961—Beginning of armed struggle against apartheid in South Africa

1963—Dissolution of Central African Federation

1963—Split of Zimbabwe African People's Union (ZAPU) and Zimbabwe African National Union (ZANU)

1964—Independence of Zambia and Malawi

1965—Unilateral Declaration of Independence (UDI) by Southern Rhodesia

1966—Beginning of liberation wars in Rhodesia and South West Africa

1974-75—Portuguese decolonization

1976—Soweto uprising

1979—Lancaster House talks over Rhodesia

1980—Independence of Zimbabwe

1983—New constitution in South Africa; mass protest led by the United Democratic Front (UDF)

1986—State of emergency across South Africa

1989—South African withdrawal from South West Africa

1990—Unbanning of anti-apartheid movements and release of political prisoners in South Africa

1990—Independence of Namibia

1994—First democratic election in South Africa

the former Rhodesian and insurgent forces. Between 1981 and 1987, in a process known as **Gukurahundi** (Shona language for "the rain that washes away the rubbish"), Mugabe's ZANU-PF politicized the security forces and used them to violently suppress the opposition ZAPU movement and to terrorize the Ndebele people of southwestern Zimbabwe. In the 1987 Unity Accord, the beleaguered leaders of ZAPU, including Nkomo, agreed for their group to be absorbed into the ruling ZANU-PF party. Mugabe became a powerful executive president and Zimbabwe became a de facto one-party state. For the next decade, there would be very little real political opposition.

Conclusion

The withdrawal of Portuguese colonial rule from Angola and Mozambique in 1974-75 represented the beginning of the end for the white minority–ruled states of Southern Africa. It enabled SWAPO insurgents to establish bases in southern Angola from where they intensified the war in northern South West Africa. ZANLA staging areas spread across Mozambique's entire western border, which helped to expand the guerrilla war in adjacent Rhodesia. This created the context in which the long and destructive conflict in Rhodesia came to an end through negotiations that resulted in a majority-rule constitution and the independence of Zimbabwe in 1980. During the 1980s, the costly South African military involvement in Angola, the dramatic escalation of protest within South Africa, and the changing international circumstances created by the winding down of the Cold War informed the independence of Namibia in 1990 and the end of apartheid in South Africa in 1994.

KEY TERMS

African National Congress (ANC) 500

apartheid 497

apartheid system 497

Bantu Authorities Act 499

Bantu Education Act 499

Bantu Women's League 500

Bantustans 505

Black Consciousness movement 504

Caprivi Strip 509

Central African Federation 510

Charlotte Maxeke 500

D.F. Malan 496

Defiance Campaign 500

F.W. de Klerk 506

Freedom Charter 500

Group Areas Act 498

Gukurahundi 517

Ian Smith 513

Industrial and Commercial Workers' Union (ICU) 496

Inkatha 506

J.M.B. Hertzog 495

Jan Smuts 494

Joice Mujuru 515

Joshua Nkomo 514

Kenneth Kaunda 512

Lancaster House talks 516

Lillian Ngoyi 501

Louis Botha 494

Mangosutho Buthelezi 506

Monkton Commission 512

National Party 495

Natives Land Act 494

Nelson Mandela 502

Ox-wagon Sentinel movement 497

P.W. Botha 505

Pan-Africanist Congress (PAC) 501

Population Registration Act 498

Rand Revolt 496

Rhodesian Front (RF) 513

Rhodesian War 516

Robert Mugabe 514

Robert Sobukwe 501

Sam Nujoma 510

Sharpeville Massacre 502

Sophiatown 498

STUDY QUESTIONS

1. Why did the withdrawal of Portuguese colonial rule from Angola and Mozambique in 1974-75 represent the beginning of the end for the white minority–ruled states of Southern Africa?

2. How did Pass Laws and Land Acts create a system of oppression against nonwhites? What types of methods did South Africans employ to resist racism and apartheid? How did women contribute to these resistance movements? Why was the Sharpeville Massacre a key turning point? What were the goals of the Black Consciousness movement? How did the Sowetu Uprising revive the anti-apartheid struggle?

3. What events led to the Namibian war for independence? Why did Western and Eastern Bloc powers turn Namibia into a Cold War conflict?

1) Why did African nationalist leaders in Southern Rhodesia embark on armed struggles to liberate themselves from white minority rule? What were the results of the Lancaster House talks?

Please see page FR-10 for the Further Readings for this chapter.
For additional digital learning resources please go to
https://www.oup.com/he/falola-stapleton1e

Independent Africa in the Cold War Era: State, Economy, and Culture, c. 1960–1990

When African countries became independent in the late 1950s and 1960s, they were expected to become constitutional liberal democracies with free market economies similar to the ones enjoyed by most former European colonial powers. However, newly independent African countries had very little familiarity with these Western-style systems as they had experienced decades of rule by colonial dictatorships that structured African economies to export raw materials. Only the British colonies in West Africa, particularly the Gold Coast (Ghana), experienced a few years of internal self-government to get ready for the transition, and this proved insufficient. In most cases, African sovereignty came suddenly and without much planning or preparation, and this resulted in weak democratic institutions. Furthermore, most African countries became independent during the height of Cold War tensions between the American-led Western alliance that advocated democracy and capitalism, and the Soviet-led Eastern Bloc that advanced the idea of a socialist revolution. The early 1960s was the era of the Cuban Missile Crisis and the threat of global nuclear annihilation. Newly sovereign African governments had the freedom to stay with the political and economic concepts passed on to them by the former colonial powers, all on the Western side of the Cold War, or to experiment with new socialist political and economic models that promised to address dire problems related to poverty and underdevelopment. Given all these factors, it is not surprising that the young democracies of Africa often did not last long. Many were replaced by corrupt and violent authoritarian regimes that vied for superpower sponsorship. This was in spite of their commitment to the **Non-Aligned Movement** (NAM), which was meant to be a central body of newly independent states in Africa, Latin America, and Asia, proclaiming neutrality in the power contention between

Dictator. This caricature of Idi Amin, president of Uganda from 1971 to 1979, shows a bloated and brooding tyrant.

521

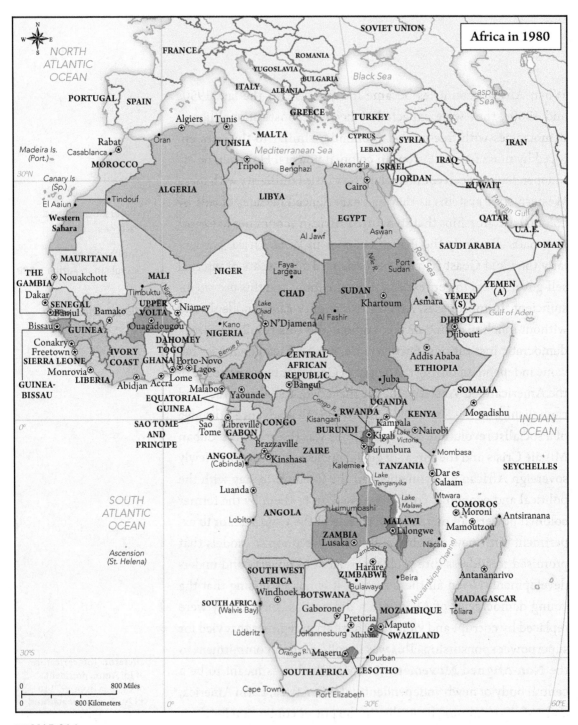

Africa in 1980

≡ **MAP 24.1**

the factional superpowers. The movement, established in 1961 as the official offspring of the Bandung conference held six years earlier, encouraged decolonization but ultimately failed in its effort to restructure the international economic system. In the same Cold War era, innovative African musicians and writers enjoyed tremendous success and began to gain global attention, but they still had to navigate problems related to the African state and economy.

Military Coups and Regimes

The term *coup d'état*, or more commonly "coup," refers to an illegal and usually sudden takeover of a government by elements of the state security forces. Very soon after gaining independence in the 1950s and 1960s, many African countries experienced military coups and were subsequently governed by undemocratic regimes composed of military personnel. Military coups became most frequent in West Africa but also took place in parts of East and Central Africa. In some African countries, from the 1960s to the early 1990s, a political culture of military coups developed, with multiple coups, counter-coups, and failed coups becoming common. In this period, examples of multiple successful military coups include three in each of Burundi, Chad, Republic of Congo, and Sierra Leone, four in each of Benin, Mauritania, Sudan, and Uganda, five in each of Upper Volta (Burkina Faso) and Ghana, and six in Nigeria. Many of these countries and others also experienced unsuccessful coup attempts.

Since the early 1960s, questions have been raised about why personnel within African militaries took the apparently drastic measure of taking over their countries' governments. Upon independence from European powers, African countries had inherited Western-style government systems, civil services, and security forces. The typical Western military was supposed to remain apolitical and subordinate to elected civilian governments. Although many of postcolonial Africa's first African military officers had been trained in European military academies, they quickly abandoned this tradition and sought to take control of the state. Justifying their actions, military coup plotters routinely decried ousted civilian leaders as incompetent and corrupt, and explained that the military was the only efficient arm of the state capable of intervening to save the country from political and economic chaos. In reality, the military regimes of Africa typically became just as (or more) inefficient, corrupt, and oppressive as the former civilian governments. New military coup plotters would often then use the same excuse to explain their actions against a previous military regime. To explain this departure from the Western apolitical military model, some observers claimed that there was an age-old "warrior tradition" in African history and that in precolonial times there was usually no difference between a society's government and military leadership and there were many historical examples of warlords. Therefore, so it followed, the newly independent African states of the 1960s and 1970s were simply going back to their historic warrior-oriented political system. Of course, this theory is impossible to prove (or disprove), and it is contradicted by the fact that a few African countries, such as Senegal, Tanzania, and Botswana, have never experienced a successful or attempted military coup.

Perhaps it is worth considering the nature of the European-led colonial militaries in Africa that were transformed, usually without much change, into the armed forces of independent African states. Formed during the late-nineteenth-century conquest period, the colonial armies of Africa were not exact copies of their parent organizations in Europe. The primary purpose of African colonial armies was to uphold the colonial regime by discouraging and suppressing rebellions. They were internal security forces. Defending a colony's borders and providing a military manpower reservoir for external emergencies, such as during the world wars, were secondary missions. In short, the colonial militaries of Africa were profoundly political institutions, and once they became national armed forces, they were easily politicized. Furthermore, not all Western militaries were/are as apolitical as they pretend. In the recently independent former French colonies, for instance, African officers who had been trained in France were well aware that the threat of a military coup had brought Charles de Gaulle to power in 1958.

An important aspect of military coups in Africa is that they rarely represented the entire command structure of the armed forces seizing state power. Coup plotters almost always represented a politicized faction of the military hierarchy and often shared common ethnic or regional origins. Some coups were led by generals, some by majors, some by junior officers and a few by enlisted soldiers. At times, civilian politicians sought to entrench themselves in power by cultivating loyalty among their ethnic kinsmen in the military who received promotions and patronage. Such policies politicized the military with the dominant faction supporting the existing government and other, less favored, factions opposing it.

The history of military coups in newly independent Sierra Leone represents a prime example of this trend. Gaining independence from Britain in 1961, Sierra Leone was a multiparty democracy in which the first government was formed by Prime Minister Sir Milton Margai and the Sierra Leone People's Party (SLPP). In 1964, Sir Milton passed away from natural causes and his brother and cabinet minister, Albert Margai, became prime minister. Attempting to secure his power, Albert Margai promoted members of his own Mende ethnic group from southern Sierra Leone within the military, including its commander, Brigadier David Lansana. Disgruntled military officers from other ethnic groups began to support the opposition All People's Congress (APC) led by Siaka Stevens. When Stevens's APC narrowly won the March 1967 elections, Brigadier Lansana staged a military coup and declared martial law to prevent the new government from assuming office. A few days later, a group of military officers calling themselves the National Reformation Council (NRC) and led by Brigadier Andrew Juxon-Smith overthrew and arrested Lansana and suspended the constitution. In April 1968, a group of army sergeants calling themselves the Anti-Corruption Revolutionary Movement (ACRM) and led by Colonel John Bangura ousted the NRC regime. Bangura's ACRM reinstated the constitution and installed the previously elected Siaka Stevens as prime minister of a civilian government. Prime Minister Stevens promoted Bangura to brigadier and appointed him commander of the military. Quickly establishing an authoritarian state, Stevens accused Bangura of plotting a coup, and in 1970 the latter was arrested, convicted of treason, and hanged. In 1971, after Stevens appointed his Limba ethnic fellow Joseph Momoh as commander of the armed forces, soldiers loyal to the late Bangura, including many from Bangura's Temne ethnic group, mutinied, but their protest was suppressed and some were imprisoned. Stevens, now a president of a republic, then took steps to prevent further coups and mutinies. From 1971 to 1973, troops from the neighboring Republic of Guinea, ruled by Sékou Touré who was a political ally of Stevens, were stationed in Sierra Leone. Furthermore, Stevens created his own paramilitary force called the State Security Division (SSD), which was separate from the military and which was focused on crushing protest. In 1975, Stevens charged a number of military officers and politicians, including Brigadier Lansana, with orchestrating a failed coup; they were subsequently executed. In 1978, Sierra Leone became a one-party state under the APC, and when Stevens retired in 1985 he was succeeded as president by former military commander Momoh. In 1992, in the context of an unfolding civil war, which will be discussed in Chapter 26, President Momoh was overthrown by a group of Sierra Leone soldiers led by Captain Valentine Strasser.

Just as they emerged from different ranks within the armed forces, military coup leaders also held different ambitions and ideologies. This is well illustrated by the history of coups and military regimes in independent Ghana. In 1957, Ghana, formerly the British-ruled Gold Coast, became the first colony in sub-Saharan Africa to gain independence. During the late 1950s and the 1960s, the government of Kwame Nkrumah suppressed opposition political parties, particularly from the Asante region, and embarked on socialist economic policies that created economic

TABLE 24.1 Military Coups in Postcolonial Africa, 1960–1975
The following African leaders were removed through military coups between 1960 and 1975:
1960 (September 14): Patrice Lumumba, prime minister of the Republic of Congo (now Democratic Republic of Congo)
1963 (January 13): Sylvanus Olympio, president of Togo
1963 (August 15): Fulbert Youlou, president of the Republic of Congo
1963 (October 28): Hubert Maga, president of Dahomey (now Benin)
1964 (January 12): Jamshid bin Abdullah Al Said, sultan of Zanzibar
1964 (February 17): Léon M'ba, president of Gabon
1965 (November 25): Joseph Kasavubu, president of the Republic of Congo (now Democratic Republic of Congo)
1965 (November 27): Sourou-Migan Apithy, president of Dahomey (now Benin)
1966 (January 1): David Dacko, president of the Central African Republic
1966 (January 3): Maurice Yaméogo, president of Upper Volta (now Burkina Faso)
1966 (January 15): Abubakar Tafawa Balewa, prime minister of Nigeria
1966 (February 4): King Mutesa II of Buganda, president of Uganda
1966 (February 24): Kwame Nkrumah, president of Ghana
1966 (July 8): Mwambutsa IV, king of Burundi
1966 (July 29): Johnson Aguiyi-Ironsi, head of state of Nigeria
1966 (November 28): Ntare V, king of Burundi
1967 (January 13): Nicolas Grunitzky, president of Togo
1967 (March 21): Siaka Stevens, prime minister of Sierra Leone
1967 (December 16): Christophe Soglo, president of Dahomey (now Benin)
1968 (April 19): Andrew Juxon-Smith, acting governor-general of Sierra Leone
1968 (September 4): Alphonse Massamba-Débat, president of the Republic of Congo
1968 (November 19): Modibo Keïta, president of Mali
1969 (May 25): Ismail al-Azhari, president of Sudan
1969 (October 21): Sheikh Mukhtar Mohamed Hussein, president of Somalia
1971 (January 25): Milton Obote, president of Uganda
1972 (January 13): Kofi Abrefa Busia, prime minister of Ghana
1972 (October 11): Philibert Tsiranana, president of Madagascar
1972 (October 26): Justin Ahomadégbé-Tomêtin, chairman of the Presidential Council of Dahomey (now Benin)
1973 (July 5): Grégoire Kayibanda, president of Rwanda
1974 (April 15): Hamani Diori, president of Niger
1974 (September 12): Haile Selassie I, emperor of Ethiopia
1975 (February 5): Gabriel Ramanantsoa, president of Madagascar
1975 (April 13): François Tombalbaye, president of Chad
1975 (July 29): Yakubu Gowon, head of state of Nigeria
1975 (August 3): Ahmed Abdallah Abderemane, president of the Comoros

chaos. Nkrumah became president of a republic in 1961 and imposed a one-party state under his rule in 1964. Under Nkrumah, Ghana's foreign policy favored the Soviet Union and attempted to fulfill the Pan-Africanist dream of a United States of Africa. In February 1966, while Nkrumah was on a diplomatic trip to North Vietnam and China, officers of the Ghanaian military and police calling themselves the National Liberation Council (NLC) took over the government. Led by General Joseph A. Ankrah, the NLC regime privatized the economy, devalued the local currency to encourage exports of cocoa, and invited multinational corporations to invest in the country. Internationally, and within the Cold War context, the NLC re-established close ties with Britain and the United States, which some observers believed had orchestrated the coup. With approval from Ghana's business and traditional elites, the NLC organized multiparty elections in 1969 and handed over power to the civilian government of Kofi A. Busia and his Progress Party (PP). Prime Minister Busia's government inherited massive economic problems caused partly by the huge government debt incurred by the previous Nkrumah government and Ghana's economic dependence on cocoa exports. Unpopular austerity measures, including frozen wages and tax increases recommended by the International Monetary Fund, made the Busia government unpopular with elites, trade unions, and the military.

In January 1972, after Busia had begun to interfere in military appointments, Lieutenant Colonel Ignatius K. Acheampong led a coup that replaced civilian rule with a military regime. During the 1970s, the Supreme Military Council (SMC), led by General Acheampong, reversed Busia's austerity measures, nationalized the assets of foreign companies, and suppressed student protest. Continued economic problems including rampant inflation prompted the SMC, in 1978, to replace Acheampong with Lieutenant General Frederick W.K. Akuffo, who formally promised to restore civilian government.

≡ **Coup leader.** Leading military coups in Ghana in 1979 and 1981, Flight Lieutenant Jerry Rawlings (1947-2020) returned the country to civilian rule in the 1990s and served two terms as an elected civilian president.

In June 1979, on the eve of transition to multiparty civilian democracy, a group of junior officers led by Flight Lieutenant **Jerry Rawlings** seized power claiming that the planned transition had not taken into account the real problems of the country. Called the Armed Forces Revolutionary Council (AFRC), the young officers who had taken charge executed previous military rulers Acheampong and Akuffo, accusing them of corruption and of tarnishing the military's reputation. In September, the AFRC handed power to the elected civilian government of Hilla Limann's People's National Party (PNP), but with a public warning that it was expected to put the interests of the people before personal enrichment. The Limann government failed to deal with the continuing economic problems and responded to a series of trade union strikes by dismissing striking public employees. Consequently, in December 1981 Flight Lieutenant Rawlings staged another coup, installing the Provisional National Defense Council (PNDC).

Criticizing past governments as ruling for the benefit of elites and using party politics to divide Ghanaians, Rawlings's PNDC regime portrayed itself as leading a populist revolution; establishing a network of committees to give ordinary people a say in decision-making in business, the military, and local administrations; and founding tribunals to punish those who engaged in corruption and opposed the revolution. Although there were many leftists within the PNDC, Rawlings initiated a pragmatic Economic Recovery Program (ERP) that included austerity measures and financial assistance from the World Bank and Western countries. By 1987, the economy had stabilized as inflation decreased, there was economic growth, and Ghana managed to pay half a billion dollars in outstanding loan payments dating back to the Nkrumah period. As the PNDC state continued currency devaluation and privatization, student groups and exiled politicians criticized it for the country's high rate of unemployment. In 1992, the PNDC managed the drafting of a new constitution, which returned Ghana to civilian rule and multiparty democracy. As civilian politicians, Rawlings and his National Democratic Congress (NDC), a new name for the PNDC, would go on to win elections in November 1992 and again in 1996.

Capitalism and Socialism in Africa

In the 1950s and 1960s, the concepts of development and underdevelopment were applied to newly independent African countries. The countries of Western Europe and North America were considered developed as they had industrial economies, primarily urban populations, high levels of healthcare and education, and generally comfortable standards of living. African countries, as well as some Asian and Latin American ones, were perceived as underdeveloped or developing due to their economic emphasis on the export of agricultural products and minerals, lack of industry, low level of healthcare and education, and relatively poor rural populations. To maintain friendly relations with the many new countries of the underdeveloped world, and in the context of the Cold War, Western powers set up international development agencies to provide funding and technical assistance. For example, the United States Agency for International Development (USAID) was launched in 1961 and the Canadian International Development Agency (CIDA) was founded in 1968. American-led international economic institutions such as the World Bank and the International Monetary Fund (IMF), both established at the end of the Second World War and based in Washington, DC, provided loans to pay for development projects. These loans did not require collateral, but they did come with conditions related to the recipient's economic policies. In the first three decades of the independence era, many African governments tried to copy Western-style development with a host of ambitious and expensive but poorly conceived economic and infrastructural programs. New African governments also paid for the perceived trappings of a sovereign state, such as fleets of limousines for senior officials, new government buildings and presidential palaces, and arms purchases for the military. Lacking a strong local business sector, African states tried to foster the creation of an African middle class by unnecessarily expanding their civil services and artificially boosting the value of the local currency to make imported consumer goods cheaper. All this was unsustainable and led many African states to take on increasingly heavy debt burdens with crippling interest payments.

Some postcolonial African governments pursued the sort of capitalist economy favored by the outgoing colonial powers and the Western world. In Côte d'Ivoire, which became independent in 1960, the government of President **Félix Houphouët-Boigny** retained close relations with former colonial power France and maintained a free enterprise economy. Investment by foreign companies was encouraged through the construction of an up-to-date Western-style business and hotel district in the city of Abidjan and through government regulations that allowed most profits to be taken out of the country. Under Houphouët-Boigny, who ruled an authoritarian one-party state, the economy of Côte d'Ivoire continued to focus on the export of agricultural products, primarily cocoa and coffee, that had been developed during colonial times. During the 1960s cocoa production tripled, and by the late 1970s it was the world's largest producer of that product. At the same time, coffee production increased by almost 50 percent, making Côte d'Ivoire the world's third-largest coffee producer, after Brazil and Columbia. Within West Africa, it became the foremost exporter of palm oil and pineapples. This approach created very favorable economic statistics. From 1960 to 1965, the economy of Côte d'Ivoire grew between 11 and 12 percent, which was the greatest increase among Africa's non-petroleum producing countries. From 1960 to 1978, the gross domestic product increased by a factor of 12, and it achieved a trade surplus. People from other West African countries, particularly Upper Volta (Burkina Faso), flocked to Côte d'Ivoire, where many found jobs in cocoa production. Working as business managers, educators, and technicians, the number of French people in the country increased from 30,000 in 1960 to 60,000 in 1980. As neighboring Ghana slipped into economic crisis under the socialist economic policies of Nkrumah, Western and African leaders praised Houphouët-Boigny as the "sage of Africa" who had produced the "Ivoirien miracle." Journalists compared his young, glamourous, and Parisian-educated wife, Marie-Thérèse Houphouët-Boigny, with American first lady Jackie Kennedy. However, the economic success of Côte d'Ivoire was short-lived. Described as "growth without development," the economy was dependent on foreign investment and expertise. In 1978, the economy began to decline as the international price of cocoa and coffee decreased sharply, and a severe drought in the early 1980s exacerbated the problem. Houphouët-Boigny responded to these problems by using the government marketing board to pay an unrealistically high price to farmers for their products, which was not sustainable, as the state lost a massive amount of money and borrowed heavily. By 1987, Côte d'Ivoire had accrued an international debt of US$10 billion, for which it became unable to make payments. Attempts to develop an offshore oil industry were hindered by the global recession of the 1980s. The Ivoirien economic "miracle" had turned into a disaster. This crisis formed the context for violent conflict that developed in Côte d'Ivoire during the 1990s and 2000s.

During the Cold War era, many African governments pursued a state-directed socialist economic agenda, believing that it would alleviate poverty and foster economic development. Many African leaders theorized that they could build upon the communal aspects

≡ **Cocoa.** A young Ivoirian boy sorts cocoa beans. Nearly 80 percent of the world's cocoa comes from West Africa, of which the Côte d'Ivoire is the largest producer.

of traditional African society, seen as lacking the class structure of Western societies, to create an indigenous form of socialism that would work well for Africa. During the 1960s and 1970s, a number of different strands of **African socialism** were developed. In many cases these philosophies became mere rhetoric to justify authoritarian rule, the creation of one-party states, and the personal enrichment of those in power.

In Senegal, during the 1960s and 1970s, President Léopold Sédar Senghor was a famous intellectual who had previously contributed to the francophone philosophy of **negritude**, which indicted colonialism and promoted a Pan-African identity (see Chapter 22). While in office, he advocated for African socialism within a cultural context, but his government did little to change the free market orientation of Senegal's economy, which was heavily dependent on groundnut exports. Under Senghor, Senegal became a one-party state, conservative Muslim elites remained influential, and close relations were maintained with France, the former colonial power.

In Zambia, which had become independent from Britain in 1964, President Kenneth Kaunda established the principle of "Zambian humanism," which combined a state-controlled economy with traditional African values. Since colonial times, the Zambian economy was almost entirely dependent upon copper mining that was conducted by foreign-owned mining companies, such as the Anglo-American Corporation. At the end of the 1960s, Kaunda orchestrated a government takeover of the Zambian mining industry, which, in 1971, was brought under the central management of the state-controlled Zambian Industrial and Mining Corporation (ZIMCO). However, Kaunda's nationalization of the mining industry was badly timed. International copper prices dropped steeply in 1973 and the government had to borrow heavily from the IMF, and by the middle of the 1980s Zambia had become the world's most indebted country relative to its GDP. During the 1980s, as a condition for continued IMF assistance, the Kaunda regime devalued its currency, removed subsidies on food, and reduced government spending. This resulted in rioting as food prices increased and public employees were retrenched.

The most well-known and substantial experiment with African socialism was attempted in Tanzania under the leadership of Julius Nyerere and his TANU government. In the 1967 Arusha Declaration, Nyerere emphasized the need to use African socialism, known by the Swahili term *Ujamaa*, meaning "brotherhood" or "extended family," as a model for development. Tanzania became a one-party state under TANU: important economic assets were nationalized, including banks, companies, processing plants, and apartment buildings; compulsory free education was provided; healthcare was increased; and a national Tanzanian identity was promoted over ethnic identities. Most famously, Nyerere's Ujamaa program involved the creation of new **Ujamaa villages**, which were cooperative projects where collective agriculture was practiced and where public services could be concentrated. During the early 1970s, the TANU regime compelled many thousands of rural Tanzanians to resettle in Ujamaa villages, and security forces were deployed to quell resistance. Since Ujamaa villages were directed to grow cash crops such as coffee, tea, tobacco, and sisal to generate revenue for the government that could be used for national development, food production was undermined. The program was further plagued by droughts, decline of prices for exports, lack of foreign investment, and Tanzania's expensive 1978–79 war with Uganda. During the 1970s, as the Ujamaa villages proved disappointingly unproductive, Tanzania sought financial assistance from the IMF and received international humanitarian assistance to feed its people. The Ujamaa villages were disbanded in the 1980s, and the return of people to their home areas caused confusion over land ownership. In 1985, Nyerere apologized for his failed economic policies and retired from the presidency. Romanticizing the Ujamaa experiment, some tout its achievements in education and healthcare while blaming its ultimate failure on imagined Western sabotage. Unfortunately, it left Tanzania, which was already poor, as one of the most impoverished countries in the world and heavily dependent on foreign aid.

During the 1950s and 1960s, governments in North Africa adopted the ideology of **Arab socialism** that advocated a state-directed economy but rejected Soviet-style communism, which was seen as anathema to the central role of Islam in Arab society. Arab socialists usually promoted Arab nationalism and Pan-Arabism, condemned the creation of Israel as a Western colonial outpost in Arab lands, and tried to chart a middle path between the two superpowers. Nevertheless, Arab socialist leaders were generally secular, which put them at odds with

☰ **African Socialists.** *Left:* President of Zambia from 1964 to 1991, Kenneth Kaunda 1924–2021 nationalized the country's copper mines, which resulted in massive economic problems. *Center:* Tanzanian women working at an Ujamaa village in Tanzania in 1974. *Right:* Julius Nyerere (1922–1999) was president of Tanzania from 1964 to 1985.

political-religious movements like the Muslim Brotherhood. In the late 1950s, the Egyptian government of Gamal Abdel Nasser, who had come to power as a result of the 1952 takeover by the Free Officers movement, nationalized major economic assets, beginning with the Suez Canal, the proceeds from which would be used to fund the construction of the **Aswan Dam**, which was central to economic development. Once the British and French backed down, ending the 1956 Suez Crisis (see Chapter 21), Nasser nationalized all other British and French industries operating in Egypt, though most of the Egyptian economy remained in the hands of private enterprise. Due to deteriorating relations with the West, Nasser increasingly turned to the Soviet Union for assistance with the Aswan Dam project and to arm the Egyptian military for a future war with Israel. Nasser remained in power until his death in 1970. In 1962, Algeria became independent under the one-party rule of the National Liberation Front (FLN), which had fought a long war against France (see Chapter 22). While the initial FLN government led by Ahmed Ben Bella focused on agricultural production through rural cooperatives, FLN military leader Houari Boumédiène seized power in 1965 and nationalized the Algerian oil industry, using the revenues to embark on state-planned industrialization. This worked well during the early 1970s, when oil prices were high, but after Boumédiène's death in 1978, as oil prices decreased, the state-directed socialist economy faltered, and during the 1980s the FLN government embarked on economic liberalization. Under Boumédiène, Algerian foreign policy supported the Non-Aligned Movement and sponsored anti-colonial liberation movements like the Palestine Liberation Organization (PLO) and South Africa's African National Congress (ANC).

A few African countries adopted the Marxist-Leninist scientific socialism advocated by the Soviet Union. The most well-known of these was Ethiopia, where, in 1974, a group of military officers overthrew the pro-Western and feudal regime of Emperor Haile Selassie and instituted a revolutionary and extremely violent Soviet-style government called the **Derg** under the leadership of Haile Mariam Mengistu. The Soviet Union delivered a massive amount of aid to Ethiopia, but mostly in the form of weapons and ammunition to

☰ **Arab socialism.** Soviet premier Nikita Khrushchev and Egyptian leader Gamal Abdal Nasser tour the Aswan High Dam in the early 1960s.

fight a war with Somalia in 1978 and insurgencies in the Eritrea and Tigray regions. A planned and bureaucratized economy was created in which the government took over all large businesses, urban properties, economic assets, and rural land, undermining the historic feudal landowners and the Ethiopian church. Rural people, once tenants to absentee landlords, were forced to move to government-operated collectives and mechanized farms where their agricultural produce was distributed by the state. Agricultural production was disrupted by poor planning, drought, and civil war in some regions. Indeed, the Derg's collectivized agriculture contributed to a catastrophic famine that occurred in 1983 and 1984. As discussed in Chapter 25, the Mengistu regime was weakened by the end of Soviet support in the late 1980s and it was overthrown by a rebel alliance in 1991.

In the former French colony of Upper Volta, army officer Captain **Thomas Sankara** led an ambitious but short-lived socialist government. Coming to power in a 1983 coup carried out by disgruntled junior officers, the charismatic Sankara saw himself as a Marxist revolutionary and the Che Guevara of Africa. His government rejected foreign assistance, repudiated debts incurred by previous despotic regimes, and sought to eliminate the influence of Western-dominated international economic institutions like the IMF and World Bank. Emphasizing national self-sufficiency and pride, Sankara renamed the country Burkina Faso or "Land of Upright Men." In rural areas, the Sankara administration stripped traditional chiefs of their authority to claim tribute and unpaid labor, and redistributed their lands to peasants who were then assisted by state irrigation and fertilization programs. Consequently, Burkina Faso became self-sufficient in food production and eventually produced a food surplus. For example, while the average wheat production in the countries of the Sahel area for 1986 was 2,500 pounds per acre, farmers in Burkina Faso grew 3,500 pounds per acre. Sankara also encouraged the production of cotton, not as a cash crop but for the local manufacture of

≡ **Socialist leader.** Thomas Sankara (1949–1987—left), president of Burkina Faso, and French president François Mitterrand (right).

clothing for the population. Making healthcare a priority, Sankara's government launched a massive vaccination program and became the first African state to publicly acknowledge the gravity of the HIV/AIDS pandemic. Without outside aid, Sankara orchestrated the building of houses, roads, and railways and embarked on a large-scale tree-planting program to counter deforestation and desertification. Although Sankara's education policies resulted in some initial success, they were derailed by striking teachers who were fired and replaced by untrained university graduates. Unusual among West African states at the time, Sankara's government promoted women's rights by outlawing forced marriages, polygamy, and female genital modification; women were also appointed to the cabinet and the military. Human rights abuses became associated with people's tribunals that conducted trials of those accused of corruption and laziness, and revolutionary defense committees that became overzealous and acted like gangs. In late 1987, Sankara was assassinated during a coup led by his deputy, Blaise Compaoré, who restored close relations with France, accepted World Bank and IMF assistance, and reversed most of Sankara's reforms. Remaining in power for the next 27 years, Compaoré was overthrown by a popular uprising in 2014.

Personalist Dictatorships

Shortly after decolonization, many African governments became **personalist dictatorships**. In this form of government, the state's leader exercises absolute power over policies and appointments, and a cult of personality is developed. The leader's image is displayed prominently and widely, he receives widespread and routine public adulation, and he is bestowed with a series of honorific titles. In this atmosphere, the leader's personal idiosyncrasies often become official policy. Personalist dictatorships are either official or unofficial one-party states where any criticism of the leader and his government is banned under threat of deadly violence. They often stage grandiose spectacles or engage in over-the-top rhetoric in an attempt to create legitimacy and to distract people from rampant corruption, nepotism, economic misery, and violence. In Cold War Africa, such leaders also took advantage of superpower rivalries to garner external support and resources.

In 1960, during the Congo Crisis (see Chapter 22), Colonel **Joseph Mobutu** overthrew Prime Minister Patrice Lumumba and orchestrated his execution. Although the American CIA sponsored Mobutu as a foil to growing Soviet interest in the former Belgian colony, he remained the military chief-of-staff and did not formally take over the government at that time. Mobutu waited until the UN had suppressed the separatist regime in the southern region of Katanga and the Congolese government, with the help of the United States and Belgium, had crushed a leftist rebellion in the east. In 1965, Mobutu staged a military coup that overthrew President Joseph Kasavubu and Prime Minister Moïse Tshombe (formerly the Katanga separatist leader) and installed himself as head of an emergency government that placed the country under martial law. While Kasavubu was allowed to retire, other politicians were executed in public, and army mutinies in the east (including one by foreign mercenaries) were put down with American help. In 1967, Mobutu created a state based on the Popular Movement of the Revolution (MPR), which became the only legal political party; membership became compulsory for all Congolese, and all power was placed in the hands of the leader. This regime was confirmed in a rigged 1970 election in which Mobutu and the MPR received almost 100 percent of the vote, voting was done in public, and the number of ballots cast exceeded the number of registered voters. Mobutu launched a state ideology called *authenticité*, which was anti-colonial and sought to promote an imagined version of African culture and a new national identity. In 1971, the name of the country changed to the Republic of Zaire, which was derived from a Portuguese version of the Kikongo word "nzere" or "nzadi," meaning "the river that swallows all rivers." This referred to the Congo River. Similarly, colonial names for cities and towns changed to African ones, with, for example, Leopoldville becoming Kinshasa, Stanleyville becoming Kisangani, and Elisabethville becoming Lubumbashi. Under *authenticité*, Mobutu's regime tried to transform Zairean culture. Forbidden to wear Western-style suits and neckties, men donned a plain-looking outfit that was similar to the uniform popularized by Mao in China. Women adopted traditional African hairstyles and clothing. Parents were forbidden from giving their children European names and many adults Africanized their names, including Joseph-Desiré Mobutu, who became Mobutu Sese Seko Kuku Ngbendu Wa Za Banga, meaning "the all-powerful warrior who, because of his endurance and inflexible will to win, goes from conquest to conquest, leaving fire in his wake." Putting away his military uniform, the renamed Mobutu Sese Seko adopted what became his trademark costume of a Mao suit, as well as a leopard-skin hat and a carved walking stick both of which were traditional symbols of authority in Southern and Central Africa. In 1974, to highlight his regime and promote his image as an international Black leader, Mobutu hosted a high profile and globally televised boxing match called "the Rumble in the Jungle" between celebrated African-American heavyweight fighters Muhammed Ali and George Foreman. Mobutu nationalized foreign-owned businesses, particularly Belgian ones, and had relatives and cronies run them for his own profit. Amassing a personal fortune of some five billion US dollars kept in Swiss bank accounts, Mobutu became notoriously corrupt and his regime was denounced as a **kleptocracy**. Using his authority primarily for personal gain, he frequently chartered

≡ **Personalist dictator.** Zaire's leader Mobutu Sese Seko (1930–1997—second from left) meets with US president Richard Nixon (second from right) in 1973.

supersonic Concord jets for international trips, built a palace in his hometown of Gbadolite, bought expensive properties in Europe, and lived a lavish lifestyle. At the same time, Mobutu's government did little to develop the country as ordinary Zairians suffered from poverty and high inflation.

Although his movement officially rejected right- and left-wing political ideologies, Mobutu was an ardent anti-communist, which meant that he enjoyed considerable support from the United States, and he made a number of personal visits to the White House. When the Angolan civil war broke out in 1975, Zaire, the United States, and apartheid South Africa all backed the National Front for the Liberation of Angola (FNLA) led by Holden Robert, Mobutu's brother-in-law, against the Soviet- and Cuban-backed Popular Movement for the Liberation of Angola (MPLA). Since Zaire was, at the time, the second-largest francophone country, France added Mobutu to its network of allies in postcolonial Africa. Despite disputes over Belgian business interests in Zaire, Brussels also remained a strong supporter of the Mobutu regime. In 1978, France and Belgium dispatched paratroopers to southern Zaire's Shaba province (formerly Katanga) to repel an incursion by Katanga rebels backed by pro-Soviet Angola. Mobutu's anti-Soviet stance also eventually earned him goodwill from China, given Sino-Soviet tensions, and improved relations between Washington and Beijing in the 1970s and 1980s.

Mobutu's arch-enemy in postcolonial Africa was Libyan leader **Muammar Gaddafi**. During a 1985 visit to Burundi, Gaddafi publicly called on the people of neighboring Zaire to rise up against their tyrant. While the two dictators were sponsored by different powers and used different rhetoric, their regimes were similarly personalist and oppressive. In 1969, Gaddafi, then a junior army officer inspired by Nasser's revolution in Egypt, led a military coup that overthrew the Western-backed and corrupt and unpopular monarchy of oil-rich Libya. Under Gaddafi, who chaired the Revolutionary Command Council (RCC), Libya became a republic and engaged in socialist-oriented reforms. During the early 1970s, Gaddafi's government initiated a **Green Revolution** that redistributed agricultural land and supported farmers, and nationalized a large portion of the oil industry, with the new revenues used to improve housing, healthcare, education, and social programs. Women's rights were addressed as men and women were made equal under the law, pay equity was introduced, new educational and job opportunities were made available to women, and child and forced marriage were outlawed. At the same time, Muslim Shari'a law became the legal system, Arabic was imposed as the official language, alcohol was forbidden, Christian churches were closed, and the country's Italian and Jewish communities were expelled. Supporting the cause of Pan-Arab unity, Gaddafi's new regime became friendly with Egypt and Sudan, and sponsored the Palestinian Liberation Organization (PLO) in its struggle against Israel, as well as other left-wing revolutionary movements such as South Africa's African National Congress (ANC) and America's Black Panther Party. Decrying imperialism, Gaddafi forced the closure of US and British military bases in Libya.

≡ **Brotherly leader and guide of the revolution.** Gaddafi carefully cultivated his public image as a Pan-Africanist. The costume he wore at the 2009 African Union conference in Ethiopia was inspired by traditional West African dress.

In 1973, Gaddafi strengthened his grip on power by declaring a popular revolution that would be guided by his new ideology, called the "Third International

Theory," that rejected Western capitalism and Eastern communism and advocated for a Pan-Arab state under Islamic principles. This philosophy was explained in Gaddafi's **Green Book**, similar to Mao's "Red Book," which his supporters carried and quoted from. Gaddafi's abolition of private property and monopolization of business led to protest. In response, he purged the military of politically unreliable officers, crushed student protests, oppressed Muslim scholars who accused him of idolatry, and had critics hanged in public. In 1977, Gaddafi changed the Republic of Libya to the Great Socialist People's Libyan Jamahiriya (state of the masses), which was supposed to be a direct democracy governed by a network of people's congresses but in reality was a dictatorship ruled by Gaddafi, who took the title "Brotherly Leader and Guide of the Revolution." At this time, Gaddafi became alienated from Egypt, which made peace with Israel following the 1973 Arab–Israeli War and allied itself with the United States, and Tripoli developed closer relations with the Soviet Union, from which it bought massive amounts of weaponry with oil money. Indeed, Libya and Egypt fought a short border war in 1977. Given the failure of his leadership in the Arab world, Gaddafi turned increasingly toward sub-Saharan Africa, sending Libyan forces to Uganda in 1979 in a failed effort to defend Idi Amin's regime from Tanzanian invasion. During the 1980s, Libyan troops invaded northern Chad, where they supported rebels fighting against the southern-based government of Hissène Habré that was backed by France, the United States, and Mobutu's Zaire. Libyan clashes with the US Navy in the Gulf of Sirte prompted Gaddafi to initiate the production of chemical weapons and to begin an ultimately unsuccessful nuclear weapons program. Furthermore, he backed more rebel and terrorist groups, and was involved in the bombing of an American civilian airliner over Scotland in 1988.

Some of Africa's personalist dictators became unstable megalomaniacs. In Uganda, in 1966, civilian Prime Minister Milton Obote had used the army, composed of fellow northerners and led by General **Idi Amin**, to remove the king of Buganda as the ceremonial president of the country. In 1971, Amin led a military coup that overthrew President Obote while he was on an overseas visit. Amin's regime murdered around 100,000 people as he oppressed the Acholi and Langi ethnic groups associated with the exiled Obote, and gradually turned on almost all elements of Ugandan society. In 1972, he expelled Uganda's Asian community and gave their businesses to Ugandans, which caused an economic crisis. Seen internationally as a buffoon, Amin promoted himself to the highest military rank of field marshal and awarded himself medals and titles including "Conqueror of the British Empire in Africa in General and Uganda in Particular." In 1975, Amin became chairman of the Organization of African Unity (OAU), and hosted the group's conference, at which he celebrated the UN International Year of the Woman by staging a beauty pageant and marrying his 19-year-old girlfriend, Sarah Kyolaba, a singer with an army band, in a lavish US $2 million ceremony in which the PLO's Yasser Arafat served as his best man. Amin was initially supported by Israel, which wanted a foothold in sub-Saharan Africa in order to frustrate Arab states further north, but he fell out with the Israelis when they refused to give him sophisticated weapons to support a planned invasion of Tanzania. A 1976 Israeli commando raid on Uganda's Entebbe airport, which rescued Israeli citizens taken captive during the hijacking of a civilian airliner by international terrorists who Amin seemed to support, fatally weakened the dictatorship. Trying to distract Ugandans from his terrible government, Amin launched an invasion of Tanzania in 1978, but his incompetent forces were quickly defeated, and a Tanzanian counter-invasion toppled his regime the next year.

In the Central African Republic (CAR), a former French colony, Colonel **Jean-Bédel Bokassa** came to power in a 1966 military coup that overthrew the civilian government of his cousin David Dacko. Bokassa was a career soldier who had fought in the Free French forces during the Second World War, had served in the French army in Indochina in the 1950s, and had become commander of the CAR military shortly after independence in 1960. With French assistance, his

≡ **Amin and Bokassa.** *Left:* Reversing the usual colonial racial hierarchy, Amin forced white Ugandans to take a pledge of loyalty to him in 1975. *Right:* Taking power in a 1966 coup in the Central African Republic, Jean Bedel Bokassa had himself crowned emperor in 1977. He was overthrown by a French military intervention in 1979.

military dictatorship was transformed into a megalomaniacal and corrupt personalist regime. In 1976, he proclaimed that the CAR was now the Central African Empire, and the next year he had himself crowned emperor in an extravagant ceremony modeled on the 1804 coronation of Napoleon I in France. Although his "empire" was among the world's poorest countries, Bokassa's coronation cost US $20 million and included a diamond-studded crown and a huge golden throne. In 1979, food shortages caused rioting in the CAR and Bokassa's security forces massacred 100 schoolchildren who had refused to buy school uniforms from a company owned by one of his wives that displayed the emperor's picture. Because of his instability and international embarrassment, France dispatched military forces to the CAR, where they overthrew Bokassa and reinstated the previous government.

While all Africa's Cold War–era personalist dictators were men, some women played key roles in support of these regimes. In 1964, Britain granted independence to the small central African country of Malawi. Initially prime minister, Dr. Hastings Kamuzu Banda quickly created a one-party state under his Malawi Congress Party (MCP), and in 1970 he was appointed president for life and called by the title Ngwazi meaning "chief of chiefs" or "conquerer." Political opponents were jailed, murdered, or forced to flee the country. As an anti-communist, Banda received international support from the West, and he warmed up to pro-western pariah regimes like apartheid South Africa and Taiwan. During the 1970s, the conservative Banda, who had worked as a medical doctor in Britain and was a member of the Scots Presbyterian Church, banned men from having beards or long hair and outlawed short skirts and bell bottom trousers, all of which were very much in fashion elsewhere. In 1964, Banda appointed **Cecilia Kadzamira** as the country's "official government hostess" and eventually as "mama" of Malawi. Before Malawi's independence, Kadzamira had worked as a nurse at Banda's medical practice and became his private secretary. Although they were never married, Kadzamira functioned as a powerful "first lady," controlling access to President Banda and becoming a leading member of his inner circle. As such, several of her close relatives were given prominent positions within the government. Furthermore, in 1985 Kadzamira became head of an organization called Chitukuko Cha Amayi muMalawi (CCAM) (Women's Development in Malawi) that cultivated support for the regime among women by encouraging them to become more involved in politics, education, religion, and family life. Given rumors that the president and "official hostess" were not getting along, Banda banned the popular Simon and Garfunkel song "Cecilia" because of the line "Cecilia, I'm down on my knees, I'm begging you please, to come home."

Culture

Music

From the 1960s to 1980s, larger-than-life artists from Nigeria and Zaire generally dominated African music. While West African highlife music had emerged from colonial Gold Coast (Ghana), musicians from postcolonial Nigeria transformed the genre (see Chapter 18). A former merchant sailor who worked as a musician in Britain during the mid- to late 1940s, Bernard Olabinjo **"Bobby" Benson** returned to his native Lagos in 1947 and formed a band called the Bobby Benson Jam Session that played Caribbean calypso and American big band swing music and introduced the electric guitar to Nigeria. During the 1950s, the group expanded and helped to popularize highlife music, and Benson opened a popular night club and hotel in Lagos. Benson's greatest hit was the 1960 song "Taxi Driver." In this era, British record companies seeking to expand their operations to Africa began establishing recording studios in Lagos. In 1954, Victor Olaiya, who had played trumpet in Benson's Jam Session Orchestra, formed his own group called the **Cool Cats** that became a famous highlife act in Nigeria influenced by recordings of African-American artist James Brown. The Cool Cats played at state balls during the 1956 visit of Queen Elizabeth II to Nigeria and the 1960 Nigerian independence celebrations, and in 1963 they shared a stage with famous African-American trumpeter Louis Armstrong during an event to mark Nigeria's transition into a republic. Olaiya's group, renamed All Stars Band, also played for the Nigerian army contingent, serving as UN peacekeepers in the Congo during the early 1960s and for the federal military during the Nigerian Civil War (1967–70).

In the late 1950s and early 1960s, **Fela Kuti**, who originated from an elite family of teachers in southwestern Nigeria, studied music in London, where he formed a band called Koola Lobitos that mixed American jazz and West African highlife. In 1963, he returned to Nigeria, where he worked as a radio producer for the Nigerian Broadcasting Corporation, played trumpet with Olaiya's All Stars Band, and recreated the Koola Lobitos. Kuti left Nigeria during the country's civil war of 1967 to 1970. In 1967, Kuti moved to Ghana where he began developing a new musical style called **Afrobeat** that combined West African highlife with American jazz and funk. Visiting Los Angeles in 1969, Kuti became politicized by the Black Power movement and the Black Panther Party, and this was reflected in his music, style, and activism. In 1970, Kuti, who renamed his band Nigeria '70 and then The Afrika '70, returned to Lagos, where he founded the **Kalakuta Republic**, which was a commune and recording studio in Lagos that he declared independent from the Federal Republic of Nigeria, as well as a separate performance venue called the

Afrika Shrine. Garnering international attention, Kuti's performances attracted visiting musical stars such as James Brown in 1970 and former Beatle Paul McCartney in 1972. Kuti, who started to sing in Nigerian Pidgin so that his words could be understood more broadly, became a critic of Nigeria's military government and in 1976 released a song entitled "Zombie," which negatively characterized Nigerian soldiers as mindlessly accepting orders from corrupt officers. Furthermore, he embarrassed the military regime of Olusegun Obasanjo by criticizing its extravagant hosting of the Second World Black and African Festival of Arts and Culture in 1977 (FESTAC 77), and stars performing at the festival, such as South African trumpeter Hugh Masekela and American musician Stevie Wonder, began to frequent the Afrika Shrine. In February 1977, just a week after FESTAC had ended and the stars had returned home, Nigerian soldiers attacked and destroyed the Kalakuta Republic, and during the violence **Funmilayo Ransome-Kuti**, a 78-year-old educator and pioneering Nigerian women's rights activist and Fela's mother, was thrown out of an upper floor window and later died from her injuries. Resonating with people in other African countries under military rule, "Zombie" was performed by Kuti and his band at a 1978 concert in Accra, Ghana, where it caused a riot and led to his expulsion from the country. After the destruction of the Kalakuta Republic, Fela Kuti became more controversial by simultaneously marrying 27 women, founding a political party called Movement of the People, attempting to run for president of Nigeria during the brief return to civilian rule in 1979, and writing provocative songs that called out international corporations and Nigerian political leaders for corruption and oppression. With the return of military rule in the early 1980s, Kuti was imprisoned for almost two years on trumped-up charges. Kuti and his group, renamed Egypt '80 in recognition of ancient Egyptian civilization's role in African history, toured North America and Europe in the 1980s and joined other international stars in opposing the apartheid system in South Africa. During the 1990s, Kuti clashed with the Nigerian military government of Sani Abacha. In 1997, the 58-year-old musician succumbed to the HIV/AIDS pandemic that was ravaging Africa. Over one million people attended his funeral in Lagos.

Many other artists added to Nigeria's rich and increasingly internationally celebrated music industry. A prominent example of the **Juju** music genre of western Nigeria, **King Sunny Adé** rose to fame in Nigeria in the 1970s, released several albums with the British-Jamaican company Island Records in the early 1980s, and received two Grammy nominations in the 1980s and 1990s.

By the early 1950s, Congolese rumba (or soukous) was popular in the Belgian Congo, where a Leopoldville-based recording industry had developed between the world wars. At this time, Congolese rumba developed two distinct genres,

≡ **Fela Kuti.** *Left:* Fela Kuti (1938–1997) was a Nigerian activist and musician who developed the "Afrobeat" style. He is shown here in 1975 with members of his band. *Right:* Funmilayo Ransome-Kuti (1900–1978) was a Nigerian women's rights activist and mother of musician Fela Kuti.

each defined by a popular band in the colonial capital of Leopoldville. Le Grand Kallé et l'African Jazz, or **African Jazz**, founded in 1953 and led by singer Joseph Athanase Tshamala Kabasele, otherwise known as Le Grand Kallé, pioneered a westernized, romantic, and soft form of Congolese rumba that was well received by the emerging African middle class and reflected its aspirations and confidence. In 1960, African Jazz traveled to Belgium, where Kabasele participated in the negotiations that led to Congo's independence, and during this trip the band first played the song "Independence Cha Cha," which introduced Congolese rumba to Europe and became a huge hit back home and in other francophone African countries.

The other major style of Congolese rumba was traditionalist, visceral, rhythmic, and highly danceable and championed by a band called OK Jazz (later renamed **TPOK Jazz**, meaning "All Mighty OK Jazz"), formed in 1956 and eventually led by guitarist and singer François Luambo Makiadi, widely known as **Franco**. In

1966, just after Colonel Mobutu came to power through a coup and had political opponents publicly hanged, Franco and TPOK Jazz released a song called "Luvumbu Ndoki" (Luvumbu the Sorcerer) that recited a local legend about an evil chief who killed his relatives. Since the song was an obvious reference to Mobutu, the new regime banned it and Franco fled to neighboring Congo-Brazzaville for a few months. Upon his return home, Franco became an important propagandist for the Mobutu dictatorship and its cultural program of *authenticité* that involved changing the country's name to Zaire and Africanizing many aspects of life. During the 1970s, Franco and TPOK Jazz toured the country with Mobutu. They composed and performed songs celebrating the regime and its authoritarian leader. As a reward, Mobutu gave Franco a thriving Kinshasa nightclub called Un, Deux, Trois and a recording company called MAZADIS that released TPOK Jazz music. Other Congolese musicians struggled to compete. Franco and his group played at international cultural events such as Zaire 74, a Black music festival that coincided with the "Rumble in the Jungle" boxing match, and FESTAC 77 in Nigeria. Although he became extremely wealthy, Franco was jailed for a few months in the late 1970s for releasing two songs that were considered obscene because of references to oral and anal sex. During the 1980s, though he retained favorable relations with Mobutu, Franco and his band lived mostly in Belgium, from where they toured West Africa and the United States and released a massive amount of music. In 1989, two years after releasing a song entitled "Beware of AIDS," Franco died in Brussels and his body

was flown back to Kinshasa, where Mobutu declared four days of national mourning and gave him a state funeral.

During the 1970s and 1980s, Congolese rumba evolved significantly and its center of gravity spread beyond Zaire. A new type of Congolese rumba developed, inspired by the wild rebel attitude of Western "rock and roll." Formed in 1969, Zaika Langa Langa (ZLL) dropped the use of wind instruments and focused entirely on snare drums, electric guitars, and synthesizers. ZLL spawned a whole

≡ **TPOK Jazz.** A record by Zaire's Congolese rumba group TPOK Jazz, picturing lead singer Franco (1938–1989—right).

family of related bands called the "Langa Langa Family." In the late 1970s, **Papa Wemba**, originally a member of ZLL, formed Viva La Musica, which maintained one branch in Zaire and another in Paris, where it gained fame in the emerging World Music scene of the 1980s by combining Congolese, Latin, and rock music. Papa Wemba, through his personal style, also gave international exposure to the flamboyant attire of the La Sape subculture of Brazzaville and Kinshasa that dated back to the colonial era. Prompted by economic problems and state control in Zaire, many Congolese rumba musicians moved to Kenya, Tanzania, Uganda, and Zambia, where they popularized the genre. Distinctive and long-lasting Swahili versions of Congolese rumba developed in Kenya and Tanzania. Many Congolese performers also traveled to francophone West Africa, particularly Togo and Côte d'Ivoire, and to Paris and Brussels, where they built a Congolese music industry. One of the most successful Congolese musicians in Paris during the 1980s was Kanda Bongo Man, whose music videos inspired the back-and-forth hip motions of the kwassa kwassa dance craze that spread across Africa.

≡ **Musical pioneer.** Beginning in the 1980s, Zairean/Congolese singer Papa Wemba (1949–2016) rose to international acclaim by combining Congolese, Latin, and rock music into a new genre called "rumba rock."

Literature

African novelists also achieved international acclaim during the early decades of the continent's independence era. Many of their works focused on the ambiguities introduced to African society through European colonial rule. Eventually becoming the most well known of all African writers, Nigeria's **Chinua Achebe** published *Things Fall Apart* in 1958, *No Longer at Ease* in 1960, and *Arrow of God* in 1964. After publishing *Weep Not, Child* in 1964, *The River Between* in 1965, and *A Grain of Wheat* in 1967, Kenya's **Ngũgĩ wa Thiong'o** endured imprisonment in the late 1970s for co-authoring a play that criticized the country's authoritarian government, and he then went into a period of exile in Britain and the United States. Although Ngũgĩ's early novels were written in English, the author became a strong advocate for cultural decolonization through using African languages with his subsequent works like 1982's *Devil on the Cross*, written in Kikuyu and translated into English. **Tsitsi Dangarembgwa**'s 1988 *Nervous Conditions* represented the first English-language novel published by a Black Zimbabwean woman, and she

subsequently became a film-maker and pro-democracy activist. Literature in francophone Africa built on the **negritude** movement of the 1930s to 1950s, in which Black intellectuals living in France, notably the poets Aimé Césaire of Martinique, Léon Damas of French Guiana, and Léopold Sédar Senghor of Senegal, promoted a distinct Black identity. Examples of celebrated postcolonial African authors who wrote novels in French include Senegal's Ousmane Sembène, who published *Les Bouts de Bois de Dieu* (God's Bits of Wood) in 1960, which focused on colonial oppression, and later works that criticized the corruption of African elites, and Senegal's **Mariama Bâ**, whose *Une si*

≡ **Kenyan writer.** Ngũgĩ wa Thiong'o, shown in this 1982 photo, was imprisoned for criticizing his country's authoritarian government.

Timeline

1951—Independence of Libya

1952—Free Officers movement takes power in Egypt

1957—Independence of Ghana

1958—Publication of Chinua Achebe's novel *Things Fall Apart*

1960—Independence for French territories such as Côte d'Ivoire, Central African Republic, and Senegal, and the Belgian Congo

1961—Independence of Sierra Leone

1961—Independence of Tanganyika (Tanzania from 1964)

1962—Independence of Uganda

1964—Independence of Zambia and Malawi

1964—Ngũgĩ wa Thiong'o publishes *Weep Not, Child*

1965—Joseph Mobutu comes to power through a military coup in the Congo

1966—Military coup in Ghana overthrows civilian government of Kwame Nkrumah

1966—Ugandan prime minister Milton Obote uses military force to usurp king of Buganda as national president

1966—Colonel Jean Bedel Bokassa leads a military coup that takes power in Central African Republic

1967—Two military coups in Sierra Leone

1967—Arusha Declaration in Tanzania

1967—Two military coups in Nigeria

1967–70—Nigerian Civil War

1968—Military coup and reinstatement of civilian government under Siaka Stevens in Sierra Leone

1969—Muammar Gaddafi comes to power by a military coup in Libya

1969—Nigerian musician Fela Kuti visits Los Angeles, United States

1970—Mobutu's regime confirmed by a rigged election in the Congo

1970—Hastings Kamuzu Banda appointed president for life of Malawi

1970s—Ujamaa program in Tanzania

1971—Military mutiny in Sierra Leone

1971—Nationalization of Zambian copper mining industry

1971—Mobutu changes the name of the Congo to Zaire and pursues policy of *authenticité*

1971—Idi Amin stages a military coup in Uganda to overthrow Milton Obote

1972—Military coup overthrows civilian government of Kofi Busia in Ghana

1973—Collapse of world prices for copper causes problems in Zambia

1973—Gaddafi declares a new revolution in Libya

1973—Egypt and Syria defeated in "October War" with Israel

1974—Military coup in Ethiopia deposes Emperor Haile Selassie

1974—Mobutu stages the "Rumble in the Jungle"

1975—Accusations of a military coup plot in Sierra Leone

1975—Mobutu's regime backs FNLA rebels in the Angolan Civil War

1977—Gaddafi changes the name of the Republic of Libya to the Great Socialist People's Libyan Jamahiriya and becomes the "Brotherly Leader"

1977—Egypt and Libya fight a border war

1977—Jean-Bédel Bokassa crowned as emperor of Central African Empire

1977—FESTAC 77 in Lagos, Nigeria; destruction of Fela Kuti's Kalakuta Republic

1978—Sierra Leone becomes a one-party state under Siaka Stevens

1978—Start of economic problems in Côte d'Ivoire

1978—French and Belgian forces intervene in southern Zaire in support of Mobutu

1978-79—War between Uganda and Tanzania. Idi Amin overthrown by Tanzanian invasion.

1979—French forces remove Bokassa from power in Central African Republic

1979—Military coup led by Jerry Rawlings in Ghana

1979—Publication of Mariama Bâ's *Une si longue lettre* (So Long a Letter)

1981—Second military coup led by Jerry Rawlings in Ghana

1983—Military coup in Burkina Faso brings Thomas Sankara to power

1985—Julius Nyerere acknowledges failure of Ujamaa policy and retires

1985—Malawi's President Banda appoints Cecilia Kadzamira as head of Chitukuko Cha Amayi muMalawi (CCAM) (Women's Development in Malawi)

1987—Thomas Sankara overthrown and killed in a military coup

1991—Fall of the Mengistu regime in Ethiopia

1992—Joseph Momoh overthrown by military coup in Sierra Leone

1992—Ghana returns to civilian multiparty democracy

longue lettre (So Long a Letter), published in 1979, and *Un Chant écarlate* (Scarlet Song), published in 1981, highlight the experience of women in relation to traditions like polygamy.

Conclusion

In the late 1950s and early 1960s, there was great optimism about the future of newly independent Africa, which was seen as becoming a prosperous member of the world community. Unfortunately, some 30 years later, at the end of the 1980s, it was clear that in many cases the African state and economy were in a mess. Many African countries had become politically unstable, undergoing a series of military coups, counter-coups, failed coup plots, and army mutinies. One-party states, military rule, and personalist dictatorships were common, with these regimes engaging in rampant corruption and oppression, and many clinging to power with the support of one or the other superpower. The many economic experiments with different types of socialism had clearly failed to solve problems around poverty and underdevelopment, and indeed had made these problems worse. At the same time, those countries that had continued the type of export capitalism left behind by the colonial rulers had not done very well, either. By the end of the Cold War, around 1990, many African countries were so heavily indebted that they could never pay off what they owed, governments struggled to pay salaries to civil servants such as teachers and medical personnel, and state infrastructure such as roads, railways, and water and electrical services had deteriorated. Conversely, cultural themes, including the rise of popular music and celebrated novels, reflected considerable success. Accelerating a process that had begun decades before, Cold War–era African musicians experienced continually changing artistic and political influences by touring other African countries as well as North America and Europe. Non-African artists, particularly stars from the African diaspora, performed in parts of Africa and similarly picked up inspiration from local acts. Popular music became an important political instrument in postcolonial Africa as some musicians used their fame as a platform to oppose authoritarian and corrupt regimes and other performers became wealthy supporting them. At the same time, African novelists began to tell African stories to the rest of the world, gaining recognition in international literary circles.

KEY TERMS

Arab socialism 531

African jazz 544

African socialism 531

Afrika Shrine 543

Afrobeat 542

Aswan Dam 533

authenticité 536

"Bobby" Benson 542

Cecilia Kadzamira 541

Chinua Achebe 547

Cool Cats 542

Derg 533

Fela Kuti 542

Félix Houphouët-Boigny 529

Franco 544

Funmilayo Ransome-Kuti 543

Green Book 539

Green Revolution 538

Idi Amin 539

Jean-Bédel Bokassa 540

Jerry Rawlings 528

Joseph Mobutu (Mobutu Sese Seko) 535

Juju 543

Kalakuta Republic 442

King Sunny Adé 543

kleptocracy 536

Mariama Bâ 547

Muammar Gaddafi 538

negritude 531

Ngũgĩ wa Thiong'o 547

Non-Aligned Movement 521

Papa Wemba 546

personalist dictatorships 535

Thomas Sankara 534

TPOK Jazz 544

Tsitsi Dangarembgwa 547

Ujamaa villages 532

STUDY QUESTIONS

1. What reasons do scholars give for the many coups d'état that occurred in Africa from the 1960s to the 1990s? Did the leaders of military coups share common goals and ideologies?

2. Which approaches did the leaders of newly independent African countries use to develop economies, infrastructure, and health resources? Who were the main proponents of African socialism?

3. What methods did dictators use to gather support? What ideologies did they espouse? How did they become involved in the international rivalries of the Cold War? What role did women play in personalist dictatorships?

4. What were the main developments in African music and literature during this period? Why did musicians like Fela Kuti and writers like Ngũgĩ wa Thiong'o gain international recognition? How did music and literature interconnect with the political sphere?

Please see page FR-11 for the Further Readings for this chapter.
For additional digital learning resources please go to
https://www.oup.com/he/falola-stapleton1e

Independent Africa in the Cold War Era: Cooperation and Conflict, 1960–1990

During the colonial era, European officials had managed relations between most African territories and restricted their interaction with other powers outside the continent. With decolonization in the late 1950s and 1960s, the increasing number of African sovereign states became free to engage with each other and with nations in more distant parts of the world. As discussed in Chapter 24, some African states allied themselves with either the United States or the Soviet Union, the two Cold War superpowers, while some tried to remain non-aligned. Furthermore, African relations with former colonial powers varied, with some governments distancing themselves and others retaining close ties. New external partners, such as Israel, Cuba, and Communist China also sought relations with postcolonial Africa. Among themselves, newly independent African states attempted to cooperate by forming an array of international governmental organizations at the continental and regional levels. Since most African countries inherited borders created by colonizers without much regard for human or physical geography, some independent African countries experienced terrible civil wars caused by separatist movements or regional power struggles. In Cold War–era Africa, civil wars were rarely isolated, as outside powers both within and outside the continent attempted to gain influence by supporting either the state or the rebels. Among African states, a tragic pattern of tit-for-tat support of rebel groups in neighboring countries became the norm. At the same time, state-versus-state wars were comparatively rare in Africa, but those that happened in the Cold War era usually became proxy conflicts for the global superpowers. Cooperation and conflict also took place in the cultural and diplomatic arenas.

Call for freedom. A 1976 poster urge independence for Zimbabwe and condemns the white-minority government of Rhodesia.

Owing to the intense and multifaceted contentions between the two Cold War blocs during this period, diplomatic cooperation and conflict represented a consistent feature of the era. One incident that brought the newly independent African states into early confrontation with the Western Bloc was the 1960 testing of an atomic bomb by the French government in the Sahara Desert of Algeria, which was still a French territory. The testing of the atomic bomb, code named Gerboise Bleue (blue rat), launched France into the club of atomic superpowers, including the United States, the Soviet Union, and Britain, as the international arms race intensified. Considered to be of higher impact compared to other powers' initial atomic tests, with the effects and fallout of the blast persisting for several decades and covering vast lands beyond the Sahara, Gerboise Bleue led to the seizure of French assets in Ghana, the recall of Morocco's ambassador to France, and condemnations from African states as well as other global leaders. The strained relationship caused by this act was, however, mended in due course, leading to renewed mutual cooperation between France and many African countries.

International Organizations

Informed by the concept of Pan-Africanism, which had emerged out of the African diaspora, discussions about the potential political unification of Africa had taken place during the Pan-African Congresses held in North America and Europe during the first half of the twentieth century (see Chapter 19). Once African countries became independent in the late 1950s and early 1960s, such discussions were no longer theoretical. In April 1958, Ghana hosted the First Conference of Independent African States, which brought together representatives from Ghana, Ethiopia, Liberia, Libya, Morocco, Sudan, Tunisia, and Egypt (United Arab Republic). Apartheid South Africa declined an invitation to attend and was the only independent African country not represented at the conference. The delegates, who were mostly foreign ministers, discussed various issues such as potential economic cooperation, peaceful resolution of disputes, and the need to assist other African territories to gain independence. Particularly, the delegates resolved that France should enter into negotiations with the FLN with a view to granting independence to Algeria. In June 1960, a Second Conference of Independent African States was held in Ethiopia and consisted of delegates from 11 independent African states; the provisional governments of the Belgian Congo, Nigeria, Somalia, and Algeria; and African nationalist groups from Northern Rhodesia (Zambia), Southern Rhodesia (Zimbabwe), Kenya, Tanganyika, Uganda, South West Africa (Namibia), and South Africa. While the representative from Ghana called for the creation of an international organization of African states, the Nigerian delegate cautioned that this proposal was premature but that African countries should cooperate. Ghana also hosted a series of All-African People's Conferences in 1958, 1960, and 1961 that, in addition to sovereign African states, included representatives from national liberation movements, opposition political parties, trade unions, and ethnic groups. Tensions between radical activists who dominated the conferences and the more conservative representatives of states, who had to worry about international diplomacy and economic consequences, led to the demise of the event.

The question of international cooperation divided the growing number of independent African states into two factions: the **Casablanca Group** and the **Monrovia Group**. The Casablanca Group, formed at a conference in Morocco in January 1961 and influenced by Pan-Africanism, promoted the concept of a formal political union or federation of African states. Prominent in the Casablanca Group were radical leaders Kwame Nkrumah of Ghana, Sékou Touré of Guinea, and Gamal Abdel Nasser of Egypt, who pressed for armed action against the continuing colonial presence in Africa and the minority settler regimes in Southern Africa. The **Monrovia Group**, established in Liberia in May 1961, preferred economic cooperation between separate and sovereign African states. The governments that formed the Monrovia Group were more conservative, and included Nigeria as well as Liberia, which had been an independent republic for over a century and was diplomatically close to the United States. Initially called the Brazzaville Group, the francophone former French colonies that remained close to France, such as Senegal, Côte d'Ivoire, Congo-Brazzaville, and Cameroon, quickly joined the Monrovia Group. Through the mediation of Ethiopian Emperor Haile Selassie, the Casablanca and Monrovia groups agreed to the creation of an Africa-wide international governmental organization.

In May 1963, at a conference in Addis Ababa, Ethiopia, representatives of 32 African states created the **Organization of African Unity (OAU)**, which would promote African solidarity, coordinate economic development efforts, protect African sovereignty and independence, eliminate the

≡ **African unity.** Rival leaders President Siad Barré of Somalia and Emperor Haile Selassie of Ethiopia meet at the tenth anniversary conference of the Organization of African Unity (OAU) in 1973.

vestiges of colonialism, and promote broad international cooperation through the United Nations. The establishment of a permanent OAU headquarters in Addis Ababa reflected Ethiopia's status as the only indigenous African state to have survived colonial conquest. While the Casablanca and Monrovia groups dissolved, the OAU core principle of non-interference in the internal affairs of member states better reflected the Monrovia vision. The Pan-African dream of leaders Nkrumah and Touré died in the faction-riven OAU. Many of the francophone states retained friendly relations with France and bristled against the anglophone countries, and the predominantly Arab and Muslim states of North Africa resisted domination by the predominantly Black and Christian countries south of the Sahara. Although the official position of the OAU was one of non-alignment in the international Cold War, some African regimes allied with the United States and others with the Soviet Union. From the late 1960s to 1990s, a series of brutal dictators, including the notorious Mobutu Sese Seko of Zaire, Idi Amin of Uganda, and Haile Mariam Mengistu of Ethiopia, served as chairpersons of the OAU, reducing its credibility. Furthermore, OAU member states were poor countries and, as such, the organization lacked funds. The OAU gained a negative reputation as a "dictator's club" and a "talking shop" that accomplished little of significance for Africa or Africans. While the OAU received praise for supporting liberation movements fighting lingering Portuguese colonialism in parts of Africa and racist white-minority states in Rhodesia and South Africa, pressure from the organization at times prompted these armed groups to launch premature military operations that failed dismally.

The founding of the OAU also led to the 1964 creation of the African Development Bank (ADB), which operated out of its headquarters in Abidjan, Côte d'Ivoire, from 1966, with a mission to provide low-interest loans for projects that reduce poverty and improve living conditions in Africa. In 1983, because of the limited economic capacity of African states, membership in the African Development Bank opened to countries outside Africa. The rise of the United States to become the third-largest shareholder in the bank, after Nigeria and Egypt, resulted in worries that it would promote Western economic interests and policies in Africa like the World Bank and IMF. The ADB suffered mismanagement, including fraud, conflicts among officials, and lack of accountability, and about 40 percent of its projects failed.

In 1959, women's rights activists from the recently or soon to be independent francophone West African countries of Guinea, Senegal, Mali, and Dahomey met in Bamako, Mali, and created the West African Women's Union. In July 1962, a year before the establishment of the OAU, the **Pan-African Women's Organization (PAWO)** was formed during a conference in Dar-es-Salaam, Tanganyika (Tanzania). Three African women were central in creating the group. Aoua Kéita from Mali had worked as a midwife and campaigned for independence as a member of the RDA in the 1950s, and she became the only female member of Mali's national assembly when the country gained independence in 1960. Jeanne Martin Cissé had been among the first female teachers in Guinea in the 1940s, joined the RDA in the late 1940s, married a senior member of Guinea's ruling party, and held senior positions in the government of Guinea. Later, in the 1970s, she became Guinea's ambassador to the UN and the first woman to chair the UN Security Council. The third woman to found PAWO was Pauline Clark from Ghana. In 1974, at another international African women's conference held in Dakar, Sen-

OFFICE OF THE PRESIDENT
SECURITY COUNCIL

≡ **Pathbreaking woman.** In 1972, Jeanne Martin Cissé (1926–2017), a Guinean educator, politician, and diplomat, became the first woman to chair the United Nations Security Council.

egal, July 31 was declared African Women's Day. Like the OAU, PAWO would eventually be criticized for serving as a vehicle to promote the wives of African dictators.

Regional Organizations

Several regional international governmental organizations emerged in parts of Africa during the Cold War. In 1967, twelve West African states agreed to form a regional organization that would comprise a common market, and the next year, at a conference in Monrovia, the West African Regional Group was established. After delays caused by the Nigerian Civil War (1967–70), renewed diplomatic efforts resulted in the May 1975 signing of the Treaty of Lagos, which established the **Economic Community of West African States (ECOWAS)** with the aim of fostering economic cooperation and integration in pursuit of growth and development. As such, ECOWAS sought to eliminate customs duties, trade restrictions, and limitations on the movement of people around the West African region, and to harmonize economic policies and create a fund to support development projects. Because of the Cold War context, which included the prospect of military attacks on West Africa such as the 1970 Portuguese raid on Conakry, ECOWAS member states signed a Protocol on Non-Aggression in 1978 and a Protocol on Mutual Assistance on Defense in 1981. These agreements created the possibility of raising an Allied West African armed force that became a reality in 1990 with ECOWAS military intervention in the First Liberian Civil War (1989-97). The major division within ECOWAS consisted of the seven francophone countries that shared a common currency linked to the French franc and the anglophone ones centered on Nigeria. As West Africa's largest economic and military power, Nigeria was seen as dominating ECOWAS and using it as an instrument of national foreign policy.

The controversy surrounding the white-minority regimes in Rhodesia and South Africa strongly influenced regional integration in Southern Africa. During the 1960s and 1970s, the governments of the newly independent majority-rule countries bordering or located close to Rhodesia and South Africa began to refer to themselves as the **Frontline States** in that they considered themselves on the frontline of a struggle against racist regimes. In 1975, the year that Portugal pulled out of Africa, the OAU formally recognized Botswana, Zambia, Tanzania, Angola, and Mozambique as the Frontline States. Julius Nyerere, president of Tanzania, chaired the Frontline States until his retirement in 1985, when Zambian president Kenneth Kaunda took that role. In 1980, when newly independent Zimbabwe joined the Frontline States, the grouping transformed into a more formal structure called the **Southern African Development Coordination Conference (SADCC)**, with its headquarters located in Gaborone, Botswana. At this time, Lesotho, Malawi, and Swaziland joined SADCC. The basic aim of both the Frontline States and SADCC was to reduce their economic dependence on apartheid South Africa so that they could more fully support anti-apartheid liberation movements. Since land-locked countries such as Zambia and Zimbabwe were dependent on import and export through South African ports, one of the main activities of the Frontline States/SADCC was to develop alternative transportation routes linked to the coasts of Tanzania and Mozambique. As a result, apartheid South Africa used covert military action to undermine these development efforts, primarily by providing training and support for the Mozambique National Resistance (RENAMO), which conducted a campaign of sabotage and guerrilla warfare in Mozambique from the late 1970s to the early 1990s. In the 1980s, Zimbabwe and Tanzania sent soldiers into Mozambique to help the government in the fight against RENAMO and to protect economic infrastructure. Not all SADCC members were equally committed to the anti-apartheid struggle. In Malawi, a member of SADCC but not a Frontline State, the authoritarian and conservative regime of Hastings Kamuzu Banda secretly supported RENAMO and facilitated South African intelligence operations. In the early 1990s, SADCC fundamentally changed as a result of the independence of Namibia, which joined the grouping in 1990, and

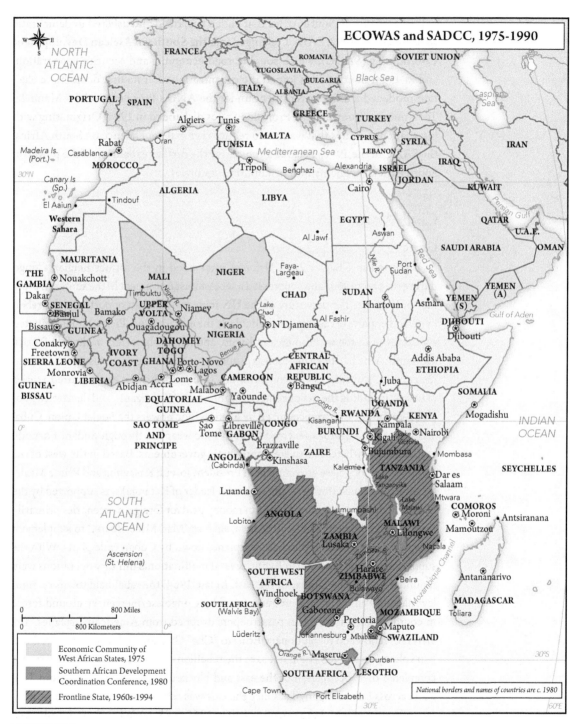

ECOWAS and SADCC, 1975-1990

Legend:
- Economic Community of West African States, 1975
- Southern African Development Coordination Conference, 1980
- Frontline State, 1960s-1994

National borders and names of countries are c. 1980

≡ **MAP 25.1**

political reforms in South Africa that ended apartheid and ushered in democratic government. In 1992, SADCC changed into the **Southern African Development Community (SADC)**, which sought broad economic and security cooperation, and in 1994, South Africa joined the organization after its first democratic election produced a unity government under the ANC's President Nelson Mandela. Their mission complete, the Frontline States disbanded in 1994. Originating with international groups that wanted to reduce regional dependence on South Africa, the SADC of the 1990s became a vehicle for the further expansion of the powerful South African economy into neighboring countries.

Civil Wars

Congo

As discussed in Chapter 22, UN forces intervened in the former Belgian Congo during the early 1960s and suppressed a secessionist movement in the southern province of Katanga. The departure of the UN force provided an opportunity for rebellion in other parts of the Congo, particularly the east. In 1964, Pierre Mulele initiated a local revolt in the western area of Kwilu, and leftist supporters of the late Patrice Lumumba, who had been deposed as prime minster and murdered just after independence, rose up in eastern Congo. The Simba (lion) rebels in the east captured a series of towns, including the major center of Stanleyville (Kisangani), and declared a People's Republic of Congo recognized by Eastern Bloc powers the Soviet Union, Cuba, and China. The **Simbas** received Eastern Bloc weapons through Sudan, Burundi, and Tanzania, where there were sympathetic governments. Based in the west of the country, the Congolese government of President Joseph Kasavubu and Prime Minister Moïse Tshombe (formerly the separatist leader of Katanga) was supported by the United States and Belgium. American money paid for foreign mercenaries primarily from France, Belgium and South Africa, such as "Mad Mike Hoare," to supplement Congolese troops and to purchase warplanes flown by Cuban exile pilots. With the suppression of the rebellion in Kwilu, several multinational military operations were mounted against the Simbas in the east. In late 1964, the rebel-held towns of Stanleyville and Paulis (Isiro) were recaptured by Congolese/mercenary ground forces in coordination with Belgian paratroopers dropped from American airplanes. The arrival of renowned revolutionary Ernesto "Che" Guevara and several hundred Cuban volunteers in 1965 could not save the rebellion as Congolese/mercenary troops completed their occupation of the east and blocked rebel supply routes from Tanzania across Lake Tanganyika. Once the east was relatively secure, Congolese military officer Joseph Mobutu staged a coup in 1965 and founded an American-backed anti-communist dictatorship that would last for the next 32 years.

☰ **Rebellion in Congo.** *Left:* Congolese troops round up prisoners suspected of being Simba rebels, August 1964. *Center:* Mercenary leader Mike Hoare (1919–2020) in the Congo in 1964. *Right:* Ernesto "Che" Guevara (1928–1967) makes a presentation to Cuban officials in March 1965 concerning his military mission to the Congo.

Nigeria

When it became independent from Britain in 1960, the populous West African country of Nigeria was divided along regional, ethnic, and religious lines. Conservative Muslim emirs, who had remained powerful as indirect rulers during the colonial era, dominated the largely Muslim north, which was home to the Hausa and Fulani ethnic groups and remained the poorest and most marginalized part of the country. The predominantly Christian south was relatively better off economically and educationally, and was split between two large ethnic groups: the Yoruba in the west and the Igbo in the east. During the 1950s, in negotiations with the British about independence, the northern leaders had been skeptical about their region becoming part of an autonomous Nigeria while eastern political leaders pushed for a united country. These positions changed after independence. In the early years of independence, the Nigerian electoral system favored the north, putting the federal government under the control of northern politicians led by Prime Minister Abubakar Balewa. In the east, people began to question why government revenues generated from their region's new oil industry were spent on developing the impoverished north. Furthermore, by the mid-1960s the Nigerian electoral system seemed to be in chaos. These problems prompted a January 1966 military coup by Igbo army officers who killed Prime Minister Balewa and other northern officials and put Igbo General Johnson Aguiyi-Ironsi in power. In July, northern military officers staged a counter-coup in which Aguiyi-Ironsi and other southerners were executed and northerner Colonel Yakubu Gowon became head of state. The massacres of easterners living in the north prompted the military officials in charge of the eastern region, led by Lieutenant Colonel Chukwuemeka Odumegwu Ojukwu, to reject Gowon's takeover and enter into ultimately failed negotiations with the new federal military government. In May 1967, Ojukwu's administration declared the independence of the oil-rich eastern region as the **Republic of Biafra**.

The secession of Biafra immediately led to the **Nigerian Civil War** (1967–70) as the federal military government embarked on an armed campaign to reincorporate the east. Major world powers supported the Nigerian government. Although they were on opposite sides of the Cold War, Britain and the Soviet Union both supported Nigeria, as they were confident it would win the struggle and they wanted access to Nigerian oil. Distracted by the Vietnam War, the United States government deferred to Britain on the Biafra issue and imposed an arms embargo on the separatist republic. Many African states, given their own potential problems with separatist movements, disapproved of Biafra, which had few international friends. France provided military assistance to Biafra as it saw a chance to replace British oil interests in the area. Biafra was also supported by apartheid South Africa and colonial Portugal, both of which needed allies in Black Africa. Desperately outnumbered and outgunned by federal forces, and eventually besieged, Biafra engaged in an international propaganda campaign to try to win public sympathy and provoke external diplomatic intervention. Biafra and its supporters portrayed the secession as necessary to protect the Christian people of Biafra, particularly the Igbo, from extermination by a genocidal northern Muslim–dominated military regime. Images of starving Biafran children circulated in Western newspapers and television reports and inspired popular sympathy for the separatist state. As a result, international humanitarian organizations and Western governments mounted relief flights into Biafra that provided food and medicine and allowed Ojukwu's

≡ **The Nigerian Civil War.** *Left:* Chukwuemeka "Emeka" Odumegwu Ojukwu (1933–2011), leader of secessionist Biafra, inspects Biafran troops during the Nigerian Civil War (1967–70). *Right:* Photographs of starving children, such as this one of a little girl, aroused worldwide sympathy for the plight of Biafrans.

regime to maintain its struggle. Although the war continued, the expanded federal forces eventually staged a final offensive that finally ended the Biafra secession in January 1970. While Gowon's government instituted a postwar reconciliation and reconstruction program and Ojukwu eventually returned from exile, many easterners resented the lack of compensation for property and money lost during the war and continued to resent the federal administration's use of oil revenues derived from their region. Except for a few years during the late 1970s and early 1980s, Nigeria remained under military rule until the 1990s. Although estimates of the death toll vary considerably, it is likely that at least two million perished during Nigeria's civil war. Most of these victims were eastern civilians who perished from hunger and disease related to displacement and the federal blockade.

Sudan

With independence from Britain and Egypt in 1956, Sudan faced similar issues around regionalism, religion, and race. During the colonial era, the British had imposed separate administrations and different policies on northern and southern Sudan. While the north remained predominantly Muslim and Arabic-speaking, the southerners converted from traditional religions to Christianity and learned English in missionary schools. After independence, Muslim Arab northerners dominated the Sudan government based in Khartoum and looked down upon the Black Christians of the marginalized south. Sudanese Arab racism towards Black southerners was also rooted in the historic enslavement of the latter. In 1955, a limited insurgency began in the south, and this escalated in the early 1960s when a new Sudanese military government actively repressed people living in the south of the country. During the 1960s and early 1970s, the Anyanya National Armed Forces, led by Joseph Lagu, tried to unify various rebel groups in the south and fought for the separation of southern Sudan. The Sudan government received support from the Eastern Bloc while the southern insurgents accepted military supplies from Israel, which sought to undermine Arab countries with which it was in conflict. In southern Sudan, the war stalemated as the rebels controlled the countryside and moved around at night to avoid observation by government warplanes that dominated the sky as government ground forces occupied towns. Taking power in a 1969 coup in Khartoum, Sudanese military leader Colonel Ja'afar Muhammad Numayri negotiated with the insurgents and achieved the 1972 Addis Ababa Agreement that ended the conflict and granted some autonomy to the south. This ended the **First Sudanese Civil War** (1955-72).

The **Second Sudanese Civil War** broke out in 1983. Islamists in the north pressured Numayri to embark on the Arabization and Islamization of the south. In the south, former rebels who had been incorporated into the Sudanese army according to the previous peace agreement refused orders from Khartoum transferring them to other parts of the country. This prompted Numayri, in June 1983, to impose direct rule over the south and make Arabic the official language of the whole country. Led by Colonel John Garang de Mabior, southern soldiers and rebels formed the Sudan People's Liberation Army (SPLA), launched another insurgency against the Khartoum administration. Since the rebels were backed by Mengistu's Ethiopia, which faced its own separatist movements, the SPLA could not advocate for secession but instead announced a goal of creating a federal Sudan in which regions would have some autonomy. During the mid- and late 1980s, the elected Islamist government of Sadiq al-Mahdi employed Arab ethnic militias to carry out mass violence against non-Muslims in the northernmost parts of southern Sudan. By 1988, Sudan was experiencing a massive refugee crisis as about three million southerners had fled to the north and 300,000 Sudanese were living in camps in Ethiopia. In 1989, another military coup in Khartoum brought Brigadier Omar Hassan Ahmad al-Bashir and an extreme Islamist faction to power. The war in the south continued as the Sudan government renewed its campaign of Islamization and Arabization. The start of the 1990s was a troubled time for the SPLA as ethnic Dinka and Nuer factions began a vicious internal struggle, and with the fall of the formerly pro-Soviet Mengistu regime in Ethiopia the movement lost its primary external sponsor. Although the global Cold War ended, the Second Sudanese Civil War continued through the 1990s and early 2000s.

Inter-State Wars

Egypt and the Arab–Israeli Conflict

During the 1960s and early 1970s, Egypt became embroiled in the **Arab–Israeli Conflict**. The global Cold War had been superimposed on the Arab–Israeli conflict, with leading Arab powers like Egypt and Syria sponsored by the Soviet Union and Israel supported by the United States. The 1956 Suez Crisis had resulted in the positioning of international UN peacekeepers in the Sinai Desert between Egypt and Israeli. However, in May 1967 clashes between Israel and Syria, which had a defense pact with Egypt, prompted Egypt's Nasser government to expel the peacekeepers and move Egyptian troops into the Sinai. While the Egyptian army comprised 200,000 men and had recently been equipped by the Soviet Union, it was unlikely that Nasser planned to invade Israel as some of his forces were in Yemen combating an insurgency. In early June 1967, Israel launched a preemptive strike against its Arab neighbors, with the Israeli Air Force destroying the warplanes of Egypt, Syria, and Jordan while they were still on the ground and Israeli ground forces defeating Egyptian troops in the Sinai and occupying the peninsula right up to the Suez Canal. The Israelis then constructed a fortified defensive line along the entire east bank of the Suez Canal.

In late 1969, fighting broke out between Egyptian and Israeli forces along the canal, and the Soviet Union and the United States negotiated a ceasefire as both countries feared being drawn into a nuclear war by their Middle Eastern allies.

Nasser died in late 1970 and was succeeded by vice president **Anwar Sadat**, another veteran of the 1952 Free Officers revolution. He purged the military of potential rivals while planning a military comeback against Israel. In October 1973, Egypt and Syria launched a massive offensive that surprised the Israelis,

≡ **Peacemakers.** Egyptian president Anwar Sadat and Israeli prime minister Menachem Begin acknowledge applause during a Joint Session of Congress in which US President Jimmy Carter announced the results of the Camp David Accords, September 1978.

who had become overconfident in their military superiority. Under cover of a large and sophisticated Soviet-supplied air defense system, Egyptian troops crossed the Suez Canal, overcame Israeli defenses, and entered the Sinai. Attempting to distract the Israelis from their war with the Syrians on the Golan Heights, Egyptian forces in the Sinai advanced beyond the protection of their air defenses and were slaughtered by Israeli armored counterattacks. The Israeli military once again pushed Egyptian troops across the canal and destroyed Egyptian air defenses. During the conflict, the Soviet Union rejected an Egyptian request for direct intervention and the United States elevated its nuclear alert status to the same level as during the 1962 Cuban Missile Crisis. Given its humiliating military defeat, in 1978 the Egyptian government signed the **Camp David Accords**, agreeing to a permanent peace with Israel in which it regained the Sinai in exchange for abandoning the cause of Palestinian liberation. In Cold War terms, Egypt ended its relationship with the Soviet Union and became a major ally of the United States. Within Egypt, the country's defection from the anti-Israeli coalition caused resentment among the Islamists of the Muslim Brotherhood, who assassinated President Sadat in 1981. Hosni Mubarak, chief of the Egyptian Air Force, succeeded Sadat and continued authoritarian rule with American support.

Angola

In Angola, which became independent in January 1975 after the departure of the Portuguese (see Chapter 22), a civil war broke out between the rebel groups that had been fighting colonial rule. This conflict drew in the Cold War superpowers and their allies. Angola was attractive to foreign forces because of its oil industry, located in **Cabinda**, a province that was disconnected from the rest of the country. The Popular Movement for the Liberation of Angola (MPLA), led by Agostinho Neto, seized the capital Luanda, which had long been its political stronghold, and received assistance from the Soviet Union, which had helped the party during the anti-colonial war. Located in remote border areas, the two other Angolan factions quickly advanced on the capital with the active assistance of the United States and apartheid South Africa. Washington wanted to prevent the Soviets from accessing Angolan oil and South Africa wanted to prevent the use of Angola as a staging area by insurgents from the South West African People's Organization (SWAPO) who were fighting for the independence of South African occupied South West Africa (Namibia). Moving down from their base in northern Angola, fighters from the National Front for the Liberation of Angola (FNLA) were supplemented by American advisors, South African airstrikes, and troops from Mobutu's Zaire. Mobutu's involvement reflected his own alliance with the United States and his personal relationship with FNLA leader Holden Roberto, who was his brother-in-law. From their home area in southern Angola, rebels from the National Union for the Total Independence of Angola (UNITA), led by Jonas Savimbi, received covert aid from the American CIA and advanced up toward Luanda along with conventional military forces from South Africa that invaded from South West Africa. In Luanda, the new and beleaguered MPLA government was saved by the direct military intervention of Cuba, armed by the Soviet Union. By the end of 1975, the Soviet-supplied MPLA-Cuban forces had destroyed FNLA and pushed UNITA and its South African allies back to southern Angola.

The MPLA regime in Angola stabilized with the continued presence of Cuban troops and Soviet military advisors and the delivery of massive amounts of Soviet weaponry. Occupying southeastern Angola, UNITA sustained its rebellion with South African and American sponsorship. As predicted, SWAPO allied with

≡ **Cold War power struggle.** UNITA rebels in Angola examine a captured Cuban (Soviet-made) tank in 1988.

the like-minded Marxist MPLA government and began to use southern Angola as a staging area to infiltrate guerrillas into the northern part of South African–occupied South West Africa. In addition, exiled South African anti-apartheid fighters from the African National Congress (ANC) established camps in Angola where they received training and weapons from the MPLA, Soviets, and Cubans. As a result, during the late 1970s and 1980s South African security forces regularly crossed into southern Angola in pursuit of SWAPO fighters but also clashed with MPLA and Cuban troops. In the late 1980s, the MPLA government launched a major Soviet-planned offensive against UNITA in southeastern Angola, but Savimbi's movement survived because of a forceful South African military intervention. However, the MPLA-Cuban defenders of the town of Quito Cuanavale halted a 1988 South African–UNITA counterattack and Cuban forces moved into southwestern Angola to threaten the border with South West Africa. This led to international negotiations that resulted in the Cubans pulling back from the border and eventually leaving Angola entirely, and in South Africa withdrawing from South West Africa. In 1990, consequently, South West Africa became independent under the new name of Namibia, with an elected SWAPO government led by President Sam Nujoma. Namibian independence occurred within the context of the end of the Cold War, as the weakening Soviet Union had pulled its advisors out of Angola in 1987 and the United States became hesitant to continue backing UNITA and the increasingly isolated apartheid South Africa. Although the Cold War dimension ended with the withdrawal of foreign powers, the **Angolan civil war** between MPLA and UNITA was essentially an internal power struggle and continued for over a decade more.

The Horn of Africa

In the Horn of Africa, the Ethiopian monarchy under Emperor Haile Selassie had been a reliable Western ally since the British had restored it during the Second World War (1939-45). During the 1950s, Selassie cultivated a close relationship with the United States by sending troops to fight against communist forces in the Korean War (1950-53) and by allowing the Americans to set up satellite communications facilities in Ethiopia. Around this time, the UN federated Eritrea to Ethiopia, thereby giving the latter control of the strategically important Red Sea coast, which could control access to the Suez Canal. With American and British help, imperial Ethiopia developed a powerful modern air force and a navy. In 1960, the colonies of British Somaliland and Italian Somaliland combined to form the independent Republic of Somalia, which quickly became a rival of adjacent Ethiopia. Inspired by the **Pan-Somali movement**, which sought to unify Somali people divided among five different East African states, independent Somalia sponsored ethnic Somali rebels in neighboring Ethiopia and Kenya during the 1960s. Since both Ethiopia and Kenya were allied to Western powers, Somalia looked increasingly to the Eastern Bloc for support. When Siad Barre came to power in Somalia in a 1969 military coup, he strengthened ties with the Soviet Union and allowed it to establish a naval base at the Red Sea port of Berbera. During the 1970s, Somalia, with Soviet assistance, developed Africa's fourth-largest armed forces. Relative to gross domestic product, it spent more on the military than any other African country. Attempting to justify his Soviet connection, Barre concocted a clumsy ideology of Somali socialism that tried to weave together Marxism and Islam.

The 1977–78 **Ogaden War** between Ethiopia and Somalia clearly illustrates the opportunistic and flexible nature of Cold War alliances in Africa. The 1974 overthrow of Emperor Haile Selassie by left-wing Ethiopian military officers provided an opportunity for Barre's Somalia to seize Ethiopia's Ogaden region containing an ethnic Somali population. Furthermore, by 1977 the Derg regime in Ethiopia, led by Haile Mariam Mengistu, was contending with an expanding insurgency in Eritrea, and its revolutionary ideology led to the expulsion American military advisors. In June and July 1977, Somalia launched an all-out invasion of Ethiopia's Ogaden region and pushed back Ethiopian ground forces. However, late that year the Soviets broke relations with Barre and established an alliance with Mengistu's Ethiopia, sending it over a billion dollars' worth of arms and ammunition and 1,000 Soviet military advisors. In addition, the Soviets had transported some 18,000 Cuban troops to Ethiopia by February 1978. Planned by a Soviet general, an Ethiopian-Cuban counteroffensive pushed Somali forces back over the border in March. For the Soviets, the larger and much more populous country of Ethiopia was a more attractive regional ally than Somalia. Before the fighting was over, Barré quickly shifted his allegiance to the United States, but the Carter administration, given its concerns over human rights, would only provide humanitarian aid. Defeat in the Ogaden War weakened Barre's grip on power within Somalia,

≡ **Castro and Mengistu.** Cuban leader Fidel Castro (center) with Ethiopian leader Haile Mariam Mengistu (right) in 1978 after their victory in the Ogaden War against Somalia.

where, by the early 1980s, several clan-based rebel groups had emerged to challenge him, leading to a very long civil war.

Chad

Civil war in postcolonial Chad turned into a complex international conflict influenced heavily by the Cold War. After Chad's independence from France in 1960, regional conflict developed between the marginalized and predominantly Muslim north and the relatively better off and primarily Christian south that dominated the government. During the late 1960s, rebels in the north acquired Eastern Bloc weapons from Algeria, Egypt, and Libya. Several thousand French troops backed the southern-based government of President François Tombalbaye, which also received weapons from the United States, Zaire, and Israel. In 1973, Muammar Gaddafi of Libya moved troops over the border into northern Chad and annexed the mineral-rich **Aouzou Strip**. This caused conflict between Libya and the Chadian government of General Félix Malloum, who came to power in a 1975 coup and, like his predecessor, enjoyed French support. The Libyan invasion of the north caused the northern rebel movement to fracture between the pro-Libyan People's Armed Forces (FAP) under Goukouni Oueddei and the anti-Libyan Armed Forces of the North (FAN) led by Hissène Habré. During the late 1970s, the FAP rebels and Libyan forces fought a coalition of the Chadian government and FAN, supported directly by France. In 1979, with a temporary withdrawal of the Libyans from northern Chad, Oueddei's FAP and Habré's FAN joined forces to overthrow Malloum as French troops did nothing. Oueddei became president of the Transitional Government of National Unity (GUNT), which included FAP and FAN, but the two factions quickly fell out and began fighting. As a result, in 1980, Oueddei signed an agreement with Gaddafi, letting Libyan troops back into northern Chad, including the Aouzou Strip. While Oueddei and Gaddafi signed a treaty agreeing to merge Chad and Libya, the two leaders fell out over the latter's backing of another Arab rebel group on the Chad–Sudan border. Oueddei demanded that the Libyans withdraw from Chad. Gaddafi, trying to win favor in the OAU, surprisingly agreed. In late 1981, the Libyan troops were replaced by OAU peacekeepers from Zaire, Nigeria, and Senegal representing the first international African attempt at peacekeeping.

In 1982, Habré's FAN, based in the Darfur region of western Sudan, invaded Chad and seized power from Oueddei, who was weakened by the departure of his former Libyan allies. The ousted Oueddei and his FAP fighters withdrew to northern Chad, where they were reinforced by Libyan troops who again crossed the border. During the mid-1980s, Chad was divided between the northern region occupied by Oueddei's loyalists (GUNT) and Libyan forces and the southern region dominated by Habré's faction, renamed the Chadian National Armed Forces (FANT), and who

≡ **Civil war in post-colonial Chad.** *Left:* A 1983 meeting of Chad's president Hissène Habré (1942–2021) with French president François Mitterrand. *Center:* Chadian soldiers pose with their Toyota Land Cruiser. *Right:* Supporters of Muammar Gaddafi rally in January 1987.

were directly supported by the French military and supplied by the United States. In 1986, Oueddei and Gaddafi fell out once again, and this resulted in reconciliation between Oueddei and Habré, who united against the Libyan invaders. During the 1987 **Toyota War**, Chadian forces mounted in Toyota pickup trucks attacked Libyan troops in northern Chad and pushed them over the border into southern Libya. In September, a Chadian lightning raid into Libya destroyed a Libyan air base, removing Libyan air power in the region. However, the Chadians abandoned plans for an offensive to recover the Aouzou Strip due to French concerns about the escalation of the conflict and Gaddafi's willingness to accept an OAU brokered ceasefire. While around 7,000 Libyans had been killed in the war and Libya lost billions of dollars worth of military equipment mostly purchased from the Soviet Union, Chad suffered less than 1,000 dead. Gaddafi, already engaged in conflicts with the US Navy in the Gulf of Sirte, blamed the United States and France for this disaster and began supporting international terrorism against the West. Making peace in 1989, Libya and Chad submitted the Aouzou Strip dispute to the International Court of Justice, which eventually awarded the territory to Chad. Backed by the United States and France, Habré's regime of the 1980s became repressive. It engaged in widespread arrest, torture, and murder of potential political opponents. In 1989, Habré accused several of his own military leaders of plotting a coup, prompting Idriss Deby, who had led operations during the Toyota War, to flee to Darfur in Sudan, where he formed a rebel group called the Patriotic Salvation Movement (MPS) backed by Libya and Sudan. In 1990, Deby's MPS crossed into Chad and seized the capital as Habré fled the country. While French troops based in Chad had initially helped the Habré government in its conflict with Deby's MPS, Paris grew tired of the brutal Habré and discontinued support. Habré fled to Senegal, where he eventually became the subject of a long legal struggle that ended in 2016 with his conviction and imprisonment for crimes against humanity.

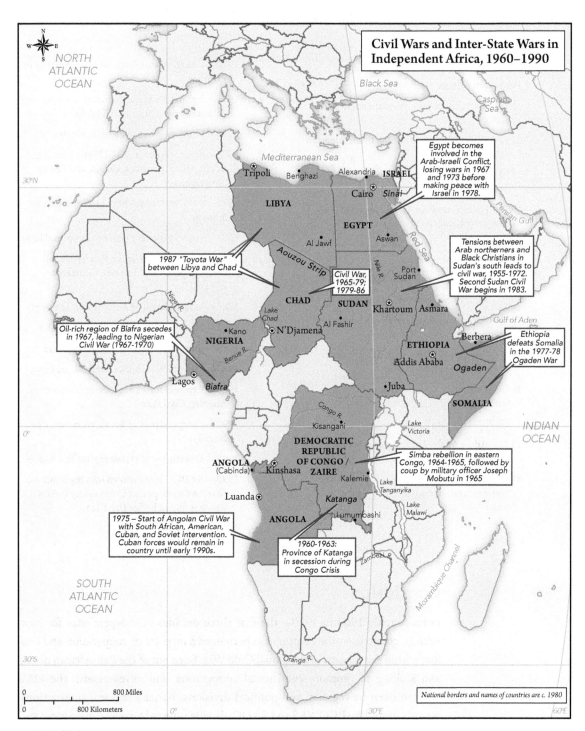

Civil Wars and Inter-State Wars in Independent Africa, 1960–1990

NORTH ATLANTIC OCEAN

Black Sea

Caspian Sea

Mediterranean Sea

Tripoli • Benghazi   Alexandria • • ISRAEL

Cairo ⊛ • Sinai

Persian Gulf

Egypt becomes involved in the Arab-Israeli Conflict, losing wars in 1967 and 1973 before making peace with Israel in 1978.

30°N

LIBYA

EGYPT

Al Jawf •

Aswan •

Aouzou Strip

Nile R.

Port Sudan •

1987 "Toyota War" between Libya and Chad

Civil War, 1965-79; 1979-86

Tensions between Arab northerners and Black Christians in Sudan's south leads to civil war, 1955-1972. Second Sudan Civil War begins in 1983.

Lake Chad

CHAD

SUDAN

Khartoum ⊛   Asmara •

Gulf of Aden

Niger R.

• N'Djamena

Al Fashir •

Oil-rich region of Biafra secedes in 1967, leading to Nigerian Civil War (1967-1970)

• Kano

NIGERIA

Benue R.

ETHIOPIA

Berbera •

Ethiopia defeats Somalia in the 1977-78 Ogaden War

Addis Ababa ⊛

Ogaden

Lagos ⊛ • Biafra

• Juba

SOMALIA

INDIAN OCEAN

0°

Congo R.

Kisangani •

Lake Victoria

DEMOCRATIC REPUBLIC OF CONGO / ZAIRE

Simba rebellion in eastern Congo, 1964-1965, followed by coup by military officer Joseph Mobutu in 1965

ANGOLA (Cabinda) • • Kinshasa

Kalemie •

Lake Tanganyika

Luanda ⊛

Katanga

Lake Malawi

1975 – Start of Angolan Civil War with South African, American, Cuban, and Soviet intervention. Cuban forces would remain in country until early 1990s.

ANGOLA

• Lumumbashi

Zambezi R.

1960-1963: Province of Katanga in secession during Congo Crisis

Mozambique Channel

SOUTH ATLANTIC OCEAN

30°S

Orange R.

| 0 | 800 Miles |
| 0 | 800 Kilometers |

National borders and names of countries are c. 1980

0°   30°E   60°E

☰ **MAP 25.2**

Timeline

1955–72—First Sudanese Civil War

1956—Suez Crisis

1958—First Conference of Independent Africa States

1960—French test atomic bomb in the Algerian Sahara

1960—Second Conference of Independent African States

1961—Formation of the Casablanca and Monrovia Groups

1963—Formation of the Organization of African Unity (OAU)

1964–65—Rebellion in Eastern Congo

1965—Mobutu seizes power in Congo

1966—African Development Bank begins operations based in Côte d'Ivoire

1967—"Six Day War" between Arab states (including Egypt) and Israel

1968—Formation of West African Regional Group

1967–70—Nigerian Civil War

1972—Addis Ababa Agreement ends First Sudanese Civil War

1973—"October War" or "Yom Kippur War" between Arab states (including Egypt) and Israel

1974—Overthrow of Emperor Haile Selassie in Ethiopia

1975—Formation of the Economic Community of West African States (ECOWAS)

1975—Formation of the Frontline States

1975—Start of Angolan Civil War, including South Africa, America, Cuban, and Soviet intervention

1977–78—Ogaden War between Ethiopia and Somalia

1978—Peace agreement between Egypt and Israel

1980—Formation of the Southern African Development Coordination Conference (SADCC)

1981—Assassination of Anwar Sadat in Egypt

1982—Hissène Habré seizes power in Chad

1983—Start of Second Sudanese Civil War

1987—"Toyota War" between Chad and Libya

1989—External forces begin to withdraw from Angolan Civil War

1990—Independence of South West Africa as Namibia

1990—Overthrow of Habré regime in Chad

1992—SADCC transformed into the Southern African Development Community (SADC), which is joined by South Africa

Conclusion

From roughly 1960 to 1990—the first three decades of independence for most African countries—the continent experienced a mixture of cooperation and conflict within the context of the global Cold War. Born out of the Pan-African dream and seeking to promote continental cooperation and development, the OAU became riven by regional and political divisions. Africa's regional international organizations like ECOWAS and SADC, despite internal tensions, were more successful in promoting their agendas, including regional integration and the end of white-minority regimes in the south. The commitment of the OAU and its members to maintaining the borders inherited from the colonial era plus the failure of separatist movements during civil wars in Nigeria and Congo meant that no successful secessionist states emerged in Cold War Africa. Although the Cold War superpowers became involved in backing different sides of Africa's inter-state wars, it is important to remember that these conflicts were motivated by local factors such as the struggle for political power in Angola and Chad and the territorial ambitions of Somalia and Libya.

KEY TERMS

Angolan Civil War 567

Anwar Sadat 565

Aouzou Strip 569

Arab–Israeli Conflict 564

Cabinda 566

Camp David Accords 565

Casablanca Group 555

Economic Community
of West African States
(ECOWAS) 557

First Sudanese
Civil War 563

Frontline States 558

Monrovia Group 555

Nigerian Civil War 561

Ogaden War 568

Organization of African
Unity (OAU) 555

Pan-African Women's
Organization (PAWO) 556

Pan-Somali Movement 567

Republic of Biafra 561

Second Sudanese Civil War 563

Simbas 560

Southern African Development
Community (SADC) 560

Southern African Development
Coordination Conference
(SADCC) 558

Toyota War 570

STUDY QUESTIONS

1. What were/are the goals of the Organization of African Unity, the African Development Bank, ECOWAS, and SADC?

2. How did regionalism, religion, and race contribute to internal divisions and civil wars in many African countries?

3. What were the main events in Egypt's involvement in the Arab–Israeli conflict? How was Soviet, Cuban, and US intervention in Africa an extension of the Cold War? What were some of the principal sites of US–Soviet rivalry in Africa? How did externally supplied military equipment influence these conflicts?

Please see page FR-11 for the Further Readings for this chapter.
For additional digital learning resources please go to
https://www.oup.com/he/falola-stapleton1e

26

Independent Africa after the Cold War: State, Economy, and Conflict

In 1989, the vast majority of African countries were governed by one-party states, military regimes, and dictatorships. By 1991, however, this situation had begun to change dramatically. The collapse of the authoritarian, communist Soviet Union and its Eastern Bloc satellites inspired political opposition groups across Africa to demand democratic reforms, including the creation of multiparty electoral systems. Western international aid to African countries, most of which had become heavily indebted and therefore dependent upon this assistance, became conditional on moves toward democracy. African dictatorships lost their superpower support as the troubled Soviet Union reduced assistance in the late 1980s and then collapsed in 1991. The consequent absence of a communist threat meant that the United States no longer needed to back anti-communist regimes.

The collapse of the Eastern Bloc at the end of the 1980s made socialism globally unfashionable. Without any rival system, Western powers like the United States promoted a **neoliberal** economic approach that consisted of free markets, deregulation, privatization, and government austerity. Beginning in the 1980s, Western international economic institutions such as the World Bank and International Monetary Fund (IMF) imposed **structural adjustment** policies on heavily indebted African states that had become dependent on continued foreign financial assistance. Structural adjustment involved devaluation of local currency, reduction in the size of the civil service, privatization of state-owned enterprises, and removal of trade barriers. While structural adjustment sought to promote Africa's historic role as a provider of raw materials for the world market, these policies resulted in higher prices for goods and increased unemployment, which reduced standards of living for ordinary people. Structural adjustment generally diminished the fragile African middle class, creating a more unequal society where most people became very poor and a few enjoyed incredible wealth.

The advent of the twenty-first century bought a number of new factors that influenced the African state and economy. The September 2001 terrorist

Activist. Known as the "woman in white," student activist Alaa Salah gained international attention in 2019 for leading protests in Sudan against the regime of Omar Al-Bashir.

attacks on the United States and the subsequent international **War on Terror** inspired strong American support for African regimes that would combat Islamist extremism. African governments whose economic policies met with Western approval, particularly around privatization, were rewarded by having large chunks of their massive foreign debts forgiven, liberating them from crippling interest payments and supposedly enabling them to alleviate poverty. Critics of this "debt relief" program point out that it encourages the type of economic policies that have generally worsened poverty in Africa and that it is simply a new form of structural adjustment. In Africa, concerns about state sovereignty became linked to economic issues. Launched in 2002, the UN-backed International Criminal Court (ICC) began to prosecute cases of war crimes, crimes against humanity, and genocide that could not be, or were not, dealt with by national courts. Since all those brought to trial at the ICC were Africans, this led to accusations that international justice was racist and that it did not apply to powerful countries such as the United States, Russia, and China, which remained outside the ICC. Reacting to the mass violence of the 1990s in places like Somalia and Rwanda, international organizations like the UN began to limit state sovereignty during the 2000s, agreeing to intervene to avoid genocide and other mass atrocities. While the OAU of the 1960s to 1990s had been strongly against interference in internal state affairs, the renamed **African Union** (AU) of the 2000s declared that intervention was sometimes necessary.

These challenges to African sovereignty were countered by increasing Chinese engagement in the continent. Beginning in the 1990s, the rise of China as a global economic superpower markedly expanded Chinese trade and relations with African countries. The acquisition of African raw materials became important for growing Chinese manufacturing and export. Many African states preferred to engage in economic deals with China. In contrast to Western governments, nongovernmental organizations (NGOs), and businesses that increasingly imposed conditions related to human rights, China maintained a policy of non-interference in the internal affairs of sovereign states.

Democratization

In many African countries, democratization happened very quickly during the 1990s. While some long-serving authoritarian rulers were able to remain in power after the transition to multiparty democracy, the new constitutions created in the early 1990s usually had presidential term limits that meant they eventually had to step aside. The first mainland African country to experience a democratic transition was West Africa's Republic of Benin. President Mathieu Kérékou had come to power in a 1972 military coup, but economic crisis and popular protest prompted him to

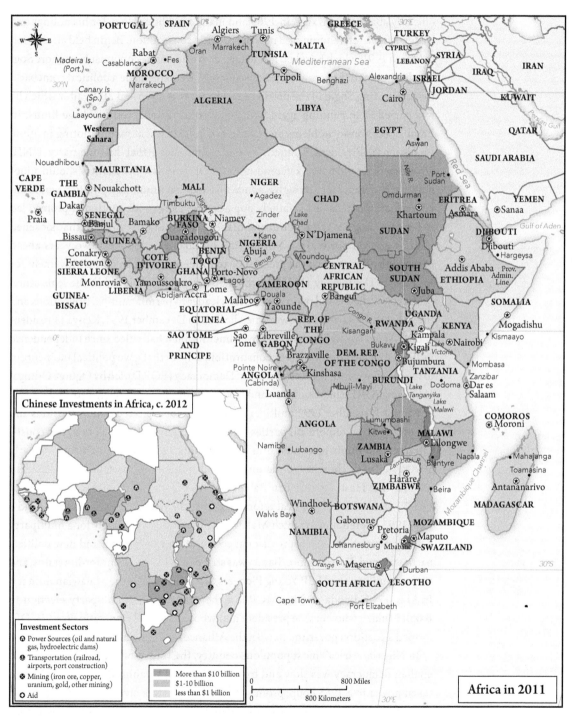

Chinese Investments in Africa, c. 2012

Investment Sectors

- ⊕ Power Sources (oil and natural gas, hydroelectric dams)
- ⊙ Transportation (railroad, airports, port construction)
- ⊗ Mining (iron ore, copper, uranium, gold, other mining)
- ○ Aid

More than $10 billion
$1-10 billion
less than $1 billion

0   800 Miles
0   800 Kilometers

Africa in 2011

≡ **MAP 26.1**

officially abandon Marxism in 1989 and make a public apology for his failings as a leader. After a referendum on a new democratic constitution, Benin held an election in March 1991, which Kérékou lost to former World Bank economist Nicéphore Soglo, who assumed the presidency. Subsequently, Kérékou made a political comeback, twice defeating Soglo in the presidential elections of 1996 and 2001, after which he was barred from running again because of constitutional term and age limits. In Zambia, economic problems and political disillusionment incited rioting in 1990. In response, President Kenneth Kaunda announced that his one-party UNIP government would hold a referendum on whether or not the country should adopt multiparty democracy. Though Kaunda insisted that a multiparty system would encourage ethnic divisions, a failed coup attempt, along with continued protest, led to his canceling the referendum and making constitutional changes that loosened UNIP's grip on power. In a November 1991 snap election, held two years ahead of schedule, Kaunda lost the presidency to Frederick Chiluba of the Movement for Multiparty Democracy (MMD), which also formed a majority in the legislature. Kaunda was the second mainland African leader to permit multiparty elections and then peacefully surrender power when he lost. In December 1991, Kenya's President Daniel Arap Moi and his KANU government, which had ruled since independence in 1964, repealed the one-party constitution, a move that gave political momentum to the new Forum for the Restoration of Democracy (FORD), led by Oginga Odinga. However, FORD split along Luo and Kikuyu ethnic lines, allowing Moi and KANU to win the December 1992 multiparty election. Moi exploited ethnic divisions and the proliferation of political parties to also win Kenya's 1997 election, but constitutional term limits prevented him from running again in 2002. During the early 1990s, Malawi's churches, trade unions, and student groups called on "President for Life" Dr. Hastings Kamuzu Banda and his one-party Malawi Congress Party (MCP) state to enact political reforms. The weakened regime relented and held a June 1993 referendum in which Malawians voted overwhelmingly for a multiparty democratic system. A new provisional constitution was drafted, and new political parties formed. Furthermore, Banda was stripped of his president-for-life status, and his party militia, the MCP Young Pioneers, was disarmed by the Malawian military. In May 1994, Banda and his MCP lost the country's first multiparty election to Bakili Muluzi, who became president and whose United Democratic Front (UDF) formed a coalition government with the Alliance for Democracy (AFORD).

In Nigeria, Africa's most populous country, the transition from military rule to civilian democracy was slow and troubled. General Ibrahim Babangida, who had taken power in a 1985 coup, promised to hand over to a civilian government, and in 1989 a new constitution was formulated. In 1990, despite a failed coup, multiparty local government elections were held. However, state elections scheduled for the next year were canceled due to widespread fraud. Though businessman M.K.O. Abiola won presidential elections in June 1993, Babangida annulled the results, which prompted rioting. Consequently, Babangida passed authority to an interim government under civilian Ernest Shonekan, but this did little to stop Nigeria's slide into an economic and political crisis that was worsened by international sanctions. In November 1993, General Sani Abacha seized control, replacing the interim government with military officers and promising civilian democratic government in 1995. Abiola declared himself president, but Abacha then had him imprisoned. In 1995, an alleged coup plot incited the Abacha regime to arrest a number of military and political leaders, including former military head of state Olusegun Obasanjo. As Abacha's administration continued to promise civilian rule within three years and organized local government elections in 1997, another supposed coup plot resulted in more arrests. In June 1998, however, Abacha died suddenly of heart failure and was replaced by General Abdulsalami Abubakar, who

released political prisoners and appointed an independent electoral commission. Abiola, arguably the legitimate president, died under mysterious circumstances just as he was about to be released from detention. In late 1998 and early 1999, multiparty elections were held for local, state, and national governmental bodies. Running as a civilian under the banner of the center-right People's Democratic Party (PDP), Obasanjo won the presidential election and was inaugurated in May 1999. He was Nigeria's first elected civilian leader in 16 years. In the Nigerian presidential election of 2003, Obasanjo retained power by defeating another former military ruler turned civilian politician, Muhammadu Buhari of the All Nigerian People's Party (ANPP). Given a limit of two presidential terms, Obasanjo could not run in the 2007 elections and subsequently became an international statesman. Later, Buhari, running under the banner of the All Progressives Congress (APC), won Nigeria's 2015 presidential election, marking the first time in the country's history that political power was transferred from one civilian party to another.

≡ **Olusegun Obasanjo** was military ruler of Nigeria from 1976 to 1979, and an elected civilian president from 1999 to 2007.

Civil Wars in West Africa

In some African countries, the collapse of Cold War–era dictatorships led to terrible civil wars during the 1990s and 2000s. Since armed factions could no longer use ideology to appeal to superpowers for military assistance, they focused more on extracting natural resources to support war efforts. The 1990s and 2000s became the era of Africa's **resource curse**, as the presence of valuable raw materials, such as minerals or hardwood, instead of fueling peace and prosperity, made it much more likely that a country would experience warfare. This, in turn, led to human suffering, population displacement, state collapse, and extreme poverty.

Liberia and Sierra Leone

The diminutive West African countries of Liberia and Sierra Leone were hard-hit by a series of interrelated civil wars in the 1990s and 2000s. In Liberia in 1980, the more than century-old rule of the Americo-Liberian elite ended with a military coup that installed Master Sergeant Samuel Doe as the country's first indigenous leader. Supported by the United States, Doe ruled Liberia oppressively and for the benefit of his own Krahn ethnic group, which stimulated resentment among other ethnic communities such as the Gio and Mano. Consequently, at the end of 1989 a rebel group called the National Patriotic Front of Liberia (NPFL), led by Charles Taylor and supported by Libya and neighboring francophone countries, invaded Liberia from Côte d'Ivoire. A rebel splinter group called the Independent National Patriotic Front of Liberia (INPFL) captured Doe and video recorded his horrific murder. The arrival of an ECOWAS intervention force, consisting mostly of Nigerian troops, prevented a complete rebel takeover. During the early 1990s, Taylor's NPFL, based at the large Firestone rubber plantation, exported iron ore and timber through the port of Buchanan. As fighting continued, the INPFL withered but was replaced by several other rebel groups such as the United Liberian Movement for Democracy (ULIMO), which itself split into two ethnically based factions that also exported resources. In 1995, after a long series of ECOWAS negotiations, a ceasefire and political transition was agreed to, although rebel groups continued to fight each other. In a 1997 election, Liberians voted Taylor into the presidency as they were afraid he would continue the war if he lost. This **First Liberian Civil War** (1989–97) resulted in 200,000 deaths, the flight of 800,000 refugees to neighboring countries, and the internal displacement of 1.2 million Liberians.

In 1985, Sierra Leone's long-time authoritarian leader Siaka Stevens was succeeded by General Joseph Momoh. Since Sierra Leone contributed some troops to the ECOWAS force in Liberia, Taylor orchestrated the formation of a rebel group inside Sierra Leone called the Revolutionary United Front (RUF) that launched an insurgency in 1991, and amid the fighting, General Momoh's own army overthrew him in a coup. Unable to capture Freetown, the RUF seized control of diamond producing areas and exported the resource through Liberian rebels such as Taylor's NPFL. In this chaotic **Sierra Leone Civil War** (1991–2002), communities formed self-defense militias that ultimately contributed to the violence. In 1995, the Sierra Leone government, also using diamond revenues, hired the international mercenary group Executive Outcomes, which delivered a severe blow to the RUF, pushing it out of many diamond mining areas. Frustrated by the government's inability to destroy the RUF, another faction of the Sierra Leone military, led by Brigadier Julius Maada-Bio, seized power at the start of 1996. While this resulted in an election that installed a civil coalition government under Ahmad Tejan Kabbah, and in the cancelation of the mercenaries' contract, yet another military faction, called the Armed Forces Revolutionary Council (AFRC), attempted to take power in the middle of 1997. This led to fighting in Freetown between an ECOWAS intervention force, the AFRC, and the RUF. In January 1999, the RUF launched "Operation No Living Thing," which involved a deadly incursion into Freetown and prompted the weak Kabbah government to make concessions to end the war. In the subsequent Lomé Peace Accord, signed in July 1999, RUF leader Foday Sankoh became a vice president and the minister of mines in exchange for a promise to disarm his rebels. The peace process was supervised by the newly arrived UN Mission to Sierra Leone (UNAMSIL), which, with 17,000 international personnel, was the world's largest UN peacekeeping mission at the time. In 2000, with the RUF refusing to disarm and taking UN hostages, the British government dispatched a robust military expeditionary force to Sierra Leone, which effectively destroyed the RUF. Almost simultaneously, Sankoh was arrested as his bodyguards had shot protestors in Freetown, and in 2003 he died while in custody awaiting trial. By early 2002, over 50,000 RUF fighters had been disarmed and the group collapsed.

In Liberia, Taylor's regime became increasingly tyrannical, and its involvement in smuggling diamonds from Sierra Leone resulted in international sanctions. The departure of ECOWAS peacekeepers from Liberia at the end of 1999 created an opportunity for new rebel groups to depose Taylor. This prompted the start of the **Second Liberian Civil War** (1999–2003). In 2000, Liberians United for Reconciliation and Democracy (LURD), comprised of oppressed Mandingo people, invaded Liberia from Guinea, where they received support from the government of Lansana Conté in exchange for cocoa, coffee, and diamonds. Within LURD, female rebels, many of whom had been raped by Taylor's fighters in the previous war or after, formed a unit called the Women's Artillery Commando, led by the courageous Black Diamond. Taylor's increasingly disreputable image drove away his international allies, Gaddafi of Libya and Blaise Compaoré of Burkina Faso, and meant that his request for ECOWAS assistance was rejected. In 2002, a new rebel group called the Movement for Democracy in Liberia (MODEL), consisting

☰ **Civil wars in Liberia.** *Left:* A rebel leader during the First Liberian Civil War (1989–97), Charles Taylor was elected as president of Liberia in 1997 and resigned at the end of the Second Liberian Civil War in 2003. In 2012, the International Criminal Court convicted him of war crimes and crimes against humanity and sentenced him to 50 years' imprisonment. *Center:* Liberian peace activist Leymah Gbowee played a key role in ending the Second Liberian Civil War in 2003. *Right:* Africa's first elected female head of state, Ellen Johnson Sirleaf served as president of Liberia from 2006 to 2018.

of former Doe regime supporters, invaded from Côte d'Ivoire. Negotiations held in Ghana produced an agreement from Taylor that he would resign and impelled the dispatch of ECOWAS peacekeepers and an American military expedition to facilitate the delivery of humanitarian aid. A peace activist group called **Women of Liberia Mass Action for Peace**, led by Leymah Gbowee, played a central role in pressuring male Liberian leaders to end the war. In August 2003, Taylor, recently indicted by the UN-backed Special Court in Sierra Leone for his involvement with the RUF, resigned and departed for exile in Nigeria. As fighting continued, some 15,000 international peacekeepers of the UN Mission in Liberia (UNMIL) began arriving and helped stabilize the new transitional government. In 2006, at the request of the recently elected Liberian president **Ellen Johnson Sirleaf**, Africa's first female head of state, Nigeria withdrew its protection of Taylor, sending him to The Hague in the Netherlands to stand trial for crimes against humanity and war crimes with regard to his activities pertaining to the Sierra Leone Civil War.

Côte d'Ivoire, Nigeria and Cameroon

The 1995 death of Felix Houphouët-Boigny, who had ruled Côte d'Ivoire for over 30 years, led to civil war in the former French colony. By the 1990s, xenophobia had become a major problem as historic migrant labor from northern countries, such as Burkina Faso and Mali, meant that about a quarter of Ivoirians were first- or second-generation immigrants, mostly concentrated in the north. This situation was further complicated by the fact that, as in many West African countries, the south was relatively better off and predominantly Christian, and the north was poorer and mostly inhabited by Muslims. With the transition to democracy, a crisis developed over who qualified to vote, and popular northern leader Alassane Ouattara was excluded from running for president because of his foreign ancestry. In 2002, in response to xenophobic violence, northern soldiers mutinied and took control of the northern region, attacking the capital of Abidjan in the south. France, long accustomed to militarily intervening in its former colonies in Africa, dispatched a force to separate the northern rebels from the supporters of President Laurent Gbagbo in the south. Rebels from the north and west eventually formed an alliance called the New Forces. Although the rebels agreed to join a unity government under Gbagbo, they withdrew from the peace process in 2004 in response to renewed violence and delays in implementing the peace accords. Both the rebels and Gbagbo's forces turned against the French soldiers, and there were anti-French riots in Abidjan. Côte d'Ivoire remained divided between the rebel-held north and the south occupied by Gbagbo's military. In 2010, five years after Gbagbo's presidential term had ended, long-delayed elections resulted in Ouattara's victory. Since Gbagbo refused to step down, the New Forces invaded Abidjan in 2011, cooperating with the French and UN to apprehend Gbagbo, who was sent to The Hague to face ICC charges of war crimes committed by his supporters. However, citing lack of evidence, the ICC dismissed the charges against Gbagbo in 2019 allowing the former president to return to Côte d'Ivoire in 2021.

As Nigeria transitioned to civilian democratic government in the 2000s, insurgency broke out in different parts of the country. In 2006, the Movement for the Emancipation of the Niger Delta (MEND) began raiding oil production facilities, and in 2009 a group called **Boko Haram** ("Western civilization is forbidden") launched an Islamist insurgency in the northeast, aligning themselves with global jihad. The Boko Haram rebellion eventually spilled over Nigeria's borders into Cameroon, Chad, and Niger impacting the entire Lake Chad Basin. Concurrently, a political movement in the southeast revived the idea of the separatist state of Biafra and was suppressed by the federal government. By 2021, a separatist movement had also emerged in western Nigeria and armed groups proliferated across the northern and central regions raiding schools and kidnapping students for ransom. Secessionism also emerged in neighboring Cameroon. In 2017, activists in anglophone western Cameroon declared the secession of **Ambazonia** from the larger state that was dominated by the francophone majority and ruled by a French-backed authoritarian regime.

Democracy and Authoritarianism in Southern Africa

A Cold War battleground from the 1960s to 1980s, Southern Africa began to stabilize after 1990. Nevertheless, transitions to democracy were not uniformly successful across the region.

South Africa, Botswana, and Namibia

Dramatic change happened in South Africa, where negotiations led to the dismantling of the white minority apartheid state, the creation of a democratic constitution, and the 1994 election of Nelson Mandela of the African National Congress (ANC) as the country's first Black president. Consistently re-elected during the late 1990s and 2000s, the ANC government suffered from corruption scandals amid economic problems and mounting public pressure to address inequity in land ownership by expropriating white commercial farmers and distributing their properties to landless Blacks. In several other Southern African countries, regular elections were held after independence, but the same political parties, despite being criticized for authoritarian behavior, were always returned to power. In Botswana, where the small population benefited from the advent of diamond production in the early 1970s, the conservative Botswana Democratic Party (BDP) won every election since independence in 1966. Since Namibia's independence in 1990, the South West African People's Organization (SWAPO) has successfully used the memory of its struggle against South African occupation to dominate electoral politics.

Mozambique

During the late 1970s and 1980s, Mozambique endured a terrible civil war between the pro-Soviet Front for the Liberation of Mozambique (FRELIMO) state and the Mozambique National Resistance (RENAMO) rebels backed by apartheid South Africa. The war ended in the early 1990s when FRELIMO dropped socialism and embraced multiparty democracy, and RENAMO entered a UN-supervised peace process and became a political party. Beginning in 1994, FRELIMO won regular elections and presided over a relatively successful reconstruction program, with RENAMO serving as parliamentary opposition. In 2004, FRELIMO's Joaquim Chissano, who had ruled since 1986, relinquished the presidency after two elected terms

≡ **Mozambique leader.** During Joaquim Chissano's tenure as the second president of Mozambique from 1986 to 2005, he ended the country's civil war in 1993 and Mozambique became a multiparty democracy. Chissano voluntarily stepped down after the end of his second elected presidential term.

even though this was not required by the constitution. After some renewed violence in the mid-2010s, RENAMO and the FRELIMO-led Mozambique government signed a peace deal in 2019.

Angola

In Angola, at the start of the 1990s, the end of the Cold War prompted negotiations between the ruling Popular Movement for the Liberation of Angola (MPLA), which abandoned socialism, and the National Union for the Total Independence of Angola (UNITA) rebels, who had lost American backing, with both sides agreeing to a UN-supervised ceasefire and democratic elections. However, upon losing the 1992 election, UNITA resumed fighting and engaged in diamond mining and smuggling through Zaire/DRC to obtain weapons, mostly from bankrupt former Soviet republics. Simultaneously, oil revenues funded the MPLA government's war effort, and briefly, in the mid-1990s, it hired South African mercenaries who had been fighting on the other side of regional conflicts just a few years before. UNITA's diamond smuggling operations were undermined during the late 1990s, when the Angolan army twice invaded Zaire/DRC and recaptured diamond producing areas inside Angola. Angolan president José Eduardo dos Santos declared that peace could only be achieved through military victory. In 2002, UNITA leader Jonas Savimbi was killed in an ambush and the remnants of his organization demobilized. At that time, some four million Angolans, one third of the population, were internally displaced and the country's medical, educational, and economic infrastructure was largely destroyed. In what some call a "negative peace," the MPLA used questionable elections to retain a firm grip on power and oil revenues.

Zimbabwe

During the 1980s, Zimbabwe experienced the increasingly authoritarian rule of Robert Mugabe and his Zimbabwe African National Union-Patriotic Front (ZANU-PF), which had been elected following the end of white minority rule and the granting of independence by Britain. From 1981 to 1987, the Shona-dominated ZANU-PF state politicized the Zimbabwe military and used it to terrorize the Ndebele people of the southwest and eliminate their Zimbabwe African People's Union (ZAPU) opposition party. This further entrenched the rule of Mugabe's ZANU-PF, and during the 1990s Zimbabwe functioned as a de facto one-party state. At the end of the 1990s, economic problems caused by structural adjustment and resentment over ZANU-PF's near dictatorial rule inspired protest from trade unions and the creation of an opposition party called the Movement for Democratic Change (MDC). To meet this challenge, Mugabe mobilized veterans of the 1970s liberation war by giving them new pension packages and allowing them to violently seize white-owned commercial farms, thus damaging agricultural

☰ **Hostile confrontation.** A mother and her two daughters are blocked from leaving their farmhouse by Zimbabwe war veterans in a rural district north of the capital of Harare in March 2000. Zimbabwe spiraled into an ever-deepening economic crisis after President Robert Mugabe urged the violent seizure of land from the country's remaining white farmers.

production and export. Amid a collapsing economy with the world's highest recorded inflation, which caused hundreds of thousands to leave the country, Mugabe's ZANU-PF clung to power through several highly disputed elections during the 2000s by employing widespread intimidation and violence. ZANU-PF's continued control was facilitated by the splitting of the MDC into two factions. Although MDC entered a temporary unity government in 2008, which stabilized the economy, ZANU-PF repression and economic problems persisted. In 2017, Zimbabwe's military, commanded by ZANU-PF loyalists, staged a coup that replaced the elderly and out-of-touch Mugabe with ZANU-PF stalwart Emmerson Mnangagwa.

Secession and Failed States in East Africa

After Ethiopia and Somalia fought each other in the 1977–78 Ogaden War, both countries experienced worsening internal conflicts.

Ethiopia

In Ethiopia during the 1980s, the Soviet-backed totalitarian regime of Haile Mariam Mengistu responded with increasing brutality to multiple insurgencies. In **Eritrea**, a former Italian colony that the UN had arbitrarily federated to Ethiopia in the 1950s, the Eritrean Liberation Front (ELF) and the Eritrean People's Liberation Front (EPLF) fought for independence. These two secessionist movements also battled each other, and by the early 1980s only EPLF remained. In the adjacent area of Tigray, the Tigray People's Liberation Front (TPLF) waged a guerrilla campaign to reform the oppressive Ethiopian state. In the context of acute drought and famine across East Africa during the mid-1980s, the Mengistu regime denied international food aid to people in rebel areas. With the decline and eventual end of Soviet military support from the late 1980s, Mengistu's forces faltered and were defeated by the EPLF at the decisive Battle of Afabet in 1988. In early 1991, Mengistu fled Ethiopia as an alliance of rebel forces occupied Addis Ababa. In May 1991, Eritrea gained independence, becoming the first successful secessionist state in postcolonial Africa. Held in 1993, a UN approved referendum within Eritrea confirmed its independence from Ethiopia. In Ethiopia, a coalition of former rebel groups under TPLF leader Meles Zenawi formed a government and gave up socialism to facilitate better relations with the West. While Zenawi's regime became increasingly authoritarian, prompting the continuation of several insurgencies, Ethiopia strongly allied with the United States in the post-2001 War on Terror. While Eritrean separatists and Ethiopian rebels had cooperated in the ouster of Mengistu, Eritrea and Ethiopia fell out and fought a border war at the end of the 1990s, with peaceful relations restored some 20 years later in 2018. The rise of Ethiopia's Prime Minister Abiy Ahmed in 2018 inspired hope as he represented the first prime minister from the marginalized Oromo ethnic group, and he made peace with Eritrea. Nevertheless, this political realignment alienated the formerly dominant TPLF from Ethiopia's central government leading to the outbreak of war in Tigray in 2020. At the same time, the completion of the Grand Ethiopian Renaissance Dam (GERD) on the Blue Nile River incited tension between Ethiopia seeking to use hydro-electric power to promote its economic development and neighboring Sudan and Egypt worrying about their water supply.

Somalia

Internally weakened by its loss in the Ogaden War, Somalia's Siad Barré dictatorship was challenged by a succession of rebellions during the 1980s. These insurgent groups, based on traditional Somali clans, were supported by Mengistu's Ethiopia, which sought to destabilize its regional rival. Barre retained power as a result of American military assistance and divisions among the rebels. Although Barre and Mengistu made peace in 1988 so they could focus on countering rebellions in their respective countries, the Somali civil war reached Mogadishu around the same time. In January 1991, Barre, who had provoked a massive uprising by ordering the bombardment of parts of Mogadishu, fled the capital and eventually went into exile. With the collapse of the Barre regime, Somalia reverted to the old colonial division between British Somaliland in the north and Italian Somaliland in the south. In May 1991, the Somali National Movement (SNM) rebels took control of the north and declared its independence as Somaliland, and in 1998 a similar process led to the proclamation of independence for Puntland in the northeast. However, no international recognition was forthcoming for these separatist states despite their relatively stable administrations. Since civil war continued in the south as armed factions fought over Mogadishu, Somalia became known as a **failed state.** Civil war and drought meant that in the early 1990s there were about one million Somali refugees in neighboring countries, and the UN predicted that one and a half million Somalis would starve to death.

With rebel leaders blocking the delivery of international food aid, which they wanted to control for profit, the UN sanctioned a primarily American military intervention called Operation Restore Hope in southern Somalia in 1992. International forces delivered food aid but mostly did not disarm the rival Somali factions. In early 1994, after the deaths of 18 American military personnel in a failed attempt to capture Somali warlords late the previous year, US forces withdrew from Somalia. The last UN peacekeepers left in early 1995 as there was no peace to keep. After the 2001 terrorist attacks, the United States provided support for the secular Somali warlords in their continuing conflict with the Islamic Courts Union (ICU), which was attempting to restore order through Sharia law. In 2006, Ethiopia, encouraged by the United States, invaded southern Somalia and pushed the ICU out of Mogadishu and other major towns. The next year, the African Union Mission in Somalia (AMISOM), consisting mostly of Ugandan and Burundian troops and paid for by the United States and the European Union, arrived to support Somalia's Transitional Federal Government (TFG) and engaged ICU insurgents. In 2009, as Ethiopian forces withdrew and moderate ICU elements joined the TFG, the former ICU youth movement **Al Shabaab** continued the war, aligning itself with global jihad. Al Shabaab attacks within Kenya, which targeted that country's tourism industry, provoked a major Kenyan military intervention in support of AMISOM in 2011. Fighting between Somalia's weak government, supported directly by AMISOM and indirectly by the United States, and Al Shabaab continued during the 2010s and into the 2020s. Around the same time, the breakdown of law and order in Somalia, the proliferation of weapons, and the destruction of the local fishing industry by foreign overfishing led to the rise of Somali piracy in the strategic waters leading

≡ **Failed state.** US soldiers conduct a nighttime sweep in a village during the political and military turmoil that characterized Somalia in the early 1990s.

into the Red Sea. This was countered by an international naval task force and the placement of armed guards on container vessels.

Sudan

Sudan's second civil war started in 1983, when the northern-dominated government in Khartoum, pressured by Islamist extremists, abandoned the previous peace agreement and launched a coercive program of Islamization and Arabization in the predominantly Christian south. In 1991, with the collapse of Ethiopia's Mengistu regime, the southern rebels of the Sudan People's Liberation Army (SPLA) lost their main sponsor and this threw the movement into chaos, prompting terrible violence between ethnic Dinka and Nuer factions. The rise to power of Omar Hassan Ahmad al-Bashir and Islamists in a 1989 coup in Khartoum intensified the war and led to state-sponsored "Arab" militias conducting genocide of non-Muslims in the Nuba Hills and parts of the south. The start of the US War on Terror, however, prompted the Bashir regime to break its links with international Islamist terrorists. While the advent of Sudan's oil industry at the start of the 2000s provided it with revenue to continue the war in the south, it also encouraged Khartoum to discuss peace as the conflict was disrupting the economy and hindering petroleum export. The outbreak of another rebellion in western Sudan's Darfur region in 2002 delayed the implementation of a negotiated peace in the south until 2005, when an autonomous government of South Sudan was created. SPLA leader John Garang was killed shortly afterward in a helicopter crash. In a 2011 referendum, the people of South Sudan voted overwhelmingly for independence, which became official in July under the presidency of the SPLA's Salva Kiir Mayardit. With international recognition, South Sudan became the second African country to successfully separate from another state in the postcolonial era. Regrettably, within two years the new state was wracked by its own civil war as fighting was renewed between ethnic factions, primarily the Dinka led by Salva Kiir and the Nuer led by Riek Machar.

Beginning in 2003, marginalized African farming communities in **Darfur** rebelled against the oppressive Bashir regime, which deployed militias from nomadic "Arab" communities as a cheap form of counterinsurgency that led to horrible atrocities and accusations of genocide. Promoted by American celebrities, the "Save Darfur" movement mobilized Western international outrage against Khartoum but did little to end the conflict. The war lingered into the 2010s as the rebel groups fragmented, Bashir lacked an incentive to negotiate as he was indicted for war crimes and genocide by the ICC, and African Union/UN peacekeepers were deployed but lacked the resources to stabilize the vast region. In 2019, the 30-year reign of Bashir ended as he was removed by his own military within the context

≡ **Refugee.** A Darfurian woman sorts and cleans millet at a refugee camp in Chad, 35 miles from the border with Sudan.

of prolonged civilian protests related to economic problems and demands for democracy. During the protests, women's rights activist Alaa Salah gained international prominence demanding that women have equal representation in Sudan's transitional state structures.

Uganda

Since independence from Britain in 1962, Uganda had been ruled by a series of increasingly oppressive regimes from the country's north (see Chapter 24). In 1971, Milton Obote was overthrown by a coup that brought Idi Amin to power; Amin was in turn ousted by the 1979 Tanzanian invasion and Obote returned to power in a disputed 1980 election. During the early and mid-1980s the National Resistance Army (NRA), led by Yoweri Museveni, fought an insurgency in southern Uganda against the Obote regime, which dispatched ill-disciplined northern troops who victimized southern civilians, driving them to the rebel cause. In 1986, Museveni's NRA soldiers captured Kampala and formed a government. Almost immediately, a series of rebel groups emerged in the north. During the 1990s, the Sudan government retaliated against the Museveni state's support for the SPLA in Sudan by backing rebels in northern Uganda. These insurgent groups included the West Nile Bank Front (WNBF) in the northwest and the Lord's Resistance Army (LRA) that terrorized people in Acholiland and aimed to create a Christian theocracy. These northern rebels, in addition to the western Ugandan insurgents of the Alliance of Democratic Forces (ADF), also used eastern Zaire/DRC as a sanctuary. This prompted Uganda to invade eastern Zaire/DRC in 1996–97 and 1998–2002, destroying the WNBF, though the ADF managed to survive by engaging in illegal mining. The end of the north vs. south civil war in Sudan in the mid-2000s meant that Khartoum stopped assisting rebels in northern Uganda. Although the LRA was negotiating with the Ugandan government, an ICC indictment of LRA leader Joseph Kony ended any chance of peace, with the rebels fleeing into the ungoverned space around the border of South Sudan, the DRC, and the CAR, where they continued to prey on civilians. While Museveni was initially seen as a new type of African leader in the 1990s, his regime became authoritarian and repressive, and in 2002 the constitution was changed to extend his term in office. In 2018, another constitutional change to eliminate presidential age limits provoked protests against the possibility that the 74-year-old Museveni would again run for election. In January 2021, Museveni won his sixth term in office with opposition leader and musician Bobi Wine decrying the result as fraudulent.

War and Genocide in Central Africa

Rwanda

During the Cold War era, independent Rwanda was ruled by two successive Hutu majoritarian regimes that oppressed and scapegoated the formerly privileged Tutsi minority. This caused an exodus of Tutsi people from Rwanda, and by 1990 there were around one million of them living in neighboring countries and some further afield in Europe and North America. In 1963–64, in retaliation for a failed incursion by armed Tutsi rebels from adjacent Burundi, the Hutu Power regime of Grégoire Kayibanda massacred around 20,000 Rwandan Tutsi civilians in what international observers considered a genocide. In 1973, economic problems led to a military coup that replaced the southern Hutu regime of Kayibanda with the northern Hutu regime of General Juvenal Habyarimana. While Habyarimana attempted to soften Rwanda's image on the issue of the Tutsi minority in order to acquire foreign aid, the regime continued to practice a Hutu Power ideology and refused to allow the return of exiles. In 1990, the Rwandan Patriotic Front (RPF), consisting of long-exiled Rwandan Tutsi who had helped Museveni's NRA take power in Uganda, deserted the Ugandan army with their weapons and invaded neighboring Rwanda. Habyarimana's regime was saved by a quick French military intervention that sought to maintain Rwanda as part of France's network of francophone African allies against what Paris perceived as an anglophone RPF threat. The war stalemated during the early 1990s, with the incompetent Rwandan military dependent on French assistance and the rebel RPF ensconced in the Virunga Mountains but lacking internal political support. Habyarimana's transition of Rwanda from a one-party state to multiparty democracy encouraged the RPF to participate in negotiations as the rebels needed to be included in a power-sharing agreement since they could not win elections. The new multiparty system also opened the political space for extreme anti-Tutsi parties. The 1993 Arusha Accord committed Habyarimana, the RPF, and other groups to form a shared government, and a small UN peacekeeping force arrived in Rwanda to supervise its implementation. Nonetheless, on the evening of April 6, 1994, Habyarimana was killed when his presidential jet was shot down by a missile just before it was about to land in Kigali. While some would later claim that the RPF assassinated Habyarimana to restart the war and take the country by force, it is far more likely that an extremist Hutu element within the government and army did not want to share power and that it staged a coup so it could exterminate the Tutsi minority. Within hours of Habyarimana's death, a systematic plan was put into effect that involved the killing of Tutsi in Kigali and then other towns and rural areas. Killings were carried out by Hutu army units but also by Hutu militias and gangs armed with machetes. The UN force was unprepared, and the murder of 10 Belgian peacekeepers by Hutu soldiers prompted the withdrawal of the entire Belgian contingent. Around the same time, France, Belgium, and Italy dispatched a force by air to the Kigali airport, from where it evacuated Western civilians and First Lady Agathe Habyarimana, a key figure in the Hutu Power elite, and her entourage. Over 100 days, from April to July 1994, around 800,000 mostly Tutsi people were murdered in Rwanda in the deadliest **genocide** since the Second World War and the fastest genocide in history. As soon as the genocide began, the predominantly Tutsi RPF, led by Paul Kagame, launched an offensive that pushed back the Rwandan army and eventually occupied the entire country. During June and July, French forces occupied west and southwest Rwanda in what they called Operation Turquoise, supposedly to create a safe zone for refugees but instead providing an avenue through which the retreating Hutu army and militias could continue killing and flee into eastern Zaire. The departure of French troops allowed the advancing RPF to complete its takeover, and it dominated the subsequent coalition government. Initially, Kagame became vice president and defense minister in an RPF-dominated unity government, but in 2000 the RPF gained formal control with Kagame as president. While Kagame and the RPF presided over successful reconstruction, much of this economic success was based on the looting of minerals in adjacent Zaire/DRC, and the new Tutsi-dominated state in Rwanda became authoritarian, imprisoning some critics for spreading alleged "genocide ideology" and sending assassins to kill others in neighboring countries. In 2015, in a familiar scenario, the Rwandan constitution was changed to remove presidential term limits, and in 2017 Kagame was elected for a third term with 98 percent of the vote.

Burundi

While Burundi had the same Hutu and Tutsi identities as Rwanda, its early postcolonial regimes were controlled by the Tutsi-dominated military. Fearing the creation of a Rwanda-style Hutu majoritarian state, Burundi's Tutsi military regime eliminated the potential Hutu political leadership by exterminating all educated Hutu and Hutu students in a 1972 genocide. Rwandan Tutsi exiles in Burundi added to

THE RWANDAN GENOCIDE

Top left: Hutu Power leader Juvenal Habyarima took power in Rwanda in a 1973 military coup and was killed when his presidential jet was shot down over Kigali in April 1994, signaling the start of the genocide against the Tutsi in Rwanda. *Top right:* Rwandan president Paul Kagame with US secretary of state John Kerry in 2013. From 1990 to 1994, Paul Kagame led the predominantly Tutsi rebel group Rwanda Patriotic Front (RPF). *Bottom left:* During the 1994 genocide in Rwanda, Tutsi often sought sanctuary in churches, where they were massacred by Hutu militia. *Bottom right:* A Hutu man accused of participating in the genocide appears before a Gacaca court in 2005. After the genocide, and building partly on a traditional legal system, Rwanda set up Gacaca courts at community level to accelerate the trails of the many suspected genocide perpetrators.

the extreme anti-Hutu atmosphere. The Tutsi military government banned references to the Tutsi and Hutu identities, claiming that they fostered racial hatred, and Hutu were excluded from higher education. In 1988, violence broke out in northern Burundi beginning with Hutu peasants killing around 300 Tutsi, which prompted the Tutsi army to slaughter around 20,000 Hutu and drive 50,000 into neighboring countries. The international pressure for democratization at the end of the Cold War prompted Burundi to create a unity government in 1991 under Tutsi military leader Pierre Buyoya, with 12 Hutu and 12 Tutsi ministers, though the latter retained control of the most important government offices. Further political liberalization resulted in the 1993 electoral victory of the predominantly Hutu and moderate Front for Democracy in Burundi (FRODEBU), with the party's leader, Melchior Ndadaye, becoming Burundi's first Hutu president. Later that year, Tutsi soldiers assassinated Ndadaye, inciting vengeful Hutu gangs to murder around 25,000 Tutsi civilians, which was followed by the Tutsi army killing at least the same number of Hutu. Around 700,000 Burundians fled to nearby countries, including 350,000 Hutu who entered Rwanda, increasing tensions there and contributing to the 1994 genocide. The 1993 assassination of Ndadaye and the return of Buyoya to power in a 1996 coup enflamed the situation in Burundi, with armed Hutu rebels fighting an insurgency against the Tutsi military regime. Drawn-out international negotiations eventually resulted in the Hutu rebel groups transforming into political parties and participating in a transition to democracy supervised first by the African Union and UN. In 2005, Pierre Nkurunziza, a former Hutu rebel leader whose father had been killed in 1972, was elected president of Burundi. Like post-genocide Rwanda, post–civil war Burundi experienced authoritarian drift. In 2015, Nkurunziza's attempt to seek an unconstitutional third presidential term led to a failed coup, violence, and international condemnation, and in 2018 a referendum made constitutional changes that would allow him to remain in power for many years. While Nkurunziza announced in 2018 that he would not seek another term in office, the 55-year old passed away in early 2020 just after his party gained electoral victory and amid the start of the COVID-19 pandemic.

Zaire/Democratic Republic of the Congo

During the early and mid-1990s, the Mobutu dictatorship in Zaire, previously backed by the United States as a bulwark against communism, engaged in prolonged political dialogue to delay democratic reforms. This situation was radically altered by the 1994 arrival of about half a million Hutu refugees from Rwanda, among whom were armed fighters who had perpetrated genocide in their home country. While the new RPF-led government in Rwanda claimed to be threatened by Hutu rebels hiding in the massive refugee camps that had developed in eastern Zaire, the Mobutu regime seemed unwilling or unable to contain Rwandan Hutu militias who were victimizing Zairean Tutsi known as Banyamulenge. In 1996, the armies of Rwanda and Uganda invaded eastern Zaire on the grounds that exiled rebel groups based there threatened their borders and the refugee camps needed to be forcefully dismantled. Rwanda and Uganda orchestrated the foundation of an allied Zairean rebel group called the Alliance of Democratic Forces for the Liberation of Congo (AFDL), consisting mostly of Banyamulenge Tutsi and led by long-exiled Congolese revolutionary Laurent Kabila, who had been active during the 1960s Congo Crisis. Rwandan and allied AFDL troops pursued Rwandan Hutu refugees almost 1,200 miles across Central Africa, massacring many of them near Mbandaka on the banks of the Congo River. Almost 200,000 Rwandan Hutu refugees disappeared in Zaire in 1996–97, leading UN investigators to accuse the Tutsi Rwandan military of genocide. In a massive blow to Mobutu, the Angolan army invaded Zaire to prevent UNITA rebels from using the country as a conduit for diamond exports. Although the Americans had backed Mobutu for three decades during the Cold War, they now supplied Rwanda and Uganda with intelligence and equipment to support their invasion. With unpaid and incompetent Zairean forces retreating before the invaders, Mobutu fled the country in 1997 and Kabila was installed as president of the renamed Democratic Republic of the Congo (DRC).

≡ **Laurent Kabila.** In 1997, Congolese/Zairean rebel leader Laurent Kabila, backed by troops from Rwanda, Uganda, and Angola, overthrew Mobutu Sese Seko and became president of the renamed Democratic Republic of the Congo. He was assassinated by a bodyguard in 2001.

Seeking political legitimacy within the DRC, Kabila quickly turned on his external backers, and in July 1998 he ordered the expulsion of all foreign troops including Rwandans. Within weeks, the Rwandan and Ugandan militaries again invaded eastern DRC, founding several local rebel groups such as the Rally for Congolese Democracy (RCD) backed by Kigali and the Movement for the Liberation of Congo (MLC) backed by Kampala. As in the **First Congo War** of 1996–97, Rwanda and Uganda justified their invasion by claiming to be in pursuit of expatriate rebels from their countries who were operating in the DRC. The beleaguered Kabila then called on the Southern Africa Development Community (SADC), which the DRC had recently joined, to defend his country from foreign invasion. While some SADC member states, like Botswana and South Africa, balked at protecting the unelected Kabila, military forces from Angola, Zimbabwe, and Namibia were dispatched to the DRC to defend against aggression by supposedly Western-backed neocolonial actors. Once again, Angolan intervention aimed to block UNITA diamond smuggling through the DRC. Furthermore, Kabila partnered with exiled Rwandan and Burundian Hutu rebels to combat Rwandan and Ugandan invasion. The presence of armies from so many African countries in the DRC inspired journalists to call this conflagration **Africa's World War**. It is also called the Second Congo War (1998–2002). The DRC became divided between the east occupied by Rwandan and Ugandan soldiers along with allied Congolese rebels, and the west and south controlled by Kabila's forces and their foreign partners. Although all the foreign armies in the DRC claimed to be pursuing their own security issues, they all became involved in pillaging the country's valuable mineral resources. Among these minerals was coltan, which was important in the burgeoning global electronics industry.

Eventually, military involvement in the DRC became diplomatically embarrassing for the foreign powers—and costly, as mineral smuggling was profitable for individual officers and politicians but not for government treasuries. US policy toward the conflict also changed as the Clinton administration, ridden by guilt for failure to act against the 1994 genocide in Rwanda, supported Rwanda and Uganda, but from 2001 the new Bush administration became critical of those countries' aggression in the DRC. At the start of 2001, Laurent Kabila was assassinated by his bodyguards, and his son, Joseph Kabila, took over and was much more cooperative in negotiations. In 2002, a series of talks led to the withdrawal of foreign state forces and the establishment of a Congolese unity government led by the young Kabila. However, foreign rebels such as the Rwandan Hutu of the Democratic Forces for the Liberation of Rwanda (FDLR) and the Uganda ADF in eastern DRC were not included in the agreements and were designated as "negative forces." A UN force and a reconstituted DRC military attempted to eliminate these groups and establish state control in the east, but this proved difficult because of the area's vast size and the lack of infrastructure. Into the 2010s and early 2020s, violence continued in eastern and northeastern DRC between UN and DRC state forces, and various Congolese militias and foreign rebel groups, most of which were involved in illegal mining and smuggling of minerals. In this context, the region became notorious as the scene of widespread sexual violence against women.

Central African Republic

For 30 years after its 1960 independence from France, the Central African Republic (CAR) was controlled by autocratic leaders from the country's predominantly Christian southern region, with the north, home to Muslim communities, remaining marginalized. France was heavily involved in these regimes. In 1979, French troops deposed the violent dictatorship of Jean Bédel Bokassa, and during the 1980s and early 1990s the military government of General André Kolingba allowed France to use the CAR as a base for interventions across Africa. In 1993, as a result of democratic reforms that France had pressured the CAR to enact, Ange-Félix Patassé was elected as the country's first president from the north. The CAR army became divided into ethnic factions as Kolingba had recruited soldiers from his own small southern Yakoma ethnic group who Patasse superseded with members of his northern Sara-Kaba community. This resulted in a series of army mutinies in the late 1990s that were suppressed by French forces, and UN peacekeepers were briefly deployed.

The 1998–2002 war in the DRC greatly influenced events in the adjacent CAR. During 2002 and 2003, General François Bozize, backed by the DRC's Kabila regime and Chad, staged a rebellion and seized power from Patasse, who was supported by DRC rebel leader Jean Pierre Bemba and Libya's Gaddafi. With the 2005 electoral victory of Bozize, who was from the south, an uprising broke out in the north, but French intervention prompted the insurgents to sign a peace agreement. In 2012, another northern rebellion began as a result of Bozize's election for a second presidential term and his failure to implement the previous peace deal. Calling themselves Seleka (union), a coalition of northern rebels took over major towns and drove Bozize out of the country. As rebel leader Michel Djotodia declared himself the CAR's first Muslim president, Christian militias called "anti-balaka" (a reference to a magical protection charm) formed in the south and began fighting the rebels and massacring Muslim civilians. International warnings that the CAR was on the verge of genocide produced a UN peacekeeping force, comprised mostly of African countries and France. While the 2014 resignation of Djotodia enabled the election of a government, much of the country remained divided between hostile armed factions separated by UN troops. Bozize returned to CAR in 2019 intending to run for president in upcoming elections but he was blocked by the country's constitutional court that cited his previous bad behavior in office.

Islamist Movements and the "Arab Spring" in North Africa and the Sahara

Civil War in Algeria

Having fought for independence from France, a goal that was achieved in 1962, Algeria's National Liberation Front (FLN) became an authoritarian regime dominated by its military. Political analysts observed that postcolonial Algeria "was not a state with an army, but an army with a state." During the 1970s and 1980s, Algeria used oil revenues to buy massive quantities of weapons from the Soviet Union, Soviet technicians and advisors worked in Algeria, and thousands of Algerians trained and studied in the Soviet Union. During this time, the Algerian government's primary security concern was potential conventional warfare with Morocco, since Algeria backed rebels in Moroccan-occupied Western Sahara. In the late 1980s, popular protests in Algeria were sparked by an economic crisis caused by the decline of oil prices; this happened as Soviet support for the FLN state declined. The regime of President Chadli Bendjedid embarked on democratic reforms, downgraded the rule of the military in government, and created a new constitution. However, the electoral success of the Islamic Salvation Front (FIS) prompted a 1992 military coup that removed Bendjedid, installed a puppet civilian government, and declared a state of emergency. With the FIS banned, the Islamist movement split into two groups, the rural-based and moderate Islamic Salvation Army (AIS) and the urban-based and radical Armed Islamic Group (GIA), which both launched an insurgency against the state and fought each other. These Islamist rebels were bolstered by the return of Algerians who had fought against the Soviet occupation of Afghanistan during the 1980s. In turn, the Algerian military bought weapons from former Soviet republics and France, and greatly expanded its paramilitary forces. During 1997 and 1998, the radical GIA massacred civilians, proclaiming that anyone not fighting the government was an apostate. Revulsion over the killings led to the AIS negotiating amnesty and peace with the Algerian state. Coming to power through a controversial election in 1999, President Abdelaziz Bouteflika presided over a peace process that granted amnesty to insurgents who had not committed murder or rape, and many fighters returned to civilian life. The decade-long **Algerian Civil War** (1992–2002) claimed the lives of at least 44,000 people. From 2001, in the context of the War on Terror, the United States provided military support to Algeria, enabling it to hunt down remaining Islamist insurgents. The fraught GIA dissolved, with a surviving faction called the Salafist Group for Preaching and Combat (GSPC) fleeing south into the Saharan areas of Mauritania, Mali, Niger, and Chad, where it took up kidnapping of foreigners and smuggling. In 2007, attempting to associate itself with global jihad, GSPC changed its name to Al-Qaeda in the Islamic Maghreb (AQIM) as the United States expanded security cooperation with Algeria and its southern neighbors. In 2019, widespread pro-democracy protests pressured Bouteflika to resign.

Mali and Niger

In postcolonial Mali and Niger, both former French colonies, the Tuareg nomads of the northern Sahara region resented control by southern-based governments and some dreamed of creating a Tuareg state called Azawad. During the early 1960s, Tuaregs in Mali rebelled against the government, but their meager arms were no match for the Soviet-equipped Malian army. By the end of the 1980s, many Malian and Nigerien Tuaregs who had escaped drought by moving north to work in Libya began to return home as the Libyan oil industry was downsizing, and some of them had gained combat experience and become radicalized during their tours in Gaddafi's military adventures in the Middle East and Afghanistan. As a result, in 1990,

Tuareg rebellions supported by the Gaddafi regime began in the northern regions of Mali and Niger. In northern Mali, the state, as part of its counterinsurgency program, armed non-Tuareg militias that attacked Tuareg communities. By 1995, both insurgencies had ended as a result of separate negotiated agreements in which the Malian and Nigerien governments promised to absorb Tuareg rebels into their armies and grant partial autonomy to parts of the north. Delays in implementing these settlements led to renewed Tuareg rebellions in Mali and Niger from 2006 to 2009, when a new set of peace deals were made. In Niger this was facilitated by the expansion of uranium mining, which gave new resources to the state. The 2011 fall of Gaddafi in Libya caused more Tuareg former members of the Libyan military to return home to Mali with their weapons, and this led to yet another rebellion. At the start of 2012, Tuareg separatists seeking to establish the new state of Azawad, along with both Tuareg and international Islamist fighters from an AQIM faction, took control of towns in northern Mali. Islamic **Shari'a law** was imposed, and historic tombs and libraries that were deemed heretical were destroyed. With the

Malian army in retreat and the Mali government toppled by a military coup, the rebels advanced toward the capital of Bamako. In January 2013, France launched Operation Serval in which French ground and air forces arrived, drove the rebels back north, and liberated northern towns. Because of the fragile condition of the Malian state, the French continued their military presence under the title of Operation Barkhane and were joined by a multinational UN force. While the secular Tuareg separatists stepped back from the conflict, the French, UN, and revamped Malian forces pursued a counterinsurgency war against Islamist rebels. By 2019, almost 180 UN peacekeepers had been killed in Mali, making it the most dangerous ongoing UN mission.

North Africa

Compared to other regions of the continent, democratization started late in North Africa and had mixed results. In 2010, as a result of economic problems and the rapid communication of social media, a series of popular protests against authoritarian governments began in the Middle East and North Africa, and became known as the **Arab Spring**. This movement started in Tunisia, where the military regime of Zine al-Abidine Ben Ali,

≡ **Shaky peace.** Malian troops join former rebels during a joint patrol in the northern Malian city of Gao in February 2017.

who had taken power in a 1987 coup, crushed the Islamist movement during the 1990s and became a reliable American ally in the War on Terror during the first decade of the 2000s. In early 2011, the Tunisian military commander refused orders for his troops to fire on protestors and Ben Ali subsequently fled the country, allowing a transition to democracy. The same year, mass protests in Egypt led to the collapse of the long-standing military regime of Hosni Mubarak and the installation of Islamist Mohammed Morsi as the country's first elected president. However, disagreements between Islamists and secularists in the government created chaos and informed a 2013 military coup in which Minister of Defence Field Marshal Abdel Fattah el-Sisi took over and imprisoned Morsi who later passed away in 2019. The new military regime violently suppressed Islamist protestors and orchestrated the transformation of Sisi into a civilian but authoritarian president. In Libya, the Gaddafi regime improved its relations with the West after the Cold War, gave up attempts to develop weapons of mass destruction, and cooperated with American anti-terrorist operations after 2001. Nevertheless, a popular rebellion against Gaddafi began in 2011, and it was supported by airstrikes from the North Atlantic Treaty Organization (NATO). With the capture and killing of Gaddafi by rebels in October 2011, Libya became divided between areas controlled by various armed militias. By 2019, conflict had developed between the eastern-based warlord regime of Khalifa Haftar, a military commander under Gaddafi who was supported by Egypt, Saudi Arabia and Russia, and a UN and Turkish-backed administration in the west around Tripoli. In 2020, after an offensive by Haftar's eastern forces failed to capture Tripoli, the factions agreed upon an internationally negotiated ceasefire.

Conclusion

After 1990, many African countries experienced profound political and economic change. The end of the Cold War caused the collapse of long-established authoritarian regimes and the rise of multiparty democracy in many African countries. Of course, authoritarianism did not entirely disappear, with some regimes surviving such as in Zimbabwe, some being re-established as in Egypt, and constitutions being modified to extend presidential terms as in Uganda and Rwanda. In general, socialism was abandoned and replaced with neoliberal economic polices that privatized economies and devalued currencies to promote Africa's historic export of raw materials. Although there were new political freedoms in many countries, ordinary people struggled with rising prices and increasing unemployment as African society became even more polarized between the few rich and the many poor. In some areas the post–Cold War political transition was extremely troubled, with

Timeline

1983–2005—Second Sudanese Civil War

1987–2006—Insurgency in northern Uganda

1989–1997—First Liberian Civil War

1990–95—Tuareg rebellions in northern Mali and Niger

1991—Fall of the Soviet Union

1991—Multiparty election in Zambia

1991—Fall of the Barre regime in Somalia and Mengistu regime in Ethiopia

1991—Independence of Eritrea

1991—Declaration of independence by Somaliland

1991–2002—Sierra Leone Civil War

1992—Multiparty election in Kenya

1992–2002—Algerian Civil War

1992—UNITA loses election in Angola and continues civil war

1992–93—Operation Restore Hope in Somalia

1993—General Sani Abacha takes power in Nigeria

1993–2005—Civil war in Burundi

1994—Genocide against the Tutsi in Rwanda

1994—Multiparty elections in Malawi and Mozambique

1994—First democratic elections in South Africa

1994–95—US and UN withdraw from Somalia

1996–97—First Congo War

1998–2002—Second Congo War (Africa's World War)

1999—End of military rule in Nigeria

1999–2003—Second Liberian Civil War

2001—Terrorist attacks on the United States— Start of US-led "War on Terror"

2002—End of Angolan Civil War

2002–2011—Côte d'Ivoire Civil War

2003—Start of insurgency in Darfur, Sudan

2004–2007—Civil war in the Central African Republic

2006—Ethiopian invasion of Somalia

2006–2009—Tuareg Rebellions in Mali and Niger

2007—African Union troops (AMISOM) arrive in Somalia

2009—Start of Al Shabaab insurgency in Somalia

2009—Start of Boko Haram insurgency in northeast Nigeria

2010—Protests in Tunisia begin the "Arab Spring"

2011—Independence of South Sudan

2011—Fall of Gaddafi regime in Libya

2011—Fall of Mubarak regime in Egypt

2012+—Civil war in Central African Republic

2012—Rebellion in northern Mali; French intervention

2013—Start of civil war in South Sudan

2013—Military coup in Egypt

2017—Military coup in Zimbabwe

2019—Protests lead to the fall of the Bashir regime in Sudan and the Bouteflika regime in Algeria numerous civil wars waged in parts of the continent during the 1990s and 2000s. Post–Cold War Africa became the scene of failed states, the world's worst genocide since the end of the Second World War, and a conflict that involved half a dozen African countries fighting over the resources of the Congo. After years of maintaining the international borders inherited from colonial rulers, postcolonial Africa experienced its first two successful secessions, resulting in the creation of Eritrea in 1991 and South Sudan in 2011. Slightly reminiscent of the Cold War, the global struggle between Western powers and international jihadists was superimposed on Africa from the 2000s and exacerbated violence in places like Somalia and Mali. Whereas Southern Africa witnessed many Cold War era conflicts, the Sahel and Horn of Africa regions experienced an upsurge of insurgency from around the 2010s onward. That said, some African countries became or already were stable democracies, such as Ghana, Senegal, and Botswana.

KEY TERMS

Africa's World War or Second Congo War (1998–2002) 596

African Union 576

Al Shabaab 588

Algerian Civil War (1992–2002) 598

Ambazonia 583

Arab Spring 599

Boko Haram 583

Darfur 590

Ellen Johnson Sirleaf 582

Eritrea 586

failed state 588

First Congo War (1996–97) 595

First Liberian Civil War (1989–97) 580

genocide 592

neoliberal 575

resource curse 580

Second Liberian Civil War (1999–2003) 581

Shari'a law 599

Sierra Leone Civil War (1991–2002) 581

structural adjustment 575

War on Terror 576

Women of Liberia Mass Action for Peace 582

STUDY QUESTIONS

1. What factors have strengthened the movement toward democratization in Africa? What obstacles have hindered Nigeria's, Zimbabwe's, Mozambique's, and Angola's transition to democracy?

2. What is the relationship between an African country's exploitable natural resources, instability, xenophobia, and jihad?

3. What led to some African countries being described as "failed states" during the 1990s and 2000s?

4. Why did genocide take place in post-colonial Rwanda and Burundi? What was the impact of genocide on those countries?

5. Why is the Second Congo War (1998-2202) known as "Africa's World War"? Why did so many countries become involved in the conflict?

6. How did the US-led War on Terror effect Africa?

7. What was the "Arab Spring"? What were its goals, and have they been achieved?

Please see page FR-13 for the Further Readings for this chapter.
For additional digital learning resources please go to
https://www.oup.com/he/falola-stapleton1e

Independent Africa after the Cold War: Health, Environment, and Culture

In the late twentieth and early twenty-first centuries, the acceleration of **globalization**, a multifaceted process involving communications and transport technology among other factors, meant more interaction between Africa and the rest of the world. While the political and economic implications of this phenomenon for Africa were discussed in Chapter 26, globalization also influenced issues related to health, environment, and culture. From the 1980s, sub-Saharan Africa became the center of the HIV/AIDS pandemic, and Africa was, by far, the worst affected continent. In the mid-2010s, the outbreak of Ebola in West Africa incited worldwide panic and from 2020, Africa experienced the COVID-19 pandemic. As growing Chinese and other foreign demand for animal products like rhino horn and elephant ivory led to the decline of these animals in the African wilderness, Western conservationists demanded a total ban on the hunting of Africa's endangered species while some African governments responded that these animals represented exploitable national resources. More broadly, climate change caused by industrial production in North America, Europe, and Asia began to take an enormous toll on non-industrialized Africa, causing devastating droughts and floods as well as human conflict. During the 1990s and 2000s, lesbian, gay, bisexual, transgender, and queer (LGBTQ+) rights campaigns in Africa drew inspiration from similar movements in North America and Western Europe, and the subsequent backlash by conservative African politicians and religious leaders received support from like-minded Western churches. Around the same time, the global women's rights movement became successful in efforts to have African states ban female genital modification (FGM) or female genital cutting (FGC), but some African women saw this as an attack on their culture—as adults, they resented

Desertification. The desert encroaches on a village in the Sahel region of Mali in 2008.

the loss of freedom of choice. Although African film production began in the colonial era, the advent of home video technology led to the stunning domestic and international success of Nigerian Nollywood movies in the 1990s and 2000s. American hip-hop music and culture arrived in Africa in the 1980s, and within a few years African versions had developed, contributing to the growth of a successful hip-hop scene across the continent.

Health Crises

Health crises are not new to African history. While African people long contended with tropical diseases like malaria, these ailments kept European colonialists out of much of Africa for many years. Eventually, colonialism introduced new diseases to Africa, such as smallpox, transmitted to the Cape's Khoisan people by the Dutch in the late 1600s and 1700s, cattle diseases like lungsickness and rinderpest that undermined East African pastoralists during the late nineteenth century, and tuberculosis in Southern Africa's mine compounds of the twentieth century. Like the bubonic plague that hit Egypt and Nubia in the 1300s (see chapter 3), Africa experienced a series of epidemics and pandemics facilitated by globalization during the twentieth and early twenty-first centuries.

Influenza

At the end of the First World War (1914-18), Africa experienced the **influenza pandemic** that emanated from ports like Freetown, Cape Town, and Mombasa, where returning soldiers landed. During a six-month period in 1918 and 1919, the pandemic killed around 2 percent of Africa's population, amounting to some 2.4 million people and giving Africa the highest average mortality rate of any continent. Most of these deaths occurred in sub-Saharan Africa, in countries with high levels of migrant labor. South Africa, Nyasaland (Malawi), Tanganyika (Tanzania), Kenya, Cameroon, the Gold Coast (Ghana), and the Gambia lost more than 5 percent of their populations. While the initial wave of the pandemic hit North Africa, providing survivors with some immunity, this did not happen in sub-Saharan Africa, making the second wave much deadlier in that zone. At the time, Western biomedicine lacked a cure or vaccine, and traditional African treatments proved useless. As most victims were between 18 and 40 years old, the influenza pandemic resulted in an economic and social catastrophe in Africa, including agricultural disruption and famine.

HIV/AIDS

From the late 1980s to the 2010s, Africa was ravaged by another pandemic: the human immunodeficiency virus/acquired immune deficiency syndrome (**HIV/AIDS**). While people who initially contracted HIV would not usually experience symptoms, the condition sometimes resulted in AIDS, which compromised the body's immune system making it vulnerable to various types of infections that caused death. Historically, it appears the disease began as simian immunodeficiency virus (SIV) in primates such as monkeys and chimpanzees. During the early twentieth century, probably somewhere in southeast Cameroon, SIV jumped from primates to humans, becoming HIV and causing AIDS. This initial transmission likely took place when human hunters were exposed to the blood of infected animals. The subsequent spread of HIV/AIDS across Africa took a few decades, facilitated by factors including Central Africa's interconnected river system, the displacement of people by colonial conquest and forced labor, coercive colonial vaccination programs that reused unsterilized syringes, the dramatic growth of African cities, and the construction of road and rail transportation systems. The development of passenger air transport in the late twentieth century meant that HIV/AIDS moved out of Africa, and at the start of the 1980s it was clinically identified in North America and Europe. It was at this point that the term "HIV/AIDS" was coined. Whereas HIV/AIDS in the Western world was thought to spread primarily through homosexual sex and intravenous drug use, in Africa the virus passed mostly through heterosexual sex and mother-to-child transmission during pregnancy, birth, or breastfeeding. The process was enabled by some aspects of African culture such as polygamy, men's tendency to have multiple sexual partners and to refuse to use condoms, hesitancy to talk about the cause of death, and in some places the expectation that widows would marry their late husband's brother. Other important factors included lack of education, lack of women's rights, poor healthcare facilities, and the fear and stigma associated with the virus that discouraged people from being tested. By 2010, some two thirds of the world's 35 million people infected with HIV lived in Africa and around 15 million of them had died. In 2011, some 70 percent of all AIDS-related deaths in the world occurred in Africa. Perhaps because of its extensive migrant labor network and developed transport infrastructure, Southern Africa was particularly hard-hit by the disease. In most Southern African countries, by 2011 at least 10 percent of the total population was HIV positive; in South Africa the figure was 17 percent, and in Botswana, Lesotho, and Swaziland the number was around 25 percent, making these the worst affected states in the world. The East African countries of Kenya, Uganda, and Tanzania were also badly impacted. Significantly lower infection rates occurred in countries in the Horn of Africa, North Africa, and West Africa, where Muslim communities held more conservative attitudes toward sex. During the 1990s and 2000s, the impact of the HIV/AIDS pandemic on sub-Saharan Africa hollowed out society as adults in their thirties and forties were most likely to die, and average life expectancy in some African countries dropped to round 45 years old. Families were deprived of primary breadwinners, children were orphaned, and older grandparents had to take on more responsibilities with fewer resources. On a broader level, the HIV/AIDS pandemic worsened poverty and hindered economic development in many parts of Africa.

South Africa became the scene of important political struggles over the HIV/AIDS pandemic. During the 1980s and early 1990s, the white minority apartheid state ignored the emerging HIV/AIDS crisis, associating it with Black South Africans and foreign Black migrant workers. At the end of the 1990s and beginning of the 2000s, in the post-apartheid era, the South African ANC government of President Thabo Mbeki accepted controversial and inaccurate theories that denied that HIV caused AIDS, claiming that deaths attributed to AIDS had been caused by poverty. South African health minister Dr. Manto Tshabalala-Msimang infamously and wrongly claimed that HIV/AIDS could be successfully treated with natural remedies such as beetroot and garlic. This "AIDS denial" policy likely contributed to the unnecessary deaths of around 300,000 South Africans. Formed in South Africa in 1998, the **Treatment Action Campaign (TAC)** employed legal action and public protest reminiscent of the anti-apartheid struggle to compel the ANC government to provide effective anti-AIDS medical treatment through the state health system and to force the pharmaceutical industry to produce cheaper versions of anti-AIDS drugs. The first major legal victory of TAC happened in late 2001 when a South African court ordered the government to provide drugs and treatments to reduce mother-to-child transition of HIV. In 2003, the South African cabinet overruled President Mbeki by declaring that "HIV causes AIDS" and the state launched a plan to use public clinics to distribute newly developed antiretroviral drugs that extend the life of people with HIV and reduce the risk of transmission. Over the next few years, TAC continued its activism, pressuring the government to speed up and expand the delivery of the drugs.

The first organized programs to counter HIV/AIDS in Africa involved trying to change people's sexual behavior. During the 1990s, some African governments, NGOs working in Africa, churches, and international donors began to promote a sex education program known as "Abstinence; Be Faithful; Use a Condom" or **ABC**. There was some criticism that conservative politicians and religious leaders in Africa and the West emphasized the A and the B, which prioritized reducing a person's number of sexual partners over prevention through condom use. Nevertheless, the ABC program achieved some success, particularly in Uganda,

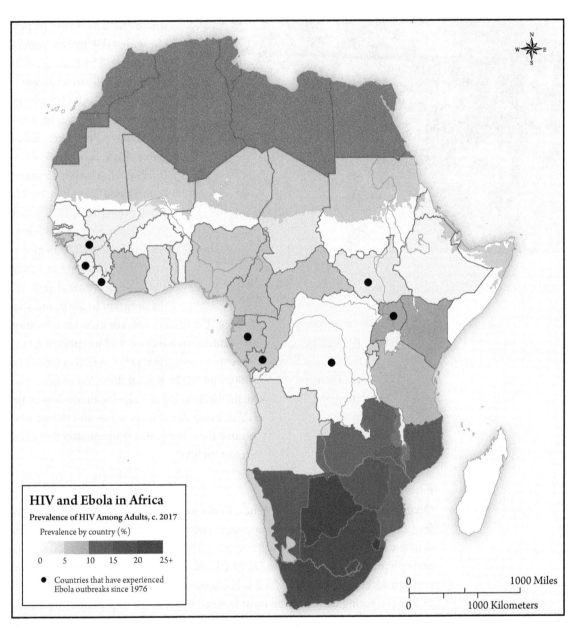

HIV and Ebola in Africa

Prevalence of HIV Among Adults, c. 2017

Prevalence by country (%)

0   5   10   15   20   25+

● Countries that have experienced
  Ebola outbreaks since 1976

0   1000 Miles

0   1000 Kilometers

≡ **MAP 27.1**

≡ **TAC.** Activists from the Treatment Action Campaign in South Africa rally during a protest march to parliament in Cape Town, South Africa, August 2007.

where the percentage of people with HIV in the population dropped from a high of 15 percent in 1991 to 5 percent in 2001. In 2003, the US administration of George W. Bush initiated the President's Emergency Plan for AIDS Relief (PEPFAR), which dramatically increased spending on the crisis, providing US$15 billion to 15 poor countries with high rates of HIV/AIDS. Twelve of these countries were in Africa. The US government renewed the program in 2008 and widened its scope to include more countries. The funds were/are used for education through the ABC strategy, provision of antiretroviral drugs and treatments for opportunistic infections, and care of patients suffering from HIV/AIDS as well as orphaned children. During the late 2000s and 2010s, the combination of education programs and more readily available medication led to a significant decline in the number of people infected with HIV in many African countries and the number of HIV/AIDS related deaths. At the same time, the rate of transmission decreased and average life expectancy also began to increase.

Ebola

Occurring in parts of equatorial Africa, **Ebola** has generated enormous international fear, though it has killed far fewer people than HIV/AIDS. Ebola is a viral hemorrhagic fever contracted through contact with bodily fluids from an infected animal or human. It causes fever and internal and external bleeding, and often results in death within a few days or weeks. Ebola outbreaks have often been traced back to a hunter eating undercooked meat from an infected bat or primate. The disease was first identified during a 1976 outbreak in rural northern Zaire (now DRC), near the Ebola River, which caused 280 deaths and was relatively quickly contained by a quarantine imposed by the Mobutu regime. In this particular case, the spread of Ebola was expedited by a clinic that reused unsterilized syringes. Later the same year, around 150 people died in a similar outbreak in southern Sudan. There were no other significant Ebola outbreaks for another 20 years. In 1995, Ebola caused the deaths of 315 people in the city of Kikwit in western Zaire, and between late 1994 and 1997 there were three less deadly occurrences in Gabon. Serious outbreaks became more frequent during the 2000s and 2010s. These included a 2000–2001 outbreak that killed 224 people in northern Uganda, a 2002–03 occurrence in western Republic of Congo that claimed the lives of 128, and a 2007 incident in western DRC that resulted in 187 deaths. There were also minor outbreaks in Gabon, western Uganda, and northern and western DRC. From December 2013 to June 2016, the most deadly and widespread Ebola epidemic occurred in West Africa, where the disease was previously unknown. It began in southern Guinea and quickly spread across the nearby tri-border area to Liberia and Sierra Leone, where there had been terrible civil wars in the 1990s and 2000s. Ebola claimed the lives of 11,310 people in West Africa. Healthcare workers were particularly vulnerable, representing 10 percent of the dead. In August 2014, the World Health Organization (WHO) declared an international public health emergency, and the next month it announced that the Ebola outbreak was the most acute public health emergency in modern history. At the same time, the UN declared that the crisis represented a threat to international peace and security. Although the poor healthcare systems of these West African states could not cope with the crisis, international medical workers arrived, and detailed tracing of anyone who had contact with an infected person, community education, and quarantines and travel restrictions eliminated the outbreak. Given international travel, there were related but small occurrences of Ebola in Nigeria, Mali, and the United States, as well as singular cases of infection in Italy, the United Kingdom, and Spain.

Besides the loss of life, Guinea, Liberia, and Sierra Leone experienced serious economic and social setbacks related to the Ebola outbreak; in Liberia and Sierra Leone it also hindered postwar reconstruction. The West African Ebola crisis also encouraged more international research into medical treatments and experimental vaccines. In August 2018, another Ebola outbreak began in northeastern DRC, an area where there is ongoing conflict between a weak state supported by a UN force and numerous

≡ **Ebola.** A health worker in Liberia, covered head to foot in protective gear, sprays people being discharged from an Ebola treatment center in Monrovia, Liberia, during the 2014 Ebola outbreak.

rebel groups engaged in illegal mining. Given this situation, it proved extremely difficult for local and international health workers to counter the epidemic that claimed around 800 lives in less than a year.

COVID-19

African countries face the unfolding Coronavirus or **COVID-19** pandemic representing the worst global health emergency in a century. Originating in China at the end of 2019, the virus spread to the rest of the world causing millions of deaths. States have imposed strict isolation measures to slow the spread of the virus, reducing stress on healthcare systems but causing dire economic problems. Given the poverty prevalent in most African countries, social isolation and lockdowns have proven very difficult or impossible to implement, as most people simply cannot work from home and weak healthcare systems cannot cope with large numbers of COVID-19 patients. In addition, African states lack the financial resources to copy the massive economic emergency packages rolled out in Europe and North America. As in other parts of the world, pandemic lockdown measures combined with other problems related to poverty and sometimes state oppression incited protests across parts of Africa. In some parts of the continent, at the start of the pandemic, recent experience with other public heath crises such as HIV/AIDS and Ebola proved useful in Africa's response to COVID-19, such as the use of local contact tracing. Reminiscent of the influenza pandemic of 1918-19, much of African seemed to escape the full brunt of the initial waves of the COVID-19 pandemic. Since elderly people were particularly vulnerable to COVID-19, some experts speculated that Africa's relatively young overall population partly explained this phenomenon. However, new variants of COVID-19 emerged making the later stages of the pandemic extremely deadly for much of Africa. The pandemic illustrates the impact of global inequity. While wealthy countries in North America and Europe purchased many millions of doses of rapidly developed vaccines and vaccinated large percentages of their populations, Africa lacked these resources and vaccination there proceeded frustratingly slowly. As the pandemic continues, international programs such as COVID-19 Global Access (Covax) attempt to provide vaccines to poor parts of the world including Africa and governments debate whether or not to lift intellectual property rules to allow the manufacture of vaccines in poor countries.

The Environment

When African countries became independent, many inherited a network of massive, state-controlled game reserves and national parks that had been created in the colonial period. These parks, many founded in the 1950s, had been cleared of indigenous people and were patrolled by armed, paramilitary gamekeepers. In Eastern and Southern Africa, game parks and reserves had become centers for a profitable safari tourism industry catering mostly to wealthy people from North America and Western Europe who wanted to see and take photographs of large African animals like elephants, rhinos, buffalo, and lions. A sub-sector of this tourism industry involved legal sport hunting in which wealthy Western hunters payed large sums to shoot rare animals and bring home part or the entire animal as a trophy. Even before independence, Africa's parks and reserves were targeted by poachers, who illegally hunted animals and harvested animal products like ivory elephant tusks and rhino horn, which were smuggled through criminal networks and sold in other parts of the world such as Europe, the Middle East, and Asia. As poaching increased steadily after independence with the connivance of corrupt government officials, the numbers of rare animals like elephants, rhino, and mountain gorillas decreased dramatically in some places and they became listed as endangered species. From the 1990s, the economic rise of China contributed to a further increase in poaching in Africa, as it created a larger market for African animal products, some of which, like rhino horn, are used in traditional Chinese medicine, and newly affluent Chinese wanted decorative carved ivory. Many East and Southern African countries responded to greater poaching by adopting military-style anti-poaching campaigns and deploying armed forces to national parks.

Launched in 1975, the **Convention on International Trade in Endangered Species of Wild Flora and Fauna (CITES)** attempted to limit the sale of certain species of animals and plants to ensure that they did not disappear from the natural environment. Almost all African countries entered this international agreement, and CITES placed restrictions on the trade in endangered species from Africa. During the 1990s and 2000s, CITES meetings witnessed angry disagreements over approaches to conservation of endangered species, particularly elephants. The number of elephants in Africa dropped from around 1.3 million in the 1940s to around

≡ **Illegal trade.** A huge pile of poached elephant ivory seized by the government burns in Nairobi, Kenya, in 2019.

600,000 in 1989. An international elephant-poaching and ivory-smuggling network developed. At the center of it was Burundi, which, from the 1965 to 1986, exported 1,300 tons of ivory, amounting to around 13,000 animals, but the country had no wild elephants. While poaching was largely to blame for the decline of elephants, there were other contributing factors, such as the reduction of their habitat, with national parks and game reserves becoming overpopulated. On the fringes of these areas, elephants clashed with a growing human population. This led to some African states culling elephants, which created large state-owned stockpiles of ivory. To counter elephant poaching, Western governments and Western-based conservative organizations demanded a complete ban on the hunting of elephants, an end to the legal sale of ivory, and the destruction of state-owned ivory stockpiles. Kenya, with its large parks and safari tourism industry, became the main proponent of this policy among African countries. Conversely, some Southern African countries, particularly Zimbabwe, Namibia, and South Africa, objected to what they saw as Western interference in sovereign African states and claimed that wildlife, including endangered species like elephants, represented a national resource that could be used to benefit their citizens, and revenues from ivory sales could support conservation. Favoring regulated elephant hunting and ivory trade, these governments maintained that a complete ban would serve to increase prices for illegal ivory by reducing the amount available, and would therefore encourage more poaching. In the late 1980s, the Zimbabwe government of Robert Mugabe introduced the **Communal Areas Management Program for Indigenous Resources (CAMPFIRE)** in which rural communities, some of which were plagued by elephants that destroyed crops and killed people, sold hunting licenses to international sport hunters to shoot elephants. Supported by funding from the US government, CAMPFIRE earned rural Zimbabweans about US$20 million between 1989 and 2001, with this money being used to build schools, clinics, and agricultural infrastructure like mills and boreholes. However, a complete ban on ivory imports adopted by the US and other countries in 2014 and the rise of an anti-hunting animal rights movement in North America and Western Europe, as well as economic and political crises in Zimbabwe, undermined CAMPFIRE and prompted a revival of poaching in Zimbabwe. In 2018, China, previously the destination for about 70 percent of ivory exports, succumbed to international pressure, imposed a complete ban on ivory sales, and launched a public awareness campaign about elephant conservation.

Climate Change

Africa's historically limited industrial production means that it produces very little of the carbon emissions that accelerate global climate change. Nevertheless, by the start of the twenty-first century, climate change was having a significant impact on

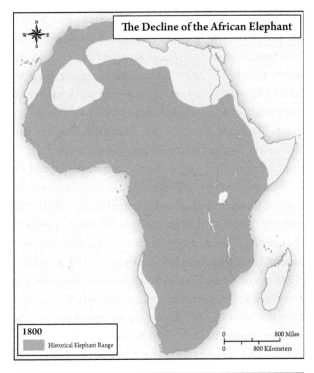

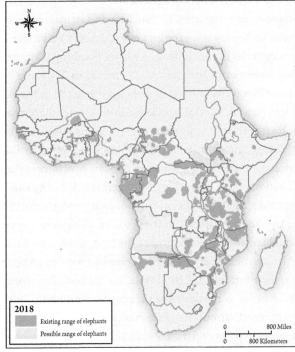

≡ **MAP 27.2**

Africa and Africans. Overall, the continent began to experience a combination of more frequent and prolonged droughts, and increased catastrophic flooding. The main impact of this trend has been to hinder food production, leading to hunger, starvation, migration, and conflict. West Africa's Sahel region, where the temperature has increased 1.5 times the global average in recent years, has been dramatically affected by **desertification** and drought caused by climate change, with millions of people in countries like Mali, Niger, Chad, and Burkina Faso experiencing food insecurity. The decreasing amount of usable land has contributed to violence between semi-nomadic herder and settled cultivator communities, and this has been further aggravated by a proliferation of weapons, the region's porous borders, and the spreading of armed jihadist, militia, and criminal groups. By the start of 2019, herder–farmer violence related to climate change in Central Nigeria had claimed more lives than the country's Boko Haram jihadist insurgency in the northeast. The shrinking of Lake Chad, which reduced in size by around 95 percent between the 1960s and late 1990s as a result of climate change and unsustainable human usage, also contributed to the Boko Haram conflict in northeastern Nigeria, Cameroon, Niger and Chad. On the other side of Africa, climate change has been linked to increasing and devastating floods. In early 2000, heavy rains and a cyclone caused the worst flooding in Mozambique in half a century, killing 700 people, leaving many tens of thousands homeless, disrupting agriculture, destroying schools and hospitals, spreading illnesses like malaria and diarrhea, and damaging reconstruction efforts that had been underway since the end of the country's civil war in the early 1990s. Subsequent cyclones caused more destructive flooding in Mozambique and in the neighboring countries of Malawi and Zimbabwe in 2007 and 2019. In addition, across the continent rising temperatures have resulted in the expansion of malaria from Africa's coastal, riverine, and lowland areas into interior highlands.

What is more, by this time, it appeared that natural resources such as gold, diamonds, copper, coltan, and petroleum—all of which are found in abundance in Africa—were more of a curse than a blessing. African governments' approach to the issue of exploitation of natural resources in their states during this period was in no way different from their attitude toward poaching and general environmental conservation. Unlike in Western countries where oil exploration conforms to strict environmental laws that seek to protect the land, water, and air, if such laws exist in oil-rich African states, they are hardly complied with by companies due to weak institutional monitoring aided by chronic corruption. The characterization of many African countries as **rentier states** is based largely on this phenomenon. Expectedly, this has raised various dissenting voices against the practices of multinational oil companies in parts of Africa. But in lieu of gaining their governments'

support, many of these voices have been snuffed out by states seeking oil revenue. The result of this is the continued environmental degradation of oil-rich territories. With environmental degradation comes loss of livelihood from fishing and farming, and deterioration of health including decreased lifespans. A reverberating instance in this macabre phenomenon is the plight of the oil-producing Niger-Delta states in Nigeria and the murder of environmental activists from the Ogoni community, including author **Ken Saro-Wiwa** by the military regime of Sani Abacha in 1995. Although the Abacha regime soon collapsed due to international sanctions and internal protest, this condemnation did not result in any changes to the environmental condition of this area. Even today, environmental degradation and the pathetic state of the people living upon these resources have been at the core of the emergence of militias and unrest in this area, as demands have morphed from peaceful protest followed by the likes of Saro-Wiwa, to violent resistance led by several warlords in the oil-rich regions of the state. In the same manner, flooding, landslides, banditry, and other negative developments have become frequent in gold, diamond, and other mining areas in Africa.

≡ **Climate change and environmental destruction.** *Left:* A man helps his wife across a flooded river north of the Mozambique capital of Maputo in February 2000. In the background, a bus that was swept away when a bridge collapsed lies wrecked in the mud. *Center:* The remains of livestock decompose in the desert during a severe drought in Niger in 2010. *Right:* Steam from boiling hot oil rises from open pools in an illegal refinery in Nigeria's Niger Delta.

Contested Culture

Homophobia and Homosexuality

Sexuality became a highly contentious topic in post–Cold War Africa. During the colonial era, some European powers had imposed legal bans on same-sex relations on their colonies in Africa and others did not. Britain transferred its own **homophobic laws** to its African colonies. While these laws were eventually scrapped in Britain, they were inherited by African postcolonial states, where they remained in the legal codes. Conversely, since France's anti-gay laws had been repealed during the French Revolution of the 1790s, the French colonial rulers who arrived in Africa in the late 1800s did not impose such laws, and therefore, after independence, former

French colonies in Africa did not have legal restrictions related to homosexuality. However, some former French colonial territories with primarily Muslim populations passed anti-gay laws after independence, including Senegal and Algeria in 1966 and Mauritania in 1983. In general, from the 1960s to 1980s, homosexuality was not a prominent topic in African public discourse or politics.

This changed in the 1990s and 2000s, when LGBTQ rights movements in Western Europe and North America gained success including legal recognition of same-sex

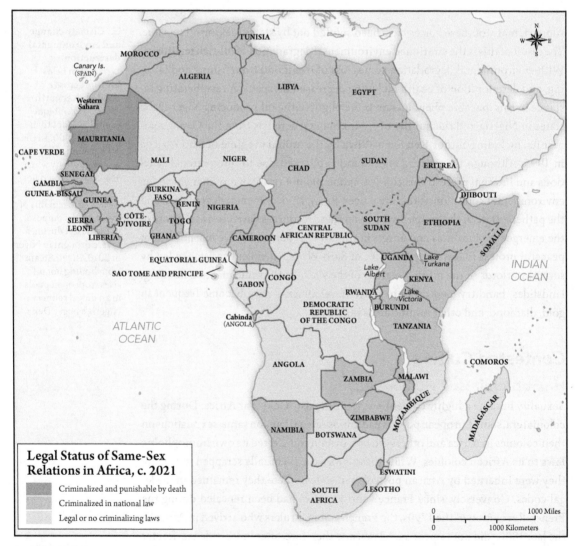

Legal Status of Same-Sex Relations in Africa, c. 2021

- Criminalized and punishable by death
- Criminalized in national law
- Legal or no criminalizing laws

≡ **MAP 27.3**

marriage. In some parts of Africa, LGBTQ activists became organized and demanded similar legal reforms, and received some attention and sympathy from the West. This inspired a homophobic backlash in many parts of Africa. The controversy was fueled by conservative Christian religious leaders from the United States who opposed same-sex marriage at home and sought allies among African Christians. In the 2000s, for instance, the worldwide Anglican Church effectively split over issues such as ordination

≡ **Gay-bashing.** A homophobic Ugandan newspaper headline published in 2010.

of LGBTQ clergy and same-sex marriage, with some US Anglican churches joining with their counterparts in parts of Africa, such as Uganda and Nigeria, to oppose these reforms. Simultaneously, other evangelical and conservative Christian churches from the US became popular in areas of Africa where they preached homophobic messages. Similarly, the expansion of fundamentalist Islam and Shari'a law in places like Sudan and northern Nigeria expanded existing anti-gay laws and technically imposed the death penalty for same-sex relations.

In an era of greater demands for democratization, many African politicians began to rally populist support by making homophobic statements, and some African governments enhanced their already homophobic legislation. President Robert Mugabe of Zimbabwe was one of the first African leaders to engage in this rhetoric, and it foreshadowed his eventual falling out with Western countries over political violence and economic collapse during the 2000s. In 1995, responding to a display set up by a gay rights organization at a Harare bookfair, Mugabe gave a homophobic speech and repeated such comments over the next few years, provoking violence against the LGBTQ community. In 1999 and 2001, British gay rights activist Peter Tatchell attracted media attention by attempting to place Mugabe under citizen's arrest for human rights abuses while he was visiting Western Europe. Subsequently, many African leaders such as Namibia's Sam Nujoma, Kenya's Daniel Arap Moi, the Gambia's Yahya Jammeh, and Uganda's Yoweri Museveni, made homophobic public statements. Some critics accused them of using homophobia to distract their people from authoritarianism and economic problems. In Uganda, where conservative American churches became popular, homophobia increased dramatically during the 2000s, with newspapers claiming that homosexuals were recruiting children, publishing the names of alleged homosexuals in Uganda, and demanding that they be hanged. In 2013, the Uganda parliament passed a law expanding the existing colonial-era ban on same-sex relations and extending punishment from up to 14 years' imprisonment to life imprisonment. The initial proposal for the law sought to impose the death penalty for same-sex relations. A few African countries that had never had anti-gay laws began to enact them, such as Burundi in 2009 and Chad in 2017, and many African states passed laws specifically prohibiting same-sex marriage. While South Africa's post-apartheid constitution guaranteed freedom of sexual orientation and South Africa became the first African country to allow same-sex marriage in 2006, homophobic violence became common in South African society. In 2019, Botswana's High Court struck down the country's ban on same-sex relationships, citing that it was discriminatory while in neighboring Zambia, a gay couple received a 15-year prison sentence. In some cases, LGBTQ people have fled aggressively homophobic states like Uganda, claiming refugee status in South Africa, North America, or Western Europe.

A public debate emerged on the position of homosexuality within African culture. Many African political and religious leaders claimed that homosexuality was inherently un-African and that it represented foreign decadence introduced to the continent by Europeans during the colonial era. When Western governments and NGOs criticized homophobic laws in Africa, some African leaders and anti-gay activists accused them of neocolonialism and of trying to impose offensive foreign values on Africans. Countering this stand, African LGBTQ activists and others maintained that homosexuality had existed and been tolerated in many precolonial African societies until it was criminalized by homophobic Western Christian missionaries and colonial rulers. Political leaders in Western Europe and North America began to talk about making international aid to African countries conditional on the removal of homophobic laws. In turn, African politicians, such as Tanzania's ardently homophobic President John Magufuli, declared that they preferred to make economic deals that did not impose these conditions, such as those with China. In 2019, homosexuality was outlawed in 34 out of 54 African countries.

Female genital mutilation/modification

During the late twentieth and early twenty-first centuries, the cultural practice, in parts of Africa, of cutting or removing part of a woman's genitalia, known as female circumcision or **female genital mutilation or female genital modification (FGM)** or female genital cutting (FGC), became extremely controversial. Although it is not mentioned in the Qur'an, Muslims in parts of Africa thought or think of the practice as a religious requirement related to female purity. In many areas it represents the central part of a traditional initiation to adulthood and is associated with membership in female secret societies such as Sande in Sierra Leone, Liberia, and Guinea. As discussed in Chapter 18, attempts by white missionaries to eradicate the practice in colonial Kenya had informed the growth of African political protest. In the 1970s, in the context of the emergence of the women's rights movement in the West, Western and African feminists began to call on international organizations and states to outlaw the practice. It was at this time that feminist scholars coined the term FGM, or "female genital mutilation," as "female circumcision" appeared insufficient to describe the violence of some of these procedures. In 1983, the UN General Assembly defined FGM as violence against women. In the 2000s, UN agencies such as WHO and the United Nations Children's Emergency Fund (UNICEF) launched programs to reduce FGM, which was seen as a human rights violation. In 2003, the African Union adopted the **Maputo Protocol** on human rights and women's rights, which included a declaration that FGM was harmful and should be eliminated. In some cases, African women were granted asylum in Western states such as the US, Canada, and Sweden, as it was claimed that FGM practiced in their home countries represented a form of persecution against women. In addition, some people from African immigrant communities in the West faced legal prosecution for performing FGM. From the 1990s to 2010s, the governments of most African countries where FGM was practiced, primarily in West, Central, and East Africa, placed legal restrictions or complete bans on the practice, though it continued in many places.

However, from around the 2000s, a new generation of African women scholars criticized Western feminist portrayals of FGM as racist and Eurocentric, objecting to the term "mutilation" as rooted in stereotypes of African societies as barbaric and primitive, and to claims that African women who performed or assisted with genital cutting were cooperating with their own oppression. Some claimed that the practice had been misunderstood and that it was not as damaging to women's health or sexuality or as oppressive as many believed and that outlawing it infantilized adult African women. In addition, these critics saw policies to eliminate the procedure as a form of Western neocolonialism and maintained that adult women should have the freedom to choose whether or not to undergo the procedure. African women have been on both sides of the debate. For example, nurse and midwife Edna Adan Ismail campaigned for the abolition of FGM/FGC in Somalia during the 1970s and 1980s and later became secessionist Somaliland's minister of health, and Sierra Leonean–American anthropologist Fuambai Ahmadu voluntarily underwent the procedure as an adult, and she continues to advocate for women's right to choose.

≡ **The FGM/FGC Debate.** *Left:* Edna Adan Ismail, nurse, midwife, and former minister in the government of Somaliland, advocated for a ban on female genital modification/cutting (FGM/C). *Right:* Sierra Leonean–American anthropologist Fuambai Ahmadu questions an outright ban on female genital modification/cutting (FGM/C).

Popular Culture

Film

The African film industry gained tremendous success during the post–Cold War era. The invention of motion pictures and the start of the film industry in Western Europe and North America in the 1890s and early 1900s corresponded with the Scramble for Africa. As such, film arrived in Africa at the start of the colonial period. War correspondents made the first newsreels during the South African War of 1899–1902, the silent films were first shown in Lagos, Nigeria, in 1903, and a short documentary was filmed in Egypt in 1907. During the 1920s, commercial cinemas were opened in urban centers and mobile cinemas toured rural areas and quickly became popular forms of entertainment and centers of social life. Africa's filmmaking industry began at the same time, with the continent's first film studio opening in Johannesburg, South Africa, in 1915, and the first sound feature film being made in Nigeria in 1926. Films were also used for propaganda. In British territories, the Colonial Film Unit, which functioned from 1939 to 1955, made and distributed short documentaries and newsreels illustrating the benefits of British rule for African audiences. During the apartheid era in South Africa, separate Afrikaner and African filmmaking industries emerged with state assistance, and the country became a cost-effective and popular location for British and American film productions.

After independence in the 1960s, the African film industry expanded with the opening of more theaters that showed a flood of foreign-made films from North

America, Europe, and Asia, and in some countries, television stations were launched. Concerned about the potential loss of African culture, African filmmakers and African governments became proactive in promoting African film productions. In 1966, the World Festival of Black Arts held in Senegal featured 26 films made in 16 African countries, and the Carthage Film Festival, held annually in Tunisia, was launched to showcase African and Arab cinema. In 1969, the Pan-African Federation of Filmmakers (FEPACI), inspired by Beninese/Senegalese film director Paulin Soumanou Vieyra who had made the first French-language African film in 1955, was formed to promote African cinema, and the biannual Pan-African Film and Television Festival of Ouagadougou (FESPACO) was inaugurated in Upper Volta (Burkina Faso) and eventually gained state sponsorship. During the 1960s, Ghana's President Kwame Nkrumah established the state-owned Ghanaian Film Industry Corporation, which sent Ghanaians to other countries to train in filmmaking and produced over 150 films and documentaries aimed at promoting national and Pan-African pride. Simultaneously, Nigerian producers, writers, and actors began making commercial films that were shown in local theaters. During the 1970s, Nigerian cinema was boosted by military ruler Yakubu Gowon's indigenization program, an economic oil boom that gave Nigerians more disposable income, and the construction of more large theaters, including the huge National Arts Theatre in Lagos. In the 1980s, in what some have called the "Golden Age" of Nigerian cinema, Nigerian filmmakers released a number of highly profitable feature films, including *Papa Ajasco* in 1984 and *Mosebolatan* in 1985. Around the same time, however, economic problems, including the devaluation of the local currency as part of structural adjustment and the proliferation of televisions, on which people would see feature films as well as television series, made cinemas less popular and undermined Nigeria's film industry, leading to the closure of many cinemas.

The advent of video recording in the late 1970s and early 1980s had a massive impact on West African filmmaking and began with people recording televised programs and selling the tapes in markets. In the late 1980s, filmmakers in Ghana and Nigeria pioneered the use of video cameras to make films that were released directly to the public on video tapes, and they became extremely popular as people could watch them at home. It is also likely that the deterioration of security in Nigeria at the time encouraged people to stop going out to theaters. One of the

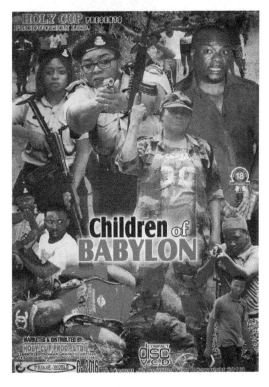

≡ **Nollywood.** A film poster for a Nollywood action thriller.

first highly successful Nigerian video films was the two-part 1992–93 thriller *Living in Bondage*, which starred actors already well known on Nigerian television. Consequently, during the 1990s and early 2000s, the Nigerian video film industry experienced explosive growth, eventually producing around 200 mostly low budget films every year and becoming the world's third-largest film industry behind the United States and India. Combining the words "Nigeria" and "Hollywood," journalists began to call the Nigerian film industry **Nollywood**. Nollywood produced films in Nigerian languages like Yoruba and Igbo for domestic audiences and the emergent Nigerian diaspora, as well as many English films for the Nigerian and international markets. While Nollywood films addressed a variety of themes, many focused on melodramatic morality tales of good versus evil and often involved supernatural forces, which appealed to ordinary people in Nigeria and other African countries. Some highbrow African film critics decried Nollywood for lowering the quality of filmmaking on the continent.

A similar but smaller video film industry also developed in neighboring Ghana, where it became called "Gollywood," and popular Ghanaian actors moved to Nigeria to work in more profitable productions there. Like America's Hollywood and India's Bollywood, Nollywood created a host of celebrated and glamorous movie stars who, beginning in 2005, were honored by Nigeria's annual African Movie Academy Awards. By 2010, nevertheless, Nollywood began to decline as rampant black-market copying and selling of videos made the industry less economically viable. This led to a resurgence of traditional and higher-quality filmmaking in Nigeria, supported by grants from the government, and the construction of new cinemas in elite shopping and entertainment centers aimed at middle- and upper-income consumers.

≡ **Film star.** In 2005, Genevieve Nnaji became the first winner of Nigeria's African Movie Academy Awards' "Best Actress in a Leading Role" category.

Music

Similar trends happened in the field of popular music. Originating in African-American urban communities in the United States and expanding into a global cultural phenomenon, **hip-hop** music and dance arrived in Africa in the 1980s. This was facilitated by the growing number of African immigrants in the United States—the number increased from 200,000 in 1990 to 800,000 in 2000—many of whom retained family links with their home countries. In many parts of Africa, young people were first exposed to hip-hop through imported audio and video cassettes played at house parties or night clubs or on local radio. The first African hip-hop artists of the 1980s were often youth from middle- or upper-class families who could afford appropriate equipment, and they usually imitated their American idols. Eventually, by the end of the 1980s, original African hip-hop styles emerged, with rapping in African languages. In francophone Africa, hip-hop arrived from not only the United States but also Europe. The large number of Senegalese immigrants in New York City and Paris influenced the early arrival of hip-hop in Senegal at the start of the 1980s. Among the early influences on Senegalese hip-hop were the group Positive Black Soul, which was formed in Dakar in 1989 and often performed in the Wolof language, and **MC Solaar**, a Senegalese-Chadian immigrant to Paris, who was one of the first African hip-hop artists to sign with a major American recording label and was considered the best French rapper. A vibrant hip-hop scene also developed in Algeria during the country's civil war of the 1990s, and Algerian artists living in France influenced French hip-hop. A successful Nigerian hip-hop music or **Naija** music industry developed hand-in-hand with the rise of Nollywood in the 1990s and 2000s. In addition, hip-hop contributed to the growth of new African musical styles such as hiplife in Ghana, which, like hip-hop, often addresses political and social issues, and Bongo Flava in Tanzania and kwaito in post-apartheid South Africa, which are types of dance music that avoid deeper commentary. By the mid-2000s, hip-hop music and culture was well known in every African country and a series of regular hip-hop festivals had been organized, including Burkina Faso's Waga Hip Hop Festival, Uganda's HipHop Summit, and Tanzania's Okoa Mtaa Festival.

≡ **Hip-hop artist.** MC Solaar performs in France in 2009.

Timeline

1969—Pan-African Federation of Filmmakers (FEPACI) established

1975—Founding of the Convention on International Trade in Endangered Species of Wild Flora and Fauna (CITES)

1976—First known Ebola outbreak occurs in Zaire (DRC)

1981—Identification of HIV/AIDS

1983—UN defines female genital mutilation (FGM) as violence against women

1980s—"Golden Age" of Nigerian cinema

1980s—Arrival of hip-hop in Africa

1980s–2000s—HIV/AIDS pandemic spreads across Africa

1989—Start of Communal Areas Management Program for Indigenous Resources (CAMPFIRE) in Zimbabwe

c. 1990+—Rise of Nollywood video film industry

1995—Homophobic statements by Zimbabwean president Robert Mugabe begins a trend among African leaders

1998—Formation of Treatment Action Campaign (TAC) in South Africa

2000—Worst flood in 50 years in Mozambique

2001—First legal victory for TAC in South Africa

2003—South African government declares "HIV causes AIDS" and launches treatment program

2003—United States government launches President's Emergency Plan for AIDS Relief (PEPFAR)

2003—African Union (AU) declares that FGM should be eliminated

2005—Beginning of African Movie Academy Awards

2007—Flooding in Mozambique

2009—Boko Haram insurgency begins in northeastern Nigeria

2010—Some 35 million people worldwide have been infected with HIV, two thirds live in Africa, and 15 million have died

c. 2010+—Decline of Nollywood video film industry

2010s—Worsening of herder–farmer violence in the Sahel

2013–16—Ebola outbreak in West Africa (Guinea, Liberia, and Sierra Leone)

2013—Uganda parliament makes same-sex relations punishable by life imprisonment

2014—US ban on ivory imports

2018—China bans ivory imports

2019—Flooding in Mozambique and neighboring countries

Conclusion

From the 1990s, in the age of globalization, Africans contested issues around health, environment, and culture. As the HIV/AIDS pandemic ravaged the continent, some South African politicians denied scientifically proven facts and were challenged in court by a social movement that compelled effective state action to save lives. In the environmental context, conservationists urged a total ban on the hunting and exploitation of endangered species that some governments saw as a valuable resource. Sexuality became a much disputed subject, with the rise of homophobia and LGBTQ activism, and arguments between Western and African feminists over FGM. Although Nollywood movies became wildly successful, critics looked down on their storylines and low-budget productions. While it is tempting to engage in pessimism about postcolonial Africa, there have been some positive developments, such as an abating of the HIV/AIDS pandemic, advancements toward an Ebola vaccine, and the growth of vibrant film and music industries, as well as the democratization discussed in Chapter 26. As with the rest of the world, the impact of climate change and COVID-19 on Africa remain a challenge.

KEY TERMS

ABC 608

Communal Areas Management Program for Indigenous Resources (CAMPFIRE) 614

Convention on International Trade in Endangered Species of Wild Flora and Fauna (CITES) 613

COVID-19 612

desertification 616

Ebola 610

female genital mutilation/modification (FGM) 620

globalization 605

hip-hop 624

HIV/AIDS 607

Homophobic Laws 617

Influenza Pandemic 606

Ken Saro-Wiwa 617

Maputo Protocol 621

MC Solaar 625

Naija 625

Nollywood 624

rentier states 616

Treatment Action Campaign (TAC) 608

STUDY QUESTIONS

1. Why did Africa countries in the late twentieth and early twenty-first centuries experience major health crises, including Ebola and COVID-19? How has South Africa's Treatment Action Campaign raised awareness of HIV/AIDS?

2. What are the main sides in the debate about conservationism in game reserves and national parks in Africa? What are the effects of climate change and environmental degradation on the livelihoods of many Africans across the continent?

3. Why is homophobia prevalent across many African countries? Why is female genital mutilation/modification (FGM) controversial for many African women?

4. What are some of the contributions of the African film industry, in particular Nollywood? How have African musicians embraced hip-hop and influenced its development?

Please see page FR-13 for the Further Readings for this chapter.
For additional digital learning resources please go to
https://www.oup.com/he/falola-stapleton1e

Thematic Conclusion to Part Two

The nineteenth century represented a remarkable moment in the history of African people. During this time, African societies experienced a plethora of rapid changes. Although the changes were largely political and economic, their effects penetrated the sociocultural fabric of the people in an unprecedented way. For centuries, African societies evolved various political and economic formations within which the people governed their own affairs. Wars were fought for expansion of territory and access to resources and trade routes. However, all of this took a different turn in the nineteenth century, as much of Africa experienced violent waves of change, with migrant groups of refugees or warriors creating new states. These processes included the conflicts that led to the creation of new and larger states in Southern Africa, such as the Zulu and Sotho kingdoms; the Yoruba Wars that gave rise to Ibadan in West Africa; and the expansion of the Maasai in East Africa. Similarly, modernizing Egypt embarked on a series of wars to achieve autonomy within the Ottoman Empire, and jihads in the Sahel region of West Africa led to the founding of the Muslim theocratic empires of Sokoto and Tukolor. Many of these conflicts resulted in the collapse of existing African states. The new powers that replaced them often waged war against each other, thereby facilitating the intrusion of Europeans into African affairs. During the early and middle decades of the nineteenth century, the European presence in Africa, previously limited to the coast, began expanding inland

Community action. In 2005, the Zimbabwean police and military demolished thousands of informal settlements in the country in an operation called Murambatsvina ("clear out the rubbish"). Among the estimated 700,000 people who lost their homes and livelihoods in a matter of weeks were a group of women in Killarney, a suburb of Bulawayo, Zimbabwe's second-largest city. The women worked together to create an *arpillera* (a patchwork quilt) to express the fear and chaos they had experienced. The *arpillera* was a joint effort to show the world the violence the community had suffered at the hands of their own government.

with the creation of Boer republics and new British settler territories in Southern Africa, French and British conquests in West Africa, and the French occupation of Algeria. In North Africa, modernization programs including the construction of the Suez Canal led to states like Egypt, Tunisia, and Morocco incurring heavy international debts, which further bolstered European dominance.

During the nineteenth century, Europe's **Industrial Revolution** led to greater demands for African raw materials like palm oil, peanuts, cotton, ivory, and rubber. While intensified trade in raw materials caused more rivalry and warfare among African powers, the proliferation of imported firearms made these conflicts more lethal and enabled some states to dominate others. In this intensely competitive environment, African states did not unify against foreign conquest but attempted to gain advantage over their local rivals by entering into alliances with increasingly intrusive European powers. The regional ambitions of African leaders prompted them to collaborate with the agents of European colonization with the thought that they were using these agents to execute and advance their own interests. By the time all these leaders realized that they had lost their independence to European conquest, neither their spiritual powers nor their obsolete firearms could save them.

The Partition of Africa

A number of factors facilitated the European **Scramble for Africa** in the late nineteenth century. The activities of Western Christian missionaries in Africa paved the way for colonial conquest by creating pockets of Westernized African Christian converts. By the end of the nineteenth century, many missionaries began to see European colonial rule as a way to accelerate their planned Christian transformation of the continent. In West Africa, the arrival or return of African-American former slaves augmented this process, as they became agents of what they saw as the spread of civilization and modernization. In places like Abeokuta in what is now western Nigeria, these returnees introduced a new Western-style administrative system and cooperated with missionaries who shared the same goals. In Sierra Leone and Liberia, African Americans formed settler societies, dominating and exploiting indigenous people. Emanating from the Second Industrial Revolution, Western technological innovations proved decisive, as advances in tropical medicine allowed Europeans to penetrate parts of Africa previously considered the "white man's grave," thereby undermining African economic intermediaries; modern weaponry like the Maxim gun subdued African resistance; and steamboats and steam-powered locomotives extracted large amounts of raw materials. The Industrial Revolution also encouraged fierce competition among European merchants and traders backed by their home governments. Africa became not only a source of raw materials for European industry but also a market for finished goods. By the second half of the nineteenth century, it became clear to all these actors, including the missionaries and formerly enslaved persons, that the only way for each of them to achieve their goals in Africa was through the occupation of these territories by various European powers. For the European merchants, it was trade; for the missionaries, it was the civilization/modernization of the people through Christianization. Formerly enslaved persons were concerned with the general and social transformation of the society with them as the anchor; European governments saw their enterprise as a means to expand their areas of influence into glorious empires. Hence, it is often said that the colonial conquest of Africa was influenced by three G's: **God, Gold, and Glory.**

Debating the reasons for the Scramble for Africa, scholars have put forth competing economic, strategic, diplomatic, and psychological theories. Economic theories focus on a range of reasons, from European powers' search for investment

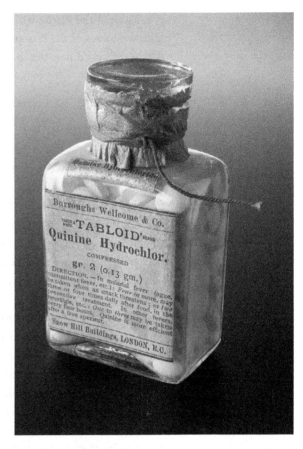

≣ **Tool of empire.** A bottle of quinine tablets. Derived from the bark of cinchona trees, which are native to South America, quinine effectively treats malaria. The use of this medicine greatly reduced mortality rates for European colonists in sub-Saharan Africa.

opportunities to their need for raw materials, and strategic theories stress certain key territorial seizures as triggering a domino effect of invasions in Africa. Psychological theories highlight the idea of "might is right," and the diplomatic theories partly view the partition as a movement towards a closer relation between the colonized and the colonial powers. In some of the opening moves of the Scramble, Britain took possession of Lagos in present-day Nigeria in 1861 and occupied Egypt in 1882, and France seized Tunisia in 1881. King Leopold II of Belgium declared interest in acquiring the Congo River Basin in the 1870s, Portugal renewed its historic claims over Angola and Mozambique, and Germany suddenly entered the race for colonies in 1884 by claiming Togo, Cameroon, South West Africa (Namibia), and German East Africa (the mainland of what is now Tanzania plus Rwanda and Burundi). This led to the Berlin Conference of 1884–85, where representatives of the European powers met to negotiate their claims to parts of Africa and coordinate the conquest of the continent.

Resistance to Colonial Conquest

Diplomatic agreements between European powers charted their scramble for African territory. While the Berlin Conference set out the principle of "effective occupation," meaning a European power had to actually send officials to part of Africa in order to ratify territorial claims, the Brussels Act of 1890 prohibited Western countries from providing weapons to African states that could be used to defend themselves against the ongoing invasions. Other specific diplomatic agreements, such as the Anglo-German Treaties of 1886 and 1890, finalized borders between the new colonial territories in Africa. In part, these treaties were also ways in which the imperial powers in Europe outmaneuvered their African counterparts, who had developed the strategy of playing one European power against the other to their own advantage. In the late 1860s, for example, Lesotho's King Moshoeshoe accepted British authority to preserve the remnants of his state from Boer expansion, and during the 1890s Samori Toure of the Mandinka Empire tried but failed to play the French off against the British. Diplomatic agreements between European powers meant that they did not clash with each other as they raced to claim African territory during the late nineteenth century. The Scramble also involved fraudulent agreements, such as when British officials, in 1889, tricked the Ndebele ruler Lobengula into signing a treaty giving them authority over the neighboring lands of the Shona people in what is now Zimbabwe. Subsequently, in 1893–94, the British South Africa Company (BSAC) invaded the Ndebele state and Lobengula died during his retreat.

Responding to European invasion, African powers employed both diplomatic and military means. The diplomatic response involved African rulers accepting "protection" from European colonial powers. For example, Lewanika of the Lozi kingdom in what is now western Zambia accepted British supremacy, Protestant leaders in East Africa's Buganda Kingdom agreed to cooperate with the British who had put them in power during a recent civil war, and Rwanda's Queen Mother Kanjogera cooperated with the Germans to install her son Musinga as king. This diplomatic approach was often informed by African leaders' desire to protect themselves from local rivals—such as the Lozi kingdom, which was threatened by Ndebele raids, and King Tofa of the Gun kingdom of West Africa's Porto Novo, who allied with the French to secure his position from neighboring Dahomey, the Yoruba states, and the British. The Yoruba states, destabilized by years of warfare among themselves and intimidated by several British military expeditions, mostly signed away their sovereignty to Britain, agreeing not to engage in treaties with other European powers.

In terms of military resistance, many African states bravely defended themselves but were defeated by European invasion. Examples of military conquest during the Scramble include the British invasions of the Asante Kingdom in 1873–74, the Zulu kingdom in 1879 and the Ngoni states in Central Africa in the 1890s, the French campaigns against the Mandinka and Tukolor empires in the 1880s and 1890s, and the German defeat of the Hehe kingdom in East Africa in the 1890s. At times, the abolition of the slave trade provided a justification for colonial conquest, as with the British takeover of Lagos in 1861, Zanzibar in 1890, the Yao and Swahili-Arabs around Lake Malawi in the 1890s, and the Sokoto Caliphate in the early 1900s, and Leopold II's subjugation of the Swahili-Arabs in eastern Congo in the early 1890s. While Ethiopia's Menelik II attempted a diplomatic settlement with the Italians in neighboring Eritrea through the 1889 Treaty of Wuchale, Ethiopia became the only African state to defend itself successfully from colonial invasion by defeating an Italian force at the 1896 Battle of Adwa. Many African leaders who resisted European conquest were killed, such as Lat Dior of Cayor in Senegal in 1886 and Koitalel of Kenya's Nandi people in 1905, and others were captured and exiled, such as Urabi Pasha of Egypt in 1882, Jaja of Opobo in eastern Nigeria in 1887, Prempeh of

≡ **African resistance.** Ethiopian forces, armed with Western firepower, and urged on by St. George (top center), mow down Italian invaders.

Asante in 1896, and Samori Toure in 1898. Although all of Africa except Ethiopia and the African-American Republic of Liberia succumbed to European invasion during the Scramble, it often took another decade or more to impose colonial rule on the people. In the early years of colonial occupation, the imposition of oppressive taxation and forced labor provoked widespread rebellions, such as the Ndebele and Shona Uprisings in 1896–97, the Sierra Leone Hut Tax Rebellion of 1898, the Maji Maji revolt of 1905 in German East Africa, and resistance by the Herero and Nama people, previously enemies, in German South West Africa in 1904–07. Some of the most tenacious and enduring resistance to colonial rule took place among decentralized communities like the Igbo of eastern Nigeria and the Nandi of Kenya.

Colonialism and "Modernization"

From the nineteenth century onward, African people experienced tremendous changes in their ways of life. Undoubtedly, the most enduring impact of colonization on Africa is the way it transformed the society from "traditional" to "modern." "Traditional" refers to all that was indigenous to the people of Africa, while the term "modern" is associated with Western civilization. Specifically, the modernization of African society was deeply rooted in the culture of the imperial power controlling the resources and people of a particular African colony. At the same time, the westernization that occurred in Africa during the colonial era did not result in European colonizers seeing Africans as their equals. As such, the transformation of the French colonies in Africa, for instance, into modernity was characterized by the French culture, which, ultimately, was meant to set them as an appendage of this culture. This modernization process sought to suppress African religions and spirituality hitherto at the center of African civilizations. Acting as the vanguard of this transformation, missionaries portrayed African societies as backward and barbaric and desperately in need of enlightenment through Christianity and Western civilization.

≡ **Civilizing and Christianizing mission.** A white missionary, guided by a radiant Christ in the background, attends to a sick African child in this c. 1916 painting.

Destroying the basis of African civilization— African religion and spirituality—then became a necessary tool for effective colonization of the people. The meticulously created visual arts, which also depicted the people's spirituality, were carted away to European museums or destroyed with little or no protest from the growing number of African Christian converts who associated these items with a supposedly primitive past. In West Africa, previously westernized African-American former slaves who returned to the region furthered this **civilizing mission**. In colonial Africa, European-style modernization meant that westernized Africans worshipped in the European way, ate European food and drank European drinks, wore European-style clothing, lived in European-style houses decorated with European furniture, and learned European languages. Within the white supremacist colonial racial hierarchy, however, westernized Africans remained subordinate to Europeans, but they were considered superior to the mass of less transformed ordinary African people. Given their formal educational qualifications, the westernized African elite gained jobs within the lower levels of the colonial bureaucracy and mission churches and therefore acquired some influence. At times, the westernized elites became rivals of traditional leaders who worked within the colonial indirect-rule administrative system and usually did not possess the same level of Western education.

Within the colonial context, the status and influence of the westernized and Christianized African elite made other people want to emulate them, therefore further encouraging religious conversion and social change. As mission Christianity spread, African marriage patterns and family life changed as polygyny was discouraged in favor of monogamy, and household gender roles were transformed to some extent. A European-style wedding, with a white dress for the bride and a dark suit and tie for the groom, became a symbol of prestige for aspiring members of the westernized African elite. Western-style education, usually operated by missionaries, also became a status symbol and a key to success within the colonial system. Schools taught practical subjects such as tailoring and carpentry but highlighted academic fields as more important. Indeed, the expansion of the colonial legal and healthcare systems meant that some members of the westernized African elite became lawyers and doctors, representing archetypes of modernity. For Africa, the colonial education system replicated the Western preference for white-collar over blue-collar professions. In addition, the importation of large quantities of Western manufactured goods into colonial Africa, often cheaper than locally produced goods and seen as markers of civilization, hindered the progress of local artisans and created a dependent economy. As a result, westernized African elites receiving regular salaries as civil servants or church employees pursued an aspirant "modern" lifestyle while blue-collar workers struggled to feed their families. In Africa's growing colonial cities, with their hotels, bars, and clubs, Western-style clothing and fashion became markers of status, with women putting on high heel shoes, lipstick, and straight-hair wigs, and men donning trousers, shirts, ties, jackets, and shiny shoes. In the same way, Western consumer items like cigarettes, chewing gum, bottled beer and liquor, body lotions, soap, and tea became popular. Popular culture in Africa, involving musical styles combining African, African-American, and European influences, as well as organized sports, also emerged in this setting. What remained of African traditions in the face of modernization largely became an adulterated version of old practices.

Colonial Economy and the State

Colonial rule restructured the African economy to meet colonial expectations and needs. The colonial powers ensured that they presided over an African economy designed for the exportation of raw materials and importation of finished industrial goods. Since the raw materials were needed to supply the emerging industries in Europe, with African states now an appendage of one colonial power or the other, the colonial powers dictated not only what materials were produced but also the price paid for them. External forces drove Africa's colonial economy, and the needs of African people counted for little. European governments enacted policies that favored their own nationals operating within the colonial economies of Africa, and these rules often disadvantaged Africans. This happened in the white settler–dominated territories like South Africa, Southern Rhodesia (Zimbabwe), and Algeria, as well as in the many tropical colonies, where the only Europeans were a few merchants, missionaries, and officials. Where settler minorities gained control of the state, African majorities experienced eviction from their ancestral lands to make way for white-dominated commercial agriculture. This dispossession boosted the profitability of settler farms as it undercut African economic competition and created a pool of cheap African migrant labor emanating from overcrowded and impoverished African reserves that held few opportunities. In the many colonies without settler minorities, colonial states maximized the profits of European companies by manipulating the prices paid to African producers for their goods. This economic system seemed reminiscent of the colonial conquest of Africa, in which European powers coordinated their efforts while division characterized the African response. While European companies operating in Africa formed syndicates and received strong support from colonial administrations, individual African traders could not compete as they lacked capital and government assistance. African farmers were compelled to sell their products at the low prices set by the colonial state as, if they refused, others would do so. The same choice confronted them each time they wanted to purchase manufactured goods as European products steadily dominated the market, pushing out locally fashioned alternatives. As we have discussed, the prestige of European-style consumer goods added to their attractiveness in colonial Africa. While some African people tried to redress this imbalance by forming farm cooperatives and trade unions, they could not change the essentially exploitative nature of the colonial economy.

To meet the industrial needs of European states, expand profit, subjugate the colonies, and further make the people dependent on the metropolitan states in Europe, there was a systematic promotion of cash crops, to the detriment of food crops. For instance, the interests of the Western chocolate industry led to the spread of cocoa farming in West Africa, particularly in western Nigeria, the Gold Coast (Ghana), and Côte d'Ivoire, where it led to the rise of a new set of local elites. Its massive production in these areas promoted labor migration that later populated small towns and villages, with a concomitant effect on the economic capacity of these regions. Similar processes happened with the spread of other cash crops like cotton and palm kernel. The need to pay taxes to the colonial state served to encourage African farmers to grow crops sold for money. Tax defaulters were put to work as unpaid labor on government projects such as road or bridge construction, and at times colonial security forces violently punished communities refusing to pay tax. **Colonialism** usually made farming synonymous with poverty and encouraged wage labor in places like mines, commercial plantations, or construction sites. Of course, some African farmers managed to become successful producers of cash crops despite the institutional disadvantages.

The colonial state imposed a legal system that controlled African workers. In some colonies, particularly settler minority–controlled territories, African workers could only move around freely if they carried an identity document or pass endorsed by an employer. This seriously hindered the ability of African workers to search for the best-paying jobs. Furthermore, the state criminalized workers' protests in demand of better working conditions and higher pay with strikes broken by police.

☰ **The fruits of empire.** This advertisement from 1910 shows Britannia greeting a young African woman who has landed her boat with a cargo of African cocoa.

Infrastructural developments at this time, even though they were beneficial to the colonized peoples, were primarily aimed at maximizing the European exploitation of the colonies. Tremendous transformation occurred in the area of communication and transportation. Newly constructed roads and railways linked the rural hinterland areas producing the export goods to the port cities from where they were transported to their destinations in Europe. Simultaneously, the colonial transport system tended not to link different parts of the African interior or different regions of Africa, minimizing the economic integration of colonial Africa.

The colonial economic and political structures imposed on Africa prevented the development of local industries and institutionalized a system whereby Africa exported raw materials and imported refined goods. This system originated with the transatlantic slave trade and "legitimate commerce," but it became entrenched during the era of colonial rule. With the Great Depression of the 1930s, African raw materials and markets became even more important for the struggling economies of European powers. The main economic actors of colonial Africa, including cash crop producers and wage laborers, produced little or nothing of what their society consumed. Altogether, despite this exploitative situation, it produced new classes of elites and wealthy Africans who rose to prominence through their engagement with the colonial economy.

Nationalism and the Decolonization of Africa

While European powers took advantage of African crises and weakness during the late-nineteenth-century Scramble, the **decolonization** of Africa in the 1950s and 1960s took place against the background of economic crisis and war in Europe. During Africa's colonial era, Europe experienced the First World War (1914–18), the Great Depression, the Second World War (1939–45), and the beginnings of the **Cold War**. After the Second World War, former great powers like Britain and France became subordinate players in a new world order dominated by two superpowers, the United States and the Soviet Union. By the 1950s, the European colonial powers were nowhere near as strong as they had been prior to 1929. The Second World War and postwar reconstruction prompted European colonial powers to accelerate the production of raw materials in Africa, but this led to more grievances and increased protest among urban workers and rural farmers. Although the role of African war veterans in anti-colonial protest is often exaggerated, Allied wartime propaganda and declarations about freedom and self-determination resonated among colonized people in Africa. Changes that took place during and immediately after the Second World War prompted the African nationalist movements to shift their demands from civil rights and better living conditions within the existing colonial system to the granting of self-government to African territories. Simultaneously, the nationalist organizations evolved from small elitist groups employing moderate tactics such as petition writing to mass movements staging large-scale street protests and political rallies. In an increasingly urbanized colonial Africa, the proliferation of media such as newspapers and radio facilitated mass **nationalism**.

In places where the colonial powers agreed to withdraw, decolonization proceeded through negotiations. However, in territories where colonial powers and/or settler regimes refused to grant reforms, African nationalist movements embarked on liberation wars to free their homelands from foreign occupation. Aiding these struggles was the establishment of the United Nations at the end of the Second World War and the organization's support for the principles of decolonization and self-determination. The slightly earlier decolonization of Asia proved influential as it inspired African nationalists to pursue independence and the Asian former colonies joined a growing anti-colonial group within the United Nations. The postwar African nationalist movement was also bolstered by the continued activities of the **Pan-Africanist** movement, particularly the 1945 Pan-African Congress in Manchester, UK, which brought together many African-American and African intellectuals and political leaders to condemn racism, colonialism, and capitalism.

Both Cold War–era superpowers officially opposed colonialism. For the Soviet Union, the collapse of the Western imperial colonies in Africa and elsewhere in Asia and Latin America was a matter of state foreign policy to limit their influence and bring about the end of capitalism. This situation provided the African nationalists with the opportunity that eluded their forebears during the partition and conquest of Africa by the colonial forces, as they could now ally with a powerful bloc interested in the liberation of their lands. In cases where African

≡ **Colonial troops.** Members of the Gold Coast (Ghana) Regiment of the Royal West African Frontier Force relax during a break sometime in the 1940s.

nationalists fought wars of liberation such as in the Portuguese colonies of Angola, Mozambique, and Guinea-Bissau, and in the settler states of Rhodesia, South West Africa, and South Africa, the insurgents received weapons, logistical support, and training from the Soviet Union and its Eastern Bloc allies. On the other side of the Cold War, the United States officially opposed colonialism and promoted **democracy**, but the colonial powers were also its main allies and therefore they all worked to stage manage a political transition that would keep former colonies in Africa within the orbit of the Western alliance and curtail the spread of communism. For both the Soviet Union and the United States, access to African resources represented an important objective during the decolonization era. While the colonial powers tried to retain control of their African territories and suppressed nationalist movements during the late 1940s and 1950s, most of them eventually gave in to African peoples' demands for independence.

By 1990, virtually all African colonies had been liberated, with the exception of South Africa, where the white supremacist apartheid regime began a negotiated transition to democracy. Many of these countries, especially ones that acquired independence through peaceful means, maintained a close relationship with their former colonial masters and retained a capitalist economy little changed from the colonial era. Some independent African countries, particularly those that had experienced violent liberation wars, distanced themselves from the Western Bloc and experimented with forms of socialism and communism.

Africa and the Age of Political Independence

The history of precolonial Africa reveals a network of constantly changing societies, with many engaged in expansion through territorial conquest and amalgamation. Many of Africa's small communities and states aspired to grow in size, but they did not get the opportunity to do so before the onset of European colonial incursion and conquest. Following the 1884–85 Berlin Conference and the European occupation of Africa through either violence, diplomacy, or trickery, the first priority of the colonial administrations in Africa was to create larger states to facilitate control and economic exploitation. Paradoxically, while the legacy of colonial imposed borders is often cited as a reason for the failure of independent African states, postcolonial African political leaders and elites have never reached a peaceful conclusion on how these boundaries could be reconfigured or state structure reorganized in a more appropriate way. Attempts toward deconstructing this physical and psychological structure have always ended in civil wars and incessant instability in these states. This cannot be isolated from the reality that colonial boundaries have become instrumental to the manipulation of ethnic identity and the exploitation of the people for political gains by the political elites. As a result, all sorts of political, social, and economic crises, including various types of violent conflict, plague postcolonial African states.

Most African states began to gain independence from around 1957, and almost all had attained autonomy by 1980. Kwame Nkrumah, the first president of Ghana, advised Africans, "Seek ye first the political kingdom and all things shall be added unto you," meaning that he hoped political independence would lead to economic independence and prosperity. However, the elements "added" to the postcolonial African state were not those Nkrumah had in mind. For many African states, the honeymoon period of independence lasted less than a decade before political decay and economic crisis set in. This also happened in Nkrumah's Ghana.

Africa's political independence did not materialize into economic independence, and hence, these states found it difficult to fund essential projects. While postcolonial states continued many colonial-era policies and laws, they often failed to maintain transport and communications infrastructure inherited from the colonial period. As such, with the increasing population and deteriorating economic and infrastructural situation, independent African states soon became plagued by the problems of unemployment, infrastructural decay, and limited opportunity for social mobility, causing genuine frustrations among the people. The situation became more complicated as the nationalists turned politicians seemed not to know what to do with the independence they had attained. Many turned the political victory of independence into a personal one, thereby using political offices for self-aggrandizement and patrimonialism. Many of them turned themselves into what has been described as "gatekeepers," using control of the government to collect "rent" for all activities going on within the state and ignoring the welfare of their people. This led to the alienation of the state and society in postcolonial Africa, and the mistrust between these two elements hindered nation building. The sense of patriotism that characterized the era around the granting of independence in many African countries quickly gave way to pessimism and disappointment. The few African leaders seeking to move beyond a Western industrial model of development were removed through military coups or assassination. The rusting railways, deteriorating telecommunications services, dilapidated structures, "debt trap" international loans, and rising poverty created a massive ticking time bomb of instability for much of postcolonial Africa.

The divisions in these states became manifest through coups, ethno-religious crises, and civil wars. Coups and counter-coups were staged because of ethnic jingoism among the political elites in collaboration with the military, and accusations of **corruption** and maladministration against the existing government. Through economic and political crises, postcolonial African countries further integrated into the world economy through loans, international aid, and other arrangements that deepened their dependence on Western countries and, more recently, China and other Asian countries. Regardless of the economic condition of African states at this time, governance was characterized by lavishness, luxury, and excessive display of privilege. As African economies continued to rely on exporting natural resources, they remained vulnerable to changing prices and demands set by interests outside the continent. In addition, postcolonial Africa remained dependent on the West for imported commodities, modernization theories, and popular culture. Although many aspects of African culture survived, anything from Europe or America became fashionable and modern. Post-independence Africa became characterized by import-dependent economies, extractive economies, predatory states, beggar states, and **prebendal** states concerned with furthering the interests of the ruling elite. These issues were facilitated by broader factors such as the global Cold War of the 1950s to 1980s and the **neoliberal** agenda imposed by structural adjustment programs (SAPs) from the 1980s onward.

The Inherited Identity: Democracy and Democratic Practices in Africa

Democracy was one of the most important legacies handed over to the post-independent states in Africa by the colonial powers. This does not mean that Africans lacked historical experience with democracy, as many precolonial societies and states practiced aspects of democratic governance, including consultation and checks-and-balances. What the colonial powers handed over to the people of Africa, therefore, was representative democracy as practiced in the West. While colonial regimes in Africa did not practice democracy, the newly independent countries of Africa were expected to adopt Western representative democratic systems with little preparation. In many cases, the candidates who won the initial elections in independent Africa were those with close ties to the outgoing

≡ **Western glamor.** A decal of the pop-singer Madonna adorns a motorcycle in a market in Segou, Mali.

colonial power. Election rigging betrayed the much talked about democratic values and principles. Democracy, which has since become the yardstick through which governments across the world legitimize their rule, if only in name, became another tool of destabilization in Africa. Election crises as a result of accusations of electoral manipulation and fraud are not uncommon in African countries. In some cases, such as in Nigeria in 1966, such corrupt practices contributed to military coups. In clear terms, the democracy handed over to the colonized population of Africa by the imperial Western powers was structured in such a way that corrupt and selfish political elites dominated it.

Many dictatorships emerged during the initial decades of Africa's independence. Despite official democratic systems, many postcolonial African dictators seemed nostalgic for the monarchical regimes of the precolonial past. They manipulated elections, changed constitutions to lengthen their tenure, and used the coercive power of the state to crush opposition. Across the continent, civil liberties and political rights, the essentials of a democratic government, were traded for the disposition of the ruling powers in the states. Institutions and respect for the rule of law, requirements of any stable democracy, were and are fragile in postcolonial African countries, prompting the rise of "strongman" politics. Both authoritarian and democratic governments in postcolonial Africa suppressed human rights, using violence to silence criticism and to further their own agendas. Democratic practice in Africa is thus defined as the instrument through which officials are "elected" every four years and the people are expected to look away after the four-year ritual. Criticism of "elected" officials became characterized as insubordination, reckless opposition, and insolence toward the authorities.

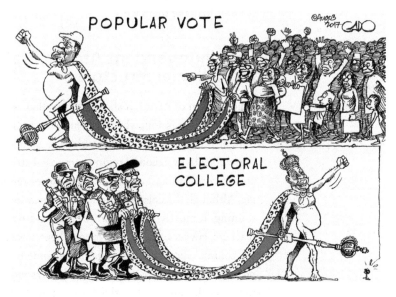

≡ **Political cartoon.** Kenyan graphic artist Godfrey "Gado" Mwampembwa has become famous for his scathing depictions of political corruption and hypocrisy. This cartoon draws on the notion of the electoral college in the United States to characterize the Kenyan general election of 2017. In the top half of the image, Gado depicts the main opposition leader, Raila Odinga, backed by what he calls the "popular vote"—the ordinary people. By contrast, in the bottom half of the image, he shows the incumbent president, Uhuru Kenyatta, backed not by the voters but by an "electoral college." However, while the electoral college in the United States is made up of elected and appointed representatives officials, Gado shows the Kenyan president supported by the leaders of the country's security forces.

In postcolonial Africa, for the most part, democracy failed to live up to its potential as it did not facilitate real political independence or the socioeconomic liberation of the people. The political elites see democracy as a conduit to perpetrate and wield state powers and boost their presence in the society, while many ordinary people see elections as a chance to cash in on electoral corruption. All this implies is that democracy in postcolonial Africa has not aided the path of nation building. At the heart of the electoral process is thuggery, assassination, money laundering, vandalism, hate speech, arson, demagoguery, and kidnappings. While one-party states and military coups have fallen out of fashion, this has not translated into the strengthening of democratic practices in many parts of contemporary Africa. All this should not be taken to mean that democracy cannot work in Africa. To reverse this trend, African states would have to invest genuinely in human capacity building. Strengthening civic education in these states and decolonizing the broader educational curriculum can be instrumental to achieving a better democratic ambience in Africa. As democracy represents a constant work in progress, African states and institutions will have to engage in constant tending of their governance systems to make them work.

Post-Independent African States and the Colonial Structure

Colonization of Africa, it should be recalled, was premised on three main points: the civilizing mission, which was justified in the name of God; wealth accumulation, or the gold factor; and the glory of holding such vast territories. To achieve these objectives, colonial regimes imposed structures of exploitation, oppression, and domination and engaged in the social re-engineering of the colonized people. Although the colonial missionary education system engaged in some artisanal training, it mostly focused on producing a westernized educated elite of clerks, teachers, lawyers, clergy, and medical personnel who managed the lower levels of the colonial state and who became dependent upon the industrialized West. This put the Christian missionary education system at the vanguard of a broad agenda to westernize and civilize the African people, and created an understanding that all useful knowledge came from Europe or the Americas. At the same time, the colonial economy made the West dependent on Africa for raw materials and made Africa dependent on the West for manufactured goods. Upon independence, African countries lacked skilled technicians such as engineers and relied on foreign experts to lead development projects such as construction of new transport infrastructure, processing plants, or dams.

Colonial boundaries and ethnic divisions represent another aspect of colonial structures. To be sure, the colonial powers did not create ethnic identities in Africa as these linguistic-cultural clusters had existed long before the colonial period. What they did instead was to promote ethnic identity as a core administrative principle and to dominate Africa through ethnic divide-and-rule tactics. The colonial powers exacerbated political divisions and rivalries among Africa's ethno-cultural groups, setting them against each other. Ethnic identity, boundaries, and structures then became another colonial construct to be decolonized by post-independent African governments. As we have noted in the previous section, the state handed over to the nationalist politicians was a colonial inherited state, and as such, the structure that sustained this state was that of authoritarian-

ism sometimes cloaked in the rhetoric of humanitarianism and democracy. Aspects of the inherited colonial state included a security apparatus designed to maintain colonial control through violence and local administrations based on the colonial indirect-rule system of ethnically oriented traditional leaders and customary law. Deconstructing these deeply entrenched elements of the old colonial system became extremely difficult, as they had taken on a life of their own.

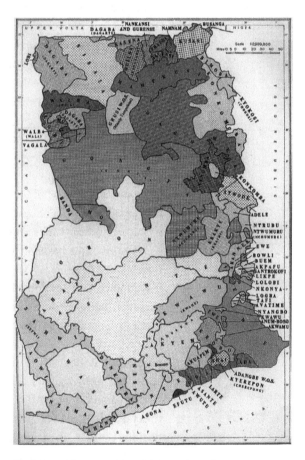

≡ **Cultural diversity.** This 1966 map shows the ethnolinguistic diversity of Ghana. The colors indicate the geographical distribution of the country's many cultural groups.

While it was easy for the governments of independent Africa to reinforce colonial structures, states that tried to change the status quo struggled to find successful alternatives. In places like Ghana, Tanzania, Guinea, Mozambique, Zambia, and Zimbabwe, attempts toward deconstructing the colonial structure led to dictatorship or authoritarian regimes. Anti-colonial leaders like Nkrumah of Ghana, Nyerere of Tanzania, and Touré of Guinea failed as they attempted to impose their agenda by force and their countries' economies deteriorated. Though the people wanted freedom and economic prosperity, they did not often understand the ideologies of these leaders and became alienated from the increasingly oppressive states. With increasing hunger, dilapidated infrastructure, rising unemployment and poverty, and the burgeoning ideological gap between the state and the society, these reforms never saw the light of day as the administrations that initiated them could not live long enough to effect the changes. Furthermore, because these governments were built around a strong figure and not institutions, there was no foundation of continuity for the decolonization projects of these radical leaders.

To understand the inherited colonial structure, it is pertinent to recall that African states achieved independence during the Cold War, and although many claimed non-alignment, they appealed to either the Eastern or Western Bloc to achieve their goals. Those African countries generally on the Western side of the Cold War, also the side of the former colonial powers, maintained free market or liberal economic systems and therefore perpetuated many colonial structures. Meanwhile, Africa's radical anti-colonial leaders sympathetic to the Eastern Bloc tried to dismantle every form of colonial structure both physical and psychological. Both types of African states became oppressive. While the pro-Western regimes repressed opposition leaders and intellectuals who wanted to deconstruct aspects of the inherited colonial state, the pro–Eastern Bloc governments silenced those calling for human rights and freedom of expression, casting them as agents of neocolonialism.

To decolonize Africa is to commence the process of nation building in these states earnestly, and as we have mentioned, these states have remained in disarray, with no consciously built national philosophy and guiding principle that resonates with the whole, or at least the majority, of the people. Therefore, the continued dichotomy between the state and the society represents the biggest obstacle to reform in the independent African states. On the individual state level, some attempts have been made toward educational, political, and economic reforms. While some left-wing postcolonial African states, like Nyerere's Tanzania, attempted to develop education systems focusing on practical skills deemed useful in national development, these "education with production" schemes generally failed as they were unpopular and the regimes that imposed them collapsed. Such states also enacted socialist economic programs, whether the domesticated "African socialism" of Kaunda's Zambia or the Soviet-style "scientific socialism" of Mengistu's Ethiopia, with nationalization of economic assets like farm land and mines. All of these socialist experiments failed in the context of the end of the Cold War, the collapse of the Soviet Union, and the rise of a global neoliberal order. The colonial structure in all of these countries has since been entrenched by the subsequent post–Cold War governments. While the colonial structures originated in the mission of the European powers in Africa, their continuation in the post-independent states ensured the further economic exploitation of the continent for the benefit of external powers and the small African ruling elite. The dependent and weak economy, disjointed educational system, and weak institutions remain the means through which the political elites in Africa perpetuate themselves in power.

Integration of African States and the Development of Regional Intergovernmental Bodies

Regional integration through the instrumentality of **intergovernmental bodies** is meant to mobilize the resources of member states to achieve a common goal that is often embedded in the set objectives of the charter establishing the intergovernmental body in question. In Africa, some attempts at regional coordination began in the era of colonial rule and were aimed at maximizing economic exploitation and colonial control. Examples include the Southern African Customs Union (SACU), created in 1910 to coordinate economic integration of South Africa, Bechuanaland (Botswana), Basutoland (Lesotho), Swaziland (Eswatini), and South West Africa (Namibia), and the African Financial Community (CFA), founded in the 1940s, which tied the currencies of France's West and Central African territories to the French franc. While both of these regional institutions survived decolonization and continue to function today, policymakers and scholars have debated the impact of such inherited colonial regional structures on postcolonial Africa.

With the independence of African states in the late 1950s and 1960s, numerous attempts were made to found regional and continental intergovernmental organizations to facilitate African development and reduce dependence on foreign powers. In 1958, the UN set up the Economic Commission for Africa to assist African countries in the establishment of regional bodies to promote the economic prosperity of member states through regional, cooperative, and integrative efforts. In the same year, Ghana's Pan-Africanist leader Kwame Nkrumah hosted the first Conference of Independent African countries to strengthen the sovereignty of the newly independent African states and aid the struggle of those still under the unpopular colonial domination. Despite disagreements between African leaders from the Pan-Africanist Casablanca Group and the state-oriented Monrovia Group, the growing number of independent African states formed the **Organization of African Unity** (OAU) in 1963 to coordinate economic development and promote African sovereignty. In 2002, in the context of the end of the Cold War and given the OAU's historic unwillingness to interfere in the internal affairs of member states and new international concerns over human rights, the continental grouping was reinvented as the **African Union** (AU) with more proactive policies. Adopting an African Peace and Security Architecture (APSA), the AU committed itself to conflict prevention and management, reserving the right to intervene in member states to protect people from mass violence. At the same time, the AU adopted a policy called the New Partnership for African Development (NEPAD), which aimed at eliminating poverty, encouraging sustainable economic growth, integrating Africa into the global economy, and promoting African women's empowerment. Furthermore, participation in NEPAD programs became dependent on member states' maintaining democratic governance monitored through an African peer-review mechanism. Nevertheless, the AU has faced criticism. APSA's heavy reliance on foreign funding and NEPAD's advancement of Western-style neoliberal economic policies has been derided as neoliberal.

Arguably, Africa's regional international organizations have experienced more success than the continental ones. Formed in 1975, the Economic Community of West African States (ECOWAS) promotes economic integration in West Africa and is on the brink of launching a regional currency called the "eco." Originating among Southern African states seeking to counter the apartheid regime in South Africa in the 1970s and 1980s, the Southern African Development Community (SADC) transformed into a broader regional grouping in the early 1990s seeking to sponsor regional economic and security cooperation. These two regional organizations each center on a major power—ECOWAS has Nigeria and SADC has South Africa—and they have launched multinational military interventions attempting to end civil wars and political turmoil in member states. Other, less robust, African regional groupings include the primarily anglophone East African Community (EAC), initially formed in 1967 but disbanded in 1977 and then recreated in 2000, and the mostly francophone Economic Community of Central African States (ECCAS), founded in 1983.

KEY TERMS

Epilogue: Future Africa

Although historians rarely agree on anything, they tend to share a common hesitancy in predicting the future. Nevertheless, the study of history can provide useful context for understanding the present and what is to come. In that spirit, history shows that the following themes will continue to be relevant in future Africa.

Politics

Despite democratization in some countries, and in the context of a rapidly changing world, Africa continues to suffer from political problems that hinder the continent's potential development and prosperity. Violence, arson, vote buying, and the rigging of election results, among other problems, characterize contemporary African politics in many places. Poor leadership sits at the center of this issue. Many African political leaders do little to address the plight of the majority, catering rather to the interests of the minority elite. Such lopsided treatment and injustice promote provincial agendas and increase divisiveness, further limiting the possibility of improving people's lives. The root of this problem is that modern African states were created by European colonial powers for the benefit of the latter, and these powers forcefully brought together different precolonial nations that had little shared history or culture. African people need to find common ground to develop for themselves the philosophies that will advance their collective course of action for the good. As continuing to build political parties around ethnicity or religion will entrench divisions, Africa needs new movements that will come up with fresh ideas and ideologies to effectively govern the state and unite the people. Political crises will abate when people are treated with justice and equity.

Economies

The future of Africa will rest on its ability to solve economic problems. Due to the failure of African leadership, issues such as poverty, unemployment, underdevelopment, poor medical conditions, hunger, and malnutrition have been difficult to eliminate. Since economic growth represents the foundation for most elements within society, failure to tackle Africa's economic challenges will render other achievements ineffective. Africa's economic plight is rooted in the way that it was incorporated into the world economy for the benefit of foreign colonial rulers, and postcolonial foreign aid and international debt forgiveness have failed to solve larger problems of poverty. Over the past two decades, the increased economic engagement of China in Africa has done little to change this situation. As such, African economies must not be driven by pressure from external actors. This is a difficult task for countries that are mostly engaged in exporting raw materials. The reality of Africa's "resource curse" should end, with the continent's natural resources used for the benefit of its people and not corrupt and unethical leaders.

Youth Demographics

Young people dominate the African population. In 2015, about 40 percent of Africa's total population was below the age of 15 years and one fifth of its people were between 15 and 24 years old. The potential for youth to change African society was demonstrated by the Arab Spring that began in North Africa in 2011, as well as by protests in Algeria and Sudan in 2019 that led to the downfall of long-standing and elderly authoritarian rulers. At the same time, persistent and dire economic problems, particularly lack of employment, inspire disappointment among African youth who move from rural areas to ever-growing cities in search of mostly nonexistent opportunities, with some tragically becoming involved in crime. Others flee their countries as illegal migrants, risking their lives to cross the Sahara Desert and the Mediterranean Sea in search of better living conditions in Europe. Although education is necessary and helpful for youth, many graduates of African universities fail to find jobs and therefore relocate to other continents where there is some chance of fulfilling their dreams. In a vicious circle, Africa's economic dilemma causes a youth brain drain, and this consequently robs the continent of the young and inventive people who might otherwise contribute to solving these problems. These trends will continue as long as Africa's wider political and economic crises remain unresolved.

Popular Culture

Africa is a zone of intense creativity in cultural fields such as music, film, and fashion. During the twentieth century, popular culture emerged as an emancipatory project to break away from the controlling influence of elite culture. In North America and Western Europe, popular culture, or pop culture, became associated with 1960s youth "counterculture," including rock music, poster and T-shirt art, and the drug scene, which rebelled against established authority. In Africa, given the lack of distinct elite and common cultures in many places, the rise of popular culture cut across all elements of society and adapted many external influences. The emergence of pop culture gives music a more important role in the awakening of the masses, fostering a shared identity among ordinary people and linking them together for common social actions. Enabled by an array of technological innovations that animated digital life, pop culture became a resistance culture used to challenge established hegemony, giving the general public a strong medium to air their opinions. At the same time, African pop culture represents an assemblage of historical artifacts and cultural legacies, all of which help to establish a common link with the African diaspora. This has been demonstrated in the global spread of soul and funk music.

The rise of popular culture in Africa ties creativity to politics. Some pop culture icons rise to the growing challenges of political upheavals, showing commitment to the project of improving the environment for everyone. When Nigeria's general elections were approaching in 2019, the musical trio of Tuface, MI, and Chidinma released a song titled "Not For Sale" to encourage a reorientation of electoral behavior. While the American entertainment industry has dominated global popular culture, including within Africa, "Not For Sale" shows African artists carving out their own space and sending their own messages. It therefore becomes obvious that pop culture can become an effective medium for promoting an African identity through the exploration of cultural norms and practices that can be exported to the rest of the world. The rise of instant global communication for ordinary people through social media presents enormous opportunities for the further dissemination of African popular culture. That said, the history of popular culture in postcolonial Africa has demonstrated that while it can serve as a voice for helpless people to express disapproval with harmful policies and to generally enrich life through entertainment, it can also be manipulated for narrow political interests and/or commercial gain. Both possibilities will continue to exist in Africa's future.

Environmental Challenges

Like the rest of the world, Africa will continue to experience environmental crises detrimental to human health and welfare. Exploitation of raw materials for export through activities like logging and mining, along with increasing urbanization, have had devastating effects on the African environment, including deforestation, loss of complex ecosystems, soil degradation, and pollution. These problems are exacerbated by poverty and lack of infrastructure. For instance, in many parts of Africa the unreliable supply of electricity means that many people cut down trees for firewood for cooking and boiling water, thereby contributing to deforestation, erosion, and air pollution. Africa has produced important environmental activists, but for the continent's mostly impoverished population, the daily struggle to survive overshadows longer-term environmental concerns. Although largely non-industrial Africa contributes little to the carbon emissions that are changing the planet's climate, poor African states and economies are not prepared to deal with consequent flooding and

desertification. In another disturbing example, recent scientific studies show that climate change is increasing the massive amount of fine dust particles from the Sahara Desert that are blown by winds across West Africa, causing severe respiratory problems and more deaths in the region than the HIV/AIDS pandemic. As of 2020, there are no concrete plans to address this problem. While attempts are being made to plant trees, develop cleaner sources of fuel for local use, and promote environmental education in parts of Africa, more needs to be done.

Technology

Though definitions vary, technology involves humans assembling components that are ultimately derived from natural resources and transforming and using them in ways that will be helpful in achieving some goal. The world has now entered the Fourth Industrial Revolution with the advent of technologies like autonomous vehicles, artificial intelligence, and an interconnected network of diverse computing devices known as the "Internet of things." Will Africa be left behind? Based on stereotypes of its supposed primitiveness, contemporary Africa is often seen as a static non-technological environment. Of course, this is not true. As this book has demonstrated, technological innovation has represented a consistently important factor in African history. This has not changed. While early-twenty-first-century Africa has the lowest Internet usage of any continent due to relatively low computer literacy and high costs, this situation is changing fast as the continent has the world's highest growth in online access. At the same time, Africa has very quickly become a boom market for cellular communications, enabling people to overcome shortcomings in older communications networks, with cellphones becoming common items in places that never had land-line phones. Cellphone banking and money transfers were pioneered in East Africa to overcome the challenge of limited access to banking facilities in rural areas, and this system has expanded to other parts of Africa, Asia, and Eastern Europe. Furthermore, new cellphone applications are being adapted to help African farmers determine the best time and place for planting, and market their crops. These same apps also widely disseminate information about health and security. Technologies such as these also have the potential to facilitate efficient and transparent elections in Africa. Rwanda presents an interesting example of an African country using technology to chart a new economic path. Attempting to transform its coffee-export economy, Rwanda's government has recently begun facilitating the development of the country as a technology hub, with plans to manufacture cellphones and laptop computers in partnership with international businesses. At the same time, Rwanda's small size and authoritarian state means that this experimental model may not be easily transferred to other African countries. Technologies can also have unforeseen negative consequences. While the Industrial Revolution of the nineteenth century ultimately led to environmental degradation and climate change, current information and communication technologies raise concerns about privacy, state surveillance, and cybercrime. There is no doubt that Africa's engagement with technology will continue into the future, but in ways that are informed by the continent's specific set of circumstances. Despite the continent's history of exploitation by external powers, the extent to which Africa's Fourth Industrial Revolution will be controlled by and serve to benefit foreign or domestic interests remains unknown.

Globalization

Facilitated by transportation and communications technology, as well as the removal of trade barriers between countries, "globalization" refers to the increasing and complex worldwide interaction and integration of people, businesses, and states. In a 2000 report, the International Monetary Fund (IMF) identified four basic aspects of globalization: trade and transactions, capital and investment movements, migration and movement of people, and the propagation of knowledge. Regardless of the possible benefits of globalization, it is important that we consider the place of Africa in the project. This is necessary because globalization can become an avenue for consuming the economic structures of others who are vulnerable because of their level of development. This is what characterized Africa's incorporation into the emerging global economy of the slave trade and colonial eras. African countries have not usually gained improved infrastructure or standards of living from their engagement with contemporary economic globalization. They will need to utilize legal and institutional agreements to enhance the potential benefits of the process and to eliminate parasitic relationships.

Concurrent with economic globalization, cultural globalization involves the worldwide diffusion of ideas through different communication media such as the Internet and television. While the dominance of Western ideas and culture through globalization has been criticized for threatening the survival of distinct African cultures, African artists have used globalization to take their African cultural productions to other parts of the world. Similar trends exist in the educational arena as African students and scholars travel to other continents to gain expertise and ideas and, in the process, economically and culturally enrich their host countries. Contrary to the entertainment industry, though, Africa's experience of educational migration is generally a one-way street as few non-African students migrate to Africa. For future Africa, globalization will continue to offer challenges and opportunities.

Migration

Most simply, "migration" means the movement from one place to another. In general, people's need to relocate is determined by "push" and "pull" factors. "Push" factors include lack of employment, limited economic opportunities, poor living conditions, desertification, drought and famine, political or religious oppression, inferior medical services, natural disasters, rampant crime, and warfare. On the flip side of the coin, "pull" factors include job and other economic prospects, better living conditions, educational opportunities, medical services, and security. For many African people, some combination of these factors is powerful enough that it prompts them to endure the loss of dignity associated with leaving their homeland to endure second-class treatment in other parts of the world, and it reinforces negative perceptions of Africa as a continent. Survival and the desire to live a better life are natural human goals. Of course, migration is not always voluntary. African people have experienced a long history of forced migration to other continents, starting with those captured and exported during the slave trade and continuing to more recent refugees from wars and economic catastrophe. In the modern context, very many African migrants have become successful in their new countries, building better lives for their children and sometimes contributing to their homeland through remittances and investments. In the short term, migration can prove beneficial for a country as it may lower unemployment and reduce demands on scarce resources. However, many African migrants have experienced exploitation and oppression in their host countries, becoming a permanent underclass, and in the long-term context, the loss of so much human potential has likely hindered African development. That said, migration will not stop in a globalized world. If African countries can improve their economy, governance, and security to facilitate dignity at home, then African migrants will be treated with dignity in other parts of the world and Africa itself will attract productive migrants from other continents.

Afrofuturism

The genesis of an emancipatory movement for the African people began with the historic Pan-Africanist movement, but today it has morphed into a call for a desirable future. **Afrofuturism** refers to a flourishing contemporary movement of African-American, African, and Black diasporic writers, artists, musicians, and theorists that especially centers on creating a better image for Black people. It is an outrightly subjective movement because of the exclusive focus given to Black welfare, progress, and essentialism. As a movement that seeks to achieve such targets for Black people who have been victims of global marginalization, Afrofuturism imagines a world where the Black family will attain a position of regard and envy for the contributions they would make to the advancement of humanity. This approach rejects social stigma that blackness somehow exists in opposition to technological narratives of progress. Rather than focusing on predictions of a utopian future, Afrofuturists consider how knowledge of past events in politics, economy, and other social issues will contribute to the project of excellence imagined for the African future. The interconnectedness of African politics, economy, and sometimes technology in the contemporary world justifies the attention given to these factors in an attempt to usher in the desired future.

Conclusion

In all, this book has looked into the various challenges confronting Africa and how they have continued to shape African society in different ways. It has demonstrated how the existing resources are either untapped or are exploited in ways that only benefit the minority, or external forces. In a world that is gravitating toward unprecedented technological, economic, and scientific advancement, Africans need to explore the untapped ingenuity that is evident in their histories because of the immense rewards that await such courageous exploration. In this spirit, efforts are required to study these African legacies so that they can be used for the benefit of people living today.

Further Reading

INTRODUCTION

Asante, Molefi Kete, *The Afrocentric Idea*. Philadelphia: Temple University Press, 1987.

Bernal, Martin, *Black Athena: The Afroasiatic Roots of Classical Civilizations*. London: Vintage, 1991.

Curtin, Philp, *On the Fringes of History: A Memoir*. Athens: Ohio University Press, 2005.

Falola, Toyin, and Jennings, C. (eds.). *Sources and Methods in African History: Spoken, Written, Unearthed*. Rochester, NY: University of Rochester Press, 2003.

Falola, Toyin (ed.). *African Historiography: Essays in Honour of Jacob Ade Ajayi*. Harlow, UK: Longman, 1993.

Henige, David, *Oral Historiography*. London: Heinemann, 1982.

Howe, Stephen, *Afrocentricism: Mythical Pasts and Imagined Homes*. New York: Verso, 1998.

Lefkowitz, Mary, *Not Out of Africa: How Afrocentrism Became an Excuse to Teach Myth as History*. New York: Basic Books, 1996.

Mudimbe, Vatentin-Yves, *The Idea of Africa*. London: James Currey, 1994.

Oliver, Rowland. *In the Realms of Gold: Pioneering in African history*. Madison: University of Wisconsin Press, 1997.

Philips, John Edward, (ed.). *Writing African history*. University of Rochester Press, 2005.

Saunders, Christopher, *The Making of the South African Past: Major Historians on Race and Class*. Cape Town: David Philip, 1988.

Vansina, Jan. *Living with Africa*. Madison: University of Wisconsin Press, 1994.

Vansina, Jan. *Oral Tradition as History*. Madison: University of Wisconsin Press, 1985.

Wright, Harrison, *The Burden of the Present: Liberal-Radical Controversy over Southern African history*. Cape Town: David Philip, 1977.

CHAPTER 1

Ansari Pour, Naser., Paster, Christoper., and Bradman, Neil, "Evidence from Y-chromosome Analysis for a Late Exclusively Eastern Expansion of the Bantu-Speaking People." *European Journal of Human Genetics* 21 (2013): 423–29.

Bocoum, Hamady (ed.). *The Origins of Iron Metallurgy in Africa: New Light on Its Antiquity*. UNESCO Publishing, 2004.

Breunig, Peter (ed.). *Nok: African Sculpture in Archaeological Context*. Frankfurt: Goethe University/National Commission of Museum and Monuments, Abuja, Nigeria, 2014.

Chan, Eva., Timmerman, Axel., Baldi, Benedetta., Moore, Andy., Lyons, Ruth., Lee, Sun-Seon., Kalsbeek, Anton., Petersen, Desiree., Rautenbach, Hannes., Fortsch, Hagen., Bornman, M.S.Rianan., and Hayes, Vanessa.. "Human Origins in a Southern African Palaeo-Wetland and First Migrations." *Nature* 575 (2019): 185–89.

Ehret, Christopher, *An African Classical Age: Eastern and Southern Africa in World History, 1000 BC to 400 AD*. Oxford: James Currey, 1998.

Hall, Martin. *Farmers, Kings and Traders: The People of Southern Africa, 200–1860*. Chicago: University of Chicago Press, 1990.

Herbertl, Eugenia. *Iron, Gender and Power: Rituals of Transformation in African Societies*. Bloomington: Indiana University Press, 1993.

Hoffecker, John F.. *Modern Humans: Their African Origin and Global Dispersal*. New York: Columbia University Press, 2017.

Montano, Valeria, Ferri, Gianmarco, Marcari, Veron-ica, Batini, Chiara, Anyaele, Okorie, Destro-Bisol, Giovani, and Comas, David "The Bantu Expansion Revisited: A New Analysis of Y-chromosome Vari-ation in Central West Africa." *Molecular Ecology* 20 (2011): 2693–708.

Stinger, Chris, and McKie, Robin, *African Exodus: The Origins of Modern Humanity.* New York: Henry Holt, 1997.

Vansina, Jan. "New Linguistic Evidence and 'the Ban-tu Expansion.'" *Journal of African History* 36, no. 2 (1995): 173–96.

CHAPTER 2

Fisher, Marjorie, Lacovara, Peter, Ikram, Salima and D'Auria, Sue *Ancient Nubia: African Kingdoms on the Nile.* Cairo: American University of Cairo Press, 2012.

Goldsworthy, Adrian, *The Fall of Carthage: The Punic Wars 265–146 BC.* Weidenfeld and Nicolson, 2012.

Hoyland, Robert, *In God's Path: The Arab Conquests and the Creation of an Islamic Empire.* Oxford University Press, 2015.

Hoyos, Dexter, *The Carthaginians.* London: Routledge, 2010.

Ikram, Salima, *Ancient Egypt: An Introduction.* Cam-bridge University Press, 2009.

Miles, Richard, *Carthage Must Be Destroyed: The Rise and Fall of an Ancient Civilization.* New York: Viking, 2010.

Naylor, Phillip, *North Africa: A History from Antiquity to the Present.* Austin: University of Texas Press, 2015.

Shaw, Ian, *The Oxford History of Ancient Egypt.* Oxford University Press, 2000.

Shepard, Jonathan, (ed.). *The Cambridge History of the Byzantine Empire, c. 500–1492.* Cambridge Univer-sity Press, 2008.

Shinnie, Peter Lewis, *Ancient Nubia.* London: Rout-ledge, 2009.

Watterson, Barbara, *Women in Ancient Egypt.* Stroud, UK: Amberley Publishing, 2013.

Wilkinson, Toby, *The Rise and Fall of Ancient Egypt.* London: Bloomsbury, 2010.

CHAPTER 3

Abun-Nasr, Jamil M. *A History of the Maghrib in the Is-lamic Period.* Cambridge University Press, 1987.

Asbridge, Thomas. *The Crusades: An Authoritative His-tory of the War for the Holy Land.* New York: Harper-Collins, 2010.

Baadj, Amar S. *Saladin, the Almohads and the Banu Ghaniya: The Contest for North Africa (12th and 13th Centuries).* Leiden, Netherlands: Brill, 2015.

Bennison, Amira. *The Almoravid and Almohad Empires.* Edinburgh University Press, 2016.

Brett, Michael. *The Fatimid Empire.* Edinburgh Univer-sity Press, 2017.

Daftary, Farhad, and Shainool Jiwa (eds.). *The Fatimid Caliphate: Diversity of Traditions.* London: I.B. Tau-ris, 2018.

Man, John. *Saladin: The Sultan who Vanquished the Cru-saders and Built and Islamic Empire.* Bantam Press, 2015.

Meri, Josef W. (ed.). *Medieval Islamic Civilization: An Encyclopedia.* New York: Routledge, 2006.

Naylor, P.C. *North Africa: A History from Antiquity to the Present.* Austin: University of Texas Press, 2015.

Spaulding, Jay. "Medieval Christian Nubia and the Is-lamic World: A Reconsideration of the Baqt Treaty." *International Journal of African Historical Studies* 28, no. 3 (1995): 577–94.

Welsby, Derek. *The Medieval Kingdoms of Nubia: Pagans, Christian and Muslims along the Middle Nile.* British Museum Press, 2002.

CHAPTER 4

Bovill, E.W. *The Golden Trade of the Moors.* London: Oxford University Press, 1968.

De Villiers, Marq, and Hirtle, Sheila. *Timbuktu: The Sahara's Fabled City of Gold.* McClelland & Stewart, 2007.

Gomez, Michael. *African Dominion: A New History of Empire in Early and Medieval West Africa.* Princeton University Press, 2018.

Hunwick, John. *Timbuktu and the Songhai Empire.* Leiden, Netherlands: Brill, 2003.

Niane, DjibrilTamsir, *Sundiata: An Epic of Old Mali.* Harlow, UK: Longman, 1994.

Law, Robin. *The Horse in West African History: The Role of the Horse in Pre-colonial West African Societies.* Oxford University Press, 1980.

Levtzion, Nehemia. *Ancient Ghana and Mali.* New York: Africana Publishing, 1980.

Levtzion, Nehemia. *Islam in West Africa: Religion, Society and Politics to 1800.* Routledge, 2018.

Lovejoy, Paul. *Transformations in Slavery: A History of Slavery in Africa.* Cambridge University Press, 1983.

McKissack, Patricia, and Frederick McKissack. *The Royal Kingdoms of Ghana, Mali and Songhai: Life in Medieval Africa.* New York: Henry Holt and Company, 1994.

Saad, Elias. *Social History of Timbuktu: The Role of Muslim Scholars and Notables 1400–1900.* Cambridge University Press, 1983.

Smith, Robert. *Warfare and Diplomacy in Pre-Colonial West Africa.* Madison: University of Wisconsin Press, 1989.

CHAPTER 5

Abun-Nasr, Jamil M. *A History of the Maghrib in the Islamic Period.* Cambridge University Press, 1987.

Kallander, Amy. *Women, Gender and the Palace Household in Ottoman Tunisia.* Austin: University of Texas Press, 2013.

Lebbady, Hasna. *Feminist Traditions in Andalusi-Moroccan Oral Narratives.* Palgrave-MacMillan, 2009.

McDougall, James. *A History of Algeria.* Cambridge University Press, 2017.

Naylor, P.C. *North Africa: A History from Antiquity to the Present.* Austin: University of Texas Press, 2015.

Ogot, Bethwell Allen, (ed.). *UNESCO General History of Africa: Africa from the Sixteenth to Eighteenth Century.* Oxford: James Currey, 1999.

Pennell, C.R. *Morocco: From Empire to Independence.* Oxford: One World, 2003.

Spaulding, Jay. *The Heroic Age in Sinnar.* Red Sea Press, 2007.

Winter, Michael. *Egyptian Society Under Ottoman Rule, 1517–1798.* London: Routledge, 1992.

Wright, John. *A History of Libya.* London: Hurst and Coy, 2012.

CHAPTER 6

Birmingham, David. *Trade and Conflict in Angola: The Mbundu and Their Neighbours Under the Influence of the Portuguese 1483–1790.* Oxford: Clarendon Press, 1966.

Curtin, Philip. *The Atlantic Slave Trade: A Census.* Madison: University of Wisconsin Press, 1969.

Eltis, David. *Economic Growth and the Ending of the Transatlantic Slave Trade.* Oxford University Press, 1987.

Green, Toby. *The Rise of the Trans-Atlantic Slave Trade in Western Africa, 1300–1589.* Cambridge University Press, 2012.

Heywood, Linda. *Njinga of Angola: Africa's Warrior Queen.* Cambridge, MA: Harvard University Press, 2017.

Law, Robin. *The Slave Coast of West Africa, 1550–1750.* Oxford: Clarendon Press, 1991.

Lovejoy, Paul. *Transformations in Slavery: A History of Slavery in Africa.* Cambridge University Press, 1983.

Manning, Patrick. *Slavery and African Life: Occidental, Oriental and African Slave Trades.* Cambridge University Press, 1990.

Miller, Joseph. *Way of Death: Merchant Capitalism and the Angolan Slave Trade 1730–1830.* Madison: University of Wisconsin Press, 1988.

Thornton, John. *The Kingdom of Kongo: Civil War and Transition, 1641–1718.* Madison: University of Wisconsin Press, 1983.

Thornton, John. *The Kongolese Saint Anthony: Dona Beatriz Kimpa Vita and the Antonian Movement, 1684–1706.* New York: Cambridge University Press, 1998.

Thornton, John. *Warfare in Atlantic Africa, 1500-1800.* New York: Routledge, 1999.

CHAPTER 7

Alpers, Edward. *Ivory and Enslaved People in East Central Africa.* University of California Press, 1975.

Campbell, Gwyn. *Africa and the Indian Ocean World from Early Times to Circa 1900.* Cambridge University Press, 2019.

Chretien, Jean-Pierre. *The Great Lakes of Africa: Two Thousand Years of History*. New York: Zone Books, 2003.

Pankhurst, Richard. *The Ethiopians: A History*. Oxford: Blackwell, 1998.

Randrianja, Solofo, and Stephen Ellis. *Madagascar: A Short History*. Chicago: University of Chicago Press, 2009.

Reid, Richard. *Political Power in Pre-colonial Buganda*. Oxford: James Currey, 2002.

Stephens, Rhiannon. *A History of African Motherhood: The Case of Uganda, 700–1900*. New York: Cambridge University Press, 2013.

Vansina, Jan. *Antecedents to Modern Rwanda: The Nyiginya Kingdom*. Madison: University of Wisconsin Press, 2004.

CHAPTER 8

Alpers, Edward. *Ivory and Enslaved People in East Central Africa*. University of California Press, 1975.

Birmingham, David. *Central Africa to 1870*. London: Cambridge University Press, 1981.

De Maret, Pierre. "Luba Roots: The First Complete Iron Age Sequence in Zaire." *Current Anthropology* 20, no. 1 (1979): 233–35.

Dlamini, Nonhlanhla. "In Search of the Early Inhabitants of Central Katanga, Democratic Republic of Congo." *South African Archaeological Society Goodwin Series* 11 (2013): 78–87.

Mainga, Mutumba. *Bulozi under the Luyana Kings: Political Evolution and State Formation in Pre-Colonial Zambia*. Lusaka: Bookworld Publishers, 2010.

Evans-Pritchard, Edward, *The Azande: History and Political Institutions*. Oxford: Clarendon Press, 1971.

Reefe, Thomas Q. *The Rainbow and the Kings: A History of the Luba Empire to 1891*. Los Angeles: University of California Press, 1981.

Roberts, Andrew. *A History of Zambia*. London: Heinemann, 1976.

Roberts, Andrew. *A History of the Bemba: Political Growth and Change in North-eastern Zambia before 1900*. London: Longman, 1973.

Schoffeleers, Matthew. "The Zimba and the Lundu State in the Late Sixteenth and Early Seventeenth Centuries." *Journal of African History* 28, no. 3 (1987): 337–55.

Vansina, Jan. *Kingdoms of the Savanna*. Madison: University of Wisconsin Press, 1966.

Vansina, Jan. *Paths in the Rainforest: Toward a History of Political Tradition in Equatorial Africa*. Madison: University of Wisconsin, 1990.

Vansina, Jan. *The Children of Woot: A History of the Kuba Peoples*. Madison: University of Wisconsin Press, 1983.

Yoder, John C. *The Kanyok of Zaire: An Institutional and Ideological History to 1895*. Cambridge University Press, 1992.

CHAPTER 9

Beach, David. *The Shona and Zimbabwe, 900–1850*. Gweru: Mambo Press, 1980.

Bhila, H.H.K. *Trade and Politics in a Shona Kingdom: The Manyika and Their African and Portuguese Neighbours, 1575–1902*. London: Longman, 1982.

Crais, Clifton, and Scully, Pamela *Sara Baartman and the Hottentot Venus: A Ghost Story and a Biography*. Princeton University Press, 2009.

Eldredge, Elizabeth *Kingdoms and Chiefdoms of Southeastern Africa: Oral Tradition and History*. University of Rochester Press, 2015.

Elphick, Richard, *Kraal and Castle: Khoikhoi and the Founding of White South Africa*. New Haven: Yale University Press, 1977.

Fontein, Joost. *The Silence of Great Zimbabwe: Contested Landscapes and the Power of Heritage*. London: Routledge, 2016.

Hall, Martin, *The Changing Past: Farmers, Kings and Traders in Southern Africa, 200–1860*. Cape Town: David Philip, 1987.

Huffman, Thomas,. *Mapungubwe: An Ancient African Civilization on the Limpopo*. Johannesburg: Wits University Press, 2005.

Huffman, Thomas. *Snakes and Crocodiles: Power and Symbolism in Ancient Zimbabwe*. Johannesburg: Wits University Press, 1996.

Mudenge, Stanley *A Political History of Munhumutapa, c.1400–1902*. Harare: Zimbabwe Publishing House, 1988.

Pikirayi, Innocent. *The Zimbabwe Culture: Origins and Decline in Southern Zambesian States*. New York: Altamira Press, 2001.

Shell, Robert, *Children of Bondage: A Social History of the Slave Society at the Cape of Good Hope, 1652-1838*. Hanover, NH: University of New England Press, 1994.

Worden, Nigel, *Slavery in Dutch South Africa*. Cambridge University Press, 1985.

CHAPTER 10

Abun-Nasr, Jamil M. *A History of the Maghrib in the Islamic Period*. Cambridge University Press, 1987.

Lambert, Frank. *The Barbary Wars: America's Independence in the Atlantic World*. New York: Hill and Wang, 2005.

Marsot, Afaf Lutfi al-Sayyid. *Egypt in the Reign of Muhammad Ali*. Cambridge University Press, 1984.

Mitchell, Timothy. *Colonizing Egypt*. Berkeley: University of California Press, 1988.

McDougall, James. *A History of Algeria*. Cambridge University Press, 2017.

Naylor, Phillip, *North Africa: A History from Antiquity to the Present*. Austin: University of Texas Press, 2015.

Pennell, C.R. *Morocco: From Empire to Independence*. Oxford: One World, 2003.

Tucker, Judith. *Women in Nineteenth Century Egypt*. Cambridge University Press, 2009.

Wright, John. *A History of Libya*. London: Hurst and Coy, 2012.

CHAPTER 11

Ajayi, Jacob FestusAde, and Smith, R.S.. *Yoruba Warfare in the Nineteenth Century*. Cambridge University Press, 1964.

Carretta, Vincent. *Equiano the African: Biography of a Self-made Man*. Athens: University of Georgia Press, 2005.

Dike, Kenneth. *Trade and Politics in the Niger Delta, 1830–1885: An Introduction to the Economic and Political History of Nigeria*. Oxford: Clarendon Press, 1956.

Everill, Bronwell. *Abolition and Empire in Sierra Leone and Liberia*. Basingstoke, UK: Palgrave-MacMillan, 2013.

Falola, Toyin. *Ibadan: Foundation, Growth and Change, 1830–1960*. Ibadan, Nigeria: Bookcraft, 2012.

Hall, Bruce, S. *A History of Race in Muslim West Africa, 1600–1960*. Cambridge University Press, 2011.

Keefer, Katrina. *Left in Our Hands: Children, Education and Empire in Early Sierra Leone*. Routledge, 2018.

Law, Robin. *The Oyo Empire, c. 1600–1836: A West African Imperialism in the Era of the Atlantic Slave Trade*. Oxford University Press, 1991.

Law, Robin (ed.). *From Slave Trade to Legitimate Commerce: The Commercial Transition in Nineteenth Century West Africa*. Cambridge University Press, 1995.

Levitt, Jeremy. *The Evolution of Deadly Conflict in Liberia*. Durham, NC: Carolina Academic Press, 2005.

Salau, Mohammed Bashir. *Plantation Slavery in the Sokoto Caliphate: A Historical and Comparative Study*. University of Rochester Press, 2018.

Sherwood, Marika. *After Abolition: Britain and the Slave Trade Since 1807*. London: I.B. Tauris, 2007.

Smaldone, Joseph. *Warfare in the Sokoto Caliphate: Historical and Sociological Perspectives*. London: Cambridge University Press, 1977.

Wilks, Ivor. *Asante in the Nineteenth Century: The Structure and Evolution of a Political Order*. Cambridge University Press, 1975.

CHAPTER 12

Alpers, Edward. *Ivory and Enslaved People in East Central Africa*. University of California Press, 1975.

Bennett, Norman. *Mirambo of Tanzania, c. 1840–1884*. London: Oxford University Press, 1971.

Campbell, Gwyn. *An Economic History of Imperial Madagascar, 1750–1895: The Rise and Fall of an Island Empire*. Cambridge University Press, 2005.

Feierman, Steven. *The Shambaaka Kingdom: A History*. Madison: University of Wisconsin Press, 1974.

Kimambo, Isaria. *A Political History of the Pare of Tanzania, 1500–1900.* Nairobi: East Africa Publishing House, 1969.

Lamphear, John. *The Scattering Time: Turkana Responses to Colonial Rule.* Oxford: Clarendon Press, 1992.

Medard, Henri, and Doyle, Shane (ed.). *Slavery in the Great Lakes Region of East Africa.* Oxford: James Currey, 2007.

Pankhurst, Richard. *The Ethiopians: A History.* Oxford: Blackwell, 1998.

Randrianja, Solofo, and Stephen Ellis. *Madagascar: A Short History.* University of Chicago Press, 2009.

Reid, Richard. *Political Power in Pre-Colonial Buganda: Economy, Society and Warfare in the Nineteenth Century.* Oxford: James Currey, 2002.

Roberts, Andrew (ed.). *Tanzania Before 1900.* Nairobi: East African Publishing House, 1968.

Sheriff, Abdul. *Enslaved people, Spices and Ivory in Zanzibar.* James Currey, 1987.

Sheriff, Abdul, Vijayalakshmi Teelock, Saada Omar Wahad, and Satyendra Peerthum (eds.). *Transition from Slavery in Zanzibar and Mauritius: A Comparative History.* Dakar: CODESRIA, 2016.

Spear, Thomas, and Richard Waller (eds.). *Being Maasai: Ethnicity and Identity in East Africa.* London: James Currey, 1993.

Vansina, Jan. *Antecedents to Modern Rwanda: The Nyiginya Kingdom.* Madison: University of Wisconsin Press, 2004.

CHAPTER 13

Delius, Peter. *The Land Belongs to Us: The Pedi Polity, the Boers and the British in the Nineteenth-Century Transvaal.* Johannesburg: Ravan Press, 1983.

Eldredge, Elizabeth, *A South African Kingdom: The Pursuit of Security in Nineteenth Century Lesotho.* Cambridge University Press, 2002.

Etherington, Norman. *Great Treks: The Transformation of Southern Africa.* London: Longman, 2001.

Giliomee, Herman. *The Afrikaners: Biography of a People.* Charlottesville: University of Virginia Press, 2003.

Hamilton, Carolyn, (ed.). *Mfecane Aftermath: Reconstructive Debates in Southern African History.* Johannesburg: Witwatersrand University Press, 1995.

Laband, John. *Rope of Sand: The Rise and Fall of the Zulu Kingdom in the Nineteenth Century.* Johannesburg: Jonathan Ball, 1995.

Mostert, Noel, *Frontiers: The Epic of South Africa's Creation and the Tragedy of the Xhosa People.* New York: Knopf, 1992.

Peires, Jeff. *The Dead Will Arise: Nongqawuse and the Great Xhosa Cattle-Killing Movement of 1856–57.* Johannesburg: Ravan Press, 1989.

Peires, Jeff. *The House of Phalo: A History of the Xhosa People in the Days of their Independence.* Johannesburg: Ravan Press, 1981.

Rasmussen, R. Kent, *Migrant Kingdom: Mzilikazi's Ndebele in South Africa.* London: Collings, 1978.

Stapleton, Timothy, *Faku: Rulership and Colonialism in the Mpondo Kingdom.* Waterloo, ON: Wilfrid Laurier University Press, 2001.

Stapleton, Timothy, *Maqoma: Xhosa Resistance to Colonial Advance.* Johannesburg: Jonathan Ball, 1994.

Thompson, Leonard, *Survival in Two Worlds: Moshoeshoe of Lesotho, 1786–1870.* Oxford: Oxford University Press, 1976.

Wylie, Dan. *Myth of Iron: Shaka in History.* Pietermaritzburg: University of KwaZulu-Natal Press, 2006.

CHAPTER 15

Hobson, John. *Imperialism: A Study.* London: Allen and Unwin, 1902.

Hochschild, Adam. *King Leopold's Ghost: A Story of Greed, Terror and Heroism in Colonial Africa.* New York: Mariner Books, 1999.

Hopkins, A.G. *An Economic History of West Africa.* London: Longman, 1973.

Jonas, Raymond. *The Battle of Adwa: African Victory in the Age of Empire.* Cambridge, MA: Harvard University Press, 2011.

Lenin, V.I. *Imperialism: The Highest Stage of Capitalism.* New York: International Publishers, 1969 (originally published 1916).

Levering Lewis, David. *The Race to Fashoda: Colonialism and African Resistance.* New York: Weidenfeld and Nicolson, 1987.

Matson, A.T. *Nandi Resistance to British Rule, 1890–1906.* Nairobi: East Africa Publishing House, 1972.

Pakenham, Thomas. *The Scramble for Africa: White Man's Conquest of the Dark Continent, 1876–1912.* New York: Harper Collins, 1991.

Perras, Arne. *Carl Peters and German Imperialism, 1856–1918.* Oxford University Press, 2004.

Porch, Douglas. *The Conquest of the Sahara.* New York: Knopf, 2005.

Robinson, Ronald, and John Gallagher. *Africa and the Victorians: The Official Mind of Imperialism.* London: MacMillan, 1961.

Vandervort, Bruce. *Wars of Imperial Conquest in Africa 1830–1914.* Bloomington: Indiana University Press, 1998.

Vanthemsche, Guy. *Belgium and the Congo, 1885–1980.* Cambridge University Press, 2012.

CHAPTER 16

Delius, Peter. *The Land Belongs to Us: The Pedi Polity, the Boers and the British in the Nineteenth Century Transvaal.* Los Angeles: University of California Press, 1984.

Gewald, Jan-Bart. *Herero Heroes: A Socio-Political History of the Herero of Namibia, 1890–1923.* Oxford: James Currey, 1999.

Heywood, Linda. *Contested Power in Angola: 1840s to the Present.* Rochester, NY: University of Rochester Press, 2000.

Laband, John. *Rope of Sand: The Rise and Fall of the Zulu Kingdom in the Nineteenth Century.* Johannesburg: Jonathan Ball Publishers, 1995.

Laband, John. *The Transvaal Rebellion: The First Boer War 1880–1881.* Harlow, UK: Pearson/Longman, 2005.

Meredith, Martin. *Diamonds, Gold and War: The British, the Boers and the Making of South Africa.* New York: Public Affairs, 2007.

Nasson, Bill. *The South African War 1899–1902.* London: Hodder Arnold, 1999.

Newitt, Malyn. *A History of Mozambique.* Bloomington: Indiana University Press, 1995.

Pakenham, Thomas. *The Boer War.* London: Weidenfeld and Nicholson, 1979.

Rotberg, Robert. *The Founder: Cecil Rhodes and the Pursuit of Power.* New York: Oxford University Press, 1988.

Shillington, Kevin. *Luka Jantjie: Resistance Hero of the South African Frontier.* New York: Palgrave-MacMillan, 2011.

Turrell, Robert V. *Capital and Labour on the Kimberley Diamond Fields, 1871–1890.* Cambridge University Press, 1987.

Van Onselen, Charles. *New Babylon New Nineveh: Everyday Life on the Witwatersrand, 1886–1914.* Johannesburg: Jonathan Ball Publishers, 2001 (originally published 1982).

CHAPTER 17

Barnes, Andrew. *Making Headway: The Introduction of Western Civilization in Colonial Northern Nigeria.* Rochester, NY: University of Rochester Press, 2009.

Bundy, Colin. *The Rise and Fall of the South African Peasantry.* Berkeley: University of California Press, 1979.

Brett, E.A. *Colonialism and Underdevelopment in East Africa: The Politics of Economic Change, 1919–39.* New York: NOK Publishers, 1973.

Falola, Toyin. *Colonialism and Violence in Nigeria.* Bloomington: Indiana University Press, 2009.

Gailey, Harry. *Lugard and the Abeokuta Uprisings: The Demise of Egba Independence.* London: Frank Cass, 1982.

Mamdani, Mahmood. *Citizen and Subject: Contemporary Africa and the Legacy of Late Colonialism.* Princeton, NJ: Princeton University Press, 1996.

Ochunu, Moses E. *Colonial Meltdown: Northern Nigeria in the Great Depression.* Athens: Ohio University Press, 2009.

Ochunu, Moses E. *Colonialism by Proxy: Hausa Imperial Agents and Middle Belt Consciousness in Nigeria.* Bloomington: Indiana University Press, 2014.

Palmer, Robin. *Land and Racial Domination in Rhodesia.* Berkeley: University of California Press, 1977.

Parsons, Timothy H. *The African Rank-and-File: Social Implications of Colonial Military Service in the King's African Rifles, 1902–1964.* Portsmouth, NH: Heinemann, 1999.

Shanguhyia, Martin, and Toyin Falola (eds.). *The Palgrave Handbook of Colonial and Post-colonial African History.* Palgrave-MacMillan, 2018.

Umar, Muhammad S. *Islam and Colonialism: Intellectual Responses of Muslims of Northern Nigeria to British Colonial Rule.* Leiden, Netherlands: Brill, 2006.

Van Onselen. Charles, *Chibaro: African Mine Labour in Southern Rhodesia, 1900–33.* London: Pluto Press, 1980.

Young, Crawford. *The African Colonial State in Comparative Perspective.* Yale University Press, 1994.

CHAPTER 18

Aderinto, Saheed. *Guns and Society in Colonial Nigeria: Firearms, Culture and Public Order.* Bloomington: Indiana University Press, 2018.

Alegi, Peter. *African Soccerscapes: How a Continent Changed the World's Game.* Athens: Ohio University Press, 2010.

Ansell, Gwen. *Soweto Blues: Jazz, Popular Music and Politics in South Africa.* New York: Continuum, 2004.

Barnes, Andrew. *Making Headway: The Introduction of Western Civilization in Colonial Northern Nigeria.* Rochester, NY: University of Rochester Press, 2009.

Collins, John. "The Early History of West African Highlife Music." *Popular Music.* 8, no. 3 (1989), 221–30.

Fleming, Tyler, *Opposing Apartheid On Stage: King Kong the Musical.* Rochester, NY: University of Rochester Press, 2020.

Kanogo, Tabitha. *African Womanhood in Colonial Kenya, 1900–1950.* London: James Currey, 2005.

Levtzion, Nehemia, and Randall Pouwels (eds.) *The History of Islam in Africa.* Athens: Ohio University Press, 2000.

Martin, Phyllis. *Leisure and Society in Colonial Brazzaville.* Cambridge University Press, 1995.

Schmidt, Elizabeth. *Peasants, Traders and Wives: Shona Women in the History of Zimbabwe, 1870–1939.* Harare: Baobab Press, 1992.

Shank, David A. *Prophet Harris: The "Black Elijah" of West Africa.* Leiden, Netherlands: Brill, 1994.

Steinhart, Edward. *Black Poachers, White Hunters: A Social History of Hunting in Colonial Kenya.* Oxford: James Currey, 2006.

Stewart, Gary. *Rumba on the River: A History of Popular Music in the Two Congos.* London: Verso, 2000.

Sundkler, Bengt. *Bantu Prophets in South Africa.* London: Lutterworth Press, 1948.

Vail, Leroy (ed.). *The Creation of Tribalism in Southern Africa.* Berkeley: University of California Press, 1991.

Webster, James B. *African Churches Among the Yoruba, 1888–1922.* Oxford: Clarendon Press, 1964.

West, Michael. *The Rise of an African Middle Class: Colonial Zimbabwe, 1895–1965.* Bloomington: Indiana University Press, 2002.

White, Luise. *The Comforts of Home: Prostitution in Colonial Nairobi.* University of Chicago Press, 1990.

CHAPTER 19

Abdi Abdulqadir, Sheik-Abdi. *Divine Madness: Mohammed Abdulle Hassan (1856–1920).* London: Zed Books, 1983.

Adi, Hakim. *Pan-Africanism and Communism: The Communist International, Africa and the Diaspora, 1919–39.* Trenton, NJ: Africa World Press, 2013.

Derrick, Jonathan. *Africa's Agitators: Militant Anti-Colonialism in Africa and the West, 1918–39.* New York: Columbia University Press, 2008.

Edgar, Robert. *The Finger of God: Enoch Mgijima, the Israelites and the Bulhoek Massacre in South Africa.* Charlottesville: University of Virginia Press, 2018.

Ellis, Stephen, and Tsepo Sechaba. *Comrades Against Apartheid: The ANC and the South African Communist Party in Exile.* London: James Currey, 1992.

Ewing, Adam. *The Age of Garvey: How a Jamaican Activist Created a Mass Movement and Changed Global Black Politics.* Princeton University Press, 2014.

Falola, Toyin, and Adam Paddock. *The Women's War of 1929: A History of Anti-Colonial Resistance in Eastern Nigeria.* Durham, NC: Carolina Academic Press, 2011.

Frederickson, George. *Black Liberation: A Comparative History of Black Ideologies in the United States and South Africa.* Oxford University Press, 1995.

Gershovich, Moshe. *French Military Rule in Morocco: Colonialism and Its Consequences.* London: Frank Cass, 2000.

Kanogo, Tabitha. *African Womanhood in Colonial Kenya, 1900–1950.* Oxford: James Currey, 2005.

Lewis, John. *Industrialization and Trade Union Formation in South Africa, 1924–1955.* Cambridge University Press, 1984.

Marshal, Jules. *Lord Leverhulme's Ghosts: Colonial Exploitation in the Congo.* London: Verso, 2018.

McCracken, John. *Politics and Christianity in Malawi, 1875–1940.* Cambridge University Press, 1977.

Odendaal, Andre. *The Founders: The Origin of the ANC and the Struggle for Democracy in South Africa.* Lexington: University of Kentucky Press, 2013.

Omissi, David. *Air Power and Colonial Control: The Royal Air Force, 1919–1939.* Manchester University Press, 1990.

O'Toole, Thomas. "The 1928–31 Gbaya Insurrection in Ubangui-Shari: Messianic Movement of Village Self-Defence?" *Canadian Journal of African Studies* 18, no. 2 (1984), 329–44.

Thomas, Martin. *The French Empire Between the Wars.* Manchester University Press, 2005.

Simons, Geoffrey Leslie. *Libya: The Struggle for Survival.* New York: Saint Martin's Press, 1993.

Strang, Bruce (ed.). *Collision of Empires: Italy's Invasion of Ethiopia and its International Impact.* London: Routledge, 2016.

Walters, Ronald. *Pan-Africanism in the African Diaspora: An Analysis of Modern Afrocentric Political Movements.* Detroit: Wayne State University Press, 1993.

CHAPTER 20

Anderson, Ross. *The Forgotten Front: The East African Campaign, 1914–1918.* Stroud, UK: Tempus, 2004.

Bierman, John, and Colin Smith. *War without Hate: The Desert Campaign of 1940–43.* New York: Penguin Books, 2002.

Byfield, Judith, Carolyn Brown, Timothy Parsons, and Ahmad Alawad Sikainga (eds.). *Africa and World War II.* Cambridge University Press, 2015.

Clothier, Norman. *Black Valour: The South African Native Labour Contingent, 1916–1918 and the Sinking of the Mendi.* Pietermaritzburg: University of Natal Press, 1987.

Echenberg, Myron. *Colonial Conscripts: The "Tirailleurs Senegalais" in French West Africa, 1857–1960.* Portsmouth, NH: Heinemann, 1991.

Fogarty, Richard. *Race and War in France: Colonial Subjects in the French Army, 1914–1918.* Baltimore: Johns Hopkins University Press, 2008.

Grundlingh, Albert. *Fighting Their Own War: South African Blacks and the First World War.* Johannesburg: Ravan Press, 1987.

Grundlingh, Albert. *War and Society: South African Black and Coloured Troops in the First World War, 1914–1918.* Stellenbosch, South Africa: SUN Media, 2014.

Jackson, Ashley. *Botswana 1939–1945: An African Country at War.* Oxford: Clarendon Press, 1999.

Jackson, Ashley. *The British Empire and the Second World War.* London: Hambledon Continuum, 2006.

Killingray, David. *Fighting for Britain: African Soldiers in the Second World War.* Rochester, NY: James Currey, 2010.

Lawler, Nancy. *Soldiers, Airmen, Spies and Whisperers: The Gold Coast in World War II.* Ohio University Press, 2002.

Lawler, Nancy. *Soldiers of Misfortune: Ivoirien Tirailleurs of World War II.* Athens: Ohio University Press, 1992.

Lunn, Joe. *Memories of the Maelstrom: A Senegalese Oral History of the First World War.* Portsmouth, NH: Heinemann, 1999.

McGregor, Andrew. *A Military History of Modern Egypt: from the Ottoman Conquest to the Ramadan War.* Westport, CT: Praeger Security International, 2006.

Nasson, Bill. *Springboks on the Somme: South Africa and the Great War, 1914–1918*. Johannesburg: Penguin, 2007.

Nasson, Bill. *World War One and the People of South Africa*. Cape Town: Tafelberg, 2014.

Page, Melvin. *The Chiwaya War: Malawians and the First World War*. Boulder: Westview Press, 2000.

Paice, Edward. *Tip and Run: The Untold Tragedy of the Great War in Africa*. London: Weidenfeld and Nicolson, 2007.

Saul, Mahir, and Patrick Royer. *West African Challenge to Empire: Culture and History in the Volta-Bani Anti-Colonial War*. Athens: Ohio University Press, 2001.

Scheck, Raffael. *Hitler's African Victims: The German Army Massacres of Black French Soldiers in 1940*. Cambridge University Press, 2006.

Samson, Anne. *World War One in Africa: The Forgotten Conflict Among the European Powers*. London: I.B. Tauris, 2013.

Schmitt, Deborah Ann. *The Bechuanaland Pioneers and Gunners*. Westport: Praeger, 2006.

Shepperson, G., and T. Price. *Independent African: John Chilembwe and the Origins, Setting and Significance of the Nyasaland Native Rising of 1915*. Edinburgh: Edinburgh University Press, 1958.

Smith, Colin. *England's Last War Against France: Fighting Vichy 1940–42*. London: Weidenfeld and Nicolson, 2010.

Stapleton, Timothy J. *No Insignificant Part: The Rhodesia Native Regiment and the East African Campaign of the First World War*. Waterloo, ON: Wilfrid Laurier University Press, 2006.

Stewart, Andrew. *The First Victory: The Second World War and the East Africa Campaign*. New Haven: Yale University Press, 2016.

Strachan, Hew. *The First World War in Africa*. Oxford University Press, 2004.

CHAPTER 21

Anderson, David. *Histories of the Hanged: The Dirty War in Kenya and the End of Empire*. London: Weidenfeld and Nicolson, 2005.

Bjerk, Paul. *Building a Peaceful Nation: Julius Nyerere and the Establishment of Sovereignty in Tanzania, 1960–64*. Rochester, NY: University of Rochester Press, 2015.

Birmingham, David. *Kwame Nkrumah: The Father of African Nationalism*. Athens: Ohio University Press, 1998.

Elkins, Caroline. *Imperial Reckoning: The Untold Story of Britain's Gulag in Kenya*. New York: Henry Holt, 2005.

Falola, Toyin, and Bola Dauda. *Decolonizing Nigeria, 1945–1960: Politics, Power and Personalities*. Austin, TX: Pan-African University Press, 2017.

Flint, J.E. "Planned Decolonization and Its Failure in British Africa." *African Affairs* 82, no. 328 (1983), 389–411.

Hargreaves, J.D. *Decolonization in Africa*. London: Longmans, 1988.

Geiger, Sudan. *TANU Women: Gender and Culture in the Making of Tanganyika Nationalism, 1955–1965*. Portsmouth, NH: Heinemann, 1997.

Louis, Wm. Roger. *Ends of British Imperialism: The Scramble for Empire, Suez and Decolonization*. London: I.B. Tauris, 2006.

Nwaubani, Ebere. *The United States and the Decolonization of West Africa, 1950–60*. Rochester, NY: University of Rochester Press, 2001.

Parsons, Timothy. *The 1964 Army Mutinies and the Making of Modern East Africa*. Westport, CT: Praeger Publishers, 2003.

Pratt, Cranford. *The Critical Phase in Tanzania, 1945–68: Nyerere and the Emergence of a Socialist Strategy*. Cambridge University Press, 1976.

Presley, Cora-Ann. *Kikuyu Women, the Mau Mau Rebellion and Social Change in Kenya*. Boulder: Westview Press, 1992.

Sherwood, Marika. *Kwame Nkrumah and the Dawn of the Cold War: The West African National Secretariat, 1945–48*. London: Pluto Press, 2019.

CHAPTER 22

Alexander, Martin S., and, J.F.V. Keiger (eds.). *France and the Algerian War, 1954–62: Strategy, Operations and Diplomacy*. London: Frank Cass, 2002.

Atangana, Martin. *The End of French Rule in Cameroon*. Lanham, MD: University Press of America, 2010.

Aussaresses, Paul. *The Battle of the Casbah: Terrorism and Counter-Terrorism in Algeria, 1955–57.* New York: Enigma Books, 2004.

Cann, John P. *Counterinsurgency in Africa: The Portuguese Way of War, 1961–1974.* Westport, CT: Greenwood, 1997.

Carney, Jay. *Rwanda Before the Genocide: Catholic Politics and Ethnic Discourse in the Late Colonial Era.* Oxford University Press, 2014.

Chafer, Tony. *The End of Empire in French West Africa: France's Successful Decolonization.* New York: Berg, 2002.

Clayton, Anthony. *The Wars of French Decolonization.* New York: Routledge, 2013.

De Witte, Ludo. *The Assassination of Patrice Lumumba.* London: Verso, 2002.

Horne, Alistair. *A Savage War of Peace: Algeria 1954–62.* New York: Review Book, 2006.

Jones, Stewart Lloyd, and Antonio Costa Pinto (eds.). *The Last Empire: Thirty Years of Portuguese Decolonization.* Bristol, UK: Intellect Books, 2003.

Lazreg, Marnia. *The Eloquence of Silence: Algerian Women in Question.* New York: Routledge, 2019.

Lemarchand, Rene. *Burundi: Ethnic Conflict and Genocide.* Cambridge University Press, 1994.

Othen, Christopher. *Katanga, 1960–63: Mercenaries, Spires and the African Nation that Waged War on the World.* Stroud, UK: The History Press, 2015.

Schmidt, Elizabeth. *Cold War and Decolonization in Guinea, 1946–58.* Athens: Ohio University Press, 2007.

Seferdjeli, Ryme. "The French Army and Muslim Women during the Algerian War(1954–62)." *Hawwa: Journal of Women in the Middle East and Islamic World* 3, no. 2 (2005), 40–79.

Van der Waals, W.S. *Portugal's War in Angola.* Rivonia, South Africa: Ashanti, 1993.

Vanthemsche, Guy. *Belgium and the Congo, 1885–1980.* Cambridge University Press, 2012.

Williams, Susan. *Who Killed Dag Hammarskjold? The UN, the Cold War and White Supremacy in Africa.* Oxford University Press, 2014.

CHAPTER 23

Cohen, Andrew. *The Politics and Economics of Decolonization in Africa: The Failed Experiment of the Central African Federation.* London: I.B. Tauris, 2017.

Dale, Richard. *The Namibian War of Independence, 1966–89: Diplomatic, Military and Economic Campaigns.* Jefferson, NC: McFarland and Company, 2014.

Davis, Stephen. *The ANC's War against Apartheid: Umkhonto we Sizwe and the Liberation of South Africa.* Bloomington: Indiana University Press, 2018.

Ellis, Stephen. *External Mission: The ANC in Exile, 1960–1990.* Oxford University Press, 2013.

Kondlo, Kwandiwe. *In the Twilight of the Revolution: The Pan-Africanist Congress of Azania (South Africa), 1959–94.* Basel, Switzerland: Basler Afrika Bibliographien, 2009.

Lan, David. *Guns and Rain: Guerrillas and Spirit Mediums in Zimbabwe.* London: James Currey, 1985.

Mandela, Nelson. *Long Walk to Freedom: The Autobiography of Nelson Mandela.* New York: Little, Brown and Company, 2008.

Martin, David, and Phyllis Johnson. *The Struggle for Zimbabwe.* New York: Monthly Review, 1981.

Moorcroft, Paul, and Peter McLaughlin. *The Rhodesian War: A Military History.* London: Pen and Sword, 2008.

Nhongo-Simbanegavi, Josephine. *For Better or Worse: Women and ZANLA in Zimbabwe's Liberation Struggle.* Harare: Weaver Press, 2000.

Sampson, Anthony. *Mandela: The Authorized Biography.* New York: Vintage Books, 1999.

Sibanda, Eliakim. *The Zimbabwe African People's Union, 1961–1987.* Trenton, NJ: Africa World Press, 2005.

Simpson, Thula. *Umkhonto we Sizwe: The ANC's Armed Struggle.* Cape Town: Penguin Books, 2016.

South African Democracy Education Trust (SADET). *The Road to Democracy in South Africa,* 7 volumes. Pretoria: University of South Africa Press.

CHAPTER 24

Baynham, Simon. *The Military and Politics in Nkrumah's Ghana.* Boulder: Westview Press, 1988.

Davidson, Basil. *The Black Man's Burden: Africa and the Curse of the Nation State.* London: James Currey, 1992.

Decalo, Samuel. *Coups and Army Rule in Africa: Studies in Military Style.* New Haven: Yale University Press, 1976.

Decker, Alicia. *In Idi Amin's Shadow: Women, Gender and Militarism in Uganda.* Athens: Ohio University Press, 2014.

Dwyer, Maggie. *Soldiers in Revolt: Army Mutinies in Africa.* Oxford University Press, 2017.

Harsch, Ernest. *Thomas Sankara: An African Revolutionary.* Athens: Ohio University Press, 2014.

Jallow, Baba (ed.). *Leadership in Post-Colonial Africa: Trends Transformed by Independence.* New York: Palgrave-MacMillan, 2014.

Kelly, Sean. *America's Tyrant: the CIA and Mobutu of Zaire.* Lanham, MD: American University Press, 1993.

Kyemba, Henry. *State of Blood: The Inside Story of Idi Amin.* New York: Paddington, 1977.

Lal, Priya. *African Socialism in Post-colonial Tanzania: Between the Village and the World.* Cambridge University Press, 2015.

Mazrui, Ali (ed.). *The Warrior Tradition in Modern Africa.* Leiden, Netherlands: Brill, 1977.

Moore, Carlos. *Fela: This Bitch of a Life.* London: Omnibus Press, 2009.

Nzongola-Ntalaja, Georges. *The Congo: From Leopold to Kabila.* London: Zed Books, 2002.

Pargeter, Alison. *Libya: The Rise and Fall of Qadaffi.* New Haven, CT: Yale University Press, 2012.

Sardanis, Andrew. *Zambia: The First Fifty Years.* London: I.B. Tauris, 2014.

Shillington, Kevin. *Ghana and the Rawlings Factor.* New York: St. Martin's Press,, 1992.

Stewart, Gary. *Rumba on the River: A History of Popular Music in the Two Congos.* London: Verso, 2000.

Titley, Brian. *Dark Age: The Political Odyssey of Emperor Bokassa.* Montreal/Kingston: McGill-Queens University Press, 1997.

White, Bob. *Rumba Rules: The Politics of Dance Music in Mobutu's Zaire.* Durham, NC: Duke University Press, 2008.

CHAPTER 25

Azevedo, Mario. *Roots of Violence: A History of War in Chad.* New York: Routledge, 1998.

De St. Jorre, John. *The Brothers' War: Biafra and Nigeria.* Boston: Houghton and Mifflin, 1972.

George, Edward. *The Cuban Intervention in Angola, 1965–1991: From Che Guevara to Cuito Cuanavale.* London: Frank Cass, 2005.

Gleijeses, Piero. *Conflicting Missions: Havana, Washington and Africa, 1959–1976.* Chapel Hill: University of North Carolina Press, 2002.

Gleijeses, Piero. *Visions of Freedom: Havana, Washington, Pretoria and the Struggle for Southern Africa, 1976–1991.* Chapel Hill: University of North Carolina Press, 2013.

Grilli, Mateo. *Nkrumaism and African Nationalism: Ghana's Pan-African Foreign Policy in the Age of Decolonization.* Palgrave-Macmillan, 2018.

Jok, Jok Madut. *Sudan: Race, Religion and Violence.* London: Oneworld Publications, 2016.

Khadiagala, Gilbert. *Allies in Adversity: The Frontline States in Southern African Security, 1975–93.* Athens: Ohio University Press, 1994.

Kufuor, Kofi Oteng. *The Institutional Transformation of the Economic Community of West African States.* New York: Routledge, 2016.

LeRichie, M., and M. Arnold. *South Sudan: From Revolution to Independence.* Oxford University Press, 2013.

Schulze, Kirsten. *The Arab–Israeli Conflict.* London: Routledge, 2017.

Stremlau, John. *The International Politics of the Nigerian Civil War.* Princeton University Press, 1977.

Tareke, Gebru. *The Ethiopian Revolution: War in the Horn of Africa.* New Haven: Yale University Press, 2009.

Van Walraven, Klaas. *Dreams of Power: The Role of the Organization of African Unity in the Politics of Africa 1963–1993.* New York: Routledge, 2018.

CHAPTER 26

Cheeseman, Nic. *Democracy in Africa: Successes, Failures and the Struggle for Political Reform.* Cambridge University Press, 2015.

Cline, Lawrence. *The Lord's Resistance Army.* Santa Barbara, CA: Praeger, 2013.

Comolli, Virginia. *Boko Haram: Nigeria's Islamist Insurgency.* London: Hurst and Company, 2015.

Ellis, Stephen. *The Mask of Anarchy: The Destruction of Liberia and the Religious Dimension of an African Civil War.* New York University Press, 2001.

Gberie, Lansana. *A Dirty War in West Africa: The RUF and the Destruction of Sierra Leone.* Bloomington: Indiana University Press, 2005.

Jok, Jok Madut. *War and Slavery in Sudan.* Philadelphia: University of Pennsylvania Press, 2001.

Keenan, Jeremy. *The Dying Sahara: US Imperialism and Terror in Africa.* Pluto Press, 2013.

Lemarchand, Rene. *The Dynamics of Violence in Central Africa.* Philadelphia: University of Pennsylvania Press, 2009.

LeRiche, Matthew, and, Matthew Arnold. *South Sudan: From Revolution to Independence.* Oxford University Press, 2012.

Mamdani, Mahmood. *When Victims Become Killers: Colonialism, Nativism and the Genocide in Rwanda.* Princeton University Press, 2001.

Noueihed, Lin, and, Alex Warren. *The Battle for the Arab Spring: Revolution, Counter-Revolution and the Making of a New Era.* New Haven: Yale University Press, 2012.

Prunier, Gerard. *Africa's World War: Congo, the Rwanda Genocide and the Making of a Continental Catastrophe.* Oxford University Press, 2009.

Prunier, Gerard. *The Rwanda Crisis: History of a Genocide.* New York: Columbia University Press, 1995.

Reyntjens, Filip. *The Great African War: Congo and Regional Geopolitics, 1996–2006.* Cambridge University Press, 2009.

Solomon, Hussein. *Terrorism and Counter-Terrorism in Africa: Fighting Insurgency from Al Shabaab, Ansar Dine and Boko Haram.* Basingstoke, UK: Palgrave, 2015.

Wallis, Andrew. *Silent Accomplice: The Untold Story of France's Role in the Rwandan Genocide.* London: I.B. Tauris, 2006.

CHAPTER 27

Ayakoroma, Barclays Foubiri. *Trends in Nollywood: A Study of Selected Genres.* Ibadan, Nigeria: Kraft Books, 2014.

Camminga, B. *Transgender Refugees and the Imagined South Africa: Bodies over Borders and Borders over Bodies.* Palgrave-MacMillan, 2018.

Clark, Misa Kibona. *Hip-Hop in Africa: Prophets of the City and Dustyfoot Philosophers.* Athens: Ohio University Press, 2018.

Crawford, Dorothy. *Ebola: Profile of a Killer Virus.* Oxford University Press, 2016.

Epprecht, Marc. *Hungochani: The History of a Dissident Sexuality in Southern Africa* (2nd ed.). Montreal and Kingston: McGill-Queens Press, 2013.

Epprecht, Marc. *Sexuality and Social Justice in Africa: Rethinking Homophobia and Forging Resistance.* London: Zed Books, 2013.

Flint, Adrian. *HIV/AIDS in Sub-Saharan Africa: Politics, Aids and Globalization.* Basingstoke, UK: Palgrave-MacMillan, 2011.

Genova, James. *Cinema and Development in West Africa.* Bloomington: Indiana University Press, 2013.

Haynes, Jonathan. *Nollywood: The Creation of Nigerian Film Genres.* University of Chicago Press, 2016.

Hernlund, Ylva, and Bettina Shell-Duncan (eds.). *Transcultural Bodies: Female Genital Cutting in Global Context.* New Brunswick, NJ: Rutgers University Press, 2007.

Mbali, Mandisa. South African *AIDS Activism and Global Health Politics.* Basingstoke, UK: Palgrave-MacMillan, 2013.

Miller, Jade. *Nollywood Central.* London: Bloomsbury Publishing, 2016.

Phillips, Howard. "Influenza Pandemic (Africa)," in: 1914-1918-online. *International Encyclopedia of* the *First World War*, ed. by Ute Daniel, Peter Ga-trell, Oliver Janz, Heather Jones, Jennifer Keene, Alan Kramer, and Bill Nasson, issued by Freie Universität Berlin, Berlin 2014-10-08. https://encyclopedia.1914-1918-online.net/article/influenza_pandemic_africa

Schauer, Jeffrey. *Wildlife Between Empire and Nation in Twentieth Century Africa*. Palgrave-MacMillan, 2019.

Somerville, Keith. *Ivory: Power and Poaching in Africa*. London: Hurst and Co., 2016.

Suich, Helen, Brian Child, and Anna Spenceley (eds.). *Evolution Innovation in Wildlife: Parks and Game Ranches to Transfrontier Conservation Areas*. London: Earthscan, 2009.

Wilson, Reid. *Epidemic: Ebola and the Global Scramble to Prevent the Next Killer Outbreak*. Washington, DC: Brookings Institute Press, 2018.

EPILOGUE

Agar, Jon, and Jacob Ward (eds.). *History of Technology, the Environment and Modern Britain*. London: UCL Press. 2018.

Bak, Hans, Frank Mehring, and Mathilde Roza (eds.). *Politics and Cultures of Liberation*. Leiden, Netherlands: Brill. 2018.

Dery, Mary. "Black to the Future: Interviews with Samuel R. Delany, Greg Tate, and Tricia Rose." In *Flame Wars: The Discourse of Cyberculture*, edited by Dery Mark, 179–222. Durham, NC: Duke University Press, 1994

"Globalization: Threat of Opportunity?" International Monetary Fund, April 2000. https://www.imf.org/external/np/exr/ib/2000/041200to.htm

Heft-Neal, Sam, Jennifer Burney, Eran Bendavid, Kara Voss, and Marshall Burke. "Air Pollution and Infant Mortality: Evidence from Saharan Dust." National Bureau of Economic Research, Working Paper 26107, July 2019, https://www.nber.org/papers/w26107

Huyssen Andreas. *After the Great Divide: Modernism, Mass Culture, Postmodernism*. Basingstoke: Macmillan, 1988.

Iheka, Cajetan, and Jack Taylor (eds.). *African Migration Narratives: Politics, Race and Space*. University of Rochester Press, 2018.

James, Paul. *Globalism, Nationalism, Tribalism*. London: Sage Publications, 2006.

Kooijman, Jaap. *Fabricating the Absolute Fake*. Amsterdam University Press, 2013.

Credits

Introduction

Introduction CO Photo Robin Batista Photography/ Alamy Stock Photo Photo I.1 Chronicle/Alamy Stock Photo Photo I.2 Miami University Libraires, Public domain, via Wikimedia Commons Photo I.3a The History Collection/Alamy Stock Photo Photo I.3b Battey, C. M. (Cornelius Marion), 1873-1927, photographer, Public domain, via Wikimedia Commons Photo I.4 Robert Sivell is the artist who painted the original oil portrait. I own the painting, and scanned it. Sandra Stowell, CC BY-SA 3.0 <https://creativecommons.org/licenses/ by-sa/3.0>, via Wikimedia Commons Photo I.5 Walter Rodney at Yale University, 1972. Photographed by Jim Alexander. Walter Rodney Collection. Atlanta University Center Robert W. Woodruff Library. Photo I.6 Fort Hare Institute of Social and Economic Research

VOLUME ONE

Part One Opener

The Michael C. Rockefeller Memorial Collection, Gift of Nelson A. Rockefeller, 1965.

Chapter One

Chapter One CO Photo Heritage Image Partnership Ltd/Alamy Stock Photo Photo 1.1a imageBROKER/ Alamy Stock Photo Photo 1.1b Olduvai_Gorge_or_ Oldupai_Gorge.jpg: Noel Feansderivative work: Aiyizo, CC BY 2.0 <https://creativecommons.org/ licenses/by/2.0>, via Wikimedia Commons Photo 1.1c The Natural History Museum/Alamy Stock Photo Photo 1.1d UPI/Alamy Stock Photo Photo 1.1e UPI/ Alamy Stock Photo Photo 1.2 Raymbetz, CC BY-SA 3.0 <https://creativecommons.org/licenses/by-sa/3.0>, via Wikimedia Commons Photo 1.3 DPK-Photo/Alamy Stock Photo Photo 1.4a Artokoloro/Alamy Stock Photo Photo 1.4b Musée du quai Branly, CC BY-SA 2.0 FR <https://creativecommons.org/licenses/by-sa/2.0/fr/ deed.en>, via Wikimedia Commons

Chapter Two

Chapter Two CO Photo Mohammed Bilel Bennouri, CC BY-SA 4.0 <https://creativecommons.org/licenses/by-sa/4.0>, via Wikimedia Commons Photo 2.1a Robert Burch/Alamy Stock Photo Photo 2.1b Danita Delimont/Alamy Stock Photo Photo 2.1c timsimages/ Alamy Stock Photo Photo 2.2 Rogers Fund, 1930 Photo 2.3 Gift of Joseph W. Drexel, 1889 Photo 2.4 Werner Forman/Universal Images Group/Getty Images Photo 2.5 HomoCosmicos/Alamy Stock Photo Photo 2.6 World History Archive/Alamy Stock Photo Photo 2.7 damian entwistle, CC BY-SA 2.0 <https://creativecommons.org/licenses/by-sa/2.0>, via Wikimedia Commons Photo 2.8 Orf3us, CC BY 3.0 <https://creativecommons.org/licenses/by/3.0>, via Wikimedia Commons Photo 2.9 AnonymousUnknown author, Public domain, via Wikimedia Commons

Chapter Three

Chapter Three CO Photo Images & Stories/Alamy Stock Photo Photo 3.1 History and Art Collection/ Alamy Stock Photo Photo 3.2 Eye Ubiquitous/Alamy Stock Photo Photo 3.3 Jack Maguire/Alamy Stock Photo Photo 3.4 I, Luc Viatour, CC BY-SA 3.0 <http:// creativecommons.org/licenses/by-sa/3.0/>, via Wikimedia Commons Photo 3.5 Aisance KALONJI, CC BY-SA 4.0 <https://creativecommons.org/licenses/by-sa/4.0>, via Wikimedia Commons

Chapter Four

Chapter Four CO Photo Bibliothèque nationale de France, Public domain, via Wikimedia Commons Photo 4.1 Images & Stories/Alamy Stock Photo Photo 4.2 Edmond Fortier (1862-1928), Public domain, via Wikimedia Commons Photo 4.3 © Shutterstock Photo 4.4 Chronicle/Alamy Stock Photo Photo 4.5a The Michael C. Rockefeller Memorial Collection, Bequest of Nelson A. Rockefeller, 1979 Photo 4.5b Bequest of Alice K. Bache, 1977

Chapter Five

Chapter Five CO Photo PVDE/Bridgeman Images
Photo 5.1 Ancient Art and Architecture/Alamy Stock
Photo Photo 5.2 Florilegius/Alamy Stock Photo Photo
5.3a Lebrecht Music & Arts/Alamy Stock Photo Photo
5.3b Erich Lessing/Art Resource, NY Photo 5.4 Georges Jansoone, CC BY-SA 3.0 <http://creativecommons.
org/licenses/by-sa/3.0/>, via Wikimedia Commons
Photo 5.5a Francisco de Zurbarán, Public domain, via
Wikimedia Commons Photo 5.5b Robert Murray/
Alamy Stock Photo Photo 5.6 Eugène Delacroix, Public
domain, via Wikimedia Commons

Chapter Six

Chapter Six CO Photo Dirk Valkenburg, Public domain,
via Wikimedia Commons Photo 6.1a Bridgeman Images
Photo 6.1b Luisa Ricciarini/Bridgeman Images Photo
6.1c Jorge de Aguiar, Public domain, via Wikimedia
Commons Photo 6.1d Bridgeman Images Photo 6.2
Bridgeman Images Photo 6.3 Gift of Ernst Anspach, 1999
Photo 6.4a "Mandingo Slave Traders and Coffle, Senegal,
1780s", Slavery Images: A Visual Record of the African
Slave Trade and Slave Life in the Early African Diaspora,
accessed March 27, 2021, http://www.slaveryimages.
org/s/slaveryimages/item/409 Photo 6.4b Rama, Public
domain, via Wikimedia Commons Photo 6.4c Plymouth
Chapter of the Society for Effecting the Abolition of the
Slave Trade, Public domain, via Wikimedia Commons
Photo 6.4d Praefecturae Paranambucae Pars Borealis,
una cum Praefectura de Itâmaracâ, JCB Map Collection.

Chapter Seven

Chapter Seven CO Photo © Photo Josse/Bridgeman
Images Photo 7.1 dave stamboulis/Alamy Stock Photo
Photo 7.2 John Dambik/Alamy Stock Photo Photo 7.3 A.
Davey from Where I Live Now: Pacific Northwest, CC
BY 2.0 <https://creativecommons.org/licenses/by/2.0>,
via Wikimedia Commons Photo 7.4a Harvey Barrison
from Massapequa, NY, USA, CC BY-SA 2.0 <https://
creativecommons.org/licenses/by-sa/2.0>, via Wikimedia Commons Photo 7.4b Edward C. Moore Collection,
Bequest of Edward C. Moore, 1891 Photo 7.5a David
Stanley from Nanaimo, Canada, CC BY 2.0 <https://
creativecommons.org/licenses/by/2.0>, via Wikimedia
Commons Photo 7.5b Georg Braun, Public domain, via
Wikimedia Commons Photo 7.6 Andrei Nekrassov/
Alamy Stock Photo Photo 7.7 Florilegius/Alamy Stock
Photo Photo 7.8 Chronicle/Alamy Stock Photo

Chapter Eight

Chapter Eight CO Photo The photo is produced as a
full-page color illustration in Memory: Luba Art and
the Making of History, Mary Nooter Roberts and
Allen F. Roberts, eds. (1996, Munich: Prestel, for the
Museum for African Art, New York), p. 35. Photo
8.1 Daderot, CC0, via Wikimedia Commons Photo
8.2 Antiqua Print Gallery/Alamy Stock Photo Photo
8.3 Unknown author, Public domain, via Wikimedia
Commons Photo 8.4 "Mode of Transporting Ivory,
Central Africa, mid-1860s", Slavery Images: A Visual
Record of the African Slave Trade and Slave Life in
the Early African Diaspora, accessed March 27, 2021,
http://www.slaveryimages.org/s/slaveryimages/
item/2850 Photo 8.5 Brooklyn Museum, CC BY 3.0
<https://creativecommons.org/licenses/by/3.0>, via
Wikimedia Commons Photo 8.6 Joerg Boethling/
Alamy Stock Photo Photo 8.7a Martin Harvey/Getty
Images Photo 8.7b Historical Images Archive/Alamy
Stock Photo

Chapter Nine

Chapter Nine CO Photo The Stapleton Collection/
Bridgeman Images Photo 9.1a Greatstock/Alamy
Stock Photo Photo 9.1b Marius Loots, CC BY-SA 3.0
<https://creativecommons.org/licenses/by-sa/3.0>,
via Wikimedia Commons Photo 9.2a Andrew Moore
from Johannesburg, South Africa, CC BY-SA 2.0
<https://creativecommons.org/licenses/by-sa/2.0>,
via Wikimedia Commons Photo 9.2b Christopher
Scott/Alamy Stock Photo Photo 9.3 Bridgeman Images
Photo 9.4 CNP Collection/Alamy Stock Photo Photo
9.5 Charles Davidson Bell, Public domain, via Wikimedia Commons

Chapter Ten

Chapter Ten CO Photo Jean-Léon Gérôme, Public
domain, via Wikimedia Commons Photo 10.1 Niday
Picture Library/Alamy Stock Photo Photo 10.2a Auguste Couder, Public domain, via Wikimedia Commons Photo 10.2b Historic Collection/Alamy Stock
Photo Photo 10.3a © Archives Charmet/Bridgeman
Images Photo 10.3b Photoglob Co., publisher, Public
domain, via Wikimedia Commons Photo 10.4a The
Picture Art Collection/Alamy Stock Photo Photo 10.4b
The History Collection/Alamy Stock Photo Photo 10.5
SOTK2011/Alamy Stock Photo

Chapter Eleven

Chapter Eleven CO Photo Look and Learn/Rosenberg Collection/Bridgeman Images Photo 11.1 British Library, CC0, via Wikimedia Commons Photo 11.2a Heritage Image Partnership Ltd/Alamy Stock Photo Photo 11.2b © The Granger Collection Ltd d/b/a GRANGER Historical Picture Archive Photo 11.3 © The Granger Collection Ltd d/b/a GRANGER Historical Picture Archive Photo 11.4 © The Granger Collection Ltd d/b/a GRANGER Historical Picture Archive Photo 11.5 © The Granger Collection Ltd d/b/a GRANGER Historical Picture Archive Photo 11.6 The History Collection/Alamy Stock Photo Photo 11.7 Historic Images/Alamy Stock Photo Photo 11.8a A. Hoen & Co.; Hoen, August, 1817-1886., Public domain, via Wikimedia Commons Photo 11.8b Library of Congress Prints and Photographs Division Washington, D.C. 20540 USA http://hdl.loc.gov/loc.pnp/pp.print Photo 11.9 Chronicle/Alamy Stock Photo

Chapter Twelve

Chapter Twelve CO Photo Collection Gregoire/Bridgeman Images Photo 12.1a Artist: Edwin R L Stocqueler (1829-1895), Public domain, via Wikimedia Commons Photo 12.1b PVDE/Bridgeman Images Photo 12.2 Chronicle/Alamy Stock Photo Photo 12.3 © National Portrait Gallery, London Photo 12.4 North Wind Picture Archives/Alamy Stock Photo Photo 12.5 © Look and Learn/Bridgeman Images Photo 12.6 DidierTais, CC BY-SA 3.0 <https://creativecommons.org/licenses/by-sa/3.0>, via Wikimedia Commons Photo 12.7a Rod Waddington, CC BY-SA 2.0 <https://creativecommons.org/licenses/by-sa/2.0>, via Wikimedia Commons Photo 12.7b Shuo Huang/Alamy Stock Photo Photo 12.7c Science History Images/Alamy Stock Photo

Chapter Thirteen

Chapter Thirteen CO Photo Public Domain Photo 13.1 © British Library Board/Robana/Art Resource, NY Photo 13.2 Bensusan Museum anon, Public domain, via Wikimedia Commons Photo 13.3a Public Domain Photo 13.3b AnonymousUnknown author, Public domain, via Wikimedia Commons Photo 13.3c Anon., Public domain, via Wikimedia Commons Photo 13.4 Smith Archive/Alamy Stock Photo Photo 13.5 Smith Archive/Alamy Stock Photo Photo 13.6 Charles Davidson Bell, Public domain, via Wikimedia Commons

Part One Thematic Conclusion

Part One TC CO Photo Florilegius/Alamy Stock Photo Photo TC.1 Public Domain Photo TC.2 Suzanne Long/Alamy Stock Photo Photo TC.3 The Michael C. Rockefeller Memorial Collection, Gift of Nelson A. Rockefeller, 1972 Photo TC.4 Creator:Dierk Lange, CC0, via Wikimedia Commons

VOLUME TWO

Part Two Opener

Oshodi Road, Lagos, Nigeria. From the series 'Metropolis'. Photo: Martin Roemers

Chapter Fourteen

Map of Africa James Monteith, Public domain, via Wikimedia Commons

Chapter Fifteen

Chapter Fifteen CO Photo © CCI/Bridgeman Images Photo 15.1 Adalbert von Rößler (†1922), Public domain, via Wikimedia Commons Photo 15.2a Chronicle/Alamy Stock Photo Photo 15.2b ullstein bild Axel-Springer-Strasse 65 Berlin Photo 15.2c Courtesy of the Library of Congress Photo 15.2d Reproduction courtesy of the Norman B. Leventhal Map & Education Center at the Boston Public Library Photo 15.3 Henri Louis Dupray, Public domain, via Wikimedia Commons Photo 15.4a Public Domain, https://commons.wikimedia.org/w/index.php?curid=336496 Photo 15.4b CPA Media - Pictures from History PO Box 10 Phra Singh Post Office Chiang Mai Photo 15.5 © National Army Museum/Bridgeman Images Photo 15.6 Public Domain Photo 15.7 Henri Gaden (1867-1939), Public domain, via Wikimedia Commons Photo 15.8a The History Collection/Alamy Stock Photo Photo 15.8b Danita Delimont/Alamy Stock Photo Photo 15.9 Pictorial Press Ltd/Alamy Stock Photo Photo 15.10 Sueddeutsche Zeitung Photo/Alamy Stock Photo Photo 15.11a J. Geiser. Algier phot., Public domain, via Wikimedia Commons Photo 15.11b Wikimedia Commons Photo 15.12a ullstein bild Axel-Springer-Strasse 65 Berlin Photo 15.12b "Colonie Belge, 1885-1959 byTshibumba. Private Collection on long-term loan to the National Museum of Natural History, Smithsonian Institution."

Chapter Sixteen

Chapter Sixteen CO Photo Courtesy of the Library of Congress Photo 16.1 The Microcosm. South African Library Anon., Public domain, via Wikimedia Commons Photo 16.2a Courtesy of the Library of Congress Photo 16.2b LSE Library, No restrictions, via Wikimedia Commons Photo 16.3 Humansdorpie at en.wikipedia, Public domain, via Wikimedia Commons Photo 16.4 Sarin Images 25 Chapel Street Brooklyn Photo 16.5 Chronicle/Alamy Stock Photo Photo 16.6 Public domain, via Wikimedia Commons Photo 16.7 Unknown authorUnknown author, Public domain, via Wikimedia Commons Photo 16.8a History and Art Collection/Alamy Stock Photo Photo 16.8b © Look and Learn/Bridgeman Images

Chapter Seventeen

Chapter Seventeen CO Photo (ca. 1899) From the admiralty, Algiers, Algeria. , ca. 1899. [Photograph] Retrieved from the Library of Congress, https://www.loc.gov/item/2001697801/. Photo 17.1 Historic Images/Alamy Stock Photo Photo 17.2 Unknown authorUnknown author, Public domain, via Wikimedia Commons Photo 17.3 indéterminé ; probablement Jules Leclercq (1848-1928), Public domain, via Wikimedia Commons Photo 17.4 Agence Roger Viollet 46 rue de la Mare Paris Photo 17.5a J. Audema, Public domain, via Wikimedia Commons Photo 17.5b Lebrecht History/Bridgeman Images Photo 17.6 Courtesy of the Library of Congress Photo 17.7 Unknown authorUnknown author, Public domain, via Wikimedia Commons Photo 17.8a People working among tobacco plants, Rhodesia. Zimbabwe, None. [Between 1890 and 1925] [Photograph] Retrieved from the Library of Congress, https://www.loc.gov/item/89714079/. Photo 17.8b Black, Chinese and White laborers in a gold mine in South Africa. , None. [Between 1890 and 1923] [Photograph] Retrieved from the Library of Congress, https://www.loc.gov/item/2001705558/. Photo 17.8c Library of Congress Photo 17.8d Library of Congress Photo 17.9 Van Altena, Edward, Public domain, via Wikimedia Commons

Chapter Eighteen

Chapter Eighteen CO Photo MARKA/Alamy Stock Photo Photo 18.1a Mary Evans Picture Library Photo 18.1b Mary Evans/Sueddeutsche Zeitung Photo Photo 18.2 Pandries, CC BY-SA 3.0 <https:// creativecommons.org/licenses/by-sa/3.0>, via Wikimedia Commons Photo 18.3 © Franco Visintainer, CC BY 3.0 <https://creativecommons.org/licenses/by/3.0>, via Wikimedia Commons Photo 18.4a Mary Evans/Sueddeutsche Zeitung Photo Photo 18.4b ©The Scout Association/Mary Evans Photo 18.5 Frans Schellekens/Contributor, Getty Images Photo 18.6a Talma, Public domain, via Wikimedia Commons Photo 18.6b Copyright Anthony Barboza photog. All rights reserved. Photo 18.7 Liberaal Archief, Public domain, via Wikimedia Commons

Chapter Nineteen

Chapter Nineteen CO Photo Balfore Archive Images/Alamy Stock Photo Photo 19.1a Bain News Service, publisher, Public domain, via Wikimedia Commons Photo 19.1b World History Archive/Alamy Stock Photo Photo 19.2a Everett Collection Inc/Alamy Stock Photo Photo 19.2b Library of Congress Photo 19.2c Library of Congress Photo 19.2d Unknown authorUnknown author, Public domain, via Wikimedia Commons Photo 19.3 By The National Archives UK, OGL v1.0, https://commons.wikimedia.org/w/index.php?curid=19967163 Photo 19.4 Unknown authorUnknown author, Public domain, via Wikimedia Commons Photo 19.5 Marion Kaplan/Alamy Stock Photo Photo 19.6 Bettmann/Contributor, Getty Images Photo 19.7 Georgios Kollidas/Alamy Stock Photo

Chapter Twenty

Chapter Twenty CO Photo (1942) Typical members of the Free French naval force and the voluntiers tirailleurs infantrymen. Libya. Libya, 1942. ?. [Photograph] Retrieved from the Library of Congress, https://www.loc.gov/item/2017872567/. Photo 20.1 The History Collection/Alamy Stock Photo Photo 20.2 Unknown authorUnknown author, Public domain, via Wikimedia Commons Photo 20.3 Bain News Service, P. (1914) Spahis in camp at Arsy after battle. , 1914. [Photograph] Retrieved from the Library of Congress, https://www.loc.gov/item/2014697873/. Photo 20.4 GRANGER 25 Chapel St. Suite 605 Brooklyn Photo 20.5 (1941) Italian naval prisoners march through Tobruk on their way to a prison camp. Tobruk Libya, 1941. March 3. [Photograph] Retrieved from the Library of Congress, https://www.loc.gov/item/2003668310/. Photo 20.6 United States Office of War Information. Overseas Picture Division. Washington Division; 1944, Public domain, via Wikimedia Commons Photo 20.7a Photograph from Martin King Photo 20.7b No 9 Army Film & Photographic Unit, Watson E (Sgt), Public domain, via Wikimedia Commons Photo 20.7c John Gordon Murphy (1920-2004) VX 64825., CC0, via Wikimedia Commons Photo 20.7d Library of Congress Photo 20.8 Terrence Spencer, Public domain, via Wikimedia Commons Photo 20.9 Peter J. Hatcher/Alamy Stock Photo

Chapter Twenty-One
Chapter Twenty-One CO Photo © Illustrated London News Ltd/Mary Evans Photo 21.1 Courtesy of Library of Congress. Photo 21.2 Abbie Rowe, Public domain, via Wikimedia Commons Photo 21.3 Keystone Press/Alamy Stock Photo Photo 21.4 Keystone Press/Alamy Stock Photo Photo 21.5 Public Domain Photo 21.6 Charleslincolnshire, CC BY-SA 4.0 <https://creativecommons.org/licenses/by-sa/4.0>, via Wikimedia Commons

Chapter Twenty-Two
Chapter Twenty-Two CO Photo Library of Congress Photo 22.1a Zdravko Pečar, CC BY-SA 4.0 <https://creativecommons.org/licenses/by-sa/4.0>, via Wikimedia Commons Photo 22.1b ullstein bild Axel-Springer-Strasse 65 Berlin Photo 22.1c By Christophe Marcheux - Own work, CC BY-SA 3.0, https://commons.wikimedia.org/w/index.php?curid=15793516 Photo 22.1d Agence France Presse/Contributor, Getty Images Photo 22.2 Courtesy of the Library of Congress Photo 22.3 Harry Pot/Anefo, CC0, via Wikimedia Commons Photo 22.4 World History Archive/Alamy Stock Photo Photo 22.5 Abbie Rowe. White House Photographs. John F. Kennedy Presidential Library and Museum, Boston Photo 22.6 Postal administration of the Kingdom of Burundi, Public domain, via Wikimedia Commons Photo 22.7a ZUMA Press, Inc./Alamy Stock Photo Photo 22.7b Keystone Press/Alamy Stock Photo Photo 22.8 Courtesy of the Library of Congress

Chapter Twenty-Three
Chapter Twenty-Three CO Photo Collection of the Smithsonian National Museum of African American History and Culture Photo 23.1a (ca. 1919) Jan Christian Smuts, -1950. , ca. 1919. [Photograph] Retrieved from the Library of Congress, https://www.loc.gov/item/2002699837/. Photo 23.1b Bain News Service,

P. (ca. 1920) Gen. J.B.M. Hertzog. , ca. 1920. [Between and Ca. 1925] [Photograph] Retrieved from the Library of Congress, https://www.loc.gov/item/2014713111/. Photo 23.1c Suidpunt, Public domain, via Wikimedia Commons Photo 23.2 South African women's services on duty in the Middle East: A South African W.A.A.F. Sergeant instructor fitting a gas mask to a beginner. Middle East, None. [Between 1940 and 1950] [Photograph] Retrieved from the Library of Congress, https://www.loc.gov/item/2011648247/. Photo 23.3a Jurgen Schadeberg/Contributor, Getty Images Photo 23.3b James Davis Photography/Alamy Stock Photo Photo 23.3c Courtesy of the Library of Congress Photo 23.3d By © Moheen Reeyad, CC BY-SA 4.0, https://commons.wikimedia.org/w/index.php?curid=71174718 Photo 23.4 Kennedy, Public domain, via Wikimedia Commons Photo 23.5a Azola Dayile, CC BY-SA 4.0 <https://creativecommons.org/licenses/by-sa/4.0>, via Wikimedia Commons Photo 23.5b Anefo, CC0, via Wikimedia Commons Photo 23.5c Pictorial Press Ltd/Alamy Stock Photo Photo 23.6 Godfrey Rubens (painter and photographer) via Wikimedia Commons Photo 23.7a Foto24/Contributor, Getty Images Photo 23.7b Unknown photographer, CC BY-SA 4.0 <https://creativecommons.org/licenses/by-sa/4.0>, via Wikimedia Commons Photo 23.8 Library of Congress Photo 23.9 Rob Bogaerts/Anefo, CC0, via Wikimedia Commons Photo 23.10 http://fototeca.iiccr.ro, Attribution, via Wikimedia Commons Photo 23.11a SPUTNIK/Alamy Stock Photo Photo 23.11b Keystone Press/Alamy Stock Photo

Chapter Twenty-Four
Chapter Twenty-Four CO Photo Valtman, E. S. (ca. 1989) Idi Amin. Uganda, ca. 1989. [Photograph] Retrieved from the Library of Congress, https://www.loc.gov/item/2002709650/. Photo 24.1 Popperfoto/Contributor, Getty Images Photo 24.2 Yefien, CC BY-SA 4.0 <https://creativecommons.org/licenses/by-sa/4.0>, via Wikimedia Commons Photo 24.3a Roland Gerrits (ANEFO), CC0, via Wikimedia Commons Photo 24.3b Getty Images Photo 24.3c Rob Bogaerts/Anefo, CC0, via Wikimedia Commons Photo 24.4 Courtesy of the Library of Congress. Photo 24.5 Keystone Press/Alamy Stock Photo Photo 24.6 Richard Nixon Presidential Library and Museum, Public domain, via Wikimedia Commons Photo 24.7 By U.S. Navy photo by Mass Communication Specialist 2nd Class Jesse

Chapter Twenty-Five

Chapter Twenty-Six

Chapter Twenty-Seven

Thematic Conclusion to Part Two

Index

Note: page numbers in *italics* reference non-text material.